Ancient China and Its Enemies

It has been an article of faith among historians of ancient China that Chinese culture represented the highest level of civilization in the greater Asia region from the first millennium B.C. throughout the pre-imperial period. This Sinocentric image – which contrasts the high culture of Shang and Chou China with the lower, "barbarian" peoples living off the grasslands along the northern frontier – is embedded in early Chinese historical records and has been perpetuated over the years by Chinese and Western historians. In this comprehensive history of the northern frontier of China from 900 to 100 B.C., Nicola Di Cosmo investigates the origins of this simplistic image, and in the process shatters it.

This book presents a far more complex picture of early China and its relations with the "barbarians" to the North, documenting how early Chinese perceived and interacted with increasingly organized, advanced, and politically unified (and threatening) groupings of people just outside their domain. Di Cosmo explores the growing tensions between these two worlds as they became progressively more polarized, with the eventual creation of the nomadic, Hsiung-nu empire in the north and Chinese empire in the south.

This book is part of a new wave of revisionist scholarship made possible by recent, important archaeological findings in China, Mongolia, and Central Asia that can now be compared against the historical record. It is the first study investigating the antagonism between early China and its neighbors that combines both Chinese historical texts and archaeological data. Di Cosmo reconciles new, archaeological evidence – of early non-Chinese to the north and west of China who lived in stable communities, had developed bronze technology, and used written language – with the common notion of undifferentiated tribes living beyond the pale of Chinese civilization. He analyzes the patterns of interaction along China's northern frontiers (from trading, often on an equal basis, to Eastern Hun–Chinese warfare during the Ch'in dynasty) and then explores how these relations were recorded (and why) in early Chinese historiography. Di Cosmo scrutinizes the way in which the great Chinese historian, Ssu-ma Chi'en portrayed the Hsiung-nu empire in his "Records of the Grand Historian" (99 B.C.), the first written narrative of the northern nomads in Chinese history. Chinese cultural definitions are explained here as the expression of political goals (for example, the need to cast enemies in a negative light) and the result of historical processes.

Herein are new interpretations of well-known historical events, including the construction of the early walls, later unified into the "Great Wall"; the formation of the first nomadic empire in world history, the Hsiung-nu empire; and the chain of events that led Chinese armies to conquer the northwestern regions, thus opening a commercial avenue with Central Asia (to become the Silk Road). Readers will come away with an entirely new, more nuanced picture of the world of ancient China and of its enemies.

Nicola Di Cosmo is Senior Lecturer in Chinese History at the University of Canterbury (Christchurch, New Zealand). He has been a Research Fellow at Clare Hall, Cambridge, and has taught at Indiana University and Harvard University. He is a contributing author of *The Cambridge History of Ancient China* (Michael Loewe and Edward Shaughnessy, eds., 1999) and *State and Ritual in China* (Joseph McDermott, ed., 1999). He is a member of the editorial boards of the *Journal of Asian Studies, Asia Major,* and the *Journal of East Asian Archaeology.*

Ancient China and Its Enemies

The Rise of Nomadic Power in East Asian History

Nicola Di Cosmo

University of Canterbury
Christchurch, New Zealand

To My Parents

PUBLISHED BY THE PRESS SYNDICATE OF THE UNIVERSITY OF CAMBRIDGE
The Pitt Building, Trumpington Street, Cambridge, United Kingdom

CAMBRIDGE UNIVERSITY PRESS
The Edinburgh Building, Cambridge CB2 2RU, UK
40 West 20th Street, New York, NY 10011-4211, USA
477 Williamstown Road, Port Melbourne, VIC 3207, Australia
Ruiz de Alarcón 13, 28014 Madrid, Spain
Dock House, The Waterfront, Cape Town 8001, South Africa

http://www.cambridge.org

First published 2002

Printed in the United Kingdom at the University Press, Cambridge

Typeface Sabon 10/12 pt.   *System* QuarkXPress [BTS]

A catalog record for this book is available from the British Library.

Library of Congress Cataloging in Publication Data

Di Cosmo, Nicola, 1957–
Ancient China and its enemies: the rise of nomadic power in
East Asian history / Nicola Di Cosmo.
p. cm.
Includes bibliographical references and index.
ISBN 0-521-77064-5
1. China–History – to 221 B.C.   I. Title.

DS741.3 .D5 2001
931–dc21   2001025577

ISBN   0 521 77064 5   hardback

Contents

Acknowledgments

So many times have I thought that this page would never be written, that it is with great relief that I can now begin to thank all the friends and people who have in one way or another given me assistance or inspiration. Because in a previous incarnation part of this book was my doctoral dissertation, my first debt of gratitude goes to the members of my doctoral committee in the then Department of Uralic and Altaic Studies at Indiana University: Christopher I. Beckwith – with whom I first discussed my idea – and Yuri Bregel, György Kara, and Elliot Sperling, who allowed me to pursue an interest that was at best tangential to the mainstream of the discipline. Lynn Struve was an exceptionally scrupulous and insightful external member. I must also thank Denis Sinor for encouraging me, while I was still a graduate student, to present papers at several conferences. I did much of the research that eventually went into this book at Cambridge University, where I was a Research Fellow in the Mongolia Studies Unit (1989–92); my sincere thanks to Caroline Humphrey and to the staff of the Mongolia Studies Unit and the Faculty of Oriental Studies for having given me valuable and much-appreciated support.

The dissertation being written, I had no intention of continuing my research in ancient Chinese history. If I have persevered, the merit belongs to Michael Loewe and Edward Shaughnessy. In different ways, they are among the best scholars I have ever worked with. Loewe's valuable works were the first that I read in this field and also the last, given the inexhaustible pace of his scholarship. Although not an Inner Asian specialist, Loewe (in collaboration with Hulsewé) has done more to enlighten our understanding of the ancient relations between China and Central Asia than any other scholar, including Pelliot and Chavannes.

Loewe and Shaughnessy's influence on this book has also been essential in a very direct way. I was thrilled when they asked me to contribute a chapter to the *Cambridge History of Ancient China*, but I accepted the task without a clear notion of how I was going to fulfill it. Having had to train myself in the basics of archaeological scholarship to write the chapter, my work for the *History* helped me to keep my interest in ancient China despite pressure "to return" to my original field, Manchu and Qing history. My participation in the making of the volume and the chance to meet the greatest scholars in the field were an invaluable psychological boost. My gratitude, then, goes to all the participants in the "Starved Rock" preparatory workshop. By the time the chapter was written, I had had some ideas that perhaps could be developed further. In talking with Ed Shaughnessy I decided to try to consolidate those ideas into a book; Ed also volunteered – a selfless act for which I am very grateful – to read a first draft. Needless to say, neither Shaughnessy nor Loewe is in any way responsible for any shortcomings of this book, but their support and encouragement have been essential to keeping me in this field long enough to finish it.

Over the years, I have become acquainted with many Early China scholars who in different ways provided me with help, advice, and useful criticism when required. Among these, I wish to mention Jessica Rawson, whose scholarship, insightfulness, and enthusiasm I have always admired. I have also profited from my acquaintance with David Keightley, Robert Bagley, and Donald Harper. Lothar von Falkenhausen has been generous with advice and assistance whenever needed, and his writings have been a source of knowledge for me. I am most indebted to Emma Bunker among the art historians working on the "barbaric" frontier. She has helped me to appreciate the visual aspect of the material culture of northern China. Others whose active research on the "northern frontier" of China has been especially valuable to me are Jenny So, Louisa Fitzgerald-Huber, Fredrik Hiebert, Victor Mair, Thomas Barfield, Gideon Shelach, Katheryn Linduff, and Yangjin Pak.

The greatest archaeologist I have known, during my time at Harvard, was the late K. C. Chang. To my eternal regret, I was just a little too late. Long before my arrival at Harvard, I had developed a revering admiration for K. C. Chang, whose books were for me, as for everyone in my generation, the formative introduction to Chinese archaeology. When I came to know K. C., a terrible illness had already started to erode his small, hard physique. Over time, we had several conversations, which I will always remember with great joy and great sadness. Yet the memory of the K. C. Chang I used to talk with will survive: probably the strongest and most generous man I have known.

Many of my former colleagues at Harvard provided me with advice and help in my work in the ancient world; I wish to thank in particular Professor Carl Lamberg-Karlovsky, with whom I had extremely rewarding talks. Of the Early China scholars, I would like to thank Bruce Brooks and the Warring States Working Group for keeping me informed about developments in the field as I was disengaging myself from my Early China studies. I owe special thanks also to Professor Denis Twitchett, whose unparalleled knowledge of Chinese history and scholarly energy, breadth, and vision are inspirational.

I am also indebted to several librarians, in particular Charles Aylmer, the Chinese Librarian at Cambridge University Library; the Librarian and staff of the Harvard–Yenching Library; and finally Martin Hejdra, the Gest Librarian at Princeton University.

My stay at the Institute for Advanced Study, where I wrote the last part of this book and tidied it up before final submission, was made especially pleasurable by the acquaintance of several scholars whose fascination for the ancient world I happen to share. Among them I should mention Professors Glen Bowersock, Oleg Grabar, and Heinrich von Staden. Last but surely not least, I must thank profusely the many valiant scholars in China who study northern China's archaeology. Some of them, like Wang Binghua and Guo Suxin, I have had the pleasure to meet personally. Without their efforts, work in this field would be impossible.

Among the institutions that provided me with teaching relief, assistance, time, and support, all or part of which I used in preparing this book, I wish to thank, first of all, at Cambridge University, the Mongolia Study Unit and Clare Hall, which allowed me to work in blissful freedom for three years; the Chiang Ching-kuo and Rockefeller Foundations, for postdoctoral grants; Harvard University, which provided me with sabbatical leave on two occasions; and, finally, the Institute for Advanced Study, which is the best working environment I have ever experienced. Cambridge University Press has been marvelous in its care and assistance. I wish to thank in particular Mary Child, Camilla Knapp, and Mike Green. It is with enduring admiration that I thank them for their patient and careful work.

Naturally I cannot ignore my wife, Lia, for her patience and support, and my son, Francesco, for having had to share my time with an "older brother" he could not see.

Whatever debts I have incurred in writing this book, responsibility for it rests solely with me. This book is by no means an arrival point; rather, it is a temporary stop on a journey that cannot be charted for sure. No doubt our understanding of the "northern frontier" of China will become increasingly rich, but this process of accumulating knowledge must be guided by a sense of history that has sometimes been obfuscated, or simply overwhelmed, by the combined weights of millenarian literary tradition and quantities of archaeological data. Trying to find its way between the Scylla of archaeology and the Charybdis of tradition, this book is an attempt to recover that sense of history. In all, I must say that (while not without its perils) it has been a marvelous voyage.

Introduction

In the time of Duke Huan of Ch'i [the position of] the son of Heaven had become humble and weak, while the feudal lords used their energies in attacking [one another]. The Southern Yi and Northern Ti engaged the Central States in battle, and the continued existence of the Central States seemed [to hang by] a thin thread [. . .] Duke Huan was troubled about the distress of the Central States and the rebelliousness of the Yi and Ti. He wished to keep alive what was dying and to preserve what was ceasing to exist, to bring esteem to [the position of] the son of Heaven and broaden civil and military occupations. Therefore the Book of Kuan-tzu grew out of this situation. (*Huai-nan-tzu*, 21:7a)[1]

It seems a shared human experience that the malleable substance at the origin of "civilizations" – a sense of cultural cohesion, shared destiny, and common origin – coagulates into a harder and stronger matter when the peoples who belong to it are confronted, at times in a threatening way, by other peoples who are seen as being different and "beyond the pale." The pale, the wall, the furrow in the soil are potentially dividing lines, demarcating the territory a community recognizes as its own, whose crossing, by an alien entity, can generate conflicts and threaten the stability of the community and, in extreme cases, cause its demise.

No wonder, then, that the antagonism between those who are "in" and those who are "out,"[2] and the criteria the community adopts to demarcate

---

[1] Adapted from Alan Rickett, trans., *Guanzi*, vol. 1 (Princeton: Princeton University Press, 1985), pp. 5–6.

[2] On the separation between "in" and "out" in the Chinese conception of world order, see Lein-sheng Yang, "Historical Notes on the Chinese World Order," in *The Chinese World Order*, ed. John K. Fairbank (Cambridge Mass.: Harvard University Press, 1968), p. 21.

not only its territory but also the characteristics that are assumed to be the very basis of its raison d'être (a faith, a race, a code of behavior, a shared set of values) are at the foundation of how a "civilization" defines itself. Although a sense of "belonging" to the community might exist prior to an external challenge, the fact of being challenged makes its members acutely aware of their common boundaries, forcing them to define cultural differences and leading them to build psychological and physical defenses. If there is one characteristic that civilizations have in common, it is their ideological need to defend themselves not just against their own enemies, but against the enemies of civilization, the "barbarians." This opposition between civilization and its enemies can be recognized as one of the great ongoing themes that we encounter in world history. Frontiers, however, are neither fixed nor exclusively defensive. With the expansion of civilization, the opening of new spaces to investigation, the acquisition of broader geographic and cultural horizons, frontiers acquire ever-different meanings. Because of their marginal yet critical status, frontiers are often gray areas, liminal zones where habitual conventions and principles can lose value, and new ones begin to appear. In this sense, the study of frontiers often promotes a critical stance toward definitions of "community," "culture," or "civilization."

The subject of the present work is the early history of China's northern frontier, the area that is understood as both crucial to a fuller understanding of ancient China and the locus of one of the great themes of Chinese history until modern times, namely, the confrontation between China and the steppe nomads. The blueprint of this "theme" was fixed in the historical literature during the Han dynasty, as the Grand Historian Ssu-ma Ch'ien composed, probably around 100 B.C., a monograph on the steppe nomadic people called Hsiung-nu, which he included in his *Shih chi* (Records of the Grand Historian). Ssu-ma Ch'ien based his history of the north on the assumption (or the pretense of it) that a chasm had always existed between China – the Hua-Hsia people – and the various alien groups inhabiting the north. That assumption is still with us, reflected in modern notions that the northern frontier has always been characterized by a set of dual oppositions – between pastoral and settled people (steppe and sown), between nomadic tribes and Chinese states, between an urban civilization and a warlike uncivilized society.

The main questions that this book explores are all about the historical realities hidden behind these dualisms: how and when did pastoral nomadism appear on the northern fringes of the Sinitic world? What was the genesis of these two opposite principles – what the medieval Arab historian Ibn Khaldun (1332–1406) called the civilization (*'umran*) of the settled and the civilization of the nomad – in Chinese history? How did the Inner Asian geographic, political, and ethnographic space become an integral part, consciously researched, of China's first comprehensive history?

Given the primary need to contextualize the cultural and political dimensions of this relationship, the historical circumstances of the northern peoples' interaction with China will form the arena of our first investigation. Two phenomena are particularly important here: the expansion of Sinitic political power into alien areas throughout much of the pre-imperial period, and the formation of the nomadic empire of the Hsiung-nu that emerges soon after the imperial unification. We need also to examine the cultural paradigm constructed by Ssu-ma Ch'ien to establish the meaning of the north within the mold of a unified vision of China's history, a paradigm that could also be used by his contemporaries and by future generations for gathering information about the north.

The main difficulty in discussing these issues is that early Chinese history is an exciting but extremely fluid field of study: new texts and artifacts regularly emerge from archaeological excavations, pushing new analyses and interpretations to the surface. Because the material excavated is varied, and the questions posed by archaeologists fan out in different directions, the interpretive "surface" is continually bubbling with novel possibilities. The historian is placed in suspension under these circumstances, as narratives are constantly being destabilized. Striving to match archaeological "narratives" and historical text-based narratives is a thankless task and often of limited use given the intrinsic incompatibility of the two sets of evidence. The textual sources often refer to an inherited tradition and, in any case, incorporate the thought process of their authors; the material evidence (as a body) is relatively accidental, and its interpretation and usefulness depend on the questions asked by modern scholars. Yet all the information available can be placed side by side to form a series of "contexts" that in their interaction may provide useful leads. Thus data collected from disparate sources "rebound" on each other within what is essentially a comparative analysis that tends to establish possible similarities, analogies, and points of contact and, by a logical process, suggests scenarios for possible solutions.

These problems have, if anything, even greater cogency in the study of China's northern frontier, where the analysis of cultural contacts must span huge geographical expanses and long periods of time. That alternative paths of inquiry exist does not mean that the historian is forever prevented from reaching any solution. To the contrary, it is the growing body of evidence itself that offers the most exciting possibilities, while demonstrating that an analysis is needed that moves away from the claustrophobic narrowness of the Chinese classical tradition (largely endorsed by the modern Western exegesis). This tradition has firmly enclosed the analysis of cultural contacts across the northern frontier between the Scylla of "sinicization" and the Charybdis of "natural" (and therefore cultureless) behavior. The "other" in the Chinese tradition seldom rose above a person regarded either as someone who was suitable material for cultural assimilation or someone

3

whose nature was hopelessly different and impermeable to civilization and thus destined to remain beyond the pale, often in unappealing or dangerous ways for the Chinese. Under these conditions, a history that critically examines cultural contacts and ethnic differences as part of the formation of various cultures is written only with great difficulty. In fact, the history of the northern frontier has frequently been reduced to a recital of mutual conquests by peoples representing two opposite principles.

This book is an attempt to expand that narrow space and to place the history of the northern frontier on the level of a cultural history, by establishing various contexts in which such a history can be articulated. Let me say from the start that these "contexts" are not meant to be exhaustive. Nor do I try to espouse a single narrative. My principal aim is to provide more than one key, in the hope of opening up different possibilities of interpretation. Hence four separate, but interconnecting, contexts are introduced here, each of which is examined as a separate *problematique* of the frontier. Partly as a consequence of the type of sources available, partly as a function of the historical discourse itself, these four contexts have been arranged in more or less chronological order. Even though these contexts (and the narratives that they produce) are still tentative and, as already noted, intrinsically unstable, this is not to say that this type of investigation necessarily leads to a blind alley. By moving from one set of evidence to the next, asking questions that emerge especially from the comparative analysis of the materials, and proposing answers that have not been previously envisaged, I hope to see a rich context emerge that will place the history of the relations between China and the north in a new light.

The book is divided into four parts, each having two chapters. Each part represents a separate narrative of the frontier. Although other scholars have treated these topics with great knowledge and competence, their results are different from mine because they base them on radically different premises. For instance, let us take two books, published in the same year, that are classics in their genre and closely relevant to the subject matter of this book, namely, Jaroslav Průšek's *Chinese Statelets and the Northern Barbarians in the Period 1400–300 B.C.* (Dordrecht, 1971) and William Watson's *Cultural Frontiers in Ancient East Asia* (Edinburgh, 1971). Průšek's control of the classical sources exceeds that of anyone else who has ever written on this topic, but he bases his narrative on certain premises (the rise of pastoral nomadism in north China, for instance) that are outside the reach of the textual tradition and that can be confirmed only by archaeological investigation. Průšek's deep erudition provides a reading that, in the end, goes far beyond the texts he so expertly analyzes, and the resulting picture remains too close to a single set of evidence to be persuasive.[3] In contrast, Watson's archaeological work is extremely rich and truly insightful, but if we look for answers to historical problems, this evidence immediately shows its limits. The same can be said of other scholarly works that have provided much enlightenment on discrete issues and problems but have remained limited to a particular period, set of sources, or scholarly tradition and disciplinary training.[4] All of them, of course, provide a generous platform onto which one can climb to look farther ahead.

The first part, devoted to archaeology, is concerned with a frontier defined through separate material cultures, the "northern" and the Chinese, that can cross borders and interact but that by and large represent two completely different traditions. The second part refers to a frontier defined not through material objects, artifacts, and burial rituals, but through written words and the ideas they convey. This is a frontier that separates peoples holding deeply divergent understandings of life, of society, of morality, and of the values that inform and define them. It is also a frontier found between those who write and those who do not (hence the one-sidedness of the evidence). The third part describes a frontier that is more properly political, one that is the result of political events, recorded in history, that led to profound transformations in the concept of frontier. From a place frequented by mythological and beastlike beings, the frontier became more concrete, a place where soldiers were deployed, merchants went to trade, and politicians sought to exploit. The fourth and last part deals with the historiography of the frontier as it was "created" in the first historical narrative in Chinese history, the *Shih-chi* of Ssu-ma Ch'ien. The influence of this early narrative cannot be overstated, as it colored deeply later understandings of the formative process of the frontier, a process whose main lines have remained largely unquestioned.

PART I. The two chapters in Part I attempt to define the archaeological context of the emergence of nomads in northern China. The first chapter

---

[3] This is not a criticism of Průšek's work, especially since Průšek did not have at his disposal the type of information we enjoy today, but rather a caveat on placing excessive faith on the written sources when trying to articulate a historical hypothesis.

[4] As a paragon of philological accuracy we could mention, for instance, A. F. P. Hulsewé and Michael Loewe, *China in Central Asia: The Early Stage, 125 B.C.–A.D. 23. An annotated translation of chapters 61 and 96 of the History of the Former Han dynasty* (Leiden: Brill, 1979); on a different level, Jenny So and Emma Bunker's archaeological expertise is brought to bear in the bold re-evaluation of the trade between China and the North in their *Traders and Raiders on China's Northern Frontier* (Seattle and London: Arthur Sackler Galley and University of Washington Press, 1995).

delineates the process through which pastoralism expanded in the Eurasian steppe zone and the emergence of cultures that had developed advanced bronze metallurgy and handicraft technologies. The introduction of horse-back riding and wheeled transportation gave these cultures further impetus and probably played a role in their ability to spread across Central Eurasia. During the early first millennium B.C. mounted nomads, recognizable as "early" or "Scythian-type" nomads, are evident in clustered cultural centers throughout Eurasia. Northern China – as we see in Chapter 2 – was by no means extraneous to this continentwide cultural process. Mixed economies practicing both agriculture and stock rearing, culturally related to the Inner Asian metallurgical complex, emerged between the world of the Shang and the bronze cultures of Central Asia, Siberia, and the Altai. At this early stage, the northern frontier societies constantly interacted with the Shang and early Chou, and, even though a frontier did exist, no sharp demarcation can be detected. In fact, China's early frontier was permeable to the introduction of forms of art and technology both from and through these neighboring northern societies.

Gradually, northern China also experienced a transition to greater reliance on animal husbandry. Here "Scythian-type" societies began to appear, characterized by expert horsemanship, martial valor, and taste for animal-style art whose formal conventions were shared across Central Eurasia. These societies, which most likely developed a degree of internal specialization, included farmers and herders and a nomadic aristocracy that seems to have achieved a dominant position. Horse riding and iron technology gradually became widespread in northern China, possibly as a result of a general evolution, among pastoral nomads, toward more sophisticated forms of social organization. The final phase of the development of this "archaeological" frontier in pre-imperial China unearths an abundance of precious objects, mostly of gold and silver, which point to a commercial role for the aristocracy and increased trade with China, dating, probably, from the fifth or fourth century B.C.

PART II. If archaeology can help us to define cultural types in terms of their way of life, technical abilities, local customs, and even spiritual realm, only through written sources can we learn about the cultural and political perspectives of the Chinese regarding the north. This issue is inextricably linked to a "culturalist" perspective that has long dominated the study of foreign relations in early China. This perspective emphasizes the sharp dichotomy between a world that is culturally superior and literate, with a common sense of aesthetic refinement, intellectual cultivation, moral norms, and ideals of social order embedded in rituals and ceremonies, and a world that lacks such achievements. The boundary between these two worlds, supported by abundant statements in the early Chinese sources, was easily interpreted as a boundary between a community that shared civilized values and a community that did not recognize those values. This interpretation has been so dominant as to preclude any other approach, even in the face of notable contradictions, such as, for instance, that a single term analogous to the European "barbarian" did not exist in ancient China. This is not to deny that the world "outside" the Central Plain was at times portrayed, in the ancient literature, as a hostile and different environment or that foreign peoples often were lumped together under an abstract concept of "otherness" and regarded as inferior, uncultured, and threatening. But we need to ask what this meant for the actual conduct of foreign relations. How can we connect these statements about cultural difference to the historical reality that produced them?

In my view, we cannot limit the discussion about the relations between Chinese (i.e., Central Plain, or Chou) states and these other political communities to a series of "cultural" statements retrieved from terse historical sources open to diverse interpretations. Such an approach would tend to establish that a system of cultural values existed, defined both as "Chinese" and in opposition to the system of "anti-values" supposedly embraced by non-Chinese peoples, regardless of the historical context in which these statements appear. But how can we accept that these statements marked a true cultural boundary without analyzing the circumstances under which they were made? To answer this question, Chapter 3 investigates the actual contexts of political relations between foreign states and Chinese states. This chapter argues that the separation between a "Hua-Hsia" Chinese cultural unity and an external barbarism, although perceived of and expressed in those terms, was actually embedded in a pattern dominated by the political and military strategies essential to the survival of the Chinese states. Moreover, those states adopted a variety of attitudes and strategies vis-à-vis the northern peoples, along a spectrum ranging from virulent opposition to alliance, political equality, and peace.

It is against a background of endemic warfare and ruthless conquest, and within a logic finely tuned to exploit every advantage that might promote the survival of the state, that we must place the statements that we find in Chinese sources stressing cultural differences. Recourse to arguments pointing to the inferiority of alien peoples served, at times, the political need to escape norms regulating interstate relations and legitimize the conquest and annexation of these peoples. At other times, the Chinese used foreign peoples as resources for strengthening the state and as allies in interstate relations.

Chapter 4 focuses on the early history of the relationship between nomads and the northern Chinese states. During the late fourth century B.C. a new type of protagonist appears in Chinese history: the mounted steppe warrior. Contemporary sources hesitatingly acknowledged the existence of horse-riding warriors, documented primarily through a famous debate in which the king of the state of Chao expounds on the necessity to adopt the methods of mounted warfare predominant in the north.

Analysis of events at this time reveals a new transformation taking place on the frontier. The incorporation of various Jung and Ti peoples by the stronger Chinese states did not exhaust the states' need to expand or to increase the resources at their disposal. In fact, the demands of the new military situation, which resulted in the need to sustain prolonged, expensive wars and in a great increase in the number of armies, may have been at the root of the northern states' expansion in the north. Offering a new interpretation for the motives behind the construction of the early "long walls" in northern China, this chapter will argue that the construction of static defense structures served to establish firm bases from which Chinese "occupation" armies could control the surrounding, non-Chinese territory. Using textual and archaeological evidence, this chapter will revisit the traditional interpretation according to which the fortified lines of defense, the precursors of the Great Wall, were built to defend the Chinese civilization (or the incipient Chinese empire) from the incursions of the nomads. Rather, walls were meant as a form of military penetration and occupation of an alien territory that the Chinese states could use in a variety of ways, including horse breeding and trade, and as a reservoir for troops and laborers. Once the Chinese began a more sustained pattern of relations with nomadic peoples, the fundamental attitude they adopted toward the nomads shows continuity with the policies and strategies that had dominated Chinese relations with the Jung and Ti, not the rupture that a purely defensive strategy (implied by the erection of "defensive walls") would entail.

PART III. The issues considered in Part II are essential to understanding the next transformation of the frontier, which coincides with the emergence of a unified nomadic power, the first such "empire" in world history and precursor to the Türk and Mongol empires. The policy of occupation and creeping expansionism practiced by the northern Chinese states in the third century B.C. was endorsed with a vengeance by the unifier of China, Ch'in Shih Huang-ti, who in 215 B.C. sent an enormous army to conquer and colonize the pasture grounds located in the Ordos region. Chapter 5 argues that the relentless pressure of the Chinese states on the northern frontier possibly acted as a catalyst for deep social transformations among the nomads. In a partial reappraisal of the genesis of the Hsiung-nu empire, I discuss in this chapter a pattern of state formation among Inner Asian nomads that aims to be consistent with the events as they are narrated in the historical sources. The rise of the Hsiung-nu empire forced radical modification of traditional approaches to "frontier management," as the Chinese were now in a position of military inferiority. A new world order thus emerged wherein the main powers split the world that they knew into two large areas of influence; although unified, China was no longer

8

hegemonic. The policy that dominated the relations between Hsiung-nu and Han in the early Former Han period was one of appeasement and accommodation in which China became a virtual tributary of the Hsiung-nu.

Chapter 6 demonstrates why this policy eventually had to be abandoned and why the Han dynasty needed to turn to more aggressive strategies. Two factors emerge: first, the ripening of conditions that on the political, military, and economic levels enabled China to invest more of its people and resources in an all-out war effort; and second and most important, the ideological shift that accompanied the realization that the *ho-ch'in* policy of appeasement did not guarantee peace. Several explanations have been offered to account for the Han endorsement of a military stance, and this chapter will explore why the *ho-ch'in* policy did not work, by looking more closely at the Hsiung-nu side. From an Inner Asian perspective, it appears that the "appeasement" policy failed owing to a structural incompatibility between Hsiung-nu and Han understandings of their mutual international obligations.

Chapter 6 ends with a survey of Han westward expansion and of the Han motives in establishing a military presence in the "Western Regions." Again, the debates are not new, and most of the opinions I express here coincide with those of other scholars. Yet my perspective emphasizes not so much the economic factors as it does the military and political ones, which seem to have prevailed in a context in which destruction of the Hsiung-nu empire as a single political entity was the overriding concern.

PART IV. A further, decisive, "transformation" of the frontier occurred in the first century B.C., when the north finally became an object of conscious historical and ethnographic inquiry. The relationship between the Hsiung-nu and China, as constructed by Ssu-ma Ch'ien in the *Shih chi*, became a polarity between two antithetical principles whose genesis coincided with the dawn of Chinese history. Together with the "crystallization" of Inner Asian history into a pattern that had not been recognized before in any way even remotely comparable to the grand scheme erected by him, the historian Ssu-ma Ch'ien opened the door to an empirical investigation of the north, made not of mythological accounts and moral precepts, but of information that was as historically rigorous as one might expect from the "Grand Historian." He selected his sources carefully, acquired much information from persons who had been closely engaged in Hsiung-nu affairs, copied memorials and diplomatic correspondence, and narrated events with precision and an abundance of detail. Part IV is based on the identification of two chief strands in Ssu-ma Ch'ien's narrative, one the collection of information vital to understanding the Chinese confrontation with the Hsiung-nu empire; the other, no less vital, the construction of a pattern that rationalized the relevance of the north in Chinese history. Chapter 7 focuses on the information that Ssu-ma Ch'ien incorporated in his monographic account of the Hsiung-nu (chapter 110), effectively starting an ethnography and a literate history of the north that also served as a model for later dynastic histories. Chapter 8 looks at how Ssu-ma Ch'ien rationalized the history of relations between the north and China into a broad pattern resting on two elements. One was the creation of a "genealogy" of northern peoples that could match the historical "genealogy" of Chinese dynasties and hegemonic states from the mythical beginning of history to the historian's time. The other was the insertion of the north and its inhabitants within the system of correspondences between the celestial and the human spheres that was believed, in Han times, to constitute cosmic order. Events such as wars or the downfalls of rulers were regarded as manifestations at the human level of the workings of that cosmic system, and, therefore, history was the "output" of a machinery of correlations that could not exclude the Hsiung-nu or more generally, foreign peoples. Thus foreign peoples and their lands become equal partners in the construction of Chinese history, whereas in the past they had been (as far as I can tell) excluded from the system of correlations and predictions upon which historical causality was ultimately based.

Our knowledge of the genesis and earliest evolution of relations between China and the north, down to the Han dynasty, is still gotten through the lens of Ssu-ma Ch'ien's "master narrative." This narrative effectively made the north into a historical protagonist. At the same time, it trapped the history of the northern frontier into a dichotomous patterns from which we have yet to free ourselves. By identifying the history of the frontier as an artifact, as a "narrative" that must be placed in a given time and intellectual milieu, and as the culmination (obviously not the end) of a long and intricate process, we can also re-establish the northern "sphere" of Chinese history as an area with its own autonomous, internally dialectical, historical, and cultural development.

PART I

CHAPTER ONE

The Steppe Highway
The Rise of Pastoral Nomadism as a Eurasian Phenomenon

Geographic Features

A Note on Terminology

The terminology for the regions inhabited by the nomadic and semi-nomadic peoples of Inner Asia in pre-historical and historical times is inherently unstable, given that geographic areas such as Central Asia, Inner Asia, the Northern Zone, and Central Eurasia are usually defined ad hoc.[1]

Because the present work is concerned mostly with what Owen Lattimore has called the "Inner Asian frontiers of China," I have adopted "Inner Asia" or "Inner Asian frontier" as a general term for the eastern part of the continental mass of Eurasia. In practice, it includes three geographical areas: in the east, Manchuria; in the center, Mongolia, including parts of Kansu, northern Shensi, and northern Shansi; and in the west, not only today's Sinkiang but also the Minusinsk Basin and the northern part of the Altai Mountains.

This central definition must be accompanied by two others. The narrower term, the so-called Northern Zone, is used, especially in China, to describe the ecological and cultural frontier between China and Inner Asia. Today this area is entirely within China's political boundaries and runs from the Liao Valley in the east, to the T'ai-hang Mountains up to the Ordos region in the center, and to the Ning-hsia–Ch'ing-hai cultural region in the west. This term often refers to the area of the Great Wall, but to avoid

---

[1] For an extensive discussion of the definition of Central Asia, see Shirin Akiner, "Conceptual Geographies of Central Asia," in *Sustainable Development in Central Asia*, ed. Shirin Akiner et al. (New York: St. Martin's Press, 1998), pp. 3–62.

anachronisms, "Northern Zone" is clearly preferable to "Great Wall Region."

The broader term, "Central Eurasia," is particularly useful for referring to the part of the Eurasian landmass that is crossed horizontally by a grassland belt stretching from western Manchuria to the Danube. Beginning in the second millennium B.C., this region saw the development of pastoral nomadic cultures that flourished from the Pontic Steppe across the Altai and to Mongolia.[2] On the Asian side, this broad expanse incorporates, the region that Alexander von Humboldt called Central Asia in 1843 and Ferdinand von Richtofen later defined as the part of continental Asia forming a closed hydrological system, with no access to the open sea. The boundaries he proposed were the Altai Mountains in the north, the Khingan Range in the east, the Pamirs in the west, and Tibet in the south.[3] Others have defined it in even broader terms, including the area running from the Caspian Sea and the Ural River Basin in the west to the Ferghana Valley and Pamir Range in the east, and from the limits of the Kazakh Steppe belt in the north to the Hindu Kush and Kopet-Dagh in the south. Today "Central Asia" has acquired a narrower meaning from its use in the former Soviet Union, and it can be said to include the territory of the Uzbek, Turkmen, Tajik, Kirgiz, and Kazak states, plus the Sinkiang (Xinjiang) Uighur Autonomous Province in northwest China, which, in ancient times, was closely connected with the rest of Central Asia.

Before we address the issue of the formation of pastoral cultures of China's Inner Asian frontier, it is necessary to survey the natural environments in which these cultures emerged, environments that placed limitations on the directions and extents of their development. The vast territory that separates China from Siberia and Central Asia can be divided into three major geographic zones: the Manchurian Plain; the steppes and forests of Mongolia; and the oases, deserts, and steppes of Sinkiang.[4]

---

[2] Denis Sinor defines Central Eurasia not only in geographical but also in cultural terms; see his *Inner Asia: A Syllabus* (Bloomington: Indiana University, 1987, 3rd rpt.), pp. 1–5.

[3] See L. I. Myroshnikov, "Appendix: A Note on the Meaning of 'Central Asia' as Used in This Book," in *History of Civilizations of Central Asia*, ed. A. H. Dani and V. M. Masson (Paris: Unesco, 1992), 1: 477–80.

[4] The following geographic survey is based primarily on: George B. Cressy, *Asia's Lands and Peoples* (New York: McGraw Hill Book Co., 1963); Robert N. Taaffe, "The Geographic Setting," *The Cambridge History of Early Inner Asia*, ed. Denis Sinor (Cambridge: Cambridge University Press, 1990), pp. 19–40; V. M. Masson, "The Environment," in *History of Civilizations of Central Asia*, 1: 29–44; Hisao Matsuda, "The T'ian-shan Range in Asian History," *Acta Asiatica* 41 (1981): 1–28.

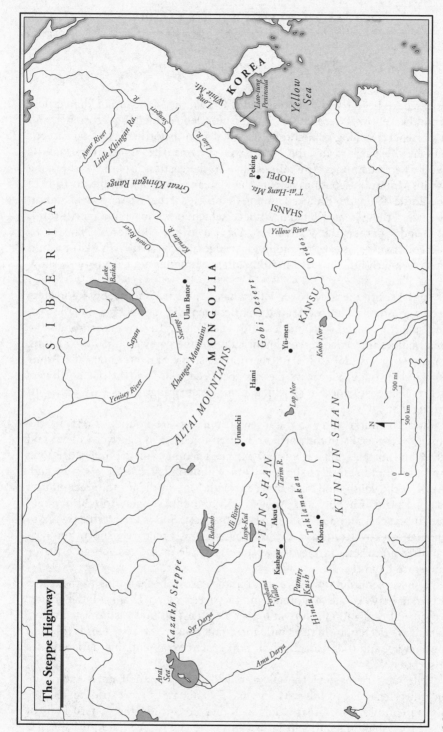

The Steppe Highway

KOREA

Yellow Sea

Liao-tung Peninsula

Long White Mt.

Amur River

Little Khingan Ra.

Sungari R.

Great Khingan Range

Liao R.

Peking

HOPEI

T'ai-Hang Mts.

SHANSI

Yellow River

Ordos

KANSU

Kerulen R.

Onon River

SIBERIA

Lake Baikal

Selenge R.

Ulan Bator

Sayan

MONGOLIA

Khangai Mountains

Gobi Desert

Yü-men

Koko Nor

Yenisey River

Hami

ALTAI MOUNTAINS

Lop Nor

KUNLUN SHAN

Urumchi

N

500 mi

500 km

Tarim R.

T'IEN SHAN

Aksu

Taklamakan

Khotan

Ili River

Issyk-Kul

L. Balkash

Kashgar

Ferghana Valley

Pamirs

Hindu Kush

Kazakh Steppe

Syr Darya

Amu Darya

Aral Sea

Map 1

15

Manchurian Plain

Located to the northeast of present-day China, the Manchurian Plain differs from the Yellow River Plain in that it is not depositional, but erosional, and it presents a rolling topography. Divided into a northern and a southern half by the Sungari and the Liao River systems, the Manchurian Plain is everywhere surrounded by mountains. To the east and southeast the Long White Mountain separates it from the Korean Peninsula. To the north rises the Little Khingan Range, running parallel to the Amur River, and to the west the Great Khingan Range, which develops on a north-south axis and separates the Manchurian Plain from the Mongolian Plateau. To the southwest, a series of mountain ranges, such as the Ch'i-lao-t'u and the Nu-lu-erh-hu, separate it from Inner Mongolia and from the Yellow River Plain.

In the south the Liao River Valley has a hundred and twenty kilometers frontage on the Gulf of Liao-tung. Between the mountains and the sea, the strip of coastal lowland leads to the Yellow River Plain through the Shan-hai-kuan, which served historically as one gateway for those seeking to enter (or invade) China. In the northeast the Sungari enters the Amur lowland through a narrow passage between hills, and in the northwest a low section of the Great Khingan mountain range gives easy access to Mongolia.

In Manchuria three natural environments are found: forest in the uplands, especially in the northern half; arable land in the river valleys; and grassland in the west. Because of the continental climate winters are long and bitter and summers short and hot. Snow falls from October through April in the south, and September through May in the north. Precipitation is concentrated in July and August, and amounts roughly to 630 millimeters in the east and 380 millimeters in the west. Soil is very fertile owing to the natural cover of grass; the growing season is relatively short, but agriculture, precarious in the dry west, is possible in the east because of the moisture from the sea.

The Manchurian uplands extend in the east from Liao-tung to the Amur River, in between the mountains and the river valleys. Thanks to the greater volume of rain and moisture at higher altitudes, we find vast forested areas, which are deciduous in the south and coniferous in the east. This is the land of hunters, and today local people still practice trapping, but agriculture is also possible.

The western part of the geographical Manchurian Plain is today the northwestern part of Inner Mongolia. The climate is more arid, unsuitable for agriculture. The Great Khingan Range constitutes the eastern limit of the Mongolian Plateau, and in fact both the environment and the lifestyle of the people here resemble those of Mongolia.[5] In terms of vegetation, the north is a forest of Siberian larch and birch, while the south is a Mongolian-type steppe. Traditionally, its inhabitants have mostly been hunters and pastoralists. The southwestern mountains are rugged and difficult to cross, serving as a natural boundary between two economic zones, the Liao Valley in the east, suitable for agriculture, and the Mongolian Steppe and Gobi Desert in the west. This mountainous area extends into northern China, in particular, the provinces of Hopei and Shansi, where the T'ai-hang mountain range acts as a natural divide running from north to south.

Moving westward from the northern part of the T'ai-hang Range, one runs into the southernmost fringes of the Gobi, that is, the Ordos Desert, circumscribed within the bend of the Yellow River. Surrounded by a rim of mountains, the Gobi is the most northern and furthest inland of all the deserts on earth, and for the most part it has a climate similar to that of a dry steppe. The ground is covered with pebbles and gravel, and it has enough water to sustain some vegetation and animal life. Extremely arid patches, with sand dunes and almost complete absence of vegetation, cover only five percent of the whole desert, mainly in the southwest.

Mongolia

Mongolia is divided into four vegetation zones, which run almost parallel to each other from east to west.[6] The southernmost part is a desert zone, which is succeeded, going north, by a desert-steppe belt. North of this is a dry steppe zone to the east and, to the west, a continuation of the desert-steppe belt in the lower elevations and, in the higher elevations, a mountain-steppe and forest-steppe zone alternating with patches of dry steppe. The northernmost zone is heavily forested, though we also find alpine meadows that provide excellent pastures interspersed with areas of Siberian taiga. The southern Gobi extends from western Inner Mongolia to eastern Sinkiang; to the north the Gobi occupies Mongolia's southern half. Mongolia also has several important mountain ranges. In the west, the Altai Mountains extend northwest to southeast, and their southeasternmost extension merges with a range known as the Gobi Altai Mountains, which forms a series of ridges crossed by intramontane valleys and basins. North of the Altai, in northwestern Mongolia, are mountain ranges that extend further north into Siberia; to the east, a large depression known as the

---

[5] Owen Lattimore, *The Mongols of Manchuria* (New York: John Day Company, 1934).

[6] An extensive introduction to the topography, hydrographic system, flora and fauna of Mongolia is included in: The Academy of Sciences MPR, *Information Mongolia* (Oxford: Pergamon Press, 1990), pp. 3–49.

Valley of Lakes is interposed between these ranges and the large mountainous area known as the Khangai Mountains. This latter area has a rolling topography, dotted by sand hills and dry river beds.

The central artery of the Khangai Mountains has a northwestern orientation, similar to that of the Altai, and is crossed by several rivers, forming a watershed between the drainage system of the Arctic Ocean Basin, into which the northern rivers flow, and the closed drainage system of Central Asia. The relief of the Khangai is smooth and gentle in its northern and northwestern parts; in the south, precipitous escarpments and breakages of the plateau are more typical. In the north-central part of Mongolia, the Khentii mountain ridge also forms a continental divide between the Pacific Ocean drainage system and the Central Asian Basin. The eastern region of Mongolia is a raised plain with abundant grassland, and an average altitude of 800 to 1,100 meters above sea level.

The major waterways of Mongolia are concentrated in the north and flow in the direction of the Arctic Basin: The Selenge is a tributary of Lake Baikal, and the Orkhon is the main tributary of the Selenge and is fed by the Tula. The rivers in the east of the country, particularly those flowing from the eastern slopes of the Khentii Mountains, belong to the Pacific Ocean drainage system; among these the Onon, a tributary of the Amur, and the Kerulen, which ends its course in the Dalai Nor lake on the western side of the Great Khingan Range, are the most important waterways and natural avenues of communication between Central Mongolia, Transbaikalia, and northern Manchuria.

Sinkiang

Sinkiang may be viewed as consisting of three major subregions: the desertic Tarim Basin in the south, the vast T'ien-shan Range in the center, and the semi-arid Zungarian Basin in the north. The Tarim Basin is drier than any other desert in China, and it includes a totally dry desert in the center, the Taklamakan, which is surrounded by a string of oases on its northern, western, and southern edges. Amongst these oases, the largest are Yarkand, Khotan, Kashgar, Aksu, Kucha, and Karashar. These oases are formed by semi-permanent water streams originating from the glaciers at the tops of the mountains encircling the Tarim Basin, that is, the T'ien-shan in the north, the Pamirs in the west, and the Kunluns in the south. Irrigation ditches allow water from the mountains to spread over the river's alluvial fan, creating relatively large stretches of farming land. Each oasis constitutes a self-enclosed system that commands some of the desert around it, an irrigated area with a principal city, barren foothills, and well-watered mountain valleys upstream.

Into this southern, more desertic region flows the main river of Sinkiang, the Tarim, which is the final destination of the streams flowing from the surrounding mountains, although many evaporate or disappear underground before reaching it. Owing to the aridity of the climate, there is no cultivation on the Tarim's banks. Eventually, the Tarim flows into the Lop Nor lake, located in the eastern part of the region. Directly to the north of Lop Nor, close to the southern slope of the Bogdo Mountain in the eastern Altai, is the Turfan depression, 266 meters below sea level. North of the Tarim Basin, the T'ien-shan extends east into China for 1,600 kilometers. Elevations reach 6,686 meters in the west and 5,089 meters in Bogda Ula, north of Turfan, in the east. The orography is rugged, although there are elevated plains and broad valleys covered with alpine meadows in some parts.

The northern half of Sinkiang is occupied by an arid zone known as Zungaria. This is a desertlike area, but it is less arid than the southern part and closer in appearance to the Gobi. Some oases are along the northern slopes of the T'ien-shan, but they are smaller and less richly irrigated than the southern ones. To the west, the T'ien-shan splits into two branches that embrace the fertile valley of the Ili River, which flows to the northwest, draining into Lake Balkash. North of the Ili, the Zungarian Gate, at 304 meters of altitude, is a deep corridor between the northern edge the T'ien-shan and the Tarbagatai Range in the northwest. This is the lowest pass in all Central Asia, and it was used by nomads as a gateway to the Kazakh Steppe. The extreme northern and northeastern limits of the region are marked by the Altai. The foothills of the Altai form a rolling plateau with excellent pastureland. The valley of the Irtysh, in the far north, between the Tarbagatai and the Altai, at an elevation of approximately 430 meters, forms another gateway to Central Asia.

In addition to these mountain chains, the southern edge of the Tarim Basin meets the Altyn Tagh mountain chain to the east, whereas the south-central and southwestern sides of the Taklamakan are blocked by the lofty Kunlun Mountains, extending down from the Tibetan Plateau. On mountain slopes, precipitation is sufficient to allow growth of a relatively dense grass cover. Indeed, the best pastures to be found in this region are on the slopes of the Altai and in the intermontane valleys and alpine meadows of the T'ien-shan; nomads can pasture their herds in these areas through the year. Forests also grow above the steppe belt, at altitudes of between 1,400 and 2,500 meters.

Finally, an important area for the development of early metallurgy and pastoral nomadic culture is defined by the Altai and Sayan Ranges, which begin near the Zungarian Gate, close to Lake Baikal, and extend east for 1,600 kilometers. The central ridges of both ranges are rolling uplands, which reach an altitude of about 2,586 meters. The Altai system, coming into Siberia from northwestern Mongolia, is enclosed between the Irtysh and Ob Rivers, where we find the Altai Mountains proper, culminating in Peak Belukha, at about 4,300 meters. East of the Ob lies the eastern Altai Range, reaching almost to the Yenisei. The two ranges of the Sayan system encircle the Minusinsk Basin: the eastern Sayan Range extends from Lake Baikal to the Yenisei, while the western Sayan Range cordons off the basin in the south. Here, too, the prevailing orography is of rolling hills. Steppe vegetation covers the lower slopes of the Altai-Sayan mountains up to some 860 meters; above it is a forest of Siberian larch, cedar, fir, pine, and birch up to and above 1,720 meters, followed by alpine meadows to the snow line at around 2,580 meters.

Sinkiang commands the communication routes between China and Central Asia. Before the advent of modern rail transportation, the caravans going west from Hsi-an (Shansi province) en route to the western êntrepots and markets reached Lan-chou and then began to cross the arid Kansu region following the base of the Nan Shan (Ch'i-liang) Range and traveling from one irrigated oasis to another. The so-called Kansu Corridor – a depression less than 80 kilometers wide and over 960 kilometers long – is dotted with oases drawing water from the Nan Shan Range. At the end of the corridor, Jade Gate (Yü-men) opened the way to Sinkiang, after passing the cities of An-hsi and Tun-huang. This area, at the western end of the Gobi, is today a barren desert, but there are signs that in antiquity the climatic conditions were more favorable and that it was then possible to travel along a line tangential to the southern edge of the Tarim Basin.[7] The better-known route, however, crossed the desert and proceeded northwest to Hami, on the eastern fringes of the T'ien-shan mountain range, and only then divided into routes to the south and to the north of the T'ien-shan Range.

To the south, two routes developed, skirting, respectively, the northern and the southern fringes of the Taklamakan Desert. They joined in the western part of the Tarim Basin, where the large oasis of Kashgar is located, and proceeded to the Terek Pass, and through this to Ferghana and Transoxiana. North of the T'ien-shan, the route passed through Urumqi, and from there, via Kulja, reached the Ili Valley and the Zungarian Pass. Finally, yet another gateway to Central Asia is located farther north, where the uninterrupted steppe belt along the base of the Altai provides a passage to the valley of the Irtysh.

[7] See Hou Can, "Environmental Changes in the Tarim Oases as Seen through Archeological Discoveries," in *Between Lapis and Jade*, ed. F. Hiebert and N. Di Cosmo, *Anthropology and Archaeology of Eurasia* (Spring 1996): 55–66; Mutsumi Hoyanagi, "Natural Changes of the Region along the Old Silk Road in the Tarim Basin in Historical Times," *Memoirs of the Research Department of the Toyo Bunko* 33 (1975): 85–113.

Pastoral Nomadism in the Steppe: Preconditions

The forests, deserts, and especially grasslands of Central Eurasia have historically been associated with the rise of pastoral nomadism. The first historical descriptions of these nomads, the Scythians, come down to us from Greek historians and geographers. Although their individual conceptions of the Asian nomads varied substantially, they clearly believed that in the prairies of Central Asia a different strain of people had developed, one whose customs and lifestyle were incompatible with those of sedentary peoples.

I praise not the Scythians in all respects, but in this greatest matter they have so devised that none who attacks them can escape, and none can catch them if they desire not to be caught. For when men have no established cities or fortresses, but all are house-bearers and mounted archers, living not by tilling the soil, but by cattle rearing and carrying their dwellings on wagons, how should these not be invincible and unapproachable.[8]

How had this different way of life arisen? In the nineteenth century, following Darwinian and positivist theories, scholars believed that nomadism was an evolutionary stage, more advanced than hunting, from which it was supposed to have sprung, but less developed than agriculture, in the progressive march of humankind toward civilization. This idea can be traced back to Lewis Henry Morgan's influence on positivistic ethnographical and sociological thought: the people who first domesticated animals became accustomed to pastoral life before learning to cultivate cereals.[9]

At the end of the nineteenth century, scholars began to criticize this viewpoint, arguing that "the domestication of animals was possible only under the conditions of a sedentary way of life."[10] The domestication of animals requires a long process of experimentation and accumulation of technical knowledge, and presupposes the existence of other sources of economic production that could allow for the surplus in fodder and grains needed to feed the animals. Thus we may conclude that plant domestication with primitive farming was probably a precondition for the domestication of animals. In the first instances of domestication of animals, which date to

---

[8] Herodotus, *Histories*, IV:46. Quoted in John Gardiner-Garden, *Greek Conceptions on Inner Asian Geography and Ethnography from Ephoros to Eratosthenes*, Papers on Inner Asia no. 9 (Bloomington: Research Institute for Inner Asian Studies, 1987), p. 5.

[9] Lewis Henry Morgan, *Ancient Society*, ed. Leslie A. White (Cambridge, Mass.: Harvard University Press, 1964), p. 290.

[10] S. I. Vejnshtein, "The Problem of Origin and Formation of the Economic-Cultural Type of Pastoral Nomads in the Moderate Belt of Eurasia," in *The Nomadic Alternative*, ed. W. Weissleder (The Hague: Mouton, 1984), p. 127.

between 7500 and 6000 B.C. in the area of the Fertile Crescent, the animals were kept as a nutritional complement to agricultural products. Some of the animals – for example, the ox, the onager, and the dog – were then used for other purposes, such as a means of transportation or as protection for domestic animals against predators.

With characteristic insight, Owen Lattimore emphasized the importance of the oasis economy for the evolution of Inner Asian steppe nomads. He hypothesized that early domestication was possible in areas where the natural environment was equally favorable to agriculture and to animal husbandry. In the steppe oases, where large herbivores captured in the steppe could be kept and fed, people gradually learned how to use them, and eventually moved out into the open steppe, thus becoming "specialized pastoralists."[11] Lattimore attributed the causes that ignited this process and "pushed" the first nomads into the steppe to an economically more efficient adaptation to the natural environment of the steppe.[12]

Although Lattimore's displacement theory is not supported by archaeological evidence, archaeologists have emphasized the importance of agricultural production in the oases, which could also spark revolutionary changes in economic patterns, social organization, and cultural development. For example, the colonization of oases was at the root of what has been called the Bactria-Margiana Archaeological Complex, as well as of the later "Oxus Civilization" of Central Asia.[13] In terms of the development of conditions suitable for the advancement of pastoralism, the oasis environment is thought to have been conducive to the appearance of a mixed farmer-pastoralist economy because the proximity of grasslands imposed fewer restrictions on stock raising than did valley agriculture, where an imbalance between humans and animals could be disastrous.[14] According to some theories, the oasis dwellers who specialized in stock breeding eventually separated themselves from their original environment and became nomadic pastoralists.[15] Yet these nomads retained close ties with farming communities, upon which they remained to an extent dependant for agricultural and handicraft products.

Extensive archaeological studies have made it clear that the line that separated early pastoral and farming communities, at least to the late Bronze

---

[11] Owen Lattimore, *Inner Asian Frontiers of China* (Boston: Beacon Press, 1962 [1940]), pp. 158–63.

[12] Ibid., pp. 63–64, 409–12.

[13] Fredrik T. Hiebert, *Origins of the Bronze Age Oasis Civilizations in Central Asia*, Bulletin 42 (Cambridge, Mass.: American School of Prehistoric Research, 1994).

[14] A. Khazanov, *Nomads and the Outside World* (Cambridge: Cambridge University Press, 1984), p. 89.

[15] Shinobu Iwamura, "Nomad and Farmer in Central Asia," *Acta Asiatica* 3 (1962): 45–50.

Age, between the second and the first millennium B.C., was not neatly defined, and even specialized pastoral nomads are known to have engaged in agriculture.[16] In the Central Asian steppes, the first mixed pastoralist-agriculturalist communities appeared following a period during the Paleolithic in which a sparse population of hunters of large game ("mega-fauna") dominated the human landscape. Organized into small societies, these communities were characterized by "relative stability, embodied in nomad base camps, and intellectual progress, reflected in a large number of prestige, symbolic innovations from statuettes to symbolic marks."[17] Pastoral cultures appeared first in the western Eurasian steppes, west of the Urals, in the mid-third millennium B.C. These pastoral communities are identified by their distinctive mound burials (*kurgan*).[18]

From the mid-third millennium B.C., the northern regions of Central Eurasia, east of the Urals, were transformed by the shift from an economy of predation to an economy of production. The steppe regions became populated with diversified communities of Neolithic hunters and fishermen as well as Bronze Age pastoralists and agriculturalists. Possibly because of a climatic desiccation that affected soil productivity, a general transition to more pronounced forms of pastoralism occurred in the steppe and semi-desert areas of Eurasia.[19] These environments created conditions favorable to the breeding of animals, and agriculture could also be practiced. Pastoralists occupied the higher alpine pastures, such as those in the T'ien-shan and the Altai regions, whereas along the lower course of the Amu Darya, in Central Asia, animal breeding co-existed with irrigated agriculture modeled after the system of irrigation of the Khorezmian civilization, at the northeastern end of the Mesopotamian world.

Although herders became gradually more mobile and the aridization of the climate made agriculture more problematic in several areas, this evolutional trajectory did not necessarily mean the abandonment of agriculture. The more common picture in central Asia during the first half of the second millennium B.C., was the development of settled agro-pastoral

---

[16] S. Vainshtein, *Nomads of South Siberia. The Pastoral Economies of Tuva* (Cambridge: Cambridge University Press, 1980), pp. 145–65.

[17] V. M. Masson, and T. F. Taylor, "Soviet Archaeology in the Steppe Zone: Introduction," *Antiquity* 63 (1989): 779–83.

[18] These have been identified with a "macro-culture" known by the name of Yama culture; see Natalia I. Shishlina and Fredrik T. Hiebert, "The Steppe and the Sown: Interaction between Bronze Age Eurasian Nomads and Agriculturalists," in *The Bronze Age and Early Iron Age Peoples of Eastern Central Asia*, ed. Victor Mair (Washington: Institute for the Study of Man, 1998), 1: 224–25.

[19] P. M. Dolukhanov, "Paléoécologie de l'Asie centrale aux ages de la pierre et du bronze," in *L'Asie centrale et ses rapports avec les civilisations orientales, des origines à l'age du fer*, Mémoires de la Mission Archéologique Française en Asie Centrale (Paris: Diffusion de Boccard, 1988), 1: 215–17.

societies that appear to have wielded considerable political and military power. In addition to the aforementioned climatic changes, the interaction between steppe peoples and more advanced agricultural cultures in the oases of Central Asia and an internal evolution toward greater economic specialization seem to have played an important role in the formation of mobile pastoral societies, such as those of the early Andronovo period (1900–1750 B.C.).[20]

According to Khazanov, the evolutionary pattern in the formation of pastoral nomads has four phases: (1) sedentary animal husbandry, (2) semi-sedentary pastoralism, (3) herdsman husbandry or distant pastures husbandry, (4) semi-nomadic pastoralism and pastoral nomadism proper.[21] David correlates these four stages with as many types of archaeological cultures, thereby proposing an evolutionary development.[22] The first phase is represented by the early horse breeders, evidence for whom has been found in the forest-steppe zone of southern Russia, at the site of Dereivka. Primitive horseback riding, presumably a development in the steppe between the Ural and the Volga in the mid-third millennium B.C., characterizes the second phase, resulting in the increased mobility of these early pastoral communities. The third phase, during the second millennium B.C., corresponds to the flourishing of the bronze culture in the steppe region and the emergence of wheeled vehicles pulled by horses. Covered wagons provided transportation and shelter during migratory moves, and light chariots may have been used in warfare and for herd control. The fourth phase, from the beginning of the first millennium B.C., corresponds to the emergence of ancient nomads, when horseback riding had already evolved into a mature stage of development. It is during the third phase, therefore, that we may assume that horses began to be ridden, but how widespread this was, and how important it was for the general social and economic life of these agro-pastoral communities, is moot. These data today have to be reconsidered in light of new evidence that places the earliest form of horseback riding in the late fourth millennium B.C.

The Horse

The role of the horse in the transition from agro-pastoralism to fully developed mounted pastoral nomadism has been considered crucial. In particular, horseback riding allowed different herding strategies, making it possible

---

[20] Shishlina and Hiebert, "The Steppe and the Sown," 1: 231.
[21] Khazanov, *Nomads and the Outside World*, pp. 19–25.
[22] T. David, "Peuples mobiles de l'eurasie: contacts d'une périphérie 'barbare' avec le monde 'civilisé,' à la fin de l'Age du Bronze et au 1er Age du Fer," in *L'Asie Centrale et ses rapports*, pp. 159–68.

for fewer people to control larger herds, and, by allowing increased mobility, leading to expansion of the political and cultural horizons of early pastoralists.[23] The horse is an animal that is notoriously difficult to tame, and according to some, the first equid to be domesticated was not the horse, but the more docile onager.[24] Nonetheless, the large number of horse remains recovered at the site of Dereivka (4200–3700 B.C.), in the south Russian Steppe, leaves no doubt that the domestication of the horse probably began in the fifth–fourth millennium B.C.[25] Among horse remains found at the Dereivka site, evidence of tooth wear caused by a hard bit, dating from before the invention of the wheel – therefore ruling out the hypothesis that the horses had been hitched to carts – indicates that the Dereivka horses were not only bred but also ridden.[26] The finding of cheek pieces made of deer antlers with holes drilled in them supports this conclusion. It is also based on the assumption that hard bits were in circulation and that their use was generalized (bit wear was found on the tooth of a single horse). Horseback riding is also assumed to have been developed to control large herds of horses. It is not clear, however, if this evidence suffices to prove that the horse was actually ridden, since horses might have been used as draft animals even in the absence of the wheel.[27] Even if the first horse breeders actually mounted the horse, the communities remained predominantly agricultural, also raising pigs, cattle, and sheep. Although the horse was the most important of the Dereivka animals, it remained so within the economic context of early agro-pastoralists.[28]

[23] David Anthony, "The Opening of the Eurasian Steppe at 2000 BCE," in *The Bronze Age and Early Iron Age Peoples of Eastern Central Asia*, 1: 94–113.

[24] J. F. Downs, "Origin and Spread of Riding in the Near East and Central Asia," *American Anthropologist* 63 (1961): 1193–1203.

[25] Dmitriy Yakolevich Telegin, *Dereivka: A Settlement and Cemetery of Copper Age Horse Keepers on the Middle Dnieper*, ed. J. P. Mallory, trans V. K. Pyatkovskiy (Oxford: B.A.R., 1986); Marsha Levine, "Dereivka and the Problem of Horse Domestication," *Antiquity* 64 (1990): 727–40.

[26] David Anthony and Dorcas Brown, "The Origin of Horseback Riding," *Antiquity* 65.246 (1991): 22-38.

[27] A striking example of this use of the horse comes from a bronze figurine adorning the handle of a dagger from the Rostonska burial, near Omsk, showing a horse bridled at the mouth pulling a human being on a pair of skis; see E. N. Chernykh, *Ancient Metallurgy in the USSR* (Cambridge: Cambridge University Press, 1992), p. 228. This use of the domesticated horse, although attested later than Dereivka, must have been possible during the Dereivka period and demonstrates that tooth wear caused by a bit, in the absence of corroborating evidence such as petroglyphs and other visual representations, is not necessarily evidence of horseback riding.

[28] Claudia Chang and Perry A. Tourtellotte, "The Role of Agro-pastoralism in the Evolution of Steppe Culture in the Semirechye Area of Southern Kazakhstan

Nonetheless, these early domesticators played an important role in the selection of the species. The Dereivka horses are not significantly different from those recovered thirty-five hundred years later, at Pazyryk, in the Altai Mountains of Kazakhstan, although they are very different from the smaller wild horses. The type of bones proves that human-controlled selection took place, and, whether or not they invented riding, these early communities must be given credit for their high level of specialization in breeding.[29] In northern Kazakhstan a settlement of the fourth–third millennium B.C. has been excavated where 99 percent of all animal remains recovered belong to horses, indicating that those people – who lived in large, semi-subterranean houses – specialized in horse breeding.[30] At this site cheek pieces have also been found, but the economic and social characteristics of this settlement do not suggest a mobile lifestyle.

A conservative interpretation would date a significant impact of early horseback riding on western and Central Asia to between the mid-third and early second millennium B.C.[31] The early horse-riding communities, however, were not properly nomadic. Although some communities were more or less mobile, riding in wheeled carts to follow their herds, their pastoralism cannot be defined as a regular cyclical migration seasonally alternating among different pasture grounds; rather, this was "herder husbandry" or at most semi-nomadism.[32] These communities also depended on agricultural production and had settlements; the migrations of some groups documented by archaeological data were most likely permanent dislocations due to causes that could have ranged from pasture exhaustion to climatic changes to external threats.[33]

---

during the Saka/Wusun Preriod (600 BCE–400 BCE)," in *The Bronze Age and Early Iron Age Peoples of Eastern Central Asia*, 1: 266.

[29] V. I. Bibikova, "On the History of Horse Domestication in South-East Europe," in Telegin, *Dereivka*, pp. 163–82.

[30] A. P. Derevyanko and D. Dorj, "Neolithic Tribes in Northern Parts of Central Asia," in *History of Civilizations of Central Asia*, 1: 185.

[31] M. A. Littauer and J. H. Crouwel, *Wheeled Vehicles and Ridden Animals in the Ancient Near East* (Leiden: Brill, 1979), pp. 45–47, 65–68. The development of horseback riding as a specialized activity, by the way, was a long process that reached completion with widespread diffusion in Inner Asia of the saddle and the stirrup at a still undefined time that might have fallen within the first half of the first millennium A.D.; see A. D. H. Bivar, "The Stirrup and Its Origin," *Oriental Art*, n.s. 1, 1 (1955): 61–65. On the stirrup, see also Lynn White, Jr., *Medieval Technology and Social Change* (Oxford: Clarendon Press, 1962), pp. 14–28.

[32] Khazanov, *Nomads and the Outside World*, p. 93.

[33] Earlier authors tended to see such large-scale migrations as evidence of the existence of pastoral nomads in the Central Asian steppe as early as the third mil-

The Aryan terminology that appears in a fourteenth-century B.C. Hittite treatise on horsemanship illustrating the training of the chariot horse suggests that such training may have been developed by steppe Indo-European peoples, perhaps the Iranian ancestors of the Achaemenian dynasty.[34] What does seem clear is that most improvements in the training and domestication of the horse were achieved by a people who were already familiar with animal breeding and who had been specializing in this economic activity, although they still practiced farming. It is also possible that the steppe environment allowed contacts among early pastoralists that favored the spread of horse-training techniques. Nevertheless, the transition to actual pastoral nomadism as practiced by horseback riders was probably not completed until the beginning of the first millennium B.C., and the first Scythian mounted archers appear on the scene only in the tenth or ninth century B.C.[35]

Andronovo's Chariots

Climatic changes may have led to the increased mobility of the steppe people starting in the third millennium B.C. In the Bronze Age the technological level of the people of the steppe region was greatly advanced by the widespread introduction of metal artifacts into all branches of production, leading to the emergence of groups skilled in metallurgy who moved about in wheeled vehicles.[36] The earliest wheeled vehicles in the Eurasian steppes were heavy wagons, dated to 2900 B.C. and attributed to the Yamnaya culture, located on the lower Dnieper.[37] Only much later, in the late third and early second millennium B.C., do wheeled vehicles appear east of the Urals, in connection with the spread of the Andronovo people. The people of this widespread and singularly successful Central Asian culture were adept at animal husbandry, and their craftsmen had mastered the art of

lennium B.C. Cf. Raphael Pumpelly, ed., *Explorations in Turkestan. Expedition of 1904. Prehistoric Civilizations of Anau*, 2 vols. (Washington: Carnegie Institution, 1908).

[34] Pentti Aalto, "The Horse in Central Asian Nomadic Cultures," *Studia Orientalia* 46 (1975): 4–7. On the linguistic evidence for the word "horse," see Juha Janhunen "The Horse in East Asia: Reviewing the Linguistic Evidence," in *The Bronze Age and Early Iron Age Peoples of Eastern Central Asia*, 1: 415–30.

[35] Franz Hančar, *Das Pferd in praehistorischer und frühistorischer Zeit* (Wien: Herold, 1956), pp. 551–63.

[36] V. Dergachev, "Neolithic and Bronze Age Cultural Communities of the Steppe Zone of the USSR," *Antiquity* 63.241 (1989): 801.

[37] Anthony, "Opening of the Eurasian Steppe," 1: 102–103.

bronze metallurgy. These metalworkers were able to manipulate alloys so that the quality of the bronze would be harder or tougher according to the specific function of the weapons and tools that they made. Later, Andronovo people, because of their long-distance migrations, may have played an important role in the development of oasis economy, a point suggested by similarities in the nomadic ceramics from distant areas.[38]

The broader utilization of mineral ores from multiple independent metallurgical sources and the expansion of the use of wheeled vehicles and bronze objects are all signs of economic development. Yet the concomitant abundance of weapons indicates that there were increasing tensions among various communities:[39] During this "second epochal type of culture," after the Neolithic revolution, it seems that "[t]he struggle for forcible redistribution of pasture and accumulated wealth [gave] rise, at a certain stage, to a type of militarization of society that found expression and progress in the production of weapons."[40]

Moreover, chariots, mostly used for war, should be distinguished from the four-wheeled wagons and two-wheeled carts used to transport people and goods. Though based on pre-existing models of wheeled vehicles, the war chariot seems to have been developed by the agro-pastoralists of the Andronovo culture.[41] The chariots were light and fast; they had spoked wheels and a rear axle supporting a box in which normally no more than two warriors could either stand, kneel, or sit.[42] Recent discoveries have revealed fully formed chariots with spoked wheels of the Sintashta-Petrovka culture, and these may date to as early as 2026 B.C.[43] These are technically and conceptually very similar to chariots found both in western Asia – at the Lchashen site in the Caucasus – and in East Asia, at the Shang royal site of An-yang. However, according to the expert opinion of Littauer and Crouwel, the Sintashta-Petrovka chariots had a gauge and especially a wheel nave that were too narrow, resulting in a very unstable structure that could not have been efficient for hunting, racing, or fighting. The inefficiency of this type of chariot is made even more evident by the probable availability of horseback riding, which clearly was a superior means of

---

[38] Hiebert, *Origins of the Bronze Age Oasis Civilization in Central Asia*, p. 135.

[39] V. M. Masson, "Les cultures anciennes d'Asie moyenne: dynamique du développement, occupation des aires écologiques, rapports culturels," in *L'Asie centrale et ses rapports*, p. 34.

[40] Masson and Taylor, "Soviet Archaeology in the Steppe Zone," p. 780.

[41] V. F. Gening, "Mogil'nik Sintashta i problema rannikh indoiranskikh plemen," *Sovetskaia Arkheologiia* 4 (1977): 53–73.

[42] Stuart Piggott, *The Earliest Wheeled Transport: From the Atlantic Coast to the Caspian Sea* (Ithaca: Cornell University Press, 1983), p. 95.

[43] David Anthony and Nikolai B. Vinogradov, "Birth of the Chariot," *Archaeology* 48.2 (1995): 38.

transportation, herd control, and warfare. Hence Littauer and Crouwel imply that chariots, which originated in the Near East, where a continuous line of development can be seen from four-wheeled carts to two-wheeled carts to light chariots, were taken on by the nomads predominantly for the symbolic of accompanying the dead to their burial place. In other words, the "prestige value" that the chariot enjoyed in the Near East prompted its construction in the steppe, not its "workaday" usefulness.[44]

The Andronovo people's unquestioned economic superiority propelled this culture across the Eurasian steppe from the Urals to South Siberia whether by horseback or by chariot, and numerous studies indicate that the chariot was imported into China from the west, through Central Asia, possibly around the thirteenth century B.C.[45] Although no definite evidence has emerged yet, it is plausible that the Andronovo culture's contacts with the eastern part of Central Asia, and especially its interaction with the archaeological context of northwestern China (present-day Sinkiang), may be responsible for the introduction into China of the chariot, whose western origin is doubted only by few. These contacts are attested to by the archaeological evidence, including similar bronze artifacts such as axes, celts shaped as spades, and other implements.[46]

The earliest Chinese chariots to have been found were discovered in burials of the Shang dynasty at An-yang; buried with the chariots were their horses and drivers, who served as sacrificial victims. This type of vehicle was used by the aristocracy for display, for hunting, and in war. It was made of a central pole, with one horse harnessed on each side, and a box – typically rectangular or oval; a spoked wheel was at each end of an axle attached crosswise to the rear end of the central pole. The chariot

[44] M. A. Littauer and J. H. Crouwel, "The Origin of the True Chariot," *Antiquity* 70 (1996): 934–39.

[45] Edward L. Shaughnessy, "Historical Perspectives on the Introduction of the Chariot into China," *Harvard Journal of Asiatic Studies* 48.1 (1988): 189–237; Stuart Piggott, "Chinese Chariotry: An Outsider's View," in *Arts of the Eurasian Steppelands*, ed. Philip Denwood, Colloquies on Art and Archaeology in Asia no. 7 (London: Percival David Foundation, 1978), pp. 32–51; Littauer and Crouwel, *Wheeled Vehicles and Ridden Animals in the Ancient Near East*. For a detailed study of the Chinese chariots of the Shang dynasty, see Magdalene von Dewall, *Pferd und Wagen im fruhen China* (Bonn: Habelt, 1964), pp. 109–77. See also Robert Bagley, "Shang Archaeology," in *Cambridge History of Ancient China*, ed. Michael Loewe and Edward L. Shaughnessy (Cambridge: Cambridge University Press, 1999), pp. 202–208.

[46] E. E. Kuzmina, "Cultural Connections of the Tarim Basin People and Pastoralists of the Asian Steppes in the Bronze Age," in *Bronze Age and Early Iron Age Peoples of Eastern Central Asia*, 1: 63–93; Ke Peng, "The Andronovo Artifacts Discovered in Toquztara County in Ili, Xinjiang," in *The Bronze Age and Early Iron Age Peoples of Eastern Central Asia*, 2: 573–80.

appears in China already fully formed.[47] There seem to have been no other wheeled vehicles, such as wagons or carts, pulled by cattle or equids, in use in China before the introduction of the chariot. Later, during the Chou dynasty, chariots were a common feature of the funerary inventory of the richest tombs, as well as forming the core of both the Chou and foreign armies.

Further Cultural Developments

Much of what happened in the second millennium B.C. is still open to question: we see the depopulation of some areas of Central Eurasia, and more contacts take place between settled farmers and mobile herders. Moreover, the movement of people, formerly occurring from west to east, seems to be partly reversed as we can also track an east-to-west movement, possibly as part of a more general migration phenomenon radiating from the Sayano-Altai region. Around the late second millennium B.C. the progress of Central Asian peoples in metallurgy was stimulated by the so-called Seimo-Turbino transcultural complex. The Seimo-Turbino became consolidated as a cultural phenomenon, including both pastoralists and mobile Neolithic hunters of the forest, in the seventeenth century B.C. Chernykh places the point of "departure" of these fast-moving people in the Sayano-Altai region, further east than the eponymous Uralic sites that lent their names to the complex. In this region the encounter of pastoral steppe cultures with metal-working forest people gave rise to a metallurgically advanced, extremely mobile, warlike society. From this part of Inner Asia the Seimo-Turbino people spread westward, a movement well documented by Chernykh based on metallographic analysis.[48]

The Rostovka site, on the Irtysh River, is representative of the eastern, or Siberian, variety of the Seimo-Turbino complex. Here bronze production, consisting of tin bronze and associated with the ancient mines of the Rudny Altai Mountains, was mostly comprised of weapons such as socketed axes, socketed spearheads, and dagger-knives. These tin bronzes eventually reached the Urals, evidence of the westward motion of the Seimo-Turbino people. A further clue to the Altai region as the original home of the Seimo-Turbino people is found in their iconography, which includes animals, such as the wild sheep, typical of the Altai and T'ien-shan regions. As they moved west they came into contact with the Andronovo people, and they may have disappeared as a separate cultural unit by the fifteenth century B.C. It is possible, however, that the Seimo-Turbino met-

[47] Yang Pao-ch'eng, "Yin-tai ch'e-tzu te fa-hsien yü fu-yüan," *K'ao-ku* 1984.6: 546–55; *K'ao-ku* 1984.6: 505–09.
[48] Chernykh, *Ancient Metallurgy in the USSR*, pp. 215–31, chapter 9.

allurgical phenomenon played an important role in the formation of Karasuk metallurgy in the Sayano-Altai region and western Mongolia.

From around the twelfth to the eighth century B.C. a new culture, known as Karasuk, came to dominate the region of South Siberia, the Yenisei and Minusinsk Basin, and the Altai extending as far as western Mongolia.[49] Like their neighbors in northern China, the Karasuk people had a mixed economy, which, although mainly based on livestock, also relied on agriculture and other supporting activities.[50] Findings of antelope and deer bones suggest extensive hunting by the Karasuk, whereas cattle and horse remains indicate that animal husbandry was their main productive activity. During the Karasuk period improved metallurgic technology resulted in important innovations, among them the bronze bit, which greatly enhanced the possibilities offered by horseback riding.

This vast cultural complex extended its influence and contacts to northern China, and the Karasuk metal inventory presents many analogies with the bronzes of the so-called Northern Zone complex. For instance, we find a type of knife with a hunched blade, similar to the "foreign" bronze knives found at An-yang and widespread across northern China, and similar to the Chinese daggers of the "Ordos" style, with a narrow guard. The pick-axes display tubular sockets for hafting such as those of the Northern Zone, though the blade's pointed cutting edge may have been derived from a Shang prototype.[51] These similarities indicate that the Northern Zone of China was in contact with a wide cultural area and possibly functioned as a clearinghouse for new technical developments into and out of China.

Early Nomadic (Scythian-type) Cultures in the Eurasian Steppe

The Karasuk people lived in felt tents, traveled in hooded carts, ate a variety of dairy products, and adapted remarkably well to a mobile way of life.[52] Yet "true" early pastoral nomads, that is, pastoralists moving with their herds according to a fixed seasonal cycle, appear only in the late Bronze and early Iron Age, a phenomenon that brought about a great expansion across Central Eurasia of mounted warlike nomads. The emergence of this new anthropological type is attested to by the iconography of tenth-century B.C. Iran and ninth-century B.C. Assyria and is confirmed by Assyrian and

---

[49] S. V. Kiselev, *Drevniaia Istoriia Iuzhnoi Sibiri* (Moscow: Nauka, 1951).

[50] A. P. Okladnikov, "Inner Asia at the Dawn of History," in *Cambridge History of Early Inner Asia*, ed. Denis Sinor (Cambridge: Cambridge University Press, 1990), pp. 85–88.

[51] The metallurgical cultures of northern China will be discussed in the next chapter.

[52] Okladnikov, "Inner Asia at the Dawn of History," pp. 94–95.

Greek sources of the ninth and eighth centuries B.C. who assign these groups names such as Cimmerians, Scythians, and Sakas.[53]

These ethnonyms are associated with the pastoral nomadic peoples who inhabited the region of the Pontic Steppe north of the Black Sea and Central Asia from the eighth century B.C. From the eastern to the western parts of the Eurasian steppe region, these early Iron Age peoples shared a cultural universe that was remarkably homogeneous, at least at the level of their material development and artistic expression. These "early nomads" or Scytho-Siberian peoples, as they are sometimes called by archaeologists, engaged in pastoral nomadism as their primary economic activity and thus their livelihood was based on cattle, sheep, and horses. Most prominent in this society was the aristocratic class of mounted warriors, specially trained as light archers, that held a privileged position over other groups. Herodotus's description of the Scythians delineates the social hierarchy of the early pastoral nomads: the Royal Scythians at the top of the ladder and the commoners, identified as "agricultural," "nomadic," or "free" Scythians, below them. In such a martial society, weapons were produced in abundance and were buried with the warriors. The horse was essential not only for herding and in battle but also for the nomads' technological development. Horse-harness components constituted a large portion of the metallurgical production of nomadic cultures. The horse was also integral to the nomads' belief system, and horse sacrifice played a prominent role in funerary rites. Another distinctive element of their culture was the "animal-art style" of nomad metalwork.

Archaeologists have adopted several of these traits for classifying early nomadic cultures. In particular, the presence of the so-called Scythian triad – weapons of bronze and iron, horse gear, and artwork in the "animal style" – in the funerary inventory has been regarded as the common denominator of steppe nomadic cultures, which are also often identified with the typical grave mounds (*kurgan*) where horse and horseman were buried together.[54] However, scholars still have no definite explanation for the

---

[53] The first historically documented steppe nomads are the Scythians, treated extensively in Greek historiography from the fifth century onward. John Gardiner-Garden has written several other works on Scythian historiography, published by the Research Institute for Inner Asian Studies (Bloomington). These are *Apollodoros of Artemita and the Central Asian Skythians* (Papers on Inner Asia no. 3, 1987); *Herodotos' Contemporaries on Skythian Geography and Ethnography* (Papers on Inner Asia no. 10, 1987); *Ktesias on Central Asian History and Ethnography* (Papers on Inner Asia no. 6, 1987); and *Greek Conceptions on Inner Asian Geography and Ethnography from Ephoros to Eratosthenes* (Papers on Inner Asia no. 9, 1987).

[54] However, it is clear that funerary rites varied widely, and the strong presence of local or regional cultural elements makes burial type a less valuable diagnostic method.

appearance of the mounted nomadic culture of the steppe around the end of the second and beginning of the first millennium B.C. This lack of consensus is all the more remarkable because of the gap of several centuries between when the prerequisites of pastoral nomadism were achieved – the dairying techniques, use of animal-driven wheeled transport, and horsemanship available in areas of Central Asia, the Kazakh Steppe, and Siberia by the second half of the second millennium B.C.[55] – and the actual appearance of the nomadic cultures, in the early first millennium B.C.[56]

Most scholars tend to privilege "internal" factors, such as overpopulation, aridization, or simply an increase in the degree of specialization and division of labor between agriculturalists and pastoralists, rather than external ones, such as invasions or cultural contacts, for the nomads' appearance. According to some scholars, pastoral nomadism evolved naturally from advanced pastoralism, and was the result of both larger herd size and the accumulated experience of a more progressive, mobile pastoral economy. Climate changes may have led to a reduction in arable land, as a result of which these formerly sedentary land cultivators and cattle breeders were obliged to become nomads. Some scholars believe that an essential contribution to the evolution of pastoral nomadism came from the forest hunters, who borrowed animals from their sedentary neighbors and then, after they began to use the horse, moved into the steppe.[57]

Yet another theory holds that, in the late second to early first millennium B.C., as a result of overpopulation, the cattle breeders and agriculturalists of the oases gave rise to groups of pastoralists who herded their animals into the surrounding deserts, which then became the "barbaric periphery of the agricultural oases."[58] As already discussed, this view is commonly associated with the "theory of displacement" (the term is Khazanov's),[59] enunciated by Lattimore, according to which pastoral nomadism emerged as an effect of the "push" on marginal populations, already settled on the edge of the steppe and in the oases, exercised by the expansion of sedentary agriculturalist societies.[60] This type of "impact-response" relationship

[55] Khazanov, *Nomads and the Outside World*, p. 94.

[56] See Vejnshtein, "Problem of Origin and Formation of the Economic-Cultural Type of Pastoral Nomads in the Moderate Belt of Eurasia," in *The Nomadic Alternative*, pp. 127–33.

[57] Ibid., pp. 130–31.

[58] Mariana A. Itina, "The Steppes of the Aral Sea in Pre- and Early Scythian Times," in *Foundations of Empire: Archaeology and Art of the Eurasian Steppes*, ed. Gary Seaman (Los Angeles: Ethnographics Press/University of Southern California, 1992), p. 50.

[59] Khazanov, *Nomads and the Outside World*, p. 89.

[60] Lattimore, *Inner Asian Frontiers of China*, pp. 328, 412.

between agriculturalists and underdeveloped "frontiersmen" is, however, not supported by current archaeological research.[61]

Finally, according to Gryaznov, in the eighth century B.C. some tribes in different parts of the steppe took to nomadism as it gradually became a more rewarding economic activity. What resulted was a generalized increase in aggressive warfare among the inhabitants of the steppe, aimed at securing territory sufficient to support nomadic herding. In search of booty and land, these tribes then attacked the sedentary peoples. Settled communities were thus compelled to turn to a nomadic life themselves, when conditions permitted, in order to effectively defend themselves. Their agricultural production was considerably reduced, preserved only at the tribes' winter pastures.[62] Rudenko, on the other hand, proposed a far more gradual transition, spanning several centuries, to "true" pastoral nomadic status.[63] Most scholars today would agree that mature pastoral nomadic cultures were built on the achievements in both technology and social and political organization of previous agro-pastoral peoples. Pastoral nomadic communities, moreover, often appear to be part of larger social configurations based on economic diversification, according to the possibilities offered by the particular environment in which they found themselves.

That there were multiple population shifts is uncontested. As a result of climatic changes and a sharp rise in aridity, Bronze Age inhabitants of the steppe started moving south, following the riverways, in search of pasture.[64] These movements were not synchronous, and reverse movement seems also to have occurred, creating a complex picture of intersecting streams and

---

[61] For a critique of the popular "diffusionist" theory, according to which the state emerged among the nomads only in conjunction with the formation of the state among the agricultural societies, see Lawrence Krader, "The Origin of the State among the Nomads of Asia," in *The Early State*, ed. Henry J. M. Claessen and Peter Skalník (The Hague: Mouton Publishers, 1978), pp. 93–107.

[62] M. P. Gryaznov, *The Ancient Civilization of Southern Siberia* (New York: Cowles Book Co., 1969), pp. 131–32.

[63] S. Rudenko, *Kul'tura naseleniia tsentral'nogo Altaia v skifskoie vremia* (Moscow: Nauka, 1960), p. 197.

[64] Scholars have noticed that by the mid-second millenium B.C. some areas of north and south Kazakhstan, Semirechiye, and northeastern Kirghizstan were apparently abandoned, only to become populated again during the early Saka period. The southern Ural steppe, which was densely populated in the Bronze Age, was also deserted by the end of the second millennium; it was repopulated in the sixth century B.C. by people from Kazakhstan and Central Asia. See V. A. Alekshin, "Problème de l'origin des cultures archéologiques du néolithique et de l'Âge du Bronze en Asie centrale (d'après les rites funéraires)," in *L'Asie centrale et ses rapports*, pp. 255–64. See also Leonid T. Yablonsky, "Some Ethnogenetical Hypotheses," in *Nomads of the Eurasian Steppes in the Early Iron Age*, ed. Jeannine Davis-Kimball et al. (Berkeley: Zinat Press, 1995), p. 243.

currents responsible for the genesis of the material culture of the steppe nomads, especially in metallurgy, and for the development of the nomads' artistic taste.

Chronology and Distribution

Scholars have believed for some time that the earliest foci of a "Scythian" culture could be found in the west, that is, in the region of the Volga River,[65] and that mounted nomadism was "imported" into the eastern steppe across Central Asia.[66] Although a logical assumption, given that a number of essential innovations (horseback riding, wheeled vehicles, metallurgy) entered Central Asia from the western and southwestern ends of the steppe, several decades of archaeological work, mainly by Soviet archaeologists after World War II, have made it increasingly clearer that at some point the process may have been led by the eastern steppe regions, including South Siberia, Tuva, the Sayano-Altai region, and western Mongolia.

Today the consensus tends to privilege Central Asia as the place of origin and dispersal of the Scytho-Siberian cultures.[67] Archaeological features of the nomadic Scythian culture were first recognized in the large *kurgan* burials of the Altai and T'ien-shan regions of the sixth to fourth century B.C. Kiselev's work in the Minusinsk Basin and Yenisei Valley in southern Siberia revealed a culture that replaced the Karasuk around the seventh century B.C., known as Tagar.[68] These were still semi-nomadic people who essentially continued the traditions of the Karasuk culture, although in the Yenisei region Tagar society supported an aristocracy similar to that of the nomads.[69]

In the Altai region and in Tuva early nomads appear possibly as early as the ninth century B.C. Gryaznov's chronology locates the beginning of the Altaic-Scythian period in the ninth century B.C. This was followed by the Maiemir period (seventh to fifth century B.C.), by the Pazyryk period (fifth to third century B.C.), and, finally, by the Shibinsk (Shibe) period (second

---

[65] Karl Jettmar, *Art of the Steppes* (New York: Crown Publishers, 1967), p. 215.

[66] Supported by linguistic evidence, Heine-Geldern has argued in favor of the thesis of an Indo-European migration that took place from the Pontic region to eastern Asia during the ninth and eighth centuries; see R. Heine-Geldern, "Das Tocharenproblem und die Pontische Wanderung," *Saeculum* 2 (1951): 225.

[67] Esther Jacobson, *The Art of the Scythians* (Leiden: Brill, 1995), pp. 29–39. For a general introduction to the history of Scythian and Sarmatian tribes, see A. I. Melyukova, "The Scythians and Sarmatians," in *Cambridge History of Early Inner Asia*, pp. 97–117.

[68] Kiselev, *Drevniaia istoriia Iuzhnoi Sibiri*, pp. 302–303.

[69] Gryaznov, *The Ancient Civilization of Ancient Siberia*, p. 217.

century B.C. to first century A.D.). From the eighth–seventh century onward two different groups in the Altai can be identified by their respective burials: the *kurgan* and the stone box. The chronology of the early nomadic cultures of the early Iron Age in the Altai that is generally accepted today follows Gryaznov's model closely and is divided into an early stage (eighth to sixth century B.C.), a middle stage (fifth to third century B.C.), and a late stage (second century B.C. to first century A.D.).[70] The chronological upper limit of the early nomads has found confirmation in the work carried out by Gryaznov and Grach at Arzhan, in Tuva. This monumental burial site, dated at the earliest to the ninth or, more possibly, to the eighth century B.C., is synchronous with the appearance across the steppe region of Inner Asia of a unitary cultural layer, that of the early Iron Age, which stretched from the Pontic area to the eastern Altai.[71] In Tuvan archaeology, this first period was also followed by a middle period – slightly earlier than elsewhere – dated to the seventh and sixth centuries B.C., and by a late period, dated from the fifth to the third century B.C. At the end of its late stage of early nomadic ("Scythian-type") evolution, Tuva entered the "Hunno-Sarmatian" period common to vast parts of Central Eurasia and generally identified with the arrival of new pastoral nomadic cultures from the east in concomitance with the expansion of the Hsiung-nu empire. Data from wooden remains from the early nomadic sites (Arzhan, Tuetka, Pazyryk, and Shibe), based on C^{14}-calibrated analysis adjusted to dendrochronological calculations (based on tree rings), confirm Gryaznov's chronology. The data also show that, given the confirmed early dating of the Arzhan *kurgan* (tenth to ninth century B.C.), the animal style typical of nomadic steppe art was probably developed as a native tradition, and not as an adaptation of Near Eastern motifs.[72]

In analyzing the cultural evolution of the early nomads, we must keep in mind that the phenomenon was not linear and that it had a vast range of regional variations based on each group's adaptation to different ecological conditions and different forms of economic development. Not all Bronze Age agro-pastoral communities became nomadic; indeed, some peoples migrated to river valleys and took up plough agriculture.[73] Moreover, early nomadic communities often showed continuity with preceding

---

[70] Nikolai A. Bokovenko, "History of Studies and the Main Problems in the Archaeology of Southern Siberia during the Scythian Period," in *Nomads of the Eurasian Steppes in the Early Iron Age*, pp. 255–61.

[71] For a map of all the early nomadic (Scythian-type) cultures of Eurasia, see M. P. Grjaznov, *Der Großkurgan von Aržan in Tuva, Südsibirien* (München: Verlag C. H. Beck, 1984), p. 77.

[72] Mark E. Hall, "Towards an Absolute Chronology of the Iron Age of Inner Asia," *Antiquity* 71 (1997): 863–74.

[73] Yablonsky, "Some Ethnogenetical Hypotheses."

Bronze Age steppe communities, in both their cultures – funerary rites, pottery, and metallurgy – and their physical aspects. During the Scythian period a plurality of cultural traditions commonly coexisted in the same general area. For instance, among the nomadic people of the seventh–sixth century B.C. in Khorezm, in the regions between the lower Syr Darya and the Amu Darya, different types of funerary rites and burial methods were practiced within a fairly consistent cultural context suggesting contacts further east, with the steppes of Kazakhstan and southern Siberia.[74] Perhaps the most plausible explanation for this phenomenon is that the nomadic communities formed in the Altai, Tuvinian, and Kazakh Steppes moved west in waves of varying speed and intensity and gradually mixed with the local people, thus generating multiple cultural combinations.

Social and Economic Development

In general, the passage from a society whose economy is mixed to a society whose economy is dominated by a nomadic element is accompanied by profound changes in social structure and organization.[75] Eventually, nomadic specialization was instrumental to the formation of more complex types of integration among peoples whose economic bases were varied and dependent upon local environmental characteristics.[76] The evolutionary trajectory of the early nomads proceeded in two directions. Internally, nomadic-dominated societies attained greater social stratification, typified by larger burials and funerary inventories marked by an abundance of prestige goods. The aristocratic warrior class is also likely to have had access to whatever surplus may have been produced under their rule, including farm products, metal tools and weapons, and perhaps even trade revenues. Externally, nomadic-dominated societies tended to have more contacts with neighboring communities, sometimes over great distances. The relationship the nomads established with these communities was one of commercial exchange and economic symbiosis but also one of latent hostility, which sometimes resulted in conflict. As the early nomads spread across Central Eurasia, their most advanced communities established themselves in a position of supremacy over non-nomadic peoples. In the northern Caucasian Steppe, for example, where signs can be found of a Scythian culture as early

---

[74] Leonid T. Yablonsky, "Material Culture of the Saka and Historical Reconstruction," in *Nomads of the Eurasian Steppes in the Early Iron Age*, pp. 201–39.

[75] G. E. Markov, "Problems of Social Change among the Asiatic Nomads," in *Nomadic Alternative*, p. 306.

[76] This case is argued in particular in Chang and Tourtellotte, "Role of Agropastoralism," 1: 264–79.

as the eighth century B.C., the nomads clearly came to dominate the local sedentary population.[77]

The formation of a military aristocracy, organized into politically authoritative clans and lineages, occurred, naturally, at different times in different places. The Arzhan complex is so large and impressive that there can be no doubt that this was the tomb of a very powerful man.[78] The creation of centers of tribal unions is visible particularly from the seventh–sixth century B.C. onward. For instance, the emergence of tribal unions in the southern Ural Steppe and Volga-Don interfluvial zone between the sixth and the fourth century B.C. can be deduced from the partition of the cemeteries into sectors, of which some were reserved for the members of a military elite, including, possibly, those with a "supra-tribal" position (i.e., a class of noblemen within a confederation of tribes).[79] The group of *kurgan*s found on the Ilek River, where larger and more complex burial structures are set apart from the others, may be one example of this social structure. Indeed, this particular site has been taken as evidence of the formation of a tribal union that had its center here, and whose aristocratic chiefs were buried with greater pomp.[80]

In the Altai region, the earliest burials are much simpler than the *kurgan*s of the Pazyryk stage.[81] More important, the Pazyryk culture presents a

---

[77] Vladimir Petrenko, "Scythian Culture in the North Caucasus," in *Nomads of the Eurasian Steppes in the Early Iron Age*, pp. 5–22.

[78] The complex, a circular mound built over an intricate wooden structure, includes seventy burial chambers whose sizes vary between 15 square meters and 150 square meters. At the center, two smaller cells are located within a larger enclosure, presumably the place of rest of the king and queen. Various noblemen, attendants, and a total of 160 horses were also buried in the structure, which has yielded an abundance of weapons, jewelry, and bronze decorations in the animal style. See Grjaznov, *Großkurgan von Aržan in Tuva, Südsibirien*; Nikolai A. Bokovenko, "The Tagar Culture of the Minusinsk Basin," in *Nomads of the Eurasian Steppes in the Early Iron Age*, p. 302.

[79] Marina Moshkova, "Sarmatians, Concluding Remarks," in *Nomads of the Eurasian Steppes in the Early Iron Age*, pp. 185–88.

[80] Vladimir Dvornichenko, "Sauromatians and Sarmatians of the Eurasian Steppes: The Transitional Period from the Bronze Age," in *Nomads of the Eurasian Steppes in the Early Iron Age*, p. 106.

[81] The Pazyryk culture is one of the better studied early nomadic "*kurgan*" cultures of Central Asia. Its chronology was recently re-worked by Hiebert, who concluded that some Pazyryk burials could have been as early as the fifth century B.C., and that similar *kurgans* in the same region date earlier and later, thereby showing a continuous tradition. See Fredrik T. Hiebert, "Pazyryk Chronology and Early Horse Nomads Reconsidered," *Bulletin of the Asia Institute*, n.s. 6 (1992): 117–29. The classic work on Pazyryk is Sergei I. Rudenko, *Frozen Tombs of*

variety of burial sites, indicating the co-existence of different social groups. The older funerary assemblage was comprised of, essentially, bronze weapons, with rare jewelery in bronze or gold, but the burial goods found in tombs of the later stage display better bronze-casting techniques; moreover, iron was used more broadly, particularly for horse gear, and gold processing was much more sophisticated.[82] Chinese silk has also been found in several burials, confirming that contacts, however indirect, occurred between the Pazyryk culture and China.[83]

Western Mongolia certainly belonged to the same cultural horizon as the Altai and Tuva regions. The Pazyryk and Uyuk cultures find a parallel here in the site at Ulangom, dated to the fifth to the third century B.C. In its central and eastern regions, Mongolia was also home to a completely different ethno-cultural group. This cultural complex is known as the slab-grave culture after the type of burial practiced, in which simple pits were lined with slabs of stone and not surmounted by a moundlike structure. The physical type of this group, distinctly Mongoloid, is also very different from the Europoid "Saka" people of the Altai. Nevertheless, in the early Iron Age these two distinct cultural and anthropological areas shared elements of material culture ranging from the shape of their arrowheads to psalia and bridle bits, animal-style motifs, and the so-called deer stones (large stone slabs engraved with stylized deer and anthropomorphic motifs).[84] This is further evidence of the vitality of a "steppe civilization" where diverse metallurgical, artistic, and possibly spiritual components were rapidly transmitted, exchanged, and absorbed from community to community. The very rapidity with which these elements spread encourages us to surmise that many groups had reached a fairly similar degree of economic, technological, and social development and that contacts among them had intensified steadily over time.

One factor that possibly affected the further political and economic development of nomadic societies was the rise and spread of iron metallurgy. Iron began to be used in Central Asia around the early first millennium B.C. Early centers of iron metallurgy were located in the southern (Anau) and Ferghana (Dal'verzhin) regions. This new technology soon

---

Siberia: The Pazyryk Burials of Iron Age Horsemen (London: Dent and Sons, 1970).

[82] Nikolai A. Bokovenko, "Scythian Culture in the Altai Mountains," in Nomads of the Eurasian Steppes in the Early Iron Age, pp. 285–95.

[83] For silk found in a recently excavated Pazyryk burial, see N. V. Polosmak, "The Burial of a Noble Pazyryk Woman," Ancient Civilizations from Scythia to Siberia 5.2 (1998): 125–63.

[84] V. Volkov, "Early Nomads of Mongolia," in Nomads of the Eurasian Steppes in the Early Iron Age, pp. 324–25.

expanded to other areas, including the steppe region. According to some scholars, iron metallurgy contributed to greater political centralization, sharper class stratification, and the formation of larger and more closely integrated socio-economic units.[85]

These larger units comprised a variety of economic activities. For instance, it is clear that across the steppe region of northern China, although pastoralism was their main activity, the nomads also hunted, whereas the regional economy included agricultural communities and trade among the different groups.[86] As already mentioned, to assess each nomadic group's economic basis we must consider its specific environment and contacts with neighboring communities. The image of the "pure" nomad is often misleading when applied to groups in this early period; thus the cattle breeders of the Altai appear to have had some semi-permanent settlements where they engaged in primitive agriculture. The tools found in their dwellings indicate that they lived in centers that supported a range of supplementary economic activities, from hoe farming to hunting, leather processing, crafting of bone and horn, and metallurgy.[87]

The presence of sedentary or semi-sedentary communities within reach of the nomads affected the exchange economy, with implications at both the social and the economic levels. For example, the settlements of the Itkil culture in the trans-Ural forest steppe region, dated between the seventh and the third century B.C., have yielded numerous remains of metallurgical production. Other metallurgical centers have been found also on the Kama and Belaya Rivers and in the forest-steppe area of the Volga River. The artifacts discovered at these sites include such typical nomadic metalwork as weapons, harnesses, cauldrons, jewelry, and mirrors, and seem to have been produced by the craftsmen of these sedentary communities for a nomadic market.[88] Evidence of the close integration of different cultural and socio-economic groups has been discovered in the region to the south of Ferghana Valley and in the highland valleys of the Altai mountain range, where between the fifth and third century B.C. the burials of nomadic and settled peoples display no differences in their funerary artifacts.[89]

In conclusion, an assessment of the economic base of the early nomads needs to take account of several factors. Among these are the intensity and frequency of contacts among neighboring communities within a region.

---

[85] G. A. Koshelenko, "L'Asie Central au début de l'age du fer: le problème des relations extérieures" in L'Asie centrale et ses rapports, pp. 171–72.

[86] Nicola Di Cosmo, "The Economic Basis of the Ancient Inner Asian Nomads and Its Relationship to China," Journal of Asian Studies 53.4 (1994): 1092–126.

[87] Bokovenko, "Scythian Culture in the Altai Mountains," pp. 285–95.

[88] Moshkova, "Sarmatians, Concluding Remarks," in Nomads of the Eurasian Steppes in the Early Iron Age, pp. 185–88.

[89] Yablonsky, "Some Ethnogenetical Hypotheses," pp. 241–52.

Even more important is the complex socio-political organization, which was likely to have been based on a hierarchy of lineages (especially within the nomadic aristocracy), of communities, such as farming settlements, and of social groups – characterized by status (free people, servants, or slaves) and by economic activity (e.g., metallurgy or other type of craftsmanship).

Material Culture

Metal objects played a critical role in the material culture of the early nomads. By the eighth century B.C. metalwork achieved a high degree of similarity across Central Eurasia. From the eighth–seventh century B.C. onward, a larger and more varied inventory of weapons dominated funerary assemblages. Common features signifying the prestige of the deceased were the design of horse harness articles, artifacts in the animal-style tradition, weapons, bronze cauldrons, and mirrors. Among the weapons, the most common were the bow and arrow, although few bows have survived.[90] Arrowheads were divided into two main categories, tanged and socketed; other weapons included daggers, swords, and spearheads.[91] Among the Sakas of the Pamir and T'ien-shan regions we find iron daggers and bimetallic daggers (iron blade with a bronze hilt) already in the necropolises of the early period (eighth to sixth century B.C.), accompanied by bronze daggers and bronze or iron arrowheads. Iron daggers continue to be found in the large *kurgans* of the Pazyryk period.[92] At the time, horse gear included bits, cheek pieces, bridle cockades, girt buckles, and strap plates; bits were made of bronze and had joined mouthpieces, and cheek pieces were made of bronze, bone, and horn.

In the burial structures of the Saka peoples of Central Asia and Kazakhstan of the seventh and sixth century B.C. we find knives made out of iron. Initially iron was used primarily for making utilitarian goods rather than luxury items.[93] Later the use of iron became more widespread, and more objects, such as horse accouterments, were made from the metal.[94] Prestige items, typically in bronze and precious metals, included ritual and ornamental objects besides weapons. Indeed, among the most valuable pieces of bronze production found throughout the nomadic world were cauldrons that had a ritual function connected with animal sacrifices,

---

[90] E. McEwen, "Nomadic Archery: Some Observations on Composite Bow Design and Construction," in *Arts of the Eurasian Steppelands*, pp. 188–202.

[91] For an inventory of Scythian armament, see Bourchard Brentjes, *Arms of the Sakas* (Varanasi: Rishi Publications, 1996), pp. 17–42.

[92] Yablonsky, "Material Culture of the Saka," pp. 201–39.   [93] Ibid.

[94] Dvornichenko, "Sauromatians and Sarmatians of the Eurasian Steppes," pp. 105–16.

possibly to cook the meat.[95] All of this is evidence of a mature martial society, with horses and riding as elements of prime economic and social importance.

The material culture also included imported items. Sauromatian bronze helmets and scale or plate armor not of local production appear in the Volga River region and southern Ural Steppes in the fifth–fourth century B.C., showing an increase in the exchange economy among neighboring communities.[96] Likewise, the Sarmatians acquired jewelry by trade with the region of Tanais (the river Don) and Phanagoria on the Bosporus.[97]

The nomadic animal art style is open to endless variations, yet preserves a remarkably unitarian aspect. The animals most often represented are mountain goats, elk, birds of prey, and boars; large felines are a favorite subject. Animal-style motifs decorate the handles of weapons and knives, metal plates, buckles, and horse gear.

Finally, gold and jewelry acquired greater relevance in funerary assemblages after the sixth century B.C. In a Saka burial of the Iron Age, excavated in eastern Kazakhstan, pieces of sheet-gold decoration are sewn on a chieftain's clothing. Advanced techniques in gold manufacturing, such as incrustation and granulation, are evidenced by artifacts, including a three-dimensional fish made from sheet gold, with its eyes and fins of inlaid turquoise, and its body adorned with granulation.[98]

Conclusion

The material culture and social organization of the early pastoral nomads of Eurasia have impressed researchers for their high degree of similarity across an immense territory. Archaeologists and art historians have stressed in particular the ritual and social significance of the horse, the abundance of weapons, and the artistic vocabulary dominated by the "animal style." Moreover, the formation of early nomadic cultures cannot be disassociated from technological advances, especially with respect to the horse and chariot, which increased the nomads' mobility and made nomads militarily superior to their settled neighbors. Their upbringing in a pastoral setting, where they acquired riding and shooting skills, and their social need to organize themselves into militarylike parties for seasonal migrations and hunting, made pastoral nomads into natural warriors.

[95] These appear throughout Central Eurasia, from the Ordos region of northern China to western Central Asia. See Miklos Erdy, "Hun and Xiongnu Type Cauldron Finds throughout Eurasia," *Eurasian Studies Yearbook* (1995): 5–94.

[96] Vladimir Dvornichenko, "Sauromatians and Sarmatians of the Eurasian Steppes," pp. 105–16.

[97] Moshkova, "Sarmatians, Concluding Remarks," pp. 185–88.

[98] Yablonsky, "Material Culture of the Saka," p. 211.

Under these circumstances, and with evidence of increasing aridization of the steppe region, pastoral nomadism remained a successful adaptation to the Inner Asian grassland environment, which allowed for not only the subsistence of the nomads but also their evolution into larger and more complex societies. Nomadic social formations retained a characteristically martial outlook and produced an aristocratic class whose main occupation seems to have been the practice of war. The emergence of such a class, probably linked to competition for pasture and to the need for defense during seasonal migrations, was a major element in the expansion of the political power of pastoral nomads over settled or semi-settled communities. In other cases, relations between nomads and agriculturalists depended upon less violent forms of economic and cultural exchange.

In a secondary stage of the development of nomadic societies, the type of items that conferred prestige on their owners, previously dominated by weapons, came to include decorative objects. This period is characterized by an elite class that cherished the rare and beautiful ornaments, such as golden plaques decorated with animals in the round and inlaid with precious stones, that signified wealth and status rather than just military prowess. This evolution reveals a shift not only in the taste but also in the social function of the nomadic elites. Together with evidence of trade, especially the importation of works of art from nearby sedentary communities, the precious art objects in the funerary inventory of the nomads suggests that the aristocracy defined itself no longer exclusively as military leaders, but as performing a range of commercial and political functions resulting in the accumulation of wealth in the form of precious metals and jewelry. The formation of a leadership that controlled the sources of wealth, such as trade and production, was arguably a necessary condition for the centralization of power and military expansion on nomadic polities. As we will see in the next chapter, a similar trend can also be observed among the pastoral nomads of northern China.

CHAPTER TWO

Bronze, Iron, and Gold
The Evolution of Nomadic Cultures on the Northern Frontier of China

Introduction: The Northern Complex

Scholars have long recognized that a cultural frontier, understood as an area of contacts among carriers of different material cultures, existed to the north of China as early as the Shang dynasty.[1] The origin of this cultural complex, its connection with China and areas in Central and northern Asia, and the characteristics of the separate cultural enclaves recognizable within it have been objects of much debate. Yet two critical questions remain unanswered: When do we begin to see a clearly delineated frontier between China and the north? More importantly, how do we define the northern frontier?[2]

China's frontier has been often understood as an ideal line dividing two ecological zones: the steppes and deserts of the north and the farmland of the south. Although this line may have shifted north or south in response to climatic variations over time, from the viewpoint of human agency this interpretation of the frontier remains fundamentally static and tells us little about cultural exchange and political interaction.[3]

---

[1] For an early and still excellent analysis of the northern frontier, see William Watson, *Cultural Frontiers in Ancient East Asia* (Edinburgh: Edinburgh University Press, 1971), pp. 96–124.

[2] This chapter is based in part on Nicola Di Cosmo, "The Northern Frontier in Pre-Imperial China," in *Cambridge History of Ancient China*, ed. Michael Loewe and Edward L. Shaughnessy (Cambridge: Cambridge University Press, 1999), pp. 885–966.

[3] Kathryn Linduff has suggested that the relationship between the Central Plain and the northern cultures emerging in the early Bronze Age evolved into one of core-periphery, thus surmising a relationship of dependency of the "frontier"

Until the third century B.C. – when a clearly demarcated political boundary between the north and China emerged with the formation of the Hsiung-nu empire (209 B.C.) – the northern frontier of China remained extremely fluid. However, at least three interconnected but independent processes played roles in defining the northern frontier: one ecological and economic, another cultural, and the last political. In this chapter, I will examine the first two of these processes, that is, the formation of pastoral nomadism in northern China, and the distinctive traits of the resulting cultures. The evidence for the analysis of the economic and cultural contexts is archaeological and is based on the divergence between the Chinese and Northern Zone's discrete metallurgical traditions. Archaeological evidence also shows that a series of "ecological frontiers" between different modes of production, social organizations, and adaptations to the environment had already developed by the mid-second millennium B.C.[4]

Metallurgy: The First Frontier

From the beginning of the second millennium B.C., beyond the core area of the Shang civilization, lay a broad belt of cultural transition between the Central Plain culture and the Bronze Age cultures of Central Asia and South Siberia. The Shang civilization was in close contact with this intermediate zone, and several Shang sites display features that can be immediately recognized as alien and intrusive. However, the process by which these adjacent but distinct cultural zones were formed is still unclear. The debate has focused on whether this cultural zone, regarded as a transitional area between the Sinitic East and the Inner Asian complex of Mongolia, South Siberia, and Central Asia, was formed through Chinese cultural diffusion to the northwest or, instead, was influenced by contacts with the North and West.[5] It is now clear that the Northern Zone (*pei-fang ti-ch'ü*) of China – largely in today's Inner Mongolia and Liaoning, and in the northern areas of Shansi, Shaansi, and Hopei – was already an independent cultural unit during the Shang dynasty and that it acted as a filter and link between the

---

upon the core. See her "The Emergence and Demise of Bronze-Producing Cultures Outside the Central Plain of China," in *The Bronze Age and Early Iron Age Peoples of Eastern Central Asia*, ed. Victor H. Mair (Washington: Institute for the Study of Man, 1998), 2: 619–43.

[4] Traditional dyadic divisions between "steppe and sown" are becoming more suspect; see J. P. Mallory, "A European Perspective on Indo-Europeans in Asia," in *The Bronze Age and Early Iron Age Peoples of Eastern Central Asia*, 1: 175–201. Recent approaches privilege a less rigid demarcation.

[5] Max Loehr, "Weapons and Tools from Anyang, and Siberian Analogies," *American Journal of Archaeology* 53 (1949): 126–44; W. Watson, *Frontiers of Ancient China*, pp. 54–56.

Central Plain and Central and northern Asia.[6] Even before the Shang dynasty, what is now northern China was home to cultures distinct from those in the core area of Central Plain civilization. These early cultures, distributed over a broad area and dating back to the late third and second millennium B.C., were responsible for the development of a closely knit metallurgical network across northern China. Of these early northern cultures, the most revealing are the Ch'i-chia culture in the northwest, the Chu-k'ai-kou culture in the north-central sector, and the Lower Hsia-chia-tien culture in the northeast.

The Ch'i-chia culture is the earliest Bronze Age culture discovered within the territory of present-day China and has been dated to the late third millennium B.C.[7] Based on typological comparison of the pottery, the Ch'i-chia culture is regarded as a continuation of the Neolithic cultures that developed in today's Ning-hsia and Kansu provinces. Although its main sites are located in Kansu,[8] the Ch'i-chia culture was broadly distributed, extending north and east into Inner Mongolia, the upper Yellow River Valley, and the upper Wei-he and Huang-shui River Valleys. Connected with earlier Neolithic cultures, such as the Ma-chia-yao, during the first half of the first millennium B.C., the Ch'i-chia people displayed cultural traits that were among the most advanced in China. Their bronze production was extensive, and they progressed from forging copper tools (knives, awls, chisels) to casting objects (knives and axes) in open molds to more complex casting using composite molds (mirrors and socketed axes).[9]

---

[6] Lin Yun, "A Reexamination of the Relationship between Bronzes of the Shang Culture and of the Northern Zone," in *Studies of Shang Archaeology*, ed. K. C. Chang (New Haven: Yale University Press, 1986), p. 272. On the relationship between Xinjiang and neighboring cultures an excellent overview is provided by Chen Kuang-tzuu and Fredrik T. Hiebert, "The Late Prehistory of Xinjiang in Relation to Its Neighbors," *Journal of World Prehistory* 9.2 (1995): 243–300. For a general survey of Northern Zone bronzes and their archaeological importance, see also Wu En, "Yin chih Chou ch'u te pei-fang ch'ing-t'ung ch'i," *K'ao-ku hsüeh-pao* 1985.2: 135–56; T'ien Kuan-chin, "Chin-nien-lai te Nei Meng-ku ti-ch'ü te hsiung-nu k'ao-ku," *K'ao-ku hsüeh-pao* 1983.1: 23.

[7] For a comprehensive examination of the Ch'i-chia culture, see Corinne Debaine-Francfort, *Du Néolithique à l'Age du Bronze en Chine du Nord-Ouest: la culture de Qijia et ses connexions* (Paris: Editions recherche sur les civilisations, 1995).

[8] That is, the sites of Huang-niang-niang-t'ai, Ch'in-wen-chia, and Ta-he-chuang. See Hu Ch'ien-ying, "Shih-lun Ch'i-chia wen-hua te pu-t'ung lei-hsing chi ch'i yüan-liu," *K'ao-ku yü wen-wu* 1980.3: 77–82, 33; and Hsieh Tuan-chü, "Shih-lun Ch'i-chia wen-hua," *K'ao-ku yü wen-wu* 1981.3: 79–80.

[9] An Zhimin [Chih-min], "The Bronze Age in the Eastern Parts of Central Asia," in *History of Civilizations of Central Asia*, vol. 1: *The Dawn of Civilization: Earliest Times to 700 B.C.*, ed. A. H. Dani and V. M. Masson (Paris: Unesco, 1992), p. 322.

The Ch'i-chia was a sedentary culture based on agriculture, with stock breeding as an important activity. Some sites yield evidence of horse domestication (for example, Ta-he-chuang and Ch'in-wei-chia), and pigs feature prominently among animal remains and funerary sacrifices.[10] The sudden appearance of advanced bronze metallurgy and the domestication of the horse in northern China strongly suggest that the Ch'i-chia people had extensive contacts with other cultures, especially those in the north and west, since no similar achievements are documented among the eastern pre-Shang cultures.

Some scholars have hypothesized that bronze metallurgy in the northwest preceded the advent of metallurgy in Central China and thus that the origins of the Ch'i-chia culture may be found in cultural processes taking place in the west.[11] A close connection may have existed between the Seimo-Turbino cultural complex and northwestern China, which would explain the transmission of South Siberian metal artifacts to the Ch'i-chia cultural area; evidence for such a connection rests mainly on socketed axes, handled knives, and the hafting method of handled awls and knives that have been unearthed at Ch'i-chia sites.[12] One ax excavated at Hsing-lin, in eastern Kansu, is a local casting but exhibits traits – such as a single loop on one side of the hafting edge – characteristic of the eastern type of the Seimo-Turbino socketed ax. A bronze knife, also found at Hsing-lin, is closely related to knives from Rostovka and Sopka, and the geometrical decoration on fragmentary handles of daggers and knives recalls Seimo-Turbino motifs. Finally, the hafting method (a metal blade inserted in a bone handle) used for an awl and a knife found at separate Hsi-ning sites is most similar to that used for metal awls and knives with bone or wood handles found in Minusinsk sites of the Okunevo period. Moreover, the same method was used by the Seimo-Turbino people. Although the precise manner in which the Ch'i-chia culture was connected with the western cultural horizon that included South Siberia, Central Asia, and Mongolia is unclear, that they were in contact seems highly likely.

[10] *K'ao-ku hsüeh-pao* 1974.2: 29–62; *K'ao-ku hsüeh-pao* 1975.2: 57–96.

[11] An Chih-min, "Shih-lun Chung-kuo te tsao-ch'i t'ung-ch'i," *K'ao-ku* 1993.12: 1110–19. It is assumed by some that metallurgy in areas to the west of Ch'i-chia, such as Sinkiang, may go back to the early second millennium B.C. The evidence comes from cutmarks on logs recovered from the cemetery of Ku-mu-kou, which are too deep and clean to have been produced by anything other than a metal tool; see Wang Binghua, "A Preliminary Analysis of the Archaeological Cultures of the Bronze Age in the Region of Xinjiang," in *Between Lapis and Jade: Ancient Cultures of Central Asia*, ed. F. Hiebert and N. Di Cosmo, *Anthropology and Archaeology of Eurasia* (Spring 1996): 70.

[12] For these comparisons see Louisa Fitzgerald-Huber, "Qijia and Erlitou, the Question of Contacts with Distant Cultures," *Early China* 20 (1995): 40–52.

The Ch'i-chia people shared cultural traits with other cultures of the northwestern regions, in Kansu, Ning-hsia, and Ch'ing-hai, which coincided with or are slightly later than the last phase of Ch'i-chia. The most important of these cultures are those of No-mu-hung in Ch'ing-hai, and Huo-shao-kou (which includes the Ssu-pa culture), Hsin-tien, and Ssu-wa in Kansu. Throughout these areas pastoral activities became gradually predominant, even though in the mixed agro-pastoral economy, farming (primarily millet), pig raising, and stock breeding (especially sheep) were closely integrated. The transition to a more clearly demarcated pastoralism did not occur everywhere in the same way: western Ch'ing-hai moved more rapidly in that direction than did Kansu or eastern Ch'ing-hai. Nevertheless the seeds were planted for the development of a relationship between people and their environment that would lead this region toward a non-urban, non-centralized way of life antithetical to the social evolution of China. Debaine-Francfort attributes this movement to a "choice" that led to an economic rupture with the earlier tradition embodied by the Ch'i-chia culture. We cannot seek the causes of this rupture in an interruption of contacts with the Chinese core regions, but must look for them in closer contacts between the Ch'i-chia and the peoples to the north and west of them.[13]

Nearly contemporary with the Ch'i-chia culture was the Chu-k'ai-kou culture, a Bronze Age cultural nucleus that developed in the north-central zone with characteristics distinct from the Central Plain civilization.[14] The importance of the Chu-k'ai-kou culture lies in its role as a possible predecessor of the so-called Northern Zone bronze culture. This culture possibly existed from the mid-third to the mid-second millennium B.C.; its territory extended out to northern and central Inner Mongolia, northern Shensi, and northern Shansi, with the Ordos region at its center.[15] The people of Chu-k'ai-kou were agriculturalists. Their main staple was millet, and they also raised sheep, pigs, and cattle. Around the end of the third millennium B.C. certain motifs appeared in their pottery decoration. They included a snake pattern and the flower-shaped edge of the *li* vessel, which archaeologists regard as characteristic of the area's later nomadic peoples.[16] Moreover,

[13] Debaine-Francfort, *Du Néolithique à l'Age du Bronze en Chine du Nord-Ouest*, pp. 340–41, 347–48.

[14] Kathryn Linduff, "Zhukaigou, Steppe Culture and the Rise of Chinese Civilization," *Antiquity* 69 (1995): 133–45.

[15] *K'ao-ku* 1988.3: 301–332; Wu En, "Chu-k'ai-kou wen-hua te fa-hsien chi ch'i yi-yi," in *Chung-kuo k'ao-ku-hsüeh lun-ts'ung* (Pei-ching: K'o-hsüeh, 1995), pp. 256–66.

[16] T'ien Kuan-chin and Kuo Su-hsin, "O-erh-to-ssu shih ch'ing-t'ung ch'i te yüan-yüan," *K'ao-ku hsüeh-pao* 1988.3: 257–75; Li Shui-ch'eng, "Chung-kuo pei-fang ti-tai te she-wen-ch'i yen-chiu," *Wen-wu* 1992.1: 50–57.

oracle bone divination (a ritual activity that came to be closely associated with Shang culture and statecraft) was already practiced in the area of the Chu-k'ai-kou culture in the first half of the second millennium.

The culture's most significant bronze objects to have been found thus far date to its last phase, Chu-k'ai-kou V, which was roughly contemporary with the early Shang (c. 1500 B.C.). These reveal an indigenous metallurgical tradition that included Shang objects, represented by *ko* (dagger-axes); Northern Zone items, such as a bronze dagger (the earliest of the kind); and even an integrally cast knife with terminal ring and upward-turned point that shows both Shang and northern features. Shang ritual vessels, such as *ting* and *chüeh*, and Shang weapons (*ko*), appear here in the Erh-li-t'ou and Erh-li-kang periods; this suggests that around the mid-second millennium B.C., there was a northward movement of Shang culture or that contacts between the local people and the Shang increased at this time.

Another early Bronze Age culture, in the northeast, is known as the Lower Hsia-chia-tien (c. 2000–1300 B.C.). Chronologically, it overlaps with the last phases of the Chu-k'ai-kou culture and with the Upper Erh-li-kang period of the Shang; geographically, it extends across southeastern Inner Mongolia, Liao-ning, and northern Hopei. The southern limit of the culture was located in Hopei, Yi-hsien, and Lai-shui counties, and the whole Peking region formed a large belt where the Lower Hsia-chia-tien and Shang cultures met. The Lower Hsia-chia-tien culture emerged at the initial phase in the transition to metalworking and produced a limited number of small objects such as rings, knives, and handles.[17] People lived in settlements and the economy was primarily agricultural, their main crop being millet. To supplement their food supply, people raised stock and hunted deer. Finally, they were able to manufacture highly polished stone and bone tools.

The Northern Zone Bronze Complex

From these three early progenitors, whose mutual relationships are far from clear, a more coherent Bronze Age cultural complex – unquestionably distinct from that of Central Plain – emerged in the Northern Zone during the Shang period. Whereas the limits of Shang political power and cultural reach can be defined more or less, the northern cultural complex is amorphous, and its boundaries cannot be clearly established.[18] The term

[17] Li Ching-han, "Shih-lun Hsia-chia-tien hsia-ts'eng wen-hua te fen-ch'i he lei-hsing," in *Chung-kuo k'ao-ku hsüeh-hui ti-yi-ts'u nien-hui lun-wen-chi 1979* (Peking: Wen-wu, 1980), pp. 163–70.

[18] On the Shang geographical and political extension, see David Keightley, "The Late Shang State: When, Where, and What?", in *The Origins of Chinese*

"Northern Zone," therefore, should not suggest a homogeneous culture, but a broad area in which different peoples shared a common metallurgical tradition, one that typified the north and marked a cultural boundary between the north and the civilization of the Central Plain.

Most characteristic of the Northern Zone complex are bronze tools and weapons, possibly indicating that the development of metallurgy was linked to the rise of military elites and to increased warfare resulting from competition for economic resources. The standard typology of the Northern Zone's complex metal inventory, provided by Lin Yun, includes daggers, knives, axes with short sockets, axes with tubular sockets, mirrors, and "bow-shaped" objects.[19]

Daggers, or short swords, are generally distinguished by their integral casting of hilt and double-edged blade and relatively narrow and straight hand guard. The early types, dated to the middle and late Shang dynasty, display a characteristic curved hilt, often decorated with geometric designs and featuring a terminal in the shape of an animal's head (horse, ram, eagle, or ibex). Other early daggers have perforated hilts or have straight hilts with grooves ending in a rattle.

Northern bronze knives, similar to knives found in Siberia and Mongolia, are also immediately recognizable. Whereas Shang knives normally have a short stem inserted into a handle of a different material, all northern-type bronze knives of this period have an integrally cast hilt. Pommels come in many shapes; the most common are the mushroom, an animal head, and various rings and loops. Geometric motifs similar to those on daggers decorate knife handles.

Clearly different from the fan-shaped ax of the Shang, the northern-type ax is typically long and thick, with a relatively narrow cutting edge. Besides the more common axes with simple sockets, its most distinctive characteristic is the type with a tubular socket set perpendicular to the blade. In early axes, the socket can be longer than the width of the body, a hafting system that is different from the predominant Shang method of attaching the handle to a protruding flat tang.[20]

Civilizations, ed. David Keightley (Berkeley: University of California Press, 1983), pp. 532–48. See also David Keightley, "The Shang: China's First Historical Dynasty," in *The Cambridge History of Ancient China*, pp. 275–77.

[19] Lin Yun, "A Reexamination," pp. 263–66.

[20] Tubular axes have been found in Hopei (Ch'ao-tao-kou and Ch'ing-lung county), in Shan-hsi, (Kao-hung, Liu-lin county, and Ch'u-chia-yü, in Shih-lou county), and at various Shang sites, such as Ta-ssu-k'ung. See *K'ao-ku* 1962.12: 644–5; Wu Chen-lu, "Pao-te hsien hsin fa-hsien te Yin-tai ch'ing-t'ung ch'i," *Wen-wu* 1972.4: 62–66; Yang Shao-shun, "Shan-hsi Liu-lin hsien Kao-hung fa-hsien Shang-tai t'ung-ch'i," *K'ao ku* 1981.3: 211–12; Yang Shao-shun, "Shan-hsi Shih-lou Ch'u-chia-yü Ts'ao-chia-yüan fa-hsien Shang-tai t'ung-ch'i," *Wen-wu* 1981.8:

Round bronze disks, usually defined as "mirrors," are also part of the northern heritage. Typically they have a smooth surface on one side; on the other, which may carry surface decoration, they have a central knob handle. A Ch'ing-hai mirror decorated on its back with a star-shaped design suggests a solar cult, possibly of Central Asian origin. Mirrors found in An-yang tombs, such as those in the tomb of Lady Fu Hao, the consort of King Wu Ting (c. 1200 B.C.), have decorative motifs that are not consonant with the artistic vocabulary of the Shang.[21] Other mirrors, found together with a *ting* vessel, curved knives, and gold earrings in Shang burials in central Shensi suggest contact with non-Chinese cultures.[22] Finally, a mirror has been found in another burial, together with two bronze *chüeh* vessels with the character Ch'iang inscribed on them.[23] This evidence connects the mirror to a distinctive northern culture, and possibly to the Ch'iang people.

Other objects regarded as characteristic of this culture include distinctive spoons and helmets. The spoons have rings on the handle with attached pendants. The helmets are undecorated; their sides come down to cover the ears, and they have a ring on the top and holes to the right and the left on the bottom.[24] One curious item is the so-called bow-shaped object, comprised of a slightly bent decorated central bar and curved lateral sections; various hypotheses have been proposed concerning its use.[25] Found in the

---

49–53; *Wen-wu* 1981.8: 46–48; Ma Te-chih et al., "Yi-chiu-wu-san-nien An-yang Ta-ssu-k'ung fa-chüeh pao-kao," *K'ao-ku hsüeh-pao* 1955.9: 25–90.

[21] Diane M. O'Donoghue, "Reflection and Reception: The Origins of the Mirror in Bronze Age China," *Bulletin of the Museum of Far Eastern Antiquities* 62 (1990): 5–25.

[22] Yao Sheng-min, "Shaan-hsi Ch'ün-hua hsien ch'u-t'u te Shang Chou Ch'ing-t'ung ch'i," *K'ao-ku yü wen-wu* 1986.5: 12–22. Note that only in the mid-seventh century did the bronze mirror become part of the Chinese native tradition.

[23] *Wen-wu* 1986.11: 7, fig. 11.5.

[24] A. Kovalev, "'Karasuk-dolche,' Hirschsteine und die Nomaden der chinesischen Annalen im Alterum," in *Maoqinggou: Ein eisenzeitliches Gräberfeld in der Ordos-Region (Innere Mongolei)*, ed. Thomas Höllman and Georg W. Kossack (Mainz: Verlag Philipp von Zabern), pp. 60–61.

[25] Bernhard Karlgren was probably wrong in considering it a kind of yoke but right in rejecting the old hypothesis that it was a "banner bell" ("Some Weapons and Tools of the Yin Dynasty," *Bulletin of the Museum of Far Eastern Antiquities*, 17 [1945]: 112). Max Loehr relates it to bows and quivers; see his "Weapons and Tools from Anyang," p. 138. However, the "bow-shaped" object appears commonly on so-called deer stones – anthropomorphic steles with carvings representing stylized deer – as a sort of pendant attached to the belt. On this basis, Lin Yun, "A Reexamination," p. 263, suggests that it was used as a "reins holder." Yet the iconography of the deer stones does not show it in combination with chariots or horses. See also Ch'in Chien-ming, "Shang Chou 'kung-hsing-ch'i' wei 'ch'i-ling' shuo," *K'ao-ku* 1995.3: 256–58.

Yin-hsü culture, whose specimens are adorned with rattles and horse heads at the ends, and in the Minusinsk region with a much simpler knob decoration, it was probably invented in the Northern Zone and thereafter transmitted to China and South Siberia.

Besides the bronze typology, the northern complex tradition also bears a typical decorative inventory, which is regarded as the telltale mark for all the art associated with non-Chinese northern peoples: the "animal style." In this artistic tradition, shared across the Northern Zone from the thirteenth century onward and common to both the Karasuk culture of South Siberia (1200–800 B.C.) and the early nomadic cultures of Central Asia, animals are variously represented on bronze vessels, weapons, and tools. In the Northern Zone, at this early stage, the style was expressed mainly by ornamental animal heads rendered in the round and attached to the ends of knife handles and dagger hilts.[26]

In terms of distribution, the Northern Zone complex has been associated with the type sites of Li–chia-ya (Ch'ing-chien county, Shensi province)[27] and Ch'ao-tao-kou (Ch'ing-lung county, Hopei),[28] and covers the broad area between the bend of the Yellow River and the Liao River drainage basin, extending across northern Hopei, Shansi, and Shensi. We know this cultural area mostly through funerary sites, which have yielded identical or closely related bronze objects, particularly daggers, knives, and axes.[29] The bronzes found at Ch'ao-tao-kou – a dagger with a decorated handle and a ram-head pommel, an ax with a tubular socket, and four knives with arched backs decorated with pommels in the form of a rattle or a ram-head knob – and at analogous sites, such as Lin-che-yü (Pao-te county, Shensi),[30] have contributed greatly to defining the Northern Zone as a distinct cultural complex.

[26] On the animal style the following works may be consulted: Karl Jettmar, *Art of the Steppes* (New York: Crown Publishers, 1967); and Anatoly Martinov, *The Ancient Art of Northern Asia*, trans. and ed. Demitri B. Shimkin and Edith M. Shimkin (Urbana: University of Illinois Press, 1991). On the origin and earliest occurrences of the animal style, see Yakov A. Sher, "On the Sources of the Scythic Animal Style," *Arctic Anthropology* 25.2 (1988): 47–60.

[27] See Katheryn Linduff et al., "An Archaeological Overview," in *Ancient Bronzes of the Eastern Eurasian Steppes*, ed. Emma Bunker (New York: Arthur Sackler Foundation, 1997), pp. 22–25.

[28] For the definition of Ch'ao-tao-kou as an archaeological culture, see Kovalev, "'Karasuk-dolche,' Hirschsteine und die Nomaden der chinesischen Annalen im Alterum," pp. 48–62.

[29] *K'ao-ku* 1962.12: 644–5.

[30] The burial ground yielded these bronze objects: a dagger with a grooved hilt and a rattle pommel, plaques with spiral designs, small rattles, small bells, a horse harness, two axes with tubular sockets, and ritual vessels. Wu Chen-lu, "Pao-te hsien hsin fa-hsien te Yin-tai ch'ing-t'ung ch'i," *Wen-wu* 1972.4: 62–66.

Evidence of interchanges between these sites and the more southern core areas of China is by no means rare, and excavated sites may need to be reassigned to one or the other cultural area based on a re-evaluation of the artifacts and the general composition of the burials. Thus, burials from Pai-fu, north of Peking, have been convincingly reclassified as a Northern Zone site.[31] Here too, as already noted for the Ch'i-chia culture, we can argue for the progressive divergence between Northern Zone and Central Plain cultures that would culminate, in the north, in the formation of a nomadic confederation at the end of the first millennium B.C. But the causes for this divergence are still not explained.[32] In fact, here we see again how a relatively small portion of a much bigger "puzzle" is magnified to give a full picture of events (in this instance, events that trace the economic, political, and social maturation of pastoral nomads). At the present stage of research, however, these events cannot be represented as a continuous evolutionary process; it is more likely that they occurred as a composite process, with multiple sources of development and interaction, to which the people of Pai-fu contributed. The most interesting aspect of this site is that Chinese *ke* blades and bronze helmets that may have belonged to charioteers have been found there.[33] The site bespeaks close commercial contacts and technology exchanges, confirming the vitality of the northern frontier throughout the Bronze Age.

Bronze weapons similar in style to the Northern Zone bronzes, and dated to the Shang and early Western Chou periods, have been found also to the east, especially in western Liao-ning.[34] Further east, however, we encounter a more varied picture, as the types of bronzes that predominate in eastern Liao-ning are quite different and mark a separate but related cultural zone. Only one type of northern-style dagger has been found in this area, together with socketed daggers not found in the rest of the Northern Zone complex. Yet the battle axes with long, narrow sockets and straight blades are similar to those found at Ch'ao-tao-kou. Unusual items, which nevertheless seem to belong to the same northern tradition, are a dagger

---

[31] Mrea Csorba, "The Chinese Northern Frontier: Reassessment of the Bronze Age Burials from Baifu," *Antiquity* 70 (1996): 564–87. Although I agree with this article's contention that Pai-fu belongs to the Northern Zone, the material it presents concerning the Caucasian faces of the people who used these burials does not convince me as to their racial identity, and does not constitute per se evidence of cultural affiliation.

[32] Csorba, "The Chinese Northern Frontier," pp. 576, 586.

[33] Wu En, "Yin chih Chou ch'u te pei-fang ch'ing-t'ung ch'I," *K'ao-ku hsüeh-pao* 1985.2: 135–56.

[34] Hsü Yü-lin, "Liao-ning Shang Chou shih-ch'i te ch'ing-t'ung wen-hua," in *K'ao-ku-hsüeh wen-hua lun-wen-chi*, ed. Su Ping-ch'i (Peking: Wen-wu, 1993), 3: 311–34; Chai Te-fang, "Chung-kuo pei-fang ti-ch'ü ch'ing-t'ung tuan-chien fen-ch'ün yen-chiu," *K'ao-ku hsüeh-pao* 1988.3: 277–99.

hilt that terminates in the shape of a human head, vessel lids, and chariot ornaments.

The considerable variety of assemblages, types of bronzes, and stylistic components suggest that several metallurgical foci existed within a broad complex. These centers interacted and influenced each other but did not fuse into a single unit. Instead, they retained their local flavor as independent and culturally distinct communities.

Early Contacts between China and the Northern Zone

Compelling evidence of contact between the Shang and the Northern Zone comes from the discovery of non-Chinese bronzes in Shang tombs excavated in the An-yang area: a bronze knife with animal-head pommel found at Hou-chia-chuang; a knife with a ring head and a Shang pickax found at Hsiao-t'un; and a pickax with a short tubular socket, unearthed with a clay tripod and a piece of jade, found at Ta-ssu-k'ung in 1953.[35] The funerary inventory from the already mentioned tomb of Fu Hao, excavated in 1976, attests to the relevance of imports from the north, as it contained a northern-style knife with an ibex head, bronze mirrors, and a bronze hairpin that had no equivalent in the Central Plain. Also, a large number of the jades found in the tomb are reported to have come from nephrite quarries in Sinkiang.[36]

Although it is generally assumed, as we have seen in the previous chapter, that the Shang chariot is a borrowing from the Andronovo people, few chariot remains have been found in the Northern Zone.[37] The presence of chariots in this region cannot be doubted, however, given their extensive documentation in the petroglyphs of the Altai region, the T'ien-shan mountains in Sinkiang, and the Yin-shan mountains in Inner Mongolia. For instance, a rock carving from the Yin-shan mountains illustrates a scene in

---

[35] Li Chi, "Chi Hsiao-t'un ch'u-t'u-te ch'ing-t'ung ch'i," *Chung-kuo k'ao-ku hsüeh-pao* 4 (1949): 1–70. These were found in tomb M164. Kovalev, "'Karasuk-dolche,' Hirschsteine und die Nomaden der chinesischen Annalen im Alterum," p. 54.

[36] Wang Ping-hua, "Hsi Han yi-ch'ien Hsin-chiang he Chung-yüan ti-ch'ü li-shih kuan-hsi k'ao-su," in Wang Ping-hua, *Ssu-chou chih lu k'ao-ku yen-chiu* (Urumqi: Hsin-chiang Jen-min, 1993), p. 167.

[37] For instance, the remains of wooden wheels found in No-mu-hung (Tu-lan county, Ch'ing-hai) and tentatively dated to the mid-second millennium B.C. (*K'ao-ku hsüeh-pao* 1963.1, pl. 3); see also Jenny F. So and Emma C. Bunker, *Traders and Raiders on China's Northern Frontier* (Seattle and London: Arthur Sackler Gallery and University of Washington Press, 1996), p. 26.

which a hunter shoots game after having dismounted from a chariot that has eight-spoked wheels and is pulled by two horses.[38] The petroglyphs, as well as the actual chariots found in the Sintashta burials, show the northern complex chariot as having essentially the same design and technical characteristics as the Chinese chariot.[39]

Yet the nature of the relationship between the Northern Zone and the bronze cultures of South Siberia remains problematic.[40] Northern Chinese cultures, like the Karasuk culture of Siberia, seem to have had mixed economies based on livestock but also relying on agriculture and other supporting activities. The bones of antelope and deer that have been found point to extensive hunting, whereas cattle and horse remains show the Karasuk people's devotion to animal husbandry. The Karasuk's metal inventory contains a variety of objects similar to the Northern Zone bronzes. We find knives with hunched backs and daggers with short guards that are similar to the Northern Zone style. Pickaxes have tubular sockets for hafting such as those of the Northern Zone, though the blade has a pointed cutting edge that may have been derived from a Shang prototype. Arrowheads also resemble those found in An-yang. Chernykh has argued for a possible symbiosis between Central Asian metallurgy and "true Chinese examples of high-quality casting," especially with respect to weapons and ritual objects. Only later did typical artifacts of this broad "Central Asian"

---

[38] Kai Shan-lin, "Ts'ung Nei Meng Yin-shan yen-hua k'an ku-tai pei-fang yu-mu min-tsu te li-shih kung-hsien," in *Ssu-chou chih lu yen-hua yi-shu*, ed. Chou Chin-pao (Urumchi: Hsin-chiang Jen-min, 1993). For other examples of chariot petroglyphs, see Edward L. Shaughnessy, "Historical Perspectives on the Introduction of the Chariot into China," *Harvard Journal of Asiatic Studies* 48.1 (1988): 202–203.

[39] See also Piggott, "Chinese Chariotry: An Outsider's View," in *Arts of the Eurasian Steppelands*, ed. Philip Denwood, Colloquies on Art and Archaeology in Asia no. 7 (London: Percival David Foundation, 1978), pp. 32–51. For an argument against the exogenous origin of the chariot in China, see Lu Liancheng, "Chariot and Horse Burials in Ancient China," *Antiquity* 67 (1993): 824–38.

[40] From the viewpoint of the development of metallurgy, the eastern zone of the steppe, with one of its most dynamic centers located in the Sayano-Altai region, embraced also Mongolia and Transbaikalia. This is what Chernykh defines as the Central Asian Metallurgical Province. The development of metallurgy and its diffusion throughout the region should probably be seen in connection with the development of nomadism, as the more technologically advanced communities may have advanced more quickly along the road of pastoral specialization, and their increased mobility may in turn have facilitated the diffusion of their technology. For the metallurgical development of this region and its extension in the Bronze Age, see E. N. Chernykh, *Ancient Metallurgy in the USSR* (Cambridge: Cambridge University Press, 1992), pp. 270–71.

zone gradually penetrate the west, thus attesting to an eastern chronological primacy.[41]

Identification of Early Nomads in the Northern Zone

A relative dearth of analysis, together with much unprocessed archaeological data, makes outlining the origins and evolution of early pastoral nomadic cultures in northern China difficult. While the Bronze and Iron Age "Scythian" cultures of the western part of Central Eurasia are fairly well established, this is not the case for the eastern part of the area. Cited among the possible causes for the transition to pastoral nomadism in northern China is the change to a more arid climate, which led to greater reliance on animal husbandry and the abandonment of a sedentary life based on farming and livestock breeding.[42] Alternatively or concurrently, researchers do not exclude the arrival from either the north or the west of migrating pastoralists who may have acted as a stimulus for the passage from agropastoralism to more specialized forms of pastoral nomadism. The extent of migrations cannot be determined based on the present state of research, but at least two originating points are possible, one in the northeast, identified with the Upper Hsia-chia-tien culture,[43] and the other in the northwest, identified with the nomadic peoples of the Sayano-Altai region and present-day Sinkiang.

It may be more productive, however, instead of looking for the origins of the appearance of Scythian-type nomads in northern China, to focus on those diagnostic elements that are characteristic of the martial pastoral nomads of the Eurasian steppe. By identifying the foci of regional nomadic cultures, and the diverse forms of technological advancement and social structure prevailing in each of them, we can construct a preliminary map of new cultural formations, whose appearance need not always depend on undocumented migrations. Only by refocusing on localized processes (but ones open to external influences) can we determine the context in which these changes occurred.

In this respect, archaeologists have assessed diachronic developments in the Northern Zone complex according to criteria that are commonly

---

[41] Chernykh, *Ancient Metallurgy in the USSR*, pp. 269–73. The similarity between the Ordos-Karasuk and the Seima-Turbino artifacts is also recognized in Karl Jettmar, "The Karasuk Culture and Its South-Eastern Affinities," *Bulletin of the Museum of Far Eastern Antiquities* 22 (1950), p. 119.

[42] Ch'iao Hsiao-ch'in, "Kuan-yü pei-fang yu-mu wen-hua ch'i-yüan te t'an-t'ao," *Nei Meng-ku wen-wu k'ao-ku* 1992.1–2: 21–25.

[43] Liu Te-cheng and Hsü Chün-chü, "Kan-su Ch'in-yang Ch'ün-ch'iu Chan-kuo mu-tsang te ch'ing-li," *K'ao-ku* 1988.5: 413–24.

assumed to be indicative of nomads, such as the relative absence of settlements, the predominance of animal bones, the remains of many sacrificed animals, and the appearance of the so-called Scythian triad – weapons, animal-style decoration, and horse harness – in grave inventories. Archaeologists also take account of the trajectory of iron use, stratigraphical evidence, and typological analysis when establishing a sequence for the development of a culture. The local characteristics of a particular culture that researchers most notice are its decorative repertoire, the shape and construction of its burials, its economy, its adaptation to the natural environment, its people's physical features, and the interaction of its inhabitants with neighboring peoples.

Periodization

Periodization of early nomadic cultures in northern China is very difficult.[44] Whereas textual evidence for the presence of mounted pastoral nomads is attested in Chinese sources at the earliest from the mid-fifth, and more clearly from the late fourth, century B.C., the archaeological record indicates an earlier arrival of pastoral people and slow expansion in the contacts between these cultures and China. Given the absence of stable chronologies, dates for the cultural evolution occurring in some of the most important early nomadic areas, such as the Ordos, must be approximate. Nevertheless, based on significant changes in the funerary assemblages, typological characteristics of specific items, and radiocarbon datings, three stages of evolution can be identified.[45]

The first stage, from the ninth to the seventh century B.C., is characterized by a greater number of horse fittings and weapons included among the burial goods found at funerary sites and by an economy increasingly dominated by animal husbandry (though agriculture continued to play an important role). During this phase, the northeastern part of the Northern Zone appears to have been especially advanced, while the central and northwestern areas do not show comparable signs of development.

The second stage, from the sixth through the fourth century B.C., begins with clear signs of the emergence of a classic nomadic steppe culture – the appearance of the "Scythian-triad" assemblage: weapons, horse gear, and

---

[44] For examples of periodization, see Wu En, "Wo kuo pei-fang ku-tai tung-wu wen-shih," *K'ao-ku hsüeh-pao* 1990.4: 409–437; and Emma Bunker, "Ancient Ordos Bronzes," in *Ancient Chinese and Ordos Bronzes*, ed. Jessica Rawson and Emma Bunker (Hong Kong: Museum of Art, 1990), pp. 291–307. See also Di Cosmo, "The Northern Frontier in Pre-Imperial China," pp. 888–93.

[45] T'ien Kuan-chin and Kuo Su-hsin, eds., *O-erh-to-ssu ch'ing-t'ung ch'i* (Peking: Wen-wu, 1986).

objects decorated in animal style. Daggers, abundant horse fittings, and animal-style plaques are found in particular in two areas of distribution: one, the north-northeastern, which encompasses the Ordos region and the intermediate zone between Inner Mongolia and Liao-ning, to the east of the T'ai-hang Mountains; and the second, the territory that spans parts of Ch'ing-hai, Kansu, and Ning-hsia.[46] Another distinctive feature of this period is the spreading of the use of iron metallurgy. Although bronze remained the dominant metal, the presence of iron tools and bimetallic weapons (especially swords with bronze hilts and iron blades) in sites where there was no previous trace of iron, suggest a later dating. Although the appearance of iron metallurgy per se does not seem to have had a crucial impact on either the technological or the social development of these communities, these cultures have a more pronounced "Scythian" character, noticeable especially in the abundance of horse trappings. It was also during this stage that the nomadic aristocracy may have risen to a position of political and military superiority over local and neighboring farmers.

The third stage is represented especially by Ordos sites, attributed to the early Hsiung-nu culture, which were in use between the third and

---

[46] Watson, in *Cultural Frontiers in Ancient East Asia*, posited the intriguing notion that the T'ai-hang mountain range constituted a boundary between the Jung and the Western Ti, and that this boundary corresponded, in the archaeological record, to two different cultural spheres, one more oriented toward the steppe culture of the nomads of Mongolia and the Altai, the other part of the mixed forest-grassland-agricultural environment of the northeast. This division is consistent with the position of the T'ai-hang Range, running along the western boundary of the Hopei province, as a watershed between the forested, maritime Manchurian zone and the continental parts of northern China. This notion is finding further support in more recent archaeological and art historical analyses of local artifacts (e.g., Bunker, *Ancient Bronzes of the Eastern Eurasian Steppes*, p. 159 and *passim*). This notion, however, is not emphasized, or even mentioned, in much Chinese archaeological literature, where the "master paradigm" is that of the Northern Zone complex, which is then broken down into local cultures often dominated by a regionalist approach. The subset of the "macroregions" to the east and to the west of the T'ai-hang Mountains is then lost, or at least overlooked. One reason for this blind spot in Chinese archaeology may be what Lothar von Falkenhausen has called the "regionalist paradigm." The archaeological "identity" of Shansi in the Chou period is closely tied to the culture of Chin, and this may have effectively excluded the cultures of northern Shansi, west of the T'ai-hang Range (which Watson relates to the Ti peoples), from the picture of the Shansi cultural past, preferring to link them to a more distant and vague "Northern Zone" or with very localized (and therefore non-regional) phenomena (see Lothar von Falkenhausen, "The Regionalist Paradigm in Chinese Archaeology," in *Nationalism, Politics and the Practice of Archaeology*, ed. Philip L. Kohl and Clare Fawcett [Cambridge: Cambridge University Press, 1995], pp. 208–10).

first century B.C. At these sites we observe a complete change in the funerary assemblage whereby the symbols of martiality have been replaced with luxurious accouterments representing a new-found wealth, possibly commercial in origin. Precious objects and ornaments seem more relevant to this culture, in terms of both sheer quantity and intrinsic value. We also find gold objects in greater numbers, gold having long been associated with the nomadic cultures, particularly with those of the western steppe, where plaques and ornaments of gold were often placed in Scythian tombs.

These three stages in the evolutionary sequence of the centers of certain northern China nomadic cultures that are assumed to be culturally related to the people who formed the Hsiung-nu empire in the late third century B.C. I am not suggesting, however, that there was a single line of evolution. Each regional focus represented a separate process and must be looked at as such. On the other hand, the high degree of similarity in the metallurgical production of all of the cultural foci in question, as well as in other aspects of these cultures, also presents a picture of exchange, borrowing, and cultural miscegenation that militates against the notion of the emergence of nomadic cultures through a series of isolated processes.

The evidence suggests that separate nomadic pastoral centers formed in the north and then came to dominate the area militarily and politically. The whirlpool of displacements, migrations, and conquests thus generated cannot be reconstructed in the absence of historical documents but cannot be doubted either, given the level of "interconnectivity" documented archaeologically. At this point several agro-pastoral peoples either disappeared altogether, converted to full-scale nomadism, or (as probably happened in the majority of cases) were forced into positions of subordination and servitude. The North remained politically agitated, but it is likely that the nomads sought to expand the political power of their groups (tribes?) over the steppe zone and, under successful clans and leaders, to forge even larger political units. These tribes were possibly those later identified in Chinese sources as both political and ethnic groups such as the Hsiung-nu, Lin Hu, Tung Hu, and Lou-fan.

First Phase: Late Western Chou and Early Spring and Autumn Period (c. Ninth–Seventh Century B.C.)

Early Nomadic Sites in the Northeast

In the Northern Zone burial sites dating from the late Western Chou and early Spring and Autumn periods contain an increasing number of animal bones – many from domesticated animals – that suggest the expansion of

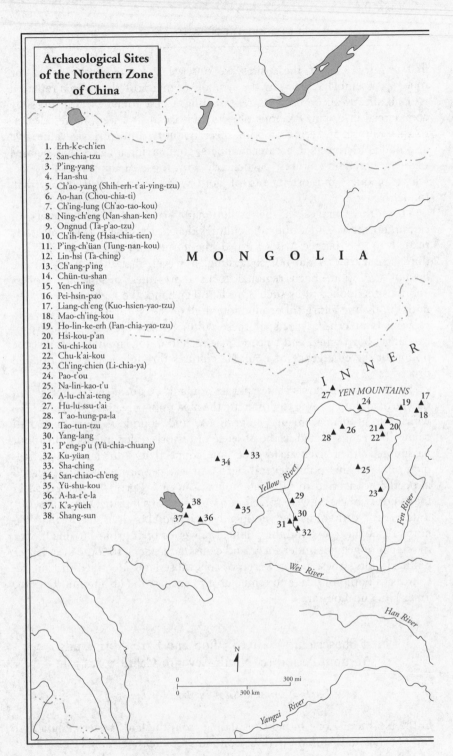

**Archaeological Sites
of the Northern Zone
of China**

1. Erh-k'e-ch'ien
2. San-chia-tzu
3. P'ing-yang
4. Han-shu
5. Ch'ao-yang (Shih-erh-t'ai-ying-tzu)
6. Ao-han (Chou-chia-ti)
7. Ch'ing-lung (Ch'ao-tao-kou)
8. Ning-ch'eng (Nan-shan-ken)
9. Ongnud (Ta-p'ao-tzu)
10. Ch'ih-feng (Hsia-chia-tien)
11. P'ing-ch'üan (Tung-nan-kou)
12. Lin-hsi (Ta-ching)
13. Ch'ang-p'ing
14. Chün-tu-shan
15. Yen-ch'ing
16. Pei-hsin-pao
17. Liang-ch'eng (Kuo-hsien-yao-tzu)
18. Mao-ch'ing-kou
19. Ho-lin-ke-erh (Fan-chia-yao-tzu)
20. Hsi-kou-p'an
21. Su-chi-kou
22. Chu-k'ai-kou
23. Ch'ing-chien (Li-chia-ya)
24. Pao-t'ou
25. Na-lin-kao-t'u
26. A-lu-ch'ai-teng
27. Hu-lu-ssu-t'ai
28. T'ao-hung-pa-la
29. Tao-tun-tzu
30. Yang-lang
31. P'eng-p'u (Yü-chia-chuang)
32. Ku-yüan
33. Sha-ching
34. San-chiao-ch'eng
35. Yü-shu-kou
36. A-ha-t'e-la
37. K'a-yüeh
38. Shang-sun

MONGOLIA

INNER

YEN MOUNTAINS

Yellow River

Fen River

Wei River

Han River

N

0   300 mi
0   300 km

Yangzi River

Map 2

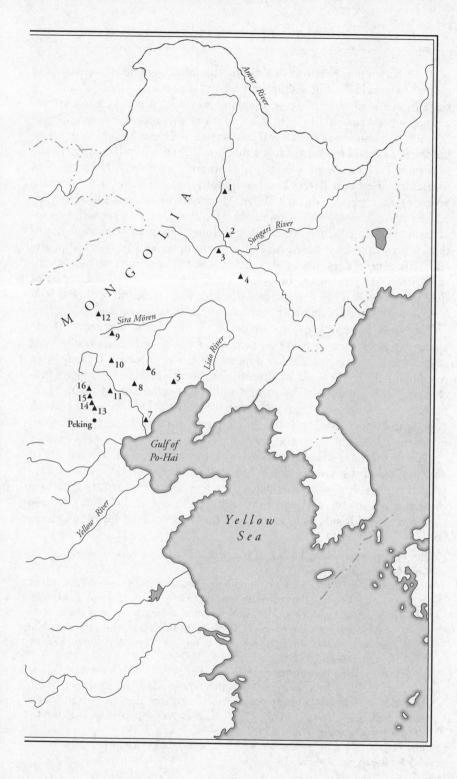

pastoral economies.[47] Horseback riding, the most significant activity of a mature pastoral nomadic culture in Eurasia, is also in evidence at an early stage in the northeastern sector, in connection with a new culture, known as the Upper Hsia-chia-tien, that appeared at the end of the second millennium B.C. and lasted for several centuries. The Upper Hsia-chia-tien geographical range extended north to the Sira Mören River Basin, up to the eastern side of the Great Khingan Mountains; its southern boundary was formed by the Luan River, Yen Mountains, and Ch'i-lao-t'u Mountains. Spanning the three provinces of Inner Mongolia, Liao-ning, and Hopei, its eastern boundary was the basin of the Liao River, and its western boundary was the area of Chao-wu-ta-meng in Inner Mongolia. Chronologies of this culture have been based on radiocarbon dates and typological analysis.[48] The general consensus today is that it lasted approximately eight centuries, from the eleventh to the fourth century B.C.; this is a long period of time that is itself subject to internal periodization, which nevertheless is at least in part certainly related to the evolution of early nomads.[49]

The most ancient sites are identified in the northern reaches of the Upper Hsia-chia-tien distribution area and seem to indicate a transitional stage, one in which this culture appears as a new, intrusive element little resembling the earlier local cultures. The horse remains in Upper Hsia-chia-tien sites are among the earliest found in northeastern China, where bronze metallurgy was extremely well developed, because of the area's abundant copper ore and the inhabitants' sophisticated metallurgical knowledge.

One of the earliest sites identified with this culture is the mining site of Ta-ching in Lin-hsi county, Inner Mongolia.[50] Radiocarbon analyses have yielded consistent datings that place the site in the tenth century B.C., thus making it one of the earliest of this culture.[51] Stone and clay molds have been found at this site, as have smelting furnaces; most of the mining tools

[47] Ts'ui Hsüan, "Nei Meng-ku hsien Ch'in shih-ch'i hsü-mu yi-ts'un shu-lun," *Nei Meng-ku she-hui k'e-hsüeh* 1988.1: 69–74.

[48] The latter has been based either on datable sites such as Nan-shan-ken, where the presence of Western Chou artifacts provide a fairly secure chronological basis, or on the stylistic evolution of distinctive cultural elements, such as the daggers with curved blades. See Chin Feng-yi, "Lun Chung-kuo tung-pei ti-ch'ü han ch'ü-jen ch'ing-t'ung tuan-chien te wen-hua yi-ts'un," *K'ao-ku hsüeh-pao* 1982.4: 387–426 (part I), and 1983.1: 39–5 (part II).

[49] The first excavation that identified the Upper Hsia-chia-tien as a separate culture took place at Ch'ih-feng, in Inner Mongolia, where distinctive features that differentiated it from the contemporary bronze culture of the Ordos region were documented. See *K'ao-ku* 1961.2: 77–81; *K'ao-ku hsüeh-pao* 1974.1: 111–44.

[50] *Wen-wu tzu-liao ts'ung-k'an* 7 (1983): 138–46.

[51] Chin Feng-yi, "Hsia-chia-tien shang-ts'eng wen-hua chi ch'i tsu-shu wen-t'i," *K'ao-ku hsüeh-pao* 1987.2: 177–208.

that have been found here are made of stone, with a very few small bronze objects (among them a drill and an arrowhead). The cemetery at Ta-p'ao-tzu in the Onggut Banner (Weng-niu-t'e-ch'i, Inner Mongolia) also belongs to the earlier phase.[52] The pottery found here seems to indicate a close connection with the north, in particular with the site of Pai-chin-pao, in Hei-lung-chiang. The earlier dates attributed to these northern sites, and the connection between the Ta-p'ao-tzu and the Pai-chin-pao pottery, suggest a southward movement of peoples associated with an economy based on hoe agriculture and hunting.

Modern-day Hei-lung-chiang, an area rich in large navigable rivers, may have been especially important as a route of communication between the northeastern region of China and Transbaikalia and Mongolia.[53] Thanks to the variety of economic activities that the Manchurian environment favored, we find evidence in the northeast of advanced metallurgical cultures with mixed economies. Farmers, fishermen, hunters, and pastoralists interacted in ways that cannot be clearly documented, but that show a tendency toward the creation of a wide and stable network of contacts through which both artistic motifs and technical innovations could travel rapidly. The development of the area, from the initial spread of bronze production in the Upper Hsia-chia-tien culture to the advent of iron metallurgy, seems to have profited from a continuous input of cultural elements from the north and the east.

Population movement may also have brought different people into contact with each other and may help explain the variety of burial practices found in Upper Hsia-chia-tien sites. Sometimes graves are simple earthern pits, and sometimes they are pits lined with stone slabs. At Chou-chia-ti cemetery, in Inner Mongolia, a funerary custom rather different from other Upper Hsia-chia-tien sites, consisting of covering the head of the deceased with sack cloth decorated with turquoise beads and bronze buttons, may indicate ethnic differences within this culture.[54] Of course, we should not

[52] Chin Feng-yi, "Hsia-chia-tien shang-ts'eng wen-hua chi ch'i tsu-shu wen-t'i"; Chu Yung-kang, "Hsia-chia-tien shang-ts'eng wen-hua te ch'u-pu yen-chiu," in *K'ao-ku-hsüeh wen-hua lun-chi*, ed. Su Ping-ch'i (Peking: Wen-wu, 1993), 1: 99–128.

[53] On the archaeology of Hei-lung-chiang, see Tan Ying-jie et al., "The Bronze Age in the Song Nen Plain," in *The Archaeology of Northeast China: Beyond the Great Wall*, ed. Sarah Milledge Nelson (London: Routledge, 1995), pp. 225–50; T'an Ying-chieh and Chao Shan-tung, "Sung Nen p'ing-yüan ch'ing-t'ung wen-hua ch'u-yi," in *Chung-kuo k'ao-ku hsüeh-hui ti-ssu-tz'u nien-hui lun-wen chi 1983* (Peking: Wen-wu, 1985), pp. 196–202; Yang Hu et al., "Hei-lung-chiang ku-tai wen-hua ch'u-lun," in *Chung-kuo k'ao-ku hsüeh-hui ti-ssu-tz'u nien-hui lun-wen chi 1979* (Peking: Wen-wu, 1980), pp. 80–96; Li Ch'en-ch'i, "Sung Nen p'ing-yüan ch'ing-t'ung yü ch'u-hsing tsao-ch'i t'ieh-ch'i shih-tai wen-hua lei-hsing te yen-chiu," *Pei-fang wen-wu* 1994.1: 2–9.

[54] *K'ao-ku* 1984.5: 417–26.

attribute all differences in burial practices to either ethnic or cultural differentiation: at Tung-nan-kou, in Hopei, the marked variations in the type
and amount of burial goods have been interpreted as a sign of social stratification.[55] In any case, animal sacrifice was integral to the burial practices
of this culture, with the prominent role of dogs in this context characteristic of northeastern cultures in general.

A further element that points to the existence of a northern Manchurian
influence on the Upper Hsia-chia-tien complex is the diffusion of iron
metallurgy, which seems to have developed first in the north and to have
filtered south only later. In Hei-lung-chiang, a region rich in forests, arable
land, and waterways, iron metallurgy can be dated to the eighth century
B.C. or even earlier, appearing at the same time as the full blossoming
of bronze production. In contrast, we find that in the Upper Hsia-chia-tien
site of Shih-erh-t'ai-ying-tzu (Ch'ao-yang county, Liao-ning), a cemetery in
use since the Western Chou, whose upper layer is dated to the early and
middle Warring States period (c. 500–350 B.C.), the metal inventory is
entirely of bronze.[56] Similarly, at T'ieh-chiang-kou, located in the eastern
part of Inner Mongolia and within the area of distribution of the Upper
Hsia-chia-tien culture, we find relatively poor burials with few bronze
artifacts.[57]

The bronze production of Upper Hsia-chia-tien sites that have been excavated includes weapons, ornaments, and horse trappings. The style is often
distinctive, and characteristic items such as the curved-blade sword indicate
the culture's vitality and autonomy. At the same time, several graves and
caches also contain Western Chou ritual bronzes and items in the typical
Ordos style, suggesting close contact between the Upper Hsia-chia-tien
people and neighboring cultures.

Within the metal inventory of the Upper Hsia-chia-tien culture we find
clear signs of its association with pastoral nomadism. At Nan-shan-ken, in
Ning-ch'eng county, Inner Mongolia – one of the most representative and
best-known sites of this culture – archaeologists have unearthed the first
iconographic evidence of horse riding in northern China, consisting of a
stirrup-shaped bronze ring adorned with the figures of two hunters on
horseback in the act of pursuing a hare.[58] The importance accorded horse

---

[55] K'ao-ku 1977. 1: 51–55.
[56] Chu Kuei, "Liao-ning Ch'ao-yang Shih-erh-t'ai-ying-tzu ch'ing-t'ung tuan-chien-
mu," K'ao-ku hsueh-pao 1960.1: 63–71.
[57] Shao Kuo-t'ien, "Ao-han ch'i T'ieh-chiang-kuo Chan-kuo mu-ti tiao-ch'a chien-
pao," Nei Meng-ku wen-wu k'ao-ku 1992.1–2: 84–90.
[58] On the Nan-shan-ken site, see Li Yi-yu, "Nei Meng Chao-wu-ta-meng ch'u-t'u-
te t'ung-ch'i tiao-ch'a," K'ao-ku 1959.6: 276–277; and K'ao-ku hsüeh-pao
1973.2: 27–39. For the illustration of the ring with the horse-rider figurine, see
K'ao-ku hsüeh-pao 1975.1: 117–140.

riding at this site is confirmed by the varied and sophisticated inventory of horse and chariot technology objects that have been found: harnesses with cheek pieces, two types of bits, tinkling bells, *luan* bells, and head ornaments and masks. Furthermore, an incised-bone plaque also recovered from Nan-shan-ken shows a hunting scene depicting chariots pulled by horses.[59] With the exceptions of the cheek pieces, which were sometimes made of bone or wood, all other horse-related items were made of bronze, suggesting that at least one of the earliest foci of the development of horseback riding on China's frontiers was located in the northeast, beginning around the eighth century B.C.

In addition, a characteristic Scythian-type assemblage has been unearthed, which also includes bronze weapons and the bones of cattle, sheep, and horses. Overall, the large increase in the quantity of remains of herbivorous animals indicates the growing importance of pastoral nomadism in the area.[60] Within this rich environment, the large number of bronze daggers, knives, axes, spearheads, arrowheads, shields, and helmets found in burials suggests that at this time a military aristocracy established itself as the dominant class over a mixed population. The military prowess and expansionism of these martial people favored the broad distribution of the Upper Hsia-chia-tien culture. The spread of nomadic pastoralism in the Northern Zone, then, should at least be partly attributed to the rise of cultural centers where nomads were dominated by a military aristocracy that later expanded its political power (and cultural influence) beyond the ethnic or economic boundaries of the original community.

At this stage mounted pastoralism was only one of the activities of these people. The Upper Hsia-chia-tien remained a predominantly sedentary society; its excavated settlements provide evidence of a farming and pig-raising economy. The houses are round and semi-subterranean, not different from those of the earlier Lower Hsia-chia-tien. This may also indicate that the earlier inhabitants continued to co-exist with the pastoral peoples. The presence of the bones of wild animals such as deer in excavated sites indicates that hunting was widely practiced. In sum, the varied ecology of the northeast, with its forests, with the fertile river valleys of southern Manchuria, and with the grassland pastures of southeastern Mongolia, allowed for different kinds of economic adaptation, of which pastoral nomadism was at first one among many. Two questions arise: what are the relationships among these various kinds of production, and what are the possible avenues that led to the development of nomadism in this region?

---

[59] *K'ao-ku* 1981.4: 304–308.

[60] Wu En, "New Chinese Archaeological Discoveries Regarding the Ancient Northern Tribes," Paper presented at the workshop "Chinese and Their Northern Neighbors," University of Pittsburgh, April 5–7, 1991.

In connection with these questions we need to consider Gideon Shelach's theory regarding chiefdom formation in the northeast during the second millennium B.C. and the transition from the Lower to the Upper Hsia-chia-tien culture. Shelach posits the appearance of small-scale chiefdoms in the area of distribution of the Lower Hsia-chia-tien culture and, in particular, in the areas of Ao-han and Ch'ih-feng. These chiefdoms compare in their social and political organization to the "chiefdoms" that appear in the Central Plain area, beginning with the Erh-li-t'ou culture (c. 1800–1600 B.C.). The difference between the Chinese and the northern chiefdoms was one of population and territorial size, rather than one of social organization, a difference also stemming from the greater ability of the Central Plain people to develop intensive agriculture. Attempting to explain a perceived gap between the collapse of the region's Lower Hsia-chia-tien culture in the mid-second millenium B.C. and the appearance, about five hundred years later, of Upper Hsia-chia-tien cultural remains,[61] Shelach rejects the expansion of Chinese influence, either direct or indirect, as the cause of radical regional transformations. He also rejects the notion that such transformations were caused by environmental changes. Instead, he proposes that the causes for the end of the chiefdoms be sought in "the social and economic environment that stimulated the development of specialized pastoralism."[62] His explanation of the emergence of pastoral nomadism in the region, while correct in its assumption that an agricultural base is needed for specialized nomadism to develop, is less convincing in its fuller formulation. In essence, Shelach argues that the intensive agriculture practiced in the northern plains of China stimulated the development of pastoral nomadism in marginal areas, where this type of farming could not have been practiced. This contention, however, runs directly counter to the statement, also reported by Shelach, that both Lower and Upper Hsia-chia-tien cultures were essentially sedentary societies depending on subsistence economies, creating the obstacle of having to explain the relationship, insufficiently developed in Shelach's argument, between Hsia-chia-tien's farming and Shang and Chou agricultural production. It seems counterintuitive to surmise the existence of exchanges in basic necessities at considerable distances when farming products were produced and could be obtained locally.[63] Still, Shelach's

---

[61] The notion that there was no habitation between the two cultures is apparently not correct. See Kuo Ta-shun, "Shih-lun wei-ying-tzu lei-hsing," in K'ao-ku-hsüeh wen-hua lun-chi, pp. 79–98.

[62] Gideon Shelach, "Social Complexity in North China during the Early Bronze Age: A Comparative Study of the Erlitou and Lower Xiajiadian Cultures," Asian Perspectives 33.2 (1994): 282.

[63] On p. 286 Shelach argues for a diffusion of Shang and Chou intensive agriculture to the northern plains, where peasants exchanged foodstuffs for pastoral products with the nomads, but he is ambiguous as to whether these exchanges

theory is important and has the undeniable merit of steering away from pernicious mechanical explanations based on climate or on notions of Chinese influence that disregard local developments.

It may be useful here to discuss the aforementioned transition, in the northwestern sector, from a predominantly agricultural to a predominantly pastoral economy, in the context of the post-Ch'i-chia cultures. Debaine-Francfort rightly suggests that economic developments in the northwest may have been influenced by contacts with areas further to the north and west, that is, Central Asia and South Siberia. The deep transformations that a people's transition to pastoral nomadism entails cannot be fully appreciated, I believe, without looking at all the areas with which the culture in question may have had contact. For the Upper Hsia-chia-tien culture, it seems to me that the appearance of pastoral nomadism, which also requires the acquisition of expert knowledge in animal husbandry and the mass production of equestrian equipment, was unlikely to have occurred in isolation. Although the transition from the Lower to the Upper Hsia-chia-tien cultures cannot yet be explained, it is possible that cultural changes, and in particular the rise in importance of pastoralism, may have been caused by more advanced pastoral or hunting-pastoral communities infiltrating, through a century-long process, from the north. This process need not be a "migration" model, but a more comprehensive model that looks to the north as well as to the south, takes into account the mobility of people over time, and recognizes the need to explain the similarities between Upper Hsia-chia-tien metallurgy and northern metallurgy. Therefore, in my view, a picture of the transition from the Lower to the Upper Hsia-chia-tien is destined to remain incomplete until the link between Upper Hsian-chia-tien and the Mongolian and Transbaikalian regions to the north is fully explored.[64]

Concerning the social and economic development of the eastern region of the Northern Zone, we should consider the likelihood that Upper Hsia-chia-tien society was a hierarchy in which an elite, possibly of nomadic warriors, ruled "classes" of miners, agricultural producers, and other people who were their subordinates, bondsmen, or tributaries. The robust

were through direct contacts between the Shang-Chou and the Hsia-chia-tien peoples, or were through "northern plains" intermediaries. In either case, the presence of settlements and farming in Hsia-chia-tien sites makes the notion of a Shang-Chou economic "spread" northward immaterial to the economic development of the area, unless it can be shown that at this time specific techniques were imported into Manchuria from China.

[64] Debaine-Francfort, *Du Néolithique à l'Age du Bronze en Chine du Nord-Ouest*, pp. 340–48. William Watson highlighted these northern connections by pointing out the similarities in the stone-lined burials (slab graves), pottery types, and other features that link Manchuria to Mongolia and Transbaikalia; see *Cultural Frontiers in Ancient East Asia*, pp. 124–41.

metallurgical production of the Upper Hsia-chia-tien (including the Ao-han area)[65] led to contact and exchanges between that culture and China and other neighboring communities. The emergence of pastoral nomadism and of an elite equestrian culture, the cultural connections with the north and west, the widespread metallurgical production, and the presence of "aristocratic" burial sites rich in bronze objects, as well as the continuation of a predominantly sedentary and agricultural lifestyle and contacts and exchanges with China, seem to indicate the presence of a much more complex social organization than is generally thought, one in which different areas constituted discrete social, economic, and political bodies that included a variety of producers and "cultures."

The Northwestern Complex

In the northwestern region, around the turn of the second to the first millennium B.C., the transition to pastoral nomadism appears to have continued as the mixed economy in which pastoral production predominated evolved into one of actual pastoral nomadism. A pattern of incipient nomadism can be detected in the evolution of the K'a-yüeh culture, distributed in Kansu and Ch'ing-hai. As in other Northern Zone areas, this long-lived culture, in existence between around 1500 B.C. and the Han dynasty, gradually evolved from a mixed farming and pastoral culture with a settled way of life to a predominantly nomadic culture. This transition is reflected in both an increased number of animal bones and sacrifices and in the composition of the animal stock. In sites of the early period, such as Shang-sun, the usual sacrificial offering was a pig, but in the middle period (A-ha-t'e-la type), pigs were replaced by cattle and horses.[66]

Partly overlapping with the K'a-yüeh culture in the Ho-hsi Corridor (an arid region in northern Kansu between the Yellow River and the steppe region of the eastern T'ien-shan) the sites of the Sha-ching culture date from the Spring and Autumn to the Warring States period.[67] The Sha-ching

---

[65] Stone molds for knives and ornaments were found at Shan-wan-tzu, in the Ao-han Banner; see Shao Kuo-t'ien, "Nei Meng-ku Ao-han-ch'i fa-hsien te ch'ing-t'ung-ch'i chi yu-kuan yi-wu," *Pei-fang wen-wu* 1993.1: 18–25.

[66] Kao Tung-lu, "Lüeh lun Ka-yüeh wen-hua," *K'ao-ku-hsüeh wen-hua lun-chi*, 3: 153–65.

[67] Its type site is Sha-ching-ts'un (Min-ch'in county), excavated in 1923–24 by Andersson; see J. C. Andersson, "Researches into the Prehistory of the Chinese," *Bulletin of the Museum of Far Eastern Antiquities* 15 (1943): 197–215. The distribution of this culture extends over Minqin, Yung-ch'ang, Ku-liang, and Yung-teng counties. See K. C. Chang, *The Archaeology of Ancient China*, 3rd ed. (New Haven: Yale University Press, 1977), pp. 407–408; *K'ao-ku yü wen-wu* 1981.4: 34–36.

people were sedentary and lived in fortified settlements surrounded by earthen walls. The type site of the culture, Sha-ching-ts'un, consists of one such fortified dwelling site; a similar settlement has been found at San-chiao-cheng (Yung-ch'ang county).[68] The walls may have been erected because the Sha-ching people had conflicts with their neighbors. Almost certainly the Sha-ching people had contacts with nomads. We have evidence for these contacts in the findings characteristic of the Ordos-type early nomadic culture – sacrifices of horses, sheep, and cattle; bronze ornaments in the animal style (eagle, deer, and dog); and a chariot axle end – unearthed at Yü-shu-kou, a site whose affiliation with the Sha-ching culture has been based on the presence of typical Sha-ching pottery.

The metallurgy of the Sha-ching people does not seem to have been especially well developed since artifacts found at excavated sites have typically been limited to small bronze items such as spearheads, arrowheads, knives, and ornaments. However, sites dated to a later period have yielded iron tools: a hoe has been found at San-chiao-cheng, and various objects at Yü-shu-kou. Some decorative features, such as the whirlwind design on an openwork ornament found both at Yü-shu-kou and in the state of Chung-shan, and the spiral design on a three-lobed object found both at Sha-ching-ts'un and in a Warring States tomb in Hopei, connect this culture to that of the Central Plain.[69] This may indicate that some of the peripheral Sha-ching sites (Yü-shu-kou marks the southern limit of its distribution) had more contacts with other cultural areas than did the Sha-ching core sites.[70]

The relationship between the different cultures found in Kansu during the first half of the first millennium B.C. is not yet fully clear, but the fortified settlements may point to a situation of enhanced warfare, in which the sedentary people were defending themselves from aggressors, possibly pastoral peoples.[71] The Sha-ching people practiced animal husbandry, as indicated by the remains of animal sacrifices, and close contact with pastoral communities may also have influenced their customs. Trade contacts with Northern Zone sites in the Ordos region and Hopei, possibly along routes already in use during the Ch'i-chia culture, is suggested by findings of imported ornaments, such as cowrie shells and turquoise beads.[72] However, excavated settlements and farming tools leave no doubt that the basis of the Sha-ching people's life remained agricultural.

---

[68] *K'ao-ku* 1984.7: 598–601. [69] Chang, *Archaeology of Ancient China*, p. 407.
[70] *K'ao-ku yü wen-wu* 1981.4: 34–36.
[71] Following Lamberg-Karlovsky's insightful suggestion, some of the earlier fortified settlements may have been erected as residences of an elite of nomadic origin. Carl Lamberg-Karlovsky, "The Bronze Age Khanates of Central Asia," *Antiquity* 68 (1994): 398–405.
[72] On the broader issue of contacts between the Ch'i-chia culture and the Central Plain, see Fitzgerald-Huber, "Qijia and Erlitou," pp. 29–39.

Second Phase: Late Spring and Autumn to Early Warring States (c. Sixth–Fourth Century B.C.)

Beginning in the seventh–sixth century B.C., an increasing number of horse fittings and ornaments seem to have been in use by peoples throughout the Northern Zone. The amount and variety of horse gear, together with evidence of horse sacrifice within funerary assemblages, betoken the growing value of the horse in both the economic and the symbolic spheres of these cultures at this time.[73] Notions of wealth, military mobility, herding techniques, and ritual observances are some of many disparate aspects of life that were transformed by the broader distribution of the horse. Yet the spread of horseback riding and the increasing social and military importance of the horse proceeded unevenly, with certain areas apparently more advanced than others.

For instance, throughout the geographic distribution of the Upper Hsia-chia-tien culture – eastern Inner Mongolia, western Liao-ning, Hopei, and the Peking area – horse fittings were prominently featured in Spring and Autumn period funerary assemblages. However, specific evidence of horse riding is not documented in some areas until the sixth century B.C., which is the date assigned to special riding bits found in Yen-ch'ing, Peking.[74] For the Central Plain we find no unequivocal evidence that horses were ridden before the fourth century B.C., when cavalry was adopted by King Wu-ling of the state of Chao.[75] In this instance, both the historical and the archaeological evidence point to a progressive "closing in" between horse-riding nomadic communities and Chinese states, partly because of the expansionist policy pursued by the northern Chou states, and partly because of the spread of pastoral nomadism in the North.

Another element of change, whose social and economic impact is more difficult to gauge on account of its limited use, is the appearance of iron. Initially, as in other parts of the Eurasian steppes, Northern Zone people

[73] Roel Sterckx, "An Ancient Chinese Horse Ritual," *Early China* 21 (1996): 47–79.

[74] Emma C. Bunker, "Unprovenanced Artefacts Belonging to the Pastoral Tribes of Inner Mongolia and North China during the Eighth–First Century B.C.," in *The International Academic Conference of Archaeological Cultures of the Northern Chinese Ancient Nations (Collected Papers)*, ed. Chung-kuo k'ao-ku wen-wu yen-chiu-so (Huhhot, 11–18 August 1992); see also So and Bunker, *Traders and Raiders on China's Northern Frontier*, p. 29.

[75] H. G. Creel, "The Role of the Horse in Chinese History," *The American Historical Review* 70.3 (1965): 649. See also C. S. Goodrich, "Riding Astride and the Saddle in Ancient China," *Harvard Journal of Asiatic Studies* 44.2 (1984): 279–306; Edouard Erkes, "Das Pferd im Alten China," *T'oung Pao* 36 (1942): 26–63.

used iron metallurgy to make tools rather than weapons and status objects, and accorded iron a position inferior to bronze and precious metals in the composition of funerary assemblages. Nevertheless, the ability to make iron tools and weapons meant an objective increase in the productive capabilities of nomadic communities. The emergence of iron metallurgy also points to the contacts between the Northern Zone and a broader cultural horizon, in particular, the far northwest (Sinkiang) and the far northeast (Hei-lung-chiang and perhaps Transbaikalia).

Present-day Sinkiang has yielded the earliest evidence of iron metallurgy within the current borders of China. This evidence includes objects such as those found at the cemetery site of Ch'a-wu-hu-kou.[76] Based on radiocarbon datings, this site, consisting of stone mounds with multiple burials encircled by a ring of stones, has been attributed to a period from the tenth to the seventh century B.C. The funerary assemblage excavated here includes objects of gold, bronze, and iron; among the bronze objects are a spearhead, horse bits, and knives with ring heads, while a bone cheek piece in the shape of a ram-head represents an early animal style. Iron objects are few and small, such as an awl and a ring. Yet evidence of horse riding and the extensive animal remains buried in sacrificial pits – sometimes together with human remains – and the absence of agricultural tools point to a culture that is clearly pastoral and nomadic. The use of iron in this region before the appearance of iron in the Central Plain is confirmed by analogous findings in Ch'ün-pa-k'e (Lun-t'ai county), the Pamirs, and the area near Urumqi.[77] Comparable iron and bronze knives found in the Chust culture in Ferghana and human skeletal remains of Europoid stock unearthed in Sinkiang point to connections between Sinkiang and the Pamirs and Ferghana regions.

The far northwest was not the only area close to the Northern Zone that had iron early on. However, the question of the spread of iron technology in South Siberia is quite complex, and there is no unified opinion. The date usually assigned to the early Iron Age in Central Asia (Transoxiana) is the beginning of the first millennium B.C., and the same date is usually applied to the early Iron Age in the steppe regions of Kazakhstan, Tuva, South Siberia, and Mongolia, even though sites of this period in the Kazakh steppe do not contain iron artifacts, and iron metallurgy developed in Mongolia only from the middle of the first millennium B.C. Nevertheless, as already mentioned, iron metallurgy seems to have

[76] "Hsin-chiang Ho-chi-hsien Ch'a-wu-hu kou-k'ou yi hao mu-ti," *K'ao-ku hsüeh-pao* 1988.1: 75–99. In Mark Hall, "Towards an Absolute Chronology for the Iron Age in Inner Asia" *Antiquity* 71 (1997): 863–74, a chronology of Saka sites dates Hsiang-pa-pai to the ninth and eighth centuries B.C.; A-la-kou should be dated no earlier than the fourth century.

[77] *K'ao-ku hsüeh-pao* 1981.2: 199–216.

existed in Tuva at least from the eighth century B.C., based on objects recovered from the Arzhan royal burial and other *kurgans* of the early nomadic period.[78]

The presence of iron allegedly as early as the end of the second millennium B.C. has been documented along the Amur River in the Maritime region of Russia, whereas by the ninth century B.C. a rich inventory of iron items including knives, daggers, and armor could be found.[79] Direct connections between this area's ferrous metallurgy and that of the Northern Zone have not yet been established for the earlier period, but there are indications that relations existed between Transbaikalia and the Chinese northeast, possibly following the ancient routes of communication through the forests of Manchuria and on the large waterways that run north to south: the Sungari, Nonni, and Liao Rivers.[80]

The best-known metal cultures in the northeast are P'ing-yang and Han-shu II, both of which present rich metal assemblages of bronze and iron. At the burial complex of P'ing-yang we find objects of bronze, iron, and gold; pottery; and tools made of bone, stone, agate, turquoise, antler,

---

[78] On the Iron Age in Central Asia, see A. Askarov, "The Beginning of Iron Age in Transoxiana," in *History of Civilizations of Central Asia*, 1: 457; A. Askarov, V. Volkov, and N. Ser-Odjav, "Pastoral and Nomadic Tribes at the Beginning of the First Millennium B.C.," in *History of Civilizations of Central Asia*, 1: 459–75; Michail Petrovič Grjaznov, *Der Großkurgan von Aržan in Tuva, Südsibirien* (München: Beck, 1984); Roman Kenk, *Grabfunde der Skythenzeit aus Tuva, Süd-Sibirien* (München: Beck, 1986). We should note that according to Martynova the presence of iron artifacts in the Shestakocvo cemetery (Minusinsk region) is a completely new phenomenon and is associated with a new cultural complex attributed to the Hunnic (Hsiung-nu) culture and dated to the last two centuries of the first millennium B.C.; see Galina S. Martynova, "The Beginning of the Hunnic Epoch in South Siberia," *Arctic Anthropology* 25.2 (1988): 74. Moreover, iron finds in other Tuvinian burials that have been dated to a much later period, that is, to the late Uyuk culture (fifth to third century B.C.), show that iron metallurgy mimicked bronze models and therefore must still have been a relatively new technique, which had not yet acquired independent status; see Nikolai Bokovenko, "Tuva during the Scythian Period," in *Nomads of the Eurasian Steppes in the Early Iron Age*, ed. Jeannine Davis-Kimball et al. (Berkeley: Zinat Press, 1995), p. 276.

[79] A. P. Derevianko, *Rannyi zheleznyi vek Priamur'ia* (Novosibirsk: Nauka, 1973); P. M. Dolukhanov et al., "Radiocarbon Dates of the Institute of Archaeology II," *Radiocarbon* 12 (1970): 130–55.

[80] At a later period, usually defined as Hunno-Sarmatian in Russian scholarship (second century B.C.–second century A.D.), there is evidence of close contacts between Hei-lung-chiang and Transbaikalia; see D. L. Brodianskii, "Krovnovsko-Khunnskie paralleli," in *Drevnee Zabaikal'e i ego kul'turnye sviazi*, ed. P. B. Konovalov (Novosibirsk: Nauka, 1985), pp. 46–50.

ivory, and shell.[81] Iron was used mostly for utilitarian projects such as tools and weapons. Bronze prevails in the artistic and decorative objects, such as animal-style plaques, buttons, and circular disks, but three earrings and two plates are in gold. Given the extensive use of metal, it is possible that this area was a center of metal production; nevertheless its people were probably non-nomadic pastoralists and specialist hunters rather than fully fledged pastoral nomads. The importance of archery, and therefore of hunting, is shown by the more than 50 bow ends and 240 arrowheads discovered as well as by the horses and dogs found buried with the human dead.

The existence of contact between the P'ing-yang culture and more southern sites and its nature are difficult to ascertain. Certain elements suggest that a southward movement may have been responsible for the introduction of iron metallurgy. Clues suggesting a southward diffusion are the funerary customs of sacrificing dogs and of covering the deceased's face with bronze buttons, which are identical with the practices found at sites located in the area near Peking, (Chou-chia-ti and Yen-ch'ing) and at the site of San-chia-tzu, attributed to the Warring States period.[82]

Along with this pastoral-hunting people, the Manchurian Plains were also home to a settled farming people whose culture is known as Han-shu II.[83] The presence of numerous clay and sandstone molds shows that this was an active center of bronze production, though the metal objects that have been found are mostly small utilitarian or decorative ones. The Han-shu II economy was based on agriculture and fishing, and a number of artifacts, from the numerous fishing hooks to boat-shaped objects to decorative fishnet motifs, show that the rivers provided a significant portion of this people's sustenance. Spears, buckles, arrowheads, and horse-shaped ornamental plaques were manufactured locally, but the iron socketed axes and iron knives found at Erh-k'o-ch'ien, which are similar to those found in the Central Plain during the Warring States period, point to a range of contacts that may have extended as far as China.[84]

---

[81] The P'ing-yang culture, dating from the late Spring and Autumn to the middle Warring States periods, has been identified in burials in southwestern Hei-lung-chiang and eastern Inner Mongolia, in particular the two burial sites of Chuan-ch'ang and Chan-tou in P'ing-yang (T'ai-lai county, Hei-lung-chiang), but no settlements associated with this culture have been found; see *P'ing-yang mu-tsang* (Peking: Wen-wu, 1990).

[82] *K'ao-ku* 1988.12: 1090–1098.   [83] *Tung-pei k'ao-ku yü li-shih* 1982.1: 136–40.

[84] An Lu and Jia Weiming, "Hei-lung-chiang Ne-ho Er-k'e-ch'ien mu-ti chi ch'i wen-t'i t'an-t'ao," *Pei-fang wen-wu* 1986.2: 2–8. Note also that in the upper layer of this culture, dated to the Warring States period, an iron dagger has been found that is very similar in shape to the bronze daggers of the Northern Zone; see Chao Shan-t'ung, "Hei-lung-chiang kuan-ti yi-chih fa-hsien de mu-tsang," *K'ao-ku* 1965.1: 45–6.

Whether the development of iron metallurgy in the Northern Zone (especially the Ordos, southern Inner Mongolia, Liao-ning, Ning-hsia, and Kansu) benefited substantially from contacts with other areas is unclear nor is it possible to establish the nature of these contacts. However, the development of iron metallurgy in the far north and west and the existence of communication routes between the Northern Zone complex and northern Manchurian cultures did establish a context in which the formation of pastoral nomadic cultures in northern China was likely to be closely linked with a broader area far from the Central Plain and only marginally affected by political and cultural processes taking place within the Sinitic cultural sphere. This broader area, marked by an early diffusion of iron metallurgy and horse riding, was home to movements of peoples, exchanges of technology, and, surely also, wars and other dramatic events of which no trace remains.

Foci of Pastoral Nomadic Cultures

NORTH-CENTRAL REGION. The appearance of early nomads in the central part of the Northern Zone was by no means instantaneous, nor was it uniform. In the period from the sixth (and even mid-seventh) to the fourth century B.C. the north-central frontier presents a fluid picture. Some sites display traits that foreshadow the appearance of a Hsiung-nu culture, while others show a lesser degree of change with respect to the previous period. Certainly people became more mobile, and several sites display signs of cultural and possibly ethnic mixtures. For instance, the site of Kuo-hsien-yao-tzu, in Inner Mongolia, features different types of burials,[85] including some that resemble those found at the site of Chün-tu-shan, near Peking. These burials include rectangular vertical earthen pits, sometimes provided with head niches and secondary platforms, wooden coffins, stone chambers, or a combination. Animal sacrifices were practiced; typically, men were buried with horses and deer or sheep, and women with cattle and sheep.

The burial assemblage found at Kuo-hsien-yao-tzu consists mostly of bronze ornaments, such as buckles, plaques, buttons, bells, rings, and earrings. Among the tools we find two knives and a pickax. Ornamental plaques with geometric or animal-style motifs are particularly abundant (with forty-four items found at a single site). Such features as the buckles and the button ornaments establish a context for this site that is typical of the Ordos region.[86] However, despite these similarities with other northern

---

[85] *K'ao-ku hsüeh-pao* 1989.1: 57–81. This is purported to be a Pei Ti site.

[86] Similar buckles were found at contemporary or later Ordos sites such as T'ao-hung-pa-la, Fan-chia-yao-tzu (Ho-lin-ko-erh), and Hsi-kou-p'an. Similar bronze bells have been found at Pei-hsin-pao. See *K'ao-ku* 1966.5: 231–42.

sites, horse fittings are not found here, although they do appear in contemporary sites such as T'ao-hung-pa-la and Mao-ch'ing-kou.

Although the people of Kuo-hsien-yao-tzu bred horses and used them in sacrifices, they do not seem to have had a highly developed horse-riding culture. Their metal inventory indicates that they were rather different from "Scythian-type" early nomads and points instead to their being a pastoral and hunting community. They had contacts with mounted nomads and were influenced by nomads' art and metallurgy, but had not yet achieved the same level of socio-economic development. It is also likely that they had trade relations with people of the Central Plain, as knife coins from the late Spring and Autumn and early Warring States periods have been found in their burials.[87] In other words, the remains left by the people of Kuo-hsien-yao-tzu may be typical of a pre-nomadic pastoral or agro-pastoral society, one that could perhaps be identified with those northern people who appear in the Chinese sources under the name of Jung or Ti.[88]

A similar center of pastoral, but not quite "early nomadic," culture is possibly recognizable at the site of Pao-t'ou in Inner Mongolia.[89] The two types of burials found here, namely, in rectangular earthen pits and in catacomb-style graves, are an unusual combination found in contemporary sites in the west, in particular at Yü-chia-chuang, in Ning-hsia. Other elements, such as a bronze semi-annular pendant, similar to a silver one found in Ku-yüan county, Ning-hsia, strongly suggest a connection between this area and the early nomads of the cultural area spanning Ning-hsia and Kansu. Objects found here are typical of early nomadic sites, for example the bronze buckles decorated in usual northern animal style, and similar to those found at Mao-ch'ing-kou (Inner Mongolia) and the three-winged arrowhead, which had a wide distribution, including Inner Mongolia, Hopei, and Liao-ning.[90] Nonetheless, Pao-t'ou is also remarkable for the

---

[87] W. Watson, *Cultural Frontiers in Ancient East Asia*, p. 102; Hsiang Ch'un-sung, "Nei Meng-ku Ch'ih-feng ti-ch'ü fa-hsien te Chan-kuo ch'ien-pi," *K'ao-ku* 1984.2: 138–44.

[88] In Chinese archaeological studies it is relatively common to identify certain northern cultures with these ancient neighbors of the Central States. See, for instance; Hsü Ch'eng and Li Chin-tseng, "Tung Chou shih-ch'i te Jung Ti ch'ing-t'ung wen-hua," *K'ao-ku hsüeh-pao* 1993.1: 1–11. This type of dependency of the archaeological work on the historical record is a classic feature of Chinese archaeology; see on this, Lothar von Falkenhausen, "On the Historiographical Orientation of Chinese Archaeology," *Antiquity* 67 (1993): 839–49.

[89] *Nei Meng-ku wen-wu k'ao-ku* 1991.1: 13–24.

[90] In Hopei, this arrowhead is found in Pei-hsin-pao, in Huai-lai county, and in Liao-ning it is found at the site of Cheng-chia-wa-tzu, Shenyang. On Pei-hsin-pao, see *K'ao-ku* 1966.5: 231–42; on Cheng-chia-wa-tzu, see *K'ao-ku hsüeh-pao* 1975.1: 141–156.

absence of some features that demarcate early nomadic sites: horse fittings, daggers, pickaxes, plaques in the Ordos tradition, and objects made of iron and gold.[91]

In contrast, some centers of "true" early nomads emerge in the north-central region at this time. These centers are characterized by typical Scythian triad funerary assemblages; one such site is Chün-tu-shan, in Yen-ch'ing county, near Peking, dated to the late Spring and Autumn and early Warring States periods.[92] The funerary assemblage, comprised mainly of horse fittings and a large number of tools and weapons – including one hundred straight-blade daggers, *ko* dagger-axes, and axes – indicates that a martial horse-riding people dominated this area. Ornaments such as plaques, belthooks, buckles, and bells are reminiscent of the Kuo-hsien-yao-tzu site, and the custom of covering the face of the deceased with sackcloth decorated with bronze buttons is shared with other sites in this area.[93] The combination of mounted nomadism with ethnic markers found in non-mounted contexts suggests the assimilation of semi-nomadic pastoralists to a fully nomadic culture and the formation of an ethnically composite society dominated by a military aristocracy possibly of northern origin.

According to the radiocarbon data, the earliest fully nomadic bronze and iron sites in the north-central area are the cemetery sites of T'ao-hung-pa-la and Mao-ch'ing-kou. Considered a late Spring and Autumn site of the sixth to fifth century B.C., T'ao-hung-pa-la may have been one of the pro-genitors of the later Hsiung-nu culture.[94] This identification is based pri-marily on the pottery found at T'ao-hung-pa-la, in particular, on the brown,

---

[91] Chinese archeologists have attributed this site to the Lin Hu, a northern people that appear in the Chinese records in the fourth–third century B.C. Because of its incomplete "Scythian triad" assemblage, however, we cannot accept the attribu-tion of this site to the Lin Hu if we take the "Hu" to be a term used to refer to early nomads. See *Nei Meng-ku wen-wu k'ao-ku* 1991.1: 13–24.

[92] *Wen-wu tzu-liao ts'ung-k'an*, 1983.7: 67–74; *Wen-wu* 1989.8: 17–35, 43. This site has been attributed to the Shan Jung, an ethnic group, probably non-nomadic, that appears in the *Ch'un ch'iu* annals beginning in the mid-seventh century B.C. (see next chapter).

[93] On mortuary practices in this area, see Yangjin Pak, "A Study of the Bronze Age Culture in the Northern Zone of China" (Ph.D. diss., Harvard University, 1995), pp. 416–20.

[94] T'ien Kuang-chin, "T'ao-hung-pa-la te Hsiung-nu mu," *K'ao-ku hsüeh-pao* 1976.1: 131–42. Rpt. in *O-erh-to-ssu ch'ing-t'ung ch'i*, ed. T'ien Kuang-chin and Kuo Su-hsin (Peking: *Wen-wu*, 1986), pp. 203–19. The site consists of seven tombs excavated in 1973. In the original report, published in 1976, T'ao-hung-pa-la was dated to the Warring States and regarded as a Hsiung-nu site on the basis of typological similarities with Hsiung-nu sites in Inner Mongolia, such as Fan-chia-yao-tzu, and the presence of iron objects. In the reprint of 1986 the site was attributed no longer to the Hsiung-nu but to the Pai Ti.

single-ear *kuan* pots, hand-made and fired at low temperature, that are regarded as a typological antecedent of the gray and more refined pottery found in Warring States period "Hsiung-nu" sites such as Hsi-kou-p'an and A-lu-ch'ai-teng.[95]

Stylistic affinities connect T'ao-hung-pa-la not only with Warring States sites but also with the earlier Upper Hsia-chia-tien sites. For instance, bronze plaques similar to those at T'ao-hung-pa-la have been found at Nan-shan-ken. Bronze daggers in the so-called antennae style (*ch'u-chiao shih*) were widespread and have been found, among other sites, at Pei-hsin-pao (Hopei) and Fan-chia-yao-tzu (Inner Mongolia), and the ring ornaments are similar to those seen in Fan-chia-yao-tzu. The T'ao-hung-pa-la metal inventory includes a pair of gold earrings of the type also seen in Nan-shan-ken and Pei-hsin-pao. Once again, this broad range of similarities between different cultural complexes within the Northern Zone underscores the fact that nomadic people may have been directly responsible for expanding the scope of human intercultural communication and commercial exchange.

The other important early nomadic site regarded by some as the "cradle" of Hsiung-nu culture is Mao-ch'ing-kou, a site that shows long and continued utilization, and one that is therefore particularly valuable for examining changes over time.[96] According to the chronology established by the main investigators of the site, T'ien Kuan-chin and Kuo Su-hsin, four phases can be recognized.[97] Phase I, dated to the late Spring and Autumn period, contains pottery and bronze items. The treatment of the body, shape of the burial, and remains of animal sacrifice present analogies with the previously discussed Kuo-hsien-yao-tzu site; other similarities include the absence of iron and the presence of a large number of bronze ornamental plaques. Differences, too, can be telling. A bronze dagger with double bird-head pommel, a bronze bit, and belthooks found at Mao-ch'ing-kou are missing from Kuo-hsien-yao-tzu. The bird head is a typical motif of the nomadic peoples of the west, in particular the Saka culture of northern Sinkiang,[98] whereas the bronze bit points to an advanced horse-riding culture. Such findings can indicate differences in a society's development toward more widespread use of horses and in its range of contacts with other cultures.

[95] On the relationship between Ordos sites and Hsiung-nu, see T'ien Kuan-chin, "Chin-nien-lai Nei meng-ku ti-ch'ü te Hsiung-nu k'ao-ku," *K'ao-ku hsüeh-pao* 1983.1: 7–24.

[96] The best study of this site is Thomas O. Höllmann and Georg W. Kossack, eds., *Maoqinggou: Ein eisenzeitliches Gräberfeld in der Ordos-Region (Inner Mongolei)* (Mainz: Philip von Zabern, 1992).

[97] T'ien Kuan-chin and Kuo Su-hsin, *O-erh-to-ssu ch'ing-t'ung ch'i*, pp. 227–315.

[98] See So and Bunker, *Traders and Raiders on China's Northern Frontier*, pp. 65–66.

The later Mao-ch'ing-kou periods, phases II, III, and IV, which span the entire Warring States era, are very different from phase I. One important development is the conspicuous use of iron, which became increasingly larger during each phase, and included, besides weapons and tools, ornamental plates. The marked differences between the burials of phase I and later burials persuaded the investigators to assign the early period to the Ti, a pre-nomadic northern people and subsequent phases to the Lou-fan, a people who appear to have been horse-riding steppe nomads culturally related to the Hsiung-nu.

Although the people of Mao-ch'ing-kou were mainly pastoral, remains of a settlement, kilns, and pottery found next to the cemetery indicate the presence of farmers in the midst of a society of the horse-riding pastoralists.[99] We do not know what relations existed between the two, but, as we have seen for northeastern nomadic cultures, the existence of small sedentary centers in an area next to burial sites belonging to nomadic people is by no means unusual. It is plausible, and indeed probable, that the economic development of the steppe depended to a great extent on the symbiotic and constructive (rather than adversarial and destructive) relationships that nomads and farmers were able to establish between themselves.

We find at Mao-ch'ing-kou an assemblage typical of an early nomadic culture and closely related to that of T'ao-hung-pa-la. The gap between the earliest occupancy and the later tombs seems to support the hypothesis of a gradual affirmation of pastoral nomadism in this area. A fully formed early nomadic culture probably existed in Mao-ch'ing-kou in the late sixth century B.C., and the finding of a knife coin in the site's upper layer also suggests that, in the fourth century B.C., there was trade with China. This site is thought to have been abandoned at the beginning of the third century B.C. as a result of occupation by Chao.

Similar to the early nomadic cultures of T'ao-hung-pa-la and Mao-ch'ing-kou is the Ordos site of Hu-lu-ssu-t'ai.[100] This site is dated to the early Warring States period (fifth–fourth century B.C.) and belongs to a group of transitional sites dated around the early to late Warring States period that also includes Fan-chia-yao-tzu and Shui-chien-kou-men.[101] The artifact assemblage found at these sites is very similar to those of T'ao-

---

[99] On this issue see Claudia Chang and Perry Tourtellotte, "The Role of Agropastoralism in the Evolution of Steppe Culture," in *The Bronze Age and Early Iron Age Peoples of Eastern Central Asia*, 1: 270–75; and Nicola Di Cosmo, "The Economic Basis of the Ancient Inner Asian Nomads and Its Relationship to China," *Journal of Asian Studies* 53.4 (1994): 1092–1126.

[100] T'a La and Liang Ching-ming, "Hu-lu-ssu-t'ai Hsiung-nu mu," *Wen-wu* 1980.7: 11–12.

[101] T'ien Kuan-chin and Kuo Su-hsin, *O-erh-to-ssu ch'ing-t'ung ch'i*, pp. 220–21.

hung-pa-la and Mao-ch'ing-kou, and the bronze tools and weapons present archaic characteristics, close to a typology found in sites attributed to the Spring and Autumn period. Horse fittings are also similar to the earlier types. At the same time, these sites also contain items that are found in later Warring States sites in the Ordos area, such as Yü-lung-t'ai, Hsi-kou-p'an, and Su-chi-kou, and that are primarily ornamental, such as decorative waist belts. Certain features in the production of traditional objects have also been standardized, as in the case of the wing-shaped dagger guard.[102]

Although precise dates for these sites require more accurate scientific evidence than typological analysis, such analysis does indicate that, possibly starting in the seventh–sixth century B.C., several areas in the north-central sector of the Northern Zone were inhabited by pastoral people; in addition, some burials, especially those dated to the sixth–fifth century B.C., possess the distinct features of the influence of militant mounted early nomads. These more advanced pastoral communities, once established, not only did not obliterate the pre-existing communities where both pastoral and agricultural activities were pursued but co-existed with them, albeit possibly in a position of supremacy. The rise of a nomadic aristocracy was probably facilitated by the existence of a socially inferior, and perhaps tribute-paying, population, which the nomadic nobility could exploit to solidify its own economic force and social role.

The question of the origins of mounted nomadism in the Northern Zone remains open.[103] Some mounted nomads may have come to this area from

---

[102] T'ien Kuan-chin, "Chin-nien-lai te Nei Meng-ku ti-ch'ü te Hsiung-nu k'ao-ku," *K'ao-ku hsüeh-pao* 1983.1: 7–24.

[103] A comprehensive review of this issue is in Wang Ming-ke, "O-erh-to-ssu chi ch'i lin-chin ti-ch'ü chuan-hua yu-mu-yeh te ch'i-yüan," *Chung-yang Yen-chiu-yüan li-shih yü-yen yen-chiu-so chi-k'an* [Bulletin of the Institute of History and Philology] 65.2 (1994): 375–44. In this article Wang Ming-ke argues that the rise of pastoral nomadism in northern China was not (or not only) a function of an independent adaptation by formerly agro-pastoral peoples to an environment particularly suitable to stock breeding. He maintains that cultural factors were more important in separating out the north from China, and that the consciousness of cultural and ethnic differences from China may have played a role in the emergence of a pastoral nomadic society. This is based on the consideration that although the preconditions for the transition to full pastoral nomadism (horse riding, for instance) had been achieved already in the early first millennium B.C., it was only several hundred years later – according to Wang – that pastoral nomads actually appear on the northern frontier, after the formation of a cultural frontier between the north and China. This thesis is engaging in the sense that specialized agriculture, by creating a surplus of cereals exchangeable for products that would be lacking in a predominantly farming society, such as animal products, might stimulate stock breeding wherever climatic conditions would allow it. From a historical point of view, however, the creation of a sharp

elsewhere, a hypothesis that rests mainly on the appearance of new types of burials, such as those using wooden and stone-slab coffins.[104] Or mounted nomadism might be the result of an internal evolution toward an increasingly specialized pastoral economy favored by external stimuli or pressures. However they might have evolved, mounted nomads must have exerted a great deal of pressure on the "periphery" formed by pre-existing semi-nomadic communities who were lagging behind in the acquisition of new technology and forms of social organization. This hypothesis is consistent with a phenomenon documented in the historical records, which reveal a sudden acceleration of pressure on the northern frontier of China from people such as the Ch'ih Ti, Pai Ti, and Shan Jung after the mid-seventh century B.C.: The expansion of the nomadic centers around this time may have been the cause of the southward movement of displaced peoples.

NORTHWESTERN ZONE. Early nomadic sites are found in the Ning-hsia–Kansu region to the west of the Wei River Valley and to the southwest of the Ordos. These are clustered in and around the areas of Ku-yüan county, in Ning-hsia,[105] and Ch'ing-yüan, in Kansu,[106] both of which appear to have been centers of diffusion of early nomadic culture comparable to Mao-ch'ing-kou and T'ao-hung-pa-la. On the basis of the funerary assemblage from several sites, and of stratigraphical analysis, we can distinguish a general process of development in the material culture of the Ku-yüan nomadic people, which shows a course similar to that found among the

demarcation between Chung-yüan agriculturalists and northern nomads remains highly speculative and is contradicted by the archaeological presence of several agricultural peoples in the arc of lands to the north of China. It is more likely that, if specialized pastoral production developed as a complementary activity to specialized farming, this "branching off" occurred within a Northern Zone economic context. In any case, Chinese sources remain mute about this process, and we run the risk of overinterpreting them by establishing cause-effect associations between factors whose mutual relationship is untestable.

[104] On Hsiung-nu burials, see S. Minyaev, "Niche Grave Burials of the Xiong-nu Period in Central Asia," *Information Bulletin. International Association for the Cultures of Central Asia* 17 (1990): 91–99; S. Minyaev, "On the Origin of the Hiung-nu," *Information Bulletin. International Association for the Cultures of Central Asia* 9 (1985): 69–78.

[105] Chung K'an, "Ning-hsia Ku-yüan hsien ch'u-t'u wen-wu," *Wen-wu* 1978.12: 86–90; Chung K'an and Han Kung-le, "Ning-hsia nan-pu Ch'un-ch'iu Chan-kuo shih-ch'i te ch'ing-t'ung wen-hua," *Chung-kuo k'ao-ku hsüeh-hui ti-ssu-tz'u nien-hui lun-wen-chi* 1983 (Peking: Wen-wu, 1985), pp. 203–13. See also the notes below.

[106] Liu Te-zhen, Hsü Chün-ch'en, "Kan-su Ch'ing-yang Ch'un-ch'iu Chan-kuo mu-tsang te ch'ing-li," *Kaogu* 1988.5: 413–24.

early nomads of the Ordos and Hopei sites. The early graves' inventory yields evidence of abundant bronze production: Weapons, animal-style ornaments, and horse and chariot fittings are all present and make this area one of the centers of "Scythian-type" pastoral nomadism in the Northern Zone. Iron metallurgy existed but was not widely used, although it is also possible that iron objects were simply not deemed fit to be included in funerary assemblages; precious metals are rare, as are chariot and horse fittings. In contrast, later graves show a net increase in ornaments, horse gear, precious objects, and iron metallurgy, a trend that parallels that seen in the Ordos.

Yet the archaeological materials from this area also reveal pronounced local characteristics and an independent path of development. The excavated sites are limited to graves, and there is no trace of permanent dwellings or settlements. Generally speaking, the funerary customs and other features in the workmanship of bone and clothing reveal local characteristics and indicate a coherent cultural complex. Yet it is possible that this area included more than one ethnic group, since throughout the area of distribution of the Ku-yüan culture there are two types of burials, "catacomb" style and earthen pit graves.[107] The use of catacomb-style graves – that is, L-shaped pits with a coffin-chamber opening on one side at the bottom of the pit – is unusual in this area but can be found in sites in northwestern China, such as Ha-ma-tun, a site of the Sha-ching culture with clear evidence of pastoralism at this time.[108] The economy of the "catacomb" people in Ku-yüan was also pastoral, as revealed by the number of sacrificed animal remains accompanying the dead, consisting of the heads, lower jaws, and hooves of horses, cattle, and sheep. A similar combination of catacomb and earthen pit graves can be seen in the possibly contemporary site of Pao-t'ou, in Inner Mongolia, which we have discussed earlier. Finally, although catacomb graves are not seen in Hsiung-nu sites of the Ordos region, they are present at Tao-tun-tzu, a Western Han site in Ning-hsia attributed to the Hsiung-nu.[109] The continuity in the types of burial found in the northwestern region during the Han period suggests that, even though there are similarities with the "Hsiung-nu" culture of the Ordos sites, local (possibly ethnic) differences were not eliminated. As a result, the term "Hsiung-nu culture" can be used in archaeology only as an umbrella term synonymous with "early nomadic culture," not in reference to a particular

---

[107] See, for instance, *K'ao-ku hsüeh-pao* 1993.1: 13–56. Here, out of twenty-nine tombs whose structure is known, one is a vertical earthen pit tomb; the remaining twenty-eight are earthen catacomb graves.

[108] *K'ao-ku hsüeh-pao* 1990.2: 205–37.

[109] Tao-tun-tzu (T'ung-hsin county, Ning-hsia) is dated to the Western Han on the basis of coins. The site comprises twenty rectangular pit graves, six catacomb graves, and one stone chamber grave. See *K'ao-ku hsüeh-pao* 1988.3: 333–56.

ethnic group or political community. Evidence of multiple burial customs within the same burial site is by no means unusual, and, as mentioned before, should be regarded as the probable result of the process of political and military change following the evolution of early nomadic communities which caused territorial displacements, partial cultural assimilation, and the fusions of different ethnic groups into larger political unions.

The possibility of regional migrations, resulting possibly from an increased militarization of the areas where strong and expansive nomadic societies appear, may be supported by the anthropological evidence from the site of Yü-chia-chuang, near the village of P'eng-p'u, dated approximately to the late Spring and Autumn.[110] Its inhabitants appear to have been north Asiatic, and different from the eastern Asiatic people that inhabited the area in the earlier Neolithic period. According to the investigators, their somatic features are consistent with an anthropological type found in northeast Asia among the Mongol, Buriat, and Tungus peoples.[111] Although this type of evidence is questioned by some archaeologists, it provides a hint that cannot be disregarded completely, since the existence of a migratory route from the Manchurian and Mongolian areas to Ning-hsia might explain the presence of cultural links between this area and the Ordos and between northeastern metallurgical cultures and the far northeast.

Burials at the important site of Yang-lang span from the early to the late Eastern Chou period.[112] Burial goods in tombs of the early period include daggers in the classic antennae style, which are usually regarded as a marker of the Western Chou and Spring and Autumn Northern Zone style, but iron remains are limited to fragments of an iron sword (tomb IM3), and horse and chariot fittings are not present in large quantity. Among the precious metals, only silver earrings are found in the earlier graves (tomb IIIM3). The abundance of bronze shows that this was a center of metallurgical production, possibly controlled by a higher social stratum; moreover, almost every grave contains funerary goods, usually more than ten objects, and several yielded over fifty.

At P'eng-p'u and Shih-la-ts'un sites, also in Ku-yüan county, we find funerary assemblages that may belong to a more advanced type of community that made a wider use of horses.[113] Iron is absent from the assem-

---

[110] The burial site of P'eng-p'u is particularly interesting because out of its thirty-one burials, twenty-seven were undisturbed prior to excavation. See *K'ao-ku hsüeh-pao* 1995.1: 79–107. This full report has been used as a reference also for the following discussion of this site.

[111] Han K'ang-hsin, "Ning-hsia P'eng-p'u Yü-chia-chuang mu-ti jen-ku chung-hsi t'e-tien chih yen-chiu," *K'ao-ku hsüeh-pao* 1995.1: 107–25.

[112] *K'ao-ku hsüeh-pao* 1993.1: 13–56.

[113] Chung K'an, "Ku-yüan hsien P'eng-p'u Ch'un-ch'iu Chan-kuo mu-tsang," *Chung-kuo k'ao-ku-hsüeh nien-chien 1988* (1989): 255–56; Lo Feng, "Ning-hsia

blage, but there are signs of advanced horse-related technology, such as bits, masks, and a bridle frontal piece of bronze. Bronze weapons and tools are still predominant, as in the early phase of Yang-lang, but the greater role played by the horse, the large selection of animal-style ornaments, and the presence of some gold finds foreshadow the type of changes in the funerary assemblage that were to take place in the mid and late Warring States period, where the preference for artistic works and precious metals in rich graves is testimony to a likely change in the social role of the aristocracy.

Finally, catacomb burials are not found in Chung-ning county, where two rectangular earthen pit graves have been excavated whose features are consistent with the north-central early nomadic sites of Chün-tu-shan and Mao-ch'ing-kou.[114] The assemblage here is typically "Scythian," with bronze weapons and ornaments, a golden plate, and horse fittings; and horses were sacrificed in burials. Because of the concurrent presence of a developed horse-riding nomadic community and of bronze weapons displaying traditional or even archaic features, this site has been dated to the early Warring States period. The significance of the presence of "early nomadic" sites with catacomb graves in close proximity with other "Scythian-type" sites with only earthen pit graves suggests that at some point different ethnic groups lived side by side and may have eventually fused into new social formations, and larger political unions.

Third Phase: Late Warring States (c. Mid-Fourth–Third Century B.C.)

The "closing in" between the northern cultures and the Chinese zone occurred during the last part of the Warring States era. From the fourth to the third centuries B.C. contacts with China became more significant. In part, the distinctive elements of early nomadic cultures, though they were still predominant and retained their northern flavor, blended with different images (trees, mountains) which substantially affected previous stylistic models.[115]

Ku-yüan Shih-la-ts'un fa-hsien yi-tso Chan-kuo mu," *K'ao-ku-hsüeh chi-k'an* 3 (1983): 130–31, 142; Lo Feng and Han Kung-le, "Ning-hsia Ku-yüan chin-nien fa-hsien te pei-fang hsi ch'ing-t'ung ch'i," *K'ao-ku* 1990.5: 403–18.

[114] *K'ao-ku* 1987.9: 773–77.

[115] Esther Jacobson, "Beyond the Frontier: A Reconsideration of Cultural Interchange Between China and the Early Nomads," *Early China* 13 (1988): 201–40. The presence of distinctive Chinese motifs in northern art have led some to believe that there was Chinese production of artistic metalwork specifically designed for the northern markets or that there were Chinese artisans among the

The nomadic sites of the fourth–third century B.C., centered in the Ordos area and generally referred to in the archaeological literature as "Hsiung-nu," exhibit a definite shift in the contents of the mortuary assemblages. Precious metals predominate in the aristocratic burials of this period, while fewer weapons were buried, and the use of iron became more common, especially for the manufacture of certain types of weapons and horse fittings. "Antennae-style" iron daggers, similar to the earlier bronze daggers, and iron swords similar to those of the Central Plain, are found both over a broader area and in larger numbers with respect to the previous period; horse bits and chamfrons were more frequently made out of iron, and the bronze pickax was replaced with an iron one.[116] Among the decorative features of this period, we see an increase in belt buckles and plates in the animal style, while other plates, round or rectangular, often depict human activities.[117] Scenes of animal combat, both realistic and stylized, became both common and artistically sophisticated, and the tendency to standardize certain features of metal artifacts became even more pronounced. To the extent that standardization may be taken as evidence of a centralized organization of the productive process, it may also be regarded as an indirect indicator of more hierarchically organized societies, within which the aristocratic stratum might have wielded greater power.

By far the most striking feature of the nomadic burials of this period is their extraordinary richness, as the funerary inventory includes at times hundreds of precious objects, including many gold and silver ornaments, at sites such as T'ao-hong-pa-la, Hsi-kou-p'an, and A-lu-ch'ai-teng.[118] In two

---

nomads. For a full illustration of this viewpoint, see So and Bunker, *Traders and Raiders on China's Northern Frontier*, chapter 4.

[116] The progressive increase in the amount of iron used can be seen by looking at Western Han sites such as Pu-tung-kou (Yi-k'o-chao-meng, Inner Mongolia), where there is a vast inventory of iron tools and weapons. Iron was reserved mostly for vessels, such as tripods and cauldrons; for weapons, such as swords, knives, and arrowheads; for horse fittings, such as bits, rings, and chamfrons; and, finally, for ornamental objects, such as belt plates. Bronze was still the principal material used for decorative and ornamental purposes.

[117] Emma Bunker, "The Anecdotal Plaques of the Eastern Steppe Regions," in *Arts of the Eurasian Steppelands*, pp. 121–42.

[118] Gold constitutes a most interesting aspect of the Northern Zone culture, because it seems to link China and the northern regions as an important medium of exchange and because of the appreciation reserved for it on both sides (an appreciation not shared for silver). On the questions of gold in ancient China and the introduction of taste for gold from the northwest, see Emma Bunker, "Gold in the Ancient Chinese World," *Artibus Asiae* 53.1/2 (1993): 27–50; and id., "Cultural Diversity in the Tarim Basin Vicinity and Its Impact on Ancient Chinese Culture," in *The Bronze Age and Early Iron Age Peoples of Eastern Central Asia*, 2: 604–18.

tombs of the late Warring States unearthed in the locality of A-lu-ch'ai-teng, located to the north of T'ao-hung-pa-la, altogether 218 gold and five silver objects were found.[119] Among the many extraordinary pieces, reproduced in the typical "Scythian" animal style, there is a unique gold headdress set, or crown, composed of four pieces: a skullcap and three headbands. Because of its richness, this site is regarded by the investigators as a royal burial of the Lou-fan people, who presumably inhabited this area during the Warring States. Finally, at Na-lin-kao-t'u in northern Shaansi, a grave attributed to the Hsiung-nu yielded a large number of gold, silver, and bronze ornamental objects,[120] even though a rare gilt silver dagger handle, possibly imported, was the only military object recovered.

The complexity of this later nomadic society is nowhere more visible than at the site of Hsi-kou-p'an, also in the Ordos area.[121] Gold and silver ornaments abound in one burial, while other assemblages present the objects normally associated with a more "classic" nomadic aristocracy, including weapons, tools, and horse equipment reminiscent of the early T'ao-hung-pa-la assemblage. At the same time, we find unmistakable evidence of agriculture: a settlement, and agricultural tools such as hoes, adzes, and pickaxes, which were also made of iron.[122]

The various types of funerary assemblages seems to indicate the existence of sharper social differentiation. The poorest members of society were buried with a few tools or weapons, while warriors continued to be buried with their weapons, and with the ornamental plaques characteristic of nomadic art. But some, presumably the most powerful chiefs, were accompanied in death by real treasures, often consisting of gold and silver artifacts. The accumulation of precious metals of course is an indication of power and wealth, but it may also point to a different origin of wealth, one no longer acquired through military ventures or the exploitation of subject peoples, but rather through commerce. While leadership in war must have remained an important function of the aristocracy, chiefs may have been increasingly involved in trade, and the precious artifacts were a form of high value currency used in commercial transactions.

This hypothesis is supported by the Chinese origin of some of these objects, which bear Chinese characters, such as golden plates and silver

[119] T'ien Kuan-chi and Kuo Su-hsin, "Nei meng-ku A-lu-chai-teng fa-hsien te Hsiung-nu yi-wu," *K'ao-ku* 1980.4: 333–38, 364, 368.

[120] Tai Ying-hsin, and Sun Chia-hsiang, "Shensi Shen-mu hsien ch'u-t'u Hsiung-nu wen-wu," *Wen-wu* 1983.12: 23–30.

[121] *Wen-wu* 1980.7: 1–10; *Nei Meng-ku wen-wu k'ao-ku* 1981: 15–27.

[122] An ax, pickax, adze, hoe, and other agricultural implements, all of iron, have been recovered from Wu-huan burials of the Han period in Hsi-cha-kou (Hsi-feng, Liao-ning). See Lin Kan, "Kuan-yü yen-chiu Chung-kuo ku-tai pei-fang min-tsu wen-hua shih te wo chien," *Nei Meng-ku ta-hsüeh hsüeh-pao* 1988.1: 3.

ornaments.[123] Moreover, some silver rein rings bear characters that have been interpreted as the marks of a workshop located in the state of Chao.[124] Chinese imports of horses, cattle, and other typical northern products such as furs, mentioned in works such as the *Chan-kuo ts'e* (see Chapter 4) may have been paid for with golden and silver objects worked in a style attractive to the nomads. Among the precious objects found in this region, the gilded bronze, golden. and silver artifacts inlaid with precious stones that have been found at Shih-hui-kou[125] bear a striking resemblance to the "Siberian" gold of Peter the Great.[126] In the same sites we find an abundance of silver, and some new animal-style motifs, which enrich an already vast gamut of modes of representation.

For all the richness of the funerary inventory, the burial structure is relatively simple. Nowhere do we find the elaborate tombs of the Altai nomads, with the subterranean wooden chamber and surface mound. Normally they are simple pit graves with or without a wooden coffin. Animal sacrifice was practiced in all the sites and included mostly horses and sheep. In Yü-lung-t'ai, a site possibly dating to the third century B.C., the number of chariot fittings, which include seven animal-shaped finials in bronze representing lambs, antelopes, deer, and horses, and two axle ends, indicate that the chariot was in use among the late nomads, but it is not clear whether this function was military or ceremonial.[127]

Finally, we should note that in the northwest an analogous process was taking place. The Yang-lang burials (Ku-yüan county) dated to the late Warring States period reveal the true blooming of nomadic culture at around that time. First, the use of iron becomes widespread and generally available for weapons, tools, and ornaments.[128] Second, gold objects appear in the funerary assemblage, though not on the scale of some Ordos sites. Finally, the amount of excavated horse gear (bits, chamfrons, bronze and bone cheek pieces, and harness ornaments) and chariot fittings (shaft ornaments, axle cuffs, and hubs) increases dramatically. Ornamental pole

---

[123] Li Xueqin, *Eastern Zhou and Qin Civilizations*, trans. K. C. Chang (New Haven and London: Yale University Press, 1985), pp. 333–35. For a discussion of Chinese exports to the steppes, see So and Bunker, *Traders and Raiders on China's Northern Frontier*, pp. 53–66.

[124] So and Bunker, *Traders and Raiders on China's Northern Frontier*, p. 59.

[125] *Nei Meng-ku wen-wu k'ao-ku* 1992.1–2: 91–96.

[126] B. B. Piotrovskij, *Tesori d'Eurasia: 2000 anni di storia in 70 anni di archeologia sovietica* (Venezia: Mondadori, 1987), pp. 114–15.

[127] *K'ao-ku* 1977.2: 111–14.

[128] In Yang Lang the following burials presented iron objects: I2 (knife and ornamental plate), I3 (sword, rings, and belt ornaments), I12 (sword with bronze hilt), I15 (knife), III4 (sword, spear, and cheek pieces), III5 (various ornaments, a horse bit, a knife and two rings), and III8 (remains of an iron object); see *K'ao-ku hsüeh-pao* 1993.1: 13–56.

tops and plaques representing animal combat are also typical of this later period.

Early nomadic sites of the Ku-yüan type share important cultural traits with the Ordos, possibly indicative of a similar type of mobile aristocratic society. Chamfrons and bits, albeit still limited in number, indicate a progressively more important role of the horse, used not only for transportation and herding but also for war. This suggests that the expansion of pastoralism and the growth in the sheer volume of herds was accompanied by the rise of a warrior class, whose social function may have also been initially related to the regulation of economic and "juridical" disputes among kin groups.

Conclusion

Northern China participated actively in what was, during the first half of the first millennium, the Central Eurasian rise of steppe pastoral nomadism. Advanced metallurgy and the development of specialized technology for the management of the horse were the most significant prerequisites for the evolution of nomadic cultures, and it is possible that pastoral nomadism was first developed in the northeastern region of the steppe belt, in a mixed environment that favored communication across different forms of ecological and economic adaptations. Contacts with areas further to the north and west, as well as the natural impetus of a flourishing culture, may have provided the right environment for the advance of pastoralism, especially along the ecological border between grassland and forest.

Throughout the ninth to the third century B.C., from western Liao-ning to Hopei, Ning-hsia, and Kansu, the herds of horses, cattle, and sheep grew, a phenomenon reflected in the higher degree of specialization achieved in these regions in the management of pastoral economies. As in other parts of Inner Asia, the growth of pastoral economies was accompanied by the rise of a militant warlike aristocracy. These military elites, by leading the political expansion of their own political communities, helped to establish more articulate relations both within the wide world of steppe pastoralism and between pastoral communities and neighboring agricultural peoples.

It is premature, at this point, to attempt to construct a model that explains the development of pastoral societies in the Northern Zone. However, we do know that this development occurred, and that such a development eventually produced increasingly larger and more powerful political units. The evidence presented thus far suggests that the areas of the Northern Zone closer to the Great Wall (from Ning-hsia and Kansu to Inner Mongolia and the northeast) underwent such an evolution, but it is important to underscore that one cannot see, in the Northern Zone as a whole, a linear evolutional continuum. At present it seems to me that two levels of analysis are either missing or not sufficiently developed. One level is the intermediate regional level between the Northern Zone complex and the local cultures.

Generally, scholars break down the Northern Zone into northwestern, north-central, and northeastern subzones, a convention to which I have also conformed. However, there are serious limitations to this method, the most significant of which is that it obscures other, possibly more relevant, parting lines, such as the cultural watersheds constituted by the T'ai-hang or by the Yin-shan mountain ranges respectively in Hopei and Inner Mongolia. In the mapping of the cultures of the Northern Zone, a regional approach needs to be developed that integrates cultural, environmental, and topographical features in an organic manner, regardless of present-day administrative divisions or abstract compass-point sectors. The second level that needs to be developed is one of comparative study among cultures within and without the Northern Zone. This is sometimes done, especially with respect to China. But clearly China was only one, and in many cases not the most important, among the cultural areas that participated in the development of various parts of the Northern Zone complex. It must be borne in mind that social and economic advancements within the Northern Zone depended greatly on a network of contacts and exchanges that included a much larger area, as each cultural area in the Northern Zone also participated independently in contacts with separate zones. Because of its natural avenues of communication (the Kansu Corridor, the Mongolian grassland and the riverways of Manchuria), and possibly because of its relatively more dense concentration of peoples with respect to other areas of northern Asia, the Northern Zone, not unlike Central Asia at the same time, became a dynamic area in which cultural clusters emerged where advancements in technology, economic production, and social organization proceeded more speedily than elsewhere.

The archaeological sites that we have labeled as "foci" for the formation of early nomads feature evident technological advances in transportation and warfare, which conceivably also reflect changes in the social and political functions of the elite, as the traditional measure of nomadic wealth, the animals they bred, became exchange commodities in an expanding trade network. Social status was expressed through the possession of more elaborate goods, such as bimetallic swords and belts made of elegant bronze plaques, and precious objects. Artifacts related to chariots, usually regarded as typical status symbols of ancient China, and to horses, which of course held primary importance in nomadic societies, came together to represent the power and wealth enjoyed in life. Advances occurred in metallurgy as well, as the use of iron became more common in the manufacture of weapons and tools; and though the social implications of the use of iron are unclear, it may be that the presence of iron agricultural tools (hoes and pickaxes, for instance) resulted in advances in farming in the northern region that would also have contributed to the enrichment of nomads, especially if we envisage the farmers as tribute-paying communities politically subordinated to the nomadic aristocracy.

A tendency toward the commercialization of relations with China can also be shown by evidence already drawn from Spring and Autumn sites in Yen-ch'ing county, near Peking, where the presence of gold is consistent and regular. Even more significantly, coins have been found that indicate a degree of monetary exchange between the Northern Zone and China. Moreover, because of the increasing importance of commerce, the nomadic aristocracy's wealth may also have been derived from its access to the routes that connected faraway communities and therefore gave them the possibility of exacting some form of payment from itinerant merchants.[129]

The pursuit of commercial interests transformed the nomadic elite, to some extent, into diplomatic and commercial agents who managed external exchanges to their own profit. It is likely that this trend reached its highest point during the late Warring States period, when a greater quantity of gold and precious objects found its way to the north. It is not unlikely that part of the people who inhabited these sites were ethnically different from the previous inhabitants, as some nomadic tribes may have descended into the Northern Zone from regions farther to the northeast and northwest. This hypothesis would explain the different artistic motifs and decorative techniques found in these later sites. Migration theories are, however, difficult to prove, and the supposed originating point of these peoples, as well as their cultural affiliation, remain moot.

The question of the emergence of a putative "pre-Hsiung-nu" culture, therefore, should be placed within the framework of a synchronic, but not necessarily linear, evolution of a pastoral aristocracy in several "core" areas. This class was not only "truly" nomadic – that is, akin to the Scythian prototype found throughout the rest of the Inner Asian steppe world – but also "new." Given our preceding discussion, we may conclude that it was likely able to manage political systems more complex than the kin group; it established its rule over societies that were ethnically and economically composite; it enhanced its economic status through the use of military resources and political influence; and it could profit from inter-tribal and interstate trade relations. During the Warring States period the nomadic political formations were probably already constituted in political bodies that were able to transcend the simple kin group, a necessary prerequisite for the creation of a "state," such as the one established by the Hsiung-nu, which was based on an elaborate hierarchical military structure around a central authority.

[129] The presence of Chinese silk at San-chia-tzu suggests that by the Warring States period Hei-lung-chiang had some relations with the Central Plain, possibly the state of Yen. See *K'ao-ku* 1988.12: 1090–98.

For the greater part of the Eastern Chou period, however, the Chinese seemed unaware of the momentous events that were occurring in the steppe region. Their relations with the inhabitants of the north were colored by the direction in which the political process internal to China was evolving. Therefore, foreign peoples appeared as pawns on the chessboard of Chinese politics, in the game for supremacy and survival played during the Spring and Autumn and Warring States periods. The following section explores the emergence within the Hua-Hsia community of cultural stereotypes and political strategies as China confronted the north in the pre-imperial period.

PART II

CHAPTER THREE

Beasts and Birds

The Historical Context of Early Chinese Perceptions of the Northern Peoples

Introduction

Is it true that, during the Spring and Autumn period, a clear consciousness emerged of a moral and cultural divide between the Chou states and a nebulous external world of alien peoples? Several passages in the *Ch'un ch'iu* and its commentaries, which later entered the *Shih chi* and other historical works, show foreigners being compared to animals and being represented as subhuman. A certain mythology of the external world and an idealized representation of geographic space in terms of its moral and political order contribute to the impression that, during the Chou period, a notion of "China" as a territory – Chou states, *chung-kuo* – and of "the Chinese" as a people – Hua or Hsia – crystallized sufficiently to make China's external boundaries deeper than internal boundaries between the various polities that comprised the Chou political and cultural universe. The evolution of an inner Chinese core differentiated from an outer non-Chinese one was already seen by Fu Ssu-nien in the opposition between the mythical Hsia dynasty and the so-called Yi peoples.[1] Nonetheless, although both the Shang and the Western Chou fought against foreign polities, the few dry records of their expeditions, triumphs, and defeats fail to convey a clear sense of this differentiation between a "Chinese" world of shared principles, revolving around a real or assumed source of moral and political authority (the Chou dynastic line), and a "barbarian" world whose inhabitants were placed at various degrees of distance from that central source.

---

[1] K. C. Chang, "Sandai Archaeology and the Formation of States in Ancient China," in *The Origins of Chinese Civilizations*, ed. David Keightley (Berkeley: University of California Press, 1983), p. 498.

The notion of a radiating civilization, shedding its light in progressively dimming quantity on the surrounding areas, was part of a worldview that surely existed during the Chou period. The boundaries of the Hua "civilization" were delineated along moral and cultural lines. The simple, diagrammatic mappings of the geographic and human space that appear in the "Yü Kung" (Tribute of Yü) chapter of the *Shu ching*, or in the *Kuo yü*, *Chou li*, and other works, were neither a means to acquire knowledge about the physical realities surrounding that community nor the result of an *inquiry* into those realities. Even when they included details possibly derived from geographic facts, these notions were framed by cosmological and ethical schemes devised, on the one hand, to demonstrate the spatial equivalence between earth and heaven and, on the other, to mark an ideal boundary between the Hua-Hsia (Chinese) community and the world outside it. This divide is common in the literature of the Warring States, and best summed up in the *Hsün-tzu*: "All the states of Hsia share the same territorial zones (*fu*) and the same customs; Man, Yi, Jung and Ti share the same territorial zones, but have different institutions."[2]

Before we consider the early texts in which we may reasonably expect to find an effort to identify these foreign lands and peoples, we should be aware that these texts have raised issues of attribution and dating that are central to current scholarship. These issues, however, will not be dealt with here. Instead, the texts in question are considered as expressions of forms of knowledge – mythological, astrological, pseudo-geographical – that were surely widespread in China during the pre-imperial period, and whose origins, albeit difficult to determine, are commonly seen as having preceded physical composition of the texts.

Two notions of geographic space were common in China's early literature: the representation of the land as a system of inscribed squares, and the representation of the world (also identified with the territory of the Chinese states) as divided into nine continents, or provinces (*chiu chou*).[3] It is in the first of these – the rich textual tradition defining geographic space as a nested succession of areas around a central seat of political and moral authority – that we find references to foreign "barbarian" peoples.[4] Generally, the prototype of this system is held to be the "Yü

---

[2] Wang Hsien-chien, *Hsün-tzu chi-chieh* (Peking: Chung-hua, 1988) 2: 329.

[3] *Shu ching* (S. Couvreur, *Chou King* [Ho Kien Fu: Imprimerie de la mission catholique, 1897], pp. 61, 86–88. Also, James Legge, *The Chinese Classics*, vol. 3: *Shoo King*, 2nd ed. (Oxford: Clarendon, 1985; rpt. Hong Kong: Hong Kong University Press, 1960), p. 149.

[4] An excellent summary is provided in *Guoyu: Propos sur le principautés I – Zhouyu*. Trans. André d'Hormon, annotations *par* Rémi Mathieu (Paris: Collège de France, 1985), pp. 66–69, n. 21.

Kung."[5] Political and ethical considerations are superimposed onto a pseudo-geographic grid in an idealized scheme whereby distance from the royal domains, located at the center, is the key element in the classification of territorial zones.[6] The farther the areas inhabited by foreign peoples are from the center, the less civilizing influence these areas receive, and the more "alien" they are. In the "Yü Kung" are five such nested square territories, each extending in all directions around the seat of imperial power for five hundred *li* beyond the closer one: the first zone is the royal domain (*tien*), the second is the land of feudal vassals (*hou*), the third is the zone of pacification (*sui*), the fourth is the zone of vassal foreigners (*yao*) where the Yi peoples live, and the fifth is the zone of uncultivated marshes (*huang*) where the Man foreigners live. Together with this five-zone tradition are other traditions, which go back to the *Chou li*, chapter 29 ("Ta ssu-ma"), where we have a nine-zone (*chiu chi*) division, and chapter 37 ("Ta hsing-jen"), with its six-zone (*fu*) arrangement of the territories around the royal domains. The peripheral zones are inhabited by a sequence of foreigners, among whom we find the Man and the Yi. The most unenlightened of these zones, which is also the farthest away, is called *fan* ("outer," and by inference, barbaric).[7] The people inhabiting these distant and benighted marshes are

---

5   The composition of the "Yü Kung" may be as late as the late Warring States period, that is, fourth–third century B.C. See Edward L. Shaughnessy, "*Shang shu*," in *Early Chinese Texts*, ed. Michael Loewe (Berkeley: Society for the Study of Early China and the Institute of East Asian Studies, 1993), p. 378. The myth of Yü's ordering of the geography of the world, a kind of "chorogenesis" through which all the potentialities of the earth were brought to light and tamed into the service of the "Son of Heaven" (and of humankind), is reported in the *Shih chi* 2, 49–77 (trans. Nienhauser, ed., *The Grand Scribe's Records*, vol. 1: *The Basic Annals of Pre-Han China by Ssu-ma Ch'ien* [Bloomington: Indiana University Press, 1994], pp. 22–32).

6   For a diagram of the geography of the "Yü Kung," see Joseph Needham, *Science and Civilization in China*, vol. 3: *Mathematics and the Sciences of the Heavens and Earth* (Cambridge: Cambridge University Press, 1959), p. 501.

7   It is well known that the term "barbarian" common in a number of European languages, does not have a single analog in the Chinese language. Yet a number of terms designating foreign peoples (Man, Yi, Ti, Jung, Ch'iang, Hu, etc.) are routinely translated as "barbarians." The distinction made in these early differentiations between *yao* peoples (allied, and possibly "absorbed," also indicated with the binome Man-Yi) and *fan* peoples (independent, and possibly hostile, also designated with the binome Jung-Ti) introduces a notion of conscious differentiation between close foreigners and far foreigners, possibly analogous to the dyadic classification of foreigners into *shu*, "tamed, cooked," and *sheng*, "raw, fierce," of later times. This distinction is hopelessly obscured when the blanket term "barbarian" is used indiscriminately. The "Ta Hsing-jen" places the states in the *fan*

exposed to gradually diminishing imperial influence, and pay tribute to the center at increasingly longer intervals of time. The *Yi Chou shu*, chapter 7, "Wang hui," has an abbreviated three-zone division, with the outer zone being that of the uncultivated marshes (*huang fu*). The nine-zone division is repeated in chapter 8, "Chih fang-shih." The *Kuo yü* (chapter 1, "Chou yü 1") presents the same basic structure and has the Ti and Jung people living in the last square zone, of the *huang fu*.[8]

It is clear, then, that in the early Chinese conception of foreign peoples, besides identifying them according to their location, which placed the Man to the south, the Yi to the east, the Jung to the west and the Ti to the north,[9] another structure existed that consistently categorized the Man and the Yi as "allied" or "assimilated" foreigners, and the Jung and Ti as outer, non-assimilated, and hostile foreigners. In the ethical and political hierarchy that these schematic representations reflect the peoples to the north and to the west were regarded as more resistant to (and therefore more distant from) the virtuous influence of the center. Yet the texts that mention these foreign peoples are expressions of an intellectual world unconcerned with the systematic exploration and empirical description of the surrounding geographical area and "ethnographic" realities.

Although similarly unconcerned with direct observation and description, the texts that allow us to understand the forms of interaction between Chou and non-Chou peoples are the ones that are "historical." As a step beyond the bare mention of "outside" peoples found in the oracle bones, and a step behind the historical accounts found in the *Shih chi*, the Chou historical texts identify in realistic terms those areas of political action and geographic space that were frequented and often occupied by foreign agents. Of course, "foreign" remains a problematic term, since its qualifications, whether cultural, political, or ethnic, need to be verified each time it is used.

This historical tradition is embodied in the *Ch'un Ch'iu* annals and its commentaries, in particular the *Tso-chuan*, which remains the richest single source for the Eastern Chou period prior to the *Shih chi*. The information relevant to foreign peoples, however, often has been read less for its historical importance – on the development of political relations, for instance – and more for its cultural dimension, that is, for what it tells us of a coa-

---

zone (*fan kuo*) outside the "nine provinces" (*chiu chou chih wai*), whereas those in the *yao* zone are by implication retained within the Chou territorial sphere. This distinction clearly supports the notion that in pre-imperial China there was a conscious realization that some foreign peoples were living inside the territory of the Chou community of states or that they could be absorbed within it.

[8] The *Kuo yü* presents some difficulty in interpreting the rings closer to the royal domains; *Kuo yü* 1 (Ssu-pu pei-yao), 3a-b. See *Guoyu*, p. 69, n. 23.

[9] *Chou li*, 33 ("Chih-fang shih"), 9a; 29 ("Ta ssu-ma"), 5a.

lescing Chinese civilization in the process of differentiating itself from a surrounding "barbarism."

A closer look at some passages on the relations between Chou and non-Chou suggests that, if these statements are taken within their historical context, they lend themselves to a different interpretation. Passages that have traditionally been used to support the view that a cultural and moral divide existed may actually reflect aspects of political change behind the foreign policy strategies of Chou states and thus need to be examined in the context of Chou foreign affairs. That is, statements concerning foreign peoples are more apt to reveal political struggles and foreign policy shifts in response to actual circumstances than to be the result of the emergence of a consciousness of cultural differentiation.

Cultural Statements in Political Context

The well-known example of the relations between the Ti people and the state of Hsing offers a suitable introduction to what I see as a necessary reevaluation of statements that, taken out of their historical context, were hastily adopted to prop up the notion of a polarized opposition between civilization and "barbarism." In 661 B.C., Kuan Chung, the famed councillor of Duke Huan, persuaded the state of Ch'i to intervene in defense of the state of Hsing, which was subject to incursions by Jung and Ti peoples. Kuan Chung's argument has been taken as plain evidence of the moral divide between Chou and non-Chou: "The Ti and the Jung are like wolves, and can never be satisfied; all the Hsia [states] are closely related, and none should be abandoned; to rest in idleness is a poison that should not be cherished."[10] According to most interpretations, this statement proves that a consciousness had been achieved among the Chou states of a clearly demarcated "us" and "them" and that such a demarcation indicates a mature notion of cultural unity within China expressed in the classic opposition between a unified Hua-Hsia community and non-Chou "barbarians."[11]

If we examine both its historical context and the text itself more closely, however, this interpretation is much less obvious. The state of Hsing, having

[10] *Ch'un-ch'iu Tso-chuan chu*, ed. Yang Po-chün (Peking: Chung-hua, 1990 [1981]) (Min 1), p. 256 [hereafter *Tso-chuan chu*] (James Legge, *The Chinese Classics*, vol. 5: *The Ch'un Ts'ew with the Tso Chuen* [London: Trübner, 1872; rpt. Hong Kong: Hong Kong University Press, 1960], p. 124).

[11] For a recent reiteration of this theme, see Cho-yun Hsu, "The Spring and Autumn Period," in *The Cambridge History of Ancient China*, ed. Michael Loewe and Edward L. Shaughnessy (Cambridge: Cambridge University Press, 1999), p. 550.

been rescued by Chin in the name of Chou "brotherhood," was attacked and conquered by Wey only a few years later, in 635 B.C. Yet not only was Wey a Chou state, it was also a state whose royal house shared the same surname with the ruler of Hsing. By invading Hsing, Wey violated the very kinship links that, allegedly, formed the internal bond uniting the Hsia political community. This constituted a blatant breach of the socio-political code of conduct on which Chin's anti-Ti posture was ostensibly based. Nevertheless, the deed was done, and in retribution Wey suffered only the verbal condemnation of later commentaries.[12]

The same year in which Hsing was annexed by Wey, the state of Chin was itself found in violation of the same principle of unity among the Central States that it had invoked. When the marquis of Chin sought to take possession of the fief of Yang-fan, the people refused to submit, claiming they were relatives of the king, and "the central states are conquered through virtue, while severity is used to intimidate the various foreign peoples (ssu yi)."[13] Unwilling to risk being alienated from the other Chou states, Chin conceded and let the people leave the city, but its action reveals the expedient nature of the principle of kinship.

The two episodes just cited suggest that the divide between the Chou and the non-Chou was defined in terms of kinship to shore up the loose federation of independent statelets that formed the Eastern Chou political community. Using lineage to underpin larger political unions is by no means unique to early China (it is a common feature of early states), and genealogical ties, whether real or fictitious, play a primary role in politics. Often the family metaphor was resorted to by some Chou state seeking hegemony within the Chou community, but the same principle could also be invoked to limit the ambition of the stronger states.

When *raison d'état* required that this principle be violated, however, Central States were ready to attack the relatives of the royal house, and they by no means shunned alliances with those allegedly outside the family, such as the Jung and the Ti. For instance, in 640 B.C. the state of Ch'i and the Ti concluded a treaty in Hsing forming a political alliance to help Hsing against Wey. Even more shocking, in 636 B.C. the Chou king attacked the state of Cheng with the help of the Ti. This was the context for another famous statement concerning the cultural differences between the Ti and the Chou community.

Those whose ears cannot hear the harmony of the five sounds are deaf; those whose eyes cannot distinguish among the five colors are blind; those whose

---

[12] *Ch'un-ch'iu Ku-liang chuan chin-chu chin-yi*, ed. Hsüeh An-chih (Taipei: Taiwan Shang-wu, 1994), p. 257.

[13] *Tso-chuan chu* (Hsi 25), p. 434 (Legge, *The Ch'un Ts'ew*, p. 196).

minds do not conform to the standards of virtue and righteousness are perverse; those whose mouths do not speak words of loyalty and faith are foolish
chatterers. The Ti conform to these four evils.[14]

These words are attributed to Fu Ch'en, a minister who opposed the pro-
Ti policy of the Chou king. However, Fu Ch'en's eloquent protest remained
unheeded. Not only did the king send the Ti to attack Cheng, he even
offered to marry the daughter of the Ti prince. Fu Ch'en remonstrated
again, this time claiming that the Ti were greedy and could never be satisfied and that marrying a Ti woman would be the king's ruin. Once again,
the king ignored this Cassandra. Yet shortly afterward Fu's prediction came
true when a coup in which the Ti gave military support to enemy faction
forced the king to flee. This political drama, however, was an internal one
at the Chou court, with the Ti playing the role of extras, eventually being
manipulated by one court faction against another. We do not know what
happened to Fu Ch'en.[15]

Fu Ch'en's disparaging depiction of the Ti was far from being a simple
statement remarking on the cultural gap between Hua and Ti. Instead, it
illustrates above all a locus classicus of Chinese history: the struggle
between the inner and outer courts, that is, between the faction of the king's
family, especially his various wives and concubines, and the faction of the
ministers. Fu Ch'en represents the minister who dutifully tries to oppose
the evil schemes of the inner court and protect a king who has allegedly
been manipulated by a faction with foreign ties.

If we were to strip this political layer from Fu Ch'en's statement about
the barbarity of the Ti, and consider it only in its "cultural" dimension, we
could still legitimately argue that Fu Ch'en's ideas of cultural purity were
not necessarily shared by other Chou people, including the king. We are
left, then, with a perception of "difference" between Chou and non-Chou
that some Chinese used for political purposes. Although I do not wish to
deny the existence of differences, Fu Ch'en's statement cannot be presented
as evidence of deep cultural cleavage between Chou and non-Chou, and
that, by inference, the Chou states were already fully conscious of their own
cultural cohesion.

Doubts about the reality of hard-and-fast cultural boundaries between
the Chou community of states and the foreigners are also raised by the *Ku-
liang* and the *Kung-yang* commentaries to the *Ch'un Ch'iu*. More than other

---

[14] *Tso-chuan chu* (Hsi 24), p. 425 (Legge, *The Ch'un Ts'ew*, p. 192).
[15] The *Tso-chuan* seems to indicate that he was captured or even perished. According to André d'Hormon's translation of the same story in the *Kuo yü*, however,
he "brought death" to the Ti, that is, he attacked and killed them. Note that
Chavannes translates the same passage: "he went to die (fighting against) the Ti."
See *Guoyu*, p. 200, and p. 208, n. 70.

sources, these commentaries reflect the view of an unbridgeable gap between the Chou states and foreigners. Statements about this gap have been presented as evidence of a closed system of interstate relations during the early Eastern Chou that excluded foreign peoples.[16] It should be noted, however, that the *Ku-liang* and the *Kung-yang* commentaries reflect ethical positions that were held much later than the events they comment on; this consideration in itself seriously dents the argument that such a sharp cultural differentiation existed during the Spring and Autumn period. What is interesting in addition, however, is that these commentaries introduce a category for referring to non-Chou peoples that is not found in the *Tso-chuan*, that is, the binome "Yi-Ti." In its most general sense, this term appears to be close to "barbarian," a word we often use in English, with considerable imprecision, to translate any item of the large inventory of Chinese names for foreign peoples.[17] Indeed, in the *Ku-liang* tradition, the Yi-Ti were those people who inhabited the reverse side of virtue and morality, to the point that it was even acceptable to punish them without paying overmuch attention to the rules of propriety otherwise supposed to regulate interstate relations: "As for Yi and Ti, one does not speak of right or wrong."[18] But who exactly were the Yi-Ti? The name itself obviously points to foreigners, but it is clear that the category could also be applied to states normally regarded as part of the Chou political and cultural system. The states of Chin, Ch'u, and Wu were all branded at one time or another as Yi-Ti because of their violation of accepted norms.

In the commentary following the record of Chin's attack against the Hsien-yü and the state of Fei (both of them "barbarians" of the White Ti confederation) of 530 B.C., the *Ku-liang* says that Chin is like the Yi-Ti because Chin joined them in waging war against the Central States.[19] This statement probably refers to the war between Chin and Chou three years earlier (533 B.C.) in which Chin had employed the Yin Jung – that is, a certain group of foreign peoples, who cannot be identified more precisely – to lay siege to the Chou city of Ying. Chin's use of foreign troops was criticized by the representative of the Chou House, who insisted that Chin would have been to blame if the Jung had been allowed to enter the Central States, arguing further that, once that had happened, the land that the ancestors had divided up and cultivated would have been abandoned to the

---

[16] Chen Shih-tsai, "Equality of States in Ancient China," *American Journal of International Law* 35 (1941): 641–50.

[17] See, for instance, Hsiao Kung-Chuan, *A History of Chinese Political Thought*, vol. 1: *From the Beginnings to the Sixth Century* A.D., trans. F. W. Mote (Princeton: Princeton University Press, 1979), pp. 137, 142.

[18] *Ch'un-ch'iu Ku-liang chuan*, p. 288.

[19] *Ch'un-ch'iu Ku-liang chuan*, p. 571. Note that according to the commentator, the appellation Yi-Ti refers to the state of Ch'u.

Jung, who would then be in a position to "administer them."[20] The Chou king's remonstrance continues: "I [the king] am to the uncle [ruler of Chin] as the crown or cap to all other garments, like the root or the spring to the tree and the river, like the ministers to the common people. If the uncle breaks the cap and destroys the crown, tears up the roots and blocks the spring, and arbitrarily casts the ministers away, then how will the Jung and the Ti have me (as ruler)?"[21]

By denying the existence of a hierarchy that subordinated the feudal states to the Chou House, Chin was implicitly questioning that a political center could exist at all. Yet if there were no political center anarchy would ensue, and the Jung and the Ti would naturally gain an advantage. In other words, the action of Chin de facto weakened the Central States, strengthening foreign forces and potentially enabling them to eventually gobble up the whole of China. In this sense, Chin's behavior indeed was no different than that of the Jung and the Ti. However, this parallel is purely political, not cultural. In the *Ku-liang* passage, the principle that separates the Central States and the Yin Jung depends on the acceptance or rejection of a certain political order. The expansionist policies of the Chou states required that the Jung and Ti be brought within the Chinese political arena, either as subjects or as allies. But if the consequences of the Jung and Ti's involvement were perceived as threatening or as damaging to the political order, then those responsible for their involvement, such as Chin in the example just mentioned, would be regarded as just like the Jung and Ti. In theory at least, the states could not subordinate the security of the Chou order to self-serving opportunism. Hence the laconic statement of the *Ku-liang* referring to Chin, in 530 B.C., as a Yi-Ti state.

Chin was not the only state to be so branded. Just one year before the Chin expedition against the Hsien-yü and Fei (i.e., 531 B.C.), the *Ch'un Ch'iu* reports that the lord of Ch'u ambushed the viscount of Ts'ai, killing him, after which the lord's son laid siege to the capital city of Ts'ai.[22] The *Ku-liang* refers to the Ch'u ruler as a Yi-Ti, on the grounds that he had tricked and killed the lord of a Central State.[23] Once again, the *Ku-liang* places a "Chinese" state in the middle of the Yi-Ti camp. As in the case of Chin, Ch'u was in violation of accepted norms through its act of treachery against the Chou state.

The state of Wu also gained an equally bad reputation. In its case, the epithet "Yi-Ti" was based on parameters that were more cultural than political. Thus *Ku-liang* contends: "The state of Wu is Yi-Ti. Its people shave

---

[20] *Tso-chuan chu* (Chao 9), p. 1309, notes that the Jung used the land for pasture. I do not see how this can be inferred from the text.

[21] *Tso-chuan chu* (Chao 9), p. 1309 (cf. Legge, *The Ch'un Ts'ew*, p. 625).

[22] *Tso-chuan chu* (Chao 11), p. 1321.   [23] *Ch'un-ch'iu Ku-liang chuan*, p. 566.

their hair and tattoo their bodies."[24] Although one might logically assume that shaving hair and tattooing bodies were Yi-Ti characteristics, since the category Yi-Ti does not refer to a single identifiable people, it likely means, quite simply, "un-Chinese." Moreover, the *Tso-chuan*, in 547 B.C., refers to Chin having taught Wu how to fight a war with chariots, including how to drive them, shoot from them, and charge the enemy with them.[25] Having shaven heads and tattoos and being unable to drive chariots were charges that could be leveled at the people of Wu but did not prevent the state from being accepted within the Chou community. Once again, we find the boundary between the Yi-Ti and the Chou anything but clearly defined.

The *Chan kuo ts'e* yields more examples of a similar nature. Several states were named as "Jung-Ti," a common binome used, as we have just seen, to denote foreign peoples outside the control of the Central Plain states. As with other common binomes, such as "Man-Yi," the two components had lost any residual ethnic significance and were simply meant to represent the general notion of "foreignness" that was used to stigmatize a behavior not consonant with commonly accepted rules. Any state could at some point be branded Jung-Ti, regardless of its geographic location – (for example, southwestern Shu)[26] – and regardless of whether it was in fact a Chou state. The following passage from the *Chan kuo ts'e* articulates this sense of cultural incompatibility about Ch'in: "Ch'in shares the same customs as the Jung and Ti; it has the heart of a tiger or a wolf; it is greedy and cruel, and cannot be trusted when it comes to making a profit; it does not behave according to protocol, righteousness, or virtuous action."[27] Accusing a state or people of immorality or lack of virtue or even of inhumanity was to make a political denunciation of unscrupulous behavior that could be applied to an enemy regardless of "ethnic" or "cultural" differences. Under such circumstances, ethnic differences were noted rarely; even when they were, they were used to underscore a moral difference and were not in themselves sufficient cause for the exclusion of a people or a state from membership in what Creel has defined as the Chou "club."[28]

Cultural differences could also function in the opposite direction, that is, a lack of culture could turn out, in some contexts, to be an advantage. This emerges in the story of Yu Yü, a Chinese renegade (a native of Chin)

---

[24] *Ch'un-ch'iu Ku-liang chuan*, p. 699.

[25] *Tso-chuan chu* (Hsiang 26), p. 1122 (Legge, *The Ch'un Ts'ew*, p. 527).

[26] *Chan-Kuo Ts'e*, annotated by Liu Hsiang, 3 vols. (Shanghai: Ku-chi, 1978), 3 (Ch'in 1), 117 (trans. J. I. Crump, Jr., *Chan-Kuo Ts'e* [Oxford: Clarendon Press, 1970], p. 67).

[27] *Chan-Kuo Ts'e* 24 ("Wei 3"), 869; cf. Crump, *Chan-Kuo Ts'e*, p. 436.

[28] Herrlee G. Creel, *The Origins of Statecraft in China: The Western Chou Empire* (Chicago: University of Chicago Press, 1970), p. 217.

who had fled to the Jung and then been sent by the king of the Jung to observe (that is, to spy on) Ch'in. Duke Mu of Ch'in questioned Yu Yü about governance among the Jung. The duke pointed out that there was still chaos from time to time in the Central States, even though they had cultural refinement, rituals, and laws, and he asked how, then, the Jung could govern without having even one of those accomplishments. Yu Yü answered that in the Central States the arts, rituals, and laws established in antiquity had deteriorated through the ages and now were being misused by those above to oppress those below, creating resentment and conflict. In contrast, the Jung had preserved their moral virtues uncorrupted, and individuals both superior and inferior were in perfect harmony. With a nice turn of phrase that played on regret, popular among philosophers with Taoist inclinations, for the loss of the ability of kings to rule "without acting" (*wu wei*), Yu Yü added that "governing the entire country is like ruling oneself. We are not aware how it is ruled. This is truly the way a sage king rules." At this point, Duke Mu asked his counselors for advice, and they concocted a plot meant to drive a wedge between the Jung king and the skillful Yu Yü. Music, held to be the pride of the Central States' higher culture, would be turned into a political tool and used first to corrupt and distract the Jung king and then to detain Yu Yü and thus create a suspicion in the mind of the king (already distracted by female musicians) against his loyal advisor. The plot worked beautifully: Yu Yü had a falling out with the Jung king and finally accepted Ch'in's invitation to serve that state. Three years later, the duke of Ch'in, with advice from Yu Yü, attacked the Jung; as a result, the duke "added twelve states under his rule, expanded his territory a thousand *li* and ruled the Western Jung as a Hegemon."[29] Whether or not this story is authentic is hard to say,[30] but it surely shows that the Central States' "culture" was not regarded in ancient China as an absolute positive value whose only function was to make a ruler more virtuous and a society more orderly. Music and other cultural features could also serve less honorable ends for a state seeking to accrue power.

That these statements are the conscious demarcation of a cultural boundary between a Chou universe and a discrete, "barbarian," non-Chou universe is cast into doubt when we become aware of their rhetorical charge and political context. When it comes to foreign peoples, the dearth of ethnographic or other data in the extant historical sources for the period, including details on matters valued by Chinese chroniclers, such as rituals and

---

[29] *Shih chi* 5, 194 (trans. Nienhauser, ed., *The Grand Scribe's Records*, vol. 1: *The Basic Annals of Pre-Han China by Ssu-ma Ch'ien* [Bloomington: Indiana University Press, 1994], pp. 100–101).

[30] This story is also reported in the *Han Fei Tzu* 3 ("Shih Kuo"), 6b-7b (Ssu-pu pei-yao) (translated in Han Fei Tzu, *Basic Writings*, trans. Burton Watson [New York and London: Columbia University Press, 1964], pp. 62–65).

genealogies, suggests a fundamental lack of interest in what we might regard as "cultural" differences. Compared to the wealth of information about political relations with non-Chou states, the scarce attention paid to foreign cultures suggests that the early Chinese chroniclers were interested almost exclusively in political events, understood as, and dominated by, ethical norms. The writers did not actively seek actual descriptions of other cultures as an intellectual pursuit. Only in the *Shih chi*, as we will see in Part IV of this book, do we find an explicit description of ethnic cultures, made as part of a new paradigm of historical knowledge.

Boundaries between presumed cultural communities in the Eastern Chou period appear to have been drawn ad hoc, according to ever-changing political circumstances. Foreign peoples existed, and were identified as such by a variety of ethnonyms, but their interaction with the Chou did not occur along polarized lines of "us" versus "them." The relatively rare statements that attempted to establish cultural or political boundaries are inadequate for us to determine the substance of the sense of cultural consolidation of the Chou community of states *against* non-Chou peoples, especially when we consider the historical context. In the sections that follow, we shall see how relations on the northern frontier cannot easily be ascribed to any given philosophical inclination, but form an eminently pragmatic body of doctrines based on the main political and military preoccupations of the period: defense and aggression, survival and expansion, and a relentless search for resources.

Peace or War?

Expressions of the political interaction between Chou states and foreigners abound but have been analyzed almost exclusively under a "moral" rubric according to a bifurcated ideological approach: If the statements stressed "peace," an attempt was carried out to educate and mold the foreigners peacefully (the Confucian-Mencian way); if the statements invoked war, then this was because these "barbarians" could only be tamed *manu militari* (the "legalist" approach). Hence the specific choices of Chinese states in their relations with non-Chinese polities have been explained by making them fit into a paradigm of foreign policy according to which political choices are dictated by moral convictions.

The so-called pacifist tendency in the relations between Chou and non-Chou has often been interpreted as deriving from a "Confucian" stress on moral cultivation, which prescribed that foreigners should be won over with virtue and exemplary behavior rather than by brute force. Nonetheless, we would be hard pressed, if asked, to show how the Chou states conformed to the teaching of a "Confucian" school of thought in their foreign policy, or how Chou relations with non-Chou peoples were inspired by a coherent set of moral principles. In the *Analects*, Confucius himself is reputed to have endorsed a militaristic view, when he lauded Kuan Chung's aggressive foreign policy: "Were it not for Kuan Chung – he is reputed to have said – we might now be wearing our hair loose and folding our clothes to the left."[31] The protection of China's cultural heritage from menacing loose-haired hordes justified the use of force.

In contrast, Mencius's well-known assertion that the foreigners did not "change" the Central States is symptomatic of how the discourse was later deflected from the political plane to the rarefied plane of cultural differences. If we look closely at his statement, Mencius clearly refers to the state of Ch'u, taken to be a "foreign" (or "barbarian" in most translations) state of the *yi* people.[32] The Mencian concept reflects an ideology of civilization, or a *mission civilizatrice*, that postulates a dialectic relationship, indeed, a struggle, between the Hua-Hsia peoples and the Yi that began with the mythical Sage Emperor Shun, whose abode was placed next to the land of the Eastern Yi. According to Mencius, this struggle ended in favor of the Hua-Hsia because of their moral superiority. These are, however, idealized forces, philosophical antinomies that transcended the historical plane and had nothing to do – at least at the moment of their formulation – with the implementation of foreign policy.

When conducting relations with non-Chou peoples, the Chou states never followed a single overriding doctrine, but were instead fluid, adaptive, and eminently pragmatic. Their foreign policy strategies evolved over time; "militaristic" or "pacifist" stances derived from differences in the process of growth of each state, being the reflection of its relative strengths and weaknesses. A clear association between foreign policies and philosophical doctrines, in particular the linkage of "Confucianism" and pacifism on the one hand and "legalism" and interventionism on the other, cannot be established before the Ch'in-Han period, and perhaps only at the time of the *Discourses on Salt and Iron*, a text attributed to Huan K'uan (first century B.C.) and written down during the reign of Emperor Hsüan-ti (74–49 B.C.).[33] Before the long period of military confrontation with the Hsiung-nu, which served as a fertile ground for the formulation of clearer doctrines of foreign relations, the lines are blurred. Indeed, for the Spring and Autumn period it is virtually impossible to identify any philosophical orientation that could be defined as either pro-war or pro-peace.

---

[31] Arthur Waley, *The Analects of Confucius* (London: Allen and Unwin, 1938), p. 185.

[32] James Legge, *The Chinese Classics*, vol. 2: *The Works of Mencius*, 2nd ed. (Oxford: Clarendon, 1895; rpt. Hong Kong: Hong Kong University Press, 1960), p. 253.

[33] Michael Loewe, "Yen t'ieh lun," in *Early Chinese Texts*, p. 477.

A series of practical doctrines emerged – couched in the moral language of the prevailing political discourse – that reflect the evolution of Chou foreign relations.[34] Given that their primary political imperatives were to survive and to expand, the Eastern Chou states articulated their foreign relations with non-Chou peoples according to the following political and strategic objectives: first, to conquer the non-Chou in order to enhance the processes of strengthening and expanding the state; second, to pursue peace when the situation required that the state's resources be preserved; third, to govern foreigners and incorporate them into the state's administrative structure in order to consolidate the state's power; and, finally, to make effective use of foreigners for military or economic purposes.

The drive of the Chou state to conquer was expressed, in the political arena, in a series of speeches and statements demonstrating how the non-Chou could, indeed why they should, be conquered. The doctrine that virtue lay in defeating the non-Chou was part of the strategy of several states that had adopted an expansionist policy in their relations with northern peoples (Jung and Ti), especially during the late seventh and sixth centuries B.C. Often, however, a state hesitated to subdue these foreigners lest the enterprise itself, even if successful, be so costly that it would weaken the state and reduce its chances of survival. A state had also to think carefully before alienating the northern peoples, whose military prowess often made them strategically important as allies. On the one hand, when peace was regarded as the wiser course of action, the Chou states established diplomatic relations; the non-Chou peoples then entered covenants and attended political conferences just as the Chou states did, and, of course, were bound by the same rules. On the other hand, when the stronger Chou states managed to incorporate non-Chou peoples, the need to govern them, and to avoid rebellions and political disruption, resulted in the creation of new administrative units and in the mobilization of these peoples, especially for military ventures.

Whether as allies or as newly conquered subjects, the non-Chou came to be seen as resources to be tapped for the aggrandizement of the state. A Chou state would adopt a "militarist" or a "pacifist" course of action depending on the analysis of the situation by a given political leader or advisor. Such an analysis dictated whether the state would resort to force or seek peace: in the end, opinions on how to deal with foreigners differed based not on philosophical doctrines and cultural leanings, but on individual perceptions of political and military realities.

The "pacifist" doctrine was adopted by a Chou state when it needed to save its resources or wished to gain allies in wars against other Chou

---

[34] "International" relations in the Spring and Autumn period are the subject of Richard Louis Walker's, *The Multistate System of Ancient China* (Hamden: The Shoestring Press, 1953).

states. The "militarist" doctrine was pursued by states that wanted to expand. Wars waged by the states of Ch'i and Chin during the Spring and Autumn period led to the territorial expansion of these states at the expense of a number of non-Chou peoples living nearby. Of course, the same logic of mutual violence underpinned the relations among the Chou states, but the inability of the Jung and Ti to become full-fledged members of the Chou "club" made them more vulnerable prey. In their wars against the Jung and Ti, the Chou states did not have to observe rules of virtuous behavior, whose violation might otherwise cause political damage to the perpetrator.

Given that in early China political concerns were invariably expressed in moral terms, when peoples not constituted as Chou states – located politically outside the range of the authority of the Chou House – entered into conflict with the Chou states, such clashes were presented as the expression of a great chasm between civilization and barbarism. If we take this literally, this rhetorical veneer flattens and ultimately obscures an undoubtedly more complex picture. The Chou states dealt with their northern and western neighbors in a variety of ways, incorporating many of them, importing some of their ways, and making them a part of their own process of military, political, and economic growth.

The Non-Chou as Conquerable

Conquering and enslaving a state's enemies was a popular way to create larger polities. A pattern of military confrontation between China and the northern peoples was already underway during the Shang (c. sixteenth century–1045 B.C.) and Western Chou (c. 1045–770 B.C.) periods. In particular, the Western Chou fought against a host of northern peoples, among whom the most prominent were the Hsien-yün and the Jung.[35] Because these peoples are held to be, in later Chinese historiography, the progenitors of the Hsiung-nu, a few words should be devoted to the early developments in their recorded encounters with the Chou.

---

[35] The term *jung* is often applied in Chinese sources to warlike foreigners. Its general meaning relates to "martial" and "military," "war" and "weapons." In the *Tso-chuan*, *jung* is also used in the sense of "war-chariot" in the phrase *yü jung* ("to drive a war chariot") and in the compound *jung ch'e* ("war chariot"). Cf. Everard D. H. Fraser and James H. S. Lockhart, *Index to the Tso-chuan* (London: Oxford University Press, 1930), p. 165. Shaughnessy attributes to the word, in the Western Chou period, the meaning of "enemy 'belligerents'" rather than "barbarians" (Edward L. Shaughnessy, "Western Zhou History," in *The Cambridge History of Ancient China*, p. 324); the "foreignness" of the Jung, however, does not seem to be in question.

The term "Jung" appears to indicate more than a single people and is regarded by some scholars not as an ethnonym but as a generic word for "bellicose" or "warlike." King Mu (956–918 B.C.) defeated the Ch'üan Jung in the twelfth year of his reign and attacked the Western Jung and the Hsü Jung the following year,[36] opening a phase of expansion under this ruler; his journey to the west was romanticized in the fourth century B.C. in the fictional account *Mu T'ien tzu chuan*.[37] The discourse reported in the *Kuo yü* apropos King Mu's expedition indicates the prevalent Chou attitude toward the Jung.[38] The discourse was pronounced by the duke of Chai, Mou-fu, who opposed attacking the Jung based on an ideal of a cosmo-political order that justified the use of force only when that order was threatened. Because the Jung were observing their station in that order, that is, were paying respect to the court and were staying in their own lands, there was no reason to attack them. But King Mu attacked them nevertheless. The tense chasm between naked political ambition and the philosophers' ideas about clockwork correspondences among human, natural, and cosmic forces needing to be kept in balance lest disaster strike, is a classic motif in the pre-imperial discussions on relations with non-Chinese states. As we will see, the Chou tended to overcome this chasm by justifying the state's conquest of foreign peoples on moral grounds.

Hostilities between the Chou and the Jung did not erupt again until the seventh year of King Yi (865–858 B.C.), when the Jung of T'ai-yüan attacked the area of the Chou capital. It was at this time that the Chou royal family gradually came to depend on other noble families to defend the realm. In 854 B.C. Kuo Kung attacked the Jung, capturing one thousand horses, but during the reign of King Li (857/53–842/28 B.C.), the dynasty began to weaken, and both the Western Jung and the Hsien-yün launched invasions deep into Chou territory.

The *Shih ching* (Classic of Poetry) contains four songs that mention military engagements between the Chou and the Hsien-yün. One of these songs, "Ts'ai ch'i," extols the deeds of Fang Shu, who apparently led as many as three thousand chariots into battle against the Hsien-yün.[39] The song "Liu yüeh" provides geographical information that allows us to place the battlefield very close to the center of the Chou state, between the lower reaches of the Ching and Lo Rivers and the Wei River Valley. Although

---

[36] *Chu-shu chi-nien* 2, 4b–5a (*Ssu-pu pei-yao*) (Legge, *The Shoo King*, "Prolegomena," p. 150).

[37] Loewe, *Early Chinese Texts*, pp. 342–46.   [38] *Guoyu*, pp. 55–58.

[39] *Shih-san ching chu-shu fu-chiao k'an-chi* ed. Juan Yüan (Peking: Chung-hua, 1980), 1: 425 (James Legge, *The Chinese Classics*, vol. 4: *The She King* [London: Trübner, 1862; rpt. Hong Kong: Hong Kong University Press, 1960], pp. 284–87).

scholars dispute the exact dates of the attacks, most place them during the reign of King Hsüan (827/25–782/80 B.C.).[40]

Toward the end of King Hsüan's reign there were repeated military engagements between the Chou state and the Jung. Particularly significant was the expedition in 790/89 B.C. (thirty-eighth year of Hsüan's reign) by Chin against the Northern Jung, and the king's expedition the following year against the Jung of the Chiang clan, who were utterly destroyed.[41] The final period of the Western Chou, under the reign of King Yu (781–771 B.C.), was marked by increasing instability on the northern frontier and by a series of attacks by the Ch'üan Jung. In 770 B.C. – the traditional date for the beginning of the Spring and Autumn period – the Chou defenses were overrun, the capital invaded, the king killed, and the court forced to move to the city of Lo.

Various Jung peoples already lived scattered over a broad area that encompassed the northern and western Wei River Valley, the Fen River Valley, and the Tai-yüan region. They were therefore distributed in today's northern Shensi, northern Shansi, and Hopei, up to the T'ai-hang Mountains.[42] With few exceptions, their attacks against the Chou do not seem to have been particularly effective. Like the Hsien-yün, they probably used chariots, but a record from 714 B.C. shows that they also fought on foot.[43] These foreign communities seem to have been organized into relatively small socio-political tribal or territorial units. Still, the "Jung" or "Ti" groups at times could coalesce into larger formations when pursuing a common political objective. In 649 B.C., for instance, the Jung of four different villages united to attack the Chou capital.[44] On that occasion, they were able to storm the city by burning down the eastern gate. These joint actions, however, were atypical for the Jung. The Ti seem to have been able to create larger unions, but they were also divided into at least two major groupings, the Ch'ih (Red) and the Pai (White) Ti. Whether "Ti" was a generic word for "northern foreigners," or a specific ethnonym, or even a political unit or a state, cannot be determined.[45] Certainly the Ti were a

---

[40] *Shih-san ching chu-shu*, 1: 424 (Legge, *The She King*, pp. 281–84).

[41] *Chu-shu chi-nien*, 2.10a; *Kuo yü* (Ssu-pu pei-yao ed.), 1 ("chou yü 1"), 9a; *Guoyu*, p. 33, n. 48.

[42] On the geography of this period, see Edward L. Shaughnessy, "Historical Geography and the Extent of Early Chinese Kingdoms," *Asia Major*, 3rd series, 2.2 (1989): 1–22.

[43] *Tso-chuan chu* (Yin 9), p. 65 (Legge, *The Ch'un Ts'ew*, p. 28).

[44] *Tso-chuan chu* (Hsi 11), p. 338.

[45] Průšek discusses at length the nature of the Ti and of their encounter with China. He attributes the appearance of the Ti and other peoples in northern China to transcontinental migrations triggered by the evolution of mounted nomadic cultures in Eurasia. See Jaroslav Průšek, *Chinese Statelets and the Northern Barbarians in the Period 1400–300 B.C.* (Dordrecht: Reidel, 1971), pp. 77–87.

political and military force to be reckoned with, recognized by the Chou as a "state" or "states" through diplomatic activity, exchange of hostages, and treaties.

As the authority of the Chou House began to wane by the mid-eighth century B.C., China was filled with many contenders for political hegemony. Relations among various political centers often resulted in wars, and in the absorption of the weaker by the stronger. Non-Chou peoples undoubtedly participated in this increasing militarization. As the Eastern Chou states vied for domination, they turned to the conquest of non-Chou peoples, particularly the Jung tribes or states, many of which seem to have been vulnerable to their attacks. This shift is nowhere clearer than with the expeditions of Duke Huan of Ch'i that were often directed against northern, non-Chou, peoples. The conquest of the Jung, wholly consistent with the process of strengthening of the Chou states, was often justified on moral or cultural grounds. Yet as we will see in a number of specific examples, once referred to their proper historical contexts, these acts of conquest leave no doubt about the purely political nature of their objectives.

The story of the military offensive launched by Chin in 666 B.C. against Jung and Ti is one of the most explicit descriptions of the fulfillment of a Chinese state's expansionist goals at the expense of non-Chou peoples:

Duke Hsien of Chin [. . .] married two women of the Jung: Hu Chi of the Great Jung, who gave him the son Chung-er, and a daughter of the Small Jung, who gave him I-wu. When Chin attacked the Li Jung their chief [*nan*, baron], gave him as wife his daughter Li Chi [. . .]. Li Chi became the favorite of the Duke, and wanted her son declared heir-apparent. In order to do this she bribed two of his favorite officials, Liang-wu of the outer court and Wu from Tung-kuan, and had them speak to the Duke to this effect: "Ch'ü-wu is the ancestral seat, P'u and the Erh-ch'ü are two frontier territories. They should have their lords residing in them. If there is no lord in your ancestral city, the people will not feel awe, if the border areas do not have a lord, this will make the Jung grow bold. That the Jung may grow bold, and that the people despise their government, are the calamities of the state. If you place the heir-apparent in charge of Ch'ü-wu, and Chung-er and I-wu in charge respectively of P'u and Erh-ch'ü, this will awe the poeple and frighten the Jung, and also symbolize the lord's [ability to] subjugate." She further made them say: "The marshes and deserts of the Ti will be to the Chin like a metropolitan area. Wouldn't it be right to expand the territory of Chin?"[46]

Marriage diplomacy and the policy of exchanging hostages had brought several Jung women to the Chin princely house and had made foreigners an important element in relations between the inner court and outer court. Although the story's focus is the court intrigue, it also reveals the position

---

[46] *Tso-chuan chu* (Chuang 28), pp. 239–40 (Legge, *The Ch'un Ts'ew*, p. 114).

at court held by the Jung: They are entirely integrated into Chin inner-court politics. The two Chin officials, goaded by the favorite wife, were able to persuade the duke to pursue a political program of indisputable astuteness. At stake were the governance of the newly conquered frontier territories and the further expansion of Chin. The plan submitted to the duke not only appealed to an ambitious expansionist ruler but also reflected some political realities. First, the Jung people who lived in the frontier territories had already been brought within the orbit of the Chin administrative and political system but remained difficult to control and potentially hostile. Second, as a result of the expansion that had brought to it the incorporation of territories inhabited by the Jung, Chin had come into contact with the Ti people. Chin's ability to keep firm control over the Jung was a necessary condition for the state's further expansion: To be accepted, a ruler had to demonstrate his ability to incorporate a variety of peoples under the same form of government. This must have been an enormous challenge for any lord of a Chou state.

The importance of the half-Jung offspring of the duke becomes evident: They were best suited to the government of the frontier because of their dual nature as both Jung and members of the feudal house. But why conquer the marshes and deserts of the Ti? Later political doctrines would make it clear that a state should not expend energy on uneconomical adventurism. At this time, the conquest of the Ti marshes and deserts seems to reflect the overriding concern of any expansionist state: to increase its power by demonstrating its ability to subjugate foreigners. Resolving the issue of control over foreign territories was an essential aspect of Chin state policy, and that meant, in practical terms, producing mixed-blood offspring for the purpose of governing new lands, this would be the right course of action.

Another example of "conquerability," repeatedly mentioned in the *Tso-chuan*, is expressed in the rule regarding the presentation of spoils of war. Here a precise line is drawn between *yi* (foreign) states and Central States for the ritual following a victorious battle. From what we can gather from scattered references, the basic doctrine maintained that, after a victory against a non-Chou state, the spoils could be offered to the king, but if the king had ordered an attack against a Chou state, then a victory was to be followed only by a report to the king on the matter, without any offer of spoils. In 663 B.C.,[47] on the occasion of a presentation of Jung spoils of war by the marquis of Ch'i to Lu,[48] the marquis was found to be in contempt of ritual. The explanation in the *Tso-chuan* is that "When the [Chou] lords obtain a victory against the four Yi, they present the booty to the king, who uses it as a warning for the Yi, but this is not so among the Central States.

[47] *Tso-chuan chu* (Chuang 31), pp. 247–48.
[48] Lu was one of the most politically prominent Central States, eventually "extinguished" by the southern state of Ch'in in 249 B.C.

The [Chou] lords do not offer booty [taken from the foreigners] to each other."

This doctrine is alluded to again in 589 B.C., when Chin tried to offer the booty taken from the state of Ch'i to the Chou king. The offer was refused with the following argument:

When Man, Yi, Jung, and Ti do not abide by the king's commands, and, being dissolute and drunken, violate the norms, if the king orders to attack them, then the spoils taken from them are presented, and the king personally receives them and congratulates, so that he would admonish those without respect and reward those with merit. If [a state] whose ruling family is related [to the Chou] violates and breaches the king's norms, and the king orders to attack them, then there is simply an announcement of the service, but no presentation of one's trophies.[49]

By this time, the presentation of spoils taken from non-Chou states was not an unusual occurrence. On two occasions, in 594 B.C. and 593 B.C., emissaries of Chin went to Chou to present the king with spoils taken from the Ti.[50]

The rules regarding the distribution of booty are especially revealing about the relationship between the House of Chou and the feudal states. Yet, they also define a clear principle of demarcation between Chou states and non-Chou peoples. Chou states established the legitimacy of a military expedition against the non-Chou by presenting the spoils to the Chou king, as an act of war sanctioned by a higher authority. When it came to rivalries among the Chou states, however, had the king accepted, through the presentation of the spoils by the winning party, the submission of people who were already his subjects, the act could be tantamount to relinquishing much of his own formal authority. The acquisition of booty from the foreigners, in contrast, shows that they were placed outside the authority of the Chou House, that they were regarded as fully conquerable, and that their submission would contribute to the growth of Chou House prestige.

As expansion into foreign lands became a more pressing concern for the Chou states, the need to seek not only political but also moral justification went hand in hand with the campaigns of conquest. In the early part of the sixth century B.C., Chin, in competition with the rival state of Ch'in, launched repeated attacks aimed at annihilating various Ti groups. These campaigns were accompanied by a search for adequate justifications so that its politicians could protect Chin from other states' accusations of deliberate aggrandizement.

---

[49] *Tso-chuan chu* (Ch'eng 2), p. 809 (Legge, *The Ch'un Ts'ew*, pp. 343, 349).
[50] *Tso-chuan chu* (Hsüan 15), p. 765; (Hsüan 16), p. 768. On the first occasion the envoy was found wanting in courtesy and, as a result, his doom was prophesied. Only in 593 B.C. was the matter carried out without incidents.

A famous instance of the moral justification for the conquest of Ti is Chin's extinction of the tribe – or state – of Lu of the Ch'ih Ti, in 594 B.C. The chief of Lu, who carried the noble title of *tzu*, was known by the name Ying Erh and had married a daughter of the lord of Chin. The real power, however, was supposedly in the hands of the experienced Lu minister Feng Shu. Allegedly, Feng Shu had the lady killed (while also wounding his chief Ying Erh, in an eye), prompting the lord of Chin to attack the Ti against the advice of some of his dignitaries. The lord was persuaded to do so, however, by the "moral argument" advanced by another advisor, a certain Po-tsung. Po-tsung maintained that Feng Shu should be punished for a range of crimes: neglecting to offer sacrifices to the ancestors, drinking, seizing the lands of the lord of Li (a Chin ally), assassinating the wife of the head of Lu, and, finally, injuring his own master. But these were mere pretexts covering a deeper political goal:

His [Feng Shu's] successor perhaps will respectfully conform to virtue and justice, and that, serving both spirits and men, will strengthen his rule. Why then wait? If we do not punish the culprit, but wait for the successor, and then punish him even though he has merits, would not it be unreasonable?[51]

Because Feng Shu was old, the lord of Chin was exhorted not to miss the opportunity to make political capital out of a moral point. Having found an excuse that could justify the use of violence and lead to expansion, Chin should use it right away, because in the future the absence of such a pretext might make justifying the "punishment" more difficult.

The lord of Chin was persuaded by the argument; he attacked the Ch'ih Ti and destroyed the Lu people. Feng Shu fled to Wei, where he probably hoped to find protection, since the Ti and the Wei had signed a peace treaty over thirty years earlier, in 628 B.C., and in the intervening years no hostilities between them were recorded.[52] Feng Shu himself might have participated in making that treaty, since he was already a prominent politician just eight years later, in 620 B.C.[53] Treaty or not, Wei turned Feng Shu over to Chin, where he was put to death, and Chin then proceeded to take possession of the Ti territories. This marked the beginning of a series of campaigns of conquest. One year later Chin annexed three other Red Ti tribes,[54] and in 588 B.C. "to punish the last remnants of the Ch'ih Ti," Chin and Wei together attacked the Chiang-kao-ju. "The Chiang-kao-ju dispersed, and the chief (*shang*) lost his people."[55] A possible interpretation is that the

---

[51] *Tso-chuan chu* (Hsüan 15), p. 762 (Legge, *The Ch'un Ts'ew*, p. 328). This is not to be confused with the Chou state of Lu.

[52] *Tso-chuan chu* (Hsi 32), p. 489.

[53] *Tso-chuan chu* (Wen 7), p. 561 (Legge, *The Ch'un Ts'ew*, p. 249).

[54] *Tso-chuan chu* (Hsüan 16), pp. 767–68.

[55] *Tso-chuan chu* (Ch'eng, 3), p. 814. The Chiang-kao-ju were a tribe that had been attacked by the Ti in 637 B.C., when the Ti were engaged in a process of

Chiang-kao-ju had broken away from the Ti as a result of Chin's attack, and the head of the entire Ch'ih Ti confederation had remained isolated. Hence Chin managed to destroy any unity that the Ti may have had in the past.

Chin's political opportunism is confirmed by the different standards adopted in different situations. In 598 B.C., during its conflict with the Ch'ih Ti, Chin made peace with some Ti people who had previously been conquered by the Ch'ih Ti and now preferred to submit to Chin. The Chin minister advised the lord of Chin to go in person to a meeting to accept the submission of these Ti people rather than request that they present themselves at the Chin court, for "if there is no virtue, the best thing is to show solicitude. Without solicitude, how can we help others? If we can be solicitous, there will be a following."[56] The reference to an absence of virtue on Chin's side – that is, presumably, the "good government" that would naturally attract subjects from near and far – can be interpreted in two ways: either Chin could not show itself as a "virtuous government" because the state's power was not great enough, or it would be useless for Chin to count on a display of magnanimous rulership because the Ti were insensitive to it. At any rate, Chin could not count on "virtuous government" to persuade the Ti to submit. On the other hand, the argument for forcing the Ti to present themselves as Chin's subjects could not be invoked because in this instance the Ti had made a friendly overture and it was in Chin's interest to seek their submission by peaceful means. Hence the pragmatic principle of "solicitude" was invoked.[57] In another instance, the Pai Ti – traditionally less hostile than the Ch'ih Ti – and Chin concluded a peace treaty in 601 B.C. that led to Chin's recruitment of these foreigners as allies in its war against Ch'in. Entering a treaty with the Ti did not pose any moral questions, and the decision to either conquer them or make a treaty with the Ti was a matter of political convenience.

Although the Ti continued to be a force to be reckoned with, they became increasingly vulnerable to the aggressive policies of the Central States. Taking advantage of a conflict between Chin and Sung, in 579 B.C. the Ti launched an attack against Chin but suffered defeat owing to lack of proper preparation.[58] In 562 B.C. Chin signed a major treaty with Ti and Jung, and in 555 B.C., for the first time, the Pai Ti submitted to the state of Lu. By this time, most peoples in the north had ceased to constitute a serious problem of foreign policy for Chin. Although battles with some minor

---

expansion, probably starting shortly before 650 B.C., that continued through the second half of the second century B.C. See *Tso-chuan chu* (Hsi 23), p. 405.

[56] *Tso-chuan chu* (Hsüan 11), p. 713 (Legge, *The Ch'un Ts'ew*, p. 310).

[57] The reference is to a quotation from the *Shih ching*: "King Wen was indeed solicitous in all" (Legge, *Shih* IV i iii, X).

[58] *Tso-chuan chu* (Ch'eng 12), p. 856.

groupings continued, they resemble mopping-up operations rather than actual wars. The only non-Chou people with which Chou states continued diplomatic relations and continued to fight were the Hsien-yü (or Hsien-yün, also a Ti people), the founders of the state of Chung-shan.

The war waged by Chin against the Hsien-yü is another example of how little propriety and virtue mattered in wars fought against foreigners. The Chin army, led by Hsün Wu, had treacherously entered the territory of the Hsien-yü by pretending it wanted to join the Ch'i army. Once inside, it had proceeded to capture the city of Hsi-yang, which was the capital of the state of Fei, and to annex Fei itself.[59] This particular action, certainly not an example of morality, did not prevent the Tso-chuan from placing the commander Hsün Wu on the high moral ground on a later occasion. Then, Hsün Wu, acting against the opinion of his advisors, who argued that he was sacrificing raison d'état to an empty moral principle, refused to obtain the surrender of the Hsien-yü city of Ku through the treachery of some of its defenders, preferring to wait until the inhabitants had been starved into submission.

By the time of the Warring States, most of the various Ti peoples who had settled along the northern Chinese territories had been absorbed into the Central States' territories. Chung-shan was attacked by Wen Hou of Wei in 408 B.C. and conquered by 406 B.C.; Wei ruled for about forty years. In 377 B.C. it regained its independence.[60] The fall of Chung-shan to Chao in 295 B.C. did not end the history of the Ti. Some of these groups were attacked by General T'ien Tan of Ch'i as late as the reign of King Hsiang (r. 283–265 B.C.),[61] but by then a different northern frontier had already started to form.

---

[59] Tso-chuan chu (Chao, 12), p. 1341 (Legge, The Ch'un Ts'ew, pp. 639, 641). From this account it seems that Fei was probably a small kingdom within a larger ethnic or political union referred to as Hsien-yü. Both Fei and the Hsien-yü were part of the much larger grouping of the Pai Ti people.

[60] This state had fortified cities and an army with a thousand war chariots and capable troops. Archaeological research has shown that, at least from the end of the fourth century B.C., Chung-shan was fully within the sphere of Chinese civilization. Its bronze production, especially at P'ing-shan, reveals its complete absorption within the culture of the Central Plain; see Li Hsüeh-ch'in, "P'ing-shan mu-tsang-ch'ün yü Chung-shan kuo te wen-hua," Wen-wu 1979.1: 37–41; translated in Chinese Archaeological Abstracts 3, ed. Albert Dien, Jeffrey Riegel, and Nancy Price (Los Angeles: The Institute of Archaeology, UCLA, 1985), pp. 804–808. Still, no matter how "Chinese" the rulers of Chung-shan were, references to their diversity indicate that for a long time their state was not accepted as one of the states of the Hua-Hsia cultural sphere. On Chung-shan see Chan Kuo Ts'e 12 ("Ch'i 5"), p. 436 (Crump, Chan Kuo Ts'e, p. 200); and Chan-Kuo Ts'e 33 ("Chung-shan"), pp. 1170–74 (Crump, Chan-Kuo Ts'e, pp. 574–76).

[61] Chan-Kuo Ts'e 13 (Ch'i 6), pp. 467–68 (Crump, Chan-Kuo Ts'e, pp. 213–14).

The campaigns of conquest against non-Chou is an overriding theme of the Eastern Chou period. As we have seen, the moral issues allegedly involved in these conflicts were, at their best, mere pretexts. Instead, the Chou states found it relatively easy to conduct military campaigns against foreign peoples, sometimes leading to their extermination, because there was no clear moral prescription against conquering them. There was, however, a political context that militated against the use of brute force. Less blunt instruments, therefore, such as alliances and peace treaties, were also adopted by the Chou states, though their final aim remained the pursuit of power.

Non-Chou as Allies

Diplomacy was an essential tool in the Chou states' struggle for supremacy. From the eighth century onward a system of interstate relations developed in China that included not only the Chou states but also non-Chou peoples, organized into bodies that participated fully in all aspects of foreign politics. At the same time, the non-Chou states were in a more vulnerable position because, as we have already seen, their participation in a treaty did not necessarily protect them in the same way that it may have protected Chou states. If realpolitik required that an ally be betrayed or an agreement overturned, this was more easily accomplished if the partner happened to be non-Chou. However, peace was a necessary ingredient in the relations between Chou and non-Chou, and thus during the Spring and Autumn period a line of foreign policy developed that justified peaceful relations with non-Chou states. This "pacifist" doctrine was not necessarily influenced by cultural and moral views, and it was more complex than the mere affirmation of the power of virtue brutality of violence. Here we shall examine what "peace" actually meant, and the passages that more clearly exemplify the pacifist orientation.

The Contexts of Peace

Peace between the Chou and non-Chou states involved a series of actions and a set of norms unrelated to issues of "benevolence" and "virtue," belonging, rather, to the realm of foreign politics. Understanding this diplomatic dimension is essential because the existence of practices that allowed agreements to be negotiated was fundamental to the formulation of any specific peace doctrine. If the non-Chou people had been entirely alienated from the political practices of the Chou states, as they are sometimes held to have been, no doctrine based on mutual trust could ever have developed. This clearly is not the case: court visits (ch'ao), blood covenants (meng), and other kinds of diplomatic exchanges forged a system of relations that included the non-Chou peoples from the very beginning.[62]

From the early Spring and Autumn period, the Chou states seem to have had little choice but to admit their powerful foreign neighbors to the highest levels of diplomatic intercourse. In 721 B.C. the state of Lu held a meeting with the Jung in which Lu rejected their request for a covenant, but in the autumn of that year Lu yielded to a second request, and peaceful relations with the Jung were established once again.[63] In the majority of cases, making peace was a three-step process: negotiation, ratification, and observance of the terms. Negotiations would be out at gatherings (hui) and concluded with a blood covenant that involved swearing an oath and other ritual practices.[64] The terms of the treaty would include most typically an agreement to cease hostility, establish good neighborly relations, render mutual aid, and form alliances against common foes.[65]

The oath that they swore would ensure, in theory, that the contracting parties respect the terms of the agreement. Although oaths were sacred, there are cases in which the Chou states wantonly violated treaties with foreign peoples. In 590 B.C., for instance, Chin mediated a peace between the Chou king and the Jung. The brother of the king, Duke K'ang of Liu, counting on the Jung's sense of security derived from the peace, was planning to attack them later. But he was warned that "to violate a covenant and deceive a great state such as Chin will lead to certain defeat."[66] He

---

[62] Roswell Britton, "Chinese Interstate Intercourse before 700 B.C.," *American Journal of International Law* 29 (1935): 616–35. On the notion of equality among early states see also Ch'eng Te-hsu, "International Law in Early China," *Chinese Social and Political Science Review* 11 (1927): 40.

[63] *Tso-chuan chu* (Yin 2), p. 20 (Legge, *The Ch'un Ts'ew*, pp. 8–9).

[64] The ritual involved in sealing a covenant has been reconstructed by Mark Lewis on the basis of the blood covenants excavated at Hou-ma. The participating people purified themselves through fasting. They erected an altar and dug a pit where an animal (generally a sheep) was sacrificed, after which they cut off its left ear and placed it into a vessel. They caught the blood in another vessel and then drank the blood. See Mark Lewis, *Sanctioned Violence in Ancient China* (Albany: State University of New York Press, 1990), pp. 43–50.

[65] Treaties between Chou and non-Chou were particularly common starting in the second half of the seventh century. Around 650 B.C., the time of expansion and growth for the Ti, several Chinese states entered peace treaties with them. In 628 B.C. Wei entered a covenant after the Ti had requested peace (*Tso-chuan chu* [Hsi 32], p. 489). In 619 B.C., the state of Lu made a covenant with the Yi-lo Jung (*Tso-chuan chu* [Wen 8], p. 567 [Legge, *The Ch'un Ts'ew*, pp. 250–51]), and in 601 B.C. Chin concluded a peace with the White Ti (*Tso-chuan chu* [Hsüan 8], p. 695).

[66] *Tso-chuan chu* (Ch'eng 1), p. 782.

proceeded to invade the Mao Jung nevertheless, and in the third month of the conflict he suffered a defeat at the hands of the Hsü Wu tribe (or lineage, *shih*). Even the guarantee of a state such as Chin had not prevented an oath with a non-Chou party from being broken.

Formal diplomatic relations also involved the brokerage of peace, so that a given state would offer its services and send mediators to solve a situation of potential conflict.[67] A state could, for instance, allow the troops of another state right of passage through its territory in the course of a military expedition. In such cases, the relative strength of the states involved determined whether permission would be given or refused. Smaller states often were too weak to deny access, although compliance might lead to the state's ruin because such requests often concealed treacherous intentions.[68] The establishment of peaceful relations was followed by the exchange of diplomatic missions, gifts, visits, and other forms of etiquette that regulated and formalized interstate relations. Not observing some of these rules could easily result in an insult and carry consequences that would eventually lead to the breach of the treaty.

The very first mention of the Jung, in the *Ch'un ch'iu*, refers to a diplomatic visit they made to Chou in 721 B.C.[69] Repaid with discourtesy by one of the Chou ministers, they abducted him while he was on a diplomatic mission to the state of Lu. Several years later (710 B.C.), the state of Lu and the Jung concluded a covenant (*meng*) "to renew the good relations of old."[70] Whether or not the two episodes are related, both point to an egalitarian relationship, in diplomacy, between Jung and Chou states. That the Jung had been treated badly justified their action against the imprudent minister and rendered Lu's covenant with them legitimate. Given that there is ample evidence that nothing barred the non-Chou from having peaceful relations with the Chou states, what were the advantages of peace for the Chou states, and how was the establishment of peaceful relations justified in political (and therefore in moral) terms?

---

[67] In 649 B.C. Chin had acted as a mediator between the Jung and the king. In 648 B.C. the lord of Ch'i sent the famed minister Kuan-chung to mediate a peace agreement between the Jung and the Chou king, and sent Hsi Peng to procure peace between the Jung and the state of Chin.

[68] During the war against the Hsien-yü, in 530 B.C., Chin treacherously attacked them after having asked and obtaining the right of passage. Moreover, in 520 B.C. soldiers of Chin took the Hsien-yü city of Ku by subterfuge, having dressed like grain merchants and hidden their armor in bundles carried on their shoulders; see *Tso-chuan chu* (Chao 22), p. 1435 (Legge, *The Ch'un Ts'ew*, pp. 691, 693).

[69] *Tso-chuan chu* (Yin 7), p. 20 (Legge, *The Ch'un Ts'ew*, p. 9).

[70] *Tso-chuan chu* (Huan 2), p. 84 (Legge, *The Ch'un Ts'ew*, p. 40).

The Doctrine of Peace

Possibly no better context for demonstrating the pragmatic nature of the Chou states' relations with non-Chou peoples exists than that of peace. Because peace in ancient China seems to have been based upon a more sophisticated level of rationalization than war – conflicts were often caused by a variety of incidental events, linked simply to the pursuit of power or to instinctive reactions to perceived threats – peace settlements and strategies can be more revealing than war when we look for the connections between moral and political reasoning. When negotiating a peace treaty with the Jung and Ti, the Chou states worked to achieve several implicit objectives. These were to increase the state's authority vis-à-vis other states, to preserve the state's economic strength by not squandering its resources in unprofitable military ventures, and to retain the state's military capability.

One of the fundamental principles of the Spring and Autumn period was that war with the non-Chou could weaken a state and therefore offer an advantage to its (Chou) enemies. Some small Chou states, engaged in a program of expansionism at the expense of non-Chou populations, were chastised for their shortsightedness. For instance, the small state of Kuo, in 660 B.C., defeated the Ch'üan Jung, yet the *Tso-chuan* describes the event as the prelude to a calamity.[71] Two years later Kuo again defeated the Jung. At this point a seer from Chin predicted certain collapse, because in the same year Kuo had been attacked by Chin and had lost the city of Hsia-yang. Kuo's failure to preserve its forces while in danger was regarded as a guarantee of disaster,[72] and indeed the statelet was eventually annexed by Duke Hsien of Chin.

Most explicit about the advantages of peace is a well-known passage in which the "pacifist" doctrine is squarely presented against the "militarist" doctrine. In 569 B.C. Chin was offered peace terms by the leader of the Wu-chung Jung, who are believed to have belonged to the Shan (Mountain) Jung.[73] A gift of leopard and tiger skins was presented to the Chin so that they would make peace with the "various Jung" (*chu jung*).[74] Chin rejected the proposal on the grounds that "the Jung and Ti know nothing of affection or friendship, and are full of greed. The best plan is to attack them."

[71] *Tso-chuan chu* (Min 2), pp. 261–62 (Legge, *The Ch'un Ts'ew*, p. 128).
[72] *Tso-chuan chu* (Hsi 2), p. 283 (Legge, *The Ch'un Ts'ew*, p. 137).
[73] Their location has been traditionally placed by some near present-day Peking, but they were probably located in the T'ai-yüan region, bordering on Chin. Other Wu-chung groups, however, appear to have inhabited the region north of the state of Yen. See Průšek, *Chinese Statelets*, p. 21, and map, 120.
[74] *Tso-chuan chu* (Hsiang 4), p. 936 (Legge, *The Ch'un Ts'ew*, p. 424).

This position, not unusual considering the previous aggressive stance adopted by Chin with non-Chou people, was however contested by Wei Chiang, who had acted as a diplomat to the Jung and had secured the Jung's terms for peace. He stated in no uncertain terms that a war with the Jung could result in the weakening of the state's hegemony: "The Jung are like wild animals: to gain them, and to lose the Hua, that cannot be!" In the rationale behind this statement, if a state allied to Chin, such as Ch'en, were to be attacked, Chin, weakened by the enterprise, could not help, thus losing not only an ally but also the trust and friendship of the other states, and its position of supremacy among the Chou states.

Wei Chiang then mentioned five reasons for making peace with the Jung, thus establishing a pacifist doctrine based on political strategy. The first advantage of peace was that the land of the Jung could be purchased. The second advantage was that the borderland people would no longer be frightened and would be able to work in the fields. A third advantage was that if the Ti and Jung were to serve Chin, other enemies of the state would be terrified and seek Chin's friendship. The fourth advantage was that by pacifying the Jung through "virtue" Chin would suffer no military losses and its weapons would be spared. And, finally, the fifth was that by relying on "virtue," people from faraway will come closer, and those close will be submissive. At this point, Chin made a covenant (*meng*) with the Jung.

Wei Chiang's argument is worthy of close examination. Besides being one of the most frequently quoted passages on early Chinese attitudes toward "barbarian" peoples, it touches on the main points constitutive of the doctrine of peace. The need for peaceful relations was determined, in Wei Chiang's thought, essentially by matters of political, economic, and military pragmatism. The first point is purely economic. Wei Chiang is careful not to deny the possibility that expansion would be beneficial, but argues that land could be purchased rather than conquered, and he implies that the first option would be, over all, less expensive than the latter. His second point stresses another economic principle: preserving agriculture in the border regions would allow Chin to reap additional revenues.[75] As for the third point, it seems that gaining the respect of foreign peoples would be politically useful for intimidating other adversaries.[76] Assuming that

[75] Opening up wastelands in the peripheral areas, especially available to frontier states, was a basic necessity for expansion. This policy found its most coherent formulation in the economic philosophy of Shang Yang of Ch'in. See Lewis, *Sanctioned Violence in Early China*, pp. 61–64; id., "Warring States Political History," in *Cambridge History of Ancient China*, p. 613. See also the excellent survey of Shang Yang's impact on Ch'in's politics in Steven F. Sage, *Ancient Sichuan and the Unification of China* (Albany: State University of New York Press, 1992), pp. 92–103.

[76] The peace treaty concluded with the Jung was of a type normally concluded between sovereign states, as the *meng* was in fact one of the most solemn types

the treaty was meant to preserve amity and non-belligerence, it also implied the availability of mutual military aid in case of need. What would frighten the other states, then, would be Chin's access to a reservoir of foreign auxiliary troops whose prowess must have been obvious to Wei Chiang's contemporaries. The fourth point is self-evident: Because the Ti were quite strong, wartime losses of people and materiel would be extensive. Why squander one's military strength? Chin, having achieved the position of "hegemon" among the Chinese states, would find it impolitic to become engaged in a potentially expensive and difficult campaign that might weaken its reaction were a crisis within the Chinese states to arise. This was necessary, and here we come to the fifth point, so that Chin could continue to control the Central Plain political sphere and retain its privileged position over the smaller states. The "virtue" of the fourth and fifth points is here synonymous, therefore, with clear-sighted governance, rather than with following moral precepts. No obvious moral or cultural values that would have prevented Chin from attacking the Jung were in Wei Chiang's doctrine. The motives were all political.

Seven years after Wei Chiang persuaded the lord of Chin to join in a covenant with the Jung (562 B.C.), Chin was at the head of a coalition of states that conquered the state of Cheng. The lord attributed this success to the peace treaty concluded with the Jung:

You advised this man of poor virtue to make peace with the Jung and Ti in order to be the leader of the central states. In eight years I have gathered the heads of state nine times, and they have been harmonious like music and agreeable to everything.[77]

This praise was the crowning achievement of Wei Chiang's strategy and the clearest indication of the advantages of peace.

There are other episodes that reveal the pragmatism of the Chou states' policies toward the non-Chou. A decision to opt for peace could be made, for instance, on the basis of the perception of the enemy's behavior. When, in 651 B.C., the Chin commander Li K'o defeated the Ti at Ts'ai-sang, he refused to pursue them because, according to him, it was "sufficient to frighten them" and not risk "provoking a gathering of the Ti." Li K'o made this decision against opposition from both the adjutant Liang-yü Mi, who maintained that by pursuing the enemy the Chin victory would be complete, and the adjutant Kuo Yi, who thought that "in a year the Ti will come [back] because we show them that we are weak."[78] Kuo Yi happened

---

of oaths, which involved the sacrifice of an animal and the use of its blood. See Britton, "Chinese Interstate Intercourse before 700 B.C.," p. 626; and Richard Louis Walker, *The Multistate System of Ancient China*, p. 82.

[77] *Tso-chuan chu* (Hsiang 11), p. 993. [78] *Tso-chuan chu* (Hsi 8), p. 322.

to be right; in the summer, the Ti attacked Chin to revenge the defeat at Ts'ai-sang. These types of consideration weighed on the side of peace. The Chin commander was afraid that an attack on the Ti deep in their territory might cause the Ti to join together in a larger force. Not pursuing them was not a matter of virtue, but one of tactics.

Peace had its advantages, but it remained a temporary solution at best. As we will see in the next section, the overriding tendency of the Warring States' rulers was to incorporate non-Chou peoples and mobilize their resources in the service of Chou states.

The Non-Chou as Resources

In the context of the deadly struggles among Chou states, the non-Chou often represented an essential military resource. In 649 B.C. several groups of Jung, called on by Tai, the son of King Hui, united to attack the imperial capital.[79] Their plot failed; Tai was punished and sought refuge in Ch'i. Relations between King Hsiang and the Jung became strained, and Ch'i had to serve as mediator between the two parties. In another instance, in 627 B.C., Chin mobilized the Chiang Jung and with their help defeated Ch'in.[80] Three years later, however, Ch'in went back on the offensive against Chin, recovered its lost territories, and became lord of the Western Jung, who acknowledged its hegemony.[81] How had Chin initially been able to use the Chiang Jung? The exact nature of their relationship emerged only later (559 B.C.) in a quarrel between the chief of the Chiang Jung and the Chin minister Fan Hsüan-tzu. Wishing to prevent the head of the Chiang Jung from participating in a large interstate conference, the Chin dignitary alleged that an ancestor of the Jung's chief had come, dressed only in straw, to seek Chin's protection from Ch'in and that he and his people were given land to cultivate; instead of showing gratitude, the Jung now spread rumors about Chin that were hurting the state's reputation among the other Chou states. Therefore, the Jung chieftain would not be allowed to attend the conference.[82]

The reply by the Jung aristocrat (a "viscount," or *tzu*) makes it clear that Chin had been using the Jung as a resource to strengthen the state. He said that at the time Ch'in was persecuting them, Duke Hui of Chin,

---

[79] *Tso-chuan chu* (Hsi 11), p. 338. This episode should probably be seen as part of a succession struggle following the accession to the throne of King Hsiang, in 651 B.C.

[80] *Tso-chuan chu* (Hsi 33), p. 498 (Legge, *The Ch'un Ts'ew*, p. 225).

[81] *Tso-chuan chu* (Wen 3), p. 530.

[82] *Tso-chuan chu* (Hsiang 14), pp. 1005–7 (Legge, *The Ch'un Ts'ew*, pp. 463–64).

who regarded the Jung as descendants of the "Four Mountains,"[83] allowed them to settle on the southern frontier, a desolate land plagued by wolves and foxes.[84] The Jung cleared this land, behaved as loyal subjects, and even gave military support to Chin against Ch'in: "if the Ch'in army did not return to its country [i.e., it was annihilated] – the Jung chief stated – this was thanks to us." He pointed out that the Jung had been a valuable aid to Chin in its military and political rise and were not to blame now if "some mistake committed by the troops of your officers have created a distance with the other [Chou] lords." Before withdrawing, the Jung chieftain remarked that "the food, drink, and clothes of us Jung are all different from those of China (Hua), we do not exchange silk with them, and our languages are not mutually understandable." This statement, so often quoted to show the cultural distance between Hua-Hsia and Jung-Ti,[85] indicates, rather, that cultural distance did not mean political distance: The Jung were an integral part of Chou politics and an additional source of soldiers and farmers.[86] Accusation leveled at Chin in 533 B.C.[87] for relying on foreign troops to strike at the heart of the Chou political system indicates that by this time foreign troops were probably being used in such large numbers that they constituted a separate force within the Central States, and their mere presence was becoming a source of anxiety.

The annexation and use of non-Chou peoples by China's larger states parallel the creation of new administrative divisions and growth in the size of armies. To take once again the example of Chin, in 632 B.C. three columns were added to the three already existing armies in order to fight the Ti.[88] In 629 B.C. the number of armies was brought to five, also to fight the Ti.[89] In 588 B.C., after the forced incorporation of Jung and Ti peoples, Chin's armies increased to six – only the Chou House could command a military force of this size[90] – and it is likely that a good many of the new

---

[83] The Four Mountains were the ministers of Emperor Yao. The Chiang surname was descended from one of them.

[84] This took place in 638 B.C. *Tso-chuan chu* (Hsi 22), p. 394 (Legge, *The Ch'un Ts'ew*, p. 182).

[85] It is ironic, in this context, that the Jung chief concluded his speech by singing the ode "Ch'ing Ying."

[86] In another episode, in 638 B.C. (*Tso-chuan chu* [Hsi 22], p. 394) Jung people of the Lu-hun division (perhaps a clan or tribe) were transferred by Ch'in and Chin to the "wilderness" (*yeh*) by the river Yi, where, presumably, there was some uncultivated land.

[87] *Tso-chuan chu* (Chao 9), p. 1309.   [88] *Tso-chuan chu* (Hsi 28), p. 474.

[89] *Tso-chuan chu* (Hsi 31), p. 487.

[90] *Tso-chuan chu* (Ch'eng 3), p. 815 ((Legge, *The Ch'un Ts'ew*, p. 353). For the difference in the number of armies between the Chou king and the states, see *Tso-chuan chu* (Hsiang 14), p. 1016.

recruits came from the conquered Jung and Ti. Some Ti also submitted spontaneously to Chou states when threatened by other Ti people, and may have offered their military services in exchange for protection.[91] Some Ti tribes were also remarkably easy to conquer, as when the state of Lu defeated the Ken-mou people, who probably belonged to the Ti "galaxy."[92] These examples and others make it clear that, by the end of the sixth century B.C., Ti peoples were fully integrated in Chinese states' military establishments.[93]

The incorporation of non-Chou peoples into the armies of Chou states, as well as the protracted fighting with them, contributed also to significant changes in Chou military tactics. By 541 B.C. the state of Chin had moved toward the transformation of its chariot army into an infantry that would be more adaptable to rugged terrain and was specifically intended to fight against Jung and Ti foot soldiers.[94] Resistance in the ranks to this transition must have been considerable because the punishment inflicted on soldiers who refused to comply was death.

As the victorious Chou states kept incorporating foreign peoples, the expansion of their polities required new systems of government to absorb them politically and administratively; thus in the seventh century B.C. the *chou* system was created as a new administrative unit meant to incorporate new subjects, many of whom were in fact non-Chou peoples.[95] The question of how to preserve their loyalty was also debated. As revealed in a Ch'u dignitary's reprimand of his lord in 538 B.C., in which he admonished the lord that arrogant or impious behavior would cause the Yi, Jung, and Ti to rebel, the ruler's ability to govern foreign peoples by fair means rather than by coercion was a fundamental attribute of his virtuousness.[96]

Conclusion

The period of the Spring and Autumn saw the rise of a new relationship between the Chou states and the non-Chou peoples. During the Shang and

---

[91] *Tso-chuan chu* (Hsüan 11), p. 710 (598 B.C.).

[92] *Tso-chuan chu* (Hsüan 9), p. 699. According to Legge, these are Yi people (Legge, *The Ch'un Ts'ew*, p. 304).

[93] A note of 529 B.C. (*Tso-chuan chu* [Chao 13], p. 1359) tells us that the Ti were used as guards by Chin, while in 491 B.C. (*Tso-chuan chu* [Ai 4], p. 1627) the Ch'u minister of war recruited Ti and Jung for a military expedition.

[94] *Tso-chuan chu* (Chao 1), pp. 1215–16. See also Raimund Theodor Kolb, *Die Infanterie im alten China* (Mainz: Philipp von Zabern, 1991), pp. 187, 255–56.

[95] Cho-yun Hsu, "The Spring and Autumn Period," p. 574; Lewis, "Warring States Political History," p. 614.

[96] *Tso-chuan chu* (Chao 4), p. 1252.

Western Chou there had been frequent episodes of warfare between the Shang (and later the Chou) on the one side and, on the other, a host of peoples located around the core areas of both dynasties. However, the principles that regulated their relations are unclear, and we are left with the image of a frontier where the force of arms reigned supreme and where foreign expeditions from Chinese states followed and were followed by the incursions of foreigners in a cycle of never-ending hostility.

Beginning with the Eastern Chou, however, the political relationship between Chou states and non-Chou peoples (whose level of political organization is difficult to assess) became more regular and formalized. This relationship developed on three levels: conquest by the Chou states of non-Chou polities, diplomatic exchange between the Chou states and the non-Chou, and incorporation of non-Chou within the domain of expanding Chou states. Whenever possible, the Chou states attempted to conquer the northern non-Chou peoples and to incorporate them. This policy was carried out in particular during the eighth, seventh, and sixth centuries B.C. by the most aggressively expansionist polities, namely, Ch'i, Ch'in, and Chin. Through diplomacy – meetings, treaties, hostage exchanges, and visits to court – the Chou states tried to preserve peace with foreign powers for as long as they could. The states' goals during times of peace included sparing their resources (people, arms, equipment, and food), demonstrating good neighborly relations, and employing foreigners in the defense of state interests. When they conquered foreigners, the states used them to increase the size of the armies, guard the borders, and open up new lands. In this way, the Jung and the Ti became essential factors in the states' competition for supremacy.

At the same time, various doctrines were formulated that informed the foreign relations of the Chou states. On a general level, especially in matters of protocol and procedures, these doctrines were observed by most of the participating polities, whether inside or outside the Chou political and cultural community. On another level, however, there were significant differences in the way the doctrines were applied to non-Chou peoples. In this respect, I have argued that although presumed differences in morality were invoked to construe the enemy as "conquerable," these moral claims were neither fixed nor applicable to every foreign polity. Closer analysis of their context suggests that they were the product of political developments rather than an indication of a developing sense of cultural cohesiveness within the Chou politico-cultural community. The application of the same moral sanctions to states that were not regarded, at least in principle, as foreign, makes it clear that the idea of a "moral" or "cultural" community was still fluid. This fluidity reflects the political context of the Eastern Chou: in foreign relations the moral discourse was fully subordinated to the diktats of war and intense military and political competition and was adapted to the exigencies of the moment.

Looking at the Chou states' relations with foreign peoples from this angle, whether a "militaristic" or "pacifist" doctrine emerged was a reflection of the objectives of a particular state at a given moment rather than evidence of a greater Chou (Chinese) cultural consciousness expressing itself in terms of "moral insiders" versus "immoral outsiders." The historical information in the *Tso-chuan* and *Kuo yü* also suggests that moral considerations were secondary to what we might call the "rational choices" of polities locked in deadly combat.

Toward the end of the fifth century B.C. the Ti and the Jung seem to have been by and large eliminated as independent polities. Those that survived, such as the state of Chung-shan, remained foreign only in name, while in fact its inhabitants had become culturally indistinguishable from those of the Chou states. The process of political absorption and cultural assimilation brought the northern Chinese states into contact with another type of ethnographic and political reality: the northern nomadic peoples. Whereas the Jung and Ti were, for the most part, farmers and shepherds or mountaineers, whose military skill the Chinese states could easily match, the northern nomads' military tactics and technology, especially as related to riding horses, posed a more serious problem. The following phase of the pre-imperial history of the northern frontier tells the story of this encounter and of its consequences for both Chinese and Inner Asian history.

CHAPTER FOUR

Walls and Horses

The Beginning of Historical Contacts between Horse-Riding Nomads and Chinese States

Introduction

No other period in pre-imperial history transformed the physical aspect and the political import of the northern frontier as much as the Warring States period (480–221 B.C.). In China, the growth of state power and the increase in the size of its armies required a constant expansion of the resources of the state, forcing each ruler to find ways to maximize his own resources and try to neutralize his adversaries' advantages. During the late Warring States period, the tendency toward territorial expansion continued steadily, with the three northern states of Ch'in, Yen, and Chao trying to extend their control over new lands and peoples. The northern frontier was made part of this process of state aggrandizement, but in contrast with the earlier centuries, the Central States were now confronted with a new and far more difficult situation.

As outlined in Chapter 3, the development of pastoral cultures in northern China brought into existence martial societies of aristocratic mounted nomads. As a new "anthropological" type, the nomads appear in Chinese sources under the name of Hu. Their lifestyle was nomadic: they raised animals, fought on horseback, and excelled at archery. Probably organized into hierarchical kin-based societies divided into lineages and tribes, the Hu would soon prove capable of creating empirelike political units. Were they new to northern China? In the fifth and fourth centuries B.C., certainly not, but our knowledge is based solely on archaeological material, and an absolute chronology is still not available.[1] As we have seen, pastoral

---

[1] For a critical appraisal of the dating of Hsiung-nu sites, see, for instance, Sophia-Karin Psarras, "Exploring the North: Non-Chinese Cultures of the Late Warring States and Han," *Monumenta Serica* 42 (1994): 1–125. It needs to be

nomadic cultures probably had matured by the seventh–sixth century B.C., though they may have then been limited to fewer centers and mixed with semi-sedentary peoples.

Judging from their later successes, these martial societies were probably better organized militarily than were the agro-pastoral communities that bordered on China. That the Jung gradually disappeared from the historical record – although their name continued to be used rhetorically or vestigially – may well be the result not only of the assimilation of these groups by the Chinese states but also of the increased power of the nomadic groups that imposed their rule over these peoples, incorporating them within their own polities.

During the late Warring States two crucial events occurred: the adoption of cavalry and the construction, in the north, of military installations known as "long walls" (*ch'ang ch'eng*). Precursors of the so-called Great Wall, long walls constituted the northern lines of military fortifications later linked in a single system by Ch'in Shih Huang-ti after he unified China. Both developments contributed to a pronounced militarization of the north and to the formation of a "harder" border. In this chapter we shall look at the historical causes of this transformation and at the emergence of direct contacts between the nomads and the Chinese states.

The Question of Hu

First Encounter

The Chou states first came into direct contact with the Hu in 457 B.C.: "Hsiang-tzu of Chao [a family of the state of Chin] annexed the Jung, conquered Tai,[2] and in this way drove out the various Hu."[3] This is repeated, slightly modified, in chapter 110 of the *Shih chi*, which reports that Hsiang-tzu[4] "crossed over Mount Kou-chu,[5] annexed Tai and came

pointed out, however, that this author's dating is based on typological evidence and is not immune from criticism (see references to Psarras's work in Emma C. Bunker et al., *Ancient Bronzes of the Eastern Eurasian Steppes from the Arthur M. Sackler Collections* [New York: Arthur Sackler Foundation, 1997]).

[2] Statelet located north of Chao in present-day western Hopei. *Chung-kuo Li-shih ti-t'u chi. The Historical Atlas of China*, ed. T'an Ch'i-hsiang [Tan Qixiang] et al. (Peking: Ti-t'u ch'u-pan-she, 1982), 1: 38, 10–4.

[3] *Shih chi* 43, 1809 (E. Chavannes, *Les mémoires historiques de Se-ma Ts'ien*, 5 vols. [Paris: Leroux, 1895–1905], 5: 81).

[4] A high minister of Chin, also known as Wu-hsü; see *Tso-chuan chu* (Ai 20), p. 475.

[5] *Shih chi chu-yi*, 2135; B. Watson, *Records*, vol. 2: 132. On the reading *kou*, see *Shih chi chu-yi*, 2316.

close to the Hu-Mo."[6] The conquest of Tai was accomplished by treacherous means, as Hsiang-tzu attracted the king of Tai and Tai functionaries to a banquet, where he had them all killed. He then sent his army to conquer Tai (of course, the use of murderous stratagems, especially in dealing with states outside the Chou community, had become a fact hardly worth noting). The Chou states' relations with Tai, including the king's ensnarement, follow the pattern of relations between Chou and non-Chou prevalent in the late Spring and Autumn period and remind us also of the Chin conquest of the Hsien-yü city of Ku, in 520 B.C. As the conquest of the various Jung and Ti peoples that had once surrounded the Chou states was coming to an end, the state of Chin pushed its borders into an area occupied by a kind of people unfamiliar to them, the Hu.

Although "Hu" may have once been used as an ethnonym, in pre-Han sources it was just a generic term for nomads,[7] which, by Han times, had become synonymous with Hsiung-nu.[8] The term "Mo," mentioned in the preceding passage together with "Hu," is an old term that occurs in the *Shih ching* and in the *Chou li* in reference to foreign neighbors.[9] Generally speaking, there is no textual basis indicating that the Hu or Mo constituted a more or less homogeneous ethnic or linguistic group. Rather, "Hu" was used as a blanket term that included mounted bowmen who practiced pastoral nomadism as their main economic activity. Therefore, Hu signifies an "anthropological type" different from the Jung and Ti, but does not imply linguistic or ethnic similarities among the different *hu*.[10] According to an anonymous letter sent to the king of Yen, and recorded in the *Chan-kuo ts'e*:

---

[6] *Shih chi chu-yi* 110, 2315–16, n. 3 (Burton Watson, trans. *Records of the Grand Historian by Sima Qian* [New York and Hong Kong: Columbia University Press and The Chinese University of Hong Kong, 1993], 2: 132).

[7] Jaroslav Průšek, *Chinese Statelets and the Northern Barbarian in the Period 1400–300 B.C.* (Dordrecht: Reidel, 1971), pp. 224–25.

[8] This is evident also from the names of border garrisons and companies engaged in fighting the Hsiung-nu in the Western Regions, such as *Ling Hu* (Those who oppress the Hu) and *Yen Hu* (Those who detest the Hu). See E. Chavannes, *Les documents chinois decouverts par Aurel Stein dans les sables du Turkestan Oriental* (Oxford, 1913), p. x. Cf. Lin Kan, *Hsiung-nu shih-liao hui-pien* (Peking, 1988), pp. 50–51; 152, no. 9; 154, no. 12; 166, no. 47; 167, no. 49.

[9] *Chou Li* 10, 1a (trans. Biot, *Tcheou-li*, 2: 264). See also A. W. Rickett, *Guanzi: Political, Economic, and Philosophical Essays from Early China*, 2 vols. (Princeton: Princeton University Press, 1985–98), 1: 388. On this term see also E. Pulleyblank, "The Chinese and Their Neighbors in Prehistoric and Early Historic Times," in *The Origins of Chinese Civilization*, ed. David N. Keightley (Berkeley: University of California Press, 1983), pp. 442–46.

[10] At the same time, the differentiation between Hu, on the one hand, and Jung and Ti, on the other, must not be taken in absolute terms; in some cases the term *jung*

The Hu and the Yüeh cannot understand one another's language and cannot communicate their ideas, but when mountainous waves arise about the boat they share, they rescue one another as though they were from a single state. The allies of Shan-tung are now as if they were crossing a river on the same boat, but when Ch'in troops reach them they will not rescue one another as though they shared a single state. Their wisdom indeed cannot match that of the than Hu and Yüeh people.[11]

Obviously the meaning of this passage cannot be that Hu and Yüeh were in mutual contact and helped each other against a common threat. Instead, the name "Yüeh" is used as a generic term for the non-Chinese peoples of the south,[12] while "Hu" describes non-Chinese peoples of the north. We can thus reasonably say that, by the end of the fourth century B.C., the term "Hu" applied to various northern ethnic groups (tribes, groups of tribes, and even states) speaking different languages and generally found living scattered across a wide territory. Their fragmentation, however, could be turned, when the need arose, into a superior form of political organization (a "state"). This explains why *hu* appears often preceded by a qualifier that we may take as a marker for a specific ethnic group, as with the Lin Hu and the Tung Hu.[13] Whether or not it had originally been an ethnonym, such a designation had been lost by the late Warring States period.

According to Lattimore, the "new names" for the northern peoples that appear in the Chinese sources reflect a change in the economic specialization of non-Chinese peoples, owing to their forcible expulsion into a more arid ecological zone. Lattimore argues that the Hu and Hsiung-nu were the Jung and Ti of old, who turned to a nomadic lifestyle once they had been pushed into the steppe by expanding Chinese polities.[14] This influential argument cannot be sustained, however, in the light of the archaeological evidence presented earlier, which shows that the transition from semi-sedentary agro-pastoralism to pastoral nomadism took place in the Northern Zone of China over a long period.

In fact, we know little about the relations between northern Chinese and nomads in the period preceding the famous dispute over "Hu" clothing –

continued, somewhat anachronistically, to appear in the sources in reference to horse-riding peoples, such as the Lin Hu and the Lou Fan; see *Shih chi chu-yi* 110, 2315.

[11] *Chan Kuo Ts'e*, 30 (Yen 2), p. 1110 (Crump, *Chan-Kuo Ts'e*, p. 516).

[12] On the Yüeh people and state, see William Meacham, "Origins and Development of the Yüeh Coastal Neolithic: A Microcosm of Culture Change on the Mainland of East Asia," in *The Origins of Chinese Civilization*, ed. David N. Keightley (Berkeley: University of California Press, 1983), pp. 147–75; Pulleyblank, "The Chinese and Their Neighbors," pp. 438–41.

[13] *Shih chi chu-yi* 43, 1322 and 1323, n. 20 (Chavannes, *Mém. hist.*, 5: 44, 81).

[14] Owen Lattimore, *Inner Asian Frontiers of China* (Boston: Beacon Press, 1962 [1940]), pp. 448–49.

that is, a type of attire suitable for riding horses – leading to the adoption of cavalry by the state of Chao, a momentous event that signaled the growing importance of the northern frontier to the process of state building among the northern states. References to incursions, submissions, wars, and court visits are lacking, but we do find scattered allusions to trade, suggesting that nomads and sedentary peoples enjoyed peaceful, though distant, relations, and seeming to contradict the established wisdom that an endemic and irreconcilable hostility existed between them.[15] Compared to the Ti and Jung of the seventh and sixth centuries B.C., the northern nomads from about 450 to 330 B.C. were a tame neighbor, far from the dangerous lot that they would later become.

Trade

One area in which relations between nomads and sedentary peoples seem to have flourished is trade, a consideration supported not only by archaeological data but also by text references. In the *Chan-kuo Ts'e*[16] there are marginal, yet clear indications that the Chou states and the Hu traded with each other, with the Hu exporting horses and furs to the Chou states.[17]

In another example, the *Mu T'ien-tzu chuan* (Biography of the Son of Heaven Mu, a text usually dated around the fourth or third century B.C.), though largely fictional, mentions information that must have originated in actual practices and customs.[18] In the course of his legendary travels,

[15] This point was convincingly argued by Lattimore, who maintained that "this frontier was the voluntarily demarcated limit of the convenient expansion of the Chinese empire; in other words it was not necessitated by the aggression of the nomads against China." See Owen Lattimore, "Herders, Farmers, Urban Culture," in *Pastoral Production and Society: Proceedings of the International Meeting on Nomadic Pastoralism, Paris 1–3 Dec. 1976*, ed. L'Equipe écologie et anthropologie des sociétés pastorales (Cambridge: Cambridge University Press, 1979), p. 481.

[16] The general view of this text is that it contains much anecdotal and fictional material, and therefore should be taken with a grain of salt when used as a historical source. Because the stories are set against a historical background that is generally regarded as pertaining to the period of the Warring States, historians have found it to be of considerable use in reconstructing a given political or social context. I concur with this view. Much has been written on the reliability of the *Chan-kuo ts'e* as a historical source; for a recent appraisal see Michael Loewe, ed., *Early Chinese Texts* (Berkeley: Society for the Study of Early China and the Institute of East Asian Studies, 1993), pp. 1–11.

[17] *Chan Kuo Ts'e*, 5 (Ch'in 3), 178 and 18 (Chao 1), 608 (Crump, *Chan-Kuo Ts'e*, pp. 55, 324).

[18] Loewe, *Early Chinese Texts*, pp. 342–46.

Emperor Mu exchanged gifts with the foreign chiefs that he encountered, possibly a common practice in relations between China and northern pastoralists during the fourth century B.C. The largest "gift" received by Son-of-Heaven Mu was in the form of cattle and sheep, numbering in the thousands, which pointed to the existence (whether he really visited them or not) of specialized pastoral peoples. Even more valuable as gifts, and always mentioned at the head of any list, were horses, numbering several hundreds. Both the Chinese and foreigners alike valued horses, which had long been used in China for military and ceremonial purposes, but it was the north that had a surplus for sale to China. A third type of gift, which appears often but not always, was cereal, such as millet, indicating that at least some northern peoples relied on agriculture as well as pastoralism; other "donations" included wine, dogs, and goats.

The gifts presented by Emperor Mu in return were primarily precious artifacts, such as deer made of silver or gold, a silver bird, necklaces of gold or precious-stone beads, pearls, gold bullion, belts adorned with precious shells, and, sometimes, fine horses in a team (four of the same color), probably meant to be hitched to a royal carriage and used for display.[19] A gift of women was used to seal an alliance, a practice that points to the role of bride giving as an instrument of diplomacy.[20]

Can these gifts find their material counterparts in the recumbent bronze deer and golden animal-style plaques so common in the late Warring State nomadic burials? For the time being, we can register only the possible convergence of archaeological findings and the travels of Emperor Mu, noting that archaeology seems to corroborate the trade mentioned in the *Mu T'ien-tzu chuan*. As romanticized as the story it presents is, this text points to a growing Chinese awareness of the economy and ecology of the northern peoples and reflects a certain amount of knowledge that must have been current in late Warring States China.

Other scattered references also make it possible for us to discern a trend in diplomatic and economic exchanges in which pastoral products were exchanged for high-value items such as silk. In chapter 129 of the *Shih chi*, we find that the land "north of Lung-men and Chieh-shih is rich in horses, cattle, sheep, felt, furs, tendons and horns."[21] The commercial value of this land was not lost on the merchant Wu-chih Lo, who became rich at the time of the First Emperor of Ch'in. He traded silk for domestic animals

---

[19] This type of gift may indicate more than a passing courtesy. The envoy of the Hsiung-nu Hsi-hu-ch'en brought two teams of four horses to the Han emperor as a present. It is possible then that this tradition of diplomatic relations already existed in the fourth century B.C. See *Shih chi* 110, 2896.

[20] See Rémi Mathieu, *Le Mu Tianzi zhuan: traduction annotée: étude critique* (Paris: Collège de France, Institut des hautes études chinoises, 1978), pp. 34–36, 158–61.

[21] *Shih chi* 129, 3254 (B. Watson, *Records*, 2: 434).

with the king of a Jung tribe, thereby increasing enormously the size of his own herds of horses and cattle, whose number "could only be estimated by the valleyful."[22] Who this king was, we do not know, but the story confirms the existence of high-volume trade in the third century B.C.

Horses were also imported at that time by Chinese states from Tai, a region referred to as Ti territory whose inhabitants had urban centers and were organized into "states." The export of horses by the Jung and the Ti peoples, to which the sources refer, may either reflect the domestic production of pastoralists or agro-pastoralists or point to a phenomenon of indirect trade, whereby these tribes were procuring horses indirectly from nomads farther north and west and selling them to China.

Finally, in addition to other objects of Chinese provenance, such as the golden plaques inscribed with characters indicating their weight, hoards of coins have been discovered in the northern territories.[23] Coins and gold are definitely indicative of a complex network of circulation of goods, although its mechanisms are not yet well understood. Yet it requires no great stretch of the imagination to assume that precious-metal artifacts and possibly silk were traded for horses and furs, and that this barter trade was supplemented by monetary trade.

The question of trade, however, must be considered not only in terms of exchange but also in terms of access to markets and communication routes. For instance, Ssu-ma Ch'ien seems to imply that the fourth-century B.C. expansion of Ch'in into the land of the Jung and Ti was meant not only to facilitate trade with the foreigners but also to open up direct and safe routes with the successor states of Chin. This expansion prevented marginal peoples, such as the Jung and Ti of Tai, from playing the role of middlemen in commercial communication among northern states and between northern states and nomads.[24] The later *Discourses on Salt and Iron (Yen T'ieh Lun)*, which possibly took place between 86 and 81 B.C., also refers to the prosperous northern trade, which included the importation of furs and animals (not just horses, but also other domestic animals such as donkeys and camels) from the Ch'iang and the Hu in exchange for a few golden trinkets and some cheap silk.[25] This argument was used, in the first century B.C., to justify the Han Wu-ti expansionist program, but there is no reason to assume that such a trade had developed only recently.

---

[22] *Shih chi* 129, 3260 (B. Watson, *Records*, 2: 440).

[23] Hoards of coins minted in Yan have been discovered near Ch'ih-feng. See Hsiang Ch'un-sung, "Nei meng-ku Ch'ih-feng ti-ch'ü fa-hsien te Chan-kuo ch'ien-pi," *K'ao-ku* 1984.2: 138–44 (*cit.*, chap. 2, n. 71).

[24] *Shih chi* 129, 3261 (B. Watson, *Records*, 2: 441).

[25] Esson M. Gale, *Discourses on Salt and Iron* (Leiden: Brill, 1931; rpt. Taipei: Ch'eng-wen, 1967), p. 14.

If we hypothesize that its trade with the north was based on China's need for horses, we must ask why exactly the horses were needed. The most obvious answer is that horses became a requirement when Chinese states began to create cavalry units. The adoption of cavalry had economic and military consequences, therefore, that are widely held to have deeply altered the relationship between the north and China.

Cavalry

The central piece of textual evidence concerning the adoption of cavalry in China is a well-known debate held in 307 B.C. at the court of King Wu-ling of the state of Chao (325–299 B.C.).[26] The debate was over the adoption of cavalry and mounted archers, inspired by the superior riding expertise of the nomads, which was staunchly supported by a far-sighted king against the conservative approach of his advisers. The debate presents a broad picture of relations between Chao and its neighbors. Moreover, it shows that promotion of this military reform was meant to strengthen the state against all of its foes rather than serve as a special measure to fight off raiding nomads.[27]

The king's main aim was to turn his own Chinese people into mounted warriors to be deployed on Chao's borders with both Chinese and nomadic states. But it is doubtful that much of his new military machine actually was used to "contain" the various *hu*, for at this time the greatest threat to the existence of Chao as an independent kingdom came from the other Central States; indeed, within a few decades, Chao was invaded and conquered by Ch'in.

The position of King Wu-ling in the debate was by no means exclusively, or even primarily, a defensive one. In fact, his rhetoric was definitely focused on the development of offensive military forces. Of the two stated goals in Chao foreign policy, namely, the completion of the territorial conquests initiated by King Wu-ling's predecessor and the establishment of defenses against Chung-shan, the first is openly expansionist. The conquest of the cities of Lin and Kuo-lang had been obtained about thirty years earlier, when Chao defeated the Lin Hu nomads,[28] and the king believed that the

---

[26] To call it a debate may be misleading. Rather, it was a spirited defence of this military reform by the king himself, as he was building consensus by requesting the approval of his ministers and members of the aristocracy. *Shih chi* 46, 1806 ff. (Chavannes, *Mém. hist.* 5: 70–1); *Chan Kuo Ts'e* 19 (Yen 2), 653–67 (Crump, *Chan-Kuo Ts'e*, pp. 296–308).

[27] *Shih chi* 43, 1806 ff.

[28] At this time, in 332 B.C., a "long wall" was erected, which extended westward from the county of Yu, in the Hsün-hua commandery, to the county of Lan, in the T'ai-yüan prefecture. Cf. Chavannes, *Mém. hist.*, 5: 64, n. 1.

time had come to consolidate those territorial gains and expand the state even further. With Machiavellian determination, the king decided to promote the change, even though people might ridicule him, not because he wished to entrench himself against raiding nomads, but because the conquest of the *hu* lands and of the state of Chung-shan was integral to his political project.

Even so, a secondary foreign policy concern of the state of Chao was indeed defensive, and stated in the following passage from the *Chan-kuo Ts'e*:

At present to the east of our state the borders lie along the Yellow, the Pao and the Lo Rivers: we share these boundaries with the states of Ch'i and Chung-shan, but command not a single boat or oarman upon them. From Ch'ang-shan to Tai and Shang-tang we border Yen and the Tung Hu in the east and Lou-fan, Ch'in and Han in the west. Along this line we do not have a single mounted archer. Therefore I have gathered boats, and sought the people who live on the rivers in order to guard our boundaries on the three rivers. I changed our garments to those of the mounted archers to guard our borders against Yen, the Three Hu, the Lou Fan, Ch'in and Han.[29]

However, the main foes do not seem to have been exclusively the nomads but also Chung-shan and the other Chinese states that surrounded Chao: Yen in the north; the Hu in the east; and the Lin Hu, the Lou Fan, Ch'in, and Han in the west. It is clear that Chao's military problems were caused not just by the nomads but also by the high level of conflict among all the states and tribes. Thus, the adoption of cavalry could be presented as a solution applicable to all of Chao's military needs, offensive and defensive.

Still another argument presented by the king is more an ideological than a strategic one. As a filial and loyal follower of his ancestors, King Wu-ling said that he too, like the ancient rulers Chien and Hsiang, who had sought glory by fighting against the Hu and the Ti, wanted to conquer those peoples' lands. By teaching his people to ride and to shoot arrows from horses, he might well attain such a goal.

The decision to introduce cavalry was controversial, and although the king claimed to be ahead of his age, he was equally sure that he would be "exposed to the hatred of the vulgar people." The criticism he feared came first from Kung-tzu Ch'eng, his own uncle, who, summoned to court, predictably accused the king, by diverging from Central States' customs, of abandoning the very traditions that had gained the admiration of the Man and the Yi. "Man" and "Yi" are doubtless terms used here for the "tamed" foreigners who have been incorporated into the Chinese states, in contrast

---

[29] *Chan Kuo Ts'e*, 19 (Yen 2), p. 657 (Crump, *Chan-Kuo Ts'e*, p. 299). Cf. also *Shih chi* 43, 1806.

to the terms – especially "Hu," but also "Jung" and "Ti" – that continued to be used loosely as ideological references to the "northern foreigners" who carried the stigma of being hostile. The gist of Ch'eng's argument, which carried with it a veiled threat, was that by trying to conquer the foreigners the state might loose the support of its own people and allies.

The king's response was pragmatic and in line with the tradition of thought that justified the use of foreigners as "resources" according to the needs of the moment. He articulated three main points: first, and most classically, the king claimed that the way of the sage lay in being able to adapt to circumstances as they change. Second, he expressed cosmopolitan concerns, arguing that it was not right to condemn what was different in other peoples or to be automatically suspicious of what one did not understand about other countries. Third, the king stated that just as he needed boats on the rivers that separated Chao from Ch'i and Chung-shan, so he also needed cavalry on the mountainous borders with Yen, the Eastern Hu, Ch'in, and Hann: it was just a matter of having the right sort of tools. He made clear his intention to imitate the enterprise of his ancestors, who had been openly bent on expansion, stating that "my ancestor Hsiang shared control of Tai with the barbarians for he intended to strike the Hu"[30] and implying that the final conquest of Chung-shan was also a concern. In the end, King Wu-ling convinced Kung-tzu Ch'eng with this argument but was still faced with criticism from other quarters.

These other arguments can be encapsulated in the notion that the ways of the ancients should not be changed, as revealed in the phrase "proper clothing is an injunction of propriety."[31] The opposition to the adoption of Hu garments on the basis of an analogy between garments and behavior was voiced by yet another advisor:

Hu clothing is not thought well of in the world, and wearing it would not be something which would instruct people and make the proprieties complete. If the garment is outlandish, the intentions become disordered; when custom is flouted, the people become rebellious. So it is that one who rules a country does not clothe himself in strange garments. The Central States have no affinity for the activities of the Man and Yi peoples, so this action of yours is not something which teaches the people and makes the proprieties complete.[32]

In his rebuttal, the king availed himself of well-known rhetorical points, observing that the ancient kings did not all have the same rules, that the emperors did not imitate one another, and that in the past laws were created according to the needs of the time and rites were established according to the circumstances. The king went on to dismiss any analogy between gar-

[30] *Chan Kuo Ts'e*, 657 (Crump, *Chan-Kuo Ts'e*, p. 299).
[31] *Chan Kuo Ts'e*, 660 (Crump, *Chan-Kuo Ts'e*, p. 300).
[32] *Chan Kuo Ts'e*, 663 (Crump, *Chan-Kuo Ts'e*, p. 302).

ments, proper behavior, and historical change; he concluded by hinting pointedly at the plain ignorance of the literatus concerning military matters, quoting the saying: "choose a charioteer for his penmanship and he will never understand your team of horses." King Wu-ling clearly saw himself as being in many ways exceptional in his grasp of his age's special needs, and he was not shy in responding to them: "a talent for following the ways of yesterday is not sufficient to improve the world of today."[33]

Out of this debate, several points can be made. The adoption of cavalry, as it is narrated in the *Chan-kuo ts'e*, does not support the conventional idea that cavalry was meant to repel attacks by nomads. If we take King Wu-ling's debating points as a valid representation of his motives, this reform had a broad agenda oriented primarily toward strengthening the state. Reasons for cavalry surely entailed the protection of the borders against all enemies, but the ultimate goal was offensive, intended specifically to subdue the nomads and the state of Chung-shan. Made necessary by deep changes in the circumstances of war and relations with foreign peoples, the adoption of cavalry was presented as something revolutionary; but in fact the king of Chao was following an older tradition in the relations between Chou and northern non-Chou states, that of tapping the foreigners as resources so as to increase one's own chances of survival and victory. Of course, King Wu-ling thereby had exposed himself to the accusation of becoming a "barbarian" himself. This accusation carried serious consequences, and it can be argued that the principal reason for the debate was the king's willingness to show that the rationale for change was not at odds with proper behavior or with a tradition that supported the strategic use of the potential for war represented by foreign peoples.

Foreign peoples must have been key to the realization of the reform not only as a source of innovative military tactics and a model to emulate but also in more practical terms. Once past the political stage, the reform needed to be implemented on the ground. How did King Wu-ling accomplish that? The adoption of cavalry probably relied heavily on local recruits, people who had lived on the frontier for a long time and were acquainted with the nomads, had traded with them, and had the warlike disposition that would make them well suited to military tasks. The *Shih chi* provides significant textual evidence in support of this hypothesis:

Yang and P'ing-yang have customarily traded with the area of Ch'in and the Ti in the west, and with Chung and Tai in the north. Chung and Tai are situated north of [the old city of] Shih. They border the land of the nomads (*hu*) and are subject to frequent raids. The inhabitants are proud and stubborn, high-spirited and fond of feats of daring and evil, and do not engage in agriculture or trade. Because the region is so close to the territory of the northern foreigners (*pei yi*), armies have been frequently sent there, and when

---

[33] *Chan Kuo Ts'e*, 663 (Crump, *Chan-Kuo Ts'e*, p. 303).

supplies were transported to them from the central states, there was a surplus [for the local people to live on]. The temperament of the local people is like that of wild sheep, they are nimble and clever, but not uniform (in their behavior). From the time when the state of Chin was still undivided they were already a source of trouble because of their violent temperament. Yet, king Wu-ling profited by disciplining them, and their folksongs and ways are still the same as the customs they developed when they were under the rule of Chao. Therefore [the merchants of] Yang and P'ing-yang carry out their business quickly in their areas and obtain whatever they want.[34]

This passage implies that the peoples of Chung and Tai became a buffer against the Hu. It also suggests that they were commercially "colonized" by the merchants of Yang and P'ing-yang, who carried out a profitable trade between Chung and Tai and the western regions of Ch'in and other non-Chou peoples. But it was in Wu-ling's time that they were incorporated within "China," henceforth constituting an economic reservoir for pastoral products and a buffer against hostile nomads. Together with other northern pastoral zones, these areas continued to be inhabited by "Jung and Ti," whose herds, according to Ssu-ma Ch'ien, were "one of the riches of the empire."[35] The commercialization of the frontier, the increased strategic interest in the north, and the need for horses are the preconditions leading to the appearance of extensive fortifications in northern China toward the end of the Warring States period, an event that radically changed the concept of the frontier and opened an entirely new phase in the relationship between China and its northern neighbors.

Wall Building

Wall building did not originate in the north, but was a military concept and a technology imported from within the Central Plain, although its function may have changed once it was transferred to another context. Ssu-ma Ch'ien attributes the construction of the earliest walls to King Hsüan of Ch'i, who surveyed the land and then built a wall on hilltops and mountain peaks; in the east this wall reached the sea, and in the west it reached Chi-chou; it was a thousand *li* long and was meant to protect Ch'i from the state of Ch'u.[36] The *Chu-shu chi-nien* (Annals of the Bamboo Books) mentions an attack against Ch'i during the reign of King

---

[34] *Shih chi* 129, 3263 (B. Watson, *Records*, 2: 442).

[35] B. Watson, *Records*, 2: 441.

[36] For an introduction to the early walls, see Ou Yen, "Wo kuo ch'ang-ch'eng te k'ao-ku fa-hsien yü yen-chiu," in *Ch'ang-ch'eng kuo-chi hsüeh-shu yen-t'ao-hui*, pp. 250–63.

Wei-lieh in which Chou forces penetrated a long wall (*ch'ang yüan*).[37] The walls built by Ch'i seem to have been essentially defensive, and to have marked state boundaries.[38] Walls were built not only by the Chinese states. The state of Chung-shan and even some Jung peoples built walls against their enemies. In the case of the Yi-ch'ü Jung, the enemy was the state of Ch'in.

These walls effectively inaugurated a new type of defensive system, possibly as a consequence of the creation of infantry armies whose maneuverability required more extensive use of, and control over, natural features. The "long" walls appear also to have been strategic fortifications aimed at asserting a state's political and military control over a given area. These areas could be strategically important not just defensively but also offensively, inasmuch as control over a mountain pass or a river ford could either block an advancing hostile army or secure passage to one's own troops. Moreover, like roads, walls provide the logistic infrastructure to facilitate communication and transportation, vital elements for armies employed in the occupation or invasion of a foreign territory. Thus military walls could be an integral part of an expansionist "offensive" project, and we can assess their function properly only in their historical context.

Another factor that may have favored the building of long walls among Chinese states was the reduced space for territorial expansion. Whereas during the Spring and Autumn period the stronger states could expand relatively easily at the expense of non-Chou communities and weaker Chou states, by the fourth century B.C. the competition had become limited to a few powerful states, thus increasing the pressure to improve both defensive and offensive capabilities.

In sharp contrast to the all-embracing cultural and political metaphor that the "Great Wall of Ten Thousand Li" has become in modern times, we know little about the genesis and earliest development of northern-border walled fortifications in China. Arthur Waldron has helped to demythologize the Great Wall as an eternal fixture of Chinese civilization, the product of imperial unification under the First Emperor of Ch'in, who joined the pre-existing northern walls, creating a barrier that supposedly would keep out the nomads. Prior to 221 B.C., the warring states of China had erected "long walls" (*ch'ang ch'eng*) both in the Central Plain and in the north; yet why these walls were erected toward the end of the Warring States period and how they functioned are still, in my view, open questions.

---

[37] *Chu-shu ch-nien*, 2.26b (James Legge, *The Chinese Classics*, vol. 3: *The Shoo King*, 2nd ed. [Oxford: Clarendon, 1985; rtp. Hong Kong: Hong Kong University Press, 1960], "Prolegomena," p. 169).

[38] Legge, *The Shoo King*, "Prolegomena," p. 173.

In the standard interpretation of the genesis of the walls, "long walls" started to be built between Chinese states sometime during the Warring States period. The states of Ch'i and Ch'u were particularly precocious, followed by the state of Wei. In the north walls were built by the states of Yen, Chao, and Ch'in between the end of the fourth and the first half of the third century B.C., as a defensive measure against nomadic peoples who were encroaching upon their territory. This measure proved effective, to the point that the northern states could keep the nomads at bay while concentrating on the struggle among themselves. Upon the unification of the empire, Ch'in Shih Huang-ti demolished the internal walls and unified the external ones, thus creating a continuous barrier between China and the northern nomadic peoples.

Yet archaeological data on the actual location of the walls and the cultural environment of the areas in which they were erected raise substantial doubts about the various binary constructions typically used to explain the historical function of the walls. The walls have been chiefly interpreted as the product of tensions between the warring states of China and a politically amorphous north, between agriculture and pastoralism, or, to put not too fine a point on it, between civilized peoples and barbarians. The study of the early walls inevitably suffers from assumptions that arose in the Chinese historical consciousness long after these walls were built, especially during the Ming dynasty, when the wall actually was a military bastion intended to ward off further Mongol invasions.

The significance of "long walls" as a factor in the history of the northern frontier has to be assessed based on the evidential texture provided by the intersecting threads of the history of wall building and of the actual cultural and political contexts in which the walls were built. In this section, I intend to examine the evidence in support of the thesis that the early walls were meant to contain invading nomads, considering it in the light not only of the walls' own history but also of the broader historical context. The result, as we will see, leads to conclusions quite different from the conventional wisdom.

The Written Evidence

References to wall-building activity by the northern states are found in Chinese historical sources, in particular the *Shih chi*. As we know, this paramount monument of Chinese historical literature was written by Ssu-ma T'an and his son Ssu-ma Ch'ien about two hundred years after the first walls were built on the northern frontier. At this time the unified nomadic empire of the Hsiung-nu had created, beginning in 209 B.C., a true political and military crisis that the Han dynasty was able to overcome only with the greatest difficulty. Without going into the details of Ssu-ma Ch'ien's

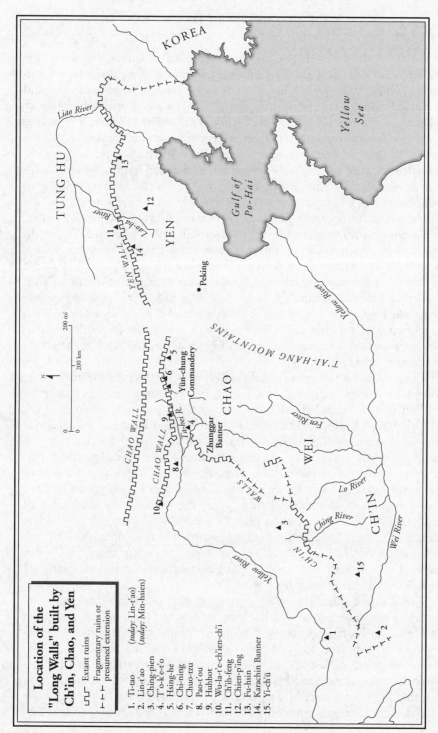

Location of the "Long Walls" built by Ch'in, Chao, and Yen

◡◡ Extant ruins

⊦–⊦ Fragmentary ruins or presumed extension

1. T'i-tao   (today: Lin-t'ao)
2. Lin-t'ao   (today: Min-hsien)
3. Ching-pien
4. To-ke-t'o
5. Hsing-he
6. Chi-ning
7. Chuo-tzu
8. Pao-t'ou
9. Huhhot
10. Wu-la-t'e-ch'ien-ch'i
11. Ch'ih-feng
12. Chien-p'ing
13. Fu-hsin
14. Karachin Banner
15. Yi-chü

Map 3

depiction of the Han–Hsiung-nu confrontation,[39] it should be noted that the historian inscribed such a confrontation in a historical model according to which "Chinese" (Hua, Hsia, Chung-yuan, Chung-kuo, etc.) and "nomads" (Jung, Ti, Hu, Hsiung-nu, etc.) constituted antithetic poles at odds since the dawn of Chinese history. This polarity between a unified north and a unified south was then projected back into the past.

Yet Ssu-ma Ch'ien's account of the late Warring States cannot be regarded as pure ideology. He recorded names and events whose multiplicity and unfolding are evidence of the political and ethnic complexity of both the north, where different groups appear to have been living, and the south, where, of course, Chinese states were still vying for power. Hence, although it is vital to remember that Ssu-ma Ch'ien's narrative of the northern frontier is not itself neutral, one cannot use this argument to dismiss *tout court* his narrative of Warring States history, which was based, we presume, on an extensive knowledge of sources available at the time. With this critical caveat in mind, I should add that historians have never truly questioned the reliability of the *Shih chi* when it comes to the Great Wall. The question I am especially concerned with is whether the *Shih chi* actually supports an interpretation according to which the walls were established as a military defense.

The state of Ch'in began to build walls on its northwestern border under King Chao-hsiang (306–251 B.C.). The pretext for Ch'in's expansion is attributed to a "scandalous" series of events. Apparently, the king of the Yi-ch'ü Jung had illicit intercourse with the Queen Dowager Hsüan, who bore him two sons. The queen dowager later deceived and killed the king of the Yi-ch'ü Jung; then she assembled the army and attacked and destroyed the Yi-ch'ü. After conquering the Jung, Ch'in also expanded to the north into the territory within the Yellow River's Great Bend (today's Ordos region). In this way, Ch'in acquired the northern commanderies of Lung-hsi, Pei-ti, and Shang. At this point, the sources say, Ch'in "built a long wall (*ch'ang ch'eng*) to guard against the Hu [i.e., nomads]." Ch'in's defense line ran from northeast to southwest, extending from the eastern part of the Yellow River's "loop" (Shang commandery) to the southern part of Kansu (Lung-hsi commandery).

The state of Yen expanded mainly in the northeast and occupied both the maritime region north of the Liao-tung Gulf and the Liao-tung Peninsula, including, to the west, a large portion of what is today Hopei province. During the reign of King Chao (311–279 B.C.), General Ch'in K'ai, who had served as a hostage among the nomads, launched a surprise attack against the Eastern Hu, who had placed their trust in him, defeated them, and forced them to retreat "a thousand *li*." Yen then "built extended fortifications (that is, the Great Wall, *ch'ang ch'eng*) from Tsao-

---

[39] This topic is treated at length in Chapter 8.

yang to Hsiang-p'ing, and established the commanderies of Shang-ku, Yü-yang, Yü-pei-p'ing, Liao-hsi, and Liao-tung in order to resist (*chü*) the nomads."[40]

The state of Chao built the northernmost line of fortifications under King Wu-ling, and possibly even earlier. Let us review the events as they appear in the *Shih chi*. King Wu-ling "in the north attacked the Lin Hu and the Lou-fan; built long walls, and made a barrier [stretching] from Tai along the foot of the Yin Mountains to Kao-ch'üeh. He then established the three commanderies of Yen-men, Yün-chung, and Tai."[41] After the conquest of Chung-shan in 295 B.C., Chao continued its drive north, advancing into today's Inner Mongolia and building a series of fortifications to the north of the Great Bend of the Yellow River in the Ho-t'ao region, where it encircles the Ordos Steppe in a wide loop, thus creating the most advanced Chinese fortified front deep into nomadic territory. The *Shih chi* also informs us that, as a consequence of the northern and western expansion of the states of Ch'in, Chao, and Yen, the "central states" came to border directly on the territory inhabited by the Hsiung-nu.[42]

This is the core textual evidence used by scholars to argue that the northern walls had a defensive purpose and had been erected as protection against nomadic attacks. However, none of these statements actually says that walls were constructed as a response to nomadic attacks on Chinese people. What they say is that the walls were built "to repel" or "to contain" the nomads *after* a substantial drive into foreign lands. The building of fortifications proceeded in tandem with the acquisition of new territory and the establishment of new administrative units. In other words, the states of Ch'in, Chao, and Yen needed to protect themselves from the nomads only after they had taken large portions of territory from other peoples and had chased the nomads away from their homelands. Surely at some point the fortifications did acquire a "defensive" function, but the context suggests strongly that this defensive role was subordinated to a grander strategy, one that was militarily offensive and territorially expansionist, pursued by all three Chinese states. To examine the context more closely, we need to zoom in on the wall itself, on its construction and its territory.

Technical Features of the Northern Walls

Chinese scholarship has been engaged for centuries in what we may regard as an antiquarian interest in the Great Wall. Issues of toponomastics, concentrating on the solution of textual problems concerning the exact location of certain portions of the Great Wall, continue to claim a central place

---

[40] *Han shu*, 3748.   [41] *Shih chi* 110, 2885.   [42] *Shih chi* 110, 2885–2886.

in modern scholarship, although these discussions have recently been based also on evidence derived from archaeological fieldwork.[43]

A survey of the early walls built by Ch'in, Yen, and Chao indicates that, together with their common features, mostly related to engineering, the walls also show differences related to topography, strategic choices, and political relations between the states and the peoples who lived around and beyond the walls. Naturally, the varying intensity and success of the archaeological surveys in the interested regions also accounts for discrepancies. (The wall of the state of Ch'in, for instance, has been more extensively researched than the walls of Chao and Yan.)

COMMON CHARACTERISTICS. As already mentioned, the northern walls were not the first walls built by Chinese states. The earliest walls had been built by the states of Wei and Ch'u and are documented in the written records and in archaeology.[44] Hence, the specific technology concerning the building of these walls was shared, in the fourth century B.C., by all states, and engineers were available to design the walls and supervise their construction.

The most important common feature of these "walls" was that they constituted an integrated system of fortifications that included not only manufactured structures but also natural barriers. These lines of fortifications made extensive use of the natural features of the surrounding topography. In mountainous terrain, along precipices and ravines or narrow gullies, the artificial structures may have been limited to a few lookout posts or to stone walls blocking a mountain pass. Across a river floodplain, rolling grasslands, or low hills, the walls were invariably built with mixed stones and earth pressed together. The "walls" also comprised ramparts and ditches, small and large forts, beacon towers, lookout platforms, watchtowers, and other structures. Typically, the walls were made of stamped earth and stones, dug out from the outer side and piled up to form the wall itself, usually on sloping terrain, so that the ground on the inner side would be considerably higher than that on the outer side. Moreover, along these walls

---

[43] For an extensive study of the archaeological context of the Great Wall in Inner Mongolia during the Warring States, Ch'in, and Han periods, see Kai Shan-lin, Lu ssu-hsien, "Nei Meng-ku ching-nei Chan-kuo Ch'in, Han ch'ang-ch'eng yi-chi," in *Chung-kuo k'ao-ku hsüeh-hui ti-yi-tz'u nien-hui lun-wen-chi 1979* (Peking: Wen-wu, 1980), pp. 212–28. For the "Great Wall" region in Ning-hsia during the same period, see "Ning-hsia ching-nei Chan-kuo Ch'in, Han ch'ang-ch'eng yi-chi," in *Chung-kuo ch'ang ch'eng yi-chi tiao-ch'a pao-kao chi*, pp. 45–51.

[44] For a selection of references to the Great Wall in written sources, see AA. VV., "Ch'ang ch'eng wen-hsien tzu-liao chi-lüeh," in *Chung-kuo ch'ang ch'eng yi-chi tiao-ch'a pao-kao chi* (Peking: Wen-wu, 1981), pp. 119–37.

the archaeologists have found, at regular or sometimes irregular intervals, mounds of stamped earth that they assume are to be the remains of elevated platforms or towers. On higher ground, such as hilltops or even mountain peaks, small stone structures have been found, in the shape of platforms, which are thought to have served as lookout posts.

On the inner side of the walls, at varying distances and intervals, we find a number of constructions, in the shape of square or rectangular enclosures, often made of stone. Such enclosures are taken to have been forts garrisoned by soldiers, and the largest among them are assumed to have been the local command stations, where high-ranking officers resided with their troops. Roads internal to the walls served to connect the various garrisons with strategically important areas. Beacon towers, also situated on the inner side of the walls, were used to communicate between the various stations. Although much of what we say about the organization of the troops along the walls is speculative, the number of structures and their spatial extension nevertheless suggest that the efficient use of the walls required a massive military presence, as well as a finely networked system of couriers, postal stations, and checkpoints.

THE CH'IN WALL. Investigations of the early Ch'in wall started with Ku Chieh-kang,[45] who visited in the 1930s the southwestern location of the walls, in the Min-hsien and Lin-t'ao districts of Kansu. Archaeological investigations were carried out in the 1970s and 1980s and important contributions to the knowledge of the Ch'in wall were published by Shih Nien-hai and others. This wall is the best known among the early northern walls, and its location has been defined with accuracy, notwithstanding some lingering controversy concerning the southwestern terminus. Its total length is estimated at 1,775 kilometers, and it actually consists of several separate "walls." Starting in southern Kansu, the line of the wall cuts through southern Ning-hsia, enters eastern Kansu, and proceeds into northern Shansi, ending its run on the bank of the Yellow River in Inner Mongolia (Zhunggar Banner). An important branch line extends eastward for 225 kilometers from south of Ching-pien, reaching almost to the Yellow River.

Three points about the walls' construction should be emphasized. First, 40 percent of the total line of the wall was built on sloping terrain: the higher ground was kept on the inside, a moat was dug on the external (and lower) side, and soil and stones were piled up into a wall. Second,

---

[45] On the Ch'in wall, see Shih Nien-hai, "Huang-he chung-yu Chan-kuo chi Ch'in shih chu ch'ang-ch'eng yi-chi te t'an-su," in *Chung-kuo ch'ang ch'eng yi-chi tiao-ch' pao-kao chi*, pp. 52–67; id., O-erh-to-ssu kao-yüan tung-pu Chan-kuo shih-ch'i Ch'in ch'ang ch'eng yi-yi t'an-suo chi," in *Chung-kuo ch'ang-ch'eng yi-chi tiao-ch'a pao-kao chi*, pp. 68–75.

fortifications have been found near ravines, crevices, and rivers encased in steep gullies. We do not find actual walls made of stamped earth, but elevated platforms and occasionally a fort blocking the entrance to a valley. This type of system accounts for 20 percent of the total length. Third, walls made of stamped earth are seen across plateaus and flat or mildly rolling plains. For construction material the builders used what was available at a location – earth, stone, or a combination of both.

On top of the walls, for its entire length, we find three to four "mounds" (elevated platforms) per kilometer, amounting to a total of approximately 6,300 mounds. Possibly, these were lookout towers and served also as lodgings for soldiers. Throughout the line of the walls, on the inner side, we encounter the ruins of forts, round watchtowers, and beacon towers. Some of these towers are especially high. Citadels and forts are distributed at a distance of three to five kilometers from each other, and their internal area may vary from 3,500 to 10,000 square meters. They are generally walled, though forts built on steep ravines and gullies do not have walls, as the natural topography provided sufficient protection. Beacon towers are located at a distance of one to two kilometers from the wall, on the inner side, and two to three kilometers from each other. In some areas watchtowers (or beacon towers) are built on high watershed crests at a distance of three to five kilometers. The dating of these constructions has been based on the style of their terracotta tiles; for example, the "cloud" decoration is typical of the Warring States period. Along the desert and hills of northern Shansi, researchers have found several roads.

The study of the toponomastics of the walls, based on the historical texts, and in particular on the *Shih chi*, has given rise to a series of controversies. The longest dispute involved the western terminus of the wall, as opinions were divided between the Min-hsien and the Lin-t'ao districts in Kansu. The majority opinion now is that, regardless of contrary evidence in the *Shih chi*, the walls actually started in Lin-t'ao (then called Ti-tao).[46] Shih Nien-hai, after a detailed examination of the course of the Ch'in wall, remarked on its strategic nature. He noticed that the meandering and tortuous line traced by the wall was due to the need to remain on higher ground. Therefore, its twists and turns follow closely the relief map of the region. In some cases the wall extends along rivers, some of which were regarded as military lines of communication. According to Shih, the Ch'in wall ended

---

[46] A contrary opinion is expressed by Shih Nien-hai, who follows the tradition in believing that the old Ch'in wall started in Min-hsien because this was the ancient location of the Lin-t'ao mentioned by Ssu-ma Ch'ien. He explains the ruins of the wall found in modern Lin-t'ao as belonging to the prefectural capital Lung-hsi, established early on to administer this territory. See Shih Nien-hai, "Huang-he chung-yu Chan-kuo chi Ch'in shih chu ch'ang-ch'eng yi-chi te t'an-su," p. 60.

in the neighborhood of today's Shih-erh-lien-ch'eng, in the T'o-k'e-t'o district (Inner Mongolia), because this was a ford of the Yellow River of strategic importance, the point at which the Ta-hei River joins the Yellow River. Following the Ta-hei one could have access to the foothills of the Yin-shan mountains and from there could reach every part of the Mongolian grassland. King Wu-ling of Chao had established the Yün-chung commandery exactly on the river Ta-hei. Hence, it was important for Ch'in to control the ford of the Yellow River to guard against possible Chao incursions. Although Shih remained faithful to the theory that the wall's purpose was to defend Ch'in against the nomads, he introduced here the notion that some of the tracts of northern walls were actually meant either to facilitate access to the steppes or to protect Ch'in from other Chinese states.

THE CHAO WALL. Investigation of the Chao wall began in the 1960s. Relying on the historical records just mentioned, Chinese archaeologists trace the beginning of the construction of the Chao wall to the reign of King Wu-ling, although they cannot provide an exact date. As for its location, the consensus is that the eastern terminus of the Chao wall is in Hsing-ho, in Inner Mongolia; then, proceeding slightly to the northwest, the wall enters the districts of Chi-ning and Chuo-tzu, then continues west passing north of Huhhot, and finally reaches Pao-t'ou. The line of the wall follows the foothills of the Ta-ch'ing and Wu-la Mountains, in the Yen-shan mountain chain. Several long stretches of the walls, especially near the Ta-ch'ing Mountains, can still be seen very clearly for several scores of kilometers.

A secondary, northern, line, not as well researched, begins north of Huhhot and ends north of the northwestern corner of the Yellow River, at the point where the river turns east. This terminus is supposed to have been the location of the fortress of Kao-ch'üeh, which appears in the sources. Along this southern tract, between Huhhot and Pao-t'ou, the wall is made of rammed earth, while some parts are made of stone. The average height is 3.5 to 4 meters. On its southern side one can see ruins of small citadels and beacon towers. Researchers are still debating the eastern and western ends of this line of fortifications, the western terminus being especially problematic, but it is possible that some ruins discovered in Wu-la-t'e-ch'ien-ch'i, west of Pao-t'ou, mark the western end.

THE YEN WALL. The Yen wall (again consisting of several separate lines of "walls") has been researched from the mid-1970s, but its entire extension has not been clearly defined yet, especially in its western part.[47] These walls,

---

[47] References to the Yen walls include: Liu Chih-yi, "Chan-kuo Yen pei ch'ang ch'eng tiao-ch'a" [An Examination of the Great Wall North of Yan during the Warring States], in *Nei Men-ku wen-hua kaogu* 1994.1: 51–53, 68; Hsiang

usually attributed to the late fourth century B.C., stretch from northern Hupei across the Jao Uda League in Inner Mongolia, and seemingly end in Liao-tung. The central portion, running approximately from the Karachin East Wing Banner in the west to the Fu-hsin district in the east, has been investigated more closely. Here we find three roughly parallel lines of fortifications: one running north of Ch'ih-feng, which is attributed to the Ch'in period; one to the south of this, running south of Ch'ih-feng, which is regarded as the northern Yen wall; and a third line further south, which is dated to the Han period. The eastern and western termini have not been conclusively ascertained yet, but a line of walls has been found as far as Liao-tung, crossing into north Korea, and tentatively attributed to the state of Yen. In the west, isolated ruins of the walls are present in various locations, and it is possible that the Yen western terminus may have been close to the Chao walls.

The construction of the Yen "walls" does not differ from that of other Warring States walls, utilizing mainly stamped earth and stone. The stone walls have a width of about four meters. At the base they are mostly built on hills and high mountain peaks. The earthen ones are slightly wider at the bottom (approximately five meters), are made of black soil, and have an external ditch. The main branch of the wall, from the Karachin Banner to Fu-hsin, has a length of 200 kilometers. Along this line researchers have discovered sixteen forts of various sizes. The largest ones appear on both banks of the Lao-ha River. One of them is surrounded by earthen walls of a length of 320 meters from east to west and 260 meters from north to south. It is assumed that these installations were used to garrison a large number of troops. The smaller forts have walls of 30 to 40 meters in length on each side and are built on high places. These were probably smaller checkpoint stations or posts for patrolling troops. Two round stone platforms have also been found on mountain tops. The distribution of these auxiliary fortifications is not as regular as it is for the Ch'in wall; moreover, no beacon towers have been found. Based on tile decorations and the presence of knife coins, pottery, and iron objects, the dating of these walls attributes them to the late warring states period.

A most interesting feature of these walls concerns the discovery, along the line of the walls, on high terrain, of several citadels and round habitations built in stone from where archaeologists have recovered artifacts attributed to the Upper Hsia-chia-tien culture. The archaeologists believe

Ch'un-sung, "Chao-wu-ta-meng Yen Ch'in ch'ang ch'eng yi-chih tiao-ch'a pao-kao," in *Chung-kuo ch'ang-ch'eng yi-chi tiao-ch'a pao-kao chi*, pp. 6–20; Chao Hua-ch'eng, "Chung-kuo tsao-ch'i ch'ang-ch'eng te k'ao-ku tiao-ch'a yü yen-chiu," in *Ch'ang-ch'eng kuo-chi hsüeh-shu yen-t'ao-hui* [Proceedings of the International Academic Symposium on the Great Wall], ed. Chung-kuo ch'ang-ch'eng hsüeh-hui (Chi-lin-shih: Chi-lin Jen-min, 1994), pp. 240–41.

that the original dwellers may have been Tung Hu, that is, a non-Chinese nomadic group that the written sources place in the northeast and against whom the state of Yen fought, "pushing them 1,000 *li* away." In other words, these dwellings may have belonged to people who fled the area after Yen attacked them. At the same time, however, the investigators also confirm that both "outside" and "inside" this line of fortifications the only cultural remains are "non-Chinese."[48] A more likely hypothesis is that these remains belonged to local people who may have been subject to Yen. From the location of their settlements it cannot be excluded that these people also performed a military service for Yen, having been either recruited or conscripted into the Yen army.

Their study of the walls' location has led Chinese archaeologists to believe that the walls did not mark an ecological boundary,[49] that is, the walls were not built to separate steppe and sown, nomad and farmer. In my opinion, they seem most consistently to have been built (far from the political and economic centers of each state) with a tactical goal in mind. This goal was to establish a strong military presence that allowed the state to control the movement of people, be they nomads, moving across plains, hills, or mountain passes; peddling merchants; transhumant populations; or hostile armies. Naturally, the walls also served a defensive purpose, but that purpose must be seen in the light of what they were actually defending.

From the location of the walls, many miles from farming settlements that could be related to either Ch'in, Chao, or Yen, and often built in a territory that could not support agriculture, we can safely exclude that the protection of Central States' agriculture was a strategic goal. It is likely then that the walls were erected to defend the surrounding non-agricultural territory and to establish lines of communication and facilitate the movements of troops as they patrolled this territory, having occupied it by forcing the local population to submit and driving away recalcitrant nomadic groups. This military presence may also have facilitated colonization of these areas by immigrants from the core regions of the states. This point comes into sharper relief as we examine the "cultural" make-up of the regions fenced in by the walls. Thus we must study the extent of the cultural presence of either Chinese (i.e., Central Plain) or non-Chinese (i.e., Northern Zone) cultures, which necessarily relies on the archaeological context, to ascertain the precise function of the walls.

---

[48] See in particular Hsiang Ch'un-sung, "Chao-wu-ta-meng Yen Ch'in ch'ang ch'eng yi-chih tiao-ch'a pao-kao," in *Chung-kuo ch'ang-ch'eng yi-chi tiao-ch'a pao-kao chi*, pp. 6–20.

[49] Tang Xiaofeng, "A Report on the Investigation on the Great Wall of the Qin-Han period in the Northwest Sector of Inner Mongolia." Trans. in *Chinese Archaeological Abstracts*, vol. 3: *Eastern Zhou to Han*, ed. Albert E. Dien et al. (Los Angeles: Institute of Archaeology, 1985), pp. 959–65.

The Archaeological Context

The northern walls were built in the middle of large stretches of grassland. From the cultural remains recovered from these areas, with the exception of some Chinese coins and other objects left in the forts by military personnel, it is obvious that the whole area of the fortifications was inhabited exclusively by non-Chinese, mostly pastoral, people.[50] Here I will present some examples of the material culture of the walls' regions, based on the Northern Zone sites discussed earlier (see Chapter 2, especially map 2, for the location of archaeological sites), that I believe to be close indicators of the broader context.

Archaeological excavations in the proximity of the section of the Yen wall near Ch'ih-feng reveal the presence, in the burial ground of T'ieh-chiang-kou (Ao-han Banner), of typological elements that place it within the general spectrum of the Northern Zone cultural area, such as the Upper Hsia-chia-tien and the so-called Ordos bronze cultures. A large number of bronze objects, such as knives with ringed handles, horse- and bird-motif ornaments, bell ornaments, buttons, earrings, and belt hooks, place this area in a cultural context that is fully outside the Central Plain sphere. The basis for dating the burial place of T'ieh-chiang-kou to the Warring States period, and to no later than 299 B.C. (date of the construction of the wall according to the written sources), rests solely on the assumption that no non-Chinese people could have remained there after the walls had been erected.

As for the Ch'in wall, its region includes some of the most important early nomadic sites of the Northern Zone cultural complex, sites that are dated to the latter part of the Warring States. The westernmost line of walls built by Ch'in is a north-to-south stretch between the districts of Lin-t'ao and Min-hsien (Kansu). Proceeding in a northeasterly direction, the Ch'in walls enter Ning-hsia, and then reach just to the north of Ku-yüan. If we consider that the territory of the Yi-ch'ü, in Shensi, was located to the east of Ku-yüan, we must assume that the wall was built after Ch'in's subjugation of this people. Archaeologically, this area is extremely rich in sites that show the continuous habitation of people whose culture and even physical

---

[50] For an investigation of the "Great Wall" territory in Inner Mongolia and its archeological cultures at an early time, see T'ien Kuang-chin, "Nei Meng-ku ch'ang-ch'eng ti-tai chu k'ao-ku-hsüeh wen-hua yü lin-ching t'ung-ch'i wen-hua hsiang-hu ying-hsiang kui-lü te yen-chiu," Nei Meng-ku wen-wu k'ao-ku 1993.1–2, pp. 16–22. A work of similar scope is Han Chia-ku, "Lun ch'ien ch'ang-ch'eng wen-hua tai chi ch'i hsing-ch'eng [On the Pre-Wall Cultural Zone and Its Formation], in Ch'ang-ch'eng kuo-chi hsüeh-shu yen-t'ao-hui, pp. 60–72, 364–65.

characteristics – according to Chinese archaeologists – were different from those of the people of the Central Plain.

The features of the Ku-yüan culture reflect, from the late Spring and Autumn period down to the late Warring States period, a fairly homogeneous cultural complex characterized by a bronze culture similar to that of the Ordos region. Among the culture's bronze objects, we find the characteristic animal-style ornamental plaques, horse and chariot fittings, and northern-style weapons.[51] Ku-yüan sites show clear connections with sites in Ch'ing-yang county (Kansu), which also show cultural affinity with the Northern Zone complex. For instance, at the site of Hung-yen, a grave and a horse-sacrifice pit were found containing bronze artifacts that have clear Ordos matches at sites such as T'ao-hung-pa-la, Hu-lu-ssu-tai, Hsi-ch'a-kou, and Yü-lung-t'ai.[52] To the west of Ku-yüan, in Ch'in-an county (Kansu), a site was discovered, also dated to the Warring States, that is unquestionably Northern Zone, and also connected with the Ordos sites of Tao-hung-pa-la, Hsi-kou-p'an, and Fan-chia-yao-tzu. Here we even find a *fu*, a sacrificial bronze cauldron of the type normally associated with northern nomads, including the Hsiung-nu. The sites in the distribution area of Ku-yüan, Ch'ing-yang, and Ch'in-an counties are all "internal" to the Ch'in wall, and prove that the region to the northwest of Ch'in was home to pastoral-martial cultures, possibly semi-nomadic or even fully nomadic, but certainly non-Chou. The Chinese presence in the area at this early time can be detected only at sites connected with the wall fortifications themselves, showing the presence of Chinese troops in an otherwise alien cultural environment.

The site of Su-chi-kou, in the Zhunggar Banner, is located between the Ch'in wall and the Chao wall in the north. This Hsiung-nu burial site of the late Warring States period is particularly astonishing for the accumulation of animal-style pole tops that have been found there. These pole tops include six with small deer statues (four standing, two kneeling), two with crane heads, one with a sheep head, one with a lion cub, two with kneeling horses, one with a wolf head, and one that is tubular. Other objects recovered include two disk ornaments with knobs and four bells.[53] Although this site was first assigned to the Han period, it is now believed to be a late Warring States site of the fourth–third century B.C. The style of its bronzes has been compared to that of the Hsiung-nu bronzes from the

---

[51] Lo Feng and Han Kung-le, "Ning-hsia Ku-yüan chin-nien fa-hsien te pei-fang-hsi ch'ing-t'ung-ch'i," *K'ao-ku* 1990.5: 403–18.

[52] Liu Te-chen, and Hsü Chin-chen, "Kan-su Ch'ing-yang Ch'un-ch'iu Chan-kuo mu-tsang te ch'ing-li," *K'ao-ku* 1988.5: 413–24.

[53] Kai Shan-lin, "Nei Meng-ku tzu-chih-ch'ü Chun-ke-erh-ch'i Su-chi-kou ch'u-t'u yi-pi t'ung-ch'i," *Wen-wu* 1965.2: 44–45.

site at Yü-lung-t'ai, also in the Zhunggar Banner. This latter site was also initially dated to the Former Han dynasty and later to the Warring States period.[54] Of extreme interest is that the Ch'in Great Wall makes a large curve around the territory of the Zhunggar Banner and, therefore, fully incorporates these sites, which are among the best-known Hsiung-nu sites of this period.

Another Warring States Hsiung-nu site is Hu-lu-ssu-t'ai. Its location and period place it just to the north of the westernmost extension of Chao's northern line of fortification.[55] Several features in its bronze inventory, including knives, axes, arrowheads, and ornamental plaques, link the metalwork of this site with that found at Yü-lung-t'ai and Su-chi-kou, showing that throughout the whole area of the Ch'in and Chao walls in the northern part of the Ordos region and beyond the Yellow River there was a relatively homogenous non-Chinese culture. Archaeologists attribute this culture to the Hsiung-nu, but it is more correctly defined simply as "early nomadic." Certainly the walls had not been built "in between" Chinese and nomads, but instead ran through an alien land inhabited by alien groups. Some of these groups were incorporated within the perimeter of the walls, some remained outside.[56]

The Frontier after the Walls Were Built

In the years following the building of the walls relations between Chinese states and northern nomads were increasingly fraught with conflict. This friction is epitomized in the story of General Li Mu of Chao, recorded in the *Shih chi*. Because this is such an important document, often used to support the notion of aggressive nomadic behavior, it is worth quoting extensively:

Li Mu was a valiant general in the northern frontier of Chao. He often stayed in the T'ai and Yen-men [prefectures] to protect them from the Hsiung-nu. He had the power to appoint officials, and all the taxes from the towns were

---

[54] T'ien Kuang-chin and Kuo Su-hsin, "Yü-lung-t'ai Chan-kuo mu," in T'ien Kuang-chin and Kuo Su-hsin, *O-erh-to-ssu ch'ing-tung ch'i* (Peking: Wen-wu, 1986), pp. 366–71.

[55] T'a La, Liang Chin-ming, "Hu-lu-ssu-t'ai Hsiung-nu mu," *Wen-wu* 1980.7: 11–12.

[56] For a discussion of the issue of "ethnic relations" in the Great Wall region, see Li Feng-shan, "Lun ch'ang-ch'eng tai tsai Chung-kuo min-tsu kuan-hsi fa-chan chung te ti-wei" [On the Position of the Great Wall Zone in the Development of the Chinese Ethnic Relations], in *Ch'ang-ch'eng kuo-chi hsüeh-shu yen-t'ao-hui*, pp. 73–85, 366–67. The position taken by this author emphasizes economic exchanges and a gradual process, since an early time, of cultural integration.

sent to the army camps to provide for the salaries of the soldiers. Every day he killed several cows to feed his soldiers, he taught his soldiers to shoot arrows and ride horses, and he carefully maintained the beacon towers. He issued a regulation that said: "If the Hsiung-nu invade the border to plunder, you must quickly enter the fortifications, and unauthorized capturing of enemies will be punished by decapitation." Every time the Hsiung-nu invaded, the soldiers lit the beacon fires, and afterwards ran for protection into the fort, and not daring to engage in battle. After having gone on in this fashion for a few years, still there were no casualties or losses. However, the Hsiung-nu thought that Li Mu was a coward, and even the soldiers sent by Chao to protect the border thought that their general was a coward. The King of Chao blamed Li Mu and sent another person to replace him as commander. Over a year later, every time the Hsiung-nu invaded the borders, the new general led the soldiers into an attack. Every time they went out to battle, they suffered many setbacks and had many people killed or injured. Therefore they could not cultivate the land or raise animals on the border. Therefore the King of Chao once again sent for Li Mu. Li Mu would not go, insisting that he was ill. The king forced him to come, and then sent him to lead the army. Li Mu said: "If the great king certainly wants to appoint me, then he should let me use my former method, then I will dare receive the order." The King allowed it. When Li Mu arrived at the border, he followed the old arrangement. For several years the Hsiung-nu did not get anything, but the people continued to believe that Li Mu was a coward. The rewards that the border soldiers used to get were no longer available, and all of them wanted to fight the Hsiung-nu. Li Mu then prepared a large army that consisted of 1,300 war chariots, 13,000 cavalry, 50,000 picked infantry and 100,000 expert archers. With the full army he carried out military exercises. Then he scattered this large force around the pastures and the countryside. The Hsiung-nu first sent a small contingent to raid the border, and Li Mu pretended to be defeated, and abandoned to the Hsiung-nu a few thousand men. The *shan-yü* [title for the chief of the Hsiung-nu] heard of this and then sent a large force to invade [Chao]. Li Mu with his large array of troops, divided into two armies, from right and left encircled and beat the Hsiung-nu, and inflicted a great defeat on them, killing hundreds of thousands of men and horses. Following this, he exterminated the Tan Lan, defeated the Tung Hu, forced the Lin Hu to surrender, and made the *shan-yü* flee far away. Ten years after this, the Hsiung-nu still did not dare come close to the cities on the border of Chao.[57]

The events related to Li Mu's military management of the frontier illustrate two points. First, Chao was continuing in its attempt to expand its northern borders; and second, the defense of the border against the nomads was becoming a more serious affair, requiring ever-larger resources. The soldiers' impatience with Li Mu's defensive approach can be interpreted, in

---

[57] *Shih chi* 81, 2249–5; *Shih chi chu-yi* 81, 1895; see also *Shih chi chu-yi* 81, 1889.

my view, as evidence of an interest of the Chao troops in advancing further into nomadic lands, or at least in plundering their territory. Otherwise the accusation of cowardly behavior would be difficult to justify in a military tradition that placed a premium on the preservation of one's own forces if no benefit could be reaped by attacking the enemy. Moreover, looking at the array of forces mobilized by Li Mu to fight the Hsiung-nu, it seems that the nomads were able by this time to concentrate their troops in fairly sizable numbers. These attacks allegedly were directed against the border cities of Chao, and the reason for those raids could be to profit from plunder or to recover lost territory, or both. It is possible that by its concentrating a large number of troops on the northern border Chao's ability to fight against other Central Plain states became seriously handicapped. At the same time, it shows that the Hsiung-nu were closest to the Chinese borders and were bearing the brunt of Chao's expansion. Li Mu's punitive action was not directed exclusively against the Hsiung-nu, but eventually reached other nomads in the area, presumably located farther from the frontier.

Like Chao, the state of Yen also had substantial contacts with the northern nomads, leading to the appearance of military people who specialized in warfare against the nomads. This applies to a Yen general named Ch'in K'ai, who was sent as hostage to the nomads. The nomads are said to have placed (or rather misplaced) their trust in him. During his captivity he learned their ways, and, as soon as he returned to Yen, he led an attack on the Tung Hu that is said to have driven them back for a thousand li.[58]

By the mid-third century B.C. the Hsiung-nu had become an important element in Central Plain politics. This passage, found in the *Chan-kuo ts'e*, refers to the reign of King Hsi, the last ruler of Yen (254–222 B.C.):

Your Highness [Prince Tan of Yen] must banish General Fan to the Hsiung-nu so that he would be killed. Then I beg that in the west you make a treaty with the Three Chin, in the south you ally with Ch'i and Ch'u and in the north you come to term with the *ch'an-yü*.[59]

Recognized as a regional power, the Hsiung-nu were conducting regular foreign relations with the Chinese states, characterized by hostage exchanges, alliances, treaties, and occasional wars. This type of relations is closely reminiscent of the system operating in the past between the Chou and the Ti, Jung, and other foreigners and suggests that the quality of Central States' foreign relations vis-à-vis the north was not affected too deeply by the fact that these new neighbors were pastoral nomads

---

[58] Cf. B. Watson, *Records*, 2: 133. Watson translates *chü hu* as "to guard against the attacks of the barbarians."

[59] *Chan Kuo Ts'e*, 31 (Yen 3), 1129 (Crump, *Chan-Kuo Ts'e*, 553).

rather than the probably semi-sedentary northerners of old (although the *hu* must have been recognized as the more accomplished soldier). Relations along the northern frontier during the late Warring States period bore little resemblance to the relations that developed between Hsiung-nu and Han after the unification of China, when the Chinese sent goods in tribute to the Hsiung-nu under the "pacification" policy known as *ho-ch'in* (see Chapter 5).

Conclusion: Configuring the Northern Walls in Late Warring States History

During the Spring and Autumn period the relationship between Chou and non-Chou peoples was characterized by two parallel tendencies: seeking expansion into the territory of Jung and Ti, and using Jung and Ti either as allies or as additional troops in the struggle against other Chou states. In the course of this process several northern states of the Jung and Ti were assimilated. Some others, however, continued their existence into the Warring States period (403–221 B.C.). The most important feature in the history of the northern frontier at this time are the instances of direct contact between Chou states and nomadic peoples, resulting from the disappearance of the Jung and Ti peoples as an independent force caused by the conquest wars waged by the Chou states against them and also possibly by the expansion of nomadic polities in the north.

The Great Wall has been cast, correctly, as marking a new phase – a new plateau – in the history of the northern frontier. However, this phase is often understood as one of worsening tensions between nomads and agriculturalists deriving from the expansion and strengthening of the nomadic economy and society in the north. Contrary to this view, I have argued that the walls' presence in the northern regions is consistent with a pattern of steady territorial growth by the states of Yen, Chao, and Ch'in, which adopted a defense technology developed among the Central States to expand into the lands of nomadic or semi-nomadic peoples and then to fence off the conquered territory from other nomadic people who either had been displaced or had grown aggressive because of the military presence of Chinese states in these regions. The walls were part of an overall expansionist strategy by Chinese northern states meant to support and protect their political and economic penetration into areas thus far alien to the Chou world. This is consistent not only with the general trends in relations with foreign peoples as they developed through the Spring and Autumn period but also with the political, economic, and military imperatives facing the Central States in the late fourth century B.C.

The "narrative" of the genesis of the northern walls formulated here, based on the discussion of various forms of evidence, forces us to reconsider the argument often brought to bear to illustrate the nature of the early relations between the nomads and Chinese. This is, in brief, the theory that the nomadic economy was dependent upon Chinese production and that nomads "traded and raided" to counterbalance this deficiency. Being exclusively reliant on animal products and unable to produce themselves an adequate source of carbohydrates, the nomads had to procure cereals by gaining access to resources outside their productive base. From this point of view, then, the quality and depth of the nomads' historical relations with the agriculturalists is explained as determined by their degree of "need" and by their ability to exchange pastoral products for agricultural ones. Naturally, this theory leads to the assumption that there was an economic frontier that in time became political and highly militarized, as the nomads had to exert pressure to extract cereals from their sedentary neighbors.

In ancient nomadic societies, however, such as the Scythians of the Pontic Steppes, it is clear that, where ecological conditions allowed them, nomads incorporated cultivators within their own society. The nomadic aristocracy formed a privileged stratum that appropriated part of the agricultural revenues by political rather than commercial means. Nomads could also trade with communities other than the Chinese states. From the archaeological remains it is clear that farming continued to be practiced in northern China outside the political control of the northern states, thus making the notion that nomads and agriculturalists were divided by sharply demarcated economic lines (defended by the walls) impossible to sustain.

In his investigation of the origin of the "great wall," Waldron finds this theory a useful fulcrum to explain why the pre-imperial Chinese states needed protection. But to the extent that the Chinese sources that refer explicitly to the building of the walls do not mention it as protection against nomadic attacks, this theory in the end rests uniquely on a series of hypothetical links "the need for cereals triggering nomadic incursions leading to the need for defences" that simply cannot be endorsed on the basis of the available evidence. Neither the adoption of mounted archery and cavalry nor the building of walls can be automatically taken as evidence of an aggressive nomadic pressure against China. The wall building undertaken by Yen took place when the state was economically and politically at the height of its power, and the state of Chao started to build walls in the far north after the adoption of cavalry by its military forces. The logical sequence that can be inferred from the historical events directly related to the walls supports the notion that it was the military expansion by Chinese states that led to the incorporation of new lands, driving out the nomads, after which the walls were built and commanderies established. Only several years after the building of walls did a Chinese state, Chao, need to defend

these borders against Hsiung-nu attacks, but these attacks are likely to have
been a reaction to a previous Chinese expansion.

Moreover, the sources yield considerable evidence that it was not the
nomads, but the Chinese states that had more interest in the commercial
development of the northern areas eventually incorporated by means of the
walls. Because these walls were built right in the middle of large stretches
of grassland used for pastoral production, it is not too great a leap of imagination to assume that a possible driving force for the expansion of Chao,
for instance, was the need to acquire horses and warriors for its nascent
cavalry.

In addition, there is no evidence to support that the walls were protecting Chinese settlements in areas traditionally inhabited by alien peoples
engaged mainly in pastoral activities. Could we assume that a massive
migration of Chinese settlers took place into these areas just before the walls
were built, so as to justify the massive investment required? There is no evidence for this scenario. In fact, relations between nomads and China down
to the end of the fourth century B.C. remain fundamentally extraneous to
the historical record. The beginning of the relationship can be dated only
to the time of the military expansion. It is therefore not surprising that the
first mention of the Hsiung-nu in the Chinese sources dates to the end of
the fourth century B.C. Although the degree of organization of the Hsiung-
nu at this early stage is unknown, since Chinese sources of this period give
us insufficient information as to their social and political structure, it
appears that by the late fourth century B.C. the Hsiung-nu were a separate
political entity.[60] Another passage from the *Shuo-yüan* refers to a swift
Hsiung-nu incursion below the territory of Lou-fan in the year 312 B.C.[61]
Although doubts have been cast on the reliability of this information,[62] and
it is possible that Ssu-ma Ch'ien's unsubstantiated statement is mistaken as
far as the Hsiung-nu's involvement in that specific episode is concerned, it
would not be anachronistic to find that nomads had begun to play a role
in Central Plain politics.

It was at this time that Chinese states began to pay attention to cavalry
and to the use of mounted warfare, although large cavalry contingents were
not being used at this time. The forts along the wall were meant to host
garrisons that controlled these still foreign areas and peoples and protected
their "tamed" inhabitants against those nomads that had been expelled. In
contrast, the argument that the walls were a protection for Chinese farming
populations against nomadic raids lacks any textual or archaeological

---

[60] Ssu-ma Ch'ien records that in 318 B.C. the Hsiung-nu were part of a joint force
with Han, Chao, Wei, Yen, and Ch'i in a military campaign against Ch'in; *Shih
chi* 5, 207.
[61] *Shuo-yüan* 1, 1a.
[62] E. G. Pulleyblank, "The Hsiung-nu," unpublished manuscript.

evidence. Such an understanding of the early functions of the walls has several historical implications. First, the expedition to the north led by Meng T'ien under Ch'in Shih Huang-ti in 215 B.C. was not *a reversal* from a defensive to an offensive strategy, which is a notion that has no textual basis but is one that we would need to endorse and somehow to explain if we were to believe that the early function of the walls was purely defensive. In fact, Ch'in's expedition to the north was not a reversal, but a continuation of a policy of colonization and militarization of the north, culminating in the unification of all the extended fortifications built earlier on.

Second, the thesis that the early walls had a fundamentally offensive function provides an insight into the process of formation of the Hsiung-nu confederacy, by making it consistent with a historical phase of increasing militarization of the region where the forts were built, subsequent strengthening of the aristocratic warrior class among the nomads, and eventual centralization of political authority into the hands of ever more powerful tribal chiefs. The military pressure exercised on the borders by various Chinese generals, such as Ch'in K'ai of Yen, Li Mu of Chao, or Meng T'ien of Ch'in, posed a territorial threat in response to which the nomadic aristocracy was able to increase its social prestige and political power.

A pattern in the relations between China and the north in the late Warring States, then, can be outlined. The northern states of Ch'in, Chao, and Yen expanded into territory belonging to alien peoples and built fortifications as a measure of military control and to facilitate the colonization of these areas. Continuing along this pattern, the state of Ch'in, after its victorious reunification of the Central Plain, sent General Meng T'ien to conquer and colonize the Ordos region. This action can be assumed to be at the root of the formation of the Hsiung-nu empire. In the next chapter we will examine the historical evidence concerning the rise of the founder of the Hsiung-nu empire, Modun, and illustrate the process of state formation of the earliest steppe empire in world history.

PART III

CHAPTER FIVE

Those Who Draw the Bow

The Rise of the Hsiung-nu Nomadic Empire and the Political Unification of the Nomads

Introduction

Before the Ch'in unification in 221 B.C., the northern states were able to "contain" the nomads, to push them away from the borders, and to inflict upon them resounding defeats, all without much trouble. In contrast, having emerged from the smoldering ashes of the Ch'in, the Han dynasty (202 B.C.–A.D. 9) was forced for decades to accept humiliating peace treaties and, being incapable of defending the borders effectively, was subject to the nomads' initiative both politically and militarily. Unless the point is made that the nomads at the time of the late Warring States period were *qualitatively* different from the Hsiung-nu of the Han period, we would have to conclude, paradoxically, that the states of Chao and Yen were more powerful and effective in their struggle against the nomads than the Han dynasty under Kao-tsu (206–195 B.C.), Wen-ti (179–157 B.C.), or Ching-ti (156–141 B.C.).

Seeking a solution to the "mystery" of the ethnic origin of the Hsiung-nu, much has been said on the linguistic affiliation of the Hsiung-nu and other possible indicators of their ethnicity. This debate, of which I present a summary in the first part of this chapter, has been so far inconclusive, and opinions as to the language and ethnicity of the Hsiung-nu remain divided. A more promising line of investigation, based on anthropological and historical questions, has concentrated on the economic and other social mechanisms that may have played a role in the formation of nomadic empires. However, these explanations have often remained divorced from a close scrutiny of the historical events.

Even though various studies have referred to the Hsiung-nu empire as a new and different type of political organization, the standard narrative is often confined to pointing out the "threat" that the nomads constituted for the Chinese, presenting the issue in terms of a greater nomadic force that endangered not only the people who lived in the frontier region but even the stability of China as a newly born empire. At the root of this manner of portraying the history of the relations between early imperial China and Hsiung-nu there is, as we have pointed out in Chapter 4, the common assumption that the military confrontation was caused first of all by pillaging inroads into Chinese territory that periodically disrupted peaceful relations.[1] According to this interpretation, such actions in turn produced a Chinese military reaction to stabilize the frontier zone. In consequence, the expedition launched by the state of Ch'in into the Ordos region after the unification of China is not understood as part of a Chinese policy of imperial expansion, but as a measure necessary "in order to keep the Hsiung-nu out of raiding range."[2] At the other end of the spectrum, the argument that the Hsiung-nu had as their ultimate goal the conquest of China, and in particular that in the process of formation of the Hsiung-nu state the leader Modun aimed to build a state power that could ultimately conquer China, has not gathered much support.[3]

The unification of the northern nomads within the Hsiung-nu empire is a phenomenon that cannot be explained by presenting it as an extreme case of one and the same pathology, namely, their inveterate aggressive behavior. This chapter will examine the events associated with the unification of the Hsiung-nu, aiming to establish the most plausible historical interpretation, and to formulate a more comprehensive hypothesis to explain the qualitative difference between the Hsiung-nu empire and the nomads of the Warring States period, and the new relationship that developed between the nomads and China at the beginning of the Han dynasty. Particular importance will be attached to two wide-ranging aspects of foreign politics: the formation of a bipolar world order, and the formulation, on the Han side, of the so-called *ho-ch'in* or "appeasement" policy. Although based in part on older conceptions of foreign policy, the tributary relationship established between China and the nomads under the aegis of *ho-ch'in* was a new development in Chinese theories of foreign policy. This policy deviated dramatically from previous rubrics in that it was no longer pursuant of a project

---

[1] Hucker maintains that the Hsiung-nu, given the possibility, "unhesitatingly raided the Han frontiers" (Charles Hucker, *China's Imperial Past: An Introduction to Chinese History and Culture* [Stanford: Stanford University Press], pp. 125–26); see also J. Gernet, *A History of Chinese Civilization* (Cambridge: Cambridge University Press, 1982), p. 119; Yü Ying-shih, "Han Foreign Relations," in *The Cambridge History of China*, vol. 1: *The Ch'in and Han Empires, 221 B.C.–220 A.D.*, ed. M. Loewe and D. Twitchett (Cambridge: Cambridge University Press, 1986), p. 385.

[2] Hucker, *China's Imperial Past*, p. 45.

[3] W. Eberhard, *A History of China* (Berkeley: University of California Press, 1977 [1960]), p. 73.

of expansion (by incorporating foreigners) or strengthening (by using foreigners as resources or allies) of the state. It was instead a defensive stance whose primary link with past conceptualizations was that it too embraced the notion of the use of a devious "stratagem" against non-equals.

The Ethnic Origin of the Hsiung-nu

The question of the ethnic origin of the Hsiung-nu has long been the subject of heated scholarly debates.[4] Attempts dating back to the nineteenth century to identify them with peoples that appear in Greek sources, such as the *Phrynoi* and *Phaunoi*, have led to blind alleys.[5] On the basis of linguistic evidence valiant efforts have been made to identify at least the linguistic affiliation of the Hsiung-nu. The identification of the Hsiung-nu with the "Tartar" race, comprising Huns, Turks, and Mongols, goes back to the eighteenth-century French literatus H. Deguignes.[6] This theory, inspired by the belief that the Hsiung-nu were the forebears of the very Huns who invaded the Roman empire, survived well into the twentieth century. Hirth, de Groot, and Shiratori all endorsed the "Turkish" equation. The ethnonym "Ti" of the Chinese sources was taken to be an early transcription of the

---

[4] In the following discussion I shall not touch on the old dispute round the relationship between Hsiung-nu and Huns. The gist of the matter is that, although archaeological evidence and descriptions of the Huns in Western sources point rather convincingly in the direction of an Asiatic component among the Huns, there is no evidence that the ruling elite of the Huns, which bore Germanic names, was related to the Asian Hsiung-nu. Whereas the names Hsiung-nu, Huna, and Hun have been recognized to have a common linguistic basis (Paul Pelliot, "A propos des Comans," *Journal Asiatique* [1920]: 141), one must make allowance for the fact that the name, unquestionably prestigious after five centuries of existence as the major nomadic power in Inner Asia, might have had multiple referents, and be equally common across Asia to designate nomads in general, or a certain nomadic tribe or statelet, or the people who spoke a certain language (whose identity is unknown to us), and may have been transferred to Western Asia and Eastern Europe in the wake of the migrations that took place in the Volkerwanderung period without a specific or even approximate relationship to the Hsiung-nu tribal chieftains and peoples of East Asia. Some of archaeological evidence relevant to the issue of the relationship between Huns and Hsiung-nu is exposed in Miklos Erdy, "Hun and Xiongnu Type Cauldron Finds throughout Eurasia," *Eurasian Studies Yearbook* (1995): 5–94.

[5] Paolo Daffinà, *Il nomadismo centrasiatico. Parte Prima* (Roma: Istituto di studi dell'India e dell'Asia orientale, 1982), pp. 87–92; cf. W. Tomaschek, "Die Strassenzuge der Tabula Peutingeriana," *Sitzungsberichte der Wiener Akademie der Wissenschaften*, 102 (1883): 205–206.

[6] H. Deguignes, *Histoire general des Huns, des Turks, des Mongols et des autres Tartares*, 5 vols. (Paris: Desaint & Saillant, 1756–58), 2: 1–124.

name of the Turks, which of course added currency to this prevailing thesis. The ancestors of the Hsiung-nu were identified with other peoples, too, such as the Hsien-yün; indeed, according to Pritsak, the Hsün-yü, Hsien-yün, Ch'üan Jung, and others all emerged from a common ethnic universe to which the Hsiung-nu also belonged.[7]

Karlgren refuted the identification of Hsiung-nu with the Hsien-yün on the basis of linguistic evidence. Haloun and Maspero denied that the tribes of northern China, such as the Ti and Jung, were "Turkish," and in fact contended that the latter were more akin to the Chinese than to Altaic peoples, a thesis later supported by Creel.[8] Ligeti was the first to question the correctness of the Altaic hypothesis for the Hsiung-nu language, and he began to follow an alternative route that took him among the South-Siberian languages of the Yenissei, in particular the Ostyak language.[9] This thesis has been further pursued by Pulleyblank, who in 1962 also concluded that the Hsiung-nu spoke a language of the Yenissei group. As a result, Altaic elements seemingly present in the language of the Hsiung-nu were interpreted as titles that were originally Siberian words but were later borrowed by the Turkic and Mongolic peoples who came to build their own states in the steppe.[10] Bailey, on the other hand, viewed the Hsiung-nu as Iranian speakers,[11] while Doerfer denied the possibility of a relationship between the Hsiung-nu language and any other known language and rejected in the strongest terms any connection with Turkish or Mongolian.[12]

---

[7] Pritsak maintained that the Hsiung-nu spoke a Turkic language similar to today's Chuvash. The "Turkish" hypothesis is also upheld by Eberhard, Bazin, and more cautiously, by Samolin; see Omeljan Pritsak, "Kultur und Sprache der Hunnen," in *Festschrift Dmytro Chyzhewskyj zum 60. Geburstag* (Berlin: Harrassowitz, 1954), pp. 238–49, and id., "Xun der Volksname der Hsiung-nu," *Central Asiatic Journal* 5 (1959): 27–34; W. Samolin, "Hsiung-nu, Hun, Turk," *Central Asiatic Journal* 3 (1957–58): 149–50. Bazin based his conclusions on the translation of a Hsiung-nu Turkic fragment in Chinese script of the fourth century A.D.; see Louis Bazin, "Une texte proto-turc du IVe siecle: le distique Hiong-nou du 'Tsin-chou,'" *Oriens* 1 (1948): 208–19.

[8] Herrlee Creel, *The Origins of Statecraft in China*, vol. 1: *The Western Chou Empire* (Chicago: University of Chicago Press, 1970), p. 200.

[9] L. Ligeti, "Mots de civilisation de Haute Asie en transcription chinoise," *Acta Orientalia Hungarica* 1.1 (1950): 140–88.

[10] E. G. Pulleyblank, "Chinese and Indo-Europeans," *Journal of the Royal Asiatic Society* (1966): 9–39; "The Chinese and Their Neighbors in Prehistoric and Early Historic Times," in *The Origins of Chinese Civilization*, ed. D. N. Keightley (Berkeley: University of California Press, 1983), p. 451.

[11] Harold W. Bailey, *Indo-Scythian Studies. Khotanese Texts* (Cambridge: Cambridge University Press, 1985), pp. 25–41.

[12] Gerhard Doerfer, "Zur Sprache der Hunnen," *Central Asiatic Journal* 17.1 (1973): 2–7.

For the time being we cannot go beyond the conclusion that the Hsiung-nu confederation was a mixture of different ethnic and linguistic groups, albeit one whose "kingly" language – to the extent that it is represented in the Chinese records – is not currently identifiable.

Following the tradition established by the *Shih chi* and later Chinese histories, most scholars in China have accepted as a working hypothesis the view that the Hsiung-nu were the descendants of a number of peoples that appear in the early sources – Jung, Ti, Hsien-yün, and so on – and, at the same time, the ancestors of the later Turks and Mongols.[13] In an influential study, Wang Kuo-wei mantained that the Kuei-fang, K'un-yi, Hsün-yü, and Hsien-yün of the Shang and Chou periods, the Jung and Ti of the Spring and Autumn period, and the Hu of the Warring States period all belonged to the same ethnic group as the Hsiung-nu.[14] This view, held also by Liang Ch'i-ch'ao and several other historians of the 1930s, was not universally accepted. Others maintained that the ancestors of the Hsiung-nu were no different from the Chinese, and in the sixth century B.C. they established a Hsien-yün state: Chung-shan. According to this interpretation, in 295 B.C. when Chung-shan was destroyed by Chao, its people moved to the central territory of Inner Mongolia and Ning-hsia, where the Hsiung-nu leader Modun subsequently became their *ch'an-yü*, and formed the Hsiung-nu confederation. The theory that the Hsiung-nu were related to the Chinese was derived from a passage in the *Shih chi*, where it is said that the Hsiung-nu were the descendants of the Hsia consort clan. However, several scholars have rejected this thesis.

In an article published in 1958, Meng Wen-t'ung maintained that Kuei-fang, Ch'üan-yi, Hun-mi, and Hsien-yün were not the real Hsiung-nu, but were related to the Hsiung-nu's ancestors. Huang Wen-pi also believed that that Kuei-fang, Hun-mi, and Hsien-yün were related to the Ch'iang family – often classified as proto-Tibetan – rather than to the Hsiung-nu ethnic group and that the Lin Hu and the Lou-fan were the only groups that gave rise to the Hsiung-nu state and constituted its inner core.

Another group of scholars, publishing in the 1940s, was inclined to believe that the Hsiung-nu were not a Far Eastern people, but had instead come from the west. Along similar lines, Lin Lü-chih tried to establish an ethnic genealogical tree that could account for all foreign peoples that appear in the sources; his history of the relations between the foreign peoples and China developed in six phases and culminated in the creation

---

[13] The inadequacy of this view was criticized by Maenchen-Helfen, in his "Archaistic Names of the Hsiung-nu," *Central Asiatic Journal* 6 (1961): 249–61.

[14] The positions of Chinese scholars were summarized in J. Průšek, *Chinese Statelets and the Northern Barbarians in the Period 1400–300 B.C.* (Dordrecht: Reidel, 1971), pp. 18–26.

of the Hsiung-nu state.[15] Ma Ch'ang-shou, in his work of 1962 hypothesized a link between Northern Ti and Hsiung-nu.[16]

In his *Complete History of the Hsiung-nu*, Lin Kan, rather than trying to establish ethnic and historical links between the Hsiung-nu and their hypothetical predecessors, explains the process of formation of the Hsiung-nu confederation within a more orthodox Marxist framework. According to Lin, during the Warring State period certain Jung and Ti tribes united and achieved a considerable degree of development; these people then "entered civilization" and established the Hsiung-nu state, while those who had been lagging behind (such as the Tung Hu) remained at a tribal stage. The Hsiung-nu state was in the end the outcome of a basically autonomous development of Jung and Ti tribes settled to the north and south of the Gobi Desert, later joined by fugitives from the state of Chung-shan. Other Jung and Ti, who had previously settled in the Yellow River plain, were subsequently absorbed by the Chinese states. The Hsiung-nu are therefore conceived of as a mixed group that incorporated all peoples (Hun-yü, Kuei-fang, Hsien-yün, Jung, Ti, and Hu) that had previously been active north and south of the Gobi.[17] As for whether the Hsiung-nu originally formed a single tribe, Lin Kan tends to identify them more closely with Hun-yü, Kuei-fang, and Hsien-yün on the basis of the phonetic resemblances.[18]

In discussing the ethnic identity of the Hsiung-nu, Chinese scholars, like their Western counterparts, have also argued about the relative plausibility of a Turkic, Mongolian, Finno-Ugrian, or Indo-European affiliation. The majority opinion is that they were of Mongol stock, but this point remains controversial. Mongol scholars have long maintained that the Hsiung-nu were proto-Mongolic people and trace the origins of the historical Mongols back to them.[19] Official historiography of the former Mongolian People's Republic maintained that as for "social development, customs and culture the Huns [i.e., the Hsiung-nu] were very close to the proto-Mongolian tribes of the Tungus group. It is quite possible that the Huns were of Mongolian origin [sic] but that subsequently, after they seized the 'Western Territory' (Eastern Turkestan, Central Asia), they were largely assimilated by Turkic tribes."[20]

---

[15] Lin Lü-chih, *Hsiung-nu shih* (Hong Kong: Chung-hua wen-hua shih-yeh kung-ssu, 1963), p. 17.

[16] Ma Ch'ang-shou, *Pei Ti yü Hsiung-nu* (Peking: San-lien, 1962).

[17] Lin Kan, *Hsiung-nu shih-liao hui-pien*, (Peking: Chung-hua, 1988), pp. 1–3.

[18] Lin Kan, *Hsiung-nu shih-liao hui-pien*, p. 4.

[19] Irincin, "Dumdatu ulus-un umaradakin-u uɣsaɣatan nuɣud bolon monggolčud-un uɣsa an ijaɣur," in *Monggol teüke-yin tuqai ügülel-üd* (Huhhot: Öbör Monggol-un Arad-un Keblel-un Qoriy-a, 1981), pp. 4–12.

[20] Ye Zhukov et al., *History of the Mongolian People's Republic* (Moscow: Nauka, 1973), p. 72.

Early State Formation

Given that the long philological and linguistic debate has remained inconclusive, simplistic solutions that posit the Hsiung-nu as the *ethnic* progenitor of Turco-Mongol empire builders have been largely discarded, and attention has shifted in recent years to economic and political processes. Because the Hsiung-nu ruled over the first historically documented Inner Asian empire, questions have been asked as to why and how the empire came about, and whether it was really an empire, or was a state or a confederation of tribes loosely kept together.

The autonomous evolution of nomadic society is sometimes held responsible for the achievement of a level of complexity and a capacity for mass mobilization comparable to those of an "early state."[21] A rather quaint hypothesis was proposed by Eberhard, who envisaged three models of nomadic societies – Tibetan, Mongol, and Turkish – each defined by a certain type of pastoral specialization. The most advanced of them, the "Turkish" type, was a society divided into tribes and specialized in horse breeding – in contrast to the sheep and cattle specialization of the Mongol and Tibetan models – and was characterized by the formation of a social and political hierarchy of tribes. These horse-breeding tribes had a migration range wider than other models, which brought them into contact with other tribes. As a consequence, these nomads developed experienced military and diplomatic leadership, which was in turn responsible for the creation of the state.[22] In reality, these models of separate specializations coupled with ethnic and linguistic affiliations cannot be tested at the level of historical analysis.

Krader studied extensively the social structures of pastoral nomads as well as problems of state formation, and assumed the existence of two mutually dependent specialized societies, the agricultural and the pastoral,

---

[21] For a definition of the early state, see Henri J. M. Claessen, "The Early State: A Structural Approach," in *The Early State*, ed. Henri J. M. Claessen and Peter Skalnik (The Hague: Mouton Publishers, 1978), pp. 533–96. Claessen divides the early states into three types: (1) "inchoate," characterized by dominant kin, family, and community, a limited number of full-time specialists, vague ad hoc taxation, and direct contacts between ruler and ruled; (2) "typical," whereby ties of kinship are counterbalanced by those of locality, the principles of heredity are counterbalanced by competition and direct appointments, and non-kin officials and title holders played a leading role in government; (3) "transitional," characterized by an administrative apparatus dominated by appointed officials, kinship ties affecting only marginal aspects of government, and prerequisites for the emergence of private ownership of the means of production, of a market economy, and of overtly antagonistic classes were already found.

[22] Wolfram Eberhard, *Conquerors and Rulers* (Leiden: Brill, 1952), pp. 69–72.

and of a continentwide exchange network between the two. Under this scheme, the development of class differentiation among the nomads is linked to the exchange of the pastoralists' surplus for agricultural goods. As the aristocracy controlled the exchange and exacted tribute from the commoners, the evolution of the state proceeded from the growing gap between these two antagonistic classes. War, plunder, and conquest are, according to Krader, abnormal conditions resulting from the interruptions of trade owing to a defective exchange mechanism.[23] The locus of political and social change is placed within the nomadic society's internal ability to generate surplus.

The attractiveness of this scheme, based on the doubtless existence of both social classes and trade in traditional pastoral societies, tends to be called into question as we fix our attention on specific instances of state formation. For instance, what was the exchange mechanism that went wrong when Modun rose to power, and what was his role in that mechanism? How was this continentwide exchange network organized? What was the volume of exchanged goods? Why is it that at certain times restrictions imposed on trade do not produce any military clash, whereas at other times the openings of border markets are immediately followed by large raiding expeditions? Can we really reduce the inhabitants of Inner Asia, divided as they were into tribes often at war among themselves, to one large specialized society of animal breeders? Finally, why is it that some Eurasian steppe nomads remained stateless?[24] These questions, generated by the historical records themselves, cannot be answered within Krader's scheme, especially because the economic basis of "nomadic" social and political units normally encompassed a variety of types of production, of which pastoral production was the most important but not the only one.

This point leads us to discuss an issue already broached in Chapter 4, namely, the hypothesis that a permanent insufficiency of nomadic production and a corresponding need for agricultural products in due course led the nomads to form political structures functional to the extraction of these products.[25] Anthropological research shows that seldom, if ever, have pastoral nomadic societies been able to prosper in isolation from other economies, in particular agriculture-based ones; moreover, historical

---

[23] Lawrence Krader, "The Origin of the State among the Nomads of Asia," in *The Early State*, pp. 93–107.

[24] On this question, see Peter Golden, "The Qipčaq of Medieval Eurasia: An Example of Medieval Adaptation in the Steppe," in *Rulers from the Steppe: State Formation on the Eurasian Periphery*, ed. Gary Seaman and Daniel Marks (Los Angeles: Ethnographics/USC, 1991), pp. 132–57.

[25] A survey of various theories on the causes of the nomadic invasions of sedentary societies can be found in Hsiao Ch'i-ch'ing, "Pei-ya yu-mu min-tsu nan-ch'in ke chung yüan-yin te chien-t'ao," *Shih-huo yüe-k'an* 1.12 (1972): 1–11.

sources are rife with accounts of nomads preying upon settled peoples. Based on these premises, this theory of "dependency" postulates that phenomena of state formation are linked to the nomads' chronic need for basic necessities lacking in their economy.[26] Because of the "non-autarchy" of pastoral economy, nomads were forced to trade with farmers or raid them. Raids, however, were small-scale enterprises until strong sedentary states imposed a new order on the frontier, making it more secure. To pressure these states into yielding to their economic demands, then, the nomads would respond by creating their own larger political entities, managed by a "supra-tribal" political class, responsible chiefly for military expeditions, and the management of the "extortion" from the military state. According to this theory, the "supra-tribal" nomadic organization would then appear as a response to the emergence of a powerful sedentary state against which small tribal bands were powerless, and which therefore "forced" the nomads to organize themselves into larger political unions.[27]

The assumption that nomads were dependent on the agricultural products of the Chinese presupposes a number of conditions, that is, that the production of nomadic social units excluded subsistence farming, that an exchange system existed between the nomads and China whereby cereals could be obtained for pastoral products, that a surplus of agricultural produce was available in China for trade with the nomads, and, finally, that there were no other sources of cereals available to the nomads besides China. This type of information normally cannot be obtained from the historical sources, so that it is next to impossible to calculate the number of nomads, and their needs, on the eve of the creation of their empire. Hence, this type of hypothesis, while it can be tested in the context of modern relations between nomadic and sedentary societies, remains speculative as an explanation of historical phenomena.

In fact, neither the written sources nor material evidence seem to substantiate this thesis. Archaeological findings show that some degree of farming was practiced among the nomads.[28] Historical sources repeatedly indicate that nomadic raiding parties, sometimes as large as armies, carried

---

[26] Among the most eloquent contributions to this important theory see Anatoly Khazanov, *Nomads of the Outside World* (Cambridge: Cambridge University Press, 1989); Thomas Barfield, *The Perilous Frontier: Nomadic Empires and China* (Oxford: Blackwell, 1989); Peter Golden, "Nomads and Their Sedentary Neighbors in Pre-Činggisid Eurasia," *Archivum Eurasiae Medii Aevi* 7 (1987–91): 41–81.

[27] See the important contribution by Barfield, expressed, for instance, in *The Perilous Frontier*, p. 37.

[28] Nicola Di Cosmo, "The Economic Basis of the Ancient Inner Asian Nomads and Its Relationship to China," *Journal of Asian Studies* 53.4 (1994): 1092–126.

away animals and people, not agricultural products.[29] Anthropological studies of traditional pastoral communities also reveal that not all the people regarded as "nomadic" had the same productive basis.[30] Further anthropological evidence indicates that even in this age of economic interdependence and ease of exchange, at least among some contemporary Inner Asian pastoral nomads consumption of cereals is minimal, and, although carbohydrates are of course essential to subsistence, they are complementary to a diet based essentially on meat and dairy products.[31] Finally, China was by no means the only source of cereals available to the nomads, because oasis and riverine farming existed from Manchuria to the Tarim Basin. An integrated network of commercial and economic relations linked together the Hsiung-nu, the city-states in the Western Regions, and the non-Chinese agro-pastoral communities who lived within the steppe. Centers of agricultural production and of other economic activities, including handicraft and trade, also appear to have existed deep in Hsiung-nu territory, far from the border with China, in northern Mongolia and Transbaikalia.[32]

These considerations call into question the historical validity of theories based on the premise that Inner Asian empires were created by nomads for the purpose of forcing agriculturalists, by the sheer power of military force (or the threat of it), to surrender products the nomads needed or desired, namely, cereals and luxury products. In reality, no such sharp demarcations between nomads and sedentary peoples can be drawn when we look at the internal economy or political organization of large "nomadic" states. Even though the core of the state may have been monopolized by the nomadic aristocracy, in areas ranging from imperial ideology to government structure, military organization, and ritual practices, nomadic and non-nomadic traditions tended to merge and to form original

[29] Hayashi Toshio, "The Development of a Nomadic Empire: The Case of the Ancient Türks (Tujue)," *Bulletin of the Ancient Orient Museum* 11 (1990): 135–84.

[30] A comparison between Khalkha, Chahar, and Daghur Mongol communities shows economic variations that range from almost exclusive animal husbandry to levels of integration of farming and pastoralism. See H. Vreeland, *Mongol Community and Kinship Structure* (New Haven: Human Relations Area Files, 1957).

[31] N. Shakhanova, "The System of Nourishment among the Eurasian Nomads: The Kazakh Example," in *Ecology and Empire. Nomads in the Cultural Evolution of the Old World*, ed. Gary Seaman (Los Angeles: Ethnographics/USC, 1989), pp. 111–17.

[32] S. Minajev, "Les Xiongnu," *Dossiers d'Archeologie* 212 (April 1996): 74–83; A. P. Davydova and V. P. Shilov, "K voprosy o zemledelii y gunnov," *Vestnik-drevnei istorii* 2.44 (1983): 193–201.

socio-political architectures.[33] While it is true that much of the history of the relations between nomads and agriculturalists along the frontier is a history of raids and wars, both sides tended to incorporate parts of the other's people, economic resources (such as land and livestock), or territory. Eventually the border zone became an area in which, no matter whether the dominant power was China or a nomadic state, local economies and cultures were neither purely nomadic nor purely sedentary but a combination of both.

Finally, taking into consideration those historical cases that may show that the nomads' need for agricultural goods might have led to state formation, we see that the Mongol conquest – arguably the most important example of a nomadic state – is regarded as an anomaly, and that Türks and Uighurs achieved predominance after a victorious rebellion against their own nomadic overlords. The only other case left, the Hsiung-nu, does show that their leadership imposed on China a tribute payment that included silk, bullion, and grains, but whether the state was created *for that purpose* is not demonstrable on the basis of the written sources, which instead point to the creation of a political coalition as a reaction against China's invasion of the nomads' territory.[34]

Another line of approach to state formation among Inner Asian peoples has emphasized the role played by sedentary states and has regarded state formation among the nomads as directly subordinate to the influence of previously established states.[35] The idea that nomads developed their states not in isolation from, but in relation to sedentary states is certainly shared widely, though different theories stress different aspects, such as the importation of the idea of universal emperorship or the utilization of the administrative knowledge developed by sedentary states. The "sacral" nature of emperorship and the notion of a "mandate" granted to the political leader by a divine entity are often believed to have been borrowed from the

---

[33] Among the most influential works on the cultural-economic differences between Khitan, Jin, and Yuan dynasties, and their bearing on "sinicization," are the writings by Yao Ts'ung-wu; see, for instance, *Yao Ts'ung-wu hsien-sheng ch'üan-chi*, vol. 5: *Liao Chin Yüan lun-wen (shang)* (Taipei: Cheng-chong shu-chü, 1981).

[34] Thomas Barfield, "The Hsiung-nu Imperial Confederacy: Organization and Foreign Policy," *Journal of Asian Studies* 41.1 (November 1981): 45–61; Nobuo Yamada, "The Formation of the Hsiung-nu Nomadic State," *Acta Orientalia Academiae Scientiarum Hungaricae* 36.1–3 (1982): 575–82.

[35] This is referred to in the anthropological literature as secondary state formation. See Barbara J. Price, "Secondary State Formation: An Explanatory Model," in Ronald Cohen and Elman R. Service, *Origins of the State: The Anthropology of Political Evolution* (Philadelphia: Institute for the Study of Human Issues, 1978), pp. 161–86.

Chinese political tradition.[36] The first evidence that, among the nomads, the notion of a king-making divine entity existed is found in Chinese sources of the second century B.C., and refers to the Hsiung-nu term *ch'eng-li*, which reflects the Turco-Mongol *tengri*. On the other hand, the Chinese term for the heavenly god, "*t'ien*," was introduced to China by the Chou at the time of their conquest of the Shang (c. 1045 B.C.). The Chou themselves belonged to a periphery that included many non-Chinese groups with whom they may have shared elements of their belief system. Moreover, in China the theory of "heaven's mandate," a form of divine legitimation of political rule, is usually attributed to the thought of Mencius, which after all does not come long before the appearance of the Hsiung-nu empire.[37] Given the absence of a relatively long period of sedimentation and experimentation during which the doctrine of "Heaven's Mandate" could have seeped through the frontier and taken root among the nomads, it is indeed possible that the notion of a sacral sanction of political rule was an ancient belief initially shared by both northerners and Chinese that eventually generated, in China, a proper doctrine of Heaven's Mandate, and, among the Hsiung-nu, the notion of a legitimizing supernatural deity.[38]

Doubtless, institutions set up by Inner Asian polities for the administration of settled people were borrowed mainly from the political traditions of China and other sedentary states. However, the issue is not as clear-cut as it might appear at first sight. A number of Inner Asian states survived, as states, without borrowing civil institutions from sedentary states; examples include the Hsiung-nu, the Türks, and the Uighurs. To say that they

---

[36] J. J. Saunders, "The Nomad as Empire-Builder: A Comparison of the Arab and Mongol Conquests," in *Muslims and Mongols*, ed. G. W. Rice (Christchurch: University of Canterbury, 1977), pp. 36–66; Herbert Franke, "From Tribal Chieftain to Universal Emperor and God: The Legitimation of the Yuan Dynasty," *Bayerische Akademie der Wissenschaften, philosophische- historische klasse, sitzungsberichte* 2 (1978): 1–85; Igor de Rachewiltz, "Some Remarks on the Ideological Foundations of Chingis Khan's Empire," *Papers on Far Eastern History* 7 (March 1973): 21–36.

[37] The doctrine according to which Heaven became the ultimate source of temporal authority may have acquired actual political relevance only at the time of Wang Mang's accession (9 A.D.). See Michael Loewe, "The Authority of the Emperors of Ch'in and Han," in *State and Law in East Asia. Festschrift Karl Bünger*, ed. Dieter Eikemer and Herbert Franke (Wiesbaden: Harrassowitz, 1981), pp. 80–111. It is interesting to note in this respect that Wang Mang's envoys attempted to have the *ch'an-yü* accept the legitimacy of Wang Mang's rule by invoking the *t'ien-ming* doctrine; see *Han shu* 94B, 3821. I am grateful to Dr. Loewe for this reference.

[38] For an identification of the Chou deity *t'ien* with the Turco-Mongol deity *tengri*, see Shirakawa Shizuka, *Kimbun tsushaku*, series "Hakutsuru bijutsukan shi" 4 (1973): 184.

were not states unless they borrowed civil institutions and acquired a state bureaucracy is a spurious argument, which is not supported by recent research on the early state.[39]

The issue of civil institutions became important only when Inner Asian states were established astride pastoral regions and sedentary areas that had already developed a tradition of political rule and bureaucratic administration. In several instances, although not always, the forms of administration employed by the "nomadic-type" polity in these areas were derived from the pre-existing civil tradition. However, if we consider the Inner Asian states to which this argument applies, such as the Khitan, Jurchen, Mongol, and Manchu states, we find that the Khitan borrowed some essential elements of their administration, such as the use of multiple capitals, from the conquered state of Po-hai.[40] This example is emblematic of the way in which the frequent assumptions that all civil traditions the nomads employed were derived from the dominant civilizations – China or Persia – tend to obscure an often more complex picture. The Jurchen certainly conformed more closely to the Chinese tradition, but in many ways they also remained faithful to the synchretic nomadic-sedentary model developed by the Liao. The Mongols in China adopted models of government developed by Uighur, Khitan, Jurchen, and Central Asian administrators, and, finally, the Manchu model of governance reflects more closely the mixed Sino-Inner Asian model rather than any purely Chinese tradition of statecraft. In general, when institutions were in fact borrowed, this process was a critical one and depended on the particular composition of the already formed Inner Asian state in question. Possibly even more important is the consideration that the borrowing occurred in a multi-cultural environment and resulted in the formation of a specific Sino–Inner Asian tradition of "mixed" institutions. Hence the postulate that the administrative knowledge developed by sedentary states was essential for the creation of Inner Asian states is only partially true, and potentially misleading.

In conclusion, the theories mentioned so far highlight important areas of investigation and offer precious insights into the mechanisms of state formation whereby the relationship between nomadic polities and central states emerge as a central factor. Yet for these theoretical schemes to be useful, the idea that Inner Asian states developed "in relation to" sedentary

---

[39] According to the typology outlined by Claessen and Skalník, these states would fall into the "typical" category of early states; cf. Henry Claessen and Skalník, "The Early State: Theories and Hypotheses," *The Early State*, p. 23, and Claessen, "The Early State: A Structural Approach," *The Early State*, pp. 589–93.

[40] Although Po-hai was largely settled, its civil tradition was different from that of the Chinese. On this state, see Johannes Reckel, "Bohai: Geschichte und Kultur eines mandschurisch-koreanischen Königreiches der Tang-Zeit," *Aetas Manjurica* 5 (Wiesbaden: Harrassowitz, 1995).

states needs to be substantiated with historical evidence that illustrates how that relationship came into being.

The Rise of Modun's Military Power

The rise of the Hsiung-nu empire unfolded in three "acts." The first was the conquest of the Ordos area, where the Hsiung-nu presumably had their pasturelands, by the Ch'in general Meng T'ien. The second was the epic, and somewhat legendary, rise of Modun to the throne of supreme chief. The third was the institution of a centralized structure of government.

Act I: General Meng T'ien, the Conqueror

Meng T'ien's expedition to the north took place in 215 B.C. The following three passages relate the main lines of this expedition:

I. Later on Ch'in destroyed the six states, and the First Emperor sent Meng T'ien to lead an army of one hundred thousand north to attack the Hu, and to completely acquire the territory south of the Yellow River. Because the Yellow River had become the [new] border, he built forty-four walled county towns overlooking the river, and filled them with people sentenced to guard the borders. Moreover, as a means of communication [he built] the Direct Road, from Chiu-yüan[41] to Yün-yang.[42] Then, taking advantage of mountain ravines, and cutting ditches through the valleys, he built border defenses in order to administer this territory, which covered ten thousand *li* from Lin-t'ao[43] to Liao-tung, and even extended, through the Yang Mountains[44] and Pei-chia,[45] beyond the Yellow River.[46]

---

[41] Name of a commandery and of its administrative center located to the west of the present-day city of Pao-t'ou, in Inner Mongolia. See *Chung-kuo Li-shih ti-t'u chi. The Historical Atlas of China*, ed. T'an Ch'i-hsiang [Tan Qixiang] et al. (Peking: Ti-t'u ch'u-pan-she, 1982) 2: 5–6, 1–6.

[42] County township, located to the northwest of present-day Ch'un-hua county, in Shansi. Sometimes this place name is used to indicate the neighboring locality of Kan-ch'üan (see earlier) (*Chung-kuo li-shih ti-t'u chi*, 2: 5–6, 4–6).

[43] County township located in present-day Min county, in Kansu (*Chung-kuo li-shih ti-t'u chi*, 2: 5–6, 4–4).

[44] Mountain range, today the Lang Mountains in Inner Mongolia (*Chung-kuo li-shih ti-t'u chi*, 2: 5–6, 1–5).

[45] Region to the north of the Great Bend of the Yellow River (Ho-t'ao area) in Inner Mongolia (*Chung-kuo li-shih ti-t'u chi*, 2: 5–6, 1–5, 6).

[46] *Shih chi* 110, 2886.

II. The First Emperor then sent general Meng T'ien with an army of three hundred thousand to the north to attack the Hu, and to invade and seize the land south of the Yellow River.[47]

III. After Ch'in unified the empire, [the emperor] sent Meng T'ien to lead an army of three hundred thousand men to the north to drive out the Jung and the Ti, and acquire the territory south of the Yellow River. He built long walls, and constructed fortifications taking advantage of passes, according to the configuration of the terrain, from Lin-t'ao to Liao-tung, stretching over a distance of more than ten thousand *li*. Then he crossed the Yellow River, and took possession of the Yang Mountains, which wind to the north like a snake.[48]

The attack on the nomads (*hu*) is explicitly mentioned in two of the passages, whereas the third refers to Jung and Ti, which in this case are simply archaic names to refer generically to northern peoples.[49] It is generally conceded that the Hsiung-nu were among the "Hu," although the absence of any reference to them may also reflect their relative lack of power and cohesion at this time. This expansion was the first deep and massive conquest of nomadic territory by a Chinese state; although it followed the pattern established already in the Warring States period, with the building of fortifications and establishment of garrisons in nomadic and semi-nomadic areas, its scale was much larger, and its effects on the Hsiung-nu probably devastating.

Act II: Modun, the Parricide

At this point we need to shift focus to the Hsiung-nu camp. The romanticized story of Modun's career and the founding of the Hsiung-nu state was

---

[47] *Shih chi* 6, 252 (E. Chavannes, *Les mémoires historiques de Se-ma Ts'ien*, 5 vols. [Paris: Ernest Leroux, 1895–1905], 2: 167).

[48] *Shih chi* 88, 2565–6.

[49] Mentioning the Jung and the Ti, and inflating the number of troops to 300,000, can be interpreted as a classical allusion to Duke Huan of the state of Ch'i, who acquired fame for the wars against Jung and Ti and, in particular, to the expedition he led in 663 or 662 B.C. In the *Ch'un ch'iu* this expedition is not reported, and the *Tso-chuan* does not offer an explanation for the omission, but the episode is condemned in the *Kung Yang* tradition (*Kung Yang chu shu*, 9, 3a). Ssu-ma Ch'ien's allusion may have meant to be a condemnation of Meng T'ien's action, which stood for authoritarian hubris and hunger for power. The two historical characters also offered material for a triangulation that was meant to have as ultimate target Han Wu-ti, also responsible for pouring enormous resources into the conquest of the north. In the colophon of the biography of Meng T'ien, in chapter 88, Ssu-ma Ch'ien charges him with showing disregard for the distress of the common people. See Ssu-ma Ch'ien, *Statesman, Patriot and General in Ancient China*, trans. Derk Bodde (New Haven: American Oriental Society, 1940), p. 62.

narrated by Ssu-ma Ch'ien. The hero, Modun, was a gifted child, but his father, *Ch'an-yü* T'ou-man, wanted the son of another of his wives to succeed him. To eliminate the competitor, he sent the young Modun to the Wu-sun people as a hostage; then he attacked the Wu-sun, hoping that they would kill their hostage in retribution. Modun escaped his fate and returned to the Hsiung-nu and his father, who was impressed with his ability as a warrior. This was to be T'ou-man's undoing. Modun gathered a group of warriors who were bound to remain absolutely loyal to him. To train them, as the story goes, Modun ordered each man to shoot Modun's favorite horse, summarily executing any who refused; then he ordered each to shoot Modun's favorite wife, but again a few hesitated, a mistake they paid for with their own lives. Once the lesson had been learned, Modun ordered his followers to shoot his father. Apparently this time no one failed to discharge his arrows.[50] Having in this way eliminated his own father, Modun became the *ch'an-yü*, and, immediately upon succeeding to the throne, proceeded to defend the Hsiung-nu from the aggression of other nomadic tribes. His success allowed him to create a large empire that would humiliate the Han dynasty in 198 B.C. and, over the next few decades, impose its rule widely: from Manchuria to northern and western Mongolia, to the Altai region, to the Tian-shan region, and beyond. Despite the legendary and romanticized elements in the account reported by Ssu-ma Ch'ien, to the extent that we accept the historical existence of Modun, we cannot exclude that his rise to power was achieved through the creation of an efficient bodyguard and the slaying of his own father.

Act III: A New Leadership

The standard narrative of the political organization of the Hsiung-nu after the rise of Modun is given in the *Shih chi*. This is the first detailed account

---

[50] One might be tempted to note a vague analogy with the terrorist method adopted by Sun-tzu to train the palace women of the king of Wu, but the similarity is only superficial. The execution of insubordinate soldiers by a general to enforce discipline is not a particularly original idea exclusive to a single story. More important, whereas the giggling of the palace women brings ridicule upon Sun-tzu, the crucial aspect in Modun's creation of his bodyguard is the preparation of his troops for a coup d'état. Sun-tzu does not ask the soldiers to kill anybody dear to him; in fact, the king of Wu requested that the lives of his concubines be spared. In the case of Sun-tzu discipline is enforced for discipline's sake, but the authority of the king over the general is not disputed. In the case of Modun, the creation of an absolutely loyal bodyguard was part of a subversive project. On these grounds we may discard the notion of a hypothetical derivation of Modun's story from Sun-tzu's. For a translation of Sun-tzu's story, see Ralph D. Sawyer, *The Seven Military Classics of Ancient China* (Boulder: Westview Press, 1993), pp. 151–53.

of the political and administrative structure of an early Inner Asian nomadic ruling elite:

[In the Hsiung-nu state] there are the Left and Right Wise Kings, Left and Right Lu-li Kings, Left and Right Generals, Left and Right Commandants, Left and Right Household Administrators and Left and Right Ku-tu Marquises. The Hsiung-nu word for "wise" is *t'u-ch'i*, therefore they often refer to the Heir Apparent as the T'u-ch'i King of the Left. Starting from the Wise Kings of the Left and Right, down to the Household Administrators, the most important ones [command] ten thousand horsemen, the least important a few thousand; altogether they are referred to as the twenty-four high dignitaries (*erh-shih-ssu ta ch'en*).[51]

Below the supreme "khan," who was endowed with the charisma of "divine" appointment, was an upper-aristocratic stratum. The twenty-four *ta ch'en* formed a supreme political council, headed by the *ch'an-yü*, which effectively ruled the empire.[52] This was not a "tribal council," but a pyramidal structure of "kings" and military commanders. By "kings" are meant, as this was a common term in Han society as well, high-ranking members of the aristocracy who had control over certain portions of the Hsiung-nu empire, territories that were in fact appanages over which they exercised a virtually independent rule. The other high dignitaries, such as the generals, commandants, and household administrators, were members of the court and held high positions, both civil and military, in the central government. Key characteristics of the government – the appanage system, the division of official posts into two halves ("left" and "right," corresponding to east and west), the decimal military structure (e.g., units divided into tens, hundreds, thousands, etc.), and the limited number of top-ranking commanders and ministers gathered in council – are all traits that can also be found in later Inner Asian states.

The term *ta ch'en*, for instance, is used in the Chinese sources to refer to the top members of the government of the Türk (T'u-chüeh) empire (A.D.

---

[51] *Shih chi chu-yi* 110, 2318 ff.; *Shih chi* 110, 2890–2.

[52] This institution is described in detail in Omeljan Pritsak, "Die 24 Ta-ch'en. Studie zur Geschichte des Verweltungsaufbaus der Hsiung-nu Reiche," *Oriens Extremus* 1 (1954): 178–202. See also Masao Mori, "Reconsideration of the Hsiung-nu State. A Response to Professor O. Pritsak's Criticism," *Acta Asiatica* 24 (1973): 20–34. Barfield's description is ambiguous, since he assumes the existence of three levels, the first of which was formed by the *ch'an-yü* and *Ku-tu* marquises, whereas the twenty-four imperial leaders formed the second tier, and the third level was formed by a large class of indigenous tribal leaders. The ambiguity arises from the fact that the *Ku-tu* marquises were not regarded to be part of the twenty-four imperial leaders, and that there is no mention of the Lu-li kings of the right and left, or of the wise kings of the right and left. See Barfield, *The Perilous Frontier*, pp. 37–38.

551–630). Of course, the T'ang chroniclers could have borrowed the term as a rhetorical device to establish a historical analogy between Hsiung-nu and Türks. There is proof that this was not their intent. The Hsiung-nu were said to have had twenty-four high dignitaries, and the Türks were said to have had twenty-eight. The numerical difference would be inconsistent with an effort to construct a historical analogy. This difference can be explained only as the result of specific information about the Türks that the Chinese chronicle was documenting; the similarity between the Hsiung-nu and the Türk government structures was because of the institutional continuity within the Inner Asian political tradition. Likewise, the decimal structure of the army continued among the Inner Asian polities that had grown into states, and in which the tribal armies had been replaced by a central army.

Finally, the following passage reveals the tribal element in the Hsiung-nu government:

The highest positions are all hereditary offices. The three clans of Hu-yen, Lan, and, more recently, Hsü-pu are their aristocratic families. [. . .] Each group has its portion of territory [. . .] but the Wise Kings of the Left and Right and the Lu-li Kings hold the largest [lands]; the Left and Right Ku-tu Marquises assist in the government. Each of the twenty-four supreme chiefs appoints his own "chiefs of thousands," "chiefs of hundreds," "chiefs of tens," subordinate vassals, ministers, commanders-in-chief, household administrators, *chü-ch'ü* and so on.[53]

Tribal and clan affiliations were a central feature of the Inner Asian political system. Only members of certain lineages could occupy the highest political offices, and, normally, supreme political power was regarded as the monopoly of a single clan, that of the "charismatic" leader who unified the many tribes into a state. Hereditary access to state positions was to endure as an essential aspect of Inner Asian politics down to the Ch'ing dynasty (1644–1911).

The Formation of the Hsiung-nu State in Historical Perspective

On the basis of examples drawn from other instances of state formation among Inner Asian peoples, the plausible details in the story of Modun's rise are his creation of a bodyguard, the coup d'état against the tribal aristocracy, and the centralization of political power. Presumably, the succession struggle occurred in a moment of crisis for Hsiung-nu society, as the expedition of Meng T'ien forced the Hsiung-nu to leave their pasturelands,

[53] *Shih chi chu-yi* 110, 2318 ff.; *Shih chi* 110, 2890–2.

and Modun's creation of an independent military force emerged out of the heightened military mobilization of Hsiung-nu society, as some men took up arms and became professional soldiers. The rise of Modun corresponded to the centralization of power, evident in the composition of the Hsiung-nu government, which Ssu-ma Ch'ien described in great detail.

Crisis, militarization, and centralization are concepts common to the political process of state formation in Inner Asia history. The initial momentum for "state building" often came from a challenge to the current leadership at a time of economic and social crisis, followed by generalized violence, and then by military mobilization. Eventually, under an effective military leader, a process of political centralization occurred that would lay the foundation for territorial and political expansion. Before we examine this process further, and focus on the Hsiung-nu in Modun's time, an explanation of each of these stages of state formation is in order.[54]

Crisis

Traditional pastoral societies were typically divided into kin groups that shared a common lineage and territory, and whose smallest social unit was the familial nucleus.[55] This social organization provided the basis for political cohesion, necessary for production, defense, migration, and war. Social stratification entailed the existence of two separate classes, the commoners and the aristocracy. Members of the aristocracy owed their privileged position to birth and personal qualities. Some lineages were recognized as being endowed with higher prestige, and the top political people usually belonged to these lineages. Social positions within the lineage depended on inherited wealth and status, as well as on individual abilities. The aristocracy provided leadership in the organization of large hunts and of raids against neighboring groups (whether nomadic or settled), which served the purpose of establishing social ranks and testing leadership skills.

Sparse, extensive pastoral production, supplemented with hunting and limited farming, allowed for little surplus, which was often exchanged with neighboring communities. This economic basis left limited margins for the formation of any class not directly involved in production; as a result, the

[54] The following sections are based in part on Nicola Di Cosmo, "State Formation and Periodization in Inner Asian History," *Journal of World History* 10.1 (Spring 1999): 1–40.

[55] Lawrence Krader, *Social Organization of the Mongol-Turkic Pastoral Nomads* (The Hague: Mouton, 1963), pp. 316–72; Elisabeth Bacon, *Obok: A Study of Social Structure in Eurasia* (New York: Wenner-Gren Foundation, 1958), pp. 106–19.

number of members of the tribal aristocracy effectively disengaged from direct production was, under normal circumstances, limited.[56] Moreover, pastoral nomadism is an extremely fragile economic system, and a number of unfavorable circumstances could easily ignite an economic crisis.[57] Historically, the delicate balance between consumption and production came to be altered when the crisis involved more than a restricted number of people; at these difficult times entire tribes and peoples mobilized for war or for large-scale migrations. The notion of crisis, then, is central to the state-building process.

Crises could be of different types. In a pastoral environment a severe winter, a drought, or an epidemic could reduce the size of their herds below the level sufficient to sustain the people. Overgrazing could reduce the fertility of the soil and nutritional value of the grass, thus forcing the people to seek better land elsewhere. Economic need, however, did not automatically produce political unity. On the contrary, among the tribal peoples and chiefdoms of Inner Asia on the eve of the emergence of a state the more common picture was one of social disaggregation, with the poorest abandoned to their own fate, and the more daring members of the tribe banding together in semi-lawless associations.

Time and again the sources indicate that when large raiding parties attacked sedentary states they took away animals and people. This need for the very products that they were supposed to produce themselves is a possible indicator of an ongoing economic crisis. On the one hand, economic need in general disrupts social relations; on the other hand, the breakdown of tribal bonds allowed for a greater degree of social mobility. Leadership ability counted more than birth or lineage, and effective leaders could prove themselves and emerge at these times, thus becoming catalysts for new forms of political organization.

A crisis situation could also be brought about by other causes. For instance, tensions between ethnic groups, or between "enslaved" and "master" tribes, could result in protracted friction, and finally explode into an all-out war. In the rebellion of the Türks against their Jou-jan overlord (A.D. 551) and in the struggle of the Jurchen against the Khitan (1115), we can identify two such crises. A crisis could also be ignited by an invasion by the regular army of a sedentary state, which would occupy and settle the land. If the established tribal leadership was unable to respond to the

---

[56] According to a census carried out in Mongolia among traditional herders in 1918, only six of the 401 families examined were considered to be members of the nobility, whereas the overwhelming majority were direct producers. See Herbert Vreeland, *Mongol Community and Kinship Structure* (New Haven: Human Relations Area Files, 1957).

[57] On this question, see the excellent synopsis in Khazanov, *Nomads of the Outside World* (Cambridge: Cambridge University Press, 1984), pp. 69–84.

challenge, an emergency situation would arise, thereby creating the conditions for the advent of new leadership.

In a social and economic crisis the political power of the military aristocracy was enhanced. Unfortunately, the beginnings of Inner Asian states are often shrouded in mystery or covered in a thick coating of legend. But generally the rise of new protagonists was marked by a disregard for traditional rules of seniority, by individual ambition, by sheer military ability, and by personal charisma. When successful, these new leaders were able to impose a new political order by dismantling the obsolete tribal hierarchies.

Returning to the Hsiung-nu, at the beginning of chapter 110 Ssu-ma Ch'ien identifies the "crisis" (*chi*) as the catalyst for political action among the nomads, and then goes on to provide an account of the rise of Modun. This offers textual support for the notion that the unification of the Hsiung-nu took place in reaction to a crisis.

Militarization

A key aspect of the "crisis," in its social and political implications, was the militarization of society. Although it is true that "nomadic-type" peoples were all accustomed to fighting, it is not true that they were constantly engaged in war. More often, their armed conflicts were limited to raiding the camp of a traditional enemy, avenging a wrong, or stealing a wife. When a crisis arose, however, the mobilization for war was not limited to the formation of small armed bands, but meant the creation of actual tribal armies and the proliferation of military leaders. Every male able to fight became a soldier and engaged in actual campaigns against nomadic foes or against the regular armies of sedentary states that were much longer and more complex than the occasional raids. When the crisis forced tribal groups to move away from their ancestral lands, their migrations also required tightly organized military escorts. As an example of the extent of militarization of Inner Asian societies at certain times, it has been calculated that when Chingis Khan rose to power the total number of adult males fit for military service was no more than fifty to one hundred thousand, yet the Mongol army in 1206 has been estimated at over one hundred thousand men. If the figures are even approximately correct, they suggest that practically every adult male had been drafted.[58]

[58] Valery P. Alekseev, "Some Aspects of the Study of Productive Forces in the Empire of Chengiz Khan," in *Rulers from the Steppe*, p. 191; Desmond H. Martin, *The Rise of Chingis Khan and His Conquest of North China* (Baltimore: The Johns Hopkins Press, 1950), pp. 12–15; Desmond H. Martin, "The Mongol Army," *Journal of the Royal Asiatic Society* (1943): 46–85.

Andreski devised three parameters to define social structures on the basis of military organization: military participation ratio, subordination, and cohesion. According to these criteria, the Inner Asian tribal society on the eve of state formation can be characterized by a high military participation ratio, a low degree of subordination, and a high degree of cohesion. Intensive warfare, among other possible factors, would produce a higher degree of subordination, resulting in a "widely conscriptive" (or "neferic") society marked by high levels of all three parameters. This is, in fact, a type of social transition attributed by Andreski to Eurasian nomads.[59]

This analytical approach is useful as long as we realize its limits. As the power and authority of the charismatic leader-to-be grew, members of defeated tribes were incorporated into the future khan's tribe, the level of subordination rose, ranks were established, and commanders were appointed. However, together with the increase in subordination, a qualitative difference in the military participation ratio also emerged. Whereas in the pre-crisis situation of "normalcy," conflicts were limited even though there was a high military participation ratio, during the period of "crisis," military ventures became, for a large part of the male population, a regular, professional activity.

The creation of the state, then, did not produce a demobilization of the military aristocracy and soldiery. On the contrary, it increased the size of the army and turned part-time soldiers into full-time soldiers. Moreover, as the royal clan strengthened its hold on power, it also tended to become larger and larger. The frequent struggles for succession must have persuaded the potential candidates to draft into their personal retinues and to retain control of as many craftsmen, servants and personal troops as possible. The proliferation of these non-producers increased the overall rate of consumption. Because production could not have increased, and in fact probably decreased owing to the impact of militarization on an already critical situation, heavy pressure emerged for the acquisition of external resources. Compared with the resources produced within their own economic bases, the political centers of steppe empires were enormously expensive.

According to tribal custom, the aristocracy exacted tribute from commoners and from subordinate or enslaved tribes. As the aristocratic class required resources far greater that those provided by the traditional economy, the ability to gain revenues external to a society's productive base was key to the emergence of the state apparatus, its survival, its foreign relations, and its projection of force beyond its political and territorial boundaries. As a solution the leaders would seek to incorporate, through military force, other peoples into the state's economy as tribute bearers, thus supplying the revenues necessary to fill the gap between the requirements

[59] Stanislav Andreski [Andrzejewski], *Military Organization and Society* (London: Routledge & Kegan Paul, 1968 [1954]), pp. 150–51.

of the state and the productive capacity of the social body. The tribute would be monopolized by the supreme leader and the clans associated with the government, in particular the khan's lineage and the consort clan. Their final objective was to strike a balance between incoming tribute and expenses for the maintenance, rewards, and stipends of the aristocratic elite, the army, and the state apparatus. The ability to extract revenues from tributary sources was an imperative for Inner Asian "nomadic-type" states and became a matter of overwhelming concern for the preservation of the unitarian structure of the state. Before we tackle this issue, however, we need to examine the political mechanism that produced the charismatic leader and the new social order.

Centralization

The sacral investiture of the "supra-tribal" leader was key to the process of political centralization. During the crisis, and coeval with the ongoing militarization of society, the leader emerged from the pool of members of the military aristocracy, either by defeating competing chiefs or by successfully defending the interests of the tribe. In that process, he acquired the support of other tribes, whose chiefs elevated him to the position of supreme leader. The electors formally relinquished their authority as tribal leaders and submitted to him. Isolated individuals could also flock to join the leader and then become part of the emergent new polity. The investiture of a "supra-tribal" leader was sacral in the sense that it conferred on the "khan" the right to proclaim himself "protected by Heaven," or "appointed by Heaven." As a result, the authority of the assembly that elected the leader (the Mongol *khuriltai*, or the *populus* in the Roman sense) was transferred to the person of the khan, who became the charismatic leader.

Although the appointment of the khan was not limited to a particular length of time, or to the solution of a crisis, sometimes a system was adopted that seems to indicate an attempt to limit the powers of the charismatic leader to a fixed period of time.[60] Türks and Khazars, for instance, had the custom of depriving the khan of air by strangulation at the time of his investiture until he reached a state of semi-conscious stupor, at which point he would be asked how long his reign would last. The period of his "dictatorship"would then be as long as the number of years "murmured" by the khan. In most cases, however, no such limitation was imposed.

---

[60] We may tentatively see an analogy here with the Roman institution of the *dictator*, a supreme military leader appointed for a limited period of time to resolve a crisis.

The sacral investiture points to the existence of an "ideology in reserve" that was activated under special circumstances.[61] Krader saw a distinct dyadic opposition between the collegial, almost socialistic relations that existed in the tribal society and the hierarchical, individualistic set of class relations that emerged with the birth of an Inner Asian state and that was imposed upon the first.[62] This distinction helps highlight the fact that, as soon as the sacral investiture takes place, a new ideology emerges, which, by requiring unconditional subordination to the khan and the imperial clan, transforms social and political relations from semi-horizontal to semi-vertical. The activation of this notion is tantamount to a social revolution, as it radically changes social and economic relations, as well as military and civil organization.

After the appointment of the khan, a new political apparatus took shape made up of permanently mobilized armies and bodyguard corps, a supra-tribal justice administration, and a body of imperially appointed military and civil officials. The first task of the khan was to ensure the loyalty of the *populus* and the establishment of a warless state (the *Pax Nomadica*), of which the royal clan would be guarantor. Having accomplished this, the khan wold need to consolidate rapidly the power of the imperial clan, which he could achieve by monopolizing revenues and redistributing them to the military aristocracy that had rallied around him. The military expansion that followed the establishment of the new statelike polity was not the result of fresh energies. Rather, it was part of the formative process of the state itself. Military activity was necessary to acquire the means to reward military leaders and to establish a hierarchy in which members of the royal clan would be in a commanding position. If the dynastic founder could not place the royal clan in firm control of the state, then the foundation of the state would forever remain weak, and the state itself might easily vanish at his death.

Although the political solution of the crisis that brought together the members of various tribes was contingency bound and therefore inherently temporary and anomalous, it resulted in the consolidation of the authority of a single or double (with the consort clan) lineage. In this sense, the newborn state resembled the tribe itself, which was often structured according to a hierarchy of lineages among which only one was supposed to provide political leaders. The perquisites of power, such as the right to hereditary succession and the right to exaction of tribute, were then transferred to the "supra-tribal," state level, and claimed by the charismatic clan. The new polity, the "tribe-state," was not a *tribal* state, that is, a state

---

[61] For the notion of an "ideology in reserve" in nomadic societies, see Philip Carl Salzman, "Introduction," in *When Nomads Settle: Processes of Sedentarization as Adaptation and Response*, ed. Philip Carl Salzman (New York: Praeger, 1980).

[62] Krader, "The Origin of the State among the Nomads of Asia," pp. 100–101.

controlled by tribal constituencies, but a state that was structured like a tribe in terms of hierarchies and access to power.

The ambiguity of the system of imperial succession in Inner Asian polities reflects, then, the ambiguity inherent in the tribe itself. Succession could be formally defined as either linear or lateral, but, in effect, any of the sons or brothers of the khan had a legitimate right to succeed him as long as the aspirant had enough support among the *populus*. This phenomenon was recognized by Joseph Fletcher, Jr., and named "bloody tanistry" after the Celtic analogy. According to Fletcher's interpretation, the tribal constituencies had the power to elect a successor by siding with the one who proved to be the most able, and the proof was provided by the leader-to-be's skill in defeating his competitors. Succession wars were necessary as a means of selection of the leader.[63]

However, once the dynastic founder had been successful in using the sacral investiture to consolidate the power of the clan, succession could in fact take place with limited bloodshed, or with no bloodshed at all, although the transmission of power by inheritance rather than by acclamation could create tension between the tribal *populus* and the new khan. External wars were often fought as a means to release that tension and to demonstrate, through victory, that the successor still enjoyed "divine" support. When there was a struggle for succession, the outcome depended not so much on the ability of the khan to please the tribal leaders as on his ability to control the government of the state. The correct management of state revenues could guarantee that members of the tribal aristocracy, now appointed to positions within the military or even within the civil administration, profited from their loyalty to the khan. In this case, the old-style tribal aristocracy, which still preserved a tribal constituency, was often powerless to oppose the central government, and it is interesting to note that time and again "nativistic" challenges were met successfully by the central governments, thanks to their greater resources.[64] The consolidation of the supreme power of the leader also required that a number of those men under arms be reorganized into permanent fighting units under the direct control of the royal clan and of the khan. However, loyal chieftains by and large retained control of their tribal troops, even though they were appointed to their positions by the khan.

Having examined in detail the process of state formation in the Inner Asian tradition, we should now turn to the Hsiung-nu polity, and analyze

---

[63] Joseph Fletcher, Jr., "Turco-Mongolian Monarchic Tradition in the Ottoman Empire," *Harvard Ukrainian Studies* 3–4 (1979–80): 236–51.

[64] A well-known historical example of a "nativistic" challenge is the struggle between the brothers Arigh Böke and Qubilai for control of the Mongol *ulus* ("state"); see Morris Rossabi, *Qubilai: His Life and Times* (Berkeley: University of California Press, 1988), pp. 53–62.

it in the light of the same tradition. The essential postulate of this type of analysis is that there be sufficient structural elements, as we have just seen, to link the formation of the Hsiung-nu empire to the later history of so-called steppe empires. These linkages do not rest exclusively on the purported "nomadic" nature of these empires, but on the similarity they display in the political process and in the social and economic transformations that accompany it.

State Formation among the Hsiung-nu

Scholars have emphasized that the Hsiung-nu emerged, as a unified polity, immediately after the unification of China, implying an influence of China on processes of state formation among the nomads.[65] Others, as we have already mentioned, saw the Hsiung-nu empire as the political outcome of a primarily economic situation, that is, the nomads' need to extract agricultural products from a powerful neighbor. Masao Mori has advanced the thesis that the Hsiung-nu state was created by an internal political process, whereby the central power of the ch'an-yü and his clan (together with the consort clan) over the other tribes was increased.[66] Others have seen the Hsiung-nu as a loose political organization that could not be termed a "state" but was rather a tribal confederation whose leader remained essentially a tribal chieftain, however outstanding.[67]

The bare sequence of events as we have already described it suggests that the struggle sustained by Modun was directed primarily against the traditional tribal aristocracy led by his father T'ou-man and was carried out by the efficient, totally loyal, disciplined bodyguard that he created and used to seize power.[68] This fits in well with the transition from a looser tribal structure to a more centralized political structure, which otherwise would be difficult to explain. This process of centralization occurred between the invasion of the Ordos by Meng T'ien (215 B.C.) and the rise of Modun to supreme leadership (209 B.C.). After the death of Meng T'ien, who was forced to commit suicide in 210 B.C., and the collapse of Ch'in, the expansion of the Hsiung-nu confederation unfolded to a large extent independently of the events in the south and was directed against the Inner Asian tribes that constituted the primary enemies of the Hsiung-nu.

---

[65] Khazanov, *Nomads of the Outside World*, p. 25.
[66] Mori Masao, "Kyôdo no kokka," *Shigaku zasshi* 59.5 (1950): 1–21.
[67] Nobuo Yamada, "The Formation of the Hsiung-nu Nomadic State," *Acta Orientalia Academiae Scientiarum Hungaricae* 36.1–3 (1982): 575–82.
[68] On the question of the Inner Asian guard corps, and their role in world history see Christopher Beckwith, "Aspects of the History of the Central Asian Guard Corps in Islam," *Archivum Eurasiae Medii Aevi* 4 (1984): 29–43.

The crisis ignited by China's push into the northern steppes was, then, the catalyst that led to the Hsiung-nu's creation of a stricter hierarchy and more cohesive military organization. According to Ssu-ma Ch'ien, before the unification, "China, the land of caps and girdles, was divided among seven states, three of which bordered the territory of the Hsiung-nu."[69] The territory of the Hsiung-nu, therefore, extended over the entire northern marches, encompassing the borders of the states of Ch'in, Yen, and Chao. Later, Meng T'ien's expedition drove the Hsiung-nu out of the Ordos region, and fortifications were set up along this new borderline; at this time, according to the *Shih chi*, "the Eastern Hu were very powerful and the Yüeh-chih were flourishing."[70] The Ch'in invasion is likely to have created a shortage of pastureland, which upset the balance of power existing at that time in the steppe and forest regions, with the main immediate effect of weakening the Hsiung-nu. The Hsiung-nu became therefore the target of other Inner Asian peoples, such as the Eastern Hu (perhaps formerly subject to the Hsiung-nu) and the Yüeh-chih. Internally, this crisis produced a drastic change of leadership, with the violent coming to power of Modun, as well as a change in the military, which can be seen in the training of an imperial bodyguard, perhaps analogous to those of the Persian, Scythian, and, later, Turco-Mongol empires.[71] Modun was therefore able to respond efficiently and swiftly to the critical situation.[72]

The internal unity of the Hsiung-nu body politic and the centralized structure were primarily meant as political and military responses to the Chinese invasion and threats from other nomads. Relying on their new military structure, the Hsiung-nu managed to defeat their Inner Asian enemies and consolidate their rule over the whole of eastern Inner Asia. At the same time, the civil war in China relieved pressure from the south, thus making it possible for Modun to concentrate his forces against his Inner Asian enemies and to recover the land taken away by Meng T'ien.[73] The rise of Modun, however, need not coincide with the creation out of nothing of a Hsiung-nu union of tribes, but with its reorganization and with a process of centralization of political and military power.[74] Hence the formation of

---

[69] *Shih chi* 110, 2886. [70] *Shih chi chu-yi* 110, 2317.

[71] The ancient *comitatus* of the Germanic tribes was also similarly structured; cf. Beckwith, "Aspects of the History of the Central Asian Guard Corps in Islam."

[72] Berthold Laufer, *Chinese Clay Figures. Part I: Prolegomena on the History of Defensive Armor* (Chicago: Field Museum of Natural History Publication no. 177, 1914), pp. 224–27.

[73] *Shih chi chu-yi* 110, 2317–18.

[74] As a loosely organized political entity, the Hsiung-nu had possibly existed for at least a century before the unification of China. They are mentioned as part of a coalition of states formed to attack Ch'in in 318 B.C., although commentators have remained skeptical about this record on account of its early date and

the Hsiung-nu empire should not be directly related to the unification of China per se. The origin of the conflict between Chinese and Hsiung-nu that would later assume the shape of a war between a defensive China and aggressive nomadic invaders must be sought, more precisely, in the expansion of China into nomadic grazing grounds followed by events that can be interpreted only within the context of steppe politics.

Hsiung-nu Expansion under Modun

After Modun became supreme leader (*ch'an-yü*), the Hsiung-nu engaged in a policy of military expansion that led them to establish their sovereignty, or at least their influence, over an immense territory encompassing the steppes, desert, and mountains from Manchuria to Central Asia. The Hsiung-nu first expanded in the east, so that the eastern (left) wing of the empire extended from the territory that would later become the Han Shang-ku commandery[75] to the land of the Hui-mo and Ch'ao-hsien.[76] This whole area had previously been inhabited by the Eastern Hu (Tung Hu), who were thoroughly defeated by Modun.[77] There is no doubt that the nomadic peoples defeated by the Hsiung-nu were responsible for paying tribute to them and that these payments, probably exacted at fixed times from the various tribal leaders, were essential for the support of the Hsiung-nu court, military machine, and general economic well-being.[78]

Before the campaign against the Yüeh-chih, in the 170s B.C., the westernmost extension of the Hsiung-nu does not seem to have gone much

isolation; see *Shih chi* 6, 207 (William H. Nienhauser et al., ed., *The Grand Scribe's Records*, vol. 1: *The Basic Annals of Pre-Han China* [Bloomington: Indiana University Press, 1994], p. 112). It is interesting, however, that the record says that the five states of Hann, Chao, Wei, Yen, and Ch'i *led* the Hsiung-nu to attack Ch'in. In other words, the Hsiung-nu were used by these states against Ch'in. In this case, the Hsiung-nu of the record need not be an imperial confederation; they could have been cavalry troops from tribes drafted in the Central States' armies or persuaded through diplomatic means to serve them. Both ways would be consistent with the Eastern Chou utilization of foreign peoples as "resources."

[75] *Chung-kuo li-shih ti-t'u chi*, 2: 9–10, 2–4.
[76] *Shih chi* 110, 2889. The Hui-mo are regarded as an ancient people that lived to the north of the Korean Peninsula (see *Shih chi chu-yi* 110, 2318). The Ch'ao-hsien kingdom was located in the northern part of the Korean Peninsula.
[77] *Shih chi* 110, 2889–90.
[78] To appreciate the importance of nomadic tributes to the Hsiung-nu we may note the argument made around 50 B.C. by Hsiung-nu leaders favorable to peace with China that, because their former tributaries (such as the Wu-huan) had recognized Chinese authority, it was better to submit to China (*Han shu* 94B, 3797).

beyond the western limit of the Yellow River Bend, although we do not know exactly how far west it extended north of the Yellow River, into present-day Inner and Outer Mongolia. The Ordos area, east of Shang commandery,[79] was occupied by the right (i.e., western) wing of the Hsiung-nu, whose territory also joined with that of the Yüeh-chih, Ti, and Ch'iang peoples.[80] In the north, Modun subjugated peoples known as the Hun-yü, Ch'ü-yi, Ting-ling, Ko-k'un, and Hsin-li, who were located in northern Mongolia and western Siberia.[81] In the south, he recovered the land previously occupied by Ch'in and pushed the border south of the Yellow River, and conquered the lands of the Lou-fan and of the king of Po-yang.[82] Modun also extended his realm to include the counties of Chu-na, located southeast of present-day Ku-yüan county, in Ning-hsia, and Fu-shih, southeast of today's Yü-lin county, in Shensi.[83] Then he invaded the territories of the former states of Yen and of Tai.[84] This means that the territory including present-day Ning-hsia, the northern parts of Shansi, Shensi, and Hopei, and the whole of Liao-ning was either controlled by the Hsiung-nu or open to their incursions.

At this time the court of the *ch'an-yü* was located in the area where the commanderies of Tai and Yün-chung were later established.[85] This was probably the *ch'an-yü*'s personal domain, and it extended from the northeastern corner of the loop of the Yellow River, north of the Ordos Desert, to the northern parts of Shansi and Hopei.[86] Another important place within the Hsiung-nu state was Lung-ch'eng, located probably southwest of Ulan Bator, in present-day Mongolia, where religious ceremonies and political gatherings were held.[87] This was the site where, in the fifth month of the

---

[79] *Chung-kuo li-shih ti-t'u chi*, 2: 5–6, 2–6/3–6.   [80] *Shih chi* 110, 2891.

[81] *Shih chi* 110, 2893; cf. also *Shih chi chu-yi* 110, 2319; *Han shu* 94A, 3753.

[82] *Shih chi* 110, 2889–90. The Lou-fan were a people located to the east outside the Great Bend of the Yellow River (*Chung-kuo li-shih ti-t'u chi*, 2: 9–10, 3–3). The Po-yang were a Hsiung-nu tribe that inhabited the territory to the south of the Great Bend of the Yellow River (*Shih chi chu-yi* 110, 2318).

[83] *Chung-kuo li-shih ti-t'u chi*, 2: 5–6, 4–5 and 3–6.

[84] *Chung-kuo li-shih ti-t'u chi*, 2: 9–10, 2–4/3–4.   [85] *Shih chi* 110, 2891.

[86] *Chung-kuo li-shih ti-t'u chi*, 2: 5–6, 1–7/2–9.

[87] *Chung-kuo li-shih ti-t'u chi*, 2: 67, 2–4; also *Shih chi chu-yi* 110, 2319. Possibly the Lung-ch'eng mentioned in this passage was not located in Outer Mongolia. Evidence against this identification, according to Wang Wei-mao, include the following points: (1) the Hsiung-nu were nomads and had no fixed settlements; (2) their political center was at that time to the south of the Gobi; (3) there are other passages that mention other Lung-ch'eng places that seem to be located in different areas. According to this author, the Lung-ch'eng mentioned in this record was located to the south of the Gobi and to the north of Shang-ku prefecture. See Wang Wei-mao, "Hsiung-nu Lung-ch'eng k'ao-pien," *Li-shih yen-chiu* 1983.2: 142–44.

year, the *ch'an-yü* performed sacrifices to the ancestors, Heaven and Earth, and to the deities.[88]

To acquire the external revenues they needed to counterbalance the militarization of society and the growing size of their courts and political apparati, the Hsiung-nu adopted a purely tributary system. Through military pressure and formal treaties they forced weaker states as well as vanquished nomadic states to pay tributes to the Hsiung-nu leadership. Besides the tribute paid by China, the city-states and other polities in the Tarim Basin paid the Hsiung-nu ruler in fixed amounts of luxury goods and staples that went to support the court and its military establishment and then "trickled down" to the more distant aristocratic lineages. Defeated nomads such as the Wu-huan were also forced to pay a price to their overlords. The tributary system soon revealed its limits, however, for the unity of the political system could survive only as long as tributes kept coming in. Considering the chronic instability of the royal clan, which could be easily disabled by its internal struggles, the state establishment was obviously extremely fragile.

Early Han Relations with the Hsiung-nu

Han Kao-tsu's Treaty of 198 B.C.

At the outset of the Han dynasty, the military situation was extraordinarily complex because of semi-independent potentates with whom the emperor vied for full political control. In 200 B.C., the seventh year of Han Kao-tsu's reign (206–194 B.C.), the Hsiung-nu attacked Hsin, the king of Hann (a northern satrapy not to be confused with the Han dynasty), at Ma-yi.[89] Hsin made a pact with the invaders, and planned a rebellion against the emperor in T'ai-yüan. The Hsiung-nu, once they had obtained the support of Hsin, led their army to the south across the Kou-chu Mountains,[90] attacked the T'ai-yüan commandery, and reached the walls of Chin-yang.[91] Kao-tsu personally led the troops to attack the Hsiung-nu and quell the rebellion of Hann, but his forces met with frigid weather, and twenty

[88] *Shih chi* 110, 2892.

[89] Ma-yi: the then-capital of the Han kingdom, it was located in present-day Shuo county, in Shansi; see *Chung-kuo li-shih ti-t'u chi*, 2: 17–18, 3–10.

[90] Kou-chu Mountains: today called Yen-men Mountains, a mountain range located to the southeast of Ma-yi, near present-day Tai county, in Shansi (*Chung-kuo li-shih ti-t'u chi*, 2: 17–18, 3–10). In ancient times it was known as one of the nine Great Fortresses (Chiu Ta Yao-sai).

[91] Chin-yang: placed to the south of present-day T'ai-yüan city, in Shansi (*Chung-kuo li-shih ti-t'u chi*, 2: 17–18, 5–10).

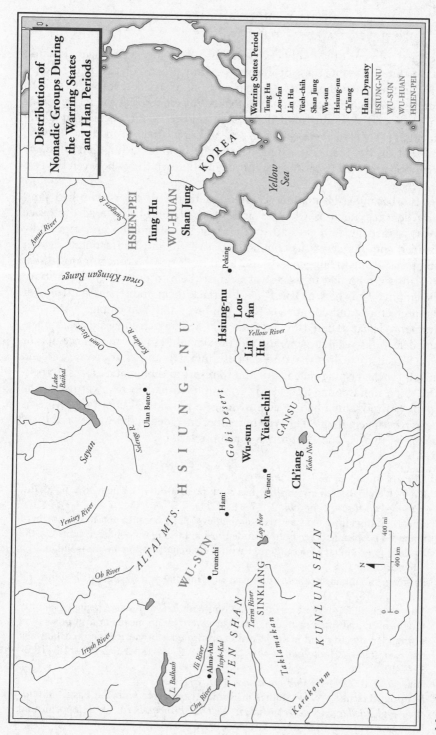

Distribution of Nomadic Groups During the Warring States and Han Periods

Warring States Period
Tung Hu
Lou-fan
Lin Hu
Yüeh-chih
Shan Jung
Wu-sun
Hsiung-nu
Ch'iang

Han Dynasty
HSIUNG-NU
WU-SUN
WU-HUAN
HSIEN-PEI

KOREA

Yellow Sea

HSIEN-PEI
Tung Hu
WU-HUAN
Shan Jung

Amur River
Sungari R.
Great Khingan Range
Onon River
Kerulen R.

• Peking

Hsiung-nu   Lou-fan

Yellow River

Lin Hu

HSIUNG-NU

Lake Baikal
• Ulan Bator
Selenge R.
Sayan

Gobi Desert

Wu-sun   Yüeh-chih

GANSU

Ch'iang
Koko Nor

Yenisey River

ALTAI MTS.   HSIUNG-NU

• Hami
• Yü-men

WU-SUN

Ob River
• Urumchi

Lop Nor

KUNLUN SHAN

Irtysh River

T'IEN SHAN
SINKIANG

Tarim River

Taklamakan

Hi River
• Alma-Ata
Issyk-Kul
L. Balkash
Chu River

Karakorum

N

400 mi
400 km
0

Map 4

or thirty percent of the soldiers are said to have lost their fingers because of frostbite.[92] Despite these problems, the army pressed on to P'ing-ch'eng.[93] Modun then moved against Kao-tsu with an army of cavalrymen said to number four hundred thousand,[94] blocked the emperor at the mountain of Pai-teng, and then surrounded the Han soldiers at the locality of P'ing-ch'eng.[95] The Han were allowed to withdraw after seven days. Having inflicted on the Han a crushing defeat, the Hsiung-nu imposed tributary conditions that led to ratification of the first-known treaty between the two powers.

Hsin became a Hsiung-nu general. Together with others who had similarly defected, such as Chao Li and Wang Huang, he ignored the peace treaty signed by Kao-tsu and the head of the Hsiung-nu and repeatedly invaded and plundered the commanderies of Tai and Yün-chung.[96] At that point, disaffected Han generals and local lords had become a major threat to Kao-tsu, who had to wage war against them to protect the integrity of the empire. Thus he sent Fan K'uai to attack them and regain control over the prefectures and counties of Tai, Yen-men, and Yün-chung.[97] After the dramatic defeat suffered by Han Kao-tsu at P'ing-ch'eng, and the numerous defections of Han generals and provincial "kings," the Han emperor was forced to realize that the Chinese infantry and charioteers were no match for the Hsiung-nu cavalry and to resort to diplomatic means. Expensive gifts, tantamount to a yearly tribute, then had to be awarded to the *ch'an-yü*, and China had to acknowledge a position of inferiority vis-à-vis its northern neighbor.[98] The type of treaty concluded at this time was termed *ho-ch'in*, that is, "peace through kinship relations."

[92] *Shih chi* 8, 384–5; *Shih chi chu-yi* 8, 214.

[93] P'ing-ch'eng: located to the northeast of present-day Ta-t'ung city, in Shansi (*Chung-kuo li-shih ti-t'u chi*, 2: 17–18, 2–11).

[94] This is an obviously exaggerated number, especially because not all the northern nomadic peoples had yet been included in the Hsiung-nu confederation. On the basis of later military encounters, I would estimate that this figure is inflated by a factor of ten.

[95] Pai-teng: mountain located to the east of P'ing-ch'eng (*Chung-kuo li-shih ti-t'u chi*, 2: 17–18, 2–11).

[96] Yün-chung and Tai: these territories, along with Yen-men, were being constantly fought over, and often shifted hands. They were by no means in firm possession of the Han dynasty and in some ways constituted a broad frontier belt between the two states (*Chung-kuo li-shih ti-t'u chi*, 2: 17–18, 2–8/2–9/2–11/3–10/2–12/3–12).

[97] *Shih chi* 110, 2894–5; *Shih chi chu-yi* 110, 2319–20.

[98] Manfred Raschke, "New Studies in Roman Commerce with the East," in *Aufstieg und Niedergang der römischen Welt, II Principat*, ed. H. Temporini and W. Haase, vol. 9.2 (Berlin: De Gruyter, 1978), p. 614.

The Ho-ch'in *Treaty Policy and the Principle of Equality*

The *ho-ch'in* policy is usually regarded as a pure and simple policy of accommodation, a means of buying peace in exchange for goods.[99] In fact, it was more than this. Although in essence this policy implicitly pacified the nomads through bribes, it also included elements that could reconcile it, in spirit if not in substance, with previous frontier policies. The architect of the *ho-ch'in* policy was Liu Ching, the councillor who had advised Kao-tsu against attacking the Hsiung-nu. The policy he proposed instead consisted of sending an imperial princess – Kao-tsu's oldest daughter – to become the legitimate consort of Modun. According to Liu Ching's plan, once a relation of kinship had been established, and Modun had become the emperor's son-in-law, then Modun's son – the heir-apparent to the Hsiung-nu throne – would be Kao-tsu's grandson and thus placed in a position of subordination to China. Liu suggested that this policy be coupled with two other strategic moves. The first was a "corruption" campaign, whereby the Han would periodically send to the Hsiung-nu those valuable things that they craved, and of which the Han had a surplus. The second was an "indoctrination" campaign, whereby the Han would send rhetoricians to the Hsiung-nu to explain the rules of proper conduct. Because, according to proper Confucian conduct, a grandson could not treat his grandfather as an equal, the superiority of the Chinese emperor to the Hsiung-nu ruler would thereby be established, and, fighting no battles, the Hsiung-nu would gradually become Han subjects. This policy was accepted in 199 B.C., and began to be implemented with the treaty of 198 B.C.[100]

The *ho-ch'in* treaty of 198 B.C. signaled Han acceptance of equal diplomatic status with the Hsiung-nu and the inauguration of a bipolar world order. Such a recognition of equal status rested on two elements: (1) a marriage alliance was contracted by the two ruling houses; and (2) the Han

---

[99] On the *ho-ch'in* policy during the early Western Han, see Ying-shih Yü, *Trade and Expansion in Han China: A Study in the Structure of Sino-Barbarian Economic Relations* (Berkeley: University of California Press, 1967), pp. 10–12; Arthur Waldron, *The Great Wall of China: From History to Myth* (Cambridge: Cambridge University Press, 1990), pp. 40–41; Luo Ta-yün, "Hsi Han ch'u-ch'i tui Hsiung-nu ho-ch'in te shih-chi," *Yün-nan Min-tsu Hsüeh-yüan Hsüeh-pao* 1985.4: 44–9; Shih Wei-ch'ing, "Kuan-yü Hsi Han cheng-fu yu Hsiung-nu ho-ch'in jo-kan wen-t'i," *Hsia-men Ta-hsüeh Hsüeh-pao* 1985.4: 21–9; Chang Ch'ang-ming, "Shih-lun Hsi Han te Han Hsiung kuan-hsi chi he-ch'in cheng-ts'e," *Chiang-huai Lun-t'an* 1983.6: 83–8. For the period after Han Wu-ti, cf. Ch'en Po, "Shih-lun Hu-han-yeh Ch'an-yü tsai yü Han "ho-ch'in" chung te chu-tao tso-yung," *Hsi-pei Ta-hsüeh Hsüeh-pao* 1990.4: 36–9.

[100] *Shih chi chu-yi* 99, 2144; *Shih chi* 99, 2179.

agreed to send a yearly tribute of silk, cloth, grain and other foodstuff.[101] Later treaties were based on the same principles, which were sometimes expressed even more emphatically; for instance, the title of *ch'an-yü* received the same diplomatic status as that of *huang-ti* (the Chinese emperor), and relations between the two rulers were defined as "brotherly." In 162 B.C. Emperor Wen wrote to the Hsiung-nu ruler in the following terms:

I and the *ch'an-yü* are the father and mother of the people, problems that have emerged in the past owing to the bad deeds of subordinate people should not ruin our brotherly happiness. I have heard people say that Heaven does not cover just one side, and Earth is not partial to anyone. I and the *ch'an-yü* should cast aside the trivial problems of the past and together follow the Great Tao.[102]

The metaphors used (father and mother, Heaven and Earth) imply complementarity between two independent entities rather than submission or even subordination of one to the other. However, diplomatic recognition of equal dignity did not reflect actual power relations in military terms: the Han also needed to pacify the Hsiung-nu with payment of a tribute. The initial treaty between Han Kao-tsu and Modun stipulated a yearly payment to the Hsiung-nu of silk, wine, and grain and marked a fundamental change in the Chinese conception of foreign relations. Such a policy, which clearly placed the Han in a position of political inferiority, was unprecedented for the Chinese. Insult was added to injury when Modun extended a marriage proposal to the empress dowager Lü Hou.[103] This

---

[101] *Han shu* 94A, 3754; *Shih chi* 110, 2895; *Shih chi chu-yi* 110, 2320.

[102] *Shih chi chu-yi* 110, 2324–5; *Han shu* 94A, 3762–3.

[103] During the reign of Emperor Hui (194–188 B.C.) Fan K'uai had suggested that the Han replied with military means to an insulting letter sent by Modun to the empress dowager Lü Hou. The text of the letter, and of Lü Hou's reply, is not recorded in the *Shih chi*, but in *Han shu* 94. The *ch'an-yü*'s letter read: "I, who am alone but still vigorous, a ruler who was born amidst lowlands and swamps, and who was raised in fields with oxen and horses, have several times approached the borders, wishing to be friendly with the Central States. You. Your Majesty, sit alone on the throne, and I, alone and restless, have no one beside me. We are both bored, and are both bereft of what could console us. I would like to exchange what I have for what I do not have." Lü Hou replied: "I who stand at the head of an impoverished domain was frightened and withdrew in order to think about the letter. I am old of age, my soul has grown decrepit. My hair and teeth have dropped out and my stride has lost firmness. You, Shan-yü, have probably heard about me. You ought not sully yourself. I, who stand at the head of an impoverished domain, am not to blame [for refusing] and should be pardoned. I have two imperial chariots and two teams of four coach horses which I present to you with two ordinary turn-outs." Cf. L. Peremolov and

affront might have spurred China to adopt a more aggressive stance in the name of preserving the honor of the country, yet for decades the *ho-ch'in* policy continued to be endorsed, and the Han withdrawal of political and diplomatic recognition from even a single Hsiung-nu leader was never seriously considered.

Although the *ho-ch'in* policy was dictated by the military inferiority of the Chinese, we should not underestimate the presence of elements that link this policy, in spirit, to those policies adopted by Chinese states toward northern peoples before unification. These elements were, first, the argument for peaceful relations to preserve the strength of the nation, and second, the exchanges of gifts and hostages and the intermarrying, which were not uncommon in the earlier relations with Ti and Jung. Even Li Ssu, the "legalist" minister of Ch'in Shih Huang-ti, had proclaimed the unsuitability of military confrontations with the nomads.[104] These precedents left ample space for more flexible diplomatic policies and seem to indicate that concerns about effectiveness were more important than displays of superiority. Even on the eve of the abandonment of this policy, at a debate held at Wu-ti's court in 135 B.C. (described in Chapter 6), the *ho-ch'in* policy was fiercely defended by Han An-kuo, and had initially obtained the consensus of the majority of ministers.

China's weakness at the time of Han Kao-tsu was, of course, the result of military developments that had made the nomads far more dangerous than they had been. Waging wars against their nomadic foes, the Hsiungnu had expanded over a territory that extended from Manchuria to the land west of the Yellow River. In the process, they had absorbed other nomadic tribes, which led to the further growth of their armed forces within a military organization made more effective by its centralized structure. On the Han side, the efficacy of Kao-tsu's army was hopelessly undermined by the soldiers' lack of experience in fighting the nomads and by the lack of discipline of the commanders, members of a nobility whose loyalty to the emperor could not be taken for granted. These factors made the Han army objectively inferior to the Hsiung-nu, and forced Kao-tsu to adopt a conciliatory attitude, which in the long run allowed the Han to buy time and to build up a strong economy and a "modern" army that would eventually enable China to fight back. Brides and bribes did not prevent the Hsiungnu from launching raids and swift attacks along the border, or from requesting repeatedly that the "tribute" paid by China be increased, but it preserved a substantial balance on the border and, compared with full-scale war, imposed a lighter burden on the state's finances. The *ho-ch'in* policy

A. Martynov, *Imperial China: Foreign-Policy Conceptions and Methods* (Moscow: Progress Publishers, 1983), pp. 64–65.

[104] Sechin Jagchid and Van Jay Symons, *Peace, War and Trade along the Great Wall* (Bloomington: Indiana University Press, 1989), pp. 56–57.

became therefore the *conditio sine qua non* for the preservation of the economic strength and territorial integrity of the reborn Chinese empire.

A New World Order

At the beginning of the second century B.C., Han and Hsiung-nu were by no means the only players on the international scene. Other protagonists included those nomadic peoples that had not been conquered by the Hsiung-nu nor had voluntarily joined them, and the small kingdoms and oasis-states of Central Asia, which became a bone of contention in the armed struggle between Han and Hsiung-nu at the time of Wu-ti (141–87 B.C.).

During the reign of Wen-ti (179–157 B.C.) the Hsiung-nu empire reached the acme of its expansion, and in a diplomatic communication to Emperor Wen the *ch'an-yü* declared:

With the assistance of Heaven, the talent of officers and soldiers, and the strength of the horses the wise king of the right has succeeded in destroying the Yüeh-chih, and in unsparingly killing them or bringing them into submission. Lou-lan,[105] the Wu-sun,[106] the Hu-chieh[107] and other twenty-six states contiguous to them are now part of the Hsiung-nu. All the people who draw the bow have now become one family and the northern region (*pei chou*) has been pacified.[108]

The same principle was confirmed a few years later, in 162 B.C., in the treaty concluded by Emperor Wen. This treaty stipulated that, in accordance with the tradition fixed by former emperors, the Hsiung-nu should rule over the nation of the archers to the north of the Great Wall, and the settled people living in the south, those who wore hats and sashes, should be ruled by the Chinese emperor.[109] This implies the recognition of a divide between a northern and a southern region that both powers had pledged to respect. This new world order can be said to conform to what we might call the principle of great-power primacy, which is rooted in the belief that posses-

---

[105] Kingdom in the Western Regions, located to the west of the Lop Nor (in Sinkiang); its king's residence was in the city of Yü-ni (*Chung-kuo li-shih ti-t'u chi*, 2: 37–38, 5–11).

[106] Pastoral people who originally occupied the area between the Kansu and Ch'ing-hai provinces and later moved to the region of the Ili River and Issik Kul. Their capital was Ch'ih-ku city (*Chung-kuo li-shih ti-t'u chi*, 2: 37–38, 4–6).

[107] People that inhabited the area between the Kansu and Sinkiang provinces and later moved to the north (*Chung-kuo li-shih ti-t'u chi*, 2: 39, 2–2).

[108] *Shih chi* 110, 2896; *Shih chi chu-yi* 110, 2321; *Han shu* 94A, 3756–3757.

[109] *Shih chi chu-yi* 110, 2324–5; *Han shu* 94A, 3762–3; *Shih chi* 110, 2902.

sion of superior military power and, in the case of China, also of moral and cultural superiority, went hand in hand with international leadership. In the relationship between the two major powers this principle was manifested in two ways: first, in the equal status of the rulers participating in this relationship; and second, in the definition not only of the borders between the two countries – which guaranteed their territorial integrity – but also of their respective "areas of influence," which in turn implied the great powers' mutual recognition of the right to keep an unchallenged political supremacy over those peoples and states included in those areas.

In the dualistic conception of foreign relations that dominated the first period of the Han dynasty, it is not surprising to see that the known world was effectively split into two halves. Hsiung-nu and Chinese rulers allowed each other not only effective authority over the people of their own state (i.e., those living within the territorial boundaries directly under the administrative, political, and military control of each ruler) but also an overlordship, or primacy, over the other independent communities and states living in the respective areas of influence. The concepts of great power primacy and areas of influence are vital for understanding the political events that took place as Han Wu-ti began to expand militarily in the Western Regions toward the end of the second century B.C. When the famous explorer and imperial envoy Chang Ch'ien was sent by Emperor Wu to seek an anti-Hsiung-nu alliance with the Yüeh-chih nomads in 139–138 B.C., he was captured by the Hsiung-nu, who expressed their displeasure in the following terms: "The Yüeh-chih lie to the north of us, how can the Han send their envoys there? If I wished to send envoys to Yüeh [a state to the south of China] would the Han allow me to do so?" Clearly Chang Ch'ien was found in violation of the agreement that defined separate areas of influence.

The Hsiung-nu's political and economic domination of Central Asia (the *hsi-yü*, or Western Regions of the Chinese records), as far as the Tarim Basin and beyond, may have been the result of their offensive againt the Yüeh-chih, who originally lived near Tun-huang and Ch'i-lien.[110] Escaping from the Hsiung-nu, they fled westward, where they attacked Ta-hsia (Bactria). Subsequently, their king established his court north of the Kuei River.[111] The Hsiung-nu exercised their supremacy over these regions in no uncertain terms. The people to the east of Samarkand were obliged to serve the Hsiung-nu, and the states of Lou-lan and Ku-shih, which lay on the trade routes, "often acted as the ears and eyes for the Hsiung-nu, enabling

[110] Territory to the east of Tun-huang and to the west of the Ch'i-lien Mountains (*Chung-kuo li-shih ti-t'u chi*, 2: 33–34, 2–3/3–5).
[111] *Shih chi* 123, 3162; *Shih chi chu-yi* 123, 2593. The Yüeh-chih settled in Transoxiana, to the north on the upper course of the Amu Darya; Kuei is the name of the Amu Darya (*Chung-kuo li-shih ti-t'u chi*, 2: 13–14, 3–2).

their troops to intercept the Han envoys."[112] The Hsiung-nu overlordship in the Western Regions was secured with ruthless means. Whenever they heard that one of their tributary states had surrendered to the Han they would immediately send a military force to attack it. After the Han began sending diplomatic missions to the Western Regions, the Chinese envoys complained that when a Hsiung-nu messenger carrying tokens of credence from the *ch'an-yü* arrived, all the states along his route provided him with relays of escorts and food and did not detain or harm him. In contrast, Han envoys could not obtain food or horses without paying for them. Clearly, then, the Hsiung-nu regarded the north as their domain, and the tribute they exacted from the subordinate polities was instrumental in the political consolidation and economic well-being of their state.

The peoples of the Western Regions, whether nomadic tribes or oasis-states, were organized in independent political communities, and their rulers regarded themselves as the sole authority over their people and territory. Because they could not compete with the two "superpowers" of the day, however, in time they were forced to establish relations with either China or the Hsiung-nu – and sometimes with both – that implied a degree of subordination. The system of international relations in which they all participated comprised therefore essentially two types of relations: those between the two great powers, and those between the great powers and the lesser states.

Lesser states acquired certain obligations when they pledged allegiance to either one of the two great powers. First, a hostage had to be sent from the lesser state to the great power's court; preferably he had to be someone eligible to inherit the throne. Then there was a tribute in kind – foodstuff, clothing, horses, and so on – to be paid regularly. The rulers of the states that pledged allegiance to the Han were also given Chinese titles to mark the type and degree of their vassal relationship. Those states that were caught in between the two powers found themselves in a most unfortunate position, with their fate often depending on sheer luck. The state of Lou-lan (Kroraina, in the Tarim Basin), for instance, had to juggle in keeping "tributary" relations with both powers, as Hsiung-nu and Han required it to send hostages to their courts. Although the Hsiung-nu at first won the diplomatic battle by being quicker in installing on the throne their protégé, the Han won the war by sending a secret agent to assassinate the unfriendly king.

One of the tactics later used by China in the struggle against the Hsiung-nu was to undermine the Hsiung-nu's authority as a "great power." This is expressed clearly in a speech by Chang Ch'ien to Wu-ti:

[112] *Han shu* 96A, 3876 (Hulsewé and Loewe, *China in Central Asia*, pp. 85–86).

Now the *ch'an-yü* has recently suffered at the hands of the Han and as a result the region occupied by the Hun-yeh king has been depopulated. The Man-yi peoples are typically greedy for Han goods. If we now take this opportunity and send rich bribes and gifts to the Wu-sun and persuade them to move farther east and occupy the region which formerly belonged to the Hun-yeh king, then the Han could conclude a treaty of brotherhood with them, and, under the circumstances, they would surely do as we say. If we could get them to obey us, it would be like cutting off the right arm of the Hsiung-nu. Once an alliance has been forged with the Wu-sun, states from Ta-hsia (Bactria) to its West could all be induced to come to court and become our outer vassals.[113]

Opening "brotherly" – that is, equal status – relations with the Wu-sun would have undermined Hsiung-nu paramountcy in the region and opened the door to Han diplomatic and political penetration. Hence the Han sent a princess to wed the Wu-sun king, so "to separate the Hsiung-nu from their allied states (*yüan kuo*) of the west."[114] One point is clear: at least until the power of the Hsiung-nu was broken, and the Chinese consolidated their control over the Western Regions, in the mid-first century B.C., relations between greater and lesser powers are the only ones that can be defined as "tributary" because they implied a degree of subordination and dependence in foreign affairs, while allowing virtually complete autonomy in internal affairs. The relations between greater powers, on the other hand, were based on the mutual recognition of equal status.

The Ho-ch'in *Policy during the Reigns of Emperors Wen and Ching*

For the new world order to be effectively preserved, a substantial equality between the two "superpowers" needed to be achieved also on the military plane. Emperor Wen began to take measures that were intended to rebuild the military forces on a more modern basis. First steps in this direction were the appointments of Palace Military Commander Chou She and Chief of Palace Attendants Chang Wu as generals "in command of a force of a thousand chariots and a hundred thousand horsemen to garrison the vicinity of Ch'ang-an and guard the capital from the nomadic invaders."[115] Clearly the *ho-ch'in* policy did not prevent the Hsiung-nu from attacking the very heart of China's political power, but Han Wen-ti was gradually adapting to the enemy's tactics and replacing infantry troops with cavalry. Although still

[113] *Shih chi* 123, 3168 (Watson, *Records*, 2: 238).
[114] *Shih chi chu-yi* 110, 2331; *Shih chi* 110, 2913.
[115] *Shih chi chu-yi* 110, 2324; *Shih chi* 110, 2901.

unable to establish military supremacy over the nomadic armies, the Chinese could successfully repel invading parties and even pursue them beyond the borders. Yet this new army fulfilled a defensive function, was concentrated around the capital, and continued to be unable to mount long-range expeditions into Hsiung-nu territory. As a result, Han Wen-ti continued to base his foreign policy on peace treaties and to send the Hsiung-nu large amounts of "millet, leaven, gold, silk, cloth, thread, floss and other articles."[116]

These treaties should have guaranteed the pacification of the border areas. In reality, no matter how many treaties were concluded, and regardless of the amount of tribute paid to the nomads, the agreements were repeatedly ignored. During the last period of Wen-ti's reign, new measures were taken to protect the borders with additional garrisons, more evenly distributed, as part of a gradual but constant reorganization of the Chinese military. This step was intended to accomplish two tasks: the reinforcement of the border garrisons and the creation of a central standing army, positioned around the capital, which could intervene whenever and wherever a major Hsiung-nu invasion might be attempted.

The Hsiung-nu ability to threaten the heart of Han political power, and the failure of the "appeasement" strategy to relieve the Han of the threats of invasion, made the situation at the frontier a virtually permanent crisis. An attack by the Hsiung-nu against the western border fortifications at Chu-na, in the winter of 166 B.C., ended with the defeat of Han forces and the death of Sun Ang, the chief commandant of Pei-ti.[117] Rather then mere raiding incursions, the Hsiung-nu attacks against the Han northern commanderies resembled migrations of tens of thousands of people, who invaded a certain area for several months; in consequence, a large number of Han troops needed to be mobilized to repel them. Here is a telling example of such a "raid":

In the winter of the sixth year of the latter part [of Emperor Wen's reign, i.e., 158 B.C.] thirty thousand Hsiung-nu invaded the Shang Commandery, and thirty thousand invaded the Commandery of Yün-chung. In order to defend against the Hsiung-nu, [the emperor] appointed the Palace Counselor Ling Mien as General of Chariots and Cavalry to garrison Fei-hu Pass;[118] the former Chancellor of Ch'u, Su Yi, was made a general and sent to guard Kou-chu; General Chang Wu was stationed at Pei-ti; the Governor of the Ho-nei Commandery Chou Ya-fu was made a general, and stationed at

---

[116] *Shih chi chu-yi* 110, 2325; *Shih chi* 110, 2903.

[117] County located to the southeast of today's Ku-yüan county, in Ning-hsia province (*Chung-kuo li-shih ti-t'u chi*, 2: 33–34, 5–9). See also *Shih chi chu-yi* 10, 261; *Shih chi* 10, 428.

[118] Mountain pass located between the present-day counties of Lai-yüan and Yü, in Hopei (*Chung-kuo li-shih ti-t'u chi*, 2: 17–18, 3–12).

Hsi-liu;[119] the Director of the Imperial Clan Liu Li was made a general and sent to Pa-shang;[120] the Marquis of Sung-tzu [Hsü Li] was sent to garrison Chi-men.[121] Several months later the Hsiung-nu left, and the armies were recalled.[122]

The northern borders were equally unstable during Emperor Ching's reign (156–141 B.C.), and the northern provinces of Yen and Yen-men were subject to continuous raids and attacks.[123] More concessions were granted to the Hsiung-nu in the peace treaties, which included the establishment of markets along the border, and possibly a permissive attitude about control over contraband trade.[124] This produced favorable results, downgrading border conflicts to minor clashes and circumscribed skirmishes; morever, from this point on the Hsiung-nu do not seem to have carried out attacks as deeply into China's territory as they had done during Wen-ti's time.

Chia Yi and Ch'ao Ts'o

The position of the statesman Chia Yi (201–169 B.C.) best exemplifies the deep ideological discomfort felt by some Han politicians with the *ho-ch'in* policy and the pressure to replace a "horizontal" system of foreign relations with a "vertical" one. Chia Yi represented the relationship between China and the Hsiung-nu with a body metaphor, whereby China was the head and the Hsiung-nu were the feet. The failure of such a "proper" relationship resulted, according to him, in the inversion of these two elements, whereby, as a consequence of "appeasement," China ended up at the bottom and the nomads on top.[125] His position argues strongly for the restoration of a hierarchical world order and the alignment of foreign policy with the idea of universal emperorship, and yields evidence of the "ideological" pressures against appeasement present within the Han political debate. His views regarding the divide between a cultured Hua-Hsia community and a cultureless foreign world cast the Hsiung-nu into a position

---

[119] Located on the northern bank of the Wei River, in Shensi, to the southeast of the city of Hsien-yang (*Chung-kuo li-shih ti-t'u chi*, 2: 15–16, 7–11).

[120] Area (also called Pa-t'ou) located to the east of Hsi-an, by the Pa river. In ancient times this was a strategic military place to control the area of Hsien-yang and Ch'ang-an (*Chung-kuo li-shih ti-t'u chi* 2: 15–16, 7–12).

[121] Place located to the northeast of the city of Hsien-yang, in Shensi (not marked in *Chung-kuo li-shih ti-t'u chi*).

[122] *Shih chi chu-yi* 10, 263–4; *Shih chi* 10, 431–2. (Watson, *Records*, 1: 304–305).

[123] *Shih chi chu-yi* 11, 277 and 279; *Shih chi* 11, 444 and 448.

[124] *Shih chi chu-yi* 110, 2326, *Shih chi* 110, 2904–905.

[125] *Han shu* 48, 2240/2241–2; Yü Ying-shih, *Trade and Expansion*, p. 11.

of polar opposition to the Han dynasty. The strongly ideological stance advocated by Chia Yi, however, was not tempered by any notion of molding the enemy through the example of virtuous behavior. For him, rituals, music, and the other achievements of the Chinese cultural sphere were not just a sign of a superior society, nor were they the "sugar-coated bullets" to be used to dazzle and corrupt, if possible, their primitive enemies. Instead, they were the means through which the two opposite "camps" came to be differentiated: those with rituals on the one side, those without on the other, with no possibility of dialogue between the two. It is interesting to note that this position, while echoing Spring and Autumn and Warring States positions, is singularly blunt in its formulation and lacks an articulation at the political level, in a situation in which it was obviously imperative that the Han find a diplomatic "voice" with which to engage the Hsiung-nu.[126] Mostly, he despised the Han defectors who would aid and abet the Hsiung-nu cause, and even go so far as to justify it. These traitors to Chinese civilization were the object of several devastating statements in which he suggested that people such as Chung-hang Yüeh, the notorious counselor of the *ch'an-yü*, should be made to kneel and then flogged. This type of highly ideological stance to an extent foreshadowed the positions assumed by Wang Mang, the "usurper" of the Hsin dynasty (9–23 A.D.), who would address the head of the Hsiung-nu (an independent, if tributary, nation) as "Submitted Caitiff of the Surrendered Slaves."[127] But Chia Yi's unwillingness to compromise appears to have been dictated more by blind, and somewhat powerless, rage than by rational thinking. Not surprisingly, his position, advocating the submission of the Hsiung-nu without suggesting how that would be accomplished, remained without influence, and the *ho-ch'in* policy continued to be carried out without being affected by it.

An entirely different view would be taken by Ch'ao Ts'o (d. 154 B.C.), the champion of centralization and relentless persecutor of separatist "subordinate kings," who seems to have been alone in addressing the issue of foreign relations in practical terms and in recognizing the unworkability of *ho-ch'in* not based on ideological grounds, but as a result of its failure to meet expectations. He clearly identified the economic and military issues at stake and made the most comprehensive contemporary military study of the relations with the Hsiung-nu. His suggestions focused on a reform of the military as a whole and on socio-economic reforms for the border

---

[126] Modern commentators tie Chia Yi's position to the *ju-chia* position of drawing the line between Hua and Yi that finds some sparse mention in Confucius's *Analects*. See Wang Hsing-kuo, *Chia Yi p'ing chuan: fu Lu Chia Ch'ao Ts'o p'ing chuan* (Nan-ching: Nan-ching Ta-hsüeh, 1992), p. 169.

[127] De Crespigny, *Northern Frontier*, p. 205.

regions and mostly hinge on the need to update military thinking and make it relevant to the current circumstances.

Ch'ao Ts'o was particularly concerned with security and the military aspect of confrontation with the nomads, and his writings deal squarely with frontier management and issues of military strategy. The following passage, from a memorial presented to Wen-ti in 169 B.C., which is also one of the first studies of the military capabilities of nomadic cavalry, illustrates the extent of Han knowledge of Hsiung-nu military matters unquestionably available to Ssu-ma Ch'ien and to his contemporaries.

The configuration of terrain and fighting ability of the Hsiung-nu differ from those of China. Going up and down mountain slopes, and crossing torrents and streams, the Hsiung-nu horses are better than the Chinese. On dangerous roads and sloping narrow passages they can both ride and shoot arrows; Chinese mounted soldiers cannot match that. They can withstand the wind and rain, fatigue, hunger and thirst; Chinese soldiers are not as good. These are the qualities of the Hsiung-nu. However, on a level terrain in the plains, using light chariots and swift cavalry, the Hsiung-nu rabble would easily be utterly defeated. Even with strong crossbows that shoot far, and long halberds that hit at a distance, the Hsiung-nu would not be able to ward them off. If the armors are sturdy and the weapons sharp, if the repetition crossbows shot far, and the platoons advance together, the Hsiung-nu will not be able to withstand. If specially trained troops are quick to release (their bows) and the arrows in a single stream hit the target together, then the leather outfit and wooden shields of the Hsiung-nu will not be able to protect them. If they dismount and fight on foot, when swords and halberds clash as [the soldiers] come into close quarters, the Hsiung-nu, who lack infantry training, will not be able to cope. These are the advantages of China. If we look at this situation, the Hsiung-nu have three advantages, while China has five.[128]

The description of the military capabilities of Han and Hsiung-nu is lucid and eloquently presented and based on a realistic appraisal of the respective strengths. This type of information has no analogies in pre-Han military writings and provided Ssu-ma Ch'ien with first-hand information. Probably there was no other politician, in his age, who had such a good grasp of the military imperatives facing China.

In the same memorial, Ch'ao Ts'o requested the formation of a corps of light cavalry to fight the Hsiung-nu because of the obvious inadequacy of infantry and chariots. He also proposed that surrendered Hsiung-nu or other nomadic peoples, such as the Yi-ch'ü, be used to guard the frontiers

[128] *Ch'ao Ts'o chi chu-yi* (Shanghai: Jen-min, 1976), p. 8. For another translation of this memorial and for its military implications, see Joseph Needham et al., *Science and Civilization in China*, vol. 5: *Chemistry and Chemical Technology, Part VI: Military Technology: Missiles and Sieges* (Cambridge: Cambridge University Press, 1994), pp. 123–25.

against other tribesmen, under the leadership of Chinese generals with experience and understanding of their customs and usages, a policy that went under the name of "using foreigners to attack foreigners" (*yi man-yi kung man-yi*).[129] This strategy, more commonly known as "using 'barbarians' to control the 'barbarians'" (*yi yi chih yi*), during the Former Han meant simply the incorporation of foreigners within the Han military forces as a defense against the northern nomads. The subsequent establishment of self-supporting military units would be key to Wu-ti's offensive strategy.

Regardless of the peace treaties and use of foreign auxiliaries, the situation at the border remained critical, while the Hsiung-nu continued to expand to the west and to the north. In the fifth month of 177 B.C. the Hsiung-nu entered undisturbed the Pei-ti[130] and Shang commanderies,[131] and withdrew only after a force of eighty-five thousand cavalry was sent to Kao-nu,[132] led by Chancellor Kuan Ying, marquis of Ying-yin. In the course of the incursion the Hsiung-nu were reported to have plundered and harassed foreign peoples (*yi*) who were used by the Han as frontier guards.[133] Whereas this is an indication that the policy suggested by Ch'ao Ts'o was already being implemented at this time, it is also clear that it was not working.[134] The Hsiung-nu offensive was carried out not by the *ch'an-yü* himself, but by a subordinate leader, bearing the title of wise king of the right.[135] The attack must have been extremely critical, as the emperor himself then visited the border areas, which ran from the Kan-ch'üan Palace[136] to Kao-nu, in order to inspect the defenses of T'ai-yüan.[137] The situation was complicated not only because of the constant Hsiung-nu pressure, but also because of the continuing disaffection of Han aristocrats,

---

[129] *Han shu* 49, 2281. Cf. also *Ch'ao Ts'o chi chu-yi*, pp. 8 ff.

[130] Commandery located in the southwestern part of the Great Bend of the Yellow River, did not cover the same territory as the prefecture bearing the same name of the Ch'in period. It administered an area that included the northeastern part of present-day Kansu, and the southeastern part of Ning-hsia. Its administrative center was at Ma-ling (*Chung-kuo li-shih ti-t'u chi*, 2: 17–18, 4–4/6–4).

[131] Commandery located in the northern part of Shensi province (*Chung-kuo li-shih ti-t'u chi*, 2: 17–18, 4–7/6–7).

[132] District located to the northeast of the present-day city of Yen-an, in Shensi (*Chung-kuo li-shih ti-t'u chi*, 2: 17–18, 6–7).

[133] These are possibly the same as the Yi-ch'ü mentioned previously.

[134] For an analysis of Ch'ao Ts'o strategy against the Hsiung-nu, see AA. VV., "Ch'ao Ts'o k'ang-chi Hsiung-nu te chan-lüeh ssu-hsiang," *Li-shih yen-chiu* 1975.1: 74–8.

[135] *Shih chi chu-yi* 110, 2320–1; *Shih chi* 110, 2895.

[136] Kan-chüan Palace: located in the Kan-ch'üan Mountains (*Chung-kuo li-shih ti-t'u chi*, 2: 15–16, 4–4).

[137] *Shih chi* 10, 425; *Shih chi chu-yi*, 10, 259–60.

ready to take advantage of the military trouble at the border to set off an insurrection.[138]

Conclusion

The Hsiung-nu appeared as a wholly new force in Chinese history, one that imposed itself upon the consciousness of Han rulers and statesmen, as well as intellectuals, military leaders, and common people, with an urgency and a sense of real threat that nomadic peoples had never elicited before. In the north, China's thus far ever-expanding cultural and political space reached a seemingly unbreachable "wall" of alien peoples and lands that could not be conquered. Even more alarmingly, the nomads were able to sap the strength and resources of the empire, whether directly, through tribute and looting, or indirectly, by attracting seditious Han leaders and forcing the empire to expend much energy and resources in the pursuit of military advantages.

In this chapter we have explored the key factors that led to the creation of the Hsiung-nu empire. The crisis following the Ch'in expedition into the Ordos and the leadership struggle that occurred at the same time, as well as the increased militarization of Hsiung-nu society, are the plausible scenario that explains the process of centralization and the creation of a wholly new political structure. However, contemporary Han military weakness, which forced Kao-tsu to enter a tributary relationship with the Hsiung-nu, also provided the bulk of those external revenues without which the Hsiung-nu leadership would not have been able to support the impressive court, military apparatus, and tribal loyalty, and which arguably were critical to the survival and expansion of the Hsiung-nu empire.

It was at this point that China accepted the reality of a world order that was essentially bipolar, even though it included several minor polities with formal independence but that were de facto in a relationship of political subordination to one or the other power. The equilibrium on which this system of international relations was based – borders guaranteed by treaty, yearly payment, diplomatic marriages, definition of areas of influence – entered a critical stage as it became apparent that the *ho-ch'in* policy no longer provided stability. Understanding the factors that contributed to the crisis will be central to our analysis of Han Wu-ti's abandonment of "appeasement" and inauguration of an aggressive foreign policy.

---

[138] For instance, following the Hsiung-nu invasion, the king of Chi-pei rebelled, and the Han court was forced to stop the army sent against the Hsiung-nu, cf. *Shih chi* 95, 2673.

CHAPTER SIX

From Peace to War

China's Shift from Appeasement to Military Engagement

Introduction

With the accession of Emperor Wu in 140 B.C., a half-century-long tradition of foreign relations based on the search for diplomatic solutions and negotiated agreements came to an end. In the phase that followed, the Han dynasty assumed an outward-looking, expansion-driven, military-oriented posture. The Han–Hsiung-nu bipolar system of foreign relations came to an end, formally, with the breakup of the Hsiung-nu empire and the formal acceptance by Hu-han-yeh *ch'an-yü* in 51 B.C. of a position of inferiority to the Han emperor Hsüan-ti (73–49 B.C.). This development was the direct result of the successful military and political campaigns during Han Wu-ti's reign (140–87 B.C.). The shift from the "peace through kinship" strategy to the military solution, which took place during the lifetime of Ssu-ma Ch'ien, is one of the momentous events of Han history, and one whose repercussions were felt at every level of political and social life. This change in the means through which relations with the Hsiung-nu were conducted led to territorial expansion, but it also created economic problems and fostered tensions between government policy makers and the court on the one side, and the literati on the other. The respective positions were represented in stark contrast in the *Discourses on Salt and Iron* held in the early first century B.C.[1]

The plain narrative of the confrontation between Han and Hsiung-nu during the reign of Han Wu-ti is well known and does not need to be

---

[1] Especially relevant to our discussion is *chüan* seven (sections 43–48) of the *Yen-t'ieh lun* (ed. *Ssu-pu pei-yao*).

repeated here;[2] moreover, parts of it will be addressed in the following chapter, as we analyze Ssu-ma Ch'ien's attitudes toward the Hsiung-nu. It should be noted that in my discussion of the Hsiung-nu I rely most heavily on the *Shih chi* and make recourse to the *Han shu* only occasionally, when it provides specific information needed for clarification. The narrative on the Hsiung-nu in the *Han shu* (chapter 94) down to about 90 B.C. is essentially parallel to that of the *Shih chi*, but the *Han shu* is much more detailed concerning several aspects of Hsiung-nu–Han relations because of the reports sent from Central Asia after the establishment of the Protectorate General in 59 B.C. (a point made most eloquently in Michael Loewe's introduction to *China in Central Asia*). However, the period after the completion of the *Shih chi* (c. 90 B.C.) has not been included in the present work other than marginally to explain some of the consequences of the events taking place in Wu-ti's time, because the main focus of this and the following (Part IV) section lies in the transformation of the frontier in Ssu-ma Ch'ien's time and in its representation in the *Shih chi*. Given this chronological limit, and given the deep differences in period, historical outlook, and personal interest taken by Ssu-ma Ch'ien and Pan Ku, taken here to be the main authors of, respectively, *Shih chi* and *Han shu*, the *Han shu* has not been included as a main source. Nonetheless, I do not wish to give the impression that the *Han shu* is not an important source. It is, unquestionably, the major source for Han history. It has less validity in this study because it is not the first account to detail the history of Han–Hsiung-nu relations; that is, it was Ssu-ma Ch'ien, not Pan Ku, who made the essential shift leading to creation of a "history" of Inner Asia within Chinese historiography. For this reason, we cannot ignore the lingering controversy concerning the authenticity of some chapters of the *Shih chi*, in particular the possible derivation of chapter 123 of the *Shih chi* from chapter 61 of the *Han shu*. This issue had been discussed by a number of scholars and, to my mind, has not yet been settled.[3] This is not surprising for a text such

[2] There are several accounts of the relations between the Han and the Hsiung-nu; the basic events are narrated in a clear and synthetic manner in Ying-shih Yü, "The Hsiung-nu," in *Cambridge History of Early Inner Asia*, ed. Denis Sinor (Cambridge: Cambridge University Press, 1990), pp. 118–49. The best study of the Chinese penetration in the Western Regions is still Anthony Hulsewé, with an introduction by M. A. N. Loewe, *China in Central Asia: The Early Stage, 125 B.C.–A.D. 23. An Annotated Translation of Chapters 61 and 96 of the History of the Former Han Dynasty* (Leiden: Brill, 1979).

[3] On this and related issues, see Hulsewé and Loewe, *China in Central Asia*, pp. 13–33; Anthony Hulsewé, "The Problem of the Authenticity of Shih-chi," *T'oung Pao* 66 (1975): 83–147; D. D. Leslie, and K. H. J. Gardiner, "Chinese Knowledge of Central Asia," *T'oung Pao* 68.4–5 (1982): 254–308; J. R. Gardiner-Gardner, "Chang Ch'ien and Central Asian Ethnography," *Papers of Far Eastern History* 33 (1986): 23–79; Yves Hervouet, "Le valeur relative de textes du

as the *Shih chi* whose transmission history remains fuzzy at best for over a thousand years. However, the controversy is relatively unimportant to this account, as it refers mainly to the biographies of Chang Ch'ien and Li Ling, who enter marginally in this work, and about whom additional information is available in other, non-suspect parts of the *Shih chi*. Most of the information discussed here is derived from chapter 110 of the *Shih chi*, which does not present textual problems of a magnitude to justify doubts about its authenticity with respect to chapter 94 of the *Han shu*. Instead, in this chapter, I will focus on two problems that to this date remain unresolved.

First, I will try to clarify the reasons for the shift from the *ho-ch'in* policy to a strategy of direct military engagement and territorial expansion. Why did the "accommodation" strategy come to an end? By analyzing the conditions of its implementation, the arguments put forth by supporters, and some aspects of the later debate, I will try to link competing orientations in Han strategic thinking with the historical context of Chinese-Inner Asian relations.

The second problem of interest is the extent to which the campaign against the Hsiung-nu was carried out by Han Wu-ti and his generals. Its duration, territorial expansion, forces employed, and expenses required are nothing short of exceptional even considering the intense military activity that had marked the history of China until then. As the Han armies marched through the deserts of Kansu and showed their insignia at the gates of the oasis-cities of the Western Regions, a new world opened to China's imagination. By reaching as far as the T'ien-shan and the Tarim Basin, Han Wu-ti's expansion dwarfed even the feats of two of the most blatantly expansionistic pre-Han rulers, Duke Huan of Ch'i and the First Emperor of Ch'in. The motivation for such an accomplishment cannot be ascribed solely to megalomania. The Han political and strategic choices and the decision to fight a protracted war occurred in a climate of changing policies aimed at consolidating imperial unity and strengthening China's economy. These measures were arguably essential in allowing the Han to sustain the war effort. Internal political events within the court, after the death of the empress dowager in 135 B.C., and the waning of her influence also were

Che-Ki et du Han-chou," in *Melanges de Sinologie offérts a Monsieur Paul Demieville, part II* (Paris: Bibliotheque de l'Istitute des Hautes Etudes Chinoises, 1974), pp. 55–76; Paolo Daffinà, "The Han Shu Hsi Yu Chuan Re-Translated. A Review Article," *T'oung-p ao* 68.4–5 (1982): 309–39; Kazuo Enoki, "On the Relationship between the *Shih-chi*, Bk. 123, and the *Han-shu*, Bks. 61 and 96," *Memoirs of the Research Department of the Toyo Bunko* 41 (1983): 1–31; Edwin G. Pulleyblank, "Han China in Central Asia," *International History Review* 3 (1981): 278–96.

factors. Han strategy in the war with the Hsiung-nu has been ascribed to these climactic changes which took place during the first twenty years of Wu-ti's role. Concurrently, however, it is essential that we take account of Inner Asian political and economic realities, which exposed the Hsiung-nu to weaknesses that the Han were able to exploit, especially in the early phases of the confrontation, with considerable success. Finally, this chapter outlines the restructuring of the northern frontier as it began to take shape in Wu-ti's period, including the new administrative organization of the frontier areas.

Why Did the *Ho-ch'in* Policy Come to an End?

The dramatic shift in foreign policy that brought China from a defensive posture based on appeasement to an offensive strategy based on a total military commitment plunged the Han into a war whose final victory, attained at enormous human and economic costs, appeared Pyrrhic to many contemporary observers, including Ssu-ma Ch'ien. Even though Han statesmen failed to recognize for a long time exactly why the Hsiung-nu kept invading their territory, they could not have failed to notice that the presumed advantages that the *ho-ch'in* policy was meant to yield were simply not being realized. The Hsiung-nu's continuous demands for payments and their frequent raids (whether or not their demands had been met) could be explained only by resorting to the cultural stereotype, born out of the Spring and Autumn tradition, of the uncouth, greedy, and violent foreigner. This was a convenient rationalization, not the least because it prepared the Chinese psychologically for the unavoidable consequence of the failure of peace: a painful and prolonged war against a powerful enemy.

As we have seen in the previous chapter, the *ho-ch'in* doctrine continued to hold sway throughout the first part of the Former Han, when the metaphors of equality and complementarity between the two sovereigns had supplied the Han with a workable, if not ideal, basis for negotiation with the Hsiung-nu. As peace failed to last, however, and the borders continued to be routinely violated, the bipolar system of foreign relations – represented in the political symbolism whereby the two rulers were portrayed as "Earth" and "Heaven," or as "brothers," and their kingdoms as two complementary universes – was no longer sustainable. Disharmonious relations became the norm, precipitating a deep crisis of the entire Han approach to relations with the Hsiung-nu. It is at this point that military solutions were invoked, and the paradigm of foreign relations subsequently shifted back to the template provided by the strategy and arguments for expansion that had their precedents in the Spring and Autumn period.

The Debates over Ho-Ch'in (135–134 B.C.)

Although an acknowledgment of the desirability of a policy shift away from *ho-ch'in* and toward the military engagement of the Hsiung-nu was already present in the positions held by Ch'ao Ts'o and Chia Yi, it is the two-phase debate held in 135 and 134 B.C. that provides the most cogent explanation of the issues at stake concerning Han relations with the Hsiung-nu at the time of Han Wu-ti,[4] and the subsequent endorsement by the ministers and high officials of the Chinese emperor's aggressive military stance.[5] The protagonists, Wang Hui and Han An-kuo, argued vigorously over whether to discontinue the *ho-ch'in* policy and attack the Hsiung-nu, or continue to "appease" them. This debate is reported in the *Han shu* as a prologue to the misguided military episode that took place at Ma-yi, a border town where Han troops were disastrously defeated in an attempt to ambush the Hsiung-nu and capture their chief.

This debate, the fullest contemporary account of the factors held responsible for the switch to an offensive strategy, began in 135 B.C., and was occasioned by the *ch'an-yü*'s request to renew the *ho-ch'in* treaty. As the emperor asked for his officials' advice, Wang Hui, a man of the northeastern region of Yen who had served for years as a border official and had a reputation as an expert in nomadic matters, expressed his point of view: "When the Han conclude a peace [agreement] with the Hsiung-nu, usually after just a few years the Hsiung-nu violate the treaty. It would be better to reject their promises and send soldiers to attack them." The military option was rejected by Hann An-kuo, an able rhetorician, who supported appeasement on the following grounds:

Fighting at a distance of a thousand *li*, the army will not gain any profit. Now, the Hsiung-nu depend upon the hooves of their own horses and cherish the feelings of birds and beasts. They move around like a multitude of birds and are difficult to capture and control. In order to conquer their territory it is not sufficient to expand. In order to capture their masses it is not enough to set up a barrier. From high antiquity they have not been subjugated. If the Han have to strive over many thousands of *li* in order to gain an advantage, men and horses will be exhausted and the Bandits will completely control them. The circumstances will necessarily be perilous. I therefore maintain that this [attacking] would not be better than *ho-ch'in*.[6]

---

[4] The following discussion is based on *Han shu* 52, 2398–2403.

[5] This exchange to a certain extent foreshadows the issues at stake in the *Debates on Salt and Iron*. See Michael Loewe, *Records of Han Administration*, vol. 1: *Historical Assessment* (Cambridge: Cambridge University Press, 1967), p. 54.

[6] *Han shu* 52, 2398.

Admittedly, there was no easy solution. On the one hand, according to Wang Hui, the *ho-ch'in* policy was not a permanent solution because previous treaties had not prevented Hsiung-nu incursions. On the other, according to Han An-kuo, attacking was no solution either: the futility of war against the northerners, who move like "birds and beasts," was an old theme, but it was reinforced here by the vivid awareness, the result of many bitter lessons, that the Hsiung-nu had a military advantage when they fought in their own territory. Han An-kuo identified clearly the source of the Han disadvantage in the logistic difficulties that would be met by Chinese armies if required to spend a long time in the field. His "pacifist" argument won the day because his sentiment was shared by the other officials, and the *ho-ch'in* treaty was temporarily renewed.

A second round of the debate took place the following year, 134 B.C., when Nie Weng-yi, a prominent man in the frontier city of Ma-yi, sent Wang Hui to court to propose a plan for ending the conflict. Nie's plan consisted of using promises of gifts to induce the *ch'an-yü* and his army to approach Ma-yi and when they did so, slaughtering them. Nie thought that such a stratagem might succeed in the climate of trust between Han and Hsiung-nu that had set in after the renewal of the peace treaty. Possibly because of the tradition of foreign relations with the northerners that, as we have seen in Chapter 4, justified the use of trickery, the violation of the treaty on which this strategy was based was not seen as ethically improper. At least in part, however, this course of action must have seemed feasible also because of the diminished value of the treaty itself as a viable means of preserving good relations and because of the Hsiung-nu's own breaches of previous agreements.

It is clear from the circumstances in which the debate was held that the emperor was aggrieved by the constant, seemingly unlimited demands of the *ch'an-yü*, who had continued to raid and plunder the border regions while waiting for the *ho-ch'in* treaty to be ratified by the Han. Once again, Han Wu-ti asked for the officials' opinion, and this time Wang Hui and Han An-kuo's positions are reported in the *Shih chi* at greater length. Because this is such an important political debate, marking the beginning of a new era not only in Han history but also in the history of the relations between China and northern nomads, I will examine the two officials' positions in detail.

Wang Hui's first point is only marginally different from his earlier position. In essence, Wang presents an argument based on the following contrast: during the Warring States period even the state of Tai could hold off the nomads, and keep them from raiding and pillaging, but Han China, although politically united and invested heavily in frontier defenses, was unable to stop the Hsiung-nu. Hence, Wang stated, no alternative remained but to attack them. Han An-kuo replied by first reminding his audience of the humiliating defeat suffered by Han Kao-tsu at

P'ing-ch'eng,[7] which led to the inauguration of *ho-ch'in*, a policy that, by providing peace, had "benefited five generations." An-kuo emphasized the idea that the empire should have territorial boundaries – "the wise and sage man regards the empire as being limited" – and that Han emperors should refrain from attempting conquest. He praised Han Wen-ti for not having conquered a single inch of Hsiung-nu territory and for having eventually renewed the peace treaty. This anti-expansionist stance was at the heart of his support for *ho-ch'in*, and he reiterated it throughout the debate.

In his rebuttal of Han An-kuo's defense of *ho-ch'in*, Wang Hui resorted to an argument reminiscent of King Wu-ling's debate for the adoption of nomadic cavalry garments:

Not so! I have heard that the Five Emperors did not follow each other's rituals, and the Three Kings did not repeat each other's music. This is not because they antagonized each other, but because every one followed what was appropriate to the epoch. Moreover, Kao-ti personally dressed in a strong armor, and armed with sharp weapons, hiding in fogs and mists, immersed in snow and frost had fought continuously for over ten years, and therefore he could not avenge the outrage of P'ing-ch'eng. Without force there is no ability, and therefore he put the hearts of the empire at rest. Today, however, there are frequent alarms along the frontiers, the soldiers are wounded and killed, and in China funerary processions follow one after the other. This is what grieves the benevolent man. For this reason I say that it is appropriate to strike.[8]

The "circumstances" required proper action, and the reason Liu Pang had been defeated and forced to accept the peace terms was that the empire was not in a position to continue to fight after the many years of civil war at the end of the Ch'in. But the peace Liu Pang had secured was simply not there anymore. An-kuo replied by arguing that a change of policy would make sense only if a higher return could be guaranteed: "if the profit is not tenfold one should not change trade, and if the achievement is not one hundredfold one should not change habits." But what would China achieve by changing course? This was anything but clear. In addition, by comparing the Yi and Ti of old with the far more powerful Hsiung-nu of his day, An-kuo captured both the essence of the changes that frontier relations had undergone and the reason why the Han now faced a more difficult situation:

From the rise of the Three Dynasties the Yi and Ti did not share the calendar or the color of garments [with us]. Without might they could not be con-

---

[7] The P'ing-ch'eng prefecture was part of the Yen-men commandery, situated east of present Ta-t'ung. See Hans Bielenstein, "The Restoration of the Han Dynasty, Vol. 3: 'The People,'" in *Bulletin of the Museum of Far Eastern Antiquities* 39, part II (1967): 86, n. 3.

[8] *Han shu* 52, 2400.

trolled, and strength alone could not make them submit, and yet, as people who cannot be shepherded (*pu mu chih min*)[9] from remote regions and inaccessible lands, they were thought as insufficient to trouble the central states. But now the Hsiung-nu are light and quick, brave and hasty soldiers, they arrive like a sudden wind and leave like a disappearing lightning. Their occupation is raising animals, they go hunting with bow and arrow; they follow their animals according to the availability of pasture, and their abode is not permanent; they are difficult to capture and control. As for the present, since long they have caused the border regions to abandon tilling and weaving in order to support the common activities of the nomads. Their strength cannot be matched in a balanced way. For this reason I say it is not convenient to attack.

If Yi and Ti were so difficult to control, even though they had no unity, how much more difficult would it be to oppose the military strength of the Hsiung-nu? An-kuo's argument displays a keen knowledge of the nomads' strengths, which he saw as lying essentially in the resources of their economy and in the alleged incorporation of the northern frontier regions within the sphere of their economic activities.

Wang Hui replied with a variation on his previous argument: brilliant men act according to the circumstances, and hence Duke Mu of Ch'in was able to defeat the Western Jung and expand his territory. Likewise, Meng T'ien was able to open up thousands of miles of land and to build fortifications so that "the Hsiung-nu did not dare water their horses in the Yellow River." From this Wang Hui concluded that the Hsiung-nu could be subjugated only by force and could not be cultivated with benevolence. China was now much stronger than the Hsiung-nu, and could afford to fight them, as they were "like an abscess which must be burst open with strong crossbows and arrows, and absolutely should not be left to fester." This argument was supported by the perceptive realization that the Hsiung-nu did not have such a firm hold over their subject peoples, and, once the first blows had been dealt to the Hsiung-nu leadership, formerly vanquished nomadic tribes, such as the Yüeh-chih, "will be able to rise [against the Hsiung-nu] and will submit [to the Han]." It was perfectly clear to Wang Hui that the political basis of the Hsiung-nu was quite unstable, and that it would be possible for the Han to exploit divisions among the nomads.

Han An-kuo began to lose ground as he continued to repeat the by now trite motif that the nomads could not be defeated in their territory: "the clash of two strong winds will weaken [them] to the point that they cannot

[9] The commentary in *Han shu* 52, 2401, renders this as "people who cannot be shepherded," which I have followed. At the same time, a lingering doubt remains as to whether this expression may refer to "people who did not tend herds," that is, people who were not pastoral nomads.

raise a hair or a feather; an arrow shot from a strong bow at the end of its flight would not be able to pierce the white plain silk of Lu," that is to say, even the strongest army would eventually weaken and be exhausted to the point that it could not accomplish anything. In this way An-kuo sought to rebuke the "hawkish" military faction ready to mount ostensibly useless expeditions that would penetrate deeply into the enemy's territory but fail to achieve their stated goals.

Piqued, Wang Hui replied that that was not what he was proposing. His position was quite different:

Now the reason why I propose to attack them is absolutely not to go out and penetrate deeply, but to go along with the wishes of the *ch'an-yü*, and induce him to come close to the border. In the meanwhile, handpicked bold caval-rymen and brave infantrymen should lie in ambush and ready for action; we shall also examine how to protect them from any dangers so that they can guard against them. Once this situation has been arranged, whether we encamp to the [Hsiungu-nu] right or to their left, whether we are positioned in front of them or cut off their rear, the *ch'an-yü* can be captured, and then all the Hsiung-nu will be certainly taken.

Wang Hui's plan for a limited military engagement won the emperor's approval. In the end, it seems that Wang Hui defeated his adversary because Han An-kuo had been unable to demostrate that *ho-ch'in* could actually guarantee peace. An-kuo's main argument was a negative one, relying on the point that deep military engagement was not desirable because it would not solve the problem and would simply result in a loss of people. This position was based on the realistic understanding, with which his contem-poraries seemed to agree, that the Han army could fight the Hsiung-nu in the nomads' own territory only for a limited time; moreover, if a war were fought on the nomads' teritory, they would simply keep moving farther and farther away, so the consequences of a prolonged war would be disastrous for the Han. Recognizing the strength of this argument, Wang Hui pro-posed a limited engagement on the frontier aimed at capturing the head of the Hsiung-nu, arguing that this act would trigger certain reactions in the enemy camp – such as the surrender of other Hsiung-nu tribesmen and the rebellion of the Yüeh-chih – that would eventually destroy the political unity of the Hsiung-nu.

The Han decided, then, to pursue the military option. Unfortunately for them, the whole plot was hopelessly botched, and at the ensuing battle at Ma-yi the *ch'an-yü* not only did not fall into the trap, but deeply humili-ated the Han armies, inflicting a resounding defeat on them. And yet, in a somewhat perverse way, this disastrous outcome must have appeared as a confirmation of Wang Hui's fundamental argument. Peace treaties with the Hsiung-nu did not work, and because the nomads continued to create a serious threat on the borders and limited military action of the type attempted at Ma-yi was not successful against them, there was no other solution but to confront them on their own terms, through full-scale military engagement.

The debates between Wang Hui and Han An-kuo make it clear that if the *ho-ch'in* policy had worked, managing to ensure the peace and prosperity of the borders, the proponents of the offensive strategy could not have prevailed; indeed, at the time majority opinion was by no means in favor of military action. That the emperor eventually followed Wang Hui's advice was because the *ho-ch'in* policy was no longer particularly effective, and even An-kuo's support for it was not particularly enthusiastic: it had come to be seen as the lesser of two evils rather than as a truly successful foreign policy. The treaty system that the Han had established with the Hsiung-nu at the time of Han Kao-tsu had been quite acceptable to the Han, and, even though some at court may not have liked it, the majority had nonetheless learned to live with it. Hence possible arguments to explain its rejection by Han Wu-ti, such as "the appeasement policy was a humiliating one" or "the Chinese were tired of paying" are immaterial to the discussion; the issue that forced the change of policy was not the *ho-ch'in* policy per se, but that it was not working.[10] Why was it not working?

Limits and Ultimate Failure of the Ho-Ch'in Policy

From a Chinese perspective, appeasement had failed because the Hsiung-nu did not respect the treaties: the *ho-ch'in* policy did not guarantee the inviolability of China's borders and the tribute payments were an investment that did not pay off. These "investments," by the way, were by no means trifling, and had come to represent a considerable burden on the Han economy, though one that could be sustained, probably, without eroding too much the factor of growth that the Han had come to enjoy down to the reign of Wu-ti.[11]

Several theories have been put forward to explain the nature of the Han–Hsiung-nu relationship during the Former Han. Generally speaking, these agree that the *ho-ch'in* policy was entered by the Han at a time of military weakness and political vulnerability but disagree as to the relative

[10] One should also note that, although the shift to an aggressive stance occurred early in Wu-ti's time, the debate between "accommodation" and warfare continued even afterwards. For another debate concerning the different tactics to be employed against the Hsiung-nu see *Han shu* 94B, 3825.

[11] For a calculation of the tribute paid to the Hsiung-nu see Bielenstein, "The Restoration of the Han Dynasty," pp. 91–92; Yü Ying-shih, *Trade and Expansion in Han China: A Study in the Structure of Sino-Barbarian Economic Relations* (Berkeley: University of California Press, 1967), pp. 45–49.

importance of "appeasement" in the larger context of the two peoples' relations. According to some, both Han and Hsiung-nu accepted the settlement solution as a tactical move that from the start was conceived not as a permanent solution but as a temporary arrangement. Whereas the Han were forced to accept a tributary relationship for lack of strength, the Hsiung-nu found it advantageous for the economic gains. But neither of them renounced to pursue their own separate interests, even though they might be in violation of the treaties. On the one hand, the Hsiung-nu did not refrain from raiding the border, and the Han, on the other hand, planned to reverse the relationship once the "family connection" established with the Hsiung-nu court had achieved the goal of relegating the ch'an-yü to a subordinate position.[12] Going even further, other historians look at ho-ch'in as pure expediency within a general context of permanent warfare, and they criticize the view that the search for peace and reconciliation actually was pursued in earnest by either of the two nations. In fact, in the early period ho-ch'in treaties sealed first the tributary status of the Han vis-à-vis the Hsiung-nu and later, after the "surrender" of the southern Hsiung-nu in 51 B.C., the Han primacy. Yet in each period the ho-ch'in treaties constituted only one side of a broader and more complex relationship.[13] Others again emphasize the economic and political advantages reaped by the Han during the early period of the ho-ch'in policy. In this perspective, the policy acquires a more holistic meaning, as it is held responsible for the economic growth and political consolidation of China, as well as for the promotion of friendly relations and "cultural exchanges."[14] But regardless of the relative weight they attributed to "appeasement" as the leading strategy pursued by both Hsiung-nu and Han until the time of Han Wu-ti, all commentators agreed that peaceful relations broke down more or less regularly, without seeking an explanation beyond the often-repeated claim that the Hsiung-nu were insatiable.

This consideration leads us to a question that is central to our understanding of the shift to an offensive foreign policy: why is it that the Hsiung-nu – if we are to believe the sources – did not abide by the terms of the agreements? This question has rarely been engaged in actual historical terms. More often, scholars have sought explanations in the analysis of broader patterns of economic and political relations between the Hsiung-nu and China. In Chapter 4 we discussed the theory that places the cause of the nomads' violent raids against the Chinese borders with China's

[12] Shih Wei-ch'ing, "Kuan-yü Hsi Han cheng-fu yü Hsiung-nu ho-ch'in jo-kan wen-t'i," *Hsia-men ta-hsüeh hsüeh-pao* 1985.4: 21–29.
[13] Chang Ch'ang-ming, "Shih-lun Hsi Han te Han Hsiung kuan-hsi chi ch'i kuan-hsi chi ho-ch'in cheng-ts'e," *Chiang-huai lun-t'an* 1983.6: 83–88.
[14] Lo Ta-yün, "Hsi Han ch'u-ch'i tui Hsiung-nu ho-ch'in te shih-chih," *Yün-nan min-tsu hsüeh-yüan hsüeh-pao* 1985.4: 44–49.

unwillingness to open its border markets or to agree on paying a fixed "tribute."[15] The problem with this theory is that it assumes the existence of a mutually exclusive relationship between "trade" and "raid," even though throughout the duration of the *ho-ch'in* policy Hsiung-nu incursions often occurred soon after China agreed to open border markets and to increase its payments. Hence, the failure of the *ho-ch'in* policy to preserve peaceful relations cannot be linked to a hypothetical failure of an existing exchange mechanism. But the question of why the nomads raided China, when tribute was being delivered and markets were open, remains unanswered, and other explanations that posit a Hsiung-nu desire to expand their land or to extort more money remain a matter of conjecture that cannot be supported by the sources.[16]

By shifting focus from the economic plane to the diplomatic and military arenas, however, it is possible to offer a different explanation. As we have seen, in the calculations of the supporters of the *ho-ch'in* policy, the use of *ho-ch'in* was not simply a choice dictated by the need to establish a modus vivendi with a more powerful state, but was a long-term strategy aimed at absorbing the next generation of the Hsiung-nu leadership within the Han court's political sphere and neutralizing the Hsiung-nu as an independent and inimical state. This strategy can even be regarded as an evolution of Spring and Autumn marriage-diplomacy policies, and it indicates that the Han were ready to wait and to sacrifice part of their revenues to achieve a long-term political objective. However, the cost of this policy proved too high once it became clear that the Hsiung-nu leadership would continue to raid the border areas and did not have the slightest intention of recognizing the Han state's superiority. *Ho-ch'in* treaties appeared to be hollow, and the whole strategy had to be called into question.

A close examination of the actual treaty violations by the Hsiung-nu suggests that in various instances it was not the *ch'an-yü* himself who violated a particular agreement, but his subordinate leaders or Chinese commanders who had defected to the Hsiung-nu.[17] Possibly, then, the central point in this matter could be identified in the discrepancy in the power that each of the parties "signing" the treaty had to guarantee that the letter of the treaty

---

[15] Sechin Jagchid and Van Jay Symons, *Peace, War and Trade along the Great Wall* (Bloomington: Indiana University Press, 1989).

[16] None of these theories can accommodate the sequence of events that we see commonly, such as the systematic withdrawal of the Hsiung-nu troops after the invasion of areas sometimes very close to the capital; or the conclusion of a *ho-ch'in* agreement after the Han had actually been able to repel the Hsiung-nu, as happened with the treaty of 174 B.C. between Wen-ti and Modun, signed in the wake of diplomatic parleys following the successful expedition of 177 B.C. against the Hsiung-nu wise king of the right.

[17] *Han shu* 94B, 3754.

would be respected by the entire body politic formally under his authority. If it can be shown that one of the parties was lacking the full authority to commute the international agreement into a "law" that each member of his people subsequently had to abide by, it would then be obvious that any strategy based on the assumption that *pacta sunt servanda* would be fundamentally flawed. In other words, to understand the causes of treaty violations one must first understand the essential premises on which such treaties were based, namely, the nature of the authority of each ruler and of the understanding of "sovereignty" by each of the parties.

Regarding China,[18] one can arguably identify four different aspects as constitutive of a notion of sovereignty in the early imperial period that would allow the Chinese side to keep an international agreement.[19] First, the position of the emperor as supreme lawgiver; second, the unity of religious sanction and political power; third, the absence of another source of authority within the political community; and fourth, the link between the political authority of the sovereign and a more or less clearly delimited political community.[20]

[18] My intent here is to give a necessarily synthetic and an admittedly cursory description of some of the elements constitutive of the notion of sovereign authority in Han China to highlight areas of difference between it and the political authority of the *ch'an-yü*. This is not intended to sum up all the elements that can be brought to bear to explain the nature of the monarch's place in Han politics and society, and even less its philosophical foundations. Rather, it is intended to highlight the most glaring structural differences between the Han's and the Hsiung-nu's notion of rulership with respect to their relative abilities to observe an international treaty.

[19] On the general issue of sovereignty in early imperial China, see Michael Loewe, "The Authority of the Emperors of Ch'in and Han," in *State and Law in East Asia. Festschrift Karl Bünger*, ed. Dieter Eikemer and Herbert Franke (Wiesbaden: Harrassowitz, 1981), pp. 80–111.

[20] A similar notion of sovereignty can be seen in practice with the emergence of the Roman Principate, especially from the second century A.D. With the transition from the Republic to the Principate the territorial boundaries of Rome became more clearly defined, and the word "empire" itself (*imperium*) acquired a territorial meaning originally absent (see Richardson, "*Imperium Romanum*: Empire and the Language of Power," *Journal of Roman Studies* 81 [1991]: 1–9). Through the branching out of the imperial administrative institutions, and the granting of the right of citizenship to all free people (including those living in distant provinces), the society and politics of the empire became somewhat more cohesive. The emperor became the head, rather than the mere agent, of the body politic. His role as supreme lawgiver placed him above the law, and his divinization ensured that no superior or alternative authority (either political or religious) could exist above him. In the opinion of F. H. Hinsley, these are all compelling arguments for the existence of a notion of sovereignty in the Roman Principate, well before a theory of sovereignty was developed by sixteenth-century European

As for the first point, in the "legalist" thought that inspired many of the political ideas of the early imperial period the notion of a divine lawgiver is simply absent. According to one of the fathers of the legalist school, Shen Tao, "law does not come down from Heaven nor does it arise from Earth. It is nothing else but something that comes forth from among men, consonant with their ideas."[21] However, Anthony Hulsewé has shown that in the early imperial period the emperor himself acquired the institutional role of supreme lawgiver. His ordinances and decrees had the authority of the law and the power to overrule customary or traditional usages. The code of laws became then the ultimate source of authority within the body politic, and the only institutional power located above it was the emperor.[22]

Second, the creation of the empire set in motion a process whereby political power and "religious" sanction were reunited and led to the establishment of the principle that the religious sanction to rule could not rest with a source of authority different from the wielder of political and military power. The doctrine of Heaven's Mandate, in which Heaven became the ultimate source of temporal authority, although foreshadowed in some of the earlier texts, such as the *Book of Songs* and the *Book of Documents*, and especially in the philosophy of Mencius, developed relatively slowly on the political plane. It acquired greater relevance, and became part of the ideology of imperial legitimacy, most probably when the process of consolidation of the authority of the emperor had been completed, and it acquired actual political relevance only at the time of Wang Mang's accession (9 A.D.).[23] The religious meaning implicit in a title such as *huang-ti* already excluded, from the very beginning of the imperial period, the idea that the ruler's religious and temporal powers could be separated.[24] Surely, by presenting themselves as repositories of knowledge essential to the correct management of state affairs, ministers and literati could attempt to appropriate the right to the correct interpretation of the "will" of Heaven.[25] The tension between the formal authority and "religious" sanction of the emperor and the informal power of his advisors could generate dissent and

thinkers; see his *Sovereignty* (Cambridge: Cambridge University Press, 1986 [1966]), pp. 27–44.

[21] A. Hulsewé, "Law as One of the Foundations of State Power in Early Imperial China," in *Foundations and Limits of State Power in China*, ed. S. Schram (London: School of Oriental and African Studies, 1987), p. 12.

[22] Hulsewé, "Law as One of the Foundations of State Power in Early Imperial China," pp. 11–32.

[23] Michael Loewe, "The Authority of the Emperors of Ch'in and Han," pp. 80–111.

[24] Derk Bodde, *China's First Unifier: Li Ssu* (Leiden: Brill, 1938), p. 31.

[25] A classic study on the political influence exercised by various officials on political affairs is Wolfram Eberhard, "The Political Function of Astronomy and Astronomers in Han China," in *Chinese Thought and Institutions*, ed. John K. Fairbank (Chicago: University of Chicago Press, 1957), pp. 37–70.

disobedience, and even lay the foundations for a dynastic change, but in general it did not produce a separation between the religious and temporal powers of the emperor.

Third, within the Han political system the emperor also represented the highest source of political authority in the state. He could issue edicts and decrees, could appoint or dismiss ministers, and was the supreme judicial authority. Such authority was, per se, unchallengeable even though the person of the emperor might be subject to criticism as inadequate to the task. The postulation that the theoretical separation between the person of the ruler and the institution of kingship was the abstract point of equilibrium of a universal socio-political order was expounded in the writings of political philosophers of the late Warring States period.[26] The centrality of emperorship to the Han political and moral universe, above and beyond the qualities of the individual ruler, gave the emperor "sovereign" authority, an authority that could not be challenged without challenging the dogma of single and undivided rulership that constituted one of the ideological tenets of the state. In the political conceptions of the early Han, as reflected, for instance, in the *Huai-nan-tzu*, the notion of law, derived largely from a legalist frame, was tempered by the concerns with moral values and interests of the people usually associated with Taoist and Confucian ideas. These attempted to subordinate the ruler himself to the rule of law and thereby curb the potential abuses of a tyrannical power.[27] These elaborations, although setting standards that the ruler was asked to observe, and therefore making the ruler "accountable," at the same time did not recognize any other authority that could legitimately promulgate laws. In other words, whereas the ruler's actions could be judged by the law, it was only the ruler who could legally issue laws. By restructuring the state bureaucracy, reducing the power of the hereditary aristocracy, and eliminating semi-independent power centers, the former Han emperors had been, by and large, successful in securing not only the ideological but also the political primacy of the imperial institution. The hierarchical system of the Han bureaucracy also ensured that policies would be implemented through a chain of subordination within which each link was responsible to the higher one.

Finally, although the principle of imperial rulership was cast in universal terms, its translation from the philosophical to the political arena implied something like a change of status. Both in practice and in principle, outside the state, which the emperor headed, the authority of the emperor during the early Han was effectively limited by the norms and prac-

---

[26] Benjamin Schwartz, *The World of Thought in Ancient China* (Cambridge, Mass.: Belknap Press, 1985), p. 40.

[27] Roger Ames, *The Art of Rulership: A Study in Ancient Chinese Political Thought* (Honolulu: University of Hawaii Press, 1983), pp. 136–41.

tices that had to be observed in foreign relations; as we have seen, this was the basis of the new world order created by Han Kao-tsu and Modun. It can be argued that as the *ho-ch'in* treaty was signed, a claim to universal rulership needed to be suppressed because it was unrealistic and contradicted the policy of negotiated accommodation. The "boundedness" of political sovereignty and its territorial limits continued to be endorsed even after the Hsiung-nu had been thoroughly defeated, and there was no longer a compelling realpolitik reason to accept such limitation. For example, in 60 B.C., during the debate over the ritual that the *ch'an-yü* Hu-han-yeh was supposed to follow as he came to court to present "tribute," Hsiao Wang-chih remarked that because the *ch'an-yü* did not follow the Chinese calendar, his nation should be referred to as an independent state, and he should thus not be treated as a tributary, but should instead be assigned a rank above that of the feudal kings.[28]

Turning to the Hsiung-nu camp, the situation appears very different. In traditional Inner Asian societies, kin bonds, reliance on customary law, and segmentation of political power among clans and tribes in steppe pastoral societies prevented the emergence of any absolute, indivisible, and legally recognized authority that would be the expression of a given political community in its entirety. The "state" among the Hsiung-nu was embodied in certain features of governmental centralization that allowed for a unified military leadership and for the existence of a center recognized both within and outside of the political community, and, as mentioned earlier, it could survive only through a process of uninterrupted, ongoing negotiation between the ruler and the other tribal leaders. Thus, among the Hsiung-nu the figure of the ruler never truly represented a pole of absolute authority in the sense evoked by the notion of sovereignty; in this system the leader was more often the first among equals, whose position of primacy rested ultimately on the consent obtained from other chieftains and members of the tribal aristocracy. This consent could be coerced, but the ultimate foundation of the charismatic leader was the voluntary consensus obtained from his closest advisors, military commanders, and family members, without whom his rise to power would be impossible. These "electors" could not be kept in a position of absolute subordination.[29]

---

[28] Burton Watson, *Courtier and Commoner in Ancient China: Selections from the History of the Former Han* (New York, Columbia University Press, 1974), pp. 212–13.

[29] On the question of sovereignty and sacral kingship in Inner Asia, see Paul Roux, "L'origine céleste de la souveraineté dans les inscriptions paléo-turques de Mongolia et de Siberie," in *The Sacral Kingship* (Leiden: Brill, 1959), pp. 231–41; Mori Masao, "The T'u-chüeh Concept of Sovereign," *Acta Asiatica* 41 (1981): 47–75; Osman Turan, "The Ideal of World Dominion among the Medieval Türks," *Studia Islamica* 4 (1955): 77–90; Peter Golden, "Imperial Ideology and

Moreover, the highest points of nomadic political integration, military might, and territorial expansion were accompanied by claims of universal rulership that, by failing to identify the state with a limited political community, posed an equally unsurmountable obstacle to the emergence of the notion of sovereignty.[30] As we have seen, Modun rose to power through his successful attempt to defend the Hsiung-nu people from the attacks of both Chinese and Inner Asian foes. Once that mission had been accomplished there was no specific reason why the *ch'an-yü* should continue to enjoy paramount political authority and "supra-tribal" power.[31]

However, together with the charismatic leader, a new stratum of aristocrats and military commanders had emerged, people who had been granted a privileged position by the *ch'an-yü* and who had a bond of personal loyalty with him. The authority they enjoyed and their enhanced military power strengthened their position among their own followers and power bases and allowed them to receive the lion's share of the tribute paid by China and other states. Members of the new aristocracy filled the ranks of the "supra-tribal" institutions; they became the emperor's bodyguard, the household administrators (*ta-tang-hu*), and the Ku-tu marquises, who acted as inspectors or police agents for the *ch'an-yü*'s government.[32] Thus, so many interests had clustered around the newly authoritative institution of the *ch'an-yü* that, as long as the internal and international situation remained favorable, most continued to profit from their initial conditional support for the charismatic leader and would not withdraw it without a compelling reason. The aristocracy's political power – previously absolute within their own tribes – had been curtailed, but the advantages of the new political structure were by no means trifling, and they could not be easily forsaken.

the Sources of Political Unity Amongst the Pre-Činggisid Nomads of Western Eurasia," *Archivum Eurasiae Medii Aevi* 2 (1982): 37–76.

[30] Modun claimed for himself the title *ch'an-yü*, "established by Heaven" (*Han shu* 3756). This claim to universal rulership became particularly evident during the Mongol period. A notable example of such a claim can be found in Hulagu's letter to King Louis IX of France. On this, see Paul Meyvaert, "An Unknown Letter of Hulagu, Il-Khan of Persia, to King Louis IX of France," *Viator* 11 (1980): 252–53; also E. Voegelin "The Mongol Orders of Submission to European Powers, 1245–1255," *Byzantion* 15 (1940–41): 378–413.

[31] Nomadic societies can well continue to function in a situation of political segmentation along tribal lines. The supra-tribal organization is not needed except in special and fairly anomalous cases. On this, see Joseph Fletcher, Jr., "Turco-Mongolian Monarchic Traditions in the Ottoman Empire," *Harvard Ukrainian Studies* 3–4, pt. I (1979–80): 236–51.

[32] Rafe de Crespigny, *Northern Frontier: The Policies and Strategy of the Later Han Empire*. (Canberra: Faculty of Asian Studies, Australian National University, 1984), pp. 177–78.

All of this does not mean that the *ch'an-yü* now enjoyed absolute authority among his people. For all the organizational skills of its first leader, Modun, the Hsiung-nu empire remained a highly tribalized state, with the Hu-yen, Lan, and Hsü-pu clans holding the highest ranks. Government posts and ranks in that structure were hereditary and remained within the aristocratic families they were granted to. On the legal plane the *ch'an-yü* certainly was not seen as the supreme "lawgiver," and customary and traditional usages remained the basis of the law, to which even the *ch'an-yü* had to conform. In the political community he remained the primus inter pares, rather than the sovereign, that is, he was the agent of the interests of the community of aristocrats by whom he was supported. That support gave him the authority to issue orders, but the implementation of those orders rested always on the consent of the other members of the elite. This consent could be extracted by force or suasion but could not be compelled through adherence to a firmly established state ideology or controlled through the machinery of a state bureaucracy. Indeed, there are many examples of internal divisions among the Hsiung-nu political community and of the limits to the scope of the authority of the *ch'an-yü*.[33] For instance, succession struggles were not uncommon, as in the case of the Lu-li king of the left, Yi-chih-hsien, who at the death of the Chün-ch'en *ch'an-yü* in 126 B.C. proclaimed himself ruler and attacked and defeated Yü-shan, the heir originally appointed by the late *ch'an-yü*.[34] Disputes between the ruler and his subordinated aristocrats could also easily lead to splits in the confederacy. In 121 B.C. the *ch'an-yü* was angry with the Hun-yeh king and the Hsiu-t'u king, who had under their jurisdictions the western territories of the Hsiung-nu empire, for losing tens of thousands of men to the Han armies, and he wanted to execute them, but this could not be accomplished by a simple imperial order.[35] Although power struggles are by no means foreign to Chinese early history, one should emphasize that the bases of the authority of the *ch'an-yü*, in terms of economic and military resources, as well as legitimacy as a sovereign, rested primarily on the web of individual liaisons and personal loyalties that he had been able to create before and during his reign.

Did these two very different notions of political authority – the Han institutional emperorship and the Hsiung-nu charismatic chieftainship – play a

[33] It is indicative that the Hsiung-nu empire appeared, from a Chinese perspective, as beset by "regionalism." See Yü Ying-shih, "Han Foreign Relations," *The Cambridge History of China*, vol. 1: *The Ch'in and Han Empires, 221 B.C.–A.D. 220*, ed. Michael Loewe and Denis Twitchett (Cambridge: Cambridge University Press, 1986), p. 392.

[34] *Han shu* 94A, 3767.

[35] Both of them became fearful and plotted to surrender to the Han (*Han shu* 94A, 3769). In 104 B.C., the great commander of the left (*tso ta tu-wei*) of the Hsiung-nu wanted to kill the *ch'an-yü* (*Han shu* 94A, 3775).

role in the arena of foreign relations and diplomatic agreements? Not only did they play a role, but their fundamental asymmetry can be regarded as the main reason for the failure of the *ho-ch'in* policy. The crux of the matter is that when treaties were concluded, their observance could not exceed the limits of the authority of each contracting party. As the Han and the Hsiung-nu notions of central authority were asymmetric, so were their respective abilities to observe the provisions of the treaties. The best evidence of this "asymmetry" is provided by the protracted raids that continued despite the Chinese delivery of "appeasement" tribute to the *ch'an-yü*. Though this evidence is not extensive, it is compelling because it explicitly refers to the perpetrators of the raids as subordinate leaders and reveals that the *ch'an-yü* was unable to force his own people to abide by the conditions of the treaty that he had ratified.

Immediately after the conclusion of a *ho-ch'in* treaty with Han Kao-tsu, Chinese generals who had defected to the Hsiung-nu invaded and pillaged the border areas, followed by Hsiung-nu generals. These two groups are said to have violated the treaty often, invading and looting the regions of T'ai, Yen-men, and Yün-chung.[36] Clearly the authority of the *ch'an-yü* was not sufficient to make them respect the agreement. When Wen-ti came to the throne, in 180 B.C., the *ho-ch'in* treaty was renewed,[37] but only four years later, in 176 B.C., the wise king of the right violated the treaty on his own initiative and invaded China. Because he had settled south of the Yellow River and was encroaching upon Chinese territory, Wen-ti issued the following edict, in which he explained the reasons for his military action against the Hsiung-nu leader:

The Han and the Hsiung-nu made a brotherly pact. For not invading and pillaging the border region we granted many precious gifts to the Hsiung-nu. Today the wise king of the right has left his state [*kuo*] and has led his people to settle in the region south of the river. This is not in accord with the agreements. He often crosses the border, capturing and killing officers and soldiers. He has taken away the Man and the Yi who protected the frontier of the Shang Commandery, and ordered them not to reside in their customary [land]. Oppressing border officials, crossing the borders and pillaging is very arrogant and does not accord with the norm. This is not the treaty [that we made].[38]

The *ch'an-yü*'s reply to these accusations shows that he was quite frustrated by the situation, though he laid part of the blame for the disturbances on the Han as well. According to him the Han border officials had "provoked" the wise king of the right by invading his territory and insulting him. Unfortunately, the wise king had thereafter failed to inform the *ch'an-yü* and had instead preferred to follow the advice of other Hsiung-nu leaders, such as

[36] *Han shu* 94A, 3754; *Shih chi chu-yi* 110, 2320.
[37] *Han shu* 94A, 3756; *Shih chi chu-yi* 110, 2320.   [38] *Han shu* 94A, 3756.

the Hou-yi-lu "marquis" Nan-chih. In the *ch'an-yü*'s assessment, the source of the problem was to be found in the hatred that existed between the wise king of the right and the Han officials, who "violated the treaty between the two rulers, departing from fraternal relations."[39] The same type of situation arose in 162 B.C., when Emperor Wen-ti once again reminded the *ch'an-yü* that wicked and evil people on his side were "severing the harmony" between the two rulers.[40]

The troubles continued during Ching-ti's reign. The *ho-ch'in* treaty concluded between Han Ching-ti and the Chün-ch'en *ch'an-yü* (159–126 B.C.) when the latter acceded to the Hsiung-nu throne was ineffecual in preserving peace. Like the previous ones, this treaty provided for the opening of border markets and stipulated the bestowal of gifts as well as a princely consort for the *ch'an-yü*, but it did not prevent the Hsiung-nu from attacking and pillaging the border regions as they pleased. Here we do not know who actually carried out the raids, but it seems likely that it was not the *ch'an-yü* himself, because the *ho-ch'in* agreement did not break down, and even the border markets continued to stay open.[41]

In another example of insubordination to the *ch'an-yü* by members of the Hsiung-nu aristocracy, when the Hu-yen-t'i *ch'an-yü* (r. 85–68 B.C.) came into office he told the Han envoys that he desired the continuation of the *ho-ch'in* agreement. However, two of the most important leaders of the Hsiung-nu politico-military establishment, the wise king of the left and the Lu-li king of the right, opposed him, thus creating a split in the Hsiung-nu polity, the results of which were told as follows:

Because [the wise king of the left and the Lu-li king of the right] did not succeed to the throne, they nurtured resentment, and led their people away, wishing to go south to surrender to the Han. But fearing they would be unable to proceed on their own, they forced the Lu-t'u king [to join], and wanted to go west to surrender to the Wu-sun, so they could plot [with them] an attack on the Hsiung-nu. The Lu-t'u king reported this, and the *ch'an-yü* sent men to investigate; the Lu-li king of the right did not confess, but reversed the charge, accusing the Lu-t'u king. All the people of the country resented this. Thereafter the two kings went to live in their territory, and did not attend the assemblies at Lung-ch'eng.[42]

What is interesting in this episode is that these two disaffected leaders first attempted to "surrender to the Han," then tried to find allies to fight against "the Hsiung-nu," and eventually decided to withdraw to their own territories. The "surrender" by Hsiung-nu leaders is nothing else but an attempt to bypass the *ch'an-yü*'s authority and set up separate *ho-ch'in* agreements with the Han. That the *ho-ch'in* ultimately became an

---

[39] *Han shu* 94A, 3756; *Shih chi chu-yi* 110, 2321.
[40] *Shih chi chu-yi* 110, 2324–5; *Han shu* 94A, 3762–3.
[41] *Han shu* 94A, 3765.   [42] *Han shu* 94A, 3782.

inducement used by the Han to break the unity of the Hsiung-nu is made clear by the history of the relations between the Han and the leader of the southern Hsiung-nu, Hu-han-yeh, who agreed to split from the confederation on the condition that he gained access to Chinese goods. This was possible because of the relative ease with which members of the Hsiung-nu aristocracy could secede from the larger political union. Going back to one's own territory was an option open to the nobility that the *ch'an-yü* had no legal power to oppose, and one that reveals the inherent weakness of his authority.

Finally, one of the most explicit mentions of the *ch'an-yü*'s lack of absolute sovereignty is contained in the speech by the Han statesman Hou Ying on the occasion of a peace treaty negotiated with the Hsiung-nu leader Hu-han-yeh in 51 B.C. Hou Ying, dismissing Hu-han-yeh's proposal that the Han demobilize their frontier forces and let him guard the border instead, said: "although China possesses the teachings of propriety and morality and has the death penalty, the masses still violate prohibitions. How then could we expect the *ch'an-yü* to keep his followers from violating the treaty?"[43] Obviously a perception existed among Chinese statesmen that the sovereignty of the *ch'an-yü* was more limited than that of the Chinese emperor.

Proceeding from the assumption that the volatility of the Hsiung-nu political leadership constituted a serious, finally insurmountable, obstacle to the implementation of the *ho-ch'in*, it would be logical to surmise that the Han appeasement strategy was meant to strengthen central authority, not to undermine it. In fact, the diplomatic correspondence from 198 B.C. to 133 B.C. supports the hypothesis that the *ho-ch'in* was specifically intended to support the Hsiung-nu ruler, by granting him not only economic resources to be used to strengthen his internal position but also the authority to control the whole Hsiung-nu people. There are numerous instances in which the language of the documents specifically excludes the existence of sources of authority other than the emperor and the *ch'an-yü*. The policy of assigning the title of *ch'an-yü* to several Hsiung-nu tribal leaders, which eventually became the classic understanding of "divide and rule," was broadly enacted by Wang Mang and during the Later Han but was never part of the Han strategy in the first part of the Former Han.[44]

---

[43] *Han shu* 94B, 3804.

[44] On Wang Mang's policies toward the Hsiung-nu, see De Crespigny, *Northern Frontier*, pp. 194–218. The policy proposed by Ch'ao Ts'o was quite different and meant simply the recruitment of foreign people to fight against other foreign peoples: it referred to a military strategy rather than to a foreign affairs policy.

The early Han emperors down to the reign of Han Wu-ti were hard-pressed militarily, and needed peace to allow the nation to recover its strength, but a durable peace could be achieved only by negotiating an agreement with a single political ruler who was able to guarantee long-term stability. Since, as we have already mentioned, the final goal of the *ho-ch'in* strategy was to make the ruling clan of the Hsiung-nu into part of the Han "family," it would be logical to assume that the Han interests would best be served by a policy of "unite and rule," whereby the Hsiung-nu leader would be made into an absolute ruler and thus could steer the whole Hsiung-nu people toward a position friendly to China. Lacking that authority, even though the Hsiung-nu ruler may have been brought under the political influence of China, other Hsiung-nu tribal leaders would surely continue to fight, and the whole *ho-ch'in* strategy would be useless. The Han willingness to accede to the *ch'an-yü*'s demand that tribute be period-ically increased may well have been a response to the hope that central authority among the Hsiung-nu would be strengthened. Unfortunately no amount of tribute could accomplish that, and the security of the frontier was constantly threatened.

In conclusion, this examination of the Han relations with the Hsiung-nu suggests that between 198 and 133 B.C. the northern territories of China were constantly under pressure because there was no absolute authority within the Hsiung-nu tribal confederation capable of guaranteeing the respect of treaty obligations. Under these circumstances, China's attempts at pacifying the Hsiung-nu through pay-offs were destined to fail. Since the power of the *ch'an-yü* was not only limited but also constantly exposed to internal challenges, peace proved aleatory. No amount of Chinese support could change the core structure of nomadic society, and because a basic notion of sovereignty could not possibly develop without being preceded by radical transformations in the nomadic state's social and political texture, the position of the ruler was destined to remain fragile. Only after the realization of the ineffectiveness of the diplomatic approach, revealed in the aforementioned position expressed by Wang Hui, was the *ho-ch'in* policy discarded and replaced by military means.

War and Expansion

The political debates over frontier issues help us to clarify the rationale for war but are less useful when we attempt to understand the goals that the Han sought to achieve. In fact, there is a clear gap between the stated objec-tives and the results that the more aggressive policy carried out by Wu-ti eventually yielded. The Han dynasty expanded territorially far beyond the boundaries held by the Chou states, and by the mid-first century B.C.

the northern hegemony of the Hsiung-nu empire was broken. The conquest of the north increased the Han administrative network in the northern border areas and strengthened and rationalized the border defense system with military garrisons, fixed fortifications, and settlements. The Han western expansion as far as the Tarim Basin led to the submission of a plethora of small states and to the establishment of commercial ties with Central Asia.

These feats were most successfully carried out between 121 and 112 B.C., and gradually consolidated during and after the reign of Emperor Wu. Yet the motives behind Han Wu-ti's decision to embark on an unprecedented program of territorial expansion are not fully clear, nor can they be clarified without our first considering the actual military capabilities of the Han, the extent to which the Hsiung-nu empire had grown, and the nature of Hsiung-nu economic and political power. A long view is required to determine, for instance, whether the Han expansion was planned or was, on the contrary, the end-product of a piecemeal process. One of the most puzzling features of Wu-ti's wars against the Hsiung-nu is that none of the stated objectives of the Han offensive seems to justify either the duration of the war or the extent to which the Han armies advanced into Hsiung-nu territory. Even the most hawkish positions expressed during the debates that accompanied the shift from a pacifist to a militarist posture did not advocate anything like the results eventually achieved. There was no military or political strategy elaborated in this period that even remotely justified the decades of military offensives, political expansion, and territorial acquisition that were in fact to follow.

Arguments in favor of the expansion were expressed post facto in the *Discourses on Salt and Iron* by the "realist" faction of the government officials. These arguments can be summarized in two points: border defense and trade opportunities. According to the "ministerial" faction, which supported military intervention, Wu-ti had been driven to expansion by the need to protect the central kingdom. The conquest of Hsiung-nu territory and the establishment of commanderies in the north and west were intended to guarantee peace in the rest of the kingdom. It was, in other words, an instance of "defensive acquisition" rather than true expansion. Moreover, the benefits to be derived from trade were enormous, because by expanding into these lands China could trade goods of which it had a surplus (and which were therefore next to worthless on the internal market), for things of value, such as gold, pack animals, furs, and other precious objects. To this, the opposite faction – the "literati" – replied polemically, with the usual critique, that in pursuing an expansionist policy, the emperor intended to increase his power and aggrandize the state at the expense of the welfare of the people, who became bankrupt in the process. As for the hypothetical commercial benefits, those imported goods were not nearly worth the Chinese products exchanged for them; once all expenses – including transportation and all phases of production – had been calculated, the cost of the Chinese goods was far higher than that of the imported items.[45]

However, neither of these relatively limited objectives could justify subduing independent polities (even those that were not hostile) and bringing distant lands, far beyond the Han frontiers, under Chinese rule. To comprehend the reasons that led the Han to displace the power of the Hsiung-nu throughout the north, and to establish their own supremacy in Central Asia, we must examine two aspects of the context in which this strategy emerged. The first is purely military: it involves the development by the Han of the ability to launch long-ranging military expeditions, and the tactical solution adopted by Han Wu-ti of consolidating territorial gains by turning the conquered regions into administrative areas, which were then incorporated within the empire. These areas supported a line of fortifications that provided logistical support to Chinese armies pushing farther and farther west, and therefore constituted the vertebral column of the Han expansion into the Western Regions.

The second aspect is strategic and refers to the discovery made by the Han that the war against the Hsiung-nu could not have been won without severing the essential economic and political links between the Hsiung-nu and other polities, in particular the kingdoms of the Tarim Basin and the Ch'iang. This strategy, which was referred to as "cutting the right arm" of the Hsiung-nu, required the direct Han intervention in the Western Regions; it was the dogged pursuance of this strategy that eventually provoked a fatal split in the Hsiung-nu leadership and marked the end of the Hsiung-nu empire.

Han Wu-ti's Offensive: Political and Technical Aspects

Even though the Han did realize that the appeasement policy was never going to guarantee peaceful relations, a switch to the offensive required certain objective military capabilities, without which the constraints on any major operations would have been so great, and the costs so high, that it is unlikely the policy shift would have ever produced positive results. The realization that the ho-ch'in policy had failed provided the rationale and the determination to pursue an offensive strategy, but such a realization by itself could not have shifted the military balance in favor of the Han overnight, as the Ma-yi disaster plainly demonstrated. What enabled China to challenge the Hsiung-nu militarily was a combination of factors

[45] E. M. Gale, *Discourses on Salt and Iron. A Debate on State Control of Commerce and Industry in Ancient China* (Leiden: Brill, 1931 [rpt. 1967]), pp. 14, 99–102.

that had been accruing slowly and that resulted in an overall increase in the Chinese offensive capabilities. Two handicaps had prevented the early Han emperors from engaging the Hsiung-nu successfully: the deep political divisions within the Han camp, and the sheer battlefield superiority of the Hsiung-nu. Both of these factors had changed considerably by the time of Wu-ti.

A primary preoccupation of Wu-ti's predecessors had been the consolidation of central authority.[46] Han Kao-tsu had been unable to concentrate his efforts against the Hsiung-nu, as he was forced to devote his attention primarily to the consolidation of the central power against the centrifugal tendencies expressed by the subordinate "kings" (*chu-hou-wang*).[47] The same policy of centralization was pursued by later emperors, engaged, sometimes strenuously, in curbing the rebellions against the Han government by the *chu-hou-wang*, such as the major challenge in 156 B.C., and the defections to the Hsiung-nu by those political and military leaders who did not want to yield personal power and prestige to the central government.

The Hsiung-nu were central actors in this "internal" Han political struggle, because the harshness of the Chinese military code, admiration for Hsiung-nu martial prowess, and, above all, the conflict of interests between central power and peripheral potentates often inspired changes of allegiance. The Hsiung-nu status as an independent power enabled them to act as a subversive political and military presence and greatly increased the threat they posed both to the integrity of China and to the survival of the Han dynasty. The stories of generals such as Lu Wan, Hann Wang Hsin, Ch'en Hsi, and others who, after the establishment of the Han dynasty, decided to rebel against Kao-tsu and join the Hsiung-nu, are unambiguous in this respect. After having rewarded his allies with fiefs, Han Kao-tsu had to strengthen the authority of the central government and, unsurprisingly, came into conflict with his former supporters' yearnings for autonomy. For instance, Ssu-ma Ch'ien reports that when the king of Yen, Lu Wan, joined Kao Tsu to wipe out the "rebellious" feudatory Ch'en Hsi, who had enlisted Hsiung-nu support against the emperor, he was advised by a Chinese defector to the Hsiung-nu to put an end to his war against Ch'en Hsi and to make peace with the Hsiung-nu, for, as soon as Ch'en Hsi had been crushed, Kao Tsu would be turning against Lu Wan himself. In his concluding

---

[46] Michael Loewe, *Crisis and Conflict in Han China, 104 BC to AD 9* (London: George Allen and Unwin, 1974), p. 59.

[47] On this question, cf. M. Loewe, "The Former Han Dynasty," in *The Cambridge History of China*, pp. 139–44; W. Eberhard, *A History of China* (Berkeley: University of California Press, 1977 [1960]), pp. 77–86; Ch'u T'ung-shu, *Han Social Structure* (Seattle: University of Washington Press, 1972), pp. 76, 165–66.

remarks to chapter 93, Ssu-ma Ch'ien states that "in the empire [these lords] aroused suspicion by their great strength, while beyond its borders they sought aid from the foreigners (man-mo), so that with each day they became further alienated from the emperor and moved deeper into danger. At last, when their position became impossible and their wisdom failed, they went over to the Hsiung-nu."[48]

Besides offering a sanctuary and a political alternative to those who came into conflict with the central authority of the emperor, the Hsiung-nu were also militarily strong. The Han had suffered numerous defeats, and their border defenses had been repeatedly broken, leaving no doubt that any military encounter with the Hsiung-nu would be costly and the outcome unpredictable. In fact, that argument provided the rationale for the long-term endorsement of the ho-ch'in policy, so that any change of policy needed to be preceded by a program for the strengthening of the Han army. By the time of Han Wu-ti, conditions regarding military technology and offensive capabilities had improved to such an extent that the Han army had become far more competitive than it had been at the time of Han Kao-tsu.

The program that made this possible focused on two parallel projects: creating an effective cavalry force and improving the effectiveness of the weapons. As noted in Chapter 4, the concept of a regular cavalry was imported into China from the northern peoples, whose armament included possibly long swords, spears, compound bows, and body armor.[49] However, the bulk of the Chinese armies in the major campaigns against the Hsiung-nu carried out by Meng T'ien and by Han Kao-tsu was still made of infantry and charioteers.[50] An explicit request to the emperor that cavalry forces be used against the Hsiung-nu can be traced to the aforementioned memorial by Ch'ao Ts'o in 169 B.C.[51] Such a request suggests that, even if the building of a cavalry was underway, it had not yet been sufficiently developed.

---

[48] Shih chi 93, 2649.
[49] Burchard Brentjes, Arms of the Sakas (Varanasi: Rishi Publications, 1996); M. Rostovtzeff, Iranians and Greeks in Southern Russia (Oxford: Clarendon, 1922), pp. 203–204; Jaroslav Průšek, Chinese Statelets and the Northern Barbarians in the Period 1400–300 B.C. (Dordrecht: Reidel, 1971), pp. 116–17.
[50] Chang Chun-shu, "Military Aspects of Han Wu-ti's Northern and Northwestern Campaigns," Harvard Journal of Asiatic Studies 21 (1966): 167.
[51] Han shu 2281; cf. also Loewe, Crisis and Conflict in Han China, p. 100; Leon Wieger, Textes historiques: histoire politique de la Chine depuis l'origine, jusqu'en 1912, 2 vols. (Hsien-hsien: Impr. de Hien-hien, 1922–23), 1: 343–44; Berthold Laufer, Chinese Clay Figures, Part I, Prolegomena on the History of Defensive Armor (Chicago: Field Museum of Natural History Publication no. 177, 1914), p. 229.

China's success depended on its ability to gain access to a sufficient number of mounts to sustain a military cavalry on a continuing basis. Traditionally, China had imported horses from the region of Tai and from the nomads, and the border markets opened between Han and nomads continued to be used by China as a gateway for the importation of horses from the reign of Kao-tsu to that of Wu-ti. However, reliance on external sources would make the military dependent on supplies that might become unavailable when they were most needed, namely in wartime. Therefore, facing for the first time the problem of raising large numbers of military mounts, the early Han emperors tried to solve it autarchically and began to breed horses within China. Attempts to that effect were carried out in areas close to the northern frontier, in regions possibly not yet placed under cultivation and inhabited by pastoral peoples.[52] The caretakers of these horse-breeding stations were not only foreigners but also possibly surrendered or captured Hsiung-nu tribesmen.[53] By Wu-ti's time, mass breeding of horses was well under way: in 140 B.C. thirty-six breeding stations were already in operation on the frontier, providing maintenance for three hundred thousand horses.[54]

After some major campaigns were launched deep into nomadic territory between 129 and 119 B.C., a shortage of horses began to be felt. The state, therefore, tried to transfer the burden of providing military mounts from the frontier areas to the whole territory of the empire by promoting the private breeding of horses to be sold to the government.[55] In addition to the horses that the state purchased from private individuals, a new tax law stipulated that up to three men in any family could be exempted from military duties by presenting one horse each for the army. Finally, a portion of the revenues from the poll tax on children (k'ou-fu) was earmarked specifically for the purchase of horses for the military.[56] Already in 146 B.C. the export of horses under ten years of age was forbidden, and horses remained a much sought-after commodity.[57]

---

[52] Later dynasties (in particular the T'ang and the Ming) relied far more on horse imports that the early Han. On the T'ang-Uighur horse trade and its importance in Chinese economy, see Christopher Beckwith, "The Impact of Horse and Silk Trade on the Economies of T'ang China and of the Uighur Empire," *Journal of Economic and Social History of the Orient* 34.2 (1991): 183–98.

[53] C. Martin Wilbur, *Slavery in China under the Former Han Dynasty 206 B.C.–A.D. 25* (Chicago, Field Museum of Natural History, 1943), pp. 109–15.

[54] Nancy Lee Swann, *Food and Money in Ancient China. The Earliest Economic History of China to A.D. 25. Han Shu 24 with Related Texts, Han Shu 91 and Shih Chi 129* (Princeton: Princeton University Press, 1950), p. 38.

[55] Swann, *Food and Money in Ancient China*, pp. 308–309, 302–304.

[56] Swann, *Food and Money in Ancient China*, p. 374.

[57] Yü, *Trade and Expansion in Han China*, pp. 119–20.

Although it would be far-fetched to suggest that the sole motive for opening and defending the route to Central Asia was to gain horses needed for the wars against the Hsiung-nu, there is no doubt that Li Kuang-li's campaign of 104–101 B.C. was chiefly intended to acquire horses of a superior breed and that high-quality stallions were included in the tributary relations between China and Central Asia.[58] In fact, horses had probably been imported from Central Asia for some time before the arrival of Han armies in the Tarim Basin, although when this trade began is uncertain.[59] Nonetheless, imported Central Asian horses could not possibly satisfy the need for military mounts, which was instead probably fulfilled chiefly through the capture of animals in Hsiung-nu territory and through the incorporation into the Han army of nomadic peoples.[60]

An efficient cavalry force does not depend solely on horses. It is also essential to be able to train special troops in shooting from horseback and in all other cavalry skills. The creation of a cavalry force, one initially intended especially as a frontier defense force, had already started in 178 B.C.,[61] and in the period between 129 and 119 B.C. the mounted soldier was in fact "the key factor" in Han military campaigns.[62] From 130 B.C. to A.D. 23 the Han army comprised two types of soldiers: the *ping*, "combat soldiers for both temporary and permanent service," who were volunteers and salaried, and the *tsu*, that is, conscripted men used chiefly for labor and guard duty.[63] Because cavalry forces were already in existence before Han

---

[58] Yü, *Trade and Expansion in Han China*, pp. 119–20; Loewe, "Introduction," in *China in Central Asia*, pp. 43–44.

[59] Yetts argued that already in the first century B.C. there were two types of horses in China; see W. Perceval Yetts, "The Horse: A Factor in Early Chinese History," in *Eurasia Septentrionalis Antiqua*, "*Minns Volume*" 9 (1934): 231–55.

[60] The "heavenly horses" imported from Ferghana seem to have been used only for rituals and in parade functions only, whereas the small sturdy Przhevalsky horse – possibly the *jung ma* of the Chinese sources – continued to be used mainly in warfare. The account of the war against Ta-yüan, at the end of which only ten "high quality" horses (*shan ma*) and three thousand "medium quality" horses (*chung ma*) were selected by the Han general to be brought back, shows that horses from Central Asia were imported in relatively small quantities, owing possibly to the difficulty of taking large herds over such a long distance. *Shih chi chu-yi* 123, 4: 2602.

[61] Swann, *Food and Money in Ancient China*, pp. 168–72.

[62] Chang Chun-shu, "Military Aspects of Han Wu-ti's Northern and Northwestern Campaigns," p. 167; Michael Loewe, "The Campaigns of Han Wu-ti," in *Chinese Ways in Warfare*, ed. Frank A. Kierman and John K. Fairbank (Cambridge Mass.: Harvard University Press, 1974), p. 101.

[63] Swann, *Food and Money in Ancient China*, pp. 50–53, 207, n. 326. Chang Chun-shu ("Military Aspects," p. 169) maintains that "Emperor Wu reformed

Wu-ti, the appearance of the *ping* does not coincide, as some have surmised, with the introduction of a new type of soldier specially trained as a mounted archer. Rather, the *ping* were specially trained combat forces used as both infantry and cavalry and were accompanied by auxiliary troops comprised of mounted nomads who were also used as frontier guards.[64]

Because adequate pasture and people skilled in horse breeding were scarce, the autarchical breeding of horses was difficult to sustain, and during the reign of Wu-ti home-bred horses, because they were either few or of poor quality, had to be increasingly replaced with horses imported or captured from the nomads. The pool of horses available at the time of the first campaigns against the Hsiung-nu nevertheless provided enough mounts to enable the Han to achieve those initial victories that gave them access to the steppe and to the resources to be found there. By the time of Han Wu-ti, cavalry had grown "into an independent arm, and finally became the most important one in the wars against the roving tribes of Central Asia."[65]

Besides cavalry, Wu-ti could also count on progress in military technology made during the earlier period. The main innovations in defensive technology seem to have been the Han adoption of ironclad armor, which replaced the copper-hide armor previously in use, and metal helmets. The wearing of body armor by horsemen was a practice that was probably borrowed by King Wu-ling from the nomads, who wore a type of cuirass made of leather obtained from their domestic animals.[66] Leather armor was also used by Chinese soldiers; ironclad armor – first introduced during the Former Han – seems to be an evolution from the leather type imported from the nomads,[67] and was also used in the fighting against the Hsiung-nu during the reign of Han Wu-ti.[68] The main offensive innovation was represented by different types of crossbows, which were more or less powerful

---

the old draft system by establishing a permanent army through the use of mercenaries." We can take Chang's statement as a supposition or educated guess, but not as based on factual evidence.

[64] Loewe, "The Campaigns of Han Wu-ti," pp. 90–96.

[65] Berthold Laufer, *Chinese Clay Figures*, pp. 229–30.

[66] Laufer, *Chinese Clay Figures*, p. 224.

[67] Édouard Chavannes, *Les documents chinois decouverts par Aurel Stein dans les sables du Turkestan Oriental* (Oxford: Impr. de l'Université, 1913), pp. xv–xvi.

[68] A Western Han suit of iron armor was found at Erh-shih-chia-tzu, in Inner Mongolia. The armor is made of plates stitched together and divided into several section for the chest, shoulder, and collar. See Anon., "Hu-he-hao-t'e Erh-shih-chia-tzu ku-ch'eng ch'u-t'u de Hsi Han t'ieh chia," *K'ao-ku* 1975.4: 249–58. Transl. "The Western Han Iron Armors Unearthed from the Remains of an Ancient City at Ershijiazi in Huhehot," in *Chinese Archaeological Abstracts*, vol. 3: *Eastern Zhou to Han*, pp. 1349–58.

according to their "pull."[69] In the Han documents excavated by Stein in Central Asia, and brilliantly studied by Chavannes, there are numerous references to the crossbow.[70] Multiple-shooting, or "repetition," crossbows and precision triggers were also developed during the first half of the Former Han dynasty, making the crossbow in general a weapon superior to the nomadic bow. Indeed, these innovations in the basic crossbow design seem to have accounted for the difficulty the nomads met when fighting an organized Chinese military detachment, even when, as in the case of Li Ling's army, the Chinese soldiers were infantry troops much less numerous then the nomadic forces.[71]

In sum, the adoption of cavalry from the northern peoples, together with indigenous technological innovations, made the Chinese army probably on the whole superior to the Hsiung-nu on the battlefield. However, one fundamental weakness remained: logistical support and supplies.[72] Han statesmen recognized that the need to feed the soldiers in the field and the cold northern weather had always constituted limitations to the mobility of Chinese armies, making it impossible to sustain an expedition for more than one hundred days.[73] Given these limitations, troops stationed far away for long periods of time had to be self-supporting. Food supplies were provided by state-sponsored military farms run by *t'ien-tsu* units (translated as "agricultural conscripts," "colonists," or "pioneers").[74]

The system of garrisoned forts and beacon fires, coupled with the construction of military roads on China's northern frontier, allowed for a rapid reaction to nomadic inroads and invasions, but this was merely for defensive purposes. Once an expedition was launched, the border regions could supply foodstuffs and logistical support only within a limited range; long-term expeditions in pursuit of retreating nomadic tribes needed to rely on what they could pillage from the enemy. In the course of the campaign slow-moving livestock and people could be, and were, captured, but the bulk of the nomadic soldiers, more mobile than the Chinese, could easily retreat into the steppe, thereby avoiding direct military confrontations. If an expedition lasted longer than expected, the Chinese soldiers were ill-prepared to face the rigors of the nomadic lands and found it impossible to survive in the steppe without supplies and logistical support. In fact, climatic factors

---

[69] Loewe, *Records of the Han Administration*, 1: 99; Joseph Needham et al., *Science and Civilization in China*, vol. 5: *Chemistry and Chemical Technology, Part VI: Military Technology: Missiles and Sieges* (Cambridge: Cambridge University Press, 1994), p. 142.

[70] On the technical and mechanical aspects of the Han crossbow see Joseph Needham et al., *Science and Civilization in China 5*, Part 6: 120–44.

[71] Loewe, "The Campaigns of Han Wu-ti," pp. 119–22.

[72] Loewe, "The Campaigns of Han Wu-ti," p. 96.   [73] *Han shu* 94B, 3824.

[74] Loewe, *Records of the Han Administration*, p. 56.

and food shortages were responsible for a larger number of Chinese casualties than were the nomadic armies.

The Han Campaigns

Following the tradition of stationary border defenses developed in the late Warring States period, the Han approached this problem investing heavily in the construction a fortified line of communication with warehouses that were intended to supply garrison forces.[75] The supply system itself included three types of storage facilities: granaries (*ts'ang*), intended for the management of grain, which were kept under strict military surveillance; storehouses (*k'u*) where money and weapons were kept; and temporary stations for the storage of money, grains, and weapons of soldiers garrisoned on the frontier.[76] As already mentioned, this support structure was linked to an overall strategy of turning the border areas, as they were conquered, into "commanderies" and other administrative divisions integrated within the military and civil bureaucracy of the Han. As these areas were brought under the control of the central government, they were either settled by Chinese people or garrisoned by Han troops and foreign troops recruited under the Han insignia. Based on this strategy and on the new-found military advantages that underpinned it, the struggle against the Hsiung-nu and the Han (re)conquest of the north conducted by Wu-ti can be divided into three phases.

FIRST PHASE (133–119 B.C.). Wu-ti's early campaigns were aimed at recovering all lands to the south of the Great Bend of the Yellow River and at consolidating Han power in those border areas that were more vulnerable to Hsiung-nu attacks. This first phase of the Han offensive is characterized by a series of attacks and counterattacks that did not achieve any lasting results and failed to establish the military supremacy of either side. They did show, however, that the Han had become able to mount extensive cam-

---

[75] The study of these installations is based on the bamboo slips excavated especially from Chü-yen and Tun-huang. See Loewe, *Records of the Han Administration*.

[76] Hsü Le-yao, "Han chien so chien ch'ang-ch'eng te hou-ch'in kung-chi hsi-t'ung," in *Ch'ang-ch'eng kuo-chi hsüeh-shu yen-t'ao-hui lun-wen chi*, ed. Chung-kuo ch'ang-ch'eng hsüeh-hui (Chi-lin-shih: Chi-lin Jen-min, 1994), pp. 116–22, 375–76. The wealth of information provided by the Chü-yen and the Tun-huang slips for the investigations of Han garrison system in the northwest has been recently augmented with the discovery of over 22,500 slips at Hsüan-ch'üan, near Tun-huang; see Wu Jeng-hsiang, "Ssu–chou chih lu shang yu yi zhong-ta k'ao-ku fa-hsien: Tun-huang hsien Hsüan-ch'üan chih," in *Ch'ang-ch'eng kuo-chi hsüeh-shu yen-t'ao-hui lun-wen chi*, pp. 283–85, 487–88.

paigns and to react to Hsiung-nu incursions. The Han could both strike deep into the steppe and attack from multiple directions. After the unfortunate episode of the defeat at Ma-yi, Han military efforts to expand into Hsiung-nu territory began in earnest in 129 B.C., with a large offensive led by four commanders.

Wei Ch'ing, general of Chariots and Cavalry (*chü-ch'i chiang-chün*),[77] set out from Shang-ku;[78] Kung-sun Ho, general of Light Chariots (*ch'ing-chü chiang-chün*),[79] departed from Yün-chung; Grand Palace Grandee (*ta-chung ta-fu*) Kung-sun Ao, appointed cavalry general, was sent from the Tai commandery; and the commandant of the Guards, Li Kuang, was made general of the Imperial Cavalry (*hsiao-ch'i chiang-chün*) and set out from Yen-men. Each of the four commanders' armies comprised ten thousand cavalry. In this expedition, as in later ones, what is surprising is the striking distance of the Chinese armies. Wei-ch'ing must have penetrated fairly deeply into Hsiung-nu territory, since he reached Lung-ch'eng, the sacred site of the Hsiung-nu sacrifices to Heaven where the *ch'an-yü* held large political gatherings. Here he killed and captured several hundred men. However, Kung-sun Ao lost seven thousand cavalry, and Li Kuang was taken prisoner, though he then managed to escape and return home. Both ransomed their lives (to avoid being executed) and were degraded to the rank of commoners. Kung-sun Ho did not achieve any merit, either; so, as Ssu-ma Ch'ien recorded, out of four generals, only one attained success.[80]

This expedition was followed by a Hsiung-nu counteroffensive, in 128 B.C., when the Hsiung-nu crossed the border in force, killing the governor of Liao-hsi[81] and invading Yen-men, where they killed or captured several thousand people. Wei Ch'ing attacked them again, and Han An-kuo was made general of skilled soldiers (*ts'ai-kuan chiang-chün*) and stationed to garrison Yü-yang,[82] a position he later quit claiming that the Hsiung-nu had

---

[77] Cf. Hans Bielenstein, *The Bureaucracy of Han Times* (Cambridge: Cambridge University Press, 1980), pp. 122–23.

[78] Commandery located in the northern part of present-day Hopei. Included the territory to the west of today's Yen-ch'ing county (Peking municipality) and to the east of the city of Ch'ang-p'ing county; cf. *Chung-kuo li-shih ti-t'u chi. The Historical Atlas of China*, ed. T'an Ch'i-hsiang [Tan Qixiang] et al. (Peking: Ti-t'u ch'u-pan-she, 1982), 2: 27–28, 3–2. Its administrative center was in Chü-yang.

[79] He was formerly a grand coachman (*t'ai-p'u*).

[80] *Shih chi* 111, 2923; *Shih-chi chu-yi* 109, 2350.

[81] Commandery located in the region to the west of the lower course of today's Ta-ling River, in Liao-ning (*Chung-kuo li-shih ti-t'u chi*, 2: 27–28, 3–5).

[82] Commandery located in the region to the east of Peking. The administrative center was Yü-yang, situated to the southwest of today's Mi-yün county (*Chung-kuo li-shih ti-t'u chi*, 2: 27–28, 3–3).

fled far away. A month later, the Hsiung-nu attacked again in force Shang-ku and Yü-yang.[83] The most significant effort aimed at achieving the "paci-fication of the north" was carried out by Wei Ch'ing, who in 127 B.C. crossed the Western River[84] and reached Kao-ch'üeh,[85] killing and captur-ing twenty-three hundred enemies. After this, he went west to pacify the region south of the Yellow River, where he inspected the "old frontier" at Yü-hsi,[86] that is, the position occupied by the Ch'in armies after Meng T'ien's offensive. Next he crossed the Tzu-ling Mountains from east to west[87] and built a bridge over the Northern River.[88] Then he attacked and defeated the Hsiung-nu local lord P'u-ni at the locality of Fu-li, killed P'u-ni's picked soldiers, and took three thousand and seventy-five scouts prisoner.[89] Even such a sweeping military action did not intimidate the Hsiung-nu, who in the following year, 126 B.C., crossed the borders again and killed the grand administrator of the Tai commandery, Kung Yu. At that time the Hsiung-nu also invaded Yen-men and abducted over a thou-sand people.[90]

As the Han armies were seeking to gain the upper hand in military matters, they also proceeded to consolidate the Han defenses along the northern border, by building a series of fortification works, by transferring in new settlers, and by establishing new administrative units in the border regions. The first change in the organization of the north was made when the Shuo-fang commandery was established in 126 B.C.[91] This strategy caused the Hsiung-nu to react angrily to what they regarded as a regular invasion of their territory. As the *Shih chi* reports, "the Hsiung-nu Wise

---

[83] *Shih chi* 108, 2864; *Shih-chi chu-yi* 108, 2293.

[84] The "Western River" indicates the section of the Yellow River that flows south to north through today's provinces of Ning-hsia and Inner Mongolia.

[85] This was an important pass across the Yin Mountain Chain (*Chung-kuo li-shih ti-t'u chi*, 2: 17–18, 1–5).

[86] Also called Yü-lin Barrier (*sai*), it was located on the northeastern corner of the Great Bend of the Yellow River, which was possibly in the northeastern corner of Shensi province (not marked in *Chung-kuo li-shih ti-t'u chi*).

[87] Tzu-ling: name of a mountain; its location is unknown. It was possibly situated to the west of present-day Heng-shan county, in Shensi (not marked in *Chung-kuo li-shih ti-t'u chi*).

[88] This is the Wu-chia River, in present-day Inner Mongolia, which once flowed into the Yellow River.

[89] Fu-li: name of a fort located to the northwest of present-day Wu-yüan county, in Inner Mongolia (not marked in *Chung-kuo li-shih ti-t'u chi*).

[90] *Shih chi* 111, 2924; *Shih-chi chu-yi* 111, 2350–1.

[91] *Shih chi* 112, 2950, and 116, 2995; *Shih-chi chu-yi* 112, 2436. Commandery established in 127 B.C. It was located across the northern portion of the Great Bend of the Yellow River, in today's Inner Mongolia. Its administrative center was at Shuo-fang (*Chung-kuo li-shih ti-t'u chi*, 2: 17–18, 1–7/3–7).

King of the Right was angry that the Han had seized the territory south of the Yellow River and had built fortifications in the Shuo-fang commandery."[92] Hence, in 125 B.C. they invaded the commanderies of Tai, Ting-hsiang,[93] and Shang, killing and carrying away several thousand Han people.[94] As the military confrontation between the two empires escalated, long-range expeditions of enormous proportions were coupled with the establishment of additional outlying administrative units and permanent forces to guard the border areas. By the spring of 123 B.C., Wei Ch'ing, at the head of six other generals and an army of over one hundred thousand cavalry, proceeded several hundred *li* north of Ting-hsiang to attack the Hsiung-nu.[95] The following year ten thousand Hsiung-nu cavalry invaded Shang-ku,[96] but in 121 B.C. General Huo Ch'ü-ping, at the head of ten thousand cavalry, setting off from Lung-hsi[97] marched for over one thousand *li*, crossed the Yen-chih Mountains,[98] and attacked the Hsiung-nu. In the summer of that year Huo Ch'ü-ping, together with the Ho-ch'i marquis Kung-sun Ao, again led a force of tens of thousands at a distance of two thousand *li* north of Lung-hsi and Pei-ti. They passed Chü-yen[99] and gave battle in the Ch'i-lien Mountains,[100] where they killed or captured over thirty thousand enemies, including seventy "small kings" and lesser chieftains.[101]

These military confrontations show that the Han had become proficient in planning and enacting long-range military campaigns and were capable of making surprise attacks on areas located deep within nomad territory. This strategy paid off, as discord began to brew within the ranks of the Hsiung-nu, and some prominent Hsiung-nu leaders started to defect to the

---

[92] *Shih chi* 110, 2907; *Shih-chi chu-yi* 110, 2328.

[93] Commandery located north of the Yellow River, in the region of today's Ho-lin-ko-erh county, in Inner Mongolia; its capital was called Ch'eng-yüeh (*Chung-kuo li-shih ti-t'u chi*, 2: 17–18, 2–9).

[94] *Shih chi* 110, 2924; *Shih-chi chu-yi* 110, 2350.

[95] *Shih chi* 110, 2907; *Shih-chi chu-yi* 110, 2328.

[96] *Shih chi* 110, 2908, *Shih-chi chu-yi* 110, 2328.

[97] Province located to the south of the upper course of the Wei River, in southern Kansu (*Chung-kuo li-shih ti-t'u chi*, 2: 33–34, 5–7/5–8) (see also above).

[98] Mountain range located in present-day Kansu, west of Yung-ch'ang county and southeast of Shan-tan county. It was known for its excellent pastures (*Chung-kuo li-shih ti-t'u chi*, 2: 33–34, 3–6).

[99] County to the southeast of today's E-chi-na Banner (Edzin-Gol), in Inner Mongolia. It lay on the main route of communication between the territory to the west of the Yellow River and the land north of the desert (*Chung-kuo li-shih ti-t'u chi*, 2: 33–34, 2–6).

[100] Mountain located in Kansu, to the south of Chiu-ch'üan city (*Chung-kuo li-shih ti-t'u chi*, 2: 33–34, 3–5).

[101] *Shih chi* 110, 2908; *Shih-chi chu-yi* 110, 2328–9.

Han, among them the Hun-yeh king. Subsequently, the areas of Lung-hsi, Pei-ti, and Ho-hsi suffered fewer Hsiung-nu raids, and the Han transferred the poor people of Kuan-tung[102] to settle in the area of Hsin-ch'in-chung[103] (south of the Yellow River), which had been seized from the Hsiung-nu and which was now being populated with Chinese people. The settlement policy also allowed for a reduction in the number of troops stationed to the north of Pei-ti.[104] The Hsiung-nu continued to attack, so in 119 B.C. the Han mounted a major expedition to hit deep into Hsiung-nu territory, and the entire Han army was mobilized. During this expedition Han troops reached the T'ien-yen Mountains[105] and the fortified town of Chao-hsin[106] before turning back. Huo Ch'ü-ping, advancing over two thousand *li* from Tai, clashed with the wise king of the left. The Han soldiers killed or captured over seventy thousand enemies, and the wise king of the left and his generals all fled. Huo Ch'ü-ping performed a *feng* sacrifice at Mount Lang-chü-hsü[107] and a *shan* sacrifice at Mount Ku-yen,[108] descended to the Han-hai, and then turned back. After this, the Hsiung-nu withdrew to the northern steppe in today's Mongolia, and their royal court was no longer located south of the Gobi.[109]

During this phase the whole military and civil administrative structure of the border regions was reorganized and gradually came to be structured on three levels: (1) the commanderies inside the defensive line (*pien-sai*); (2) an intermediate area outside the defensive line populated mainly by non-Chinese peoples but still under the formal control of the Han bureaucracy; and (3) the territories that were outside the limits of Han control but that had accepted some form of subordination to the Han.[110] To the first level belonged the two commanderies of Shuo-fang and Wu-yüan, set up in 127

---

[102] Region to the east either of the Han-ku Pass (*Chung-kuo li-shih ti-t'u chi*, 2: 15–16, 4–8) or of T'ung-kuan, a district in Shensi province (not marked in *Chung-kuo li-shih ti-t'u chi*).

[103] This indicates the region south of the Great Bend of the Yellow River, in Inner Mongolia (*Chung-kuo li-shih ti-t'u chi*, 2: 17–18, 1–6/3–6).

[104] *Shih chi* 110, 2909–10; *Shih-chi chu-yi* 110, 2329.

[105] Range located in Outer Mongolia, to the southeast of today's Khangai Mountains.

[106] Hsiung-nu city built by Chao Hsin, located to the west of the T'ien-yen Mountains.

[107] Mountain located to the east of present-day Ulan Bator (*Chung-kuo li-shih ti-t'u chi*, 2: 39, 2–4.)

[108] Mountain located to the west of the Lang-chü-hsü Mountains (*Chung-kuo li-shih ti-t'u chi*, 2: 39, 2–4).

[109] *Shih chi* 110, 2910–11; *Shih-chi chu-yi* 110, 2329–30.

[110] This third level was most probably established towards the end of the reign of Wu-ti (see below). Cfr. Bielenstein, *The Bureaucracy of Han Times*, pp. 109–13.

B.C. in the region north of the Yellow River after the Han conquered those nomadic lands in the areas of Ordos, Tai, and Yen. The second level of border administration began to be established before 119 B.C. and comprised areas that lay beyond the effective reach of the Chinese military colonies but were still regarded as subject to Chinese administration. These territories were defined as Dependent States (*shu-kuo*), and their chief officer was the director of Dependent States (*tien-shu-kuo*).[111] The Dependent States were inhabited by a largely non-Chinese, nomadic population that had "surrendered" (or simply switched allegiance from the Hsiung-nu to the Chinese) and were intended to be a buffer between the Chinese defense line and the Hsiung-nu and Ch'iang tribesmen.[112] From 121 to 28 B.C. their administrative structure included a chief commandant of a Dependent State (*shu-kuo tu-wei*), with one assistant (*ch'eng*), one or more captains (*hou*) and battalion commanders (*ch'ien-jen*),[113] and a prefect of the Nine Successive Interpreters (*chiu-yi ling*).[114]

SECOND PHASE (119–104 B.C.). At the end of the period just discussed most of the objectives that Wu-ti had set out to accomplish ten years earlier had been achieved. The northern border had been secured, the Hsiung-nu had been pushed farther to the north, and the Han were no longer paying a tribute. Yet the military campaigns were proceeding unabated, and some of the most resounding Han successes were obtained between 119 and 112 B.C. The Han government continued its policy of generally strengthening and restructuring the state economy, increasing state control over the financial resources of the country, and thus possibly allowing the military campaigns to continue. The establishment of the salt and iron monopolies in 119 B.C. signaled the beginning of a wide range of economic reforms, and the timing may indicate that the rationalization and centralization of the financial administration may have been made more urgent because the war effort had depleted state resources. As events after 119 B.C. show, the Han emperor and his advisers were no longer satisfied with their initial objectives and were determined to continue to fight with a broader agenda. The goal of defeating the Hsiung-nu militarily, already achieved, was replaced by a plan for the annihilation of Hsiung-nu political power, to be

---

[111] This post was inherited from the Ch'in administration, but its authority was increased in 121 B.C.; see Bielenstein, *The Bureaucracy of Han Times*, p. 11. On the establishment of the *shu-kuo* and their relationship to the central government, see Loewe, *Records of the Han Administration*, 1: 61–63.

[112] Bielenstein, *The Bureaucracy of Han Times*, p. 109.

[113] Bielenstein has the term "millarian"; I follow here C. Hucker, *A Dictionary of Official Titles in Imperial China* (Stanford: Stanford University Press, 1975), no. 903.

[114] Bielenstein, *The Bureaucracy of Han Times*, p. 84.

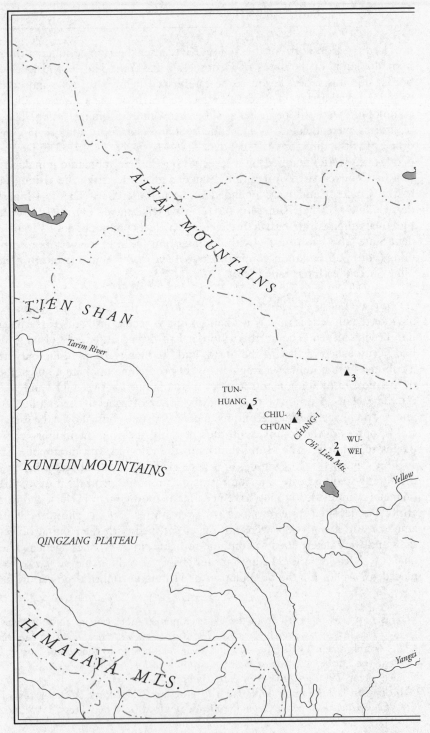

Map 5

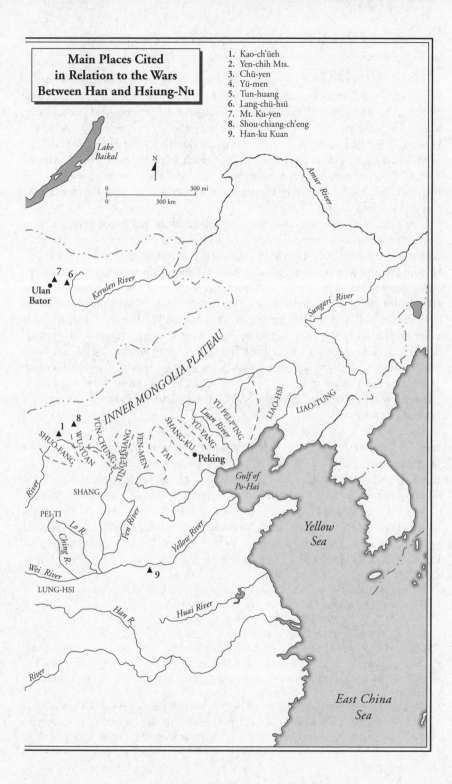

**Main Places Cited
in Relation to the Wars
Between Han and Hsiung-Nu**

1. Kao-ch'üeh
2. Yen-chih Mts.
3. Chü-yen
4. Yü-men
5. Tun-huang
6. Lang-chü-hsü
7. Mt. Ku-yen
8. Shou-chiang-ch'eng
9. Han-ku Kuan

*Lake
Baikal*

N

| 0 | | 300 mi |

| 0 | | 300 km |

Amur River

7 6

**Ulan
Bator**

Kerulen River

Sungari River

INNER MONGOLIA PLATEAU

1 8

Luan River

YU PEI-PING

LIAO-HSI

LIAO-TUNG

SHUO-FANG

YÜN-CHUNG

WU-YÜAN

TING-HSIANG

YEN-MEN

SHANG-KU

YÜ-YANG

TAI

River

SHANG

Peking

*Gulf of
Po-Hai*

PEI-TI

Lo R.

Fen River

Yellow River

Ching R.

Yellow River

Wei River

9

LUNG-HSI

*Yellow
Sea*

Han R.

Huai River

River

*East China
Sea*

accomplished through a campaign leading to their "international" isolation, both political and economic. By 110 B.C., after several other campaigns, the Han had established the new commandery of Chiu-ch'üan, which had the strategic purpose of cutting the routes of communication between the Hsiung-nu and the Ch'iang. In the north the Han expanded its areas under cultivation to Hsien-lei,[115] which became the new frontier.[116] The Hsiung-nu were forced to retreat far into the northern steppe and forests, abandoning not only the region south of the Yellow River but also the areas south of the Gobi.

The administrative expansion also continued in this phase, with a total of fourteen border commanderies established in the northern and southern regions of the empire between 112 and 108 B.C., thus consolidating the territorial gains. Westward expansion and an increasing number of military and commercial expeditions to Central Asia proceeded together with the establishment of a defensive line from east to west. This line consisted of permanent, self-supporting garrisons that controlled the movement of the nomadic tribes, signaled a warning in case of danger, engaged in agricultural production, and protected the lines of communication. The defensive line also provided steady and reliable logistical support for the Chinese expeditionary forces and included garrisons such as those along the Edsin-gol that reached out to the lakes of Chü-yen and penetrated deeply into nomadic territory.[117]

THIRD PHASE (104–87 B.C.). At this point, the way was paved for further Han expansion into the Western Regions. In 104 B.C. the Han dispatched the Erh-shih general Li Kuang-li west to attack Ferghana, and ordered General Kung-sun Ao to build the "City for Receiving Surrender" (Shou-chiang-ch'eng).[118] Han diplomats then came into contact with the kingdoms of the Tarim Basin. Wang Hui, an envoy who allegedly had been insulted by the people of Lou-lan, was sent to help Chao P'o-nu attack and defeat Lou-lan.[119] Subsequently a line of forts and stations was built from Chiu-

---

[115] Hsien-lei: name of a locality in the vicinity of today's T'a-ch'eng county, in Sinkiang (not marked in *Chung-kuo li-shih ti-t'u chi*).

[116] *Shih chi* 110, 2913; *Shih-chi chu-yi* 110, 2331.

[117] Loewe, *Records of the Han Administration*, 1: 55–56, 184, map 3.

[118] *Shih chi* 110, 2915; *Shih-chi chu-yi* 110, 2333; The "City for Receiving Surrender," which was built to welcome the Hsiung-nu noblemen who surrendered to the Han, was located in today's Inner Mongolia, to the north of the Yin Mountains (*Chung-kuo li-shih ti-t'u chi*, 2: 39, 2–4).

[119] On this see Hulsewé and Loewe, *China in Central Asia*, pp. 86–90. On the location of Lou-lan see Enoki Kazuo, "The Location of the Capital of Lou-lan and the Date of the Kharosthi Documents," *Memoirs of the Research Department of the Toyo Bunko* 22 (1963): 125–71.

ch'üan to the Yü-men Pass,[120] and Superintendent of the Imperial House-hold Hsü Tzu-wei left the Wu-yüan[121] frontier post and journeyed several thousand *li*, building fortresses, walled outposts, and a line of watch sta-tions that stretched to Mount Lu-ch'ü.[122] At the same time, the Han sent the chief commandant of Archers Carrying Heavy Bows, Lu Po-te, to build fortifications in the Chü-yen Marshes.[123]

Key to the Han expansion was the Chiu-ch'üan commandery, located in a strategic position in the Kansu Corridor.[124] In 102 B.C. the Hsiung-nu wise king of the right invaded Chiu-ch'üan and Chang-yi and abducted several thousand people,[125] and in 99 B.C. the Han dispatched the Erh-shih general Li Kuang-li at the head of thirty thousand cavalry out of Chiu-ch'üan to attack the wise king of the right in the T'ien Shan.[126] This campaign ended in disaster when, after an initial success, Li Kuang-li was surrounded by the Hsiung-nu; he barely survived, and his army was all but wiped out. In the same year, Li Ling also set out from Chiu-ch'üan at the head of five thou-sand special infantry troops. His valorous campaign also ended in defeat. He was confronted by an overwhelming number of enemy troops and even-tually surrendered to the Hsiung-nu.[127] Two years later the Han again dis-patched Li Kuang-li, this time at the head of sixty thousand cavalry and one hundred thousand infantry. The Hsiung-nu responded by moving all their families and property to the north of the Hsü-wu River,[128] while the *ch'an-yü* waited to the south of the river with one hundred thousand cavalry.[129] The last engagement between Li Kuang-li and the Hsiung-nu

---

[120] *Shih chi* 123, 3172, *Shih-chi chu-yi* 123, 2598; Yü-men (Jade Gate) is located to the northwest of Tun-huang, in Kansu (*Chung-kuo li-shih ti-t'u chi*, 2: 33–34, 2–2).

[121] Commandery located in Inner Mongolia, to the north of the Great Bend of the Yellow River (*Chung-kuo li-shih ti-t'u chi*, 2: 17–18, 2–7).

[122] This was the name of the northern extension of today's Lang Mountains, in Inner Mongolia (not marked in *Chung-kuo li-shih ti-t'u chi*).

[123] *Shih chi* 110, 2916 *Shih-chi chu-yi* 110, 2333.

[124] Commandery located in present-day Kansu province, east of the Shu-le River, and west of Kao-t'ai county; its administrative center was Lu-fu, today's Chiu-ch'üan city (*Chung-kuo li-shih ti-t'u chi*, 2: 33–34, 3–4).

[125] *Shih chi* 110, 2916–7, *Shih-chi chu-yi* 110, 2334; Chang-yi was a commandery established in 111 B.C. Its administrative center was in Lu-te. It included the ter-ritory to the west of today's Yung-shang, and to the east of Kao-t'ai, in Kansu (*Chung-kuo li-shih ti-t'u chi*, 2: 33–34, 3–6).

[126] *Shih chi* 110, 2917. *Shih-chi chu-yi* 110, 2334.

[127] On Li Ling's campaign see Loewe, "The Campaigns of Han Wu-ti," pp. 119–22.

[128] *Chung-kuo li-shih ti-t'u chi*, 2: 39, 2–4. This is today the Tula River, in the north of Mongolia.

[129] *Shih chi* 110, 2918. *Shih-chi chu-yi* 110, 2335.

occurred in 90 B.C. On this occasion he was captured, having apparently lost heart because of the execution of his family at home. Eventually he was put to death by the Hsiung-nu.[130] After 99 B.C. the heyday of Han expansion was over, and in subsequent years a different attitude emerged again, one more favorable to compromise. On their side, the Hsiung-nu were beset by internal discord, ineffective leadership, natural calamities, and the secession and sometimes open rebellion of chieftains and former tributaries.[131] This state of affairs led to the maturation of the conditions for a peaceful settlement between Hsüan-ti and Hu-han-yeh Ch'an-yü in the 50s B.C. The gains obtained by China during the period of Wu-ti, and especially the presence of the Han in the Western Regions, were consolidated and rationalized.

The administration of the Western Regions was formalized with the creation of the four commanderies of Chiu-ch'üan, Chang-yi, Tun-huang, and Wu-wei. The first two were established in 104 B.C., the third shortly after (certainly before 91 B.C.), and the fourth between 81 and 67 B.C.[132] These commanderies were placed under the control of a grand administrator (t'ai-shou) with both civil and military responsibilities, aided by a commandant (tu-wei). It was also stipulated that where the need arose more than one tu-wei might be appointed and assigned to different districts within the same commandery.

A third level in the administration of border territories, also mentioned earlier, was probably instituted during this period: the pao (protectorates) system, which presumably covered "an area that lay outside the main line of communications and defences."[133] Under Wu-ti additional posts were established for conducting relations with foreign peoples, such as the colonel protecting the Ch'iang (hu Ch'iang hsiao-wei) and the colonel protecting the Wu-huan (hu Wu-huan hsiao-wei).[134] In 60 B.C., after the heyday of the Han thrust into Central Asia, the post of protector general (hsi-yü tu-hu) of the Western Regions was created, followed in 48 B.C. by a new supernumerary military post, the Wu and Chi colonelcy (wu-chi hsiao-wei),[135] stationed near Turfan. Later, other special officers were established, including the commandant of agriculture (nung tu-wei), who was in charge of the agricultural production in the border prefectures, and the comman-

---

[130] Biographical information on Li Kuang-li is contained in *Han shu* 97A and *Shih chi* 49. For his campaign in Central Asia, see Hulsewé and Loewe, *China in Central Asia*, pp. 228–36, especially n. 926. On the intrigue that led to his family's execution see Loewe, *Crisis and Conflict*, pp. 45, 53–54.

[131] De Crespigny, *The Northern Frontier*, pp. 186–87.

[132] Loewe, *Records of the Han Administration*, 1: 62.

[133] Loewe, *Records of the Han Administration*, 1: 64.

[134] Bielenstein, *The Bureaucracy of Han Times*, p. 110.

[135] On the *wu-chi hsiao-wei*, see Hulsewé and Loewe, *China in Central Asia*, p. 79, n. 63.

dant of passes (*kuan tu-wei*).[136] By the end of Wu-ti's reign the Han had consolidated their authority in the northern and western territories, thus replacing the Hsiung-nu as the pre-eminent "superpower."

The Question of the Western Regions

Few issues in the history of the Former Han have been as rich a source for scholarly hypotheses and speculation as the discussion on the motives that dragged the Han into the Western Regions. As mentioned earlier, the Han advance into the west needs to be comprehended at a level beyond the purely tactical one. The Chinese advance can surely be explained fully only within the context of the Hsiung-nu wars, but it is difficult to see it solely as a natural extension of the declared Han need to protect the frontier regions. Although protection of the border regions was certainly one of the Han's initial goals, the war escalated into a total war, and the Han's ultimate goal became the destruction of the Hsiung-nu empire. The Western Regions were important for the Hsiung-nu as an economic base, and the Han's chief objective in conquering them was to deprive the nomads of this source of strength and support. To place this interpretation in its proper context, however, we should first examine some other theories proposed to explain why the Chinese armies colonized today's Sinkiang.

The first Chinese expedition to Central Asia, led by Chang Ch'ien, was sent in 139/138 B.C., although this dating remains controversial.[137] Thus the diplomatic initiative to find allies in the war against the Hsiung-nu preceded direct military operations, which began only in 133 B.C. However, Chang Ch'ien's mission was intercepted by the Hsiung-nu, and when he finally reached the Yüeh-chih, he found them unwilling to oppose the Hsiung-nu. The initial contacts with Central Asia, therefore, did not produce the expected results in military cooperation, but the exploration of the routes is likely to have contributed considerably to the decision to undertake a military offensive, as it was from this point that the Chinese started to learn in detail about the political composition of this region, the wealth it produced, and the hegemonic position of the Hsiung-nu over the area.[138]

The famed Silk Road explorer Sir Aurel Stein believed that the Chinese expansion into Central Asia was motivated by the need to find new markets for the silk produced in China.[139] Others have surmised that the chief

[136] Loewe, *Records of the Han Administration*, 1: 61.
[137] Hulsewé and Loewe, *China in Central Asia*, p. 209, n. 774.
[138] Hulsewé and Loewe, *China in Central Asia*, p. 211.
[139] Aurel Stein, *Serindia. Detailed Report of Explorations in Central Asia and Westernmost China* (Oxford: Clarendon Press, 1921), 1: 406.

catalyst for Chinese expansion into the Tarim Basin was the struggle with the Hsiung-nu for control of the trade routes in order to find a commercial outlet in the West for China's silk surpluses.[140] These arguments have gained widespread support and continue to appear in recent publications.[141] Lattimore distanced himself from this approach, however, and endorsed the notion that the Han was in fact dragged into Central Asia because of a growing demand for Chinese luxury products, suggesting also that the economic possibilities offered by the oases for a "prosperous, intensive, irrigated agriculture" created favorable conditions for self-supporting Chinese military settlements. Because of their economic similarity to China, and despite the geographic distance, the oases and pasturelands of Central Asia occupied by the Han had a higher degree of cohesion with the main body of China than did the areas peripheral to the steppe.[142]

These views presuppose the existence of a commercial network in Central Asia in the second century B.C. capable of supporting and managing a complex trade network. Yet at the beginning of Wu-ti's reign there is no evidence of anything in Central Asia comparable to the intercontinental trade that would develop over the land and sea routes during the period stretching from the first century B.C. to the third and fourth centuries A.D.[143] Not until Wu-ti's reign did the Chinese became cognizant of the possibilities for trade between China and Central and western Asia, even though these opportunities do not seem to have enjoyed universal appeal.[144]

Han economic involvement in modern Sinkiang was a consequence of events and factors that were primarily political. The earliest Chinese exports to Central Asia seem to be evidence of exchanges of gifts and tribute as a means of political leverage rather than evidence of commercial items within

---

[140] Frederick J. Teggart, *Rome and China. A Study of Correlations in Historical Events* (Berkeley: University of California Press, 1939), pp. 148–233; Peter Boodberg, "Turk, Aryan and Chinese in Ancient Asia," in *Selected Works of Peter A. Boodberg*, ed. Alvin P. Cohen (Berkeley: University of California Press, 1979), pp. 9–12.

[141] Jagchid and Symons, *Peace, War and Trade*, pp. 30, 65.

[142] Owen Lattimore, *Inner Asian Frontiers of China* (Boston: Beacon Press, 1962 [1940]), pp. 500–506.

[143] Manfred Raschke, "New Studies in Roman Commerce with the East," in *Aufstieg und Niedergang der romischen Welt, II Principat*, ed. H. Temporini and W. Haase (Berlin: W. de Gruyter, 1978), 9.2: 622–37. It seems that the formative period for a continental route regularly frequented by professional merchants and substantially different from the haphazard or occasional flow of trade that had existed thus far, should be dated to this period; see Liu Xinru, *Ancient India and Ancient China: Trade and Religious Exchanges, AD 1–600* (Delhi: Oxford University Press, 1988), pp. 1–22.

[144] John Ferguson, "China and Rome," in *Aufstieg und Niedergang der romischen Welt. II Principat*, 9.2: 581–603.

the framework of a burgeoning international trade.[145] Thus in the sequence of events extending from military expansion to formal commercial relations with the nomadic and sedentary peoples of Ta-yüan (Ferghana or Sogdiana)[146] and Ta-hsia (Bactria), the "flag" did not "follow the trade." On the contrary, the whole conquest of the Western Regions was due to the unforeseen outcomes of military and political developments,[147] and the exploration of Central Asia was primarily a strategic move within the wider context of the political and military confrontation between Han and Hsiung-nu.[148] Among the motives for this course of action were the desire to find allies in the West so that a "pincher" offensive could be carried out against the Hsiung-nu from both ends of the Central Asian steppe and the desire to isolate the Hsiung-nu from potential allies such as the Ch'iang. A third motive may have been related to Wu-ti's desire for "exotic" goods from Central Asia. These motives, however, do not actually explain why the Western Regions were such a crucial strategic objective for the Han even after they had repeatedly beaten the Hsiung-nu.

The Western Regions as a Hsiung-nu Power Base

It has been pointed out that Wu-ti may have intended to establish a direct connection with Central Asia to undermine Hsiung-nu prestige and authority in that region. Many of the region's peoples recognized themselves as Hsiung-nu tributaries, and if China could act as a counterweight to Hsiung-nu power, the latter's influence would be drastically reduced. But were these dwellers in the relatively sparse oases truly vital to Hsiung-nu power, and, if so, how? Unless we understand the relationship between the Hsiung-nu and the oasis people, we cannot properly assess how Han conquest of the region affected the war between the two empires.

In Hulsewé's most perceptive answer to this question, "the only reason for the Chinese expansion in Central Asia was the desire to stop the invasions of the Hsiung-nu, or, as the ancients said, to 'cut off their right arm',

[145] Raschke, "New Studies in Roman Commerce with the East," p. 611.

[146] Hulsewé and Loewe, *China in Central Asia*, p. 273.

[147] Loewe, "The Campaigns of Han Wu-ti," pp. 84–85; id., "Introduction," in *China in Central Asia*, p. 40; Yü Ying-shih, "The Hsiung-nu," pp. 131–33; Raschke, "New Studies in Roman Commerce with the East," pp. 615–17; M. C. Webb, "The Flag Follows Trade: An Essay on the Necessary Interaction of Military and Commercial Factors in State Formation," in *Ancient Civilization and Trade*, ed. J. A. Sabloff and C. C. Lamberg-Karlovsky (Albuquerque: University of New Mexico Press, 1975), pp. 179–94.

[148] Leslie and Gardiner, "Chinese Knowledge of Central Asia," pp. 254–308; J. R. Gardiner-Gardner, "Chang Ch'ien and Central Asian Ethnography," *Papers of Far Eastern History* 33 (1986): 23–79.

i.e., to deprive them of their western bases."[149] The territorial conquests of the Han were dictated by the military necessity to cut off the Hsiung-nu from those areas that supplied them with provisions: the Kansu Corridor, the oases of Central Asia, and southern Manchuria.[150] The "provisions" should be understood, I believe, as agricultural goods and the products of urban craftsmen.

We have already seen how, before Han Wu-ti's offensive, the Hsiung-nu managed to acquire large amounts of goods by relying on the frontier markets, raids into Chinese territory, and *ho-ch'in* payments.[151] As Han Wu-ti took the offensive, the Hsiung-nu could no longer count on the "tribute" products or on exchanges at the frontier markets, which were also disrupted; at the same time, they suffered heavy losses of animals and pastureland. As the Hsiung-nu retreated, moving their political center farther and farther to the north, they had to rely more heavily on the agricultural settlements in Central Asia and in southern Siberia.[152] The oases of Sinkiang were close to those centers, had a long history of contacts with nomadic peoples, and were rich enough to support a sizeable urban population. They came to represent the main (though probably not the only) source of supply for agricultural and other products for the Hsiung-nu after the nomads lost the revenues from China, especially after the campaigns of Wei Ch'ing and Huo Ch'ü-ping forced the Hsiung-nu to transfer their political and military center to the northwest. The Chinese military and political presence in Central Asia therefore became vital to the Han overall strategy of weakening the nomads and was accomplished mainly through the establishment of farming colonies managed by the military. These military-agricultural settlements had multiple functions: to prevent the Hsiung-nu from gaining access to agricultural products, to serve as advanced logistic support for Chinese expeditionary armies, and to protect the trade that China was starting to organize with the west.

The close economic ties between the Hsiung-nu and the Western Regions are evident from several passages in the *Shih chi*. In chapter 110 there is mention of the Han strategy "to create a split between the Hsiung-nu and the states to the west which had up to this time supported them."[153] These

---

[149] A. F. P. Hulsewé, "Quelques considérations sur le commerce de la soie au temps de la dynastie des Han," in *Mélanges de Sinologie offerts à Paul Demiéville, II* (Paris: Bibliothèque de l'Institut des Hautes Etudes Chinoises, 1974), p. 120.

[150] Hulsewé, "Quelques considérations sur le commerce de la soie," p. 125.

[151] Yü, *Trade and Expansion in Han China*, pp. 99–105.

[152] The Hsiung-nu royal residence was transferred north of the Gobi sometime after 119 B.C. and, in 106/105 B.C., it was moved once more, this time to the upper reaches of the Orkhon River, in Mongolia. See Daffinà, *Il Nomadismo Centrasiatico*, p. 61.

[153] *Shih-chi chu-yi* 110, 2331–2.

"states" included not only nomadic but also sedentary populations. Arguably, once the cessation of the *ho-ch'in* policy brought to an end the payment of tribute from China, the Hsiung-nu aristocracy became increasingly dependent on other states, whose military inferiority was uncontested, to replace the lost income. In addition, these areas could provide the farmland to support Hsiung-nu troops, who could, if the circumstances required it, turn themselves into farmers, as they did in the following case: "In the time of Emperor Chao the Hsiung-nu took the further step of sending four thousand cavalrymen to work the land at Chü-shih, and after his accession Emperor Hsüan despatched five commanders with troops to attack the Hsiung-nu. Those who were working the land at Chü-shih fled in alarm and Chü-shih resumed relations with Han."[154] Although the Hsiung-nu had other settlements in the steppes that also provided them with farming and handicraft products – as demonstrated by the excavations of burial sites, such as Noin Ula,[155] or of the fortified settlement of Ivolga[156] – it is unlikely that these centers had very large productive bases.

[154] Hulsewé and Loewe, *China in Central Asia*, p. 185.

[155] This is located in the northern part of Mongolia (about 100 kilometers north of Ulan Bator); other important burial sites are those of Sudzhinsk and Deretsuj, both situated in Transbaikalia, in the Buriat Mongol A.S.S.R. On the Noin Ula *kurgans*, see S. I. Rudenko, *Kul'tura Khunnov i noinulinskie kurgany* (Moskva-Leningrad: Nauka, 1962); A. Salmony, "The Small Finds of Noin Ula," *Parnassus* 8 (1936), 2: 15–20; W. P. Yetts, "Discoveries of the Kozlov Expedition," *Burlington Magazine* 48 (1926): 168–85; K. V. Trever, *Excavations in Northern Mongolia, 1924–1925* (Leningrad: Memoirs of the Academy of History of Material Culture 3, 1932).

[156] The Ivolga *gorodishche* was a Hsiung-nu fortified village located near Ulan Ude (in the Buryat A.S.S.R.). Russian archaeologists began working on it in the 1920s. The extensive excavations at the Ivolga site yield ample information on the agricultural activities of the Hsiung-nu. This village had primarily an agricultural and handicraft economy, although the raising of domestic animals, hunting, and fishing also played important roles. The village's specific function, within the context of a nomadic society, was to supplement the steppe peoples with those products, such as grains, textiles, and various artifacts, that a pure nomadic economy could not supply. Villages such as this were "trading centers" in the steppe, where the wandering nomads could acquire the products they needed and "overcome the narrow economic basis of nomadic economy." The population of the village "was composed of settled Hsiung-nu, of the aboriginal population conquered by the Hsiung-nu, and of alien craftsmen from the ranks of deserters and prisoners of war." From craniological investigation, however, it appears that the population of the village was racially homogeneous and belonged to the South-Siberian branch of the Mongoloid race. See A. V. Davydova, "The Ivolga Gorodishche. A Monument of the Hsiung-nu Culture in the Trans-Baikal Region," *Acta Orientalia Academiae Scientiarum Hungaricae* 20 (1968): 209–45. A complete bibliography on this archaeological complex is available in

Conclusion

During Wu-ti's reign the Han offensive not only inflicted serious military losses on the Hsiung-nu, but also disrupted the "tribute system" of the Hsiung-nu empire, which had thus far been the cornerstone for the political cohesion among the various tribes united by the charismatic leader Modun. A crucial blow to the nomads' power was the severance of their tributary relations with the sedentary regions of Central Asia, from which the Hsiung-nu had been able to acquire the type of tributary and commercial goods no longer available from China. At the same time, large portions of nomadic grazing land to the north of the Yellow River and in the west were seized by the Chinese, putting an additional strain on the nomadic economy. In the long run, those pressures brought about the political disintegration of the Hsiung-nu as a unified steppe empire. Although the forward strategy of Wu-ti paid some dividends in foreign policy, and the newly conquered territories were incorporated within the structure of the Han administration, the strategy also almost bankrupted the Han because of the rapid depletion of the state's finances.

The relevance of the Hsiung-nu to Han politics and society during the lifetime of Ssu-ma Ch'ien can hardly be overestimated. Besides the chapter that is specifically devoted to them, the *Shih chi* deals extensively with the Hsiung-nu in the imperial annals, in the biographies of important political figures, and in the economic chapters (e.g., chapters 30 and 129). Because of the wars' impact on Chinese society and because of the objective threat the Hsiung-nu posed, the nomadic "factor" required extensive treatment. It is not surprising, therefore, that in the *Shih chi* the Hsiung-nu are main characters, not "extras": they were a new phenomenon that needed to be explained, or at least to be brought within the boundaries of a world vision that could account for their existence and make them into the object of historical investigation. However, as momentous as they may have been, the various aspects of the relations between the Han and the Hsiung-nu do not fully explain, in themselves, the method of investigation adopted by the Grand Historian. How Ssu-ma Ch'ien created, without any discernible model or precedent, an ethnic and a political history of the Hsiung-nu, is the object of the next section of this book.

Davydova's book *Ivolginskii kompleks (gorodishche i mogil'nik) – pamiatnik khunnu v Zabaikal'e* (Leningrad: Isd-vo Leningradskogo Universiteta, 1985). On the presence of agriculture among the Minusinsk early nomads, see also M. P. Zavitukhina, "The Tagar Culture," and "The Tashtyk Culture," in AA. VV., *Frozen Tombs. The Culture and Art of the Ancient Tribes of Siberia*, (London, 1978), p. 94. On the economy of the early nomads, see Nicola Di Cosmo, "Ancient Inner Asian Nomads: Their Economic Basis and Its Significance in Chinese History," *The Journal of Asian Studies* 53.4 (1994): 1092–1126.

PART IV

CHAPTER SEVEN

In Search of Grass and Water

Ethnography and History of the North in the *Historian's Records*

Introduction

This section is dedicated to an analysis of *how* the history of the Hsiung-nu came to be written by Ssu-ma Ch'ien. As discussed in Part III, the Hsiung-nu had become a phenomenon whose effects on Han life – military, economic, and political – could not be ignored. However, by itself that consideration is surely insufficient to establish how the historian constructed his narrative of the northern nomads, and how he was able to incorporate this narrative within the general scope of his *opus magnum*.

The issue is important, at the very least, in two respects: there is no obvious precedent that Ssu-ma Ch'ien could have used for inspiration, and the pattern established by Ssu-ma's Hsiung-nu narrative became the model for representations of northern peoples and Inner Asian states in the subsequent Chinese historical literature.[1] As we will see, two orientations can be detected in accounts of the Hsiung-nu, and of Inner Asia in general: one empirical, descriptive, and data oriented, the other normative, ideological, and influenced by currents of contemporary thought. Both orientations were consistent not only with the declared goals of the historian but also with the general thinking of an age, the early Han, inclined to the construction of universal cosmological paradigms and unified historical patterns. Hence the account of the Hsiung-nu appears as a combination of various contemporary concerns and intellectual pursuits.

---

[1] See, for instance, Michael R. Drompp, "The Hsiung-nu *Topos* in the T'ang Response to the Collapse of the Uighur Steppe Empire," *Central and Inner Asian Studies* 1 (1987): 1–46; and David B. Honey, "History and Historiography on the Sixteen States: Some T'ang *Topoi* on the Nomads," *Journal of Asian History* 24.2 (1990): 161–217.

I have therefore divided the materials on the Hsiung-nu into two different sets of data. The first, in this chapter, presents information on the lifestyle, history, and ethnography of the nomads, much of which must have been acquired through direct investigation. The second refers to the position of the Hsiung-nu and Inner Asia in general as metaphysical agents and new ingredients of cosmological architectures. As is well known, Ssu-ma's *Shih chi* is far from being a consistent historical narrative. In addition to its internal contradictions, the narrative is often overlaid with concerns that deviate from any mimetic description of events. These are not only moral concerns but also, more broadly, cosmological concerns that stem from a particular philosophical tradition based on construction of a unitarian vision of the cosmos and of the principles regulating it. The narrative on Inner Asia is not exempt from these "normative" concerns, which will be discussed in Chapter 8.

To appreciate the "empirical" strain in Ssu-ma Ch'ien's construction of the Hsiung-nu narrative, however, we must first look at the role of the historian, at what Ssu-ma was trying to achieve, and at the general interpretations that have been offered concerning the role of early Han historiography. These questions are essential to understand the likely intellectual and methodological frame that informed at least part of the Hsiung-nu narrative. Hence I will begin this discussion with some brief considerations concerning the position of the historian and of history writing in early China.

The Role of the Historian (Shih) in Early China

The traditional interpretation of the *Shuo-wen*, followed by Kwang-chih Chang and others, attributes the meaning of "archivist" to the ancient graph for *shih*.[2] The existence of a class of functionaries who specialized in writing about historical matters is documented as early as the Shang dynasty (c. 1600–1045 B.C.), but the different meanings assigned to the word *shih* do not fundamentally affect the question of the role of the historian in pre-imperial times.[3] Wang Kuo-wei in China and Naito Torajirô in Japan came to the conclusion that the character *shih* ("historian") originally represented a hand holding a vessel used to contain tallies at archery contests and that the official designated by this character in Shang times

2 Kwang-chih Chang, *Art, Myth and Ritual. The Path to Political Authority in Ancient China*. (Cambridge, Mass.: Harvard University Press, 1983), p. 232, fig. 61 'f.' In the same work (p. 280), however, we also find an identical graph, reproduced in a chart of flags from Hayashi Minao's article "Chugoku senshin jidai no hata," whose assigned meaning is a hand that is holding a standard.

3 Chang, *Art, Myth and Ritual*, pp. 91–92.

was the one initially charged with the duty of keeping track of hits at these contests.[4] Archaeologists and specialists in early Chinese history generally agree that there must originally have been a class of people who specialized in the engraving of oracle bones and in the practice of writing; thus the ancient *shih* could have been an "engraver" or, simply, "one who could write."[5]

The existence of a category of *shih* functionaries as "makers of books" is shown by the inscription on a recently discovered *p'an* basin,[6] where it is recorded that the vessel was made by order of a *shih* "named Ch'iang whose lineage specialized in *tso ts'e*, the making of 'bamboo books.' "[7] This points again to the historian as someone engaged above all in the "craft of writing," an activity that had to be performed at different levels of the bureaucracy and was intimately connected with political and ritual functions. Highly esteemed because of the magical and ritual powers attributed to the written word in early China, this occupation later acquired special relevance because of the moral, political, and ideological implications inherent in preserving the past. The writings of the first historians, therefore, were used to assist the ruler in the performance of sacrificial rites; the divination records these functionaries inscribed on animal scapulas and turtle shells represent instances of their recording specific events.[8]

By the time of the Chou dynasty the *shih* had acquired important duties that included assisting with astronomical and astrological affairs, especially through the selection of auspicious and inauspicious days for the performance of particular duties and rituals; accompanying the ruler to sacrifices, on military expeditions, or to diplomatic meetings; and attending archery contests. Historians under the Chou were also invested with the authority

---

[4] Burton Watson, *Ssu-ma Ch'ien, Grand Historian of China* (New York: Columbia University Press, 1958), p. 70. For a different hypothesis, see Shirakawa Shizuka, "Shaku shi," in id., *Kokotsubungaku ronshu* (Kyoto: Hoyu shoten, 1955), 1: 1–66; and Leon Vandermeersch, *Wangdao: ou, La voie royale: recherches sur l'esprit des institutions de la Chine archaique*, 2 vols. (Paris: Ecole Française d'Extrême-Orient, 1977–80).

[5] According to K. C. Chang, many historians believe that the "earliest historiographers were also religious, possibly shamanistic figures." Yet characters that specifically indicate shamans, such as *shih* and *wu*, were already used at a very early stage and exclude the possibility of an identity of functions between the historian and the priest. Therefore, the thesis of an originally religious (possibly shamanistic) role of the *shih*, albeit highly attractive and full of interesting implications, can be accepted only as a hypothesis.

[6] T'ang Lan, "Lüeh-lun Hsi-Chou wei shih chia-tsu chiao-ts'ang t'ung-ch'i te chung-yao yi-yi," *Wen-wu*, 1978.3: 14, 19–24.

[7] Chang, *Art, Myth, and Ritual*, p. 91.

[8] C. S. Gardner, *Chinese Traditional Historiography* (Cambridge, Mass.: Harvard University Press, 1938), pp. 7–9.

to judge the morality of actions by the ruler.[9] The writing of annals was a later development that probably arose when historians had to keep a record of the official activities of rulers for future reference.[10] According to the Confucian tradition, the *wang* of the Spring and Autumn period was always flanked by a "right" and a "left" *shih*, with the duty of recording, respectively, the "deeds" and the "words" of the ruler.[11] In this respect the position of the *shih* was comparable to that of the medieval chronicler of the West or perhaps of the "logographer" of ancient Greece.

In the Warring States period, the Confucian tradition ascribed a moral value to the work of the historian by charging the past with the preeminent quality of being the repository of human experience.[12] Thus historians were invested with a moral authority derived not only from their knowledge of the past but also from their institutional role as interpreters, or judges, of the past.[13] As the functions of the *shih* came to involve rituals, such as the selection of auspicious days or the interpretation of planetary movements, the definition of the profession of the *shih* came to mean not only someone who could write but also someone who was engaged in the acquisition and control of an ever more complex and esoteric body of knowledge. Astronomy, the calendar, and the recording of human events all fell within the realm of historical knowledge and were glued together by the universal belief in the co-terminal existence, close relationship, and mutual influence of the human and heavenly worlds.[14]

History Writing during the Early Han

The dual function of the *shih* as recorder of both heavenly and human events was institutionalized during the Former Han dynasty (206 B.C.–A.D. 9),

[9] H. G. Creel, *Shen Pu-hai. A Chinese Political Philosopher of the Fourth Century B.C.* (Chicago: University of Chicago Press, 1974), p. 85

[10] B. Watson, *Ssu-ma Ch'ien*, p. 70.

[11] Otto Franke, "Der Ursprung der chinesischen Geschichtschreibung," *Sitzungsberichte der prüßischen Akademie der Wissenschaften* 23 (1925): 276–309.

[12] A. F. Wright, "On the Uses of Generalization in the Study of Chinese History," in *Generalizations in the Writing of History*, ed. L. Gottschalk (Chicago: University of Chicago Press, 1963), p. 37; Creel, *Shen Pu-hai*, p. 85.

[13] On the Confucian position on history, see Roger Ames, *The Art of Rulership: A Study in Ancient Chinese Political Thought* (Honolulu: University of Hawaii Press, 1983), pp. 1–6. But other schools of thought also exhibited similar concerns. For instance, Mo Tzu said that "the sources of our knowledge live in what is written on bamboo and silk, what is engraved on metal and stone, and what is cut on vessels to be handed down to posterity" (Chang, *Art, Myth and Ritual*, p. 89).

[14] Benjamin Schwartz, *The World of Thought in Ancient China*, (Cambridge, Mass.: Harvard University Press, 1985), p. 353.

when the *shih* became a high-ranking officer in the central administration of the state, who specialized also in astrological matters.[15] The duties of the T'ai-shih-ling (usually translated as Grand Historian or Prefect Grand Astrologer) included drawing up the annual calendar, memorializing about the monthly calendar on the first day of each month, finding auspicious days for state rituals, and keeping a record of portents and omens. He was also supposed to supervise the tests given for the appointment of the Masters of Documents, that is, the imperial secretaries, who were required to know a large number of characters and different styles of writing.[16]

After inheriting the position of Grand Historian from his father, Ssu-ma Ch'ien did not limit himself to data collecting and memorializing on auspicious days. He also allegedly continued, privately, the labor of his father, Ssu-ma T'an, in compiling a history that was not simply a collection of documents, but had a worldview, was politically "engaged," and did not refrain from interpretation and moral judgments. The project for a universal history of China down to the Han, usually attributed to the son in its mature formulation, was grandiose, but the search for the reasons Ssu-ma Ch'ien undertook it have so far failed to yield a satisfactory explanation.

Ssu-ma Ch'ien's work and thought defy easy characterization, and attempts to see him as the exponent of a given school of thought – Confucianism, Taoism, or something else – have not been particularly successful in interpreting the genesis of the *Shih chi*. A theory that has had considerable currency has pointed out the proximity of Ssu-ma Ch'ien to the so-called Huang-Lao thought. Ssu-ma Ch'ien's intellectual position has been seen as a synthesis of ideas drawn from the Huang-Lao tradition and the cosmological elements of Han Confucianism, in particular those linked to the *yin-yang* theory.[17] But the Grand Historian also criticized popular Taoist political ideals that ran counter to the notion of the centralized state, a position possibly attributable to his upbringing, which presumably stressed the "Confucian" ethos for civil service (his father having been, like him, a Grand Historian, from the beginning of his career he always remained close to the government and the palace).[18] The presence of elements belonging to different philosophical traditions and the syncretic tendencies detectable in the *Shih chi* are supported by Ssu-ma Ch'ien himself, who declared, in his

---

[15] Paul Pelliot, "L'édition collective des oeuvres de Wang Kouo-wei," *T'oung pao* 26 (1929): 118.

[16] Hans Bielenstein, *The Bureaucracy of Han Times* (Cambridge: Cambridge University Press, 1980), p. 19.

[17] Lai Hsin-hsia, "Ts'ung Shih Chi k'an Ssu-ma Ch'ien te cheng-chih ssu-hsiang," *Wen shih che* 1981.2: 56.

[18] This is the case, for instance, of the Taoist belief in "small states and poor people"; see Wu Ju-yu, "Ssu-ma Ch'ien te ju tao ssu- hsiang pien-hsi,"in *Jen-wen tsa-chih* 1984.3: 87.

famous letter to Jen An, that he wanted "to form a single school of thought" (*ch'eng yi chia chih yen*).[19] Arguably, it is in his endeavor to unify and resolve the many variances and lacunae of an as yet not unified historical past within a coherent whole that the author found a major raison d'être for his monumental work.

To gain an understanding of Han historiography, the relationship between history writing before Ssu-ma Ch'ien and the *Shih chi* has emerged as an obvious but nonetheless engaging issue. Both Édouard Chavannes and Burton Watson placed Ssu-ma Ch'ien's work within the so-called Confucian historiographical tradition, of which the *Shih chi* represented a more advanced evolutionary stage. According to Chavannes, Ssu-ma Ch'ien's main advance was his organization of already existing material within a historical context; therefore, Ssu-ma Ch'ien was a *compilateur* rather than an original thinker.[20] This was possible, according to the French sinologist, owing to a general flourishing of literary activity – a *renaissance des lettres* – during the reigns of Wen-ti and Wu-ti.[21] This interpretation leads us to two conclusions. First, Ssu-ma Ch'ien could not be considered the "father" of Chinese historiography because his own conception of history had been generated by the Confucian one. Second, based on contextual similarities, a genetic relationship is assumed to have existed between the *Shih chi* and works such as the *Spring and Autumn Annals* and the *Tso-chuan*, for which the Han historian is regarded as the conscious interpreter and follower.[22]

Seeking to justify the radical differences between the *Ch'un Ch'iu* and the *Shih chi* in conception, structure, and philosophy of history, Piet van der Loon proposed an evolutionary scheme according to which Chinese historiography developed in three stages. Before Confucius there was a "ritual" historiography; then, with and after Confucius, there was a shift toward a "moralizing" use of history; and finally, with Ssu-ma Ch'ien, there

---

[19] This statement has been the object of close scrutiny by numerous exegetes of the *Shih chi*. For instance, see Wu Chung-kuang, "Ssu-ma Ch'ien 'ch'eng i chia chih yen' shuo," *Jen-wen tsa-chih* 1984.4: 80. This sentence has also been interpreted as "to complete the words of a single family," with reference to the filial attitude shown by Ssu-ma Ch'ien to his father Ssu-ma T'an, who is credited with being the one to begin writing the *Shih chi*. Others have pointed out that the meaning of this statement resides in Ssu-ma Ch'ien's effort to give the *Shih chi* an independent status as a literary work by selecting different elements from several schools of thought and by using sources that belonged to different traditions; see Pai Shou-i, "Shuo 'ch'eng i chia chih yen,'" in *Li-shih yen-chiu* 1984.1: 55–60. To me it seems that the general thrust of these interpretations is to stress the unitarian outlook and syncretic effort present in the *Shih chi*.

[20] Édouard Chavannes, *Les mémoires historiques de Se-ma Ts'ien* (Paris: Ernest Leroux, 1895–1905) 1985, 1: clvi–clvii.

[21] Chavannes, *Mém. hist.*, 1: cviii.   [22] B. Watson, *Ssu-ma Ch'ien*, pp. 89–93.

came "systematic" history. Systematic history appeared after China had become a centralized power, capable of "transmitting the experience of statecraft."[23] This position attempts to reconcile the images of Ssu-ma Ch'ien as both "continuator" and "innovator."

The relationship between the appearance of the *Shih chi* and broad-ranging social and political changes occuring in Ssu-ma Ch'ien's time is brought into focus by the arguments stressing the new social and political conditions created in China after its political unification and the consequent "need" for an improved organization of historical knowledge. According to Hulsewé, the Chinese historian on the one hand reorganized the historical materials of the past in "better co-ordinated frames"; on the other hand, new methods and forms were produced by the unification of the empire under the Han, which were to remain standards for official history writing for the following two thousand years.[24] Dzo Ching-chuan's theory, along the same line of thought, can be summarized in the following three points: (1) as interest in the destiny of the human community grew along with the increase in the number of those who took part in politics, the ancient formulas for the presentation of historical data appeared more and more to be insufficient to satisfy the greater demand; (2) there arose a need for better organization of the old oral and written traditions; and (3) enhanced organization of historical knowledge could be realized when a new *Weltanschauung* was introduced in China with the birth of a unified empire.[25] In sum, Dzo considered history writing the fruit of the empire's

[23] Piet Van der Loon, "The Ancient Chinese Chronicles and the Growth of Historical Ideals," in *Historians of China and Japan*, ed. W. G. Beasley and E. G. Pulleyblank (London: Oxford University Press, 1961), p. 29.

[24] A. F. P. Hulsewé, "Notes on the Historiography of the Han Period," in *Historians of China and Japan*, p. 33. Very often we read that Ssu-ma Ch'ien set the pattern for the historical literature of the next two thousand years. Although the *Shih chi* did provide a model for later Standard Histories, this does not mean that no changes occurred thereafter. The major developments can be summarized as follows: (1) Fixing the boundaries of each work so that it focused on the history of a single dynasty (the *Han shu* being the first properly dynastic history); (2) appointing to official positions scholars whose task was to compile the history of the previous dynastic period; and (3) from the T'ang onward, ensuring that normally the compilation of dynastic histories was done by a committee rather than by a single person or by a family of historians; see Lien-sheng Yang, "The Organization of Chinese Official Historiography: Principles and Methods of the Standard Histories from the T'ang through the Ming Dynasty," in *Historians of China and Japan*, pp. 44–45.

[25] Ching-chuan Dzo, *Se-ma Ts'ien et l'historiographie chinoise* (Paris: Publications Orientalistes de France, 1978), p. 38. In this position we can recognize an echo of what has been arguably the most influential Western theory on early Chinese historiography, expressed by Balazs in the famous formula that "history was

creation and the establishment of Confucian dogma, which called for more "didactic, moralistic, bureaucratic compilations."[26] He saw Ssu-ma Ch'ien as the initiator of history written for use by state officials.[27] This "sociological" interpretation of early Chinese historiography has enjoyed considerable favor among scholars writing in the West, whether they have seen it as an offshoot of "orthodox political morality,"[28] as a tool to fit the needs of the bureaucratic class, or as a mirror of correct moral conduct.[29]

Yet the *Shih chi* was not intended as a bureaucratic compilation, was not necessarily written for state officials. The implied audience for Ssu-ma Ch'ien's labor is to this day a matter of conjecture. Some scholars have tried to go beyond an interpretation that stressed either the political morality of the *Shih chi* or its bureaucratic nature. Various arguments have been proposed to explain what might have induced Ssu-ma T'an and his son to embark on writing the *Historian's Records*, but the motives and conditions under which the work might have matured – consciousness of history's meaningfulness for the present, potential access to recorded materials, stimuli drawn from the lacunae and disorder of the previous historical tradition, and personal ambition – remain subjective interpretations, difficult to evaluate without there being some evidence provided by the author himself.[30]

Some sentences in the letter of self-justification sent by Ssu-ma Ch'ien to his friend Jen An have been raised to the status of a manifesto, or public declaration of intent, and naturally have been the objects of close scrutiny. These are "to gather the old traditions scattered all over the empire"

written by officials for officials"; see Etienne Balazs, "L'histoire comme guide de la pratique bureaucratique," in *Historians of China and Japan*, pp. 78–94 (trans. in English as "History as a Guide to Bureaucratic Practice," in Etienne Balazs, *Chinese Civilization and Bureaucracy* [New Haven: Yale University Press, 1964]).

[26] David Johnson, "Epic and History in Early China: The Matter of Wu Tzu-hsü," *Journal of Asian Studies* 2 (1981): 271.

[27] Dzo, *Se-ma Ts'ien et l'historiographie chinoise*, p. 136.

[28] C. B. Sargent, "Subsidized History," *Far Eastern Quarterly* 3.1 (1943): 134–38.

[29] Homer Dubs, "The Reliability of Chinese Histories," *Far Eastern Quarterly* 6.1 (1946): 31; Hans Bielenstein, "The Restoration of the Han Dynasty. With Prolegomena on the Historiography of the *Hou Han Shu*," *Bulletin of the Museum of Far Eastern Antiquities* 26 (1954): 81.

[30] F. Kierman, *Ssu-ma Ch'ien's Historiographical Attitude as Reflected in Four Late Warring States Biographies* (Wiesbaden: O. Harrassowitz, 1962). For a critique of Kierman's theory, see also Antony Hulsewé, "Reviews of *Gestalten aus der Zeit der chInesischen Hegemoniekämpfe aus Szu-ma Ts'ien's Historischen Denkwürdigkeiten*, by Erich Haenisch; *Ssu-ma Ch'ien's Historiographical Attitude as Reflected in Four Late Warring States Biographies*, by F. Kierman Jr.; 'The Restoration of the Han Dynasty, II,' by Hans Bielenstein," *T'oung Pao* 52 (1965–66): 182–99.

(*wang-lo t'ien-hsia fang-shih chiu wen*); "to research the conduct of affairs" (*k'ao chih hsing shih*); "to examine the patterns that lead to success and failure, and to rise and fall" (*chi ch'i ch'eng-pai hsing-huai chih li*); "to investigate the interaction – or boundary – between Heaven and Man" (*chiu t'ien jen chih chi*); "to comprehend the changes of the past and present" (*t'ung ku chin chih pien*), and the aforementioned "to form a single school of thought" or "to complete the words of a single family" (*ch'eng yi chia chih yen*).[31] The first two sentences have been investigated more thoroughly, in some cases leading scholars to conclude that the *Shih chi* "represents the union between 'interpretation' and 'criticism' in the tradition of Chinese historiography."[32] Whether there is such a convergence is doubtful, in the light of the ambiguity inherent in the use of terms such as "interpretation" and "criticism" in an early Han intellectual context. Noteworthy for our purpose are the stress on the dual function of the historian as someone who has to investigate both heavenly and human phenomena, the sense that history changes according to "patterns," and the holistic or synchretic vision of an intellectual pursuit.

The philosophy of history of Ssu-ma Ch'ien is enclosed in a few key terms, in particular, *li* (pattern, order, cause) and *pien*, "change," whereby some kind of disappearance of the old and appearance of the new seems to be implied. The sentence *t'ung ku chin chih pien* suggests that there is a sense of "law" that needs to be derived from the investigation of "change,"[33] which the historian must use to penetrate the general patterns

---

[31] *Han shu* 62: 2735. Watson's translation of the last three sentences is: "[I wish] to examine into all that concerns heaven and man, to penetrate the changes of the past and present, completing all as the work of one family" (B. Watson, *Ssu-ma Ch'ien*, p. 66).

[32] Yü Ying-shih, "The Study of Chinese History. Retrospect and Prospect," trans. Thomas H. C. Lee and Chun-chieh Huang, in *The Translation of Things Past. Chinese History and Historiography*, ed. George Kao (Hong Kong: Chinese University Press, 1982), p. 11. Chinese Marxist historians have interpreted Ssu-ma Ch'ien's claim for a separation between *t'ien* and *jen* as indirect evidence of a materialistic orientation, consisting of the historian's denial of Heaven's intervention in shaping the fate of individuals or states, and in his attention to economic relations rathern than to "supernatural" explanations; see La Chang-yang," Lun Ssu-ma Ch'ien te li-shih che-hsüeh," in *Ssu-ma Ch'ien yen-chiu hsin-lun*, ed. Shih Ting and Ch'en K'e-ch'in (Cheng-chou: Ho-nan jen-min,1982), p. 84; Jen Chi-yu, "Ssu-ma Ch'ien te che-hsüeh ssu-hsiang," in *Ssu-ma Ch'ien yü ⟨Shih Chi⟩ lun-chi*, ed. Li-shih yen-chiu pien-chi-pu (Hsi-an: Shaansi jen-min ch'u-pan-she, 1982), p. 105.

[33] "Change" was regarded as a "law" (*fa*) of history generating a type of "config-uration" characteristic of each particular phase (*hsing*); as such, "change" was regarded as a key principle of the Ch'un-ch'iu period. See *Ch'un-ch'u fan-lu*, ch. 63 ("Wu-hsing pien-chiu"), 10a, 183a, 130a.

of historical development. Such "laws" of history preside over and determine the specific character of each historical phase.[34] The concept of *li*, adopted by Ssu-ma Ch'ien to indicate the causes or patterns that determine the unfolding of human (historical) events – success and failure, rise and fall – was also a term that had particular significance in astronomy because the calendar was supposed to embody the *li* of the natural world and was key to cosmological conceptions associated with divinatory techniques.[35]

These concepts pertained to both sides of the activity of the historian-astronomer, that is, to his investigation of heavenly movements as well as to his attention to human developments, and they point to the same essential pursuit of a knowledge based on empirical observation. This form of knowledge, somewhat similar to what the Greek called *autopsy*, "seeing things for oneself," had as its preliminary goal the description and recording of noteworthy occurrences. In other words, the central concern of Ssu-ma Ch'ien, in the investigation of historical change, may have consisted of the definition of those characteristics of the "revolutions" from one epoch to the next that determine the special quality of a historical period and that can be regarded as the unique attributes of each "change."[36] The same concept, at least during the Han period, could be associated also with astronomical phenomena, as we find in the following passage of the *Huai-nan Tzu*, "when there is a great danger for the state, there are changes (*pien*)

[34] This is what Yang defines as *shih*, namely, the particular circumstances (the "trend" or "momentum") of that historical period; see Yang, Yen-ch'i, "Ssu-ma Ch'ien te li-shih ssu-hsiang" in *Ssu-ma Ch'ien he Shih chi*, ed. Liu Nai-he (Peking: Pei-ching ch'u-pan-she, 1987), pp. 41–58.

[35] Ho Peng Yoke, *Li, Qi and Shu. An Introduction to Science and Civilization in China* (Hong Kong: Hong Kong University Press, 1985), pp. 153, 27. For the concept of *li* as universal order, or pattern, in the *Huai-nan Tzu*, see Charles Le Blanc, *Huai-nan Tzu. Philosophical Synthesis in Early Han Thought*, (Hong Kong: Hong Kong University Press, 1985), p. 133. Note that in the same sentence Chavannes translates *li* as "causes" (*Mém. hist.*, 1: ccxxxvii). According to Needham, *li* means: "natural pattern, the veins in jade, to cut jade according to its natural markings; principle, order, organization"; see Joseph Needham, *Science and Civilization in China*, vol. 2: *History of Scientific Thought* (Cambridge: Cambridge University Press, 1956), p. 228.

[36] Although the premises are different, this notion of change is not far from that found in the theory of "relative circularity" put forth by Ohama Akira, who maintained that, although Ssu-ma Ch'ien regarded history as a continuous circular movement, there was room for deviation and crises. He concluded that "the most important point in the conception of history of Ssu-ma Ch'ien is not the system of laws in history, but rather its transformation"; see Ohama Akira, "Shiba Sen no rekishi kan," in his *Chûgoku. rekishi. unmei: Shiki to Shitsu* (Tokyo: Keiso Shobo, 1975), pp. 185–89.

in the heavenly signs (*t'ien-wen*)."[37] *Pien* was a universal analytical concept applicable to the observation of natural and astronomical phenomena, as well as to historical ones.

At the time of Ssu-ma Ch'ien, the figure of the astronomer had not yet been separated from that of the historian; Ssu-ma Ch'ien himself was both. As Nakayama points out, "in China the term *shih* comprehended both pursuits. Ssu-ma Ch'ien [...] is best known as an official historian charged with the compilation of court documents, but in his post as T'ai-shih-ling he was also responsible for maintaining astrological records."[38] Indeed, in his capacity as Grand Historian Ssu-ma Ch'ien took part in all activities related to the observation of astronomical phenomena and the preparation of the calendar, that is, the two basic pursuits of Chinese astronomy.[39]

Terms like *hsing*, *li*, and *pien* express the same level of cognitive experience, theoretical assumptions, and world vision whether they refer to human or celestial phenomena. It seems reasonable to suggest that the Grand Historian's activity had not only a theoretical but also a methodological affinity with that of the astronomer (or astrologer). In other words, we can presume that history, being epistemologically intertwined with astronomy, partook of the same heuristic assumptions and methodological tenets. The empirical recording and systematic organization of data was essential to both. This may have been true of an older period as well, but it is only with Ssu-ma Ch'ien that we find a systematic investigation and organization of history, and it is therefore Ssu-ma Ch'ien (and perhaps Ssu-ma T'an, to the extent that we can identify his contribution to the *Shih chi*) who was responsible for the application of a method derived from the tradition of the astronomer-astrologer to historical inquiry.

The "revolutionary" aspect of Ssu-ma Ch'ien's activity as a historian must rest, at least in part, on the application of methods of empirical investigation and observation of natural and human phenomena, which guided astronomical calculations long before him, to the description and rationalization of historical phenomena, and in particular of those new phenomena that emerged at the time of the unification of the empire.[40] At least one

---

[37] *Huai-nan Tzu*, 20: 2a.

[38] Shigeru Nakayama, *Academic and Scientific Traditions in China, Japan and the West* (Tokyo: University of Tokyo Press, 1984), p. 4.

[39] Xi Zezong, "Characteristics of China's Ancient Astronomy," *History of Oriental Astronomy*, ed. G. Swarup et al. (Cambridge: Cambridge University Press, 1987), p. 39. He also took part in the famous calendrical reform of 104 B.C. and was at the head of the state astronomers in charge on the observation of the sky; see Homer Dubs, "The Beginnings of Chinese Astronomy," *Journal of the American Oriental Society* 78.4 (1958): 298.

[40] Some light on this subject has been shed by Tu Sheng-yün, who takes empirical observation to be the basis of Ssu-ma Ch'ien's understanding of a number of astronomical questions, ranging from the simple identification of stars and planets to

aspect of his work as historian can be regarded as the observational, or documentary, stage, which was aimed at *describing* the various phases or facts inherent to a certain topic. Recording historical events, and providing an accurately documented description of them, was the main duty of Ssu-ma Ch'ien as a historian, just as observing and recording celestial movements was the first duty of Ssu-ma Ch'ien as an astronomer.[41] As Ssu-ma Ch'ien himself stated in his "manifesto" letter to Jen An, the historian-astronomer was primarily called on to register and explain those phenomena that indicated transformation and change.

How does this prolonged excursus on methodological issues affect our discussion of Ssu-ma Ch'ien's treatment of Inner Asia? I believe it is not simply the existence of the Hsiung-nu "phenomenon" but more precisely the search for observable phenomena and the amplification of the describable world that informed the historian's quest that led to the incorporation, within the *Shih chi*, of an unprecedented wealth of information on Inner Asia. Although knowledge of "nomadic peoples" through military confrontation, trade, and diplomatic relations must have been current in China for at least two centuries before Ssu-ma Ch'ien, the appearance of a united steppe empire at the doorstep of China was still a fairly recent phenomenon, one that not only had grave repercussions at the state's economic and political levels but was also unprecedented in Chinese history. The great concern caused by the novel formation of a unified, powerful nomadic empire, and the many wars fought by the Han against it, qualified the Hsiung-nu as a topic worthy of investigation. But it was the application of the astronomer's method to this topic that generated the "paradigm shift" from the moralistic or chronachistic accounts of the past to the historically and ethnographically rich report that Ssu-ma Ch'ien was able to produce. If other Han works of the same period failed to produce anything even remotely comparable, this is because Ssu-ma Ch'ien was concerned with and trained in the empirical acts of observing and recording to

the study of their movements for the sake of perfecting the calendar and the sundial. According to Tu, "his [Ssu-ma Ch'ien's] research in the natural sciences trained his thought and methods," a statement that has deep implications for understanding his historical method; see Tu Sheng-yün, "Ssu-ma Ch'ien te t'ien-wen-hsüeh ch'eng-chiu he ssu-hsiang," in *Ssu-ma Ch'ien he Shih Chi*, pp. 222–48.

[41] Descriptive does not mean "objective." I do not mean to imply here that the narrative provided by Ssu-ma Ch'ien is free from ideological overlay. To the contrary, the system of thought that the Grand Historian seems to subscribe to weighed heavily in his construction of historical narratives. The "rationalization" of the phenomenon within the accepted code of values provided by correlative thought in its Han Confucian formulation will be briefly tackled in chapter 8.

a degree that only an astronomer could have achieved. As we will see, the information he included in the *Shih chi* covered a large spectrum, from the ethnographic to the economic, and from the cultural to the political and military.

The Hsiung-nu Described

Within a few years after Meng T'ien's titanic expedition to the Ordos (215 B.C.), the north ceased to be, for the Chinese intellectual, either the habitat of wondrous beings or an abstract philosophical construct. Soldiers and laborers were dispatched to build and protect the extensive northern fortifications, and colonists were sent to open up the new land. The north became a new frontier not only on the political but also on the cognitive level. As its geographic horizon expanded, China's need for knowledge increased. The military disaster at P'ing-ch'eng and the humiliating peace terms that the Han had to submit to added yet another dimension to the problem of the north, which also appeared, suddenly, as an unprecedented threat to the very existence of the Chinese nation. China needed "experts" to manage the north. The debate on foreign relations that developed in China starting from the early Han was based on knowledge that, although sometimes couched in a language replete with classical allusions, had been acquired only recently. This knowledge was mastered by military experts and politicians who specialized in foreign and, in particular, northern affairs. A new breed of soldier emerged, specially trained to fight against the Hsiung-nu. Statesmen studied frontier management and submitted memorials to the throne proposing incentives and relief measures for the people sent to colonize the region.

By Ssu-ma Ch'ien's time, knowledge about the Hsiung-nu and other nomadic peoples in the north and west had been accumulating for sixty years thanks to war, trade, and diplomacy. Chang Ch'ien's expedition to Ferghana had brought back invaluable information, directly relevant to the opening of political and economic contacts between China and the states of the Tarim Basin and beyond. More important, Ssu-ma Ch'ien's early treatment of foreign countries opened the way to incorporation in the *Han shu* of even more detailed information, which became available after the establishment of the Protector General's Office (c. 60 B.C.). Would we now have this wealth of knowledge without Ssu-ma Ch'ien's earlier investigation? The question may be idle, but only to a point; it may be useful to focus on the issue that, before the *Shih chi*, there were no intellectual "containers" in which factual historical and geographical data could be stored and transmitted. Ssu-ma Ch'ien introduced empirical criteria for the collection of this type of information and the recording of historical events.

His achievements, in the areas of ethnographic enquiry, geographical documentation, and historical accuracy, are all the more remarkable considering that during his lifetime older conceptions had by no means been jettisoned by the intellectual community.

In this chapter, I will examine the type of sources from which Ssu-ma Ch'ien may have drawn his information on the Hsiung-nu and then move on to analyze the three core features of the "descriptive" phase of the Grand Historian's treatment of Inner Asia: first, Ssu-ma's representation of Hsiung-nu society, including the nomads' way of life, customs, cults, and military and social organization; second, Ssu-ma Ch'ien's attitude toward the effects, on both politics and the economy, that the wars against the Hsiung-nu had on China; and third, Ssu-ma's treatment of geographical knowledge and trade, which reflects a more general interest of the historian in the possibilities that its expanding frontiers offered China. On this last point, I will not deal with specific geographical questions, but with the manner in which the regions beyond the limina of the Chinese community are represented in the *Shih chi*, and how the changes undergone by the northern and western borders affected Chinese society.

Sources

PERSONAL ACQUAINTANCE.   Ssu-ma Ch'ien, like Herodotus in Greece, was regarded as one of the most widely traveled men of his time.[42] Most probably, considering that he had very little written material to rely upon, Ssu-ma Ch'ien collected a considerable amount of geographic and ethnographic information either by interrogating travelers or by traveling himself. When he was twenty, he journeyed through southern China, possibly for as long as four or five years. Then, after entering the civil service as a petty official (*lang-chung*), he took part in several expeditions to the west and to the south.[43] Moreover, in his capacity as *lang-chung* and, later on, as Grand Historian, he continued to travel as a member of Emperor Wu's retinue, following the ruler on inspection tours or when he traveled to perform ritual ceremonies. Especially relevant to this study is the travel that Ssu-ma Ch'ien undertook in the year 110 B.C., when he accompanied Wu-ti on a journey to inspect the northern border. There, as he says in the biography of Meng

---

[42] On Ssu-ma Ch'ien's travels, see B. Watson, *Ssu-ma Ch'ien*, p. 48; Shih Ting, "Ssu-ma Ch'ien yu-li kao," in *Ssu-ma Ch'ien he Shih chi*, pp. 126–44; Nieh Shih-ch'iao, *Ssu-ma Ch'ien lun-kao* (Peking: Pei-ching shih-fan ta-hsüeh, 1987), pp. 12–24.

[43] On this title, see Rafe de Crespigny, *Official Titles of the Former Han Dynasty as Translated and Transcribed by H. H. Dubs.* An index compiled by Rafe de Crespigny (Canberra: Centre of Oriental Studies, 1967), p 15.

T'ien, Ssu-ma Ch'ien visited the long walls built by the Ch'in general allegedly to contain the Hsiung-nu.[44]

ORAL ACCOUNTS BY CHINESE PEOPLE. Just as Iordanes based his account of the Huns, in *Getica*, on the information provided by Priscus, long-time resident at the court of Attila, so did Ssu-ma Ch'ien rely on the written and oral accounts of people who lived among the Hsiung-nu or, by being employed in diplomatic or military missions, had acquired intimate knowledge of them. One of the first was Ch'in K'ai, who was a hostage among the Hsiung-nu even before the unification.[45] Hostage exchange was a provision regularly applied to treaties and an integral part of diplomatic relations between states during the Warring States and during the Ch'in-Han period.[46]

The Hsiung-nu, particularly during the first phase of the Han dynasty, were a safe haven for rebellious Chinese leaders and dissatisfied military commanders. Most famous is Chung-hang Yüeh (also read Chung-hang Shuo), who fled to the Hsiung-nu and provided them with inside knowledge on how to conduct political negotiations with the Chinese. A speech reported in the *Shih chi* in which he replied to the Chinese envoys' claims of superior virtue contains much information on Hsiung-nu life and habits. This speech may have been recorded by the same Chinese officials who had gone to the Hsiung-nu court and who later circulated at the Han court, where Chung-hang Yüeh was regarded as a renegade and a traitor. It is worth quoting from, for behind the Confucian rhetoric that Chung-hang Yüeh used to turn the tables on the Han diplomats, there is a close description of the Hsiung-nu society:

The Hsiung-nu clearly make warfare their [main] occupation; since the old and weak cannot fight, the best food and drink are given to the strong and healthy, who then become the defense and protection [of the nation]; in this way both fathers and sons can live long in security. Can one really say that the Hsiung-nu despise old people? [...] According to Hsiung-nu custom, people eat the meat of their animals, drink their milk, and wear [clothes made with] their hides; the animals eat grass and drink water, therefore they move about in seasonal cycles. This is why in critical times they practice riding and shooting, while in peaceful times they enjoy themselves without other engagements. Their communal laws are not burdensome, and are easy to

---

[44] *Shih chi* 88, 2570; Shih Ting, "Ssu-ma Ch'ien yu-li kao," 138; Derk Bodde, *Statesman, Patriot and General in Ancient China* (New Haven: American Oriental Society, 1940), pp. 62–63.

[45] *Shih chi* 110, 2885–86.

[46] *Han shu* 94A, 3772; *Shih chi chu-yi* 2331. On hostage keeping, see Lien-sheng Yang, "Hostages in Chinese History," *Harvard Journal of Asiatic Studies* 15 (1952): 507–21.

implement. The relationship between ruler and subject is relaxed and simple, so that ruling the whole country is just like [ruling over] a single person. When a father, son or brother dies, they take their [i.e., the dead persons'] wives as their own, because they hate to see a lineage die out. Therefore, even when the Hsiung-nu meet with turmoil, the ancestral clan is always preserved.[47]

Prisoners of war were another source of information. Every battle produced for the victor, on either side, large numbers of prisoners that were taken back to the victorious countries and used in several capacities, as slaves, servants, or soldiers. In particular if they were persons of rank, returnees must have provided valuable information, and Ssu-ma Ch'ien was personally acquainted with military men who had extensive first-hand knowledge of the Hsiung-nu, such as General Li Kuang and Su Chien, who was a subordinate commander under Wei Ch'ing in the war against the Hsiung-nu.[48]

CONTEMPORARY WRITTEN DOCUMENTS AND REPORTS.   Because the Hsiung-nu had already been for several years a topic of heated debate at the Han court, documents existed that Ssu-ma Ch'ien could and did mine to gather the information he needed. Among these, the most most important, and also the best known, are the memorials by Ch'ao Ts'o, which we have discussed in previous chapters.

HSIUNG-NU PEOPLE IN CHINESE SOCIETY.   Surrendered or captured Hsiung-nu who had entered China constituted an additional source of information for Ssu-ma. Two Hsiung-nu can be regarded as representative of the nomads' presence in China. One was the person who traveled to Central Asia with Chang Ch'ien, a Hsiung-nu slave called Kan Fu. Over the thirteen years of Chang Ch'ien's travels and captivity among the Hsiung-nu, Kan Fu proved a loyal and resourceful aide to the Chinese explorer, and he must have gained considerable notoriety to have been mentioned in Chinese sources together with his famous master. The other person was Chin Mi-ti, heir apparent to the throne of the Hsiung-nu king of Hsiu-ch'u, who was captured by another Hsiung-nu chief, turned over to the Chinese, and employed as a slave inside the Yellow Gate Palace to tend horses under the supervision of the eunuchs.[49]

---

[47] *Shih chi* 110, 2899–2900; *Shih chi chu-yi* 110, 2323 (Burton Watson, trans., *Records of the Grand Historian by Sima Qian* [New York and Hong Kong: Columbia University Press and The Chinese University of Hong Kong, 1993], 2: 143–44).

[48] *Shih chi* 111, 2946.

[49] C. Martin Wilbur, *Slavery in China under the Former Han Dynasty, 206 B.C.– A.D. 25* (Chicago: Field Museum of Natural History, 1943), pp. 306–307.

Ethnography of the Hsiung-nu

It is possible that Ssu-ma Ch'ien might have been regarded as a "barbarophile" by his contemporaries. In reporting the well-known apology for the Hsiung-nu allegedly made by Chung-hang Yüeh, Ssu-ma Ch'ien showed a view distinct from the orthodox faith shared by many of his contemporaries in the superiority of the Han rituals and civilization.[50] Although the Hsiung-nu may have been cruel, greedy, and arrogant, they also had their own ways and traditions, and Ssu-ma Ch'ien's sympathies may have gone to those who, like himself, tried to understand them. Between Li Kuang, the general who had trained his soldiers to fight the Hsiung-nu using their own methods, and the more orthodox Ch'eng Pu-chih, the historian undoubtedly preferred Li Kuang.[51] Ssu-ma Ch'ien, however, feared censorship, and in the colophon to chapter 110 he admitted that he was not free to speak openly. Even more significantly, Pan Ku did not mention Ssu-ma Ch'ien's name at the close of the chapter on the Hsiung-nu (94) in the *Han shu*, when he discussed policies for dealing with the Hsiung-nu, such as those proposed by Tung Chung-shu. Pan Ku quotes the *Shu ching*, *Shih ching*, and *Spring and Autumn Annals* but does not mention the *Shih chi*, although the first part of Pan Ku's chapter is almost a verbatim copy of chapter 110 of the *Shih chi*.

Pan Ku was clearly at odds with his predecessor's views, and the fact that he explicitly supported a more militant, forward policy is further evidence of Ssu-ma Ch'ien's pacifist leanings.[52] In Pan Ku's description of the Hsiung-nu, contrary to that of Ssu-ma Ch'ien, we find strong derogatory expressions, such as that the Hsiung-nu had human faces but hearts of beasts. These two almost antithetical approaches arose from differences in methods and aims. Whereas Ssu-ma Ch'ien lived through a period of sharp confrontation between the nomads and China (one that required China's urgent understanding of its neighbors), in Pan Ku's age the Hsiung-nu had become less threatening, China was more confident of its own power as a unified empire, and a stricter Confucian orthodoxy had asserted itself. Pan Ku's aim was to explain, and perhaps intervene in, the internal political debate on foreign policy, rather than to investigate the nature of the Hsiung-nu. Ssu-ma Ch'ien's approach, in contrast, developed out of the experience

---

[50] *Shih chi chu-yi* 110, 4: 2323–24.   [51] *Shih chi* 109, 2869.

[52] On Pan Ku's theory of foreign relations, see Wang Gungwu, "Early Ming Relations with Southeast Asia: A Background Essay," in *The Chinese World Order*, ed. John K. Fairbank (Cambridge: Harvard University Press, 1968), p. 41; Chusei Suzuki, "China's Relations with Inner Asia: The Hsiung-nu, Tibet," in *The Chinese World Order*, p. 183.

and knowledge he had gathered while traveling, which made the historian recognize that the Hsiung-nu constituted, in his age, an unsolved historical problem, an anomaly that China had to face in the process of asserting itself as a politically and culturally unified entity.

Various aspects of the Hsiung-nu way of life are carefully reported in the *Shih chi*, including their social organization, rituals, and religious beliefs. Characteristic of the historian's narrative in this respect is the objectivity of his observations and its remarkable freedom from the prejudices quite common among Chinese intellectuals and politicians. In Ssu-ma's description of Hsiung-nu customs we can therefore distinguish two types of information. The first type, direct, is information that Ssu-ma Ch'ien provided himself, whereas the second, indirect, is information reported by him as other people's opinion. In the latter case, it is possible that Ssu-ma Ch'ien was expressing his own thoughts using other people's names to avoid blame or to add greater weight to the opinions expressed. Nevertheless, both contribute to give us a fairly accurate picture of Hsiung-nu customs. For this analysis, "ethnographic" material on the Hsiung-nu has been divided into the following categories: pastoral nomadism, burial customs, society and laws, military training and war, state sacrifices and ritual, and language.

PASTORAL NOMADISM. Ssu-ma Ch'ien's account of the Hsiung-nu is the first ever "ethnographic" account of nomadic peoples in Chinese history even though pastoral nomadism, as a specialized economic activity, had established itself in the steppe region to the north of China several centuries before the Han. Ssu-ma Ch'ien's account is clearly based on a detailed knowledge of pastoral economy:

Most of their domestic animals are horses, cows, sheep, and they also have rare animals such as camels, donkeys, mules, hinnies and other equines known as *t'ao-t'u* and *tien-hsi*.[53] They move about according to the availability of water and pasture, have no walled towns or fixed residences, nor any agricultural activities, but each of them has a portion of land.[54]

This description of nomadic life, which became cliché in following Chinese histories, presents some interesting points. First, Ssu-ma Ch'ien is very specific in listing all the animals bred by the nomads. This conforms to the reality of pastoral life in places such as traditional Mongolia, where the five animals commonly bred were horses, cows, sheep, goats, and camels. The donkey and crossbred equines that cannot be readily recog-

---

[53] On these animals, see Namio Egami, "The Kuai ti, the Tao you, and the Dao xi: The Strange Animals of the Xiongnu," *Memoirs of the Research Department of Toyo Bunko* 13 (1951): 87–123.
[54] *Shih chi* 110, 2879 (cf. B. Watson, *Records*, 2: 129).

nized were also part of the zoological inventory of the nomads. The breeding and herding techniques for these animals, each of which requires a special type of knowledge and care, could not have been a matter of rapid evolution, and they strongly indicate that a mature pastoral nomadic economy had existed in northern China for centuries. Second, in pointing out that "each of them has a portion of land," Ssu-ma Ch'ien seems to be referring to individual nomads, though this is not to exclude that he meant families and clans, because land rights were customarily recognized, in pastoral societies, on the basis of lineage. Ssu-ma Ch'ien's phrase, which may imply the existence of "private property," should be interpreted as meaning that the Hsiung-nu recognized for individuals and families the right to make use of specific pastures for their herds, even though the land was not fenced and could not be purchased or sold.

If landed property rights, in whatever guise, existed among the Hsiung-nu, it is unlikely that their movement in search of water and grass could be a random one; Ssu-ma Chien's statement that they had a "portion of land" indicates that migrations were confined to a given territory and implies the notion of cyclicality, which is the most essential aspect of nomadic economy. To my knowledge, this is the first written indication that the Chinese had understood the seasonal regularity of the movement of the herds. The search for water and grass symbolizes the nomadic lifestyle. In describing how General Li Kuang organized his campaigns against the Hsiung-nu, it was said that "he would make camp wherever he found water and grass." This expression suggests that he had adopted nomadic tactics of warfare to fight against the Hsiung-nu.[55]

BURIAL CUSTOMS.

In burials they use inner and outer coffins, gold and silver [ornaments], clothes and fur coats; however, they do not erect earthen mounds or plant trees, nor do they use mourning garments. When a ruler dies, his ministers and concubines are sacrificed in numbers that can reach several tens or even hundreds of people.[56]

Ssu-ma's description of burial customs is particularly interesting in view of recent archaeological discoveries. A number of Warring States sites attributed to the Hsiung-nu, in particular Hsi-kou-p'an and A-lu-chai-teng, contain large quantities of gold and silver ornaments. This funerary inventory differs from those of earlier nomadic sites in northern China in the absence of weapons. The *Shih chi* statement seems to confirm the attribution to the Hsiung-nu of burials that feature large quantities of gold and silver ornaments.

[55] *Shih chi* 109, 2869 (cf. B. Watson, *Records*, 2: 119).
[56] *Shih chi* 110, 2892 (cf. B. Watson, *Records*, 2: 137).

The issue arising from the piece of information related to the presence of an inner and outer coffin is more complex. Whereas the Hsiung-nu burials in Inner Mongolia, unlike those of the nomads of South Siberia or those of the Saka and Wu-sun of Sinkiang, are not marked by an external mound, the inner and outer coffin is present only in a few of the Hsiung-nu burials identified so far, which are far outnumbered by the more typical vertical earthen pits. In contrast, the double coffin is a standard Chinese method of burial. Therefore, the reference to the double coffin could lead us to believe that, according to Ssu-ma Ch'ien, the Hsiung-nu had borrowed a Chinese custom and were being made to appear indebted to China even though, in reality, that was not the case. It is true, however, that in sites such as Mao-ch'ing-kou, we find a double coffin.[57] Moreover, it is possible that a number of wooden coffins have disappeared simply because of decay. In fact, though not frequent, the pit with a coffin placed in a timber frame (a second coffin) with no overgrave setting has been identified by archaeologists as one of the Hsiung-nu burial structures. The hypothesis proposed by archaeologists such as Minyaev, who believe that different burial structures reflected social stratification, would indicate that Ssu-ma Ch'ien was not referring to all Hsiung-nu burials, but only to those of the aristocracy, which were more elaborate than those of commoners.[58] His information was partly inaccurate, though, since in Inner Mongolia there are a number of rich Hsiung-nu burials, undoubtedly belonging to prominent people, with no double coffin. Nevertheless, it cannot be taken as a statement that lacked historical reality, whose only purpose was to show a cultural borrowing from China.

The last statement, referring to the killing of many scores of people sacrificed at the death of the ruler, also does not find direct confirmation in Hsiung-nu archaeology. However, no "imperial" Hsiung-nu grave has so far been found, and therefore the evidence available is simply insufficient to either prove or disprove this statement. We may add that among the Mongols it was customary to kill all people who witnessed the funeral and burial place of a khan, to protect the secrecy of the location of the grave. If such a tradition existed also among the Hsiung-nu, this might explain in part Ssu-ma Ch'ien's mention of a sacrifice en masse, though the specific mention of ministers and concubines would not be correct.

SOCIETY AND LAWS. Hsiung-nu society was, to the status-conscious Chinese, a remarkably egalitarian society, with little differentiation between

---

[57] Thomas O. Höllmann and Georg W. Kossack, eds., *Maoqinggou: Ein eisenzeitliches Gräberfeld in der Ordos-Region (Innere Mongolei)* (Mainz: Verlag Philipp von Zabern, 1992): Table 15, A.

[58] S. Minyaev, "On the Origin of the Hsiung-nu," *Information Bulletin. International Association for the Cultures of Central Asia* 9 (1985): 69–78.

commoners and "aristocracy," as we have already seen in the memorial by Chung-hang Yüeh cited earlier. Ssu-ma Ch'ien's description of Hsiung-nu laws indicates the same type of existence unencumbered by burdensome social constraints:

According to their laws, those who draw the sword one foot [out of the scabbard] are sentenced to death; those who steal lose their properties; those guilty of minor offences are flogged, those guilty of major ones are sentenced to death. The longest period in jail does not exceed ten days; the imprisoned men in the whole country are very few.[59]

Finally, "They have no written language, and customary laws are only verbal."

The relatively freer and simpler existence of the Hsiung-nu is not contrasted unfavorably with Chinese society. On the contrary, behind the plain description of these simple social and legal rules, one might see a veiled criticism of the cumbersome legal system put into place by Ch'in Shih Huang-ti and his legalist advisers. Although the Han rejected laws and punishments as the only tool of social order and cohesion, the daily life of a Chinese subject was by no means free. Ssu-ma Ch'ien's own opposition to the excessive recourse to laws and punishment was openly stated in his praise of the early Han, when "the meshes of the law were spread so far apart that a whale could have passed through."[60] In Wu-ti's time, instead, the laws had become increasingly stricter and more oppressive, and myriads of people were executed, often on trumped-up charges. Even more worrying was the realization that the proliferation of laws and the increased use of punishments did not protect the subjects from abuse and unlawful action, often brought about by the very people who were supposed to enforce the law. As Ssu-ma Ch'ien states in his final remarks to chapter 122, "from the time of Zhang Tang [Chang T'ang]'s death on, the net of laws was drawn tighter and tighter, and harsh penalties became increasingly frequent, so that that the work of government officials was gradually hampered and brought to a standstill."[61] Yet, harsher laws and punishments were regarded by him as a necessary evil, to be preferred to the total absence of them, which would only favor unbridled tyranny. This was certainly a gloomy picture of his own times, in comparison with which the simpler life of the nomads must have seemed to match in some way the ideal of an effortless social machine, uncoercive and yet fully functioning by virtue of its own simplicity.

In this game of contrasting images, the historian paints a society, the Han, that has still to find the measure of its own values, morality, and

---

[59] *Shih chi* 110, 2879; *Shih chi chu-yi* 110, 2313 (cf. B. Watson, *Records*, 2: 137).
[60] *Shih chi* 122, 3131 (cf. B. Watson, *Records*, 2: 380).
[61] B. Watson, *Records*, 2: 407.

norms of social interaction.[62] The "holier-than-thou" stance of the Chinese envoys to the Hsiung-nu is not only ridiculed by Chung-hang Yüeh but also questioned by Ssu-ma Ch'ien. This type of introspective, self-critical attitude toward his own society is not overt, but transmitted to the reader through the laconic description of a different system. Ssu-ma Ch'ien's description of the Hsiung-nu is not value free. If on the one hand his effort to document other social realities demonstrates a new openness to the outer world, on the other it is also anchored to a well-defined ethical basis, of which the reader must be conscious. It is in the silent contrast between the description of the "different" and the consciousness of one's own cultural dimension that the historical narrative finds its true and most powerful message. The egalitarian, simple, harsh but fair, and above all free existence of the nomads acquires a special attractiveness only by contrast with that of the Chinese subject, whose life is fettered by many laws and endangered by cruel punishments and whimsical law enforcers.

MILITARY TRAINING AND WARFARE. The Hsiung-nu military superiority, at least in the use of cavalry, was evident to all the Chinese, but whereas Ch'ao Ts'o and other theorists were interested in finding ways to beat the Hsiung-nu on the battlefield, Ssu-ma Ch'ien was interested in finding the reasons for their strength. In the description of the progress of the young nomads from children shooting small animals to physical maturity, the secret of their equestrian proficiency and excellent marksmanship was plainly explained:

As children they are able to ride sheep, and can shoot birds and mice with bow and arrow. As they grow a little older, they can shoot foxes and hares, which they use for food. Thus as adults they are strong enough to bend a bow, and all can serve as cavalry soldiers. It is their custom to make their living in times of peace by herding the domestic animals and hunting the wild ones, but in critical situations everyone practices military skills in order to set off on invasions. This is their inborn nature.[63]

---

[62] In the *Huai-nan-tzu*, a text compiled during the reign of Wu-ti, considerable thought is devoted to the law, a topic that had been for a long time a central pillar of Chinese political philosophy. Whereas laws were considered necessary by the authors of the *Huai-nan-tzu*, an effort is devoted to smoothing their edges and confining their potentially oppressive use, by recourse to the principle of "rightness," that is, consistency with what is desirable to the people. The search for a balance between the "legalist" framework that informed the government structure, with its laws and punishments, and the Confucian and Taoist emphasis of moral principles must have been deeply felt in contemporary Han society. On this, see Ames, *The Art of Rulership*, pp. 138–40.

[63] *Shih chi* 110, 2879; *Shih chi chu-yi* 110, 2313 (cf. B. Watson, *Records*, 2: 129).

It was truly their way of life, intimately connected with animals, whether they rode, herded, or hunted them, that produced exceptional mounted warriors. The expression "this is their inborn nature" (ch'i t'ien-hsing yeh) which could also be translated as "this is their natural behavior," is, in a way, meant to reassure those who might have thought that these enemies, almost invincible until Wu-ti's time, were endowed with special powers. Ssu-ma Ch'ien brings a disturbing and even mysterious fact back onto a plane of rational understanding by clarifying, step by step, the essence of nomadic military training, and how this was the result of a different, but nonetheless natural, process of growth due to the pursuit of specific activities.

In the description of Hsiung-nu armament and tactics, Ssu-ma Ch'ien does not indulge in long-winded comparisons with the Chinese. His narrative is remarkably objective, and "moral" considerations are kept to a minimum. He describes their weapons ("they use bows and arrows as their long-range weapons, and swords and spears as their short-range weapons")[64] and their habits when it comes to going to war:

At the beginning of a [military] enterprise, they observe the stars and the moon; if the moon is rising they attack, if it is waning they retreat. [. . .] They are skilled in the use of troops that lure the enemy into an ambush. As they see the enemy they look for booty, [behaving] like a flock of birds. When they meet with hardship and defeat, they disintegrate and scatter like clouds. Those who bring back from battle the body of a dead [Hsiung-nu] gain complete possession of the dead man's household and properties.[65]

The analogy of foreign enemies with beasts and birds ultimately goes back to the classics, but in Ssu-ma Ch'ien's age it was also a common way to refer specifically to the Hsiung-nu. In the memorial presented by Chu-fu Yen to Wu-ti there are references to quasi-contemporary documentary sources on policy making regarding the Hsiung-nu, which, on account of the similarities with the Shih chi's narrative, are very likely among the sources used by Ssu-ma Ch'ien. It is said, for instance, that Li Ssu reprimanded Ch'in Shih Huang-ti for sending troops into the Ordos by saying, "it is impossible. The Hsiung-nu have no fixed cities or forts and no stores of provisions or grain. They move from place to place like flocks of birds and are just as difficult to catch and control."[66] Chu-fu Yen's memorial also quoted a warning that Kao-tsu had received from an imperial secretary on the eve of his defeat at P'ing-ch'engch'eng: "It is the nature of the Hsiung-nu to swarm together like so many beasts, and to disperse again like a flock of birds. Trying to catch them is like grabbing a shadow. In spite of all Your

---

[64] Shih chi chu-yi 110, 2313; Shih chi 110, 2879.
[65] Shih chi 110, 2892 (cf. B. Watson, Records, 2: 137).
[66] Shih chi 112, 2954 (cf. B. Watson, Records, 2: 194).

Majesty's noble virtue, I fear any attempt to attack the Hsiung-nu will only lead to danger."[67]

Ssu-ma Ch'ien's description of the nomads' behavior in battle is accompanied by expressions of moral disapproval:

During a battle, if this is going well for them, they will advance, otherwise they will retreat. They do not regard running away as something shameful; they only care about *li* (profit) and do not know of *li* (propriety) and *yi* (righteousness).[68]

When they fight in battle, those who have cut [enemy] heads or captured prisoners are presented with a cup of wine, and all the booty they have taken is also given to them; the people they capture are made into slaves. Therefore, in battle each man pursues his own gain.[69]

The statement about the Hsiung-nu's shameless pursuit of loot parallels the *Tso chuan* statement that the Ti are not ashamed of running away.[70] The "barbarians'" greediness, while it can be related to a pre-existing cliché, is set here in a much less ideological context, as if Ssu-ma Ch'ien was relating common knowledge among the military people of his age. It is, in other words, an opinion that is not necessarily derivative of the classic tradition but is a prejudice of his own age, when the Chinese military people prided themselves on fighting "by the rules" and abiding by notions of honor and selflessness. The Hsiung-nu had a different set of rules, and Ssu-ma Ch'ien's disconcerted judgment is similar to the cultural stance adopted by the Greeks and Romans when they described the fighting methods of the steppe nomads.[71] The ideal of the simplicity of "barbarian" life, opposed to the rule-laden Chinese life, is proposed again, with reference to the military, in the biography of General Li Kuang. His troops were loosely organized, never kept in formation; when they camped there were few rules, and record keeping was kept to a minimum; the only precaution he took was to send out scouts on patrol. In contrast, the more traditional Ch'en Pu-shih kept his men constantly busy, enforced a harsh discipline, and had his officers constantly writing reports. Ssu-ma Ch'ien's comment is that both generals were successful, and were not going to be caught unprepared, but the enemy was more afraid of Li Kuang's tactics, and the soldiers were happier to serve under him.

[67] *Shih chi* 112, 2955 (cf. B. Watson, *Records*, 2: 195).
[68] *Shih chi* 110, 2879; *Shih chi chu-yi* 110, 2313 (cf. B. Watson, *Records*, 2: 129).
[69] *Shih chi* 110, 2892 (cf. B. Watson, *Records*, 2: 137).
[70] *Ch'un Ch'iu Tso chuan chu*, 1: 322.
[71] Denis Sinor, "The Greed of the Northern Barbarians," in *Aspects of Altaic Civilizations II*, ed. Larry V. Clark and Paul A. Draghi (Bloomington: Indiana University, 1978), pp. 171–82.

STATE SACRIFICES AND RITUALS. Besides the structure of the Hsiung-nu government, the *Shih chi* also illustrates other aspects of Hsiung-nu political life, such as their state sacrifices and ritual practices.[72] In many ways, these rituals are reminiscent of Chinese ceremonies.

At dawn the Shan-yü leaves his camp and makes obeisance to the sun as it rises, and in the evening he makes a similar obeisance to the moon. [...] When they sit the place of honor is on the left side, toward the north. The *wu* and *chi* days [i.e., the fifth and sixth of the ten-day week] are their favorite ones. [...] Every year in the first month the important people hold a restricted meeting at the Shan-yü's court, and perform sacrifices. In the fifth month they have a large gathering at Lung-ch'eng, where they sacrifice to the ancestors, Heaven and Earth, and to their divinities. In autumn, when the horses are fat, they hold a large meeting in which they encircle a forest (*tai lin*)[73] and calculate the number of people and livestock.[74]

From this passage we infer that the Hsiung-nu were using a calendar based on the ten heavenly stems. They worshipped Heaven, the ancestors, and their deities on the *wu* (fifth stem) and *chi* (sixth stem) days. These stems corresponded to the element earth and represented the middle, fortune, and blessing. Politically, they represented the power to govern the tribes on the four sides. In the *Lü-shih ch'un-ch'iu* and *Li-chi* it is explicitly stated that the element earth corresponded to the center, and its days were *wu* and *chi*. In the chapter "T'ien-wen" of the *Huai-nan Tzu* it is also said that "the centre was the Earth; it was ruled by the Yellow Emperor who controlled and restrained the four quarters; its planetary god was Chen-hsing, its animal symbol was the yellow dragon; its note on the musical scale was *kung*; its days were *wu* and *chi*."[75] The similarities raise the question of whether there was any Hsiung-nu borrowing from the Chinese political

[72] On the religion of the Hsiung-nu, see Hsieh Chien (Jiann), "Hsiung-nu tsung-chiao hsin-yang chi ch'i liu-pien" [The Religious Beliefs of the Hsiung-nu and Their Later Development] in *Li-shih yü-yen yen-chiu so chi-k'an* 12.4 (1971): 571–614. Important information on the rituals and sacrifices mentioned in the foregoing passages is summarized in de Crespigny, *The Northern Frontier*, pp. 507–508, n. 15.

[73] *Shih chi* 110, 2893. There are different interpretations of the meaning of *tai lin*. Some say it means "to encircle a forest" (in the process of performing a sacrifice), others that it just means "forest," and others claim that it is a geographical name (see *Shih chi chu-yi* 110, 2319). De Groot locates it in the region of the Han city of Ma-yi, in the Yen-men commandery; see J. J. M. De Groot, *Chinesische Urkunden zur Geschichte Asiens I: die Hunnen der vorchristlichen Zeit* (Berlin and Leipzig: W. de Gruyter, 1921), pp. 59–60.

[74] *Shih chi* 110, 2892 (cf. B. Watson, *Records*, 2: 137).

[75] Quoted in Chen Ching-lung, "Chinese Symbolism among the Huns," in *Religious and Lay Symbolism in the Altaic World*, ed. Klaus Sagaster (Wiesbaden: Harrassowitz, 1989), p. 67.

tradition, or whether Ssu-ma Ch'ien was deliberately referring to an accepted symbology of sovereignty to stress the concept that the Hsiung-nu were an independent nation.[76] This issue is somewhat involved, because we do not have any corroborating source that may clarify the situation. The Turco-Mongol people adopted in part the Chinese calendar, but that may also have been a later development. But the expression of "bringing the calendar" to foreign countries in Chinese sources is synonymous with political and cultural expansionism. In this passage, however, no relationship of subordination can be detected, and we can only speculate on the possible implications. As this passage, taken in its entirety, seems to be consistent with the "descriptive" narrative mode, we can formulate three hypotheses. First, the Hsiung-nu, under the influence of Chinese advisers such as Chung-hang Yüeh, had started to make use of Chinese symbols of royalty such as the calendar. Second, the source that Ssu-ma Ch'ien had relied on for this information, possibly some Hsiung-nu captive or envoy, being familiar with the Chinese rituals, had added that information to enhance the prestige of the Hsiung-nu court. Third, an autochthonous calendrical tradition similar to the Chinese actually existed among the Hsiung-nu.

LANGUAGE. The *Shih chi* reports an unprecedented number of Hsiung-nu words. To be sure, these are still rather few, and they are insufficient to provide conclusive evidence of the type of language actually spoken by the nomads.[77] Nonetheless, the words' inclusion represents a new level of sophistication in the information that Chinese historical sources provide on different cultures.

Very few "Hsiung-nu" words appear in works anterior to the *Shih chi*. In the *Yi Chou shu*, chapter 36, "K'o Yin," we find words such as *ching-lu*, the Scythian dagger known in Greek sources by the name of *akinakes*, and, in chapter 59, "Wang Hui," there are two words that indicate some type of horse, *t'ao-t'u* and *chüeh-t'i*.[78] The portions of the *Yi Chou shu*

[76] On the development and use of the calendar among ancient Turco-Mongol peoples, see Louis Bazin, *Les Systemes Chronologiques dans le Monde Turc Ancien* (Budapest: Akadémiai Kiadó, 1991).

[77] The possible etymology of Hsiung-nu words is discussed in the following works: J. Benzing, "Das 'Hunnisches,'" in *Philologia Turcica Fundamenta* (Wiesbaden: Franz Steiner, 1959), 1: 685–87; E. G. Pulleyblank, "The Hsiung-nu Language," *Asia Major*, n.s. 9 (1962): 239–65; G. Doerfer, "Zur Sprache der Hunnen," *Central Asiatic Journal* 17.1 (1973): 1–50; O. J. Maenchen-Helfen, *The World of the Huns* (Berkeley: University of California Press, 1973), pp. 372–73; O. Pritsak, "The Hsiung-nu Word for 'Stone,'" in *Tractata Altaica* (Wiesbaden: Harrassowitz, 1976), pp. 479–85; H. Bailey, *Indo-Scythian Studies. Khotanese Texts VII* (Cambridge: Cambridge University Press, 1985), pp. 25–41.

[78] On *ching-lu*, see Jaroslav Průšek, *Chinese Statelets and the Northern Barbarians in the Period 1400–300 B.C.* (Dordrecht: Reidel, 1971), p. 133.

where these words appear, however, are, like the bulk of *Yi Chou shu* itself, not ancient, dating to around 300 B.C.[79] This date may possibly mark the beginning of the acquisition of knowledge about northern languages in China, a knowledge that appears to have increased considerably by the time of Ssu-ma Ch'ien.

Inner Asian words appear in the *Shih chi* and *Han shu* in various contexts. Titles are the most common, such as "queen" (*yen-chih*) or the various "kings" at the court of the *ch'an-yü*.[80] These could not be translated into Chinese without incurring some ideological or terminological difficulty. Another type of words is those usually defined as "cultural" words, that is, words specific to a given culture and lifestyle. Examples of these words are "wagon" (*fen-wen*), "bag" or "basket" (*chia-tou*), the already mentioned "dagger" (*ching-lu*), "tent," possibly a yurt, (*ch'iung-lu*), and "kumiss" (*lo*), another type of fermented mare's milk was called *t'i-hu*, "dried curd" (*mi-li*), and "fat" or "butter" (*su*).

Geographic Expansion and Trade

In the *Shih chi* place names, distances, and topographical information all appear to conform to a high standard of accuracy, and for the first time geographic information beyond the boundaries of the Central Plain became a necessary ingredient of the historical narrative.[81] Ssu-ma Ch'ien's

---

[79] Edward Shaughnessy, "The I Chou shu," in *Early Chinese Texts*, pp. 229–33.

[80] The word *wang*, usually translated as "king," was a common one in Han society and indicated a variety of peoples, including the *chu-hou-wang*, the sons of the emperor, probably better translated as "princes," and other nobles.

[81] There is extensive scholarship on the correct identification of place names. The toponomastics of foreign lands is naturally important in assessing the level of information possessed by the Chinese during the Han dynasty and also the linguistic identity of the people living in those distant regions. However, in the context of Ssu-ma Ch'ien's approach to foreign peoples, my objective is to look at the organization of geographical information rather than attempt to identify names of localities and regions. Most of the geographical research on Inner Asia has concentrated on chapter 123, on the Western Regions. Important studies include A. F. P. Hulsewé, "The Problem of the Authenticity of Shih-chi," *T'oung Pao*, 66 (1975): 83–147; A. F. P. Hulsewé and Michael Loewe, *China in Central Asia. The Early Stage, 125 B.C.–A.D. 23. An Annotated Translation of the Chapters 61 and 96 of the History of the Former Han Dynasty* (Leiden: Brill, 1979); J. R. Gardiner-Gardner, "Chang Ch'ien and Central Asian Ethnography," *Papers of Far Eastern History* 33 (1986): 23–79; D. D. Leslie and K. H. J. Gardiner, "Chinese Knowledge of Central Asia," *T'oung Pao* 68.4–5 (1982): 254–308; Edwin G. Pulleyblank, "Chinese and Indo-Europeans," *Journal of the Royal Asiatic Society* (1966): 9–39; and id., "Han China in Central Asia," *International*

rationalistic attitude was no longer satisfied with a vision of the geographic space as an accessory to mythology and a repository of legendary and fantastic accounts, whose images no longer responded to the increased data and precision demanded by the new political situation of a unified and expanding empire. The motives for the transition from a mythological geography to an "exploratory geography" should be sought in a direction different from the literary tradition.[82] The main factors that contributed to the "discovery" of foreign regions and peoples (as consciously investigated and realistically described agents in historical events) can be summarized as follows.

First, after 221 B.C. Chinese intellectuals and statesmen could finally reconcile the notion of a common culture with that of political and administrative unity. The passage from a state of fragmentation to one of unification and centralization embodied in the concept of *t'ien-hsia* was the essential precondition for the development of geographical knowledge. To be able to look beyond its "national" boundaries, China had to become a single political body and thus abandon the inward-looking attitude characteristic of the segmented community of the Warring States period.[83] The vastness of the territory under a central administration, the increased control imposed by the Han emperors over regional centers of power, and the amplification of the bureaucracy are all elements that called for a more precise knowledge of the land.

Second, China's territory had been increasingly expanding into foreign lands ever since the last phase of the Warring States period.[84] The military push that took place in that phase on the one hand brought the Chinese people into closer contact with foreigners, and was responsible, especially along the frontiers of the northern states, for the creation of amalgams of different ethnic groups. On the other hand, the military reorganization of the frontier, especially in terms of fortifications, road building, and establishing garrisons for guarding strategic places, had called for a better and

History Review 3 (1981): 278–96; Yves Hervouet, "Le valeur relative de textes du Che-Ki et du Han-chou," in *Melanges de Sinologie offérts a Monsieur Paul Demieville, part II* (Paris: Bibliothèque de l'Institute des Hautes Etudes Chinoises, 1974), pp. 55–76; Paolo Daffinà, "The Han Shu Hsi Yu Chuan Re-Translated. A Review Article," *T'oung-pao* 68.4–5 (1982): 309–39; and Kazuo Enoki, "On the Relationship between the *Shih-chi*, Bk. 123 and the *Han-shu*, Bks. 61 and 96," *Memoirs of the Research Department of Toyo Bunko* 41 (1983): 1–31.

[82] R. Mathieu, "Fonctions et moyens de la géographie dans la Chine ancienne," *Asiatische Studien* 36.2 (1982): 139.

[83] Mathieu, "Fonctions et moyens de la géographie dans la Chine ancienne," p. 125.

[84] Particularly significant is the expansion of Ch'in in the southwest. On the conquest of the states of Shu and Pa and their significance in the unification of the Chinese empire, see Steven Sage, *Ancient Sichuan and the Unification of China* (Albany: State University of New York Press, 1992), pp. 107–17.

more precise knowledge of the terrain. From what we know from Ssu-ma Ch'ien's accounts, maps were already used by the Ch'in in the year 227 B.C.[85] Although this does not exclude the development of cartography long before then, it seems that the most remarkable advancements in map making – or at least our knowledge of it – do indeed go back to the early imperial period.[86] Two Han military maps found at Ma-wang-tui's tomb no. 3 testify to the high level of technical specialization reached in this field. The maps include not only indications of encampments and fortifications (with the names of the commanding officers), watchtowers, and storehouses for military supplies but also roads, topographical features, names of counties, mountains, rivers and residential areas.[87] Geographical knowledge, as a fundamental component of military science, started to be extended into the territory beyond the borders also as a consequence of the vast program of foreign campaigns launched by Ch'in Shih Huang-ti.

Third, together with the military expansion that especially marked the reign of Han Wu-ti came other forms of contact with non-Chinese peoples, namely, exploration and trade over longer distances. Chang Ch'ien's mission to Central Asia marked only the beginning of official contacts with faraway kingdoms. Lands and peoples previously located in the realm of myth started to acquire names, specific topographical and physical characteristics, social and economic features; in a word, they entered the realm of history.

Chang Ch'ien was followed not only by the military men but also by a stream of envoys, adventurers, and merchants eager to travel to the new "Eldorado" in search of economic profit. Behind them followed the military men and finally the poor peasants, exiled criminals, and other people who formed the rank and file of the Han colonists in the Western Regions. Besides the members of diplomatic missions, many of them served under Han flags, and others were employed as slaves.[88] Moreover, Hsiung-nu who had surrendered were given financial aid to resettle in China along the northern frontier. Given this situation, there can be no gainsaying the impact that the interaction between Chinese and foreigners abroad, the

[85] *Shih chi* 34, 1561; 60, 2110; 69, 2248; 81, 2440.

[86] Mathieu, "Fonctions et moyens de la géographie dans la Chine ancienne," p. 150; Édouard Chavannes, "Les deux plus anciens spécimens de la cartographie chinoise," *Bulletin de l'École Français d'Éxtrême Orient* 5 (1903): 241; Rickett, *Guanzi*, pp. 387–91.

[87] A. G. Bulling, "Ancient Chinese Maps. Two Maps Discovered in a Han Dynasty Tomb from the Second Century B.C.," *Expedition* 20.2 (1978): 16–25; Cao Wanru, "Maps 2,000 Years Ago and Ancient Cartographical Rules," in *Ancient China's Technology and Science*, comp. Inst. of History of Natural Sciences, Chinese Academy of Social Sciences (Beijing: Foreign Languages Press, 1983), pp. 251–55.

[88] Wilbur, *Slavery*, pp. 109–17.

military campaigns, and the physical presence of foreigners in China had on the accretion of new and reliable geographical information, and its close relationship to the documentation of historical events.

The first treatise on geography (Ti-li chih, "land patterns" or "the earth's system") in Chinese historiography appears in the *Han shu*,[89] compiled by Pan Ku (A.D. 32–92), which therefore stands as an original contribution by Pan Ku. The *Shih chi*, however, develops a notion of empirical topography different from the schematic representations of old, which reflects an earlier tendency toward an accurate description of the land and its relevance especially to economic matters. A great deal of the geographic information can be found in several chapters of the *Shih chi*, in particular chapter 129 ("The Money-makers"), and chapter 29 ("The Treatise of the Yellow River and Canals"), as well as the description of Central Asia in chapter 123 ("Ta Yüan").[90]

Several passages are devoted to the description of the trade contacts that the people of the steppe regions had with China. Information about trade before Ssu-ma Ch'ien is limited to what we can infer from the *Yü kung*, from a few passages in the *Chan-kuo ts'e*, and from some parts of the *Mu T'ien-tzu chuan*, which mention the importation of horses and furs, or the existence of large herds of cattle and horses among China's neighboring peoples.[91] However, actual information about trade and merchants can be found only in the *Shih chi*, and in particular in chapter 129. Here the importance of trade opportunities in Inner Asia for both states and individuals is explicit. The transfer of the capital of Ch'in to the city of Yüeh resulted in the incorporation of the herds of the Jung and the Ti – believed to be one of the treasures of the empire – into the Ch'in economy and in the opening up of communication and trade with other states in the west.[92] In the areas of Yang and P'ing-yang, to the east of the Yellow River, the people were accustomed to trading with the Ti, though their lands, bordering on the Hsiung-nu, were often subject to raids. In this no-man's-land a mixed society had developed, where "the inhabitants have mingled with the foreigners, and their customs are by no means uniform."[93]

The story of a merchant called Ch'iao T'ao is emblematic of the opportunities created as the Ch'in and the Han dynasties pushed the frontier farther north. Ch'iao T'ao took advantage of these circumstances and accu-

[89] Cf. Anne Birrell, *Chinese Mythology* (Baltimore: Johns Hopkins University Press, 1993), p. 244.

[90] Wang Ch'eng-tsu, *Chung-kuo ti-li-hsüeh shih* (Peking: Shang-wu, 1988), p. 41.

[91] *Chan Kuo Ts'e* 3 ("Ch'in 1") 178; 18 ("Chao 1"), 608 (J. I. Crump, Jr. trans., *Chan-Kuo Ts'e*, pp. 55, 324); Rémi Mathieu, *Le Mu Tianzi zhuan: traduction annotée: étude critique* (Paris: Diffusion de Boccard, 1978), pp. 127–29.

[92] *Shih chi* 129, 3261 (cf. B. Watson, *Records*, 2: 441).

[93] *Shih chi* 129, 3263 (cf. B. Watson, *Records*, 2: 442).

mulated wealth in the form of animals, such as horses and cattle by the thousands, in addition to a large quantity of cereals, suggesting that the trade that he oversaw consisted mainly of grain sold in exchange for animals and pastoral products. Another merchant able to increase his wealth by trading with foreigners was Wu-chih Lo, who raised domestic animals, then sold them for silks and other goods that he sent as gifts to the king of a Jung state. The king repaid the gift with animals worth ten times the original cost. Eventually, this type of commerce made him so wealthy that he counted his animals only by the number of valleys occupied by the herds. This example shows not only that trade existed between China and foreign peoples but also that Chinese merchants were well aware of commercial practices in a tribal setting, where gifts could yield a high return.

The same type of trade in the shape of gift exchange is alluded to in passages of the *Mu T'ien-tzu chuan*, where it is related that the Chief of Western Mo gave Mu T'ien-tzu 300 fine horses, 10,000 cattle and sheep, and 1,000 cartloads of millet. In exchange, Mu T'ien-tzu gave him 29 golden necklaces, 30 belts of shells, 300 pouches of pearls, and 100 plants of cinnamon and ginger. Upon taking leave, Mu T'ien-tzu even saluted "in the Mo fashion."[94] The situation described here, which unambiguously points to a barter trade, must have been fairly common in fourth century B.C. China, around the time of composition of this work, and indicates the existence of long-established commercial relations between China and the north.

The establishment of direct contacts with Central Asia under Han Wu-ti, and the beginning of official trade, was described by Ssu-ma Ch'ien as the opening of a land of opportunities for many Chinese subjects, in particular for those who had criminal records and few scruples. In the Western Regions great fortunes could be made, and even the lowliest could find fortune. The number of commercial missions to the west multiplied rapidly in concomitance with military operations in the region, and the flux of trade grew to the point that those foreign countries were flooded with Chinese goods, especially silk. In consequence, Han merchandise was devalued, and Han merchants and traders could no longer buy the coveted western products, particularly horses. At this point, the Han resorted to military means, and took by force what they could no longer obtain by trade. According to Ssu-ma Ch'ien, the responsibility for this state of affairs rested mainly with the emperor, whose inexhaustible greed for foreign products resulted in granting imperial credentials to travel to the Western Regions to more and more people, many of whom acted purely in self-interest and had no qualms about enriching themselves by illicit means, in the process tainting the reputation of the Han.[95]

---

[94] Mathieu, *Le Mu Tianzi zhuan*, p. 58.
[95] Hulsewé and Loewe, *China in Central Asia*, pp. 221–22.

To this it must be added that among the soldiers sent to the west on military campaigns were many foreigners, ex-convicts, and criminals gathered from every corner of the empire. For instance, the expeditionary army led by generals Kuo Ch'ang and Wei Kuang was composed of freed criminals from the metropolitan area and twenty to thirty thousand soldiers from Pa and Shu, and the army led by Li Ling was formed by "6,000 horsemen recruited from the dependent states, and some tens of thousands of men of bad reputation gathered from the provinces and kingdoms."[96]

The Economic Impact of the Hsiung-nu Wars

In the military confrontation between the Han and the Hsiung-nu, Ssu-ma Ch'ien became a faithful observer of a dramatic escalation that caused widespread misery and threatened to plunge the nascent empire into economic chaos. While one may not wish to exaggerate the degree of hardship caused by the Hsiung-nu wars, and while the effort may have been, in the long run, less costly than the payments exacted by the Hsiung-nu through the *ho-ch'in* treaties, these wars were seen, by a portion of the Han intelligentsia, to which Ssu-ma Ch'ien belonged, with great anxiety, as documented both in *Shih chi* chapter 30 and *Han shu* chapter 24.[97] As the conflict against the Hsiung-nu "became fiercer day by day, men set off to war carrying their packs of provisions, while those left at home had to send more and more goods to keep them supplied [. . .] the common people were exhausted and began to look for some clever way to evade the taxes."[98] Besides the provisions for the troops, gifts had to be given to victorious Chinese generals and soldiers, as well as to Hsiung-nu who had surrendered. A project for the large-scale raising of horses proved very costly. In 121 B.C. the total military expenditures "amounted to over ten billion cash," and in 119 B.C. "the government treasuries were so depleted that the fighting men received hardly any of their pay."[99] Various projects for irrigation and for the embankment of the Yellow River had to be left unfinished for lack of funds. Only the merchants, "taking advantage of the frequent changes in currency, had been hoarding goods to make a profit."[100] Ssu-ma Ch'ien could not approve of such military-oriented policies, and his

[96] *Shih chi* 123, 3171, 3174. The horsemen from the dependent states were nomadic people who had accepted Han suzerainty.

[97] Throughout the Hsiung-nu wars, for instance, the need for mounts constituted a major expenditure, which strained Han resources; see Nancy Lee Swann, *Food and Money in Ancient China* (Princeton: Princeton University Press, 1950), pp. 37–38.

[98] *Shih chi chu-yi* 30, 1034. [99] *Shih chi chu-yi* 30, 1037.

[100] *Shih chi chu-yi* 30, 1040.

thoughts on the matter may have been akin to those expressed in a long quote ostensibly taken from a memorial by Chu-fu Yen that criticized the costly wars and concluded that "warfare extended over a long period of time gives rise to rebellion, and the burden of military service is apt to lead to disaffection, for the people along the border are subjected to great strain and hardship until they think only of breaking away."[101]

Ssu-ma Ch'ien's presentation of the difficulties faced by his countrymen in the struggle to survive the consequences of the war gives a fairly accurate sense of the impact of Inner Asia on China's economy and society. Several passages illustrate vividly the magnitude of the conflict, which dragged on for years, involved innumerable people, and imposed an unprecedented burden on the people.

[After the episode at Ma-yi] the Hsiung-nu broke the peace treaty and invaded the northern border; the battles followed one another and the troops could not be disbanded. The whole empire (*t'ien-hsia*) bore the brunt of this effort. As the military conflict escalated, those who went out on the expeditions had to carry their own supplies; those who remained at home had to send provisions. Those inside and those outside (the border) both suffered, and had to contribute supplies. The common people were impoverished and exhausted, and tried to find some cunning ways to evade the law. The available resources were consumed and soon became insufficient. Therefore, those who gave their own properties were appointed to official posts, and those who contributed goods were granted amnesty, and the [normal] system for selecting officials fell into desuetude.[102]

Already at the time of Emperor Wen relations with Inner Asia were considered to be a major economic burden. According to Ssu-ma Ch'ien,

[At the time of Emperor Wen] the Hsiung-nu were frequently raiding the northern borders, and many border garrisons were set up. The grain produced on the border was not sufficient to feed the troops. Therefore the government enlisted those who could supply grain and transport it to the border garrisons, and granted them honorary titles; these titles could reach as high a rank as *ta-shu-chang*.[103]

As this passage shows, the source of distress was not the yearly tribute paid by China to the Hsiung-nu, but the need to keep a large body of troops as permanent border garrisons. Guidelines concerning the settlement of border troops had been amply discussed by statesmen such as Ch'ao Ts'o and remained a central issue in the "Salt and Iron" discussion on frontier policies.

Providing an image different from the China bursting with pride, confidence, and economic prosperity normally associated with the reign of Han

---

[101] *Shih chi* 112, 2955; *Shih chi chu-yi* 112, 2379.
[102] *Shih chi chu-yi* 30, 1034.   [103] *Shih chi chu-yi* 30, 1032.

Wu-ti, Ssu-ma Ch'ien also provides evidence of the famine that struck China in 120 B.C.[104]

The next year [120 B.C.] the lands to the east of the Mountains suffered from floods and many people were starving. Therefore the emperor dispatched envoys to empty the granaries of the provinces and kingdoms in order to help the poor. Still, that was not sufficient. Then he encouraged the great and wealthy people to lend money to the poor. But it was still impossible to provide enough assistance; then he transferred the poor people to the area east of the Pass and resettled them in the region of New Ch'in,[105] to the south of Shuo-fang. Over seventy thousand people were all given food and clothing by central government officials.[106] [. . .] The expenses of the resettlement were so huge that they could not be calculated. Therefore the government granaries were completely exhausted.[107]

This situation affected the focus and implementation of Han policies in the north, because people hit by the famine were transferred, as a relief measure, to the northern frontier, thereby increasing the demographic pressure on the areas bordering on nomadic territories. The increased Han presence in the north provided the rationale and the labor to conquer, occupy, put to cultivation, and defend larger and larger portions of nomadic land.

Economic distress was caused also by the huge cost of offering rewards to victorious Chinese troops and surrendered Hsiung-nu people, as it is recorded in the following passages:

[In 123 B.C.] the Great General [Wei Ch'ing] led six generals in another attack on the Hsiung-nu (hu), killing or capturing nineteen thousand of them. Soldiers who had cut heads or captured prisoners were presented with over two hundred thousand catties of gold. The several tens of thousands of prisoners[108] also received rich rewards, and were provided with food and clothing by the government. But the Han soldiers and horses that were lost amounted to over one hundred thousand, and the cost of the [lost] weapons and suits of armor, as well as the expenses for the tranportation of provisions cannot be calculated.[109]

---

[104] On famines during the Former Han, cf. Fang Ch'ing-ho, "Hsi Han te tsai-huang" Shih-yüan 7 (1976): 12.

[105] The territory within the Great Bend of the Yellow River that Meng T'ien had occupied was called New Ch'in by Ch'in Shih Huang-ti. The name remained in use also during the Han dynasty.

[106] These officials are indicated as hsien-kuan, literally, "district officers" (cf. B. Watson, Records, 2: 87). I am following here the interpretation of the Shih chi chu-yi.

[107] Shih chi chu-yi 30, 1038.

[108] This number seems to contradict the previous figure.

[109] Shih chi chu-yi 30, 1035.

[In 121 B.C.] the General of Swift Cavalry Huo Ch'ü-ping twice in a row attacked the Hsiung-nu (*hu*) seizing forty thousand heads. That fall the Hun-yeh[110] king led several tens of thousands of people to surrender. Consequently the Han dispatched twenty thousand carriages to receive them. When they arrived at the capital they received gifts, and rewards were bestowed upon soldiers who had distinguished themselves. That year the expenditures amounted to over ten billion cash.[111]

The Han strategy for which these excerpts provide evidence was to encourage greed to foster the military activism of Han generals and soldiers and to reward the prisoners to tempt the enemy to defect. However, the concurrent need to settle more people in the new territories and to defend these areas against the Hsiung-nu counterattacks created a circular problem. A larger area called for more soldiers to defend it, but a larger military presence often made local production insufficient, so that the need again arose to colonize new land. At the same time, economic pressure built up in the interior, so that military enterprises, wasteful of both human and financial resources, became widely unpopular. Moreover, it was unclear what advantage these campaigns brought to the general populace. For Ssu-ma Ch'ien, at least, prolonged wars were able only to produce loss of life and to destroy the wealth of the country.

The economic effects of the wars against the Hsiung-nu not only were a crucial part of Ssu-ma Ch'ien's historical research but formed perhaps the most important criticism directed toward his government and ruler and foreshadowed the position of the "scholars" in the *Discourses on Salt and Iron*. Ssu-ma Ch'ien's description of the hardships suffered by the Chinese people must be placed in the context of the political debate over the role of the state itself, and the extent of its power. Frontier defense was naturally a major theme, because it involved complex decisions concerning military expenses, recruitment of troops, settlement of people on the border, and payment of premiums to both surrendered enemies and victorious troops. In his implicit criticism of Han Wu-ti, Ssu-ma Ch'ien avoided the high tones of Confucian philosophy that fill the rhetoric of the "scholars" in the *Discourses on Salt and Iron*, but, as an "objective" witness and reporter of events, he tried to provide room for those voices raised to denounce the distress of the common people. It was thanks to the historian's ability to present not so much the "moral" argument, but the historical evidence for it, that we are able, through the vivid images of the *Shih chi*, to place the political debate in its actual historical context. By providing the empirical foundations to a given

---

[110] Hun-yeh is the same name of a Hsiung-nu tribe that lived in the territory to the west of the Yellow River, today part of Kansu province.

[111] *Shih chi chu-yi* 30, 1037.

moral, logical, or political argument, the descriptive mode plays a fundamental role in defining the nature of historical knowledge and its social
function.

Conclusion

Ssu-ma Ch'ien's description of the Hsiung-nu and representation of the
history of the northern nomads is entirely different from previous and contemporary descriptions; typically, in early Chinese written sources descriptions of the north are embedded in a web of metaphysical theories and
mythological beliefs that bear no relation to their ethnographic or geographic reality. The *Shan-hai ching* (Classic of Mountains and Seas) is the
well-known representative work of a literary and oral tradition in which
foreign peoples and lands reflect an imaginary universe of fabulous, fantastic, or legendary beings. Here peoples are listed whose unworldly attributes might have inspired the illustrators of medieval bestiaries. For instance,
demons (*kuei*), people with the heads of beasts and the bodies of men, and
people with human faces and limbs and the bodies of fish are said to inhabit
the northern metropolitan territories described in chapter 12; in the "northern overseas territories" of chapter 8 we find people without bellies (Wu-
ch'ang) living close to people with hollow eyes (Shen-mu); and chapter 7
describes the country of the one-eyed men to the east of the Jou-li people,
who have one hand and one foot.[112] Mathieu's granting plausibility to this
work's geographical layout as corresponding to real topographical features
and regarding it as a pioneering work prompted by the "conquest of new
territories and exploration of new lands"[113] are questionable. The author
admits that the toponyms are problematic (the same name is used for more
than one geographical location, or different names indicate the same place),
that there are lacunae and omissions, and that the descriptions are technically insufficient – all of which tend to discredit the *Shan-hai ching* as a
work of "scientific" geography.[114]

The tradition of the *Shan-hai ching* was alive in the Han and later periods
and was very much present in Ssu-ma Ch'ien's days. Chapter 4 of the *Huai-
nan Tzu* on topography derives much of its geographical and mythological

---

[112] Rémi Mathieu, *Études sur la mythologie et l'ethnologie de la Chine ancienne.
Traduction annotée du Shanhai Jing* (Paris: Diffusion de Boccard), pp. 485–89,
418, 414.

[113] Mathieu, *Études sur la mythologie et l'ethnologie de la Chine ancienne*, p. xvii.

[114] Mathieu, *Études sur la mythologie et l'ethnologie de la Chine ancienne*, p. cii.
Hervouet denies any scientific value to the geographic and ethnographic data
that we find in the *Shan-hai ching*; cf. Yves Hervouet, *Un poéte de cour sous les
Han: Sseu-ma Siang-jou* (Paris: Presses universitaires de France, 1964), p. 307.

material from the *Shan-hai ching*.[115] Its contents have little to do with the actual exploration and description of the geographic space but are consistent with the incorporation of archaic beliefs and mythology in an overarching system of cosmic correspondences. In this respect the "geography" of the *Huai-nan-tzu* is a pure abstraction produced through the blending of cosmological, numerological, and mythological ingredients. In section VI of chapter 4, on the regions beyond the "nine provinces" (i.e., beyond China), we find again a long list of fantastic beings and strange countries. Although some of these localities may have remote connections with vague geographical notions, they are clearly divorced from any empirical knowledge.[116] The abstract and purely "ideological" use of geographical and ethnographical categories can be exemplified by this passage:

The north is a dark and gloomy place, where the sky is closed up. Cold and ice are gathered there. Insects in the larval and pupal stages lie concealed there. The bodies of the men of the north are tightly-knit, with short necks, broad shoulders, and low buttocks; their bodily openings are all connected to their genitals. The bones belong to the north. The color black governs the kidneys. The people there are like birds or beasts but are long-lived. That region is suitable for legumes and there is an abundance of dogs and horses.[117]

Here we have some realistic elements (the cold of the north and the abundance of dogs and horses) inserted in a surreal, mythological framework. Other elements derived from what seems to be a genuine knowledge of foreign peoples can be found in chapter 11, where it is said that "the Hu people see hempseed and do not know that it can be made into linen. The Yüeh people see downy hair, and do not know that it can be made into felt."[118] What transpires from this is that the Hu (northern nomads) knew how to make felt, which is perfectly true, and that the Yüeh produced good linen, which is equally possible, but the whole sentence is used as a rhetoric device to illustrate the superior knowledge of China vis-à-vis the limited knowledge of foreigners. In the same chapters a few notes on the different customs of the foreigners are used to make a moral point.[119] In every case the description of those foreign customs is never treated as an independent subject, and this type of knowledge is always

[115] John Major, *Heaven and Earth in Early Han Thought* (Albany: State University of New York Press, 1993), p. 191.

[116] Major, *Heaven and Earth*, pp. 161–63.

[117] *Huai-nan-tzu* 4, 10a/11b; I have followed the translation by Major (*Heaven and Earth*, pp. 184–85) with a slight modification.

[118] *Huai-nan-tzu* 11, 2b; cf. Benjamin E. Wallacker, *The Huai-nan-Tzu Book Eleven: Behavior, Culture and the Cosmos* (New Haven: American Oriental Society, 1962), p. 30.

[119] *Huai-nan-tzu* 11, 9a; cf. Wallacker, *The Huai-nan-tzu Book Eleven*, p. 35.

subordinated to philosophical considerations of either a cosmological or an ethical nature.

Other short pieces of information about foreign peoples, which contain grains of factual information, appear in the "Yü kung." Among them we can distinguish the Yi who wear fur clothes, the Yi of Lai, the Yi of Huai, the Yi of the islands (Tao Yi) who wear grasses, and the Ho Yi with their tributary gifts of metal goods to the court of Yao.[120] Possibly pastoral peoples are the felt-wearing Hsi-ching people and the felt-wearing Western Jung people of K'un-lun. According to Birrell, the "tribute of Yü" constitutes a document that is part history, part mythology, and part idealized political theory.[121] However, these representations hardly amount to any serious ethnographic information, nor do they incorporate a narrative history of the type that we find in the *Shih chi*.

In fact, Ssu-ma Ch'ien consciously distanced himself from this tradition, as he endorsed a rational method based on the verification of sources and on the examination of ethnographic and geographic realities, an approach he explicitly states in the concluding remarks to chapter 123:

At present, since Chang Ch'ien returned from his mission to Central Asia, the source of the Yellow River has been investigated; but where can we see the K'un-lun Mountains that the "Basic Annals" [*pen chi*] spoke about? Therefore, if we talk of the nine continents, mountains and rivers, the "Book of Documents" is the one that comes closest to the truth. But, as for the strange beings illustrated in the "Basic Annals of Yü" and in the *Shan-hai ching*, I do not dare speak about them.[122]

This passage constitutes the most direct evidence of the historian's quest for a non-mythological, observable, and empirically testable knowledge of foreign lands. This quest – and the critique to the tradition from which it sprang at least in part – constitutes the foundation for treating Inner Asia and its people as objects of historical investigation, subject to criteria of credibility as well as of, arguably, an empirical search for reliable evidence. Moreover, the history of the northern people was no longer limited to recording a certain event, such as a battle and the resulting victory or loss, but was extended to the very causes of historical change.

At the same time, Ssu-ma Ch'en was neither alien nor invulnerable to the strong intellectual currents of his own times, and especially to the cosmological thought that sought explanations in the mechanics of heavenly designs and in universal equilibria that encompassed heaven, nature, and human agency. The larger historical processes had to conform to certain

---

[120] Couvreur, *Chou King*, pp. 62–76 *passim*. Note that the term "Yi" is used as a generic term for foreigners.

[121] Birrell, *Chinese Mythology*, pp. 243–44.

[122] *Shih chi* 123, 3179; *Shih chi chu-yi* 123, 2604.

patterns that would help humans understand better the world they lived in as well as their position in the greater scheme of things to which they believed they belonged. In the next chapter, we will see how the treatment of Inner Asia reflects this "normative" orientation of the historian's work.

CHAPTER EIGHT

Taming the North
The Rationalization of the Nomads in Ssu-ma Ch'ien's Historical Thought

Introduction

The Hsiung-nu chapter of the *Shih chi* was unprecedented in its presentation of a detailed and realistic account of the nomads to the north of China. However, another aspect of the historiography of the northern nomads must be considered before we can complete our analysis of the northern frontier as it was "formalized" in the *Shih chi*. Together with his presentation of a full description of the Hsiung-nu empire and the regions of Inner Asia, Ssu-ma Ch'ien was faced with the task of having to "explain" it in terms consistent with his own vision of history. To integrate the Inner Asian nomads (as with any other phenomenon that was truly anomalous and new in Chinese history) within a unified historical frame, Inner Asia had to be understood, or "rationalized," both according to the intellectual canons of his own age and according to those principles of historical investigation that Ssu-ma Ch'ien set for himself. This "rationalization" of Inner Asia required the seamless juncture of the history of the Hsiung-nu in the flow of Chinese history, following primarily the principle of "comprehensiveness" (*t'ung*). In addition, the investigation of the relationship between "heaven" and "man," where "man" obviously had to include all the terrestrial events worthy of being recorded required that Inner Asia be included – for the first time in Chinese historiography – into the system of correlations between celestial and human occurrences that formed such an important pillar of Han thought.[1] In the *Tso-chuan*, as we have seen, there are

---

[1] Possibly the earliest mention of a specific office connected with judicial astrology and based on the *fen-yeh* system can be found in the *Chou li*; see *Chou li* 26 ("Pao-chan-shih"), 9a–10b (SPPY); (trans. Biot, *Le Tchou Li* [Paris: L'Imprimerie Nationale, 1851], 2: 113–16).

passages that can be interpreted in the sense of a temporary opposition between two opposite principles – civilization and the lack of it – but those passages certainly do not articulate a vision of history whereby the north and the Central Plain are turned into two metaphysical principles eternally at war with one another.

Placing the northern nomads within the realm of "prescriptive" history, where the shape and nature of change is sourced to the intricate web of correlations at the foundations of yin-yang and five-phase thought, is evidence of a fuller appreciation of the role of Inner Asia as a genuine part of Chinese history. Indeed, this impression is further supported by the historical reconstruction of the genealogy of the northern peoples as a principle "antagonistic" and yet complementary to the Hua-Hsia civilization from its very origins. The notion of a yin-yang opposition of the two sides (the north and the south) that pervades some of the passages concerning Inner Asia appears to be a product of the Han period, although possibly as a development based on concepts of antagonistic polarization inherited from an earlier time.[2]

The system of "allocated fields" (fen-yeh), that is, the partitioning of sky and earth stemming from the cosmo-political necessity of establishing correspondences between celestial zones and earthly regions,[3] had developed by the Warring States period into a set of correspondences between constellations and specific Eastern Chou states. The duty of the astronomers of the various states was to formulate prognostications relative to their kingdoms on the basis of the observation of the movements of planets in the portion of sky (or Lunar Lodge) assigned to each. Each lodge represented a political division of the earth, and the astrological prognostications referred to the states in whose corresponding Lunar Lodge astronomical phenomena were observed. However, during this period Inner Asian regions do not seem to have been included in these heavenly correspondences.

Among the astronomical manuscripts found at Ma-wang-tui, a silk scroll book written, according to some estimates, between 403 and 206 B.C.,[4] illustrates a system of prognostications of human matters based on the shape and movement of comets. It is significant for our discussion that all

---

[2] This notion is reflected, for instance, in the language of a treaty concluded by Emperor Wen with the Hsiung-nu in 162 B.C., where the two rulers are compared to the "mother" and "father" of all the people.

[3] K. Yabuuti, "Chinese Astronomy: Development and Limiting Factors," in *Chinese Science. Explorations of an Ancient Tradition*, eds. S. Nakayama and N. Sivin (Cambridge, Mass.: M.I.T. Press, 1973), p. 92.

[4] T'ien-fu Ku, "A Summary of the Contents of the Ma-wang-tui Silk-Scroll Book 'Assorted Astronomical and Meteorological Prognostications,'" *Chinese Studies in Archaeology*, 1 (1979): 57; Michael Loewe, "The Han View of Comets," *Bulletin of the Museum of Far Eastern Antiquities* 52 (1980): 3.

the prognostications are correlated to historical events (especially military ones) concerning the Warring States. The space beyond the political boundaries of the Hsia-Chou community was simply not included in the cosmological vision represented in this type of predictive astronomy. The author of the work did not seem to have believed that the inhabitants of those regions had any real bearing on the political vicissitudes of the Central States.

In the literature of the Han period we find contradictory evidence. We may take into consideration, for instance, the *Huai-nan-tzu*, a text that reflects beliefs and conceptions about geography and ethnography that must have been current at the time of Ssu-ma Ch'ien. In section VI of chapter 4 of the *Huai-nan-tzu*, when the regions beyond the "nine provinces" (i.e., beyond China) are discussed, we find again a long list of fantastic beings and strange countries. As Major points out, "these strange lands must be treated with great care, for they belong to a type of literature in which terrestrial and mythical geography blend together."[5] But the inclusion of Inner Asian peoples in correlative metaphysical systems was not uncommon during the Han. Statesmen such as Ch'ao Ts'o, who were actively engaged in foreign policy, referred to the northern nomads within this framework:

The territory of the Hu and Mo is a place of accumulated *yin* (i.e., very cold), the tree bark is three inches thick, and the thickness of ice reaches as many as six feet. They eat meat and drink kumiss. The people have a thick skin, and the animals have much fur, so the nature of people and animals is such that they are adapted to cold. The Yang and the Yüeh have little *yin* and much *yang*. Their people have a thin skin, their birds and animals have thin furs, and their nature is to withstand heat.[6]

In Ssu-ma Ch'ien's time correlative correspondences could also inform the "explanation" of a given historical event. Even the pragmatic Ch'ao Ts'o could reach the conclusion that "the Ch'in garrison soldiers," being neither extremely *yin* nor extremely *yang*, "were not accustomed to these climates, so the soldiers on duty died on the frontier, and those transported there died on the road."[7] This approach to historical causality was part of the intellectual climate in which Ssu-ma Ch'ien lived. But in the *Shih chi* this normative perspective is applied to Inner Asia and to the Hsiung-nu in a more systematic fashion, to the point that the northern nomads, especially after they acquired a far more threatening "imperial" dimension,

[5] J. S. Major, *Heaven and Earth in Early Han Thought* (Albany: State University of New York Press, 1993), p. 190.

[6] "Ch'ao Ts'o chi chu-yi" Tsu, *Ch'ao Ts'o chi chu-yi* (Shanghai: Shanghai Jen-min, 1976), pp. 15–16.

[7] Ibid., p. 16.

became the true alter-ego of China, a phenomenon that could not be ignored, but needed to be addressed and made into a coherent, fully investigated, agent of "history."

Ssu-ma Ch'ien's inclusion of the nomadic north in a set of astrological correlations was not aimed primarily at establishing some principle of causality that would concretely offer an explanation for a given historical event, but was a way of integrating the northern nomads with the rest of Chinese history. By making the north subject to the same rules, patterns, and laws that were thought to explain events in Chinese history, one of which was the dialectic relationship between "heaven and man," he made the north be part of a universal and integrated vision of history. Placing the Hsiung-nu in a "genealogical" relationship to Chinese history was probably even more important: the emergence of the Hsiung-nu phenomenon was explained in the context of a set of known historical categories – the various northern peoples of old – and organized into an "invented" genealogy that would result in the construction of a fictitious ethnic tie with the past. In this way, the new and ominous phenomenon lost its threatening charge.

With the exception of the ethnic genealogy of the Hsiung-nu, whose appearance at the beginning of chapter 110 is clearly meant to show continuity between the present and the past, the "normative" passages on the northern nomads are not arranged in any systematic way. However "patchy" their distribution within the *Shih chi*, there is nevertheless clear evidence of an effort to transform the north from a morally unsavory and historically amorphous place into an essential component of Chinese history. By assigning to Inner Asia certain historical and cosmological values, the historian brought Inner Asia into a wider rationalistic vision according to which the ominous north could be "explained" and somehow controlled. This "ideological" operation, together with the empirical collection of data, paved the way for the incorporation of the northern peoples into the Chinese historiographical tradition. From the *Shih chi* onward, this historiographical tradition became the repository of *both* Chinese and Inner Asian history.

Ethnogenealogy of the Hsiung-nu

Ssu-ma Ch'ien wrote the ethnogenealogy of the Hsiung-nu based entirely on the sources of the classical tradition. The Hsiung-nu emerge from it as the final link in a long chain of foreign peoples who had previously played prominent roles in Chinese history. In forging an association between the Hsiung-nu and their predecessors, Ssu-ma Ch'ien's only "objective" criterion can be found in the geographical location of these foreigners, who inhabited, generally speaking, the area to the north of China.

Of course, linking together in a genealogical sequence and historical chain a number of peoples, unchanging in their essential characteristics, who inhabited roughly the same area, cannot be accepted as a valid construction of the history of Inner Asia, considering that, over the course of more than a millennium, many of those foreigners were absorbed by Chinese states, or moved elsewhere, or simply disappeared. That at some time there were peoples who inhabited the northern regions would not necessarily make them the ancestors of the Hsiung-nu. In addition, according to both Ssu-ma Ch'ien and to other sources, the Hsiung-nu were not the only inhabitants of those regions: what was, then, the relationship between other nomads, such as the Lou-fan, the Tung Hu, and the Lin Hu, and the earlier inhabitants of the north, the Jung and Ti peoples who were regarded as ancestors of the Hsiung-nu?

A phonetic similarity between Hsiung-nu and ethnonyms such as Hun-yü and Hsien-yün may have also played a role in Ssu-ma Ch'ien's creation of linkages with the northerners of the past records, but no such proximity existed for the more prominent names in the genealogy, such as the Jung and the Ti. In general, the "ethnogenealogy" presented by Ssu-ma Ch'ien is based not on "anthropological" or documentary evidence, but on a historical correlation that aimed to establish a precise connection with the past and to demonstrate that the Hsiung-nu filled the same antithetical position to China that had previously been played by other foreigners.

It is unclear whether this construction was purely Ssu-ma Ch'ien's invention. It is more likely that Ssu-ma Ch'ien set into writing and detailed historically a perception widespread among his Han contemporaries. For instance, we find this notion plainly expressed in the following passage from a memorial by Chu-fu Yen:

It is not only our generation which finds the Hsiung-nu difficult to conquer and control. They make a business of pillage and plunder, and indeed this would seem their inborn nature. Ever since the times of Emperor Shun and the rulers of the Hsia, Shang, and Chou dynasties, no attempt has ever been made to order or control them; rather, they have been regarded as beasts to be pastured, not as members of the human race.[8]

Such reconstructions of the Hsiung-nu's remote past have a highly normative function and fulfill two goals: making the unknown seem familiar, and establishing a certain subject as one worthy of investigation (and therefore worthy of record keeping). The creation of a connection with foreign peoples of old is an example of a process of reduction to known categories. These identifications served the purpose of depriving the new enemy of his

---

[8] *Shih chi* 112, 2955; Burton Watson, trans., *Records of the Grand Historian by Sima Qian* (New York and Hong Kong: Columbia University Press and The Chinese University of Hong Kong, 1993), 2: 196.

most frightening feature, the mysterious nature of his threat, by a process of *reductio ad notum.*[9] For although nomads had been in fairly close contact, and sometimes in conflict, with the northern states of Ch'in, Chao, and Yen from the fourth century B.C. onward, a unified steppe empire had come into existence only about seventy years before Wu-ti ascended the throne. The lack of knowledge about the details of the genealogy of the Hsiung-nu royal house, admitted by Ssu-ma Ch'ien, shows clearly that he had no records available to him that could yield detailed information concerning the past history of the Hsiung-nu as a distinct ethnic or tribal unit and could explain their sudden power.

In sum, Ssu-ma Ch'ien strove to establish a genetic relationship between the Hsiung-nu and past northerners to explain where they had come from. The creation of a tradition that could link the Hsiung-nu with the remotest past was essential for making their imposing and troubling presence into a known quantity in the larger scheme of Chinese (and human) history. On the methodological plane, historical correlations allowed the historian to incorporate and rationalize the historical event. And, in addition to providing the means for a "rational" historical explanation, on the ideological level the genealogy constructed for the Hsiung-nu intended to demonstrate how over the course of its history China had been able by the force of civilization or by the force of arms to conquer the "barbarians" and to neutralize political and military threats from the north. The passages chosen by Ssu-ma Ch'ien to illustrate the past relations between China and the northern "nomads" are emblematic in this respect. Their purpose is to show that these foreign threats were very serious but that they had always been overcome. Indeed, the historian represents the unfolding of the Chinese march into foreign territories almost as a "manifest destiny." This particular notion is evidently derived from Mencius's doctrine, which attributes to the great ancestors of Chinese civilization the ability not only to domesticate nature but also to conquer and transform alien peoples.[10]

A close examination of the relevant portions of chapter 110 makes the dual purpose of the Hsiung-nu "ethnogenealogy" all the more clear. In the passages that follow Ssu-ma Ch'ien begins with the period from the mythical origins of the Hsia dynasty to the Chou conquest (passages I–III). Here we find mostly generic names for foreigners, which are used anachronistically; the presence of northern peoples whose names are known from much later records is dated back to the time of Yao and Shun and attention is also focused on the Ch'üan Jung of the Western Chou period, who invaded

[9] O. Maenchen-Helfen, "Archaistic Names of the Hsiung-nu," *Central Asiatic Journal* 6 (1961): 249–61.

[10] James Legge, *The Chinese Classics*, vol. 2: *The Works of Mencius*, 2nd ed. (Oxford: Clarendon, 1895; rpt. Hong Kong: Hong Kong University Press, 1960), p. 253.

the capital and forced the Chou to move east (passages IV–V). After the semi-mythical beginnings of Chinese history, the more plentiful records available for the Eastern Chou period allow Ssu-ma Ch'ien to stand on firmer documentary ground. The next link in the genealogy are the Shan Jung, followed by people identified by the generic terms of Jung and Ti (passages VI–VII). As we have seen in Chapter 3, these were umbrella terms used in the Chinese records to indicate a variety of different political and perhaps ethnic groupings. A precise link between them and the Hsiung-nu could not be established, except by attributing to them the same historical role with respect to China. This post facto genealogical connection both resulted from and fulfilled the need to explain and legitimize the historical role played by the Hsiung-nu.

In the opening statement of chapter 110 Ssu-ma Ch'ien assigns to the Hsiung-nu a "Chinese" origin and defines some of their reputed ancestors as pastoral nomads:[11]

I. The ancestor of the Hsiung-nu was a descendant of the ruling clan of the Hsia dynasty, named Shun-wei. As early as the time of emperors Yao and Shun and before there were people known as Shan Jung, Hsien-yün, and Hsün-yü; they lived in the northern marches (*man*) and moved around following their herds.[12]

Here we have two "postulates" that are essential for the composition of the genealogy. The "Chinese" origin of the Hsiung-nu makes them into a legitimate component of Chinese history from the very beginning and also makes them "part of the family" along the lines of a rhetoric of kinship already seen in the *ho-ch'in* treaties. Establishing kinship linkages is an essential element for giving a historical protagonist legitimacy and credibility. The mention of people to whom Ssu-ma Ch'ien attributes a pastoral nomadic identity adds to the kinship bond a cultural dimension that is the second crucial element necessary to establish a link between past and present. Associations between the sage kings of antiquity and foreign peoples were by no means foreign to the Chinese tradition. Mencius regarded Shun as "a man of the Eastern Yi (people)," and King Wen as a Western Yi. The Ch'iang people had been associated with the Chiang family name, whose members were said to be the descendents of Shen Nung[13] and

---

[11] All of the passages that follow are from *Shih chi* 110, 2879–82; see also *Shih chi chu-yi* 110, 2313.

[12] Cf. Watson, *Records*, 2: 129.

[13] Legge, *The Works of Mencius*, p. 316; *Tso-chuan chu* (Ai 9), 1653 (James Legge, *The Chinese Classics*, vol. 5: *The Ch'un Ts'ew with the Tso Chuen* [London: Trübner, 1872; rpt. Hong Kong: Hong Kong University Press, 1960], p. 819). Cf. also *Chung-kuo min-tsu shih*, ed. Wang Chung-han, p. 121.

are also mentioned among the peoples who joined the Chou against the Shang.[14]

The term "northern marches" refers to one of the zones of the concentric geographical schemes discussed earlier, and to a conception of space dominated by the notion of a central locus of political and moral authority whose beneficial effect on the surrounding lands decreases proportionally to the distance from it. Ssu-ma Ch'ien placed the ancestors of the Hsiung-nu in an area unaffected by Chinese civilization. The term *man* (here translated with "marches") was also the name of a type of foreigners that inhabited a faraway zone, which reminded the reader of the geographical scheme of the "Yü Kung," in which the Man people were located in the "wild" (*huang*) domain, that is, the zone farthest from the center of civilization.[15] Kinship closeness and cultural distance are then established at the outset as the two chief principles adopted to explicate both the continuity of the relationship between the Hsiung-nu and China and the tension generated by their presence.

II. At the end of the Hsia dynasty Kung Liu left his post as Minister of Agriculture and moved to the land of the Western Jung, were he founded the city of Pin. Some three hundred years later the Jung and Ti attacked Kung Liu's descendant, the Great Lord Tan-fu. Tan-fu fled to the foot of Mount Ch'i [. . .] this was the beginning of the Chou state.[16]

The story of the king of T'ai's (Tan Fu) trouble with foreign peoples is found in Mencius, too, whose account hints at the tribute paid by Tan Fu to the Ti. First Tan Fu gave them skins and silks, then cattle and horses, and finally pearls and gems, but none of these gifts was sufficient to hold them back and prevent their incursions. Eventually the Chinese king had to leave the area.[17] The same theme is present in the ode "Mien" of the *Shih ching*, which tells of a struggle between Tan-fu and foreign peoples (*k'un-yi*). Ssu-ma Ch'ien used the myth according to which ancestral rulers traveled to new territories and fought with alien peoples to illustrate one aspect of the process of domestication of the alien and hostile environment outside the bounds of China. The challenge was not a new one, and the sage kings had showed how to deal with it.[18] The results are made known in the following passage:

[14] James Legge, *The Chinese Classics*, vol. 3: *The Shoo King*, 2nd ed. (Oxford: Clarendon, 1895; rpt. Hong Kong: Hong Kong University Press, 1960), p. 301.

[15] Chapters 29 and 33. In the *Chou li*, however, the Man live in the sixth domain (*chi* or *fu*), i.e., an intermediate zone that comes before the Yi, thus implying a lesser degree of barbarism.

[16] Cf. Watson, *Records*, 2: 130.   [17] Legge, *The Works of Mencius*, pp. 174–76.

[18] James Legge, *The Chinese Classics*, vol. 4: *The She King* (London: Trübner, 1862; rpt. Hong Kong: Hong Kong University Press, 1960), p. 439.

III. One hundred years later Ch'ang, the Earl of the West of the Chou, attacked the Ch'üan-yi clan. Some ten years later King Wu overthrew the Shang ruler Chou, and established his residence at Lo-yi; he re-settled in the regions of Feng and Hao, and pushed the Jung and Ti to the north of the Ching and Lo rivers;[19] they would bring tribute to the court at appointed times. Their land was known as "barren domains."

It is emblematic of Ssu-ma Ch'ien's ideological approach, and of his construction of a sharp divide between Chinese and "barbarians," that, while reporting King Wu's victory against the Shang, he does not mention that the Chou had, among their allies, also Western Yi peoples.[20] The *huang fu* (barren domains) of this passage refer specifically, once again, to the "Yü Kung," where both rivers, Ching and Lo, are mentioned and suggests a gradual expansion of the "civilized" space, which culminates in the following statement:

IV. About two hundred years later, when the power of the Chou was declining, King Mu attacked the Ch'üan Jung, captured four white wolves and four white deer and returned. From this time on the people of the "barren domains" no longer travelled to court.

The Ch'üan Jung, who were later to displace the Chou royal house, are placed here as the main antagonists of King Mu. Here the reference is to the *Bamboo Annals*, which report that King Mu pushed the Jung northward, to the region of T'ai-yüan.[21] Ssu-ma Ch'ien represents this as the beginning of a "loss" of China's authority in the north, coinciding, apparently, with the decline of the power of the Chou, which resulted in a new historical cycle when the northerners climbed to a position of power.

V. Two hundred years after the time of King Mu [. . .] the Ch'üan Jung took away from the Chou the region of Chiao-huo, settled between the Ching and Wei rivers, and invaded and plundered the Central States. Duke Hsiang of Ch'in came to the rescue of the Chou court [. . .]

The episode narrated here refers to the last year of King Yu, 771 B.C., when the capital itself was attacked and, as a consequence, the Chou court was forced to move east. This was by all accounts a disastrous defeat for the Chou, as King Yu and his son were both killed. The counterattack of Duke Hsiang happened five years later, under King P'ing.[22] The wars con-

[19] These were two large northern affluents of the river Wei, in Shansi. Lo was located to the east and Ching to the west.
[20] *Chu-shu chi-nien* 2 ("Chou Wu Wang"), 1a; (Legge, *The Shoo King*, "Prolegomena," p. 144).
[21] *Chu-shu chi-nien* 2 ("Mu Wang"), 5a; (Legge, *The Shoo King*, "Prolegomena," p. 151).
[22] *Chu-shu chi-nien* 2 ("P'ing Wang"), 12a; (Legge, *The Shoo King*, "Prolegomena," p. 158).

tinued for several decades, a period in which the northerners (this time identified with the Shan Jung) continued to threaten the heart of China's political power. What follows at this point is a series of passages in which Ssu-ma Ch'ien lists all the major wars between Chou states and foreigners. In every instance the pattern is the same: every foreign attack is effectively resisted by the Chou states, who defend civilization againt the constant pressure of these alien enemies. There is no mention here of the expansion of the Chou states.

VI. Sixty-five years later the Shan Jung crossed the state of Yen and attacked Ch'i. Duke Li of Ch'i [r. 730–698 B.C.] fought with them in the suburbs of his capital.[23] Forty-four years later the Shan Jung attacked Yen. Yen asked for help from Duke Huan of Ch'i [r. 685–643 B.C.], who went north and attacked the Shan Jung, who left.[24] Twenty years later the Jung and the Ti reached Lo-i and attacked King Hsiang of Chou. King Hsiang fled to the city of Fan in Cheng.[25] [. . .] After this some Jung and Ti settled in the Lu-hun area, reaching out to the east as far as [the state of] Wei, invading, plundering and ravaging the Central States. The Central States were in great distress; therefore poets made lyrics which said "we defeated the Jung and Ti," "we attacked the Hsien-yün and reached Ta-yüan," "we sent out many rumbling chariots, and built walls in the northern region."[26] [. . .] Duke Wen of Chin repelled the Jung and Ti, who then settled to the west of the Yellow River, between the rivers Yin and Lo. They were called Red Ti and White Ti.

The ethnogenealogy and history of the north ends with the victory of Duke Mu of Ch'in. The implication is that at the end of the seventh century

---

[23] This passage is reported in the *Tso-chuan*, which mentions an attack by the Pei Jung against the state of Ch'i taking place in 706 B.C. *Tso-chuan chu* (Huan 6), p. 113.

[24] According to the dates from the *Ch'un-ch'iu* and *Tso-chuan*, Duke Huan conducted his first campaigns against the northern peoples in 668 B.C. (*Tso-chuan chu* [Chuang 26], p. 223). Then, in 664 B.C., the Shan Jung attacked Yen, which at that point required and obtained the help of Duke Huan, who launched an expedition and in 663 B.C. came back with much booty. *Tso-chuan chu* (Chuang 30), pp. 246–47; (Chuang 31), p. 249.

[25] The Jung attack on the Chou capital is recorded, in the *Ch'un-ch'iu*, in the 11th year of Duke Hsi (i.e., 649 B.C.). In 644 B.C. the king informed Ch'i of the problems caused by the Jung, who must have infiltrated and settled on territories interposed between separate states. *Tso-chuan chu* (Hsi 11), p. 338.

[26] The *Ch'un-ch'iu* dates the Ti attack against the state of Wei to the year 639 B.C. (*Tso-chuan chu* [Hsi 21], p. 388). However, this development seems to have resulted from "Central Plain" interstate politics, since the previous year Ch'i had made a treaty with the Ti against Wei. As for the quotation from the *Shih ching*, which collates stanzas from separate poems, such phrases were cliché in Ssu-ma Ch'ien's age, as we find them quoted in a number of philosophical writings, such as Mencius.

the Chinese states had again gained the upper hand, and that various peoples of the north had been conquered. Others remained independent but were scattered, divided into small tribes, and could not be unified.

VII. Duke Mu of Ch'in [659–621 B.C.] obtained [the help of] Yu Yü and the eight states of the Western Jung submitted to Ch'in. These are the Mien-chu, Kun Jung, Ti, and Yüan, which were located to the west of Lung; and the Yi-ch'ü, Ta-li, Wu-chih and Ch'ü-yen, which were located to the north of the Ch'i and Liang Mountains, and Ching and Ch'i rivers. Moreover, to the north of Chin there were the Lin Hu and the Jung of Lou-fan. To the north of Yen there were the Tung Hu and the Shan Jung. These people were all living in their valleys, separated from each other, and each had a ruler. In every place they would not gather together more than a hundred warriors. Nobody had succeeded in unifying all of them.

The Hsiung-nu of the Ch'in and Han periods, however, had inaugurated a new cycle. The nomads had been unified, were extremely powerful, and once again were threatening China. What Ssu-ma Ch'ien was conveying was the existence of a pendular, or cyclical pattern in the alternation of power between north and south.

In conclusion, in tracing the ethnogenealogy of the Hsiung-nu back to the primordial stages of Chinese history, Ssu-ma Ch'ien drew not only a cultural but also a political line between the two camps. On the one side we find the Jung, Ti, and various other peoples; on the other, the Central States. From a historical viewpoint, as we have seen in Chapter 4, this demarcation line never existed because the political picture was extremely fluid, and alliances between Chinese states and alien peoples were common throughout the Eastern Chou. Although anachronistic (and consciously so), the representation of the Central States and northern peoples as opposite political realities served Ssu-ma Ch'ien's purpose of showing that a northern threat had faced China since the mythical beginning of its existence.

Inner Asia and Correlative Cosmology

In chapter 27 of the *Shih chi*, the "Treatise on the Heavenly Officials," for the first time in the history of Chinese cosmological thinking, the peoples of Inner Asia are made a part of that all-inclusive vision of the universe. Ssu-ma Ch'ien's incorporation of a much broader range of geographic and ethnographic data is accompanied by a corresponding expansion of the system of "anthropo-cosmic" correlations. Thus the northern nomads are placed in a system of astrological correlations that makes them "dependent" upon the movement of certain heavenly bodies.

The Hsiung-nu are first mentioned in connection with the constellations of the Western Palace, in particular the Pleiades. The "Heavenly Route" (*t'ien-chieh*) constellation is said to be the cosmic equivalent of the frontier lines that mark the boundary between the the Hsiung-nu and China. The nomadic countries of the north manifest the characteristics of the *yin* principle, whereas in the south there are those kingdoms that reveal the characteristics of the *yang* principle.

[The Lodge of] Mao[27] is called Mao-t'ou: this is the star of the Hu [i.e., the Hsiung-nu], and presides over funerary matters.[28] The Lodge of Pi[29] is called Han-ch'e, and symbolizes military engagements on the borders, it presides over hunting with bows and arrows. [...] Between the Lodges of Mao and Pi there is the T'ien-chieh [Heavenly Route] constellation; to the *yin* [northern] side of it there are the *yin* countries, to its *yang* [southern] side there are the *yang* countries [i.e., the Central States, China].[30]

The heavenly bodies corresponding to the Central States (in the *yang* region), were the Sun, Jupiter, Mars, and Saturn. These were located to the south of the Heavenly Route, and presided over by the Lodge of Pi. In contrast, the northwest was inhabited by the peoples whose clothes were made of felt and furs, and who used bows and arrows; this was the *yin* region, the female principle associated with coldness and darkness, whose corresponding planets were the Moon, Venus, and Mercury, located to the north of the Heavenly Route and presided over by the Lodge of Mao.

From this analogy, whereby the inhabitants of the western and northern lands – described as having the stereotypical attributes of nomadic peoples – are identified with the *yin* principle, and the Chinese are identified with the *yang* principle, we can also infer that, among all the foreigners that surrounded China, the northerners occupied a special position in such a dialectically construed China versus north polarity. Being the "*yin*" people, they occupied a position that was the anthropological and historical opposite to, and at the same time the complementary principle of, China's "civilization."

In *Shih chi*, chapter 27, the southern peoples of Yüeh, Shu, and Pa are also assigned certain astrological values, but Ssu-ma Ch'ien does not give to their position the same prominence as the northern nomads. The use of the basic correlational pattern to explain the significance of the northern

---

[27] One of the 28 Lunar Lodges, it is the fourth of the seven western lodges, and corresponds to the constellation of the Pleiades.

[28] Literally: "gatherings with white garments." White was the color for mourning.

[29] The Lodge of Pi corresponded to the constellation of the Hyades.

[30] *Shih chi* 27, 1305–1306; *Shih chi chu-yi* 27, 937 (E. Chavannes, *Les mémoires historiques de Se-ma Ts'ien*, 5 vols. [Paris: Ernest Leroux, 1895–1905], 3: 351–52).

nomads' relation to China is particularly evident in the historian's concluding remarks to chapter 27:

The Grand Historian says: From the time when people first came into existence, has there ever been a time when rulers of states have not observed the sun, the moon and the many stars and planets? Then, since the time of the Five Emperors and Three Dynasties, they have continued to keep records, and have clarified them. Inside there were those who wear caps and sashes; outside there were the Yi and Ti peoples. The Central States were divided into twelve regions. If we raise our heads, we observe phenomena in the sky, if we lower it, we take as models the many living beings on the earth. In the sky there are the sun and the moon, on the earth there are the *yin* and *yang* (principles). In the sky there are the Five Planets, on the earth there are the Five Phases. In the sky we have the different Lodges, on the earth regions and prefectures. The Brilliant Triad [i.e., the Sun, Moon and Stars] are the vital essence of the *yin* and *yang* (combination); the origin of this energy is on the earth; the wise man unites and harmonizes them.[31]

By fully integrating the Yi and the Ti at one end of the binary combinations that were thought to form the cosmic patterns of a dialectically conceived universe, Ssu-ma Ch'ien guaranteed these foreign peoples a perennial place within the cosmology and history of China.

Formulation of Prognostications Involving Northern Peoples

In the *Shih chi*, the correlation between heavenly bodies and foreign peoples found an application also in the area of astrological predictions. The movement of the planet Venus, which presided over war and conflicts, was thought to affect the relationship between the northern peoples and China. The movements and relative positions of the stars of the Northern Palace were also linked, on the human plane, to foreign wars and military expeditions, while the position of Venus in the sky was thought to influence the relative strength of the opposite armies, thus allowing prognostications to be made as to the likely outcome of a military encounter between the nomads and China.

When it [Venus] appears in the west and it is proceeding towards the east, this is auspicious for the western countries; if it appears in the east going west, this is a good omen for the eastern countries. If Venus appears in the west and misses its ordinary course, then the foreign countries will be defeated. If it appears in the east and loses its regular course, then China will be defeated. If it appears in the west at dusk on the *yin* [i.e., northern] side, then the *yin* [northern] soldiers will be strong. If it appears at the time of the evening

[31] *Shih chi* 27, 1343; *Shih chi chu-yi* 27, 954 (Chavannes, *Mém. hist.*, 3: 401).

meal, they will be a bit weaker. At midnight they will reach the point of medium weakness, and at day-break they will reach their maximum weakness; this is the time when it is said that the *yin* principle is subdued by the *yang*. If Venus appears in the east during the day on the *yang* side, then the *yang* soldiers shall be strong; if it appears at the chant of the rooster they will be a bit weaker; at midnight they reach the point of medium weakness, and dusk is the time of their maximum weakness; this is when it is said that the *yang* principle is subdued by the *yin*. If Venus is hidden [below the Equator line] and soldiers are sent out [on an expedition], the troops will meet with disaster. If it appears to the south of the Lodge of Mao,[32] then the South will vanquish the North. If it appears to the north of Mao then the North will vanquish the South; if it appears exactly in Mao, then the eastern countries will profit. If Venus appears to the north of *yu*,[33] the North will defeat the South; if it appears to the south of *yu*, the South will defeat the North; if it appears exactly in *yu*, then the western countries will be victorious.[34]

It is by no means surprising that Ssu-ma Ch'ien, in his capacity as astrologer, applied the principles of correlative cosmology to make historical agents part of universal patterns of interaction. Because correlative thought is based on the belief that celestial phenomena affect events on earth, knowledge about correspondences involving Inner Asia was also supposed to provide guidance in matters such as military campaigns against the foreigners. For instance, Mercury was the planet associated with the Man-Yi peoples – a generic literary term for foreigners that could include also the Hsiung-nu. In Ssu-ma Ch'ien's treatise the position of Mercury determined the course of the war between Chinese and foreign armies; according to it, soldiers were mobilized, advanced, or withdrawn, and battles were won or lost:[35]

When Mercury appears in the east, and it is large and white, if troops have been sent abroad, they should be recalled. If it remains constantly in the east, and its color is red, China will be victorious; if it appears in the west and its color is red, then the foreign countries will be victorious. If there are no troops abroad and it is red, then soldiers should be mobilized. If it appears in the east in conjunction with Venus, and they are both red and emit rays, foreign countries will suffer a great defeat, and China will win. If it appears in the east in conjunction with Venus, and they are both red and radiant, foreign countries will benefit. When the five planets stay in one half of the sky, and

[32] In the twelve branch system *mao* corresponds to the east.

[33] *Yu* is also one of the twelve branches, and represents the west.

[34] *Shih chi* 27, 1326; *Shih chi chu-yi* 27, 944–45 (Chavannes, *Mém. hist.*, 3: 377–78).

[35] For the association between Mercury and the Man-Yi, see *Shih chi* 27, 1330; *Shih chi chu-yi* 27, 947.

gather on the eastern side, China shall triumph; if they gather on the western side, foreign countries will gain the upper hand in war.[36]

In actual war situations, military commanders did not take much notice of these astrological matters, but it is possible that astrological criteria were observed when choosing an auspicious day to start a campaign or that they were invoked to justify the outcome of a given event.

Some of Ssu-ma Ch'ien's notions of correlations between heaven and earth show archaic elements of the mythical geography discussed earlier, such as the *fen-yeh* system of correlation between portions of the sky and corresponding regions on the earth. Ssu-ma Ch'ien expanded this system – which during the Eastern Chou included only the Chinese states – to encompass foreign areas, and in particular the lands of nomadic peoples, as can be seen in the following passage:

After Ch'in annexed the three states of Chin, Yen and Tai, all that extended to the south of the Yellow River and Han-shan became the Kingdom of the Middle, which is situated in the south-eastern part of [the land] within the Four Seas; this [region] belongs to the *yang* principle. The *yang* corresponds to the Sun, and to Jupiter, Mars and Saturn; prognostications are made when these [heavenly bodies] appear to the south of the T'ien-chieh [Heavenly Route] constellation. The Lodge of Pi presides over it. The north-western part [of the land within the Four Seas] is the region of the Hu, Mo, Yüeh-chih and of all other peoples who wear felt and furs and draw the bow; it belongs to the *yin* principle, which corresponds to the Moon, Venus and Mercury. Prognostications are made when these [heavenly bodies] appear to the north of the T'ien-chieh constellation; the Lodge of Mao presides over it. Therefore, the mountain chains and the rivers are orientated on a north-eastern gradient, and their system is such that their 'head' is located in the regions of Lung and Shu, and their tails enter Po-hai and Chieh-shih. Therefore, again making prognostications based on Venus [for the time when] Ch'in and Chin excelled in warfare, [we find that] Venus presided over the Central States. Conversely, if we take the time when the Hu and Mo made frequent incursions, and make prognostications based on Saturn, we find that Saturn appears and disappears in a restless and rapid manner, and often dominates [the actions of] foreign peoples. These are the general rules.[37]

The extension of those categories to new political and historical circumstances is also present in another passage referring to divination based on the shape of clouds:

The clouds that represent the northern peoples are similar to herds of animals and tents; the clouds that represent the southern foreigners have the shape of boats and square sails.[38]

[36] *Shih chi* 27, 1328; *Shih chi chu-yi* 27, 946 (Chavannes, *Mém. hist.*, 3: 380–81).
[37] *Shih chi* 27, 1347; *Shih chi chu-yi* 27, 956 (Chavannes, *Mém. hist.*, 3: 405–406).
[38] *Shih chi* 27, 1338; *Shih chi chu-yi* 27, 951 (Chavannes, *Mém. hist.*, 3: 395).

To the best of my knowledge, there is no evidence that northern peoples (and foreign peoples in general) were the subject of "meteorological fore-casting" of the type just quoted in any of the works that Ssu-ma Ch'ien may have used as sources for chapter 27, although the observation of the clouds as a means of prediction was known before Ssu-ma Ch'ien. However, one of the Warring States astrological manuscripts excavated at Ma-wang-tui clearly shows that clouds were associated with a historical "space" that did not include foreign peoples. In this particular source analogies are estab-lished with Chinese states such as Chao, Han, and Wei, and predictions, such as the one relative to the battle between Wu and Ch'u, remain con-fined to the wars among Chinese states.[39]

In the *Tso-chuan*, the appearance of comets is also used to formulate political predictions, but these predictions are strictly limited to the Chinese geographical and political sphere.[40] Although we cannot exclude the possi-bility that texts now lost may have already applied astrological forecasting to foreign peoples, at the present state of research, it appears that Ssu-ma Ch'ien was the first astrologer to have crossed the boundaries of the Chinese political and cultural sphere to include the non-Chinese, and the northern nomads in particular, in the correlative cosmological apparatus.

Besides the essential shift to the inclusion of foreigners within the system of astral correspondences, Ssu-ma Ch'ien also presents specific cases of prognostications related to Inner Asia, linked with astronomical and natural phenomena. Although rare, these occurrences make it clear that the histo-rian employs the "prescriptive" approach to Inner Asia to explain or justify certain events. In this way, the defeats and the victories that had dotted the history of the relations between China and Inner Asia since the foundation of the empire, and in particular the extensive campaigns launched by Han Wu-ti, could be reported by the historian in terms that were acceptable to the intellectual elite of his age. The following passages are representative of this method.

The first summarizes the relationship between China and Inner Asia from the time of Ch'in Shih-huang-ti to the Han conquest of Ferghana:

At the time of Ch'in Shih Huang in fifteen years there were four sightings of comets; the longest lasted eighty days, and it was so long that it appeared across the entire length of the sky. After that, by force of arms, Ch'in destroyed the six kings and unified the central states, and abroad expelled the four foreign nations. [. . .] When the Han rose to power the Five Planets appeared in conjunction in the Lodge of Tung-ching. At the time when Han Kao-tsu was surrounded (by the Hsiung-nu) at P'ing-ch'eng, a lunar halo

---

[39] Ku, T'ien-fu. "A Summary of the Contents of the Ma-wang-tui Silk-Scroll Book 'Assorted Astronomical and Meteorological Prognostications,'" *Chinese Studies in Archaeology*, 1 (1979): 61–62.

[40] *Tso-chuan* (Chao 17), p. 1390 (Legge, *The Ch'un Ts'ew*, p. 668).

enveloped the Lodges of Shen and Pi in seven layers. [. . .] During the *yüan-kuang* (134–129 B.C.) and the *yüan-shou* (122–117 B.C.) reign periods [of Han Wu-ti], the Banner of Ch'ih-yu appeared twice; it was so large as to cover half of the sky. After this the imperial armies were sent out four times, punitive expeditions against Yi and Ti lasted many years, and the wars against the Hsiung-nu were very fierce. At the time of the demise of the state of Yüeh (112 B.C.) Mars had entered the Dipper; when Ch'ao-hsien was subjugated (109 B.C.) a comet appeared on the defensive line along the Yellow River. When our armies conquered Ta-yüan (104–101 B.C.) a comet appeared in Chao-yao. These were all clearly visible great celestial phenomena.[41]

The next passage refers to the perceived relationship between Wen-ti's disregard of his duties, and the occurrence of new disturbances with the Hsiung-nu. Evidently Ssu-ma Ch'ien interpreted the Hsiung-nu invasion as a consequence of a series of events whose connection was not logical, but ideological. It was Wen-ti's neglectful behavior toward the proper conduct of rites that created a disruption in the order of things that then "caused" the event. The relationship between "cause" and "effect" is established by mentioning the two facts next to each other, but the event of the Hsiung-nu invasion is not meant as a "historical record" per se, but as evidence of the incorrect behavior of the emperor, a line of reasoning based on the Confucian dogma of the proper handling of rites.

From this point on [i.e., after the execution of Hsin-yüan P'ing], Emperor Wen neglected matters concerning changing the calendar system and the color of garments, and making sacrifices to the spirits. He sent sacrificial officials to administer [the temples and the altars of] the Five Emperors at Wei-yang and Ch'ang-men, and to perform the rites on prescribed occasions, but he himself did not go.[42] The following year, the Hsiung-nu invaded the borders several times, and troops were mobilized for garrison and defense duties. In the last years [of his reign] the harvest was often poor.[43]

A "classic" example of association between a historical event and the observation of a heavenly "anomaly" is the following:

On the day *hsin-hai* of the seventh month [of the year 144 B.C.] there was an eclipse of the sun. In the eighth month the Hsiung-nu invaded Shang prefecture.[44]

---

[41] *Shih chi* 27, 1348–49; *Shih chi chu-yi* 27, 957 (Chavannes, *Mém. hist.*, 3: 407–408).

[42] The term for "sacrificial officials" is *tz'u kuan*. I assume it refers to the *tz'u-ssu* officials. See Charles Hucker, *A Dictionary of Official Titles in Imperial China* (Stanford: Stanford University Press, 1985), n. 7570.

[43] *Shih chi* 28, 1383–84; *Shih chi chu-yi* 28, 988 (Chavannes, *Mém. hist.*, 3: 461).

[44] *Shih chi* 11, 446; *Shih chi chu-yi* 11, 278.

Here the linkage between the eclipse and the Hsiung-nu invasion is rendered by the proximity between two sentences, which implies a correlation between "warning" and event.

The last example shows a relationship, again by appositional association of two sentences, between the Chinese invasion of the Ferghana region, in Central Asia, and a plague of locusts:

In the same year [104 B.C., the Han] attacked Ta-yüan [Ferghana] in the West. Many locusts appeared. Ting Fu-jen and Yü Ch'u of Lo-yang put a curse on the Hsiung-nu and Ta-yüan using shamanistic rituals.[45]

A possible interpretation of this passage is that the anomalous natural phenomenon of the locusts was regarded as a consequence of the Han offensive against the Western Regions, which may have been regarded by Ssu-ma Ch'ien as "wrong" and likely to cause a natural disturbance. However, it is also possible that the association was meant to imply that the Hsiung-nu and the people of Ta-yüan used magic arts to conjure up a plague against the Han and that the two *fang-shih* were used to neutralize it.[46] Moreover, the curse may have just been an extra "aid" to the Chinese expeditionary forces that was intended to weaken the enemy at a time when the Han were facing unexpected difficulties. We should also note that these events are told immediately after the recording of the crucial event of the adoption of a new calendar, in 104 B.C., and that all four events – the new calendar, the military expeditions, the locusts, and the curse – may be related in some way. Whatever the key to the comprehension of this passage, a linkage between a natural event and a historical one that was taking place outside China's borders shows that correlations between the human and the "natural" spheres had been extended to Inner Asia.

[45] *Shih chi* 28, 1402; *Shih chi chu-yi* 28, 1001 (Chavannes, *Mém. hist.*, 3: 515).
[46] On the *fang-shih* see B. I. Schwartz, *The World of Thought in Ancient China* (Cambridge Mass.: Belknap Press, 1985), pp. 375–78.

Conclusion

In this book I have aimed to establish a basis for the study of the early relations between China and Inner Asia. Looking for a beginning often means approaching the goal from multiple avenues. Hence, I have examined the archaeological record, which can yield information lost to the written sources; the textual materials, which required placing the information provided by them in their historical contexts; and the ancient historians' methods and intentions, which can enlighten us of the intellectual and historical background of historiography. In my conclusions, even when presented as partial critiques of earlier theories, I have tried primarily to offer interpretations that are consistent with the evidence not only internal to a single set of sources but also drawn from multiple sources.

Yet the subject of this book is crossed by too many open questions, and thus arguments can be only offered tentatively; there is no doubt that much will need to be corrected as more materials and new interpretations become available. Archaeology is the area in which most of these advances may be expected in the short term, for the materials already accumulated are vast (and growing daily) and new archaeological projects are being negotiated and carried out as we write. Moreover, the study of historiography in China is far from obsolete; finally, texts excavated from ancient graves are adding new dimensions to our knowledge of the early history of China, and of its social and intellectual life.

The picture of the early history of the relations between China and Inner Asia that I have presented is a composite formed by four related and yet relatively independent narratives, each of which not only corresponds to a distinct "phase" in a historical process of change of the frontier but also presents a special quality determined by the particular sources and problems that we must consider. These four narratives are not fully compatible, and seeking to present a single "master narrative" would have forced such over- and underinterpretations of the sources that it would eventually have presented a dramatically impoverished picture of an otherwise truly complex phenomenon. To preserve that complexity, the four "narratives" have been kept to a certain extent separate and independent.

The first "instantiation" of a recognizable frontier between China and the north can de detected in the earliest archaeological records since we see, already in the second millennium B.C., that people inhabiting the "north" begin to develop their own cultural norms, social structures, and religious beliefs. Yet this early frontier cannot be represented as one between a "Sinitic" sphere and a northern, more or less uniform, cultural block. This block must be broken down into separate focuses of political and economic activity and into discrete cultural areas. This frontier, moreover, did not appear in isolation. Indeed, its emergence is a function of the permeability of the north to multiple external influences and of its own internal dynamism. Finally, relations between northern peoples and the core areas of Chinese civilization do not occur with the same intensity at all times and places. Further research will be needed to identify the factors that most influenced the relationship, and the lines along which it developed.

The second "frontier" I endeavored to analyze is one that tends to separate China (the Chou community) from the world outside by means of a cultural barrier. The image of a "civilized" world pitched against a barbaric wilderness is, however, only a partial, and an ideologically loaded, interpretation of the relations between China and the north, which, as several scholars have noted, does not exhaust the range of relations between Chinese and northern peoples. In reality, these "cultural" statements, if analyzed in their contexts, reflect some important elements constitutive of the Chinese political realities in the Spring and Autumn period. In particular, as we have seen, they can be interpreted as an expression of the Chou states' expansionist strategies and search for new resources. This is, then, a frontier determined to a large extent by the ebullient politics of the Eastern Chou period. Of what was happening on the Inner Asian side, however, little is known. What we can detect is limited to the existence of scattered polities, some of them possibly quite large and powerful, which in the long run could not sustain the competition with the stronger Chinese states and, one after the other, succumbed to and were incorporated by the growing Central Plain states. This frontier cannot be recognized as one dictated by ecological conditions or deeply different lifestyles. Differences among the Hua-Hsia peoples, Jung, Ti, and Yi surely existed, but similar cultural distinctions also existed among Chinese states, and, as the example of the culturally "sinicized" Chung-shan state proves, cultural gaps could be filled even though a community retained a foreign "ethnic" name. This political frontier reached its maximum northward expansion at the end of the Warring States period, with the construction of the northern "walls." Although they represent the maximum expansion of Chinese power before the unification of China, they are also the first step towards the creation of a much "harder" frontier, which will emerge with the encounter between "true nomads" and Chinese, in the third century B.C.

The third "frontier" is the frontier of treaties and tributes, diplomatic correspondence, and bridal exchange between the two "superpowers" of the age: the Hsiung-nu, who had unified the nomadic tribes, and the Han dynasty, ruling over a unified China. Whereas the previous "narrative" was, in the last instance, created by Chinese politics as a spin-off of interstate relations, this frontier "narrative" assigns to Inner Asia a much more central role. The transformation of frontier relations that followed the appearance of the Hsiung-nu empire should not be seen as yet another (more virulent) example of the age-long competition between the nomadic north and the sedentary south. Instead, the dynamics that led to the formation of a unified nomadic confederacy are examined from a perspective that takes into account other instances of state formation in an Inner Asian context. This analysis indicates that the probable cause for the emergence of a statelike structure lay in a political mechanism already in existence within the tribal society of the nomads, which allowed for the centralization of political and military power at times of crisis. This mechanism of social survival was "triggered" by the growing threat posed to the Hsiung-nu by the Ch'in invasion of the Ordos territories. The initial impetus of the unification, however, was directed not against China but against other nomads, who were defeated and assimilated, or allowed to join. As the frontier started to be defined in territorial and political terms as a boundary between Hsiung-nu and China, frontier relations started to be regulated through court-to-court correspondence, diplomatic missions, and exchanges of tribute. Trade relations were also subject to stricter supervision, and their implementation carried out according to international agreements. The frontier, therefore, marked the limits of the political influence of the two states. If this frontier in part coincided with an ecological boundary between a predominantly steppic zone and a predominantly agricultural zone, this is because the nomads had recovered previously lost pastureland and, secondarily, because their raids into Chinese territory did not take the shape of migrations: the Hsiung-nu, who cannot have been originally a very numerous people, preferred to expand to the west and to the north, in territories with which they had possibly had contacts for a long period of time. When the Chinese counterattacked during the time of Wu-ti, that ecological boundary was once again violated as the Han troops pushed the borders of the dynasty far beyond the traditional extension of China.

Finally, the fourth "frontier" is the one created by the historian himself, Ssu-ma Ch'ien. Two elements contributed to the appearance of the "master narrative" of the north that to this day, partly consciously, partly unconsciously, informs our knowledge and conceptualization of the frontier: the great expansion of historical knowledge collected and transmitted by

Ssu-ma Ch'ien, and the particular frame in which he inserted it. The detailed descriptions of the Hsiung-nu makes them come alive, with their horses and animals, bows and arrows, simple laws and martial ardor. These are the ancient nomads as we know them, and this is the history that needs to be constantly tapped to study not only the early but also the later relations between China and the nomads. But Ssu-ma Ch'ien also strove to insert the nomads in a general frame of history that finally placed the northern peoples in a position central to historical knowledge as was understood then, that is, as part of a larger order of cosmic and human actions mutually influencing each other. This last narrative gives to the history of the northern frontier independent status as an object of investigation, but at the same time it places the north in a position whose only referent is China: the history of the nomads came into existence, as it were, because it was relevant to China. This polarity has within itself the power to generate a false causal relationship, namely, that not only Ssu-ma Ch'ien's narrative, but also very the history of the Hsiung-nu, and perhaps of the nomads, came into existence as a product of the timeless frontier relationship between nomads and China. Without denying that the frontier was a place vibrant with exchanges and mutual stimuli, we need to recognize that Ssu-ma Ch'ien's narrative "interprets" history according to his own age's beliefs and his own intent, and therefore we need to approach it critically. This is not a simple task, because virtually all we know about the rise of the Hsiung-nu and the transformation of the frontier in the Ch'in-Han transition derives, in a historical sense, from the *Shih chi*, as does the model itself of a monograph on the Hsiung-nu. In the last part of my book I introduced the distinction between the descriptive and the normative aspects of Hsiung-nu history as a first attempt to use this source critically and to identify its different strands.

In sum, this book, by seeking to identify processes that appear to be beneath and behind the creation of historical paradigms – be they ideological, ethical, or "cosmological" – endorses a perspective that is consciously directed toward the acquisition, first of all, of a better understanding of ancient Inner Asian history. Naturally, this affects deeply also our understanding of Chinese history, as the two are intimately related, but while the depths of China's complex early history have been plumbed for some time (and continue to be plumbed at an extraordinary rate), Inner Asian history is still virgin territory.

At present, research carried out on Inner Asian topics, for example, on the origin of pastoral nomadism, on the development of trade, or the "rise and fall" of northern cultures, is based on a perspective very often subordinated to the history of China. Thus the development of intensive agriculture and state institutions in the Central Plain are often held to be the main stimulus to social and economic developments identifiable in the north, at least from the point in time in which the Chinese civilization emerged as the dominating cultural force in East Asia. There is no denying that the Shang and Chou civilizations had contacts with the north, and surely a dialectical relationship was established, as we have seen, early on. But surely too these relations were subject to variations in time, space, and intensity; moreover, they cannot be regarded as "exclusive" as northern peoples had also contacts among themselves (the archaeological record is explicit about this) and with other cultures elsewhere in Asia. The full realization of the complexity of China's northern "history" should generate questions that would take account of dynamics of cultural and social developments that cannot be assumed to have been derivative or secondary.

Finally, the Inner Asian perspective also allows us to question traditional interpretations of Chinese history. In this book I have re-examined, for instance, the question of the origin of the Great Wall. The conclusion I have reached is at odds with the standard narrative of a wall that was protecting China against barbarous invaders but possibly is closer to a historical analysis that does not take the timeless opposition between the martial north and the civilized south as an obligatory blueprint. Clearly, a reconceptualization of Inner Asian history needs to account for both the advantages and the limitations that Chinese sources present and try to eschew as much as possible those positions that would excessively subordinate the historical narrative to the frame of reference provided by the Chinese sources.

Glossary

A

A-ha-t'e-la 阿哈特拉
A-lu-ch'ai-teng 阿魯柴登
An-yang 安陽
Ao-han 敖漢

C

Ch'a-wu-hu-kou 察吾乎溝
Chan-kuo Ts'e 戰國策
Chan-tou 戰斗
ch'an-yü (shan-yü) 單于
Ch'ang (Earl of the West) 昌
ch'ang ch'eng 長城
Chang Ch'ien 張騫
Chang Wu 張武
ch'ang yüan 長垣
Ch'ang-an 長安
Ch'ang-men 長門
Ch'ang-p'ing (county) 昌平
Chang-yi (commandery) 張掖
ch'ao (court visit) 朝
Chao (state) 趙
Chao Li 趙利
Chao P'o-nu 趙破奴
Ch'ao Ts'o 晁錯
Chao-hsin 趙信
Ch'ao-hsien 朝鮮
Ch'ao-tao-kou 抄道溝
Ch'ao-yang 朝陽

Chao-yao 招搖
Ch'en (state) 陳
Ch'en Hsi 陳豨
Cheng (state) 鄭
ch'eng (assistant) 丞
Cheng-chia-wa-tzu 鄭家窪子
ch'eng-li 撐犁
Ch'eng Pu-chih 程不識
ch'eng yi chia chih yen 成一家之言
Ch'eng-yüeh 成樂
chi (crisis) 急
chi 畿 of *fu* 服
chi (heavenly stem) 己
chi ch'i ch'eng-pai hsing-huai chih li 稽其成敗興壞之理
ch'i t'ien-hsing yeh 其天性也
Ch'i (state) 齊
Ch'i (Mt.) 岐
Ch'i-chia 齊家
Ch'i-lao-t'u (Mountains) 七老圖
Ch'i-lien (Mountains) 祁連
Chi-men 棘門
Chi-ning 集寧
ch'ien-jen 千人
Ch'ih 赤 Ti
Ch'ih-feng 赤峰
Ch'ih-yu (astronomical term) 蚩尤
Chia Yi 賈誼
chia-tou 夾兜
Chiang 姜
Ch'iang 羌
Chiang Jung 姜戎
Chiang-kao-ju 廥咎如
Chiao-huo 焦穫
Chieh-shih 碣石
Chin (state) 晉
Ch'in (state) 秦
Ch'in K'ai 秦開
chin Jung chih chih 今戎制之
Chin Mi-ti 金日磾
Ch'in Shih Huang-ti 秦始皇帝
Ch'in-an 秦安
Ch'in-wei-chia 秦魏家
Chin-yang 晉陽
Ching (river) 涇
Ch'ing Ying 青蠅
Ch'ing-chien (county) 清澗
ch'ing-chü chiang-chün 輕車將軍

320

ching-lu 徑路
Ch'ing-lung 青龍
Ching-pien 靖邊
Ching-ti (Han emperor) 景帝
Ch'ing-yang 慶陽
chiu chi (nine zones) 九畿
chiu chou (nine continents) 九州
chiu t'ien jen chih chi 究天人之際
Chiu-ch'üan (commandery) 酒泉
chiu-yi ling 九譯令
Chiu-yüan 九原
ch'iung-lu 穹盧
chou 州
Chou li 周禮
Chou She 周舍
Chou Ya-fu 周亞夫
Chou-chia-ti 周家地
Ch'u (state) 楚
chü hu 拒胡
chu jung 諸戎
chü-ch'i chiang-chün 車騎將軍
Chu-chia-yü 褚家峪
ch'u-chiao shih 觸角式
chü-ch'ü (Hsiung-nu title) 且渠
Chu-fu Yen 主父偃
chu-hou-wang 諸侯王
Chu-k'ai-kou 朱開溝
Chu-na 朝那
Chü-shih 車師
Chu-shu chi-nien 竹書紀年
Ch'ü-wu 曲沃
Chü-yen 居延
Ch'ü-yen 朐衍
Chü-yang 沮陽
Ch'ü-yi 屈射
Ch'üan Jung 犬戎
Chuan-ch'ang 磚廠
Ch'üan-yi 畎夷
chüeh 爵
chüeh (vessel) 鼎
chüeh-t'i 駃騠
Ch'un Ch'iu 春秋
chün-ch'en (Hsiung-nu title) 軍臣
Ch'ün-pa-k'e 群巴克
Chün-tu-shan 軍都山
Chung 種
Chung-erh 重耳

Chung-hang Yüeh 中行説
Chung-kuo 中國
Chung-ning 中寧
Chung-shan 中山
Chuo-tzu 卓資

D

Duke Huan 桓 of Ch'i
Duke Hsien 獻 of Chin
Duke Hui 惠 of Chin
Duke K'ang 康 of Liu 劉
Duke Li 厘 of Ch'i 齊
Duke Mou-fu 謀父 of Chai 祭
Duke Mu 穆〔繆〕of Ch'in
Duke Wen 文 of Chin

E

E-chi-na 額濟納
Emperor Mu 穆
Erh-ch'ü 二屈
Erh-k'o-ch'ien 二克淺
Erh-li-kang 二里崗
Erh-li-t'ou 二里頭
Erh-shih 貳師 general
erh-shih-ssu ta ch'en 二十四大臣

F

fa (law) 法
fan 藩蕃
Fan Hsüan-tzu 范宣子
Fan K'uai 樊噲
Fan-chia-yao-tzu 范家窯子
fang 防
Fang Shu 方叔
fang-shih 方士
Fei 肥
Fei-hu Pass 飛狐
Fen (river) 汾
fen-wen 幀輻
fen-yeh 分野
feng (sacrifice) 封
Feng (region) 鄷
Feng Shu 鄷舒
fu (zone) 服
Fu Ch'en 富辰
Fu Hao 婦好

Fu-hsin 阜新
Fu-li 符離
Fu-shih 膚施

H

Ha-ma-tun 蛤蟆墩
Han An-kuo 韓安國
Han Fei-tzu 韓非子
Han Wu-ti 漢武帝
han-ch'e (astronomical term) 罕車
Han-shu (culture) 漢書
Hann (state) 韓
Hann Wang Hsin 韓王信
Hao 鄗
Heng-shan 恒山
Ho Yi 和夷
Ho-ch'i 合騎 marquis Kung-sun Ao
ho-ch'in 和親
Ho-hsi 河西
Ho-lin-ko-erh 和林格爾
Ho-t'ao (commandery) 河套
hou (captain) 侯
Hou Ying 侯應
Hou-chia-chuang 侯家莊
Hou-yi-lu 後義盧 Marquis Nan-chih 難支
Hsi-ch'a-kou 西岔溝
Hsi-feng 西豐
Hsi-kou-p'an 西溝畔
Hsi-liu 細柳
Hsi-yang 昔陽
hsi-yü 西域
hsi-yü tu-hu 西域都護
Hsia (dynasty) 夏
Hsia-chia-tien (culture) 夏家店
Hsia-yang (city) 下陽
Hsiang-p'ing 襄平
Hsiang-tzu 襄子 of Chao
Hsiao Wang-chih 蕭望之
hsiao-ch'i chiang-chün 驍騎將軍
Hsiao-t'un 小屯
Hsien-lei 舷雷
Hsien-yü 鮮虞
Hsien-yün 獫狁
Hsin-ch'in-chung 新秦中
hsin-hai 辛亥
Hsin-li 薪犁
Hsin-tien 辛店

Hsin-yüan P'ing　新垣平
hsing (phase)　行
Hsing (state)　刑
Hsing-ho　興和
hsiu-t'u (Hsiung-nu title)　休屠
Hsiung-nu　匈奴
Hsü Tzu-wei　徐自為
Hsü Jung　徐戎
Hsü-pu (Hsiung-nu clan)　須卜
Hsü-wu　徐吾 tribe (*shih*　氏)
Hsüan　宣 (Queen Dowager of Ch'in)
Hsüan-ti (Han emperor)　宣帝
Hsün Wu　荀吾
Hsün-tzu　荀子
Hsün-yü　獯粥
Hu Chi　狐姬
hu Ch'iang hsiao-wei　護羌校尉
hu Wu-huan hsiao-wei　護烏桓校尉
Hu-chieh　呼揭
Hu-han-yeh (Hsiung-nu chief)　呼韓邪
Hu-lu-ssu-t'ai　呼魯斯太
Hu-Mo　胡貉
Hu-shen-ha-pao T'ai-shan　虎什哈炮台山
Hu-yen (Hsiung-nu clan)　呼衍
Hu-yen-t'i (Hsiung-nu ruler)　壺衍鞮
Hua-Hsia　華夏
Huai-lai　懷來
Huai-nan-tzu　淮南子
Huan K'uan　桓寬
huang　荒
Huang Wen-pi　黃文弼
Huang-niang-niang-t'ai　皇娘娘台
huang-ti　皇帝
hui (gathering)　會
Hui-mo　穢貉
Hun-mi　葷彌
Hun-yeh　渾邪
Hun-yü　渾庾
Huo Ch'ü-ping　霍去病
Huo-shao-kou　火燒溝

J

Jen An　任安
Jung　戎
jung ch'e　戎車

K

K'a-yüeh 卡約
Kan Fu 甘父
Kan-ch'üan 甘泉
k'ao chih hsing shih 考之行事
Kao-ch'üeh (commandery) 高闕
Kao-hung 高紅
Kao-nu 高奴
Kao-t'ai 高臺
Kao-tsu (Han emperor) 高祖
Ken-mou 根牟
King Chao 昭 of Ch'in
King Chao 昭 of Yen
King Chao-hsiang 昭襄 of Ch'in
King Chien 簡 of Chou
King Hsi 喜 of Yen
King Hsin 信 of Hann 韓
King Hsiang 襄 of Chou
King Hsüan 宣
King Hsüan 宣 of Ch'i 齊
King Hui 惠
King Li 厲
King of Po-yang 白羊
King of Tai 代
King P'ing 平 of Chou
King Wei-lieh 威烈
King Wen 文 of Chou
King Wu Ting (Shang) 武丁
King Yi 夷
King Yu 幽 of Chou
ko 戈
Ko-k'un 鬲昆
K'o-yin-chieh 克殷解
Kou-chu (Mount) 句注
k'ou-fu 口賦
k'u 庫
Ku (city) 鼓
Ku Chieh-kang 顧頡剛
Ku-liang 古浪
Ku-liang 穀梁
Ku-shih 姑師
Ku-tu (Hsiung-nu title) 骨都
Ku-yen (Mount) 姑衍
Ku-yüan (county) 固原
kuan (pot) 罐
kuan tu-wei 關都尉

Kuan Chung 管仲
Kuan Ying 灌嬰, Marquis of Ying-yin 陰潁
Kuan-tung (place) 關東
kuei (demons) 鬼
Kuei (river) 媯
Kuei-fang 鬼方
Kun Jung 緄戎
K'un-lun 昆侖
K'un-yi 昆夷
kung (musical note) 宮
Kung Yu 恭友
Kung Liu 公劉
Kung-sun Ho 公孫賀
Kung-sun Ao 公孫敖
Kung-tzu Ch'eng 公子成
Kung-yang 公羊
Kuo (state) 虢
Kuo Ch'ang 郭昌
Kuo Kung 虢公
Kuo Yi 虢射
Kuo-hsien-yao-tzu 崞縣窰子
Kuo-lang (city) 郭狼
Kuo-yü 國語

L

Lai-shui 淶水
Lan (Hsiung-nu clan) 蘭
Lang (Mount) 狼
Lang-chü-hsü (Mount) 狼居胥
lang-chung 郎中
li (mile) 里
li (propriety) 禮
li (tripod) 鬲
li (pattern) 理
Li Jung 驪戎
Li Chi 驪姬
Li K'o 里克
Li Kuang 李廣
Li Kuang-li 李廣利
Li Ling 李陵
Li Mu 李牧
Li Ssu 李斯
Li-chi 禮記
Li-chia-ya 李家崖
Liang Ch'i-ch'ao 梁啓超
Liang-ch'eng 涼城
Liang-p'ing 梁平

Liang-wu 梁五
Liang-yü Mi 梁由靡
Liao-hsi (commandery) 遼西
Liao-tung (commandery) 遼東
Lin (city) 藺
Lin Hu 林胡
Lin Lü-chih 林旅芝
Lin Kan 林幹
Lin-che-yü 林遮峪
Lin-hsi 林西
Lin-t'ao 臨洮
Ling Mien 令勉
Liu Pang 劉邦
Liu Li 劉禮
Liu yüeh 六月
Liu Ching 劉敬
Liu-lin 柳林
lo 酪
Lo 雒
Lo (river) 洛
Lo-yang 洛陽
Lo-yi (city) 雒邑
Lou-fan 樓煩
Lou-lan 樓蘭
Lu (state) 魯
Lu Po-te 路博德
Lu Wan 盧綰
Lu (chiefdom) 潞
Lü Hou (Han Empress Dowager) 呂後
Lu-ch'ü (Mount) 盧朐
Lu-fu 祿福
Lu-hun 陸渾
Lu-li king (Hsiung-nu title) 谷蠡
Lü-shih ch'un-ch'iu 呂氏春秋
Lu-t'u king (Hsiung-nu title) 盧屠
luan (bells) 鑾
Luan (river) 灤
Lun-t'ai 輪台
Lung (region) 隴
Lung-ch'eng 籠城
Lung-hsi (commandery) 隴西
Lung-men 龍門

M

Ma Ch'ang-shou 馬長壽
Ma-chia-yao 馬家窯
Ma-wang-tui 馬王堆

Ma-yi 馬邑
Man 蠻
Man-Mo 蠻貉
Mao (Lunar Lodge) 昴
Mao Jung 茅戎
Mao-ch'ing-kou 毛慶溝
Mao-t'ou (atronomical term) 髦頭
Marquis of Sung-tzu 松茲侯
meng (covenant) 盟
Meng T'ien 蒙恬
Meng Wen-t'ung 蒙文通
mi-li 宋亂
Mi-yün 密雲
Mien 綿
Mien-chu 綿諸
Min-ch'in 民勤
Min-hsien 岷縣
Mo 貉
Modun (Mao-tun) 冒頓
Mu T'ien tzu chuan 穆天子傳

N

Na-lin-kao-t'u 納林高兔
nan (baron) 男
Nan-shan-ken 南山根
Nieh Weng-yi 聶翁壹
Ning-ch'eng 寧城
No-mu-hung 諾木洪
nung tu-wei 農都尉

P

Pa 巴
Pa-shang 霸上
Pai 白 Ti
Pai-chin-pao 白金寶
Pai-fu 白浮
Pai-teng 白登
pan (basin) 盤
Pan Ku 班固
Pao (river) 薄
Pao-chang-shih 保章氏
Pao-t'ou 包頭
Pao-te 保德
pei chou 北州
Pei Yi 北夷
Pei-chia 北假
pei-fang ti-ch'ü 北方地區

Pei-hsin-pao 北辛堡
Pei-ti (commandery) 北地
pen-chi 本記
P'eng-p'u 彭堡
Pi (Lunar Lodge) 畢
pien 變
pien-sai 邊塞
Pin (city) 豳
ping 兵
P'ing-ch'eng 平城
P'ing-ch'üan 平泉
P'ing-shan 平山
P'ing-yang (culture) 平洋
P'ing-yang 平陽
Po-hai 渤海
Po-tsung 伯宗
Prince Tan 丹 of Yen
P'u 蒲
pu mu chih min 不牧之民
P'u-ni 浦尼
Pu-tung-kou 補洞溝

S

San-chia-tzu 三家子
San-chiao-ch'eng 三角城
Sha-ching 沙井
Sha-ching-ts'un 沙井村
shan (sacrifice) 禪
Shan Jung 山戎
Shan hai ching 山海經
Shan-hai-kuan 山海關
Shan-tan (county) 山丹
shang (chief) 上
Shang (commandery) 上
Shang-ku (commandery) 上谷
Shang-sun 上孫
Shang-tang 上黨
Shen (Lunar Lodge) 參
Shen Nung 神農
Shen-mu 沈目
Shi-erh-t'ai-ying-tzu 十二台營子
shih (circumstances) 勢
shih (historian) 史
shih (lineage) 氏
shih (to serve) 事
Shih (city) 石
Shih Nien-hai 史念海

Shih ching 詩經
Shih-erh-lien-ch'eng 十二連城
Shih-hui-kou 石灰溝
Shih-la-ts'un 石喇村
Shih-lou 石樓
Shou-hsiang-ch'eng 受降城
Shu 蜀
Shu ching 書經
shu-kuo 屬國
shu-kuo tu-wei 屬國都尉
Shu-le (river) 疏勒
Shui-chien-kou-men 水澗溝門
Shun 舜 (Yü 虞)
Shun-wei 淳維
Shuo-fang (commandery) 朔方
Shuo-yüan 説苑
ssu yi 四夷
Ssu-pa (culture) 四壩
Ssu-ma Ch'ien 司馬遷
Ssu-ma T'an 司馬談
Ssu-wa (culture) 寺洼
su 酥
Su Chien 蘇建
Su Yi 蘇意, Chancellor of Ch'u 楚
Su Ping-ch'i 蘇秉琦
Su-chi-kou 速機溝
sui 綏
Sun Ang 孫卬
Sung (state) 宋

T

ta ch'en 大臣
Ta ssu-ma 大司馬
Ta hsing-ren 大行人
Ta-ch'ing (Mountain) 大青
Ta-ching 大井
ta-chung ta-fu 大中太夫
Ta-he-chuang 大何莊
Ta-hei (river) 大黑
Ta-hsia (Bactria) 大夏
Ta-li 大荔
Ta-ling (river) 大凌
Ta-p'ao-tzu 大泡子
ta-shu-chang (title) 大庶長
Ta-ssu-k'ung (site) 大司空
ta-tang-hu (Hsiung-nu title) 大當戶

Ta-yüan 大宛
Tai (commandery) 代
Tai (name) 帶
tai lin 帶林
T'ai-hang 太行
T'ai-lai 泰來
t'ai-p'u 太仆
T'ai-shih-ling 太史令
t'ai-shou 太守
T'ai-yüan (commandery) 太原
Tan-fu 亶父
Tao Yi 島夷
T'ao-hung-pa-la 桃紅巴拉
t'ao-t'u 騊駼
Tao-tun-tzu 倒墩子
te 德
t'i-hu 醍醐
ti-li chih 地理志
Ti-tao 狄道
T'ieh-chiang-kou 鐵匠溝
tien 甸
T'ien 天
T'ien Tan 田單
T'ien-chieh 天街
t'ien-hsia 天下
T'ien-shan 天山
tien-shu-kuo 典屬國
tien(t'o)-t'i 驒騱
t'ien-tsu 田卒
T'ien-yen (Mountains) 闐顏
t'ien-wen 天文
ting (vessel) 鼎
Ting Fu-jen 丁夫人
Ting-hsiang (commandery) 定襄
Ting-ling 丁零
T'o-k'e-t'o 托克托
T'ou-man (Tumen) 頭曼
Ts'ai (state) 蔡
Ts'ai ch'i 采芑
ts'ai-kuan chiang-chün 材官將軍
Ts'ai-sang 采桑
ts'ang 倉
Tsao-yang 造陽
Tso-chuan 作傳
tso-ts'e (maker of bamboo books) 作冊
T'u-ch'i (Hsiung-nu title) 屠耆
T'u-chüeh 突厥

tu-wei 都尉
Tun-huang (commandery) 敦煌
t'ung 通
Tung Hu 東胡
Tung Chung-shu 董仲舒
t'ung ku chin chih pien 通古今之變
Tung-ching (Lunar Lodge) 東井
Tung-kuan 東袯
T'ung-kuan 潼關
Tung-nan-kou 東南溝
tzu (viscount) 子
Tzu-ling (Mountain) 梓領

W

wang (king, prince) 王
Wang Huang 王黃
Wang Hui 王恢
Wang Kuo-wei 王國維
Wang Mang 王莽
wang-lo t'ien-hsia fang-shih chiu wen 網羅天下放失舊聞
Wen Hou 文侯 of Wei 魏
Wei (river) 渭
Wei (state) 魏
Wei Chiang 欄絳
Wei Ch'ing 衛青
Wei Kuang 衛廣
Wei-yang 渭陽
Wen-ti (Han emperor) 文帝
Weng-niu-t'e-ch'i 翁牛特旗
Wey (state) 衛
wu (Heavenly stem) 戊
Wu 五
Wu-ch'ang 無腸
wu-chi hsiao-wei 戊己校尉
Wu-chia 烏加
Wu-chih Lo 烏氏裸
Wu-chih 烏氏
Wu-chung 無終 Jung
Wu-huan 烏桓
Wu-la-t'e-ch'ien-ch'i 烏拉特前旗
Wu-ling, King of Chao 武靈
Wu-sun 烏孫
Wu-ti (Han emperor) 武帝
wu wei 無為
Wu-wei (commandery) 武威
Wu-yüan (commandery) 五原

Y

Yang (Mountains) 陽
Yang (area) 楊
Yang-lang (site) 楊郎
yao 要
Yao 堯 (T'ang 唐)
yeh 野 (wilderness)
Yen (state) 燕
Yen t'ieh lun 鹽鐵論
yen-chih (Hsiung-nu title for queen) 閼氏
Yen-chih (Mountain) 焉耆
Yen-ch'ing 延慶
Yen-men (commandery) 雁門
yi (rigtheousness) 義
yi man-yi kung man-yi 以蠻夷攻蠻夷
yi yi chih yi 以夷制夷
Yi 伊 (river)
Yi of Huai 淮
Yi of Lai 萊
Yi-chih-hsien 伊稚斜
Yi Chou shu 逸周書
Yi-ch'ü Jung 義渠戎
Yi-hsien 易縣
Yi-k'o-chao-meng 伊克昭盟
Yi-wu 夷吾
Yin Jung 陰戎
Yin (river) 圁
Yin-hsü 殷虛
Yin-shan 陰山
yin-yang 陰陽
Ying Erh 嬰兒
yu 酉
Yu Yü 由余
Yü Ch'u 虞初
Yü Kung 禹貢
yü jung 御戎
Yü-chia-chuang 于家莊
Yü-hsi 榆谿
Yü-lin 榆林
Yü-lung-t'ai 玉隆太
Yü-men 玉門
Yu-pei-p'ing (commandery) 右北平
Yü-shan 於單
Yü-shu-kou 榆樹溝
Yü-yang (commandery) 漁陽
yüan kuo 援國
yüan-kuang (reign title) 元光

yüan-shou (reign title) 元狩
Yüeh 越
Yüeh-chih 月氏
Yün-chung (commandery) 雲中
Yün-yang 雲陽
Yung-ch'ang 永昌
Yung-teng 永登

Select Bibliography

AA. VV. "Radiocarbon Dates of the Institute of Archaeology II." *Radiocarbon* 12 (1970): 130–55.

"Ch'ang ch'eng wen-hsien tzu-liao chi-lüeh." In *Chung-kuo ch'ang-ch'eng yi-chi tiao-ch'a pao-kao chi*. Peking: Wen-wu, 1981, pp. 119–37.

"Ning-hsia ching-nei Chan-kuo Ch'in, Han ch'ang-ch'eng yi-chi." In *Chung-kuo ch'ang-ch'eng yi-chi tiao-ch'a pao-kao chi*. Peking: Wen-wu, 1981, pp. 45–51.

Aalto, Pentti. "The Horse in Central Asian Nomadic Cultures." *Studia Orientalia* 46 (1975): 1–9.

Academy of Sciences MPR. *Information Mongolia*. Oxford: Pergamon Press, 1990.

Akiner, Shirin. "Conceptual Geographies of Central Asia." In *Sustainable Development in Central Asia*, ed. Shirin Akiner et al. New York: St. Martin's Press, 1998, pp. 3–62.

Alekseev, Valery P. "Some Aspects of the Study of Productive Forces in the Empire of Chengiz Khan." In *Rulers from the Steppe*, ed. Gary Seaman and Daniel Marks. Los Angeles: Ethnographics Press/The University of Southern California, 1991, pp. 186–98.

Alekshin, V. A. "Problème de l'origin des cultures archéologiques du néolithique et de l'Âge du Bronze en Asie centrale (d'après les rites funéraires). In *L'Asie centrale et ses rapports avec les civilisations orientales des origines a l'Age du Fer*. Paris: Diffusion de Boccard, 1988, pp. 255–64.

Ames, Roger T. *The Art of Rulership: A Study in Ancient Chinese Political Thought*. Honolulu: University of Hawaii Press, 1983.

An Chih-min. "Shih-lun Chung-kuo te tsao-ch'i t'ung-ch'i." *K'ao-ku* 1993.12: 1110–19.

An Lu and Chia Wei-ming. "Hei-lung-chiang Ne-ho Er-k'e-ch'ien mu-ti chi ch'i wen-t'i t'an-t'ao." *Pei-fang wen-wu* 1986.2: 2–8.

An Zhimin [Chih-min]. "The Bronze Age in the Eastern Parts of Central Asia." In *History of Civilizations of Central Asia*. Vol. 1: *The Dawn of Civilization: Earliest Times to 700 B.C.*, ed. A. H. Dani and V. M. Masson. Paris: Unesco, 1992, pp. 319–36.

Andersson, J. C. "Researches into the Prehistory of the Chinese." *Bulletin of the Museum of Far Eastern Antiquities* 15 (1943): 197–215.

Andreski [Andrzejewski], Stanislav. *Military Organization and Society*. London: Routledge & Kegan Paul, 1968 [1954].

Anthony, David. "The Opening of the Eurasian Steppe at 2000 BCE." In *The Bronze Age and Early Iron Age Peoples of Eastern Central Asia*, ed. Victor H. Mair. Washington: Institute for the Study of Man, 1998, vol. 1, pp. 94–113.

Anthony, David W., and Dorcas R. Brown. "The Origin of Horseback Riding." *Antiquity* 65.246 (1991): 22–38.

Anthony, David, and Nikolai B. Vinogradov. "Birth of the Chariot." *Archaeology* 48.2 (1995): 36–41.

Askarov, A. "The Beginning of Iron Age in Transoxiana." In *History of Civilizations of Central Asia*. Vol. 1: *The Dawn of Civilization: Earliest Times to 700 B.C.*, ed. A. H. Dani and V. M. Masson. Paris: Unesco, 1992, pp. 441–58.

Askarov, A., V. Volkov, and N. Ser-Odjav. "Pastoral and Nomadic Tribes at the Beginning of the First Millennium B.C." In *History of Civilizations of Central Asia*. Vol. 1: *The Dawn of Civilization: Earliest Times to 700 B.C.*, ed. A. H. Dani and V. M. Masson. Paris: Unesco, 1992, pp. 459–75.

Bacon, Elisabeth. *Obok: A Study of Social Structure in Eurasia*. New York: Wenner-Gren Foundation, 1958.

Bagley, Robert. "Shang Archaeology." In *Cambridge History of Ancient China*, ed. Michael Loewe and Edward L. Shaughnessy. Cambridge: Cambridge University Press, 1999, pp. 124–231.

Bailey, H. W. *Indo-Scythian Studies. Khotanese Texts VII*. Cambridge: Cambridge University Press, 1985.

Balazs, Etienne. "L'histoire comme guide de la pratique bureaucratique." In *Historians of China and Japan*, ed. W. G. Beasley and E. G. Pulleyblank. London: Oxford University Press, 1961, pp. 78–94. [Trans. as "History as a Guide to Bureaucratic Practice," in Etienne Balazs, *Chinese Civilization and Bureaucracy*. New Haven: Yale University Press, 1964.]

Barfield, Thomas. "The Hsiung-nu Imperial Confederacy: Organization and Foreign Policy." *Journal of Asian Studies* 41.1 (November 1981): 45–61.

The Perilous Frontier: Nomadic Empires and China. Cambridge, Mass.: Blackwell, 1989.

Bazin, Louis. "Une texte proto-turc du IVe siecle: le distique Hiong-nou du 'Tsin-chou.'" *Oriens* 1 (1948): 208–19.

Les Systemes Chronologiques dans le Monde Turc Ancien. Budapest: Akadémiai Kiadó, 1991.

Beckwith, Christopher I. "Aspects of the History of the Central Asian Guard Corps in Islam." *Archivum Eurasiae Medii Aevi* 4 (1984): 29–43.

"The Impact of the Horse and Silk Trade on the Economies of T'ang China and of the Uighuir Empire." *Journal of the Social and Economic History of the Orient* 34.2 (1991): 183–98.

Benzing, J. "Das 'Hunnisches.'" In *Philologiae Turcicae Fundamenta*, vol. 1, ed. Jean Deny. Wiesbaden: Franz Steiner, 1959.

Bibikova, V. I. "On the History of Horse Domestication in South-East Europe." In Dmitriy Yakolevich Telegin, *Dereivka: A Settlement and Cemetery of Copper*

Age Horse Keepers on the Middle Dnieper, ed. J. P. Mallory and trans. V. K. Pyatkovskiy. Oxford: British Archaeological Reports, 1986, pp. 163–82.

Bielenstein, Hans. *The Bureaucracy of Han Times*. Cambridge: Cambridge University Press, 1980.

"The Restoration of the Han Dynasty. With Prolegomena on the Historiography of the *Hou Han Shu*." *Bulletin of the Museum of Far Eastern Antiquities* 26 (1954): 1–209.

"The Restoration of the Han Dynasty, Vol. 3: 'The People.'" *Bulletin of the Museum of Far Eastern Antiquities* 39, part II (1967): 1–198.

Birrell, Anne. *Chinese Mythology: An Introduction*. Baltimore: Johns Hopkins University Press, 1993.

Bivar, A. D. H. "The Stirrup and Its Origin," *Oriental Art*, n.s. 1, 1 (1955): 61–65.

Bodde, Derk. *China's First Unifier: Li Ssu*. Leiden: Brill, 1938.

Statesman, Patriot and General in Ancient China. New Haven: American Oriental Society, 1940.

Bokovenko, Nikolai A. "History of Studies and the Main Problems in the Archaeology of Southern Siberia during the Scythian Period." In *Nomads of the Eurasian Steppes in the Early Iron Age*, ed. Jeannine Davis-Kimball et al. Berkeley: Zinat Press, 1995, pp. 255–61.

"Scythian Culture in the Altai Mountains." In *Nomads of The Eurasian Steppes in the Early Iron Age*, ed. Jeannine Davis-Kimball et al. Berkeley: Zinat Press, 1995, pp. 285–95.

"The Tagar Culture of the Minusinsk Basin," In *Nomads of the Eurasian Steppes in the Early Iron Age*, ed. Jeannine Davis-Kimball et al. Berkeley: Zinat Press, 1995, pp. 299–314.

"Tuva during the Scythian Period." In *Nomads of the Eurasian Steppes in the Early Iron Age*, ed. Jeannine Davis-Kimball et al. Berkeley: Zinat Press, 1995, pp. 265–81.

Boodberg, Peter. "Turk, Aryan and Chinese in Ancient Asia." In *Selected Works of Peter A. Boodberg*, ed. Alvin P. Cohen. Berkeley: University of California Press, 1979, pp. 9–12.

Brentjes, Burchard. *Arms of the Sakas*. Varanasi: Rishi Publications, 1996.

Britton, Roswell. "Chinese Interstate Intercourse before 700 B.C." *American Journal of International Law* 29 (1935): 616–35.

Brodianskii, D. L. "Krovnovsko-Khunnskie paralleli." In *Drevnee Zabaikal'e i ego kul'turnye sviazi*, ed. P. B. Konovalov. Novosibirsk: Nauka, 1985, pp. 46–50.

Bulling, A. G. "Ancient Chinese Maps. Two Maps Discovered in a Han Dynasty Tomb from the Second Century B.C." *Expedition* 20. 2 (1978): 16–25.

Bunker, Emma C. "The Anecdotal Plaques of the Eastern Steppe Regions." In *Arts of the Eurasian Steppelands*, ed. Philip Denwood. Colloquies on Art and Archaeology in Asia no. 7. London: Percival David Foundation, 1978, pp. 121–42.

"Ancient Ordos Bronzes." In *Ancient Chinese and Ordos Bronzes*, ed. Jessica Rawson and Emma Bunker. Hong Kong: Museum of Art, 1990, pp. 291–307.

"Unprovenanced Artifacts Belonging to the Pastoral Tribes of Inner Mongolia and North China during the Eighth–First Century B.C." In *The International Academic Conference of Archaeological Cultures of the Northern Chinese*

Ancient Nations (Collected Papers), ed. Chung-kuo k'ao-ku wen-wu yen-chiu-so. Huhhot, 11–18 August 1992.

"Gold in the Ancient Chinese World." *Artibus Asiae* 53.1–2 (1993): 27–50.

"Cultural Diversity in the Tarim Basin Vicinity and Its Impact on Ancient Chinese Culture." In *The Bronze Age and Early Iron Age Peoples of Eastern Central Asia*, ed. Victor H. Mair. Washington: Institute for the Study of Man, 1998, vol. 2, pp. 604–18.

Cao Wanru. "Maps 2,000 Years Ago and Ancient Cartographical Rules." In *Ancient China's Technology and Science*, ed. Inst. of History of Natural Sciences, Chinese Academy of Social Sciences. Beijing: Foreign Languages Press, 1983, pp. 251–55.

Cartier, Michael. "Barbarians through Chinese Eyes: The Emergence of an Anthropological Approach to Ethnic Differences." *Comparative Civilizations Review* 6 (Spring 1981): 1–14.

Chai Te-fang. "Chung-kuo pei-fang ti-ch'ü ch'ing-t'ung tuan-chien fen-ch'ün yen-chiu." *K'ao-ku hsüeh-pao* 1988.3: 277–99.

Chan Kuo Ts'e. 3 vols. Annotated by Liu Hsiang. Shanghai: Ku-chi, 1978.

Chang, Claudia, and Perry A. Tourtellotte. "The Role of Agro-pastoralism in the Evolution of Steppe Culture in the Semirechye Area of Southern Kazakhstan during the Saka/Wusun Preriod (600 BCE–400 BCE)." In *The Bronze Age and Early Iron Age Peoples of Eastern Central Asia*, ed. Victor H. Mair. Washington: Institute for the Study of Man, 1998, vol. 1, pp. 264–79.

Chang, K. C. *The Archaeology of Ancient China*, 3rd ed. New Haven: Yale University Press, 1977.

Art, Myth and Ritual. The Path to Political Authority in Ancient China. Cambridge, Mass: Harvard University Press, 1983.

"Sandai Archaeology and the Formation of States in Ancient China: Processual Aspects of the Origin of Chinese Civilization." In *The Origins of Chinese Civilizations*, ed. David Keightley. Berkeley: University of California Press, 1983, pp. 495–521.

Chang Ch'ang-ming. "Shih-lun Hsi Han te Han Hsiung kuan-hsi chi ch'i kuan-hsi chi ho-ch'in cheng-ts'e." *Chiang-huai lun-t'an* 1983.6: 83–88.

Chang Chun-shu. "Military Aspects of Han Wu-ti's Northern and Northwestern Campaigns." *Harvard Journal of Asiatic Studies* 21 (1966): 68–173.

Chao Hua-ch'eng. "Chung-kuo tsao-ch'i ch'ang-ch'eng te k'ao-ku tiao-ch'a yü yen-chiu." In *Ch'ang-ch'eng kuo-chi hsüeh-shu yen-t'ao-hui lun-wen*, ed. Chung-kuo ch'ang-ch'eng hsüeh-hui. Chi-lin-shih: Chi-lin Jen-min, 1994.

Chao Shan-t'ung. "Hei-lung-chiang kuan-ti yi-chih fa-hsien de mu-tsang." *K'ao-ku* 1965.1: 45–6.

Ch'ao Ts'o chi chu-yi. Shanghai: Jen-min, 1976.

Chavannes, Édouard. *Les mémoires historiques de Se-ma Ts'ien*. 5 vols. Paris: Ernest Leroux, 1895–1905.

"Les deux plus anciens spécimens de la cartographie chinoise," *Bulletin de l'École Français d'Éxtrême Orient* 5 (1903): 214–47.

Les documents chinois decouverts par Aurel Stein dans les sables du Turkestan Oriental. Oxford: Impr. de l'Université, 1913.

Chen Ching-lung. "Chinese Symbolism among the Huns." In *Religious and Lay Symbolism in the Altaic World, Proceedings of the Twenty-seventh Meeting of the Permanent International Altaistic Conference*, ed. Klaus Sagaster. Wiesbaden: Harrassowitz, 1989, pp. 62–70.

Chen Kuang-tzuu, and Frederick T. Hiebert. "The Late Prehistory of Xinjiang in Relation to Its Neighbors." *Journal of World Prehistory* 9.2 (1995): 243–300.

Ch'en Po. "Shih-lun Hu-han-yeh Ch'an-yü tsai yü Han 'ho-ch'in' chung te chu-tao tso-yung." *Hsi-pei Ta-hsüeh Hsüeh-pao* 1990.4: 36–39.

Chen Shih-tsai. "Equality of States in Ancient China." *American Journal of International Law* 35 (1941): 641–50.

Ch'eng Te-hsu. "International Law in Early China." *Chinese Social and Political Science Review* 11 (1927): 38–55, 251–70.

Chernykh, E. N. *Ancient Metallurgy in the USSR*. Cambridge: Cambridge University Press, 1992.

Ch'iao Hsiao-ch'in. "Kuan-yü pei-fang yu-mu wen-hua ch'i-yüan te t'an-t'ao." *Nei Meng-ku wen-wu k'ao-ku*. 1992.1–2: 21–25.

Ch'in Chien-ming. "Shang Chou 'kung-hsing-ch'i' wei 'ch'i-ling' shuo." *K'ao-ku* 1995.3: 256–58.

Chin Feng-yi. "Lun Chung-kuo tung-pei ti-ch'ü han ch'ü-jen ch'ing-t'ung tuan-chien te wen-hua yi-ts'un," *K'ao-ku hsüeh-pao* 1982.4: 387–426 (part I), and 1983.1: 39–35 (part II).

"Hsia-chia-tien shang-ts'eng wen-hua chi ch'i tsu-shu wen-t'i." *K'ao-ku hsüeh-pao* 1987.2: 177–208.

Chu Kuei. "Liao-ning Ch'ao-yang Shih-erh-t'ai-ying-tzu ch'ing-t'ung tuan-chien-mu." *K'ao-ku hsueh-pao* 1960.1: 63–71.

Ch'u T'ung-shu. *Han Social Structure*. Seattle: University of Washington Press, 1972.

Chu Yung-kang. "Hsia-chia-tien shang-ts'eng wen-hua te ch'u-pu yen-chiu." In *K'ao-ku-hsüeh wen-hua lun-chi*, ed. Su Ping-ch'i. Peking: Wen-wu, 1993, vol. 1, pp. 99–128.

Ch'un-ch'iu Ku-liang chuan chin-chu chin-yi. Ed. Hsüeh An-chih. Taipei: Taiwan Shang-wu, 1994.

Ch'un-ch'iu Tso-chuan chin-chu chin-yi. 3 vols. Ed. Li Tsung-tung and Wang Yun-wu. Taipei: T'ai-wan shang wu, 1973.

Ch'un-ch'iu Tso-chuan chu, ed. Yang Po-chün. Peking: Chung-hua, 1990 [1981].

Chung K'an. "Ning-hsia Ku-yüan hsien ch'u-t'u wen-wu." *Wen-wu*, 1978.12: 86–90.

"Ku-yüan hsien P'eng-p'u Ch'un-ch'iu Chan-kuo mu-tsang." *Chung-kuo k'ao-ku-hsüeh nien-chien 1988* (1989): 255–56.

Chung K'an, and Han Kung-le. "Ning-hsia nan-pu Ch'un-ch'iu Chan-kuo shih-ch'i te ch'ing-t'ung wen-hua." *Chung-kuo k'ao-ku hsüeh-hui ti-ssu-tz'u nien-hui lun-wen-chi 1983*. Peking: Wen-wu, 1985, pp. 203–13.

Chung-kuo li-shih ti-t'u chi. The Historical Atlas of China, ed. T'an Ch'i-hsiang [Tan Qixiang] et al. Peking: Ti-t'u ch'u-pan-she, 1982.

Claessen, Henri J. M. "The Early State: A Structural Approach." In *The Early State*, ed. Henri J. M. Claessen and Peter Skalnik. The Hague: Mouton Publishers, 1978, pp. 533–96.

Couvreur, S. *Chou King*. Ho Kien Fou: Imprimerie de la Mission catholique, 1897.

Creel, Herrlee G. "The Role of the Horse in Chinese History." *The American Historical Review* 70.3 (1965): 647–72.

The Origins of Statecraft in China. Vol. 1: *The Western Chou Empire*. Chicago: University of Chicago Press, 1970.

Shen Pu-hai. A Chinese Political Philosopher of the Fourth Century B.C. Chicago: University of Chicago Press, 1974.

Cressy, George B. *Asia's Lands and Peoples*. New York: McGraw Hill Book Co., 1963.

Crump, J. I., Jr. *Chan-Kuo Ts'e*. Oxford: Clarendon Press, 1970.

Csorba, Mrea. "The Chinese Northern Frontier: Reassessment of the Bronze Age Burials from Baifu." *Antiquity* 70 (1996): 564–87.

Daffinà, Paolo. "The Han Shu Hsi Yu Chuan Re-Translated. A Review Article." *T'oung-pao* 68.4–5 (1982): 309–39.

Il nomadismo centrasiatico. Parte Prima. Roma: Istituto di studi dell'India e dell'Asia orientale, Università di Roma, 1982.

David, T. "Peuples mobiles de l'eurasie: contacts d'une périphérie 'barbare' avec le monde 'civilisé', à la fin de l'Age du Bronze et au 1er Age du Fer." In *L'Asie centrale et ses rapports avec les civilisations orientales des origines a l'Age du Fer*. Paris: Diffusion de Boccard, 1988, pp. 159–68.

Davydova, A. V. "The Ivolga Gorodishche. A Monument of the Hsiung-nu Culture in the Trans-Baikal Region." *Acta Orientalia Academiae Scientiarum Hungaricae* 20 (1968): 209–45.

Ivolginskii kompleks (gorodishche i mogil'nik) – pamiatnik khunnu v Zabaikal'e. Leningrad: Izd-vo Leningradskogo Universiteta, 1985.

Davydova A. V., and V. P. Shilov. "K voprosy o zemledelii y gunnov." *Vestnik drevnei istorii* 2.44 (1983): 193–201.

De Crespigny, Rafe. *Official Titles of the Former Han Dynasty as Translated and Transcribed by H. H. Dubs*. An Index compiled by Rafe de Crespigny. Canberra: Centre of Oriental Studies in association with Australian National University Press, 1967.

Northern Frontier: The Policies and Strategy of the Later Han Empire. Canberra: Faculty of Asian Studies, Australian National University, 1984.

De Groot, J. J. M. *Chinesische Urkunden zur Geschichte Asiens I: die Hunnen der vorchristlichen Zeit*. Berlin and Leipzig: W. de Gruyter, 1921.

Debaine-Francfort, Corinne. *Du Néolithique à l'Age du Bronze en Chine du Nord-Ouest: la culture de Qijia et ses connexions*. Paris: Editions recherche sur les civilisations, 1995.

Deguignes, H. *Histoire general des Huns, des Turks, des Mongols et des autres Tartares*, 5 vols. Paris, Desaint & Saillant, 1756–58.

Derevianko, A. P. *Rannyi zheleznyi vek Priamur'ia*. Novosibirsk: Nauka, 1973.

Derevyanko, A. P., and D. Dorj. "Neolithic Tribes in Northern Parts of Central Asia." In *History of Civilizations of Central Asia*. Vol. 1: *The Dawn of Civilization: Earliest Times to 700 B.C.*, ed. A. H. Dani and V. M. Masson. Paris: Unesco, 1992, pp. 169–89.

Dergachev, V. "Neolithic and Bronze Age Cultural Communities of the Steppe Zone of the USSR." *Antiquity* 63.241 (1989): 793–802.

Dewall, Magdalene von. *Pferd und Wagen im fruhen China*. Bonn: Habelt, 1964.

Di Cosmo, Nicola. "The Economic Basis of the Ancient Inner Asian Nomads and Its Relationship to China." *Journal of Asian Studies* 53.4 (1994): 1092–126.

"The Northern Frontier in Pre-Imperial China." In *Cambridge History of Ancient China*, ed. Michael Loewe and Edward L. Shaughnessy. Cambridge: Cambridge University Press, 1999, pp. 885–966.

"State Formation and Periodization in Inner Asian History." *Journal of World History* 10.1 (Spring 1999): 1–40.

Doerfer, G. "Zur Sprache der Hunnen." *Central Asiatic Journal* 17.1 (1973): 1–50.

Dolukhanov, P. M. "Paléoécologie de l'Asie centrale aux ages de la pierre et du bronze," in *L'Asie centrale et ses rapports avec les civilisations orientales, des origines à l'age du fer*. Mémoires de la Mission Archéologique Française en Asie Centrale. Paris: Diffusion de Boccard, 1988, pp. 215–21.

Dolukhanov P. M., et al. "Radiocarbon Dates of the Institute of Archaeology II." *Radiocarbon* 12 (1970): 130–55.

Downs, J. F. "Origin and Spread of Riding in the Near East and Central Asia." *American Anthropologist* 63 (1961): 1193–203.

Drompp, Michael R. "The Hsiung-nu *Topos* in the T'ang Response to the Collapse of the Uighur Steppe Empire." *Central and Inner Asian Studies* 1 (1987): 1–46.

Dubs, Homer. "The Beginnings of Chinese Astronomy." *Journal of the American Oriental Society* 78.4 (1958): 295–300.

"The Reliability of Chinese Histories." *Far Eastern Quarterly* 6.1 (1946): 23–43.

Dvornichenko, Vladimir. "Sauromatians and Sarmatians of the Eurasian Steppes: The Transitional Period from the Bronze Age." In *Nomads of the Eurasian Steppes in the Early Iron Age*, ed. Jeannine Davis-Kimball et al. Berkeley: Zinat Press, 1995, pp. 101–4.

Dzo, Ching-chuan. *Se-ma Ts'ien et l'historiographie chinoise*. Paris: Publications Orientalistes de France, 1978.

Eberhard, Wolfram. *Conquerors and Rulers*. Leiden: Brill, 1952.

A History of China. Berkeley: University of California Press, 1977 [1960].

"The Political Function of Astronomy and Astronomers in Han China." In *Chinese Thought and Institutions*, ed. John K. Fairbank. Chicago: Chicago University Press, 1957, pp. 37–70.

Egami, Namio. "The Kuai ti, the Tao you, and the Dao xi: The Strange Animals of the Xiongnu." *Memoirs of the Research Department of Toyo Bunko* 13 (1951): 87–123.

Enoki, Kazuo. "On the Relationship between the *Shih-chi*, Bk. 123 and the *Han-shu*, Bks. 61 and 96." *Memoirs of the Research Department of the Toyo Bunko* 41 (1983): 1–31.

Erdy, Miklos. "Hun and Xiongnu Type Cauldron Finds throughout Eurasia." *Eurasian Studies Yearbook* (1995): 5–94.

Erkes, Edouard. "Das Pferd im Alten China." *T'oung Pao* 36 (1942): 26–63.

Falkenhausen, Lothar von. "On the Historiographical Orientation of Chinese Archaeology." *Antiquity* 67 (1993): 839–49.

"The Regionalist Paradigm in Chinese Archaeology." In *Nationalism, Politics and the Practice of Archaeology*, ed. Philip L. Kohl and Clare Fawcett. Cambridge: Cambridge University Press, 1995, pp. 198–217.

Fang Ch'ing-ho. "Hsi Han te tsai-huang." *Shih-yüan* 7 (1976): 12.

Ferguson, John. "China and Rome." In *Aufstieg und Niedergang der römischen Welt*, vol. 9.2, ed. Hildegard Temporini and Wolfgang Haase. New York: W. de Gruyter, 1978, pp. 581–603.

Fitzgerald-Huber, Louisa. "Qijia and Erlitou, the Question of Contacts with Distant Cultures." *Early China* 20 (1995): 40–52.

Fletcher, Joseph, Jr. "Turco-Mongolian Monarchic Tradition in the Ottoman Empire." *Harvard Ukrainian Studies* 3–4 (1979–80): 236–51.

Franke, Herbert. "From Tribal Chieftain to Universal Emperor and God: The Legitimation of the Yuan Dynasty." *Bayerische Akademie der Wissenschaften, philosophische-historische klasse, sitzungsberichte* 2 (1978): 1–85.

Franke, Otto. "Der Ursprung der chinesischen Geschichtschreibung." *Sitzungsberichte der prüßischen Akademie der Wissenschaften* 23 (1925): 276–309.

Fraser, Everard D. H., and James H. S. Lockhart. *Index to the Tso Chuan.* London: Oxford University Press, 1930.

Gale, Esson M. *Discourses on Salt and Iron.* Leiden: Brill, 1931; rpt. Taipei: Ch'engwen, 1967.

Gardiner-Gardner, J. R. "Chang Ch'ien and Central Asian Ethnography." *Papers of Far Eastern History* 33 (1986): 23–79.

Gardiner-Garden, John. *Apollodoros of Artemita and the Central Asian Skythians.* Papers on Inner Asia no. 3. Bloomington: Research Institute for Inner Asian Studies, 1987.

Greek Conceptions on Inner Asian Geography and Ethnography from Ephoros to Eratosthenes. Papers on Inner Asia no. 9. Bloomington: Research Institute for Inner Asian Studies, 1987.

Herodotos' Contemporaries on Skythian Geography and Ethnography. Papers on Inner Asia no. 10. Bloomington: Research Institute for Inner Asian Studies, 1987.

Ktesias on Central Asian History and Ethnography. Papers on Inner Asia no. 6. Bloomington: Research Institute for Inner Asian Studies, 1987.

Gardner, C. S. *Chinese Traditional Historiography.* Cambridge, Mass.: Harvard University Press, 1938.

Gening, V. F. "Mogil'nik Sintashta i problema rannikh indoiranskikh plemen." *Sovetskaia Arkheologiia* 4 (1977): 53–73.

Gernet, Jaques. *A History of Chinese Civilization.* Cambridge: Cambridge University Press, 1982.

Golden, Peter. "Imperial Ideology and the Sources of Political Unity Amongst the Pre-Činggisid Nomads of Western Eurasia." *Archivum Eurasiae Medii Aevi* 2 (1982): 37–76.

"Nomads and Their Sedentary Neighbors in Pre-Činggisid Eurasia." *Archivum Eurasiae medii Aevi* 7 (1987–91): 41–81.

"The Qipčaq of Medieval Eurasia: An Example of Medieval Adaptation in the Steppe." In *Rulers from the Steppe: State Formation on the Eurasian Periphery,* ed. Gary Seaman and Daniel Marks. Los Angeles: Ethnographics/University of Southern California, 1991, pp. 132–57.

Goodrich, C. S. "Riding Astride and the Saddle in Ancient China." *Harvard Journal of Asiatic Studies* 44.2 (1984): 279–306.

Grjaznov, Michail Petrovič. *Der Großkurgan von Aržan in Tuva, Südsibirien.* München: Beck, 1984.

Gryaznov, M. P. *The Ancient Civilization of Southern Siberia.* New York: Cowles Book Co., 1969.

Guoyu: Propos sur le principautés I – Zhouyu. Trans. André d'Hormon, annotations par Rémi Mathieu. Paris: Collège de France, 1985.

Hall, Mark E. "Towards an Absolute Chronology of the Iron Age of Inner Asia." *Antiquity* 71 (1997): 863–74.

Han Chia-ku. "Lun ch'ien ch'ang-ch'eng wen-hua tai chi ch'i hsing-ch'eng." In *Ch'ang-ch'eng kuo-chi hsüeh-shu yen-t'ao-hui lun-wen*, ed. Chung-kuo ch'ang-ch'eng hsüeh-hui. Chi-lin-shih: Chi-lin Jen-min, 1994, pp. 60–72, 364–65.

Han Fei Tzu. *Basic Writings*, trans. Burton Watson. New York and London: Columbia University Press, 1964.

Han K'ang-hsin. "Ning-hsia P'eng-p'u Yü-chia-chuang mu-ti jen-ku chung-hsi t'e-tien chih yen-chiu." *K'ao-ku hsüeh-pao* 1995.1: 107–25.

Hančar, Franz. *Das Pferd in praehistorischer und frühistorischer Zeit.* Wien: Herold, 1956.

Hayashi Toshio. "The Development of a Nomadic Empire: The Case of the Ancient Türks (Tujue)." *Bulletin of the Ancient Orient Museum* 11 (1990): 164–84.

Heine-Geldern, R. "Das Tocharenproblem und die Pontische Wanderung." *Saeculum* 2 (1951): 225–55.

Hervouet, Yves. *Un poéte de cour sous les Han: Sseu-ma Siang-jou.* Paris: Presses universitaires de France, 1964.

"Le valeur relative de textes du Che-Ki et du Han-chou." In *Melanges de Sinologie offérts a Monsieur Paul Demieville, part II.* Paris: Bibliotheque de l'Istitute des Hautes Etudes Chinoises, 1974, vol. 20, pp. 55–76.

Hiebert, Fredrik T. "Pazyryk Chronology and Early Horse Nomads Reconsidered." *Bulletin of the Asia Institute*, n.s. 6 (1992): 117–29.

Origins of the Bronze Age Oasis Civilizations in Central Asia. Bulletin 42. Cambridge, Mass.: American School of Prehistoric Research, 1994.

Hinsley, H. *Sovereignty.* Cambridge: Cambridge University Press, 1986 [1966].

Höllmann, Thomas O., and Georg W. Kossack, eds. *Maoqinggou: Ein eisenzeitliches Gräberfeld in der Ordos-Region (Inner Mongolei).* Mainz: Philip von Zabern, 1992.

Honey, David B. "History and Historiography on the Sixteen States: Some T'ang *Topoi* on the Nomads." *Journal of Asian History* 24.2 (1990): 161–217.

Hou Can. "Environmental Changes in the Tarim Oases as Seen through Archeological Discoveries." In *Between Lapis and Jade*, ed. F. Hiebert and N. Di Cosmo, *Anthropology & Archeology of Eurasia* 34.4 (Spring 1996): 55–66.

Hoyanagi, Mutsumi. "Natural Changes of the Region along the Old Silk Road in the Tarim Basin in Historical Times." *Memoirs of the Research Department of the Toyo Bunko* 33 (1975): 85–113.

Hsiang Ch'un-sung. "Chao-wu-ta-meng Yen Ch'in ch'ang ch'eng yi-chih tiao-ch'a pao-kao." In *Chung-kuo ch'ang-ch'eng yi-chi tiao-ch'a pao-kao chi.* Peking: Wen-wu, 1981, pp. 6–20.

"Nei Meng-ku Ch'ih-feng ti-ch'ü fa-hsien te Chan-kuo ch'ien-pi." *K'ao-ku* 1984.2: 138–44.

Hsiao Ch'i-ch'ing. "Pei-ya yu-mu min-tsu nan-ch'in ke chung yüan-yin te chien-t'ao." *Shih-huo yüe-k'an* 1.12 (1972): 1–11.

Hsiao Kung-Chuan. *A History of Chinese Political Thought.* Vol. 1: *From the Beginnings to the Sixth Century* A.D., trans. F. W. Mote. Princeton: Princeton University Press, 1979.

Hsieh Chien (Jiann). "Hsiung-nu tsung-chiao hsin-yang chi ch'i liu-pien." *Li-shih yü-yen yen-chiu so chi-k'an* 12.4 (1971): 571–614.

Hsieh Tuan-chü. "Shih-lun Ch'i-chia wen-hua." *K'ao-ku yü wen-wu* 1981.3: 79–80.

Hsü Ch'eng and Li Chin-tseng. "Tung Chou shih-ch'i te Jung Ti ch'ing-t'ung wen-hua." *K'ao-ku hsüeh-pao* 1993.1: 1–11.

Hsu, Cho-yun. "The Spring and Autumn Period." In *The Cambridge History of Ancient China*, ed. Michael Loewe and Edward L. Shaughnessy. Cambridge: Cambridge University Press, 1999, pp. 545–86.

Hsü Le-yao. "Han chien so chien ch'ang-ch'eng te hou-ch'in kung-chi hsi-t'ung." In *Ch'ang-ch'eng kuo-chi hsüeh-shu yen-t'ao-hui lun-wen* ed. Chung-kuo ch'ang-ch'eng hsüeh-hui. Chi-lin-shih: Chi-lin Jen-min, 1994, pp. 116–22, 375–76.

Hsü Yü-lin. "Liao-ning Shang Chou shih-ch'i te ch'ing-t'ung wen-hua." In *K'ao-ku-hsüeh wen-hua lun-wen-chi*, ed. Su Ping-ch'i. Peking: Wen-wu, 1993, vol. 3, pp. 311–34.

Hu Ch'ien-ying. "Shih-lun Ch'i-chia wen-hua te pu-t'ung lei-hsing chi ch'i yüan-liu." *K'ao-ku yü wen-wu* 1980.3: 77–82, 33.

Hucker, Charles. *China's Imperial Past: An Introduction to Chinese History and Culture*. Stanford: Stanford University Press, 1975.

A Dictionary of Official Titles in Imperial China. Stanford: Stanford University Press, 1985.

Hulsewé, A. F. P. "Notes on the Historiography of the Han Period." In *Historians of China and Japan*, ed. W. G. Beasley and E. G. Pulleyblank. London: Oxford University Press, 1961, pp. 31–43.

"Reviews of *Gestalten aus der Zeit der chinesischen Hegemoniekämpfe aus Szuma Ts'ien's Historischen Denkwürdigkeiten*, by Erich Haenisch; *Ssu-ma Ch'ien's Historiographical Attitude as Reflected In Four Late Warring States Biographies*, by F. Kierman Jr.; 'The Restoration of the Han Dynasty, II,' by Hans Bielenstein." *T'oung Pao* 52 (1965–66): 182–99.

"Quelques considérations sur le commerce de la soie au temps de la dynastie des Han." In *Mélanges de Sinologie offerts à Paul Demiéville, II*. Paris: Bibliothèque de l'Institut des Hautes Etudes Chinoises, 1974, pp. 117–35.

"The Problem of the Authenticity of Shih-chi." *T'oung Pao* 66 (1975): 83–147.

" Law as One of the Foundations of State Power in Early Imperial China." In *Foundations and Limits of State Power in China*, ed. S. R. Schram. London: School of Oriental and African Studies, 1987, pp. 11–32.

Hulsewé, A. F. P., and Michael Loewe. *China in Central Asia: The Early Stage, 125 B.C.–A.D. 23. An Annotated Translation of Chapters 61 and 96 of the History of the Former Han Dynasty*. Leiden: Brill, 1979.

Irincin. "Dumdatu ulus-un umaradakin-u uγsaγatan nuγud bolon monggolčud-un uγsaγan ijaγur." In *Monggol teüke-yin tuqai ügülel-üd*. Huhhot: Öbör Monggol-un Arad-un Keblel-un Qoriy-a, 1981, pp. 4–12.

Itina, Mariana A. "The Steppes of the Aral Sea in Pre- and Early Scythian Times." In *Foundations of Empire: Archaeology and Art of the Eurasian Steppes*, ed. Gary Seaman. Los Angeles: Ethnographics Press/University of Southern California, 1992, pp. 49–58.

Iwamura, Shinobu. "Nomad and Farmer in Central Asia." *Acta Asiatica* 3 (1962): 44–56.

Jacobson, Esther. "Beyond the Frontier: A Reconsideration of Cultural Interchange Between China and the Early Nomads." *Early China* 13 (1988): 201–40.

The Art of the Scythians. Leiden: Brill, 1995.

Jagchid, Sechin and Van Jay Symons. *Peace, War and Trade along the Great Wall.* Bloomington: Indiana University Press, 1989.

Janhunen, Juha. "The Horse in East Asia: Reviewing the Linguistic Evidence." In *The Bronze Age and Early Iron Age Peoples of Eastern Central Asia,* ed. Victor H. Mair. Washington: Institute for the Study of Man, 1998, vol. 1, pp. 415–30.

Jen Chi-yu. "Ssu-ma Ch'ien te che-hsüeh ssu-hsiang." In *Ssu-ma Ch'ien yü ⟨Shih Chi⟩ lun-chi,* ed. Li-shih yen-chiu pien-chi-pu. Hsi-an: Shaansi jen-min ch'u-pan-she, 1982, pp. 105–18.

Jettmar, Karl. *Art of the Steppes.* New York: Crown Publishers, 1967.

"The Karasuk Culture and Its South-Eastern Affinities." *Bulletin of the Museum of Far Eastern Antiquities* 22 (1950): 83–123.

"The Origins of Chinese Civilization: Soviet Views." In *The Origins of Chinese Civilization,* ed. D. N. Keightley. Berkeley: University of California Press, 1983, pp. 217–36.

Johnson, David. "Epic and History in Early China: The Matter of Wu Tzu-hsü." *Journal of Asian Studies* 40.2 (1981): 255–71.

Kai Shan-lin. "Nei Meng-ku tzu-chih-ch'ü Chun-ke-erh-ch'i Su-chi-kou ch'u-t'u yi-pi t'ung-ch'i." *Wen-wu* 1965.2: 44–45.

"Ts'ung Nei Meng Yin-shan yen-hua k'an ku-tai pei-fang yu-mu min-tsu te li-shih kung-hsien." In *Ssu-chou chih lu yen-hua yi-shu* ed. Chou Chin-pao. Urumchi: Hsin-chiang jen-min, 1993.

Kai Shan-lin, and Lu ssu-hsien. "Nei Meng-ku ching-nei Chan-kuo Ch'in, Han ch'ang-ch'eng yi-chi." In *Chung-kuo k'ao-ku hsüeh-hui ti-yi-tz'u nien-hui lun-wen-chi 1979.* Peking: Wen-wu, 1980, pp. 212–28.

Kao Tung-lu. "Lüeh lun Ka-yüeh wen-hua." *K'ao-ku-hsüeh wen-hua lun-chi,* vol. 3, pp. 153–65.

K'ao-ku 1961.2:77–81. "Nei Meng-ku Ch'ih-feng Yao-wang-miao, Hsia-chia-tien yi-chih shih-chüeh chien-pao."

1962.12:644–5. "Hopei Ch'ing-lung hsien Ch'ao-tao-kou fa-hsien yi p'i ch'ing-t'ung ch'i."

1966.5:231–42 "Hopei Huai-lai Pei-hsin-pao Chan-kuo mu."

1975.4:249–58. "Hu-he-hao-t'e Erh-shih-chia-tzu ku-ch'eng ch'u-t'u de Hsi Han t'ieh chia." [Trans. "The Western Han Iron Armors Unearthed from the Remains of an Ancient City at Ershijiazi in Huhehot." In *Chinese Archaeological Abstracts.* Vol. 3: *Eastern Zhou to Han,* ed. Albert Dien, Jeffrey T. Riegel, and Nancy T. Price. Los Angeles: UCLA Institute of Archaeology, 1985, pp. 1349–58.]

1977.1:51–55. "Hopei P'ing-ch'uan Tung-nan-kou Hsia-chia-tien shang ts'eng wen-hua mu-tsang."

1977.2:111–14. "Nei Meng-ku Chun-ko-erh ch'i Yü-lung-t'ai te Hsiung-nu mu."

1981.4:304–8. "Nei Meng-ku Ning-ch'eng-hsien Nan-shan-ken 102-hao shih-kuo-mu."

1984.5:417–26. "Nei Meng-ku Ao-han-ch'i Chou-chia-ti mu-ti fa-chüeh chien-pao."

1984.7:598–601. "Kansu Yung-ch'ang San-chiao-ch'eng Sha-ching wen-hua yi-chih t'iao-ch'a."

1984.6:505–9."Yin-hsü hsi-ch'ü fa-hsien yi-tso ch'e-ma k'eng."

1987.9:773–77."Ning-hsia Chung-ning hsien ch'ing-t'ung tuan-chien mu ch'ing-li chien-pao."

1988.12:1090–98. "Ch'i-ch'i-ha-erh shih Ta-tao San-chia-tzu mu-tsang ch'ing-li."

1988.3:301–32. "Nei Meng-ku Chu-k'ai-kou yi-chih."

K'ao-ku hsüeh-pao 1963.1:17–44. "Ch'ing-hai Tu-lan hsien No-mu-hung Ta-li-t'a-li-ha yi-chih tiao-ch'a yü shih-chüeh."

1973.2:27–39. "Ning-ch'eng-hsien Nan-shan-ken te shih-kuo-mu."

1974.1:111–44. "Ch'ih-feng Yao-wang-miao, Hsia-chia-t'ien yi-chih shih-chüe pao-kao."

1974.2:29–62. "Kan-su Yung-ching Ta-he-chuang yi-chih fa-chüeh pao-kao."

1975.1:117–40. "Ning-ch'eng-hsien Nan-shan-ken yi-chih fa-chüeh pao-kao."

1975.1:141–56. "Shen-yang Cheng-chia-wa-tzu te liang-tso ch'ing-t'ung shih-tai mu-tsang."

1975.2:57–96. "Kan-su Yung-ching Ch'in-wen-chia Ch'i-chia wen-hua mu-ti."

1981.2:199–216. "P'a-mi-erh kao-yüan ku mu."

1988.1:75–99. "Hsin-chiang Ho-chi-hsien Ch'a-wu-hu kou-k'ou yi hao mu-ti."

1988.3:333–56. "Ning-hsia T'ung-hsin Tao-tun-tzu Hsiung-nu mu-ti."

1989.1:57–81. "Liang-ch'eng Kuo-hsien-yao-tzu mu-ti."

1990.2:205–37. "Yung-ch'ang San-chiao-ch'eng yü Ha-ma-tun Sha-ching wen-hua yi-ts'un."

1993.1:13–56."Ning-hsia Ku-yüan Yang-lang ch'ing-t'ung wen-hua mu-ti."

1995.1:79–107. "Ning-hsia P'eng-p'u Yü-chia-chuang mu-ti."

K'ao-ku yü wen-wu 1981.4:34–36. "Kan-su Yung-teng Yü-shu-kou te Sha-ching mu-tsang."

Karlgren, Bernhard. "Some Weapons and Tools of the Yin Dynasty." *Bulletin of the Museum of Far Eastern Antiquities* 17 (1945): 101–44.

Keightley, David. "The Late Shang State: When, Where, and What?" In *The Origins of Chinese Civilizations*, ed. David Keightley. Berkeley, University of California Press, 1983, pp. 532–48.

"The Shang: China's First Historical Dynasty," In *The Cambridge History of Ancient China*, ed. Michael Loewe and Edward L. Shaughnessy. Cambridge: Cambridge University Press, 1999, pp. 232–91.

Kenk, Roman. *Grabfunde der Skythenzeit aus Tuva, Süd-Sibirien*. München: Beck, 1986.

Khazanov, Anatoly. *Nomads and the Outside World*. Cambridge: Cambridge University Press, 1984.

Kierman, Frank A. *Ssu-ma Ch'ien's Historiographical Attitude as Reflected in Four Late Warring States Biographies*. Wiesbaden: O. Harrassowitz, 1962.

Kiselev, S. V. *Drevniaia Istoriia Iuzhnoi Sibiri*. Moscow: Nauka, 1951.

Kolb, Raimund Theodor. *Die Infanterie im alten China*. Mainz: Philipp von Zabern, 1991.

Koshelenko, G. A. "L'Asie centrale au début de l'age du fer: le problème des relations extérieures." In *L'Asie centrale et ses rapports avec les civilisations orientales des origines a l'Age du Fer*. Paris: Diffusion de Boccard, 1988, pp. 171–72.

Kovalev, A. " 'Karasuk-dolche,' Hirschsteine und die Nomaden der chinesischen Annalen im Alterum." In *Maoqinggou: Ein eisenzeitliches Gräberfeld in der Ordos-Region (Innere Mongolei)*, ed. Thomas Höllman and Georg W. Kossack. Mainz: Verlag Philipp von Zabern, pp. 48–62.

Krader, Lawrence. "The Origin of the State among the Nomads of Asia." In *The Early State*, ed. Henry J. M. Claessen and Peter Skalník. The Hague: Mouton Publishers, 1978, pp. 93–107.

Social Organization of the Mongol-Turkic Pastoral Nomads. The Hague: Mouton, 1963.

Ku, T'ien-fu. "A Summary of the Contents of the Ma-wang-tui Silk-Scroll Book 'Assorted Astronomical and Meteorological Prognostications.'" *Chinese Studies in Archaeology* 1 (1979): 56–74.

Kuo Ta-shun. "Shih-lun wei-ying-tzu lei-hsing." In *K'ao-ku-hsüeh wen-hua lun-chi*, ed. Su Ping-ch'i. Peking: Wen-wu, 1987, pp. 79–98.

Kuzmina, E. E. "Cultural Connections of the Tarim Basin People and Pastoralists of the Asian Steppes in the Bronze Age." In *The Bronze Age and Early Iron Age Peoples of Eastern Central Asia*, ed. Victor H. Mair. Washington: Institute for the Study of Man, 1998, vol. 1, pp. 63–93.

La Chang-yang. "Lun Ssu-ma Ch'ien te li-shih che-hsüeh." In *Ssu-ma Ch'ien yen-chiu hsin-lun*, ed. Shih Ting and Ch'en K'e-ch'in. Cheng-chou: Ho-nan Jen-min, 1982, pp. 59–92.

Lai Hsin-hsia. "Ts'ung Shih Chi k'an Ssu-ma Ch'ien te cheng-chih ssu-hsiang." *Wen shih che* 2 (1981): 53–61.

Lamberg-Karlovsky, Carl. "The Bronze Age Khanates of Central Asia." *Antiquity* 68 (1994): 398–405.

Lattimore, Owen. *The Mongols of Manchuria*. New York: The John Day Company, 1934.

Inner Asian Frontiers of China. Boston: Beacon Press, 1962 [1940].

"Herders, Farmers, Urban Culture." In *Pastoral Production and Society. Proceedings of the International Meeting on Nomadic Pastoralism, Paris 1–3 Dec. 1976*, ed. L'Equipe écologie et anthropologie des sociétés pastorales. Cambridge: Cambridge University Press, 1979, pp. 479–90.

Laufer, Berthold. *Chinese Clay Figures. Part I: Prolegomena on the History of Defensive Armor*. Chicago: Field Museum of Natural History Publication no. 177, 1914.

Le Blanc, Charles. *Huai-nan Tzu. Philosophical Synthesis in Early Han Thought*. Hong Kong: Hong Kong University Press, 1985.

Legge, James. *The Chinese Classics*. Vol. 2: *The Works of Mencius*. 2nd ed. Oxford: Clarendon, 1895; rpt. Hong Kong: Hong Kong University Press, 1960.

The Chinese Classis. Vol. 3: *The Shoo King or the Book of Historical Documents*. 2nd ed. Oxford: Clarendon, 1895; rpt. Hong Kong: Hong Kong University Press, 1960.

The Chinese Classics. Vol. 4: *The She King*. London: Trübner, 1862; rpt. Hong Kong: Hong Kong University Press, 1960.

The Chinese Classics. Vol. 5: *The Ch'un Ts'ew with the Tso Chuen*. London: Trübner, 1872; rpt. Hong Kong: Hong Kong University Press, 1960.

Leslie, D. D., and K. H. J. Gardiner. "Chinese Knowledge of Central Asia." *T'oung Pao* 68.4–5 (1982): 254–308.

Levine, Marsha. "Dereivka and the Problem of Horse Domestication." *Antiquity* 64 (1990): 727–40.

Lewis, Henry Morgan. *Ancient Society*, ed. Leslie A. White. Cambridge, Mass.: Harvard University Press, 1964.

Lewis, Mark. *Sanctioned Violence in Ancient China*. Albany: State University of New York Press, 1990.

"Warring States Political History." In *Cambridge History of Ancient China*, ed. Michael Loewe and Edward L. Shaughnessy. Cambridge: Cambridge University Press, 1999, pp. 687–50.

Li Ch'en-ch'i. "Sung Nen p'ing-yüan ch'ing-t'ung yü ch'u-hsing tsao-ch'i t'ieh-ch'i shih-tai wen-hua lei-hsing te yen-chiu." *Pei-fang wen-wu* 1994.1: 2–9.

Li Chi. "Chi Hsiao-t'un ch'u-t'u-te ch'ing-t'ung ch'i." *Chung-kuo k'ao-ku hsüeh-pao* 4 (1949): 1–70.

Li Ching-han. "Shih-lun Hsia-chia-tien hsia-ts'eng wen-hua te fen-ch'i he lei-hsing." In *Chung-kuo k'ao-ku hsüeh-hui ti-yi-ts'u nien-hui lun-wen-chi 1979*. Peking: Wen-wu, 1980, pp. 163–70.

Li Feng-shan. "Lun ch'ang-ch'eng tai tsai Chung-kuo min-tsu kuan-hsi fa-chan chung te ti-wei." In *Ch'ang-ch'eng kuo-chi hsüeh-shu yen-t'ao-hui lun-wen*, ed. Chung-kuo ch'ang-ch'eng hsüeh-hui. Chi-lin-shih: Chi-lin Jen-min, 1994, pp. 73–85, 366–67.

Li Shui-ch'eng. "Chung-kuo pei-fang ti-tai te she-wen-ch'i yen-chiu." *Wen-wu* 1992.1: 50–57.

Li Xueqin. *Eastern Zhou and Qin Civilizations*. Trans. K. C. Chang. New Haven and London: Yale University Press, 1985.

Li Yi-yu. "Nei Meng Chao-wu-ta-meng ch'u-t'u-te t'ung-ch'i tiao-ch'a." *K'ao-ku* 1959.6: 276–77.

Ligeti, L. "Mots de civilisation de Haute Asie en transcription chinoise." *Acta Orientalia Academiae Scientiarum Hungaricae* 1.1 (1950): 140–88.

Lin Kan. *Hsiung-nu shih-liao hui-pien*. Peking: Chung-hua, 1988.

"Kuan-yü yen-chiu Chung-kuo ku-tai pei-fang min-tsu wen-hua shih te wo chien." *Nei Meng-ku ta-hsüeh hsüeh-pao* 1988.1: 1–13.

Hsiung-nu shih. Huhhot: Nei Meng-ku Jen-min, 1978.

Lin Lü-chih, *Hsiung-nu shih*. Hong Kong: Chung-hua wen-hua shih-yeh kung-ssu, 1963.

Lin Yun, "A Reexamination of the Relationship between Bronzes of the Shang Culture and of the Northern Zone." In *Studies of Shang Archaeology*, ed. K. C. Chang. New Haven: Yale University Press, 1986.

Linduff, Katheryn. "Zhukaigou, Steppe Culture and the Rise of Chinese Civilization." *Antiquity* 69 (1995): 133–45.

"The Emergence and Demise of Bronze-Producing Cultures Outside the Central Plain of China." In *The Bronze Age and Early Iron Age Peoples of Eastern Central Asia*, ed. Victor H. Mair. Washington: Institute for the Study of Man, 1998, vol. 2, pp. 619–43.

Linduff, Katheryn, with Emma C. Bunker and Wu En. "An Archaeological Overview." In Emma C. Bunker, with Trudy S. Kawami, Katheryn M. Linduff, and Wu En. *Ancient Bronzes of the Eastern Eurasian Steppes*. New York: Arthur Sackler Foundation, 1997, pp. 18–98.

Li-shih yen-chiu 1975.1:74–78. "Ch'ao Ts'o k'ang-chi Hsiung-nu te chan-lüeh ssu-hsiang."

Littauer, M. A., and J. H. Crowel. *Wheeled Vehicles and Ridden Animals in the Ancient Near East*. Leiden: Brill, 1979.

"The Origin of the True Chariot." *Antiquity* 70 (1996): 934–39.

Liu Chih-yi. "Chan-kuo Yen pei ch'ang ch'eng tiao-ch'a." *Nei Men-ku wen-hua kaogu* 1994.1: 51–53, 68.

Liu Te-cheng, and Hsü Chün-chü. "Kan-su Ch'in-yang Ch'ün-ch'iu Chan-kuo mu-tsang te ch'ing-li." *K'ao-ku* 1988.5: 413–24.

Liu, Xinru. *Ancient India and Ancient China: Trade and Religious Exchanges* A.D. *1–600*. Delhi: Oxford University Press, 1988.

Lo Feng. "Ning-hsia Ku-yüan Shih-la-ts'un fa-hsien yi-tso Chan-kuo mu." *K'ao-ku-hsüeh chi-k'an* 1983.3: 130–31, 142.

Lo Feng and Han Kung-le. "Ning-hsia Ku-yüan chin-nien fa-hsien te pei-fang hsi ch'ing-t'ung ch'i." *K'ao-ku* 1990.5: 403–18.

Lo Ta-yün. "Hsi Han ch'u-ch'i tui Hsiung-nu ho-ch'in te shih-chih." *Yün-nan min-tsu hsüeh-yüan hsüeh-pao* 1985.4: 44–49.

Loehr, Max. "Weapons and Tools from Anyang, and Siberian Analogies." *American Journal of Archaeology* 53 (1949): 126–44.

Loewe, Michael. *Records of Han Administration*. 2 vols. Cambridge: Cambridge University Press, 1967.

"The Campaigns of Han Wu-ti." In *Chinese Ways in Warfare*, ed. Frank A. Kierman and John K. Fairbank. Cambridge, Mass.: Harvard University Press, 1974, pp. 67–122.

Crisis and Conflict in Han China, 104 B.C. *to* A.D. *9*. London: George Allen and Unwin, 1974.

"The Han View of Comets." *Bulletin of the Museum of Far Eastern Antiquities* 52 (1980): 1–31.

"The Authority of the Emperors of Ch'in and Han." In *State and Law in East Asia. Festschrift Karl Bünger*, ed. Dieter Eikemer and Herbert Franke. Wiesbaden: Harrassowitz, 1981, pp. 80–111.

"The Former Han Dynasty." In *The Cambridge History of China*. Vol. I: *The Ch'in and Han Empires, 221* B.C.–A.D. *220*, ed. Denis Twitchett and Michael Loewe. Cambridge: Cambridge University Press, 1986, pp. 103–222.

ed. *Early Chinese Texts: A Bibliographical Guide*. Berkeley: The Society for the Study of Early China and the Institute of East Asian Studies, University of California, 1993.

Lu Liancheng. "Chariot and Horse Burials in Ancient China." *Antiquity* 67 (1993): 824–38.

Luo Ta-yün. "Hsi Han ch'u-ch'i tui Hsiung-nu ho-ch'in te shih-chi." *Yün-nan Min-tsu Hsüeh-yüan Hsüeh-pao* 1985.4: 44–49.

Ma Ch'ang-shou. *Pei Ti yü Hsiung-nu*. Peking: San-lien, 1962.

Ma Te-chih et al. "Yi-chiu-wu-san-nien An-yang Ta-ssu-k'ung fa-chüeh pao-kao." *K'ao-ku hsüeh-pao* 1955.9: 25–90.

Maenchen-Helfen, Otto. "Archaistic Names of the Hsiung-nu." *Central Asiatic Journal* 6 (1961): 249–61.

Maenchen-Helfen, Otto J. *The World of the Huns*. Berkeley: University of California Press, 1973.

Major, John S. *Heaven and Earth in Early Han Thought*. Albany: State University of New York Press, 1993.

Mallory, J. P. "A European Perspective on Indo-Europeans in Asia." In *The Bronze Age and Early Iron Age Peoples of Eastern Central Asia*, ed. Victor H. Mair. Washington: Institute for the Study of Man, 1998, vol. 1, pp. 175–201.

Markov, G. E. "Problems of Social Change among the Asiatic Nomads." In *The Nomadic Alternative*, ed. Wolfgang Weissleder. The Hague: Mouton, 1978, pp. 305–11.

Martin, Desmond H. "The Mongol Army." *Journal of the Royal Asiatic Society* (1943): 46–85.

The Rise of Chingis Khan and His Conquest of North China. Baltimore: The Johns Hopkins Press, 1950.

Martinov, Anatoly. *The Ancient Art of Northern Asia*, trans. and ed. Demitri B. Shimkin and Edith M. Shimkin. Urbana: University of Illinois Press, 1991.

Martynova, Galina S. "The Beginning of the Hunnic Epoch in South Siberia." *Arctic Anthropology* 25.2 (1988): 61–83.

Maspero, Henri. "L'astronomie chinoise avant les Han." *T'oung Pao* 26 (1929): 267–359.

Masson, V. M. "Les cultures anciennes d'Asie moyenne: dynamique du développement, occupation des aires écologiques, rapports culturels." In *L'Asie centrale et ses rapports avec les civilisations orientales des origines a l'Age du Fer*. Paris: Diffusion de Boccard, 1988, pp. 31–35.

"The Environment." In *History of Civilizations of Central Asia*. Vol. 1: *The Dawn of Civilization: Earliest Times to 700 B.C.*, ed. A. H. Dani and V. M. Masson. Paris: Unesco, 1992, pp. 29–44.

Masson, V. M., and T. F. Taylor, "Soviet Archaeology in the Steppe Zone: Introduction." *Antiquity* 63 (1989): 779–83.

Mathieu, Rémi. *Le Mu Tianzi zhuan: traduction annotée: étude critique*. Collège de France, Institut des hautes études chinoises. Paris: Diffusion de Boccard, 1978.

"Fonctions et moyens de la géographie dans la Chine ancienne." *Asiatische Studien* 36.2 (1982): 125–52.

Études sur la mythologie et l'ethnologie de la Chine ancienne. Traduction annotée du Shanhai Jing. Collège de France, Institut des hautes études chinoises. Paris: Diffusion de Boccard, 1983.

Matsuda, Hisao. "The T'ian-shan Range in Asian History." *Acta Asiatica* 41 (1981): 1–28.

McEwen, E. "Nomadic Archery: Some Observations on Composite Bow Design and Construction." In *Arts of the Eurasian Steppelands*, ed. Philip Denwood. Colloquies on Art and Archaeology in Asia n. 7. London: Percival David Foundation, 1978, pp. 188–202.

Meacham, William. "Origins and Development of the Yüeh Coastal Neolithic: A Microcosm of Culture Change on the Mainland of East Asia." In *The Origins of Chinese Civilization*, ed. David N. Keightley. Berkeley: University of California Press, 1983, pp. 147–75.

Melyukova, A. I. "The Scythians and Sarmatians." In *Cambridge History of Early Inner Asia*, ed. Denis Sinor. Cambridge: Cambridge University Press, 1990, pp. 97–117.

Meyvaert, Paul. "An Unknown Letter of Hulagu, Il-Khan of Persia, to King Louis IX of France." *Viator* 11 (1980): 245–59.

Minajev, S. "Les Xiongnu." *Dossiers d'Archeologie* 212 (April 1996): 74–83.

Minyaev, S. "On the Origin of the Hiung-nu." *Information Bulletin. International Association for the Cultures of Central Asia* 9 (1985): 69–78.

"Niche Grave Burials of the Xiong-nu Period in Central Asia." *Information Bulletin. International Association for the Cultures of Central Asia* 17 (1990): 91–99.

Mori, Masao. "Kyôdo no kokka." *Shigaku zasshi* 59.5 (1950): 1–21.

"Reconsideration of the Hsiung-nu State. A Response to Professor O. Pritsak's Criticism." *Acta Asiatica* 24 (1973): 20–34.

"The T'u-chüeh Concept of Sovereign." *Acta Asiatica* 41 (1981): 47–75.

Moshkova, Marina. "Sarmatians, Concluding Remarks." In *Nomads of the Eurasian Steppes in the Early Iron Age*, ed. Jeannine Davis-Kimball et al. Berkeley: Zinat Press, 1995, pp. 185–88.

Myroshnikov, L. I. "Appendix: A Note on the Meaning of 'Central Asia' as Used in This Book." In *History of Civilizations of Central Asia*. Vol. 1: *The Dawn of Civilization: Earliest Times to 700 B.C.*, ed. A. H. Dani and V. M. Masson. Paris: Unesco, 1992, pp. 477–80.

Nakayama, Shigeru. *Academic and Scientific Traditions in China, Japan and the West*. Tokyo: University of Tokyo Press, 1984.

Needham, Joseph. *Science and Civilization in China*. Vol. 2: *History of Scientific Thought*. Cambridge, Cambridge University Press, 1956.

Science and Civilization in China. Vol. 3: *Mathematics and the Sciences of the Heavens and Earth*. Cambridge: Cambridge University Press, 1959.

Needham, Joseph, and Robin D. S. Yates. *Science and Civilization in China*. Vol. 5: *Chemistry and Chemical Technology, Part VI: Military Technology: Missiles and Sieges*. Cambridge: Cambridge University Press, 1994.

Nei Meng-ku wen-wu k'ao-ku 1981:15–27. "Hsi-kou-p'an Hsiung-nu mu-ti tiao-ch'a-chi."

1991.1:13–24. "Pao-t'ou Hsi-yüan Ch'un-ch'iu mu-ti."

1992.1–2:91–96. "Yi-chin-huo-lo-ch'i Shih-hui-kou fa-hsien de O-erh-tuo-ssu shih wen-wu."

Nieh Shih-ch'iao. *Ssu-ma Ch'ien lun-kao*. Peking: Pei-ching Shih-fan Ta-hsüeh, 1987.

Nienhauser, William H., Jr., ed. *The Grand Scribe's Records*. Vol. 1: *The Basic Annals of Pre-Han China by Ssu-ma Ch'ien*. Bloomington: Indiana University Press, 1994.

The Grand Scribe's Records. Vol. 7: *The Memoirs of Pre-Han China by Ssu-ma Ch'ien*. Bloomington: Indiana University Press, 1994.

O'Donoghue, Diane M. "Reflection and Reception: The Origins of the Mirror in Bronze Age China." *Bulletin of the Museum of Far Eastern Antiquities* 62 (1990): 5–183.

Ohama, Akira. *Chûgoku. rekishi. unmei: Shiki to Shitsu*. Tokyo: Keiso Shobo, 1975.

Okladnikov, A. P. "Inner Asia and the Dawn of History." In *Cambridge History of Early Inner Asia*, ed. Denis Sinor (Cambridge: Cambridge University Press, 1990), pp. 41–96.

Ou Yen. "Wo kuo ch'ang-ch'eng te k'ao-ku fa-hsien yü yen-chiu." In *Ch'ang-ch'eng kuo-chi hsüeh-shu yen-t'ao-hui lun-wen*, ed. Chung-kuo ch'ang-ch'eng hsüeh-hui. Chi-lin-shih: Chi-lin Jen-min, 1994, pp. 250–63.

Pai Shou-i. "Shuo 'ch'eng i chia chih yen.' " *Li-shih yen-chiu* 1984.1: 55–60.

Pak, Yangjin. "A Study of the Bronze Age Culture in the Northern Zone of China." Ph.D. diss., Harvard University, 1995.

Pelliot, Paul. "À propos des Comans."*Journal Asiatique* 15 (1920): 125–85.

"L'édition collective des oeuvres de Wang Kouo-wei." *T'oung pao* 26 (1929): 113–82.

Peng, Ke. "The Andronovo Artifacts Discovered in Toquztara County in Ili, Xinjiang." In *The Bronze Age and Early Iron Age Peoples of Eastern Central Asia*, ed. Victor H. Mair. Washington: Institute for the Study of Man, 1998, vol. 2, pp. 573–80.

Peremolov, L., and A. Martynov. *Imperial China: Foreign-Policy Conceptions and Methods*. Moscow: Progress Publishers, 1983.

Petrenko, Vladimir. "Scythian Culture in the North Caucasus." In *Nomads of the Eurasian Steppes in the Early Iron Age*, ed. Jeannine Davis-Kimball et al. Berkeley: Zinat Press, 1995, pp. 5–22.

Piggott, Stuart. "Chinese Chariotry: An Outsider's View." In *Arts of the Eurasian Steppelands*, ed. Philip Denwood. Colloquies on Art and Archaeology in Asia no. 7. London: Percival David Foundation, 1978, pp. 32–51.

The Earliest Wheeled Transport: From the Atlantic Coast to the Caspian Sea. Ithaca: Cornell University Press, 1983.

P'ing-yang mu-tsang. Peking: Wen-wu, 1990.

Piotrovskij, B. B. *Tesori d'Eurasia: 2000 anni di storia in 70 anni di archeologia sovietica*. Venezia: Mondadori, 1987, pp. 114–15.

Polosmak, N. V. "The Burial of a Noble Pazyryk Woman." *Ancient Civilizations from Scythia to Siberia* 5.2 (1998): 125–63.

Price, Barbara J. "Secondary State Formation: An Explanatory Model." In *Origins of the State: The Anthropology of Political Evolution*, ed. Ronald Cohen and Elman R. Service. Philadelphia: Institute for the Study of Human Issues, 1978, pp. 161–86.

Pritsak, Omeljan. "Kultur und Sprache der Hunnen." In *Festschrift für Dmytro Chyzhewskyj zum 60. Geburstag*. Berlin: Harrassowitz, 1954, pp. 238–49.

"Die 24 Ta-ch'en. Studie zur Geschichte des Verweltungsaufbaus der Hsiung-nu Reiche." *Oriens Extremus* 1 (1954): 178–202.

"Xun der Volksname der Hsiung-nu." *Central Asiatic Journal* 5 (1959): 27–34.

"The Hsiung-nu Word for 'Stone.' " In *Tractata altaica*, ed. Walther Heissig. Wiesbaden: Harrassowitz, 1976, pp. 479–85.

Průšek, Jaroslav. *Chinese Statelets and the Northern Barbarians in the Period 1400–300 B.C.* Dordrecht: Reidel, 1971.

Psarras, Sophia-Karin. "Exploring the North: Non-Chinese Cultures of the Late Warring States and Han." *Monumenta Serica* 42 (1994): 1–125.

Pulleyblank, E. G. "The Hsiung-nu Language." *Asia Major*, n.s. 9 (1962): 239–65.

"Chinese and Indo-Europeans." *Journal of the Royal Asiatic Society* (1966): 9–39.

"Han China in Central Asia." *International History Review* 3 (1981): 278–96.

"The Chinese and Their Neighbors in Prehistoric and Early Historic Times." In *The Origins of Chinese Civilizations*, ed. David Keightley. Berkeley: University of California Press, 1983, pp. 411–66.

"The Hsiung-nu." Unpublished manuscript.

Pumpelly, Raphael, ed. *Explorations in Turkestan. Expedition of 1904. Prehistoric Civilizations of Anau: Origins, Growth, and Influence of Environment.* 2 vols. Washington: Carnegie Institution, 1908.

Rachewiltz, Igor de. "Some Remarks on the Ideological Foundations of Chingis Khan's Empire." *Papers on Far Eastern History* 7 (March 1973): 21–36.

Raschke, Manfred. "New Studies in Roman Commerce with the East." In *Aufstieg und Niedergang der römischen Welt, II Principat*, ed. Hildegard Temporini and W. Haase, vol. 9.2. Berlin: W. de Gruyter, 1978, pp. 614–1361.

Reckel, Johannes. *Bohai: Geschichte und Kultur eines mandschurisch-koreanischen Königreiches der Tang-Zeit.* Aetas Manjurica 5. Wiesbaden: Harrassowitz, 1995.

Richardson, J. S. "*Imperium Romanum*: Empire and the Language of Power." *Journal of Roman Studies* 81 (1991): 1–9.

Rossabi, Morris. *Qubilai: His Life and Times.* Berkeley: University of California Press, 1988.

Rostovtzeff, Michael Ivanovitch. *Iranians and Greeks in Southern Russia.* Oxford: Clarendon, 1922.

Roux, Paul. "L'origine céleste de la souveraineté dans les inscriptions paléo-turques de Mongolia et de Siberie." In *The Sacral Kingship*. Leiden: Brill, 1959, pp. 231–41.

Rudenko, S. *Kul'tura naseleniia tsentral'nogo Altaia v skifskoie vremia.* Moscow: Nauka, 1960.

Rudenko, S. I. *Kul'tura Khunnov i noinulinskie kurgany.* Moskva-Leningrad: Nauka, 1962.

Rudenko, Sergei I. *Frozen Tombs of Siberia: The Pazyryk Burials of Iron Age Horsemen.* London: Dent and Sons, 1970.

Rickett, Allyn W. *Guanzi: Political, Economic, and Philosophical Essays from Early China.* 2 vols. Princeton: Princeton University Press, 1985–98.

Sage, Steven F. *Ancient Sichuan and the Unification of China.* Albany: State University of New York Press, 1992.

Salmony, A. "The Small Finds of Noin Ula." *Parnassus* 8.2 (1936): 15–20.

Salzman, Philip Carl. "Introduction." In *When Nomads Settle: Processes of Sedentarization as Adaptation and Response*, ed. Philip Carl Salzman. New York: Praeger, 1980.

Samolin, W. "Hsiung-nu, Hun, Turk." *Central Asiatic Journal* 3 (1957–58): 143–50.

Sargent, C. B. "Subsidized History." *Far Eastern Quarterly* 3.1 (1943): 134–38.

Saunders, J. J. "The Nomad as Empire-Builder: A Comparison of the Arab and Mongol Conquests." In *Muslims and Mongols: Essays on Medieval Asia by J. J. Saunders*, ed. G. W. Rice. Christchurch: University of Canterbury, 1977, pp. 36–66.

Sawyer, Ralph D. *The Seven Military Classics of Ancient China*. Boulder: Westview Press, 1993.

Schwartz, Benjamin I. *The World of Thought in Ancient China*. Cambridge, Mass.: Belknap Press of Harvard University Press, 1985.

Shakhanova, N. "The System of Nourishment among the Eurasian Nomads: The Kazakh Example." In *Ecology and Empire. Nomads in the Cultural Evolution of the Old World*, ed. Gary Seaman. Los Angeles: Ethnographics/University of Southern California, 1989, pp. 111–17.

Shao Kuo-t'ien. "Ao-han ch'i T'ieh-chiang-kuo Chan-kuo mu-ti tiao-ch'a chien-pao." *Nei Meng-ku wen-wu k'ao-ku* 1992.1–2: 84–90.

"Nei Meng-ku Ao-han-ch'i fa-hsien te ch'ing-t'ung-ch'i chi yu-kuan yi-wu." *Pei-fang wen-wu* 1993.1: 18–25.

Shaughnessy, Edward L. "Historical Perspectives on the Introduction of the Chariot into China," *Harvard Journal of Asiatic Studies* 48.1 (1988): 189–237.

"Historical Geography and the Extent of Early Chinese Kingdoms." *Asia Major*, 3rd series, 2.2 (1989): 1–22.

"Western Zhou History." In *Cambridge History of Ancient China*, ed. Michael Loewe and Edward L. Shaughnessy. Cambridge: Cambridge University Press, 1999, pp. 292–351.

Shelach, Gideon. "Social Complexity in North China during the Early Bronze Age: A Comparative Study of the Erlitou and Lower Xiajiadian Cultures." *Asian Perspectives* 33.2 (1994): 261–92.

Sher, Yakov A. "On the Sources of the Scythic Animal Style." *Arctic Anthropology* 25.2 (1988): 47–60.

Shih Nien-hai. "Huang-he chung-yu Chan-kuo chi Ch'in shih chu ch'ang-ch'eng yi-chi te t'an-su." In *Chung-kuo ch'ang-ch'eng yi-chi tiao-ch'a pao-kao chi*. Peking: Wen-wu, 1981, pp. 52–67.

"O-erh-to-ssu kao-yüan tung-pu Chan-kuo shih-ch'i Ch'in ch'ang ch'eng yi-yi t'an-suo chi." In *Chung-kuo ch'ang-ch'eng yi-chi tiao-ch'a pao-kao chi*. Peking: Wen-wu, 1981, pp. 68–75.

Shih san ching chu shu fu chiao k'an chi. Ed. Juan Yüan. Peking: Chung-hua, 1980.

Shih Ting. "Ssu-ma Ch'ien yu-li kao." In *Ssu-ma Ch'ien he Shih chi*, ed. Liu Nai-he. Peking: Pei-ching ch'u-pan-she, 1987, pp. 126–44.

Shih Wei-ch'ing. "Kuan-yü Hsi Han cheng-fu yü Hsiung-nu ho-ch'in jo-kan wen-t'i." *Hsia-men ta-hsüeh hsüeh-pao* 1985.4: 21–29.

Shirakawa Shizuka. "Shaku shi." *Kokotsu kinbungaku ronsô* 1 (1955): 1–66.

Kimbun tsushaku. Kobe: Hakutsuru bijutsukan, 1962, p. 84.

Shiratori, K. "Sur L'origine des Hiong-nou." *Journal Asiatique* 102 (1923): 71–81.

Shishlina, Natalia I., and Fredrik T. Hiebert, "The Steppe and the Sown: Interaction between Bronze Age Eurasian Nomads and Agriculturalists." In *The Bronze Age and Early Iron Age Peoples of Eastern Central Asia*, ed. Victor H. Mair. Washington: Institute for the Study of Man, 1998, vol. 1, pp. 222–37.

Sinor, Denis. "The Greed of the Northern Barbarians." In *Aspects of Altaic Civilizations II*, ed. Larry V. Clark and Paul A. Draghi. Bloomington: Indiana University, 1978, pp. 171–82.

Inner Asia: A Syllabus. Bloomington: Indiana University, 1987 [3rd rpt.].

So, Jenny, and Emma C. Bunker. *Traders and Raiders on China's Northern Frontier*. Seattle and London: Arthur Sackler Gallery and University of Washington Press, 1995.

Stein, Aurel. *Serindia. Detailed Report of Explorations in Central Asia and Westernmost China*. 5 vols. Oxford: Clarendon Press, 1921.

Sterckx, Roel. "An Ancient Chinese Horse Ritual." *Early China* 21 (1996): 47–79.

Suzuki, Chusei. "China's Relations with Inner Asia: The Hsiung-nu, Tibet." In *The Chinese World Order*, ed. John K. Fairbank. Cambridge: Harvard University Press, 1968, pp. 180–97.

Swann, Nancy Lee. *Food and Money in Ancient China. The Earliest Economic History of China to A.D. 25. Han Shu 24 with Related Texts, Han Shu 91 and Shih Chi 129*. Princeton: Princeton University Press, 1950.

T'a La, and Liang Chin-ming. "Hu-lu-ssu-t'ai Hsiung-nu mu." *Wen-wu* 1980.7: 11–12.

Taaffe, Robert N. "The Geographic Setting." *The Cambridge History of Early Inner Asia*, ed. Denis Sinor. Cambridge: Cambridge University Press, 1990, pp. 19–40.

Tai Ying-hsin, and Sun Chia-hsiang. "Shensi Shen-mu hsien ch'u-t'u Hsiung-nu wen-wu." *Wen-wu* 1983.12: 23–30.

T'an Ying-chieh, and Chao Shan-tung. "Sung Nen p'ing-yüan ch'ing-t'ung wen-hua ch'u-yi." In *Chung-kuo k'ao-ku hsüeh-hui ti-ssu-tz'u nien-hui lun-wen chi 1983*. Peking: Wen-wu, 1985, pp. 196–202.

Tan Yingjie and Chao Shan-tung. "Sung Nen p'ing-yüan ch'ing-t'ung wen-hua ch'u-yi." In *Chung-kuo k'ao-ku hsüeh-hui ti-ssu-tz'u nien-hui lun-wen chi 1983*. Peking: Wen-wu, 1985, pp. 196–202.

Tan Ying-jie et al. "The Bronze Age in the Song Nen Plain." In *The Archaeology of Northeast China: Beyond the Great Wall*, ed. Sarah Milledge Nelson. London: Routledge, 1995, pp. 225–50.

T'ang Lan. "Lüeh-lun Hsi-Chou wei shih chia-tsu chiao-ts'ang t'ung-ch'i te chung-yao yi-yi." *Wen-wu*, 1978.3: 14, 19–24.

Tang Xiaofeng. "A Report on the Investigation on the Great Wall of the Qin-Han Period in the Northwest Sector of Inner Mongolia." Trans. in *Chinese Archaeological Abstracts*. Vol. 3: *Eastern Zhou to Han*, ed. Albert E. Dien et al. Los Angeles: Institute of Archaeology, 1985, pp. 959–65.

Teggart, Frederick J. *Rome and China. A Study of Correlations in Historical Events*. Berkeley: University of California Press, 1939.

Telegin, Dmitriy Yakolevich. *Dereivka: A Settlement and Cemetery of Copper Age Horse Keepers on the Middle Dnieper*, ed. J. P. Mallory, trans. V. K. Pyatkovskiy. Oxford: British Archaeological Reports, 1986.

T'ien Kuang-chin. "Chin-nien-lai te Nei Meng-ku ti-ch'ü te Hsiung-nu k'ao-ku." *K'ao-ku hsüeh-pao* 1983.1: 7–24.

"T'ao-hung-pa-la te Hsiung-nu mu," *K'ao-ku hsüeh-pao* 1976.1:131–42. Rpt. in *O-erh-to-ssu ch'ing-t'ung ch'i*, ed. T'ien Kuang-chin and Kuo Su-hsin. Peking: Wen-wu, 1986, pp. 203–19.

"Nei Meng-ku ch'ang-ch'eng ti-tai chu k'ao-ku-hsüeh wen-hua yü lin-ching t'ung-ch'i wen-hua hsiang-hu ying-hsiang kui-lü te yen-chiu." *Nei Meng-ku wen-wu k'ao-ku* 1993.1–2: 16–22.

T'ien Kuang-chin, and Kuo Su-hsin. "Nei Meng-ku A-lu-chai-teng fa-hsien te Hsiung-nu yi-wu." *K'ao-ku*, 1980.4: 333–38, 364, 368.

"Yü-lung-t'ai Chan-kuo mu." In *O-erh-to-ssu ch'ing-tung ch'I*, ed. T'ien Kuang-chin and Kuo Su-hsin. Peking: Wen-wu, 1986, pp. 366–71.

"O-erh-to-ssu shih ch'ing-t'ung ch'i te yüan-yüan." *K'ao-ku hsüeh-pao* 1988.3: 257–75.

eds. *O-erh-to-ssu ch'ing-t'ung ch'i.* Peking: Wen-wu, 1986.

Tomaschek, W. "Die Strassenzuge der Tabula Peutingeriana." *Sitzungsberichte der Wiener Akademie der Wissenschaften* 102 (1883).

Trever, K. V. *Excavations in Northern Mongolia, 1924–1925.* Leningrad: Memoirs of the Academy of History of Material Culture 3, 1932.

Ts'ui Hsüan. "Nei Meng-ku hsien Ch'in shih-ch'i hsü-mu yi-ts'un shu-lun." *Nei Menggu shehui kexue* 1988.1: 69–74.

Tu Sheng-yün. "Ssu-ma Ch'ien te t'ien-wen-hsüeh ch'eng-chiu he ssu-hsiang." In *Ssu-ma Ch'ien he Shih Chi*, ed. Liu Nai-he. Peking: Pei-ching ch'u-pan-she 1987, pp. 222–48.

Tung-pei k'ao-ku yü li-shih 1982.1:136–40. "Ta-an Han-shu yi-chih fa-chüeh te chu-yao shou-huo."

Turan, Osman. "The Ideal of World Dominion among the Medieval Türks." *Studia Islamica* 4 (1955): 77–90.

Vainshtein, S. *Nomads of South Siberia. The Pastoral Economies of Tuva.* Cambridge: Cambridge University Press, 1980.

Van der Loon, Piet. "The Ancient Chinese Chronicles and the Growth of Historical Ideals." In *Historians of China and Japan*, ed. W. G. Beasley and E. G. Pulleyblank. London: Oxford University Press, 1961, pp. 24–30.

Vandermeersch, Leon. *Wangdao ou, La voie royale. Recherches sur l'esprit des institutions de la Chine archaique.* 2 vols. Paris: Ecole Française d'Extreme-Orient, 1977–80.

Vejnshtein, S. I. "The Problem of Origin and Formation of the Economic-Cultural Type of Pastoral Nomads in the Moderate Belt of Eurasia." In *The Nomadic Alternative*, ed. W. Weissleder. The Hague: Mouton, 1984, pp. 127–33.

Voegelin, E. "The Mongol Orders of Submission to European Powers, 1245–1255." *Byzantion* 15 (1940–41): 378–413.

Volkov, V. "Early Nomads of Mongolia." In *Nomads of The Eurasian Steppes in the Early Iron Age*, ed. Jeannine Davis-Kimball et al. Berkeley: Zinat Press, 1995, pp. 319–33.

Vreeland, Herbert. *Mongol Community and Kinship Structure.* New Haven: Human Relations Area Files, 1957.

Waldron, Arthur. *The Great Wall of China: From History to Myth.* Cambridge: Cambridge University Press, 1990.

Waley, Arthur. *The Analects of Confucius.* London: Allen and Unwin, 1938.

Walker, Richard Louis. *The Multistate System of Ancient China.* Hamden: The Shoestring Press, 1953.

Wallacker, Benjamin E. *The Huai-nan-Tzu Book Eleven: Behavior, Culture and the Cosmos.* New Haven: American Oriental Society, 1962.

Wang Binghua [Wang Ping-hua]. "A Preliminary Analysis of the Archaeological Cultures of the Bronze Age in the Region of Xinjiang." In *Between Lapis and Jade: Ancient Cultures of Central Asia*, ed. F. Hiebert and N. Di Cosmo, *Anthropology and Archaeology of Eurasia* 34.4 (Spring 1996): 67–86.

Wang Ch'eng-tsu. *Chung-kuo ti-li-hsüeh shih*. Peking: Shang-wu, 1988.

Wang Gungwu. "Early Ming Relations with Southeast Asia: A Background Essay." In *The Chinese World Order*, ed. John K. Fairbank. Cambridge, Mass.: Harvard University Press, 1968, pp. 34–62.

Wang Hsing-kuo. *Chia Yi p'ing chuan: fu Lu Chia Ch'ao Ts'o p'ing chuan*. Nanching: Nan-ching ta hsueh, 1992.

Wang Ming-ke. "O-erh-to-ssu chi ch'i lin-chin ti-ch'ü chuan-hua yu-mu-yeh te ch'iyüan." *Chung-yang yen-chiu-yüan li-shih yü-yen yen-chiu-so chi-k'an* [Bulletin of the Institute of History and Philology] 65.2 (1994): 375–44.

Wang Ping-hua. "Hsi Han yi-ch'ien Hsin-chiang he Chung-yüan ti-ch'ü li-shih kuanhsi k'ao-su." In Wang Ping-hua, *Ssu-chou chih lu k'ao-ku yen-chiu*. Urumchi: Hsin-chiang jen-min, 1993, pp. 164–82.

Wang Wei-mao. "Hsiung-nu Lung-ch'eng k'ao-pien." *Li-shih yen-chiu* 1983.2: 142–44.

Watson, Burton. *Ssu-ma Ch'ien, Grand Historian of China*. New York: Columbia University Press, 1958.

Courtier and Commoner in Ancient China: Selections from the History of the Former Han. New York: Columbia University Press, 1974.

trans. *Records of the Grand Historian by Sima Qian*. 3 vols. New York and Hong Kong: Columbia University Press and The Chinese University of Hong Kong, 1993.

Watson, William. *Cultural Frontiers in Ancient East Asia*. Edinburgh: Edinburgh University Press, 1971.

Webb, M. C. "The Flag Follows Trade: An Essay on the Necessary Interaction of Military and Commercial Factors in State Formation." In *Ancient Civilization and Trade*, ed. J. A. Sabloff and C. C. Lamberg-Karlovsky. Albuquerque: University of New Mexico Press, 1975, pp. 179–94.

Wen-wu 1980.7:1–10. "Hsi-kou-p'an Hsiung-nu mu."

1981.8:46–48. "Hu-pei Sui-hsien fa-hsien Shang-tai ch'ing-t'ung ch'i."

1986.11:1–18. "Shan-hsi Ling-shih Ching-chieh-ts'un Shang mu."

1989.8:17–35, 43. "Pei-ching Yen-ching Chün-tu-shan Tung Chou Shan Jung pu-lo mu-ti fa-chüeh chi-lüeh."

Wen-wu tzu-liao ts'ung-k'an 1983.7:138–46. "Liao-ning Lin-hsi hsien Ta-ching ku t'ung-k'uang 1976 nien shih-chüeh chien-pao."

1983.7:67–74. "Luan-p'ing hsien Hu-shih-ho P'ao-t'ai-shan Shan-jung mu-ti te fa-hsien."

White, Lynn, Jr. *Medieval Technology and Social Change*. Oxford: Clarendon Press, 1962.

Wieger Leon. *Textes historiques: histoire politique de la Chine depuis l'origine, jusqu'en 1912*. 2 vols. Hsien-hsien: Impr. de Hien-hien, 1922–23.

Wilbur, C. Martin. *Slavery in China under the Former Han Dynasty, 206 B.C.–A.D. 25*. Chicago: Field Museum of Natural History, 1943.

Wright, A. F. "On the Uses of Generalization in the Study of Chinese History." In *Generalizations in the Writing of History*, ed. Louis Gottschalk. Chicago: University of Chicago Press, 1963.

Wu Chen-lu. "Pao-te hsien hsin fa-hsien te Yin-tai ch'ing-t'ung ch'i." *Wen-wu* 1972.4: 62–66.

Wu Chung-kuang. "Ssu-ma Ch'ien 'ch'eng yi chia chih yen' shuo." *Jen-wen tsa-chih* 1984.4: 76–80.

Wu En. "Yin chih Chou ch'u te pei-fang ch'ing-t'ung ch'i." *K'ao-ku hsüeh-pao* 1985.2: 135–56.

"Wo kuo pei-fang ku-tai tung-wu wen-shih." *K'ao-ku hsüeh-pao* 1990.4: 409–37.

"New Chinese Archaeological Discoveries Regarding the Ancient Northern Tribes." Paper presented at the workshop "Chinese and Their Northern Neighbors," University of Pittsburgh, April 5–7, 1991.

"Chu-k'ai-kou wen-hua te fa-hsien chi ch'i yi-yi." In *Chung-kuo k'ao-ku-hsüeh lun-ts'ung*. Pei-ching: K'o-hsüeh, 1995, pp. 256–66.

Wu Jeng-hsiang. "Ssu-chou chih lu shang yu yi zhong-ta k'ao-ku fa-hsien: Tun-huang hsien Hsüan-ch'üan chih." In *Ch'ang-ch'eng kuo-chi hsüeh-shu yen-t'ao-hui lun-wen*, ed. Chung-kuo ch'ang-ch'eng hsüeh-hui. Chi-lin-shih: Chi-lin Jen-min, 1994, pp. 283–85, 487–88.

Wu, Ju-yu. "Ssu-ma Ch'ien te ju tao ssu- hsiang pien-his." *Jen-wen tsa-chih* 1984.3: 81–87.

Xi, Zezong. "Characteristics of China's Ancient Astronomy." In *History of Oriental Astronomy*, ed. G. Swarup et al. Cambridge: Cambridge University Press, 1987.

Yablonsky, Leonid T. "Material Culture of the Saka and Historical Reconstruction." In *Nomads of the Eurasian Steppes in the Early Iron Age*, ed. Jeannine Davis-Kimball et al. Berkeley: Zinat Press, 1995, pp. 201–39.

"Some Ethnogenetical Hypotheses." In *Nomads of the Eurasian Steppes in the Early Iron Age*, ed. Jeannine Davis-Kimball et al. Berkeley: Zinat Press, 1995, pp. 241–52.

Yabuuti, K. "Chinese Astronomy: Development and Limiting Factors." In *Chinese Science. Explorations of an Ancient Tradition*, ed. Shigeru Nakayama and N. Sivin. Cambridge, Mass.: M.I.T. Press, 1973, pp. 91–103.

Yamada, Nobuo. "The Formation of the Hsiung-nu Nomadic State." *Acta Orientalia Academiae Scientiarum Hungaricae* 36.1–3 (1982): 575–82.

Yang Hu, T'an Ying-chieh, and Chang T'ai-hsiang. "Hei-lung-chiang ku-tai wen-hua ch'u-lun." In *Chung-kuo k'ao-ku hsüeh-hui ti-ssu-tz'u nien-hui lun-wen chi 1979*. Peking: Wen-wu, 1980, pp. 80–96.

Yang Shao-shun. "Shan-hsi Liu-lin hsien Kao-hung fa-hsien Shang-tai t'ung-ch'i." *K'ao ku* 1981.3: 211–12.

"Shan-hsi Shih-lou Ch'u-chia-yü Ts'ao-chia-yüan fa-hsien Shang-tai t'ung-ch'i." *Wen-wu* 1981.8: 49–53.

Yang, Lien-sheng. "The Organization of Chinese Official Historiography: Principles and Methods of the Standard Histories from the T'ang through the Ming Dynasty." In *Historians of China and Japan*, ed. W. G. Beasley and E. G. Pulleyblank. London: Oxford University Press, 1961, pp. 44–59.

Yang, Pao-ch'eng. "Yin-tai ch'e-tzu te fa-hsien yü fu-yüan." *K'ao-ku* 1984.6: 546–55.

Yang, Yen-ch'i. "Ssu-ma Ch'ien te li-shih ssu-hsiang." In *Ssu-ma Ch'ien ho Shih chi*, ed. Liu Nai-he. Peking: Pei-ching ch'u-pan-she, 1987, pp. 41–58.

Yao Sheng-min. "Shaan-hsi Ch'ün-hua hsien ch'u-t'u te Shang Chou Ch'ing-t'ung ch'i." *K'ao-ku yü wen-wu* 1986.5: 12–22.

Yao Ts'ung-wu. *Yao Ts'ung-wu hsien-sheng ch'üan-chi.* Vol. 5: *Liao Chin Yüan lun-wen (shang).* Taipei: Cheng-chung shu-chü, 1981.

Yen-t'ien lun. By Huan K'uan. *Ssu-pu pei-yao* edition. Peking: Chung-hua shu-chü, 1936.

Yetts, W. P. "Discoveries of the Kozlov Expedition." *Burlington Magazine* 48 (1926): 168–85.

Yetts, W. Perceval. "The Horse: A Factor in Early Chinese History." *Eurasia Septentrionalis Antiqua "Minns Volume"* 9 (1934): 231–55.

Yoke, Ho Peng. *Li, Qi and Shu. An Introduction to Science and Civilization in China.* Hong Kong: Hong Kong University Press, 1985.

Yü, Ying-shih. *Trade and Expansion in Han China: A Study in the Structure of Sino-Barbarian Economic Relations.* Berkeley: University of California Press, 1967.

"The Study of Chinese History. Retrospect and Prospect." In *The Translation of Things Past. Chinese History and Historiography*, ed. George Kao, and trans. Thomas H. C. Lee and Chun-chieh Huang. Hong Kong: Chinese University Press, 1982, pp. 7–26.

"Han Foreign Relations." In *The Cambridge History of China.* Vol. 1: *The Ch'in and Han Empires, 221 B.C.–A.D. 220*, ed. M. Loewe and D. Twitchett. Cambridge: Cambridge University Press, 1986, pp. 377–472.

"The Hsiung-nu." In *Cambridge History of Early Inner Asia*, ed. Denis Sinor. Cambridge: Cambridge University Press, 1990, pp. 118–49.

Zavitukhina, M. P. "The Tagar Culture," and "The Tashtyk Culture," in AA. VV., *Frozen Tombs. The Culture and Art of the Ancient Tribes of Siberia.* London: British Museum Publications, 1978, pp. 78–100.

Zhukov, Ye. *History of the Mongolian People's Republic.* Moscow: Nauka, 1973.

Index

ho-ch'in treaty
and kinship, 300
violated by Hsiung-nu leaders,
224–25
Horses
domestication, 24–27
at Kuo-hsien-yao-tzu, 75
horseriding, 62
Hou-chia-chuang, 54
Hsi-kou-p'an, 79, 84, 85
Hsia-yang, city of Kuo, 119
Hsiang-p'ing, 143
Hsiang-tzu, minister of Chin, 128–29
Hsiao-t'un, 54
Hsien-yü, 100, 115
city of Ku, 115, 129
Hsien-yün, 107, 109, 298
Hsin-tien culture, 48
Hsing, state of, 97–98
Hsing-lin, 47
Hsiung-nu, 130, 151–52
armament and tactics, 277
as ancestors of the Mongols, 166
before the Ch'in dynasty, 154
behavior in battle, 278
Chinese origin of, 300
in Chinese society, 270
and Central Asia, 196
domination of the Western regions,
249
early relation with the Han, 190
ethnic origin, 163
expansion in Inner Asia, 189
genealogical "history," 298–99
government, 178
Han generals defecting to, 230
and *ho-ch'in* treaty, 216–17
language, 280–81
linguistic affiliation, 164
location of court, 189
military training, 276
notion of sovereignty, 226
raids against Chinese borders, 201
related to the Hsien-yün, 164
relationship to other northern
peoples, 165–66
sacrifices and rituals, 279–80
state formation, 186

territory invaded by China, 143
violation of treaties, 217
see also southern Hsiung-nu
Hsiung-nu culture
archaeological culture, 81
burials, 273
defined, 99
laws, 274–75
Hsiung-nu state
political and administrative
structure, 177
ruling clans, 178
Hsi-yang, capital of Fei, 115
Hsün-tzu, 94
Hsün Wu, 115
Hu
early trade with China, 131
first mentioned, 128
as a generic name for "mounted
nomads," 127
synonymous with Hsiung-nu, 129
Hu-han-yeh, Hsiung-nu ruler, 226
Hu-lu-ssu-t'ai, 78–79
as a Hsiung-nu site, 152
Hu-Mo, 129
Hua-Hsia, 90, 93, 94
culturally different from Ti, 97
Huai-nan-tzu
description of the northern peoples,
291
mythological geography, 296
notion of "law" in, 220
huang fu (barren domains)
inhabited by northern peoples,
302
hui, gatherings, 117
Hulsewé, Anthony
on early imperial laws, 219
on Ssu-ma Ch'ien, 261
on the Western regions, 249–50
Hun-yü, 189
Huo Ch'ü-ping, 239
Huo-shao-kou, 48

Inner Asia, defined, 13
in correlative cosmology, 304 ff.
Inner Asian nomads
state formation, 171